Why You Need to Know VBA

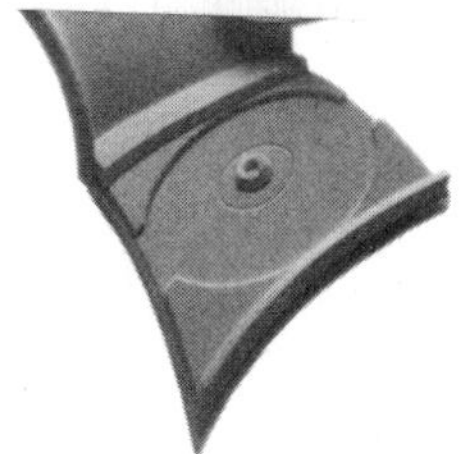

- To automate tasks with templates and macros
- To develop applications to run alongside AutoCAD
- To add menu commands and toolbar buttons to the AutoCAD window, for running your macros
- To change AutoCAD's environment settings from a macro
- To easily find your way around the AutoCAD object model
- To add hyperlinks to drawings
- To build complex solids from simple ones using code
- To macro-ize extrusion and revolution in drawings
- To use code to shade or render drawings
- To exchange data between AutoCAD and applications from the Microsoft Office family
- To use AutoCAD 2000i's new Internet features for transferring files on the Internet
- To automate Internet file transfers using a VBA interface to ensure efficient, error-free transfers.
- To use the Publish to Web Wizard for automatically creating HTML files for Web pages

Mastering AutoCAD VBA

Marion Cottingham

SYBEX®

San Francisco • Paris • Düsseldorf • Soest • London

Associate Publisher: Cheryl Applewood
Contracts and Licensing Manager: Kristine O'Callaghan
Acquisitions and Developmental Editor: Raquel Baker
Editor: Carol Henry
Production Editor: Nathan Whiteside
Technical Editor: Steve Hansen
Book Designer: Franz Baumhackl
Electronic Publishing Specialist: Jill Niles
Proofreaders: Nancy Riddiough, Nanette Duffy, Laurie O'Connell, Emily Hsuan
Indexer: Ted Laux
CD Coordinator: Erica Yee
CD Technician: Kevin Ly
Cover Designer: Design Site
Cover Illustrator: Sergei Loobkoff, Design Site

Library of Congress Card Number: 2001087093

ISBN: 0-7821-2871-8

Manufactured in the United States of America

10 9 8 7 6 5 4 3 2 1

Software License Agreement: Terms and Conditions

The media and/or any online materials accompanying this book that are available now or in the future contain programs and/or text files (the "Software") to be used in connection with the book. SYBEX hereby grants to you a license to use the Software, subject to the terms that follow. Your purchase, acceptance, or use of the Software will constitute your acceptance of such terms.

The Software compilation is the property of SYBEX unless otherwise indicated and is protected by copyright to SYBEX or other copyright owner(s) as indicated in the media files (the "Owner(s)"). You are hereby granted a single-user license to use the Software for your personal, noncommercial use only. You may not reproduce, sell, distribute, publish, circulate, or commercially exploit the Software, or any portion thereof, without the written consent of SYBEX and the specific copyright owner(s) of any component software included on this media.

In the event that the Software or components include specific license requirements or end-user agreements, statements of condition, disclaimers, limitations or warranties ("End-User License"), those End-User Licenses supersede the terms and conditions herein as to that particular Software component. Your purchase, acceptance, or use of the Software will constitute your acceptance of such End-User Licenses.

By purchase, use or acceptance of the Software you further agree to comply with all export laws and regulations of the United States as such laws and regulations may exist from time to time.

Reusable Code in This Book

The authors created reusable code in this publication expressly for reuse for readers. Sybex grants readers permission to reuse for any purpose the code found in this publication or its accompanying CD-ROM so long as all three authors are attributed in any application containing the reusable code, and the code itself is never sold or commercially exploited as a stand-alone product.

Software Support

Components of the supplemental Software and any offers associated with them may be supported by the specific Owner(s) of that material but they are not supported by SYBEX. Information regarding any available support may be obtained from the Owner(s) using the information provided in the appropriate read.me files or listed elsewhere on the media.

Should the manufacturer(s) or other Owner(s) cease to offer support or decline to honor any offer, SYBEX bears no responsibility. This notice concerning support for the Software is provided for your information only. SYBEX is not the agent or principal of the Owner(s), and SYBEX is in no way responsible for providing any support for the Software, nor is it liable or responsible for any support provided, or not provided, by the Owner(s).

Warranty

SYBEX warrants the enclosed media to be free of physical defects for a period of ninety (90) days after purchase. The Software is not available from SYBEX in any other form or media than that enclosed herein or posted to www.sybex.com. If you discover a defect in the media during this warranty period, you may obtain a replacement of identical format at no charge by sending the defective media, postage prepaid, with proof of purchase to:

SYBEX Inc.
Customer Service Department
1151 Marina Village Parkway
Alameda, CA 94501

(510) 523-8233
Fax: (510) 523-2373
e-mail: info@sybex.com
WEB: HTTP://WWW.SYBEX.COM

After the 90-day period, you can obtain replacement media of identical format by sending us the defective disk, proof of purchase, and a check or money order for $10, payable to SYBEX.

Disclaimer

SYBEX makes no warranty or representation, either expressed or implied, with respect to the Software or its contents, quality, performance, merchantability, or fitness for a particular purpose. In no event will SYBEX, its distributors, or dealers be liable to you or any other party for direct, indirect, special, incidental, consequential, or other damages arising out of the use of or inability to use the Software or its contents even if advised of the possibility of such damage. In the event that the Software includes an online update feature, SYBEX further disclaims any obligation to provide this feature for any specific duration other than the initial posting.

The exclusion of implied warranties is not permitted by some states. Therefore, the above exclusion may not apply to you. This warranty provides you with specific legal rights; there may be other rights that you may have that vary from state to state. The pricing of the book with the Software by SYBEX reflects the allocation of risk and limitations on liability contained in this agreement of Terms and Conditions.

Shareware Distribution

This Software may contain various programs that are distributed as shareware. Copyright laws apply to both shareware and ordinary commercial software, and the copyright Owner(s) retains all rights. If you try a shareware program and continue using it, you are expected to register it. Individual programs differ on details of trial periods, registration, and payment. Please observe the requirements stated in appropriate files.

Copy Protection

The Software in whole or in part may or may not be copy-protected or encrypted. However, in all cases, reselling or redistributing these files without authorization is expressly forbidden except as specifically provided for by the Owner(s) therein.

To all my students, past and present, who have inspired me more than they'll ever know.

—Marion Cottingham

Acknowledgments

I would like to thank all my supporters from the University of Western Australia, especially those from the Computer Science and Software Engineering department. In particular, thanks to Dr. Sandra Penrose for her helpful advice; Professor Barry Brady (Executive Dean of the Faculty of Engineering and Mathematical Sciences) for allowing me study leave to engage in the scholarly activity of writing this book; Professor Alan Robson (Deputy Vice-Chancellor) for his indirect support; and Colin Campbell-Fraser (Director of Public Affairs) for his encouragement.

Thanks goes to everyone at Sybex who worked on this book, especially to the Associate Publisher Cheryl Applewood for giving me the opportunity to write it, and Development Editor Raquel Baker who kept me on track until the book went into its production phase. Thanks go to Production Editor Nathan Whiteside, who helped me to keep to deadlines with his insatiable appetite for chapters. He coordinated the whole project and made the book happen on time.

Thanks to the Editor Carol Henry for her excellent editing, enthusiasm, and suggestions…from start to finish. She truly made this a better read and kept me company during the twilight hours while I worked sixteen hours ahead of her hanging upside down at the other side of the world. Thanks to the Technical Editor Steve Hansen for his comments and expert advice that also have made this a better book.

Thanks to Manufacturing Specialist Steve Melville and to Electronic Publishing Specialist Jill Niles, who put my words onto the printed page, and to Indexer Ted Laux, who has made all the material in the book easy to find.

Finally, thanks to Autodesk for producing AutoCAD, which is such a powerful software package that is fun to use and has made defunct the phrase "and now back to the drawing board!"

Contents at a Glance

Contents

Introduction

Autodesk first included Microsoft's Visual Basic for Applications (VBA) in AutoCAD Release 14. Combining the power of AutoCAD and Visual Basic provides endless opportunities for creating impressive customized applications ranging from streamlining the routine tasks you currently perform using AutoCAD to creating drawings in seconds that would normally take hours. The book takes you step-by-step through how to create macros to automate the routine tasks you currently do in AutoCAD. It shows you how to create powerful Windows applications so that you can run your macros at the click of a button. You'll quickly learn how much fun it is to build graphical user interfaces (GUIs) by simply dragging and dropping controls from a toolbox to a UserForm—you already do much the same thing when you develop drawings using AutoCAD.

The material in this book is compatible with AutoCAD 14, AutoCAD 2000, and AutoCAD 2000i.

I'm sure you'll enjoy developing code with all the pop-up help provided by the Visual Basic for Applications Integrated Development Environment (VBA IDE). If you're lucky enough to be using AutoCAD 2000i with its new updated Heidi® graphics engine, you have access to its revolutionary Internet/intranet tools that enable you to publish drawings on the Web to speed up your design review process. You'll enjoy the improvements to the Array interface that help you preview your results, and the extension to the 3D Orbit feature that allows lights, materials, and textures support while orbiting. You'll also find that you can now ask questions of the Help facility, rather than having to guess at the name of a command, method, or property. And you'll also notice an Active Assistant on display to provide additional help.

If you are not using AutoCAD 2000i and would like more information about it, go to Autodesk's AutoCAD Product Center at the following URL. Here you can get product information, view an interactive demonstration, or (in the United States and Canada) order a free demo CD.

```
http://www3.autodesk.com/adsk/index/0,,303942-123112,00.html
```

Who Should Read This Book

This book assumes that the reader is already a casual user of AutoCAD and knows its fundamentals (opening and closing drawing files, interactively creating drawings, and so forth). The material in this book extends this knowledge by showing how to perform the same tasks from VBA code, and how to enhance AutoCAD by customizing additional interfaces that make it easier to perform some tasks.

To the reader who wants to learn how to code macros in VBA, this book assumes no prior knowledge of VBA or any other programming language. It is the ideal book for AutoCAD users to learn how to write code to automate routine tasks. This book provides you with the stepping stones needed to develop your very own macros and applications that run inside AutoCAD.

To the reader who has VBA programming experience from other applications, you'll learn about the numerous objects and collections that AutoCAD has to offer and the methods and properties these contain.

Since most examples show how to perform a task first from the AutoCAD window and then from VBA code, readers with no coding experience will quickly see the relationships between how they perform a task in the AutoCAD window and the objects they need to use in code to perform the same task. The reader with coding experience will quickly see the relationships of the objects they use in code, to the drawing objects, options, and settings required for the AutoCAD window.

What You Can Do with VBA

Endless numbers of tasks are just waiting to be automated using VBA. After you've taken the time to develop a macro or an application and have fully tested that it works correctly, the code is guaranteed to perform correctly and reliably every time you use it. Just think of the timesaving possibilities of running your code instead of going through the same sequence of actions over and over again. Using VBA, many tasks can be completed with one or two mouse clicks—you can't beat that. Freeing up your time on the menial tasks lets you concentrate more on the complex tasks that require your artistic abilities.

As you make your way through this book and become more experienced at programming, you'll get more and more ambitious and find lots of things that are suitable for automating. Just about any task that you do manually in AutoCAD can be automated using VBA. This book takes you by the hand and gently guides you deeper into the "mysteries" of coding. Because of the VBA IDE's easy-to-use features, programmers no longer need to be gurus. You'll be amazed at just how quickly you start developing full-blown Windows applications that run smoothly alongside AutoCAD.

What's In This Book

This book takes you through the practical steps of creating powerful and time-saving VBA macros and applications. The focus is on automation aimed at saving time, increasing productivity, and producing complex drawings at the click of a button. The book is divided into five parts:

Part 1: VBA Macros and the Visual Basic Editor

Part 1 shows you how to develop your first application and takes you on a quick tour of the Visual Basic Editor. You'll also be introduced to some VBA programming concepts that you'll find useful as a reference as you progress through the book.

Chapter 1 provides step-by-step instructions for developing a simple application that requires a GUI, containing controls from the VBA Toolbox that are coded to respond to a user's actions.

Chapter 2 shows you how to create macros that can run on their own or be used to start an application. You'll learn to make the most of the IDE's powerful editing features.

Chapter 3 takes you on a quick tour of the IDE, showing you how to access its various windows. You'll also see how to display some of the toolbars, and how to make the best use of the Help facility.

Chapter 4 covers all the programming concepts you need for getting well underway as an AutoCAD VBA programmer. You'll find it useful to have all this information in one location rather than dispersed throughout the book—it's much easier to come back to later.

Part 2: Drawing Lines and Solid Areas Using VBA Macros

Part 2 is your tutor for using objects from the AutoCAD Object Model—lines, circles, and freeform shapes—and how to fill areas with color.

Chapter 5 shows the hierarchical structure of the AutoCAD Object Model. You'll see how to access its objects from code. You'll work through what's required to communicate with users via message boxes, and learn how to send a command to the AutoCAD command line from a macro.

Chapter 6 covers drawing lines and setting their attributes (linetype, color, and thickness) from a macro. You'll also see how to scale drawing objects from a macro.

Chapter 7 demonstrates drawing circles and freeform shapes and filling them with color. The points defining the freeform shapes are selected by the user, and the values of the coordinates are passed to a macro.

Part 3: Reusability and Customization

In Part 3, you'll fashion an AutoCAD template and create a new drawing document from code. You'll see how to design a new group of menu commands and toolbar buttons in the AutoCAD window to run your macros, and how to read and write data to a file.

Chapter 8 shows how to set the AutoCAD environment settings and make a template drawing from a macro. It compares macros and templates from the point of view of reusability, and introduces User Coordinate System (UCS) concepts applicable to AutoCAD VBA programming.

Chapter 9 describes the process of creating a new drawing document from a macro and how to create polar and rectangular arrays. You'll also see how to display text from a macro, and how to format numbers, dates, and times.

Chapter 10 introduces you to the many debugging features found in the IDE. It talks about various kinds of errors you may encounter. You'll see how you can watch the values of variables change as the code is executed.

In Chapter 11, you'll add a new group of menu commands to the AutoCAD window and create toolbar buttons for quick access to these new commands.

Chapter 12 discusses how to transfer data to and from files, and how to add a Common Dialog control to display the Windows Open and Save As dialog boxes.

Part 4: 2D Drawing Techniques

Part 4 discusses interactive drawing techniques using the snap and grid features. You'll see how to group objects and set group attributes.

Chapter 13 discusses interactive drawing techniques for increased precision, including grid and snap. It tells you how to create and manipulate a spline curve, and how to animate the movement of a drawing object.

Chapter 14 demonstrates the grouping of objects into layers or blocks so that they can be handled as single entities. It shows how to freeze and thaw layers and how to lock and unlock them.

Part 5: 3D Drawing Techniques

Part 5 describes the creation and drawing of 3D solids and how to view them from different angles using the 3D Orbit control.

In Chapter 15, you'll create a range of primitive solids and combine them using union, intersection, and subtraction operators. You'll also see how to create solids using extrusion and revolution, how to remove hidden lines, and how render solids with full color—from your VBA macro.

In Chapter 16, you'll explore the exchange of data among other Microsoft applications, using objects from Excel, Access, and Word as examples.

Chapter 17 discusses AutoCAD 2000i's latest Internet features. You'll see how to launch your Web browser from code, validate URL addresses, and open and save drawings on the Internet. You'll use the Publish to Web Wizard that creates the HTML files for your very own Web pages. You'll also see how to add hyperlinks to a drawing.

This book also features two bonus chapters (18 and 19) on the CD, which extend your skills in several areas. See "What's On the CD" later in this Introduction.

Appendices

The book's appendices provide easy-reference tools to help you find the AutoCAD information you need—when you need it.

Appendix A presents the AutoCAD Object Model so you can see how to access objects throughout the hierarchy. It also gives you a look at several other Microsoft-family object models so that you can see the strong similarities between them.

Appendix B lists all the ASCII symbols in a handy, one-stop reference table for your convenience.

AutoCAD Versions Compatible with This Book

Readers using AutoCAD 14, 2000, 2000i, and even future versions of the program will all benefit from this book. It is written to be as universally applicable as possible, since the VBA concepts and language hardly change between versions of AutoCAD. Each new release brings new objects providing additional functionality. For the most part, the new releases are upward-compatible, in that any macros written for one version will normally run without problems on a later release. So the code in the listings throughout this book and on the CD will likely be happy to run without problems for several years to come.

The screenshots throughout this book were taken using AutoCAD 2000i.

Conventions Used in This Book

This book uses a number of conventions to present information in as readable a format as possible. Tips and Warnings appear from time to time to call attention to special highlights.

Tips provide extra information that will be helpful in completing the task at hand.

Warnings alert you to situations where particular care must be taken to avoid problems.

This book takes advantage of several font styles and conventions used for the programming code. **Bold font** in text indicates something that you type at the keyboard. A `monospaced font` is used for code listings and code snippets, for URLs, and for filenames. In code lines, a continuation arrow (↵) indicates that the code line wraps down to the next line due to space limitations of the book. When a continuation arrow is present, you do not have to add a line break if you are typing the code yourself.

Have fun unlocking the power of VBA!

What's On the CD-ROM

The accompanying CD contains all the numbered code listings you'll find throughout this book. With the CD, you can quickly access the code without having to enter it yourself from scratch. Just transfer the code to the Visual Basic Editor, and then you can run the macros and try out any changes you wish to make.

Also on the CD is Adobe Acrobat Reader, for your convenience in easily accessing the bonus chapters, which are in .PDF format.

Bonus Chapters

The CD also includes two bonus chapters with additional exercises to build your 2D and 3D drawing skills.

Chapter 18: Once you've learned the basics of 2D drawing techniques, you can build on these skills with the exercises in Chapter 18, which demonstrate how to plot a drawing using the Plot Table Wizard, and how to change a Paper Space viewport from a macro. You can also build your VBA skills with the exercise on how to change a Paper Space viewport from a macro.

Chapter 19: Exercises in this chapter build on the 3D drawing skills developed in Part 5. They cover rendering and lighting effects, including using macros to accomplish hidden-line removal, shading, and rendering of 3D solids. You'll see how to control the level of smoothness at which a surface is rendered, and how to change the lighting—all from macros.

Part 1

VBA Macros and the Visual Basic Editor

In This Part

Developing a Simple VBA Application

AUTOCAD VBA

Chapter 1

In this chapter, you will learn how to create a simple VBA application through a series of tutorials. You will learn how to employ visual tools to create the graphical user interface, and write code to execute simple commands. You will also explore the basics of the Visual Basic environment by using its features to create practical code that you can reuse for repetitive tasks.

If you consider yourself an intermediate user of AutoCAD VBA and have already written some successful VBA code, you may want to skip this chapter—or even just skim over the entire Part I, depending on your experience. The material covered in Chapter 4, "VBA Programming Concepts," will always be useful to you as a reference.

This chapter covers the following topics:

- Advantages of using VBA with AutoCAD
- The AutoCAD VBA environment
- Developing your first application

Advantages of Using VBA with AutoCAD

Visual Basic for Applications (VBA) is a programming environment created by Microsoft that is built into applications to automate operations. It provides tools that you can drag and drop to build a graphical user interface (GUI), and a programming language that you can use to interact with AutoCAD objects. Using VBA with AutoCAD allows you to customize your AutoCAD application in seemingly unlimited ways. In this book, you'll see how simple it is to automate repetitive tasks. With the time saved, you'll be free to concentrate on applying your artistic talents and engineering skills to make your drawings more intricate.

Once you start writing VBA code, you'll quickly realize just how easy it is to access objects from the AutoCAD and VBA object libraries. You'll soon be able to call on the power of these objects while gaining a deeper insight into AutoCAD's features. As you start to see the benefits that VBA macros and applications can provide, you'll want to spend your extra time customizing even more tasks. Before you know it, you'll have a whole library of reusable macros and applications at your fingertips!

A macro *is a group of code statements, usually not very long or complicated, that is useful in automating a repetitive task. In your work at the computer, most likely you've used them already without realizing it.*

An application *is a program that has been created to perform a specific task. This can be something very simple, such as prompting the user for their name and password, or something very substantial and complex such as AutoCAD itself.*

Another not-so-obvious advantage of learning AutoCAD VBA is that your skills are transferable to a growing number of other applications that have VBA capability. These applications include all those in the Microsoft Office family of applications, such as Access, Word, and Excel, in addition to Microsoft Visual Basic itself and about two hundred other licensees.

VBA interfaces with applications by communicating and controlling objects through the application's object libraries, rather than by having any special connection to the application's inner workings. All you need to know are the names of the objects involved, and you can access their functionality with VBA code. You'll find the object names meaningful and easy to remember, such as ThisDrawing (an object in AutoCAD), ThisDocument (an object in Word), and ThisWorkbook (an object in Excel). As you enter the names of objects in your code, the editing features of VBA's Integrated

Development Environment (IDE) offer you drop-down lists of elements particular to the type of object you've entered. You'll see how this works in Chapter 2.

You can use a macro to automate just about anything, but it is probably most productive to start with the tasks you have to do time and time again. Why not think about those boring, uninspiring jobs you hate doing the most, and start with them! These are probably tasks that are time consuming and error prone, so implementing them in macros or applications will not only increase your productivity but lift your spirits by removing some of the tedious tasks that make you yawn just by thinking about them. (Such as adding all the required bits and pieces of information for starting a new drawing; or perhaps you've found that you regularly draw the same items over and over again.)

After you've successfully developed VBA code that works in the ways you want it to, it's guaranteed to perform correctly and reliably each time you run it. Now *there's* an incentive to learn VBA! So let's begin by examining the interface where you will write your code—the Visual Basic Editor.

The AutoCAD VBA Environment

The *Visual Basic Editor* is the integrated environment in which you develop all your VBA code. As you can see from Figure 1.1, the IDE has its own graphical user interface. Its windows provide all the tools required for creating, editing, debugging, and running your macros and applications. With this much functionality, the IDE is almost a standalone application, except that it can only be opened from the AutoCAD window and does not remain open after AutoCAD has been closed.

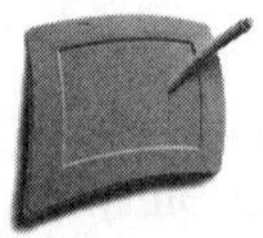

The term VBA Editor *is often used synonymously with the IDE even though the IDE provides more than just editing features.*

The VBA IDE can be opened from the AutoCAD window in a variety of ways:

- Type **vbaide** next to the command prompt in the command line.
- Choose Tools ➜ Macro ➜ Visual Basic Editor.
- Use the key-combination (shortcut) Alt+F11.

In the examples throughout this book, I've used menu commands in instructions. Most commands can also be accessed through a toolbar button or a key-combination, so occasionally I give an alternative access method as a reminder that there are other ways to invoke commands. The access method you use is up to your personal preference.

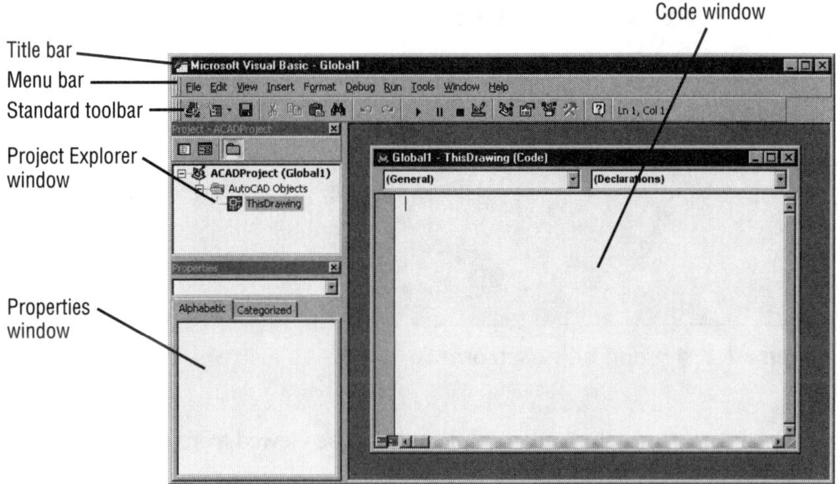

Figure 1.1 *AutoCAD's VBA environment*

Chapter 3 takes you on a guided tour of the IDE and discusses some of its features in more detail.

Creating UserForm Modules

A *module* is just a container for VBA code, and a *UserForm module* is a window (or dialog box) that can be considered a powerful extension to the AutoCAD GUI. You decide what controls to place on your UserForm in order to perform the tasks required by your application. You can place labels and text boxes in which users can enter the information that your program needs in order to run. You can use option buttons and check boxes to give users the chance to select the items they require. In fact, just about any control you've seen in the applications running under Windows is available for use in the VBA IDE.

Adding a UserForm Module to Your Application

To add a UserForm module to your application:

1. Start AutoCAD and choose Tools ➜ Macro ➜ Visual Basic Editor. The VBA IDE opens.
2. Choose Insert ➜ UserForm. UserForm1 appears, containing a title bar with a Close button, as shown in Figure 1.2.

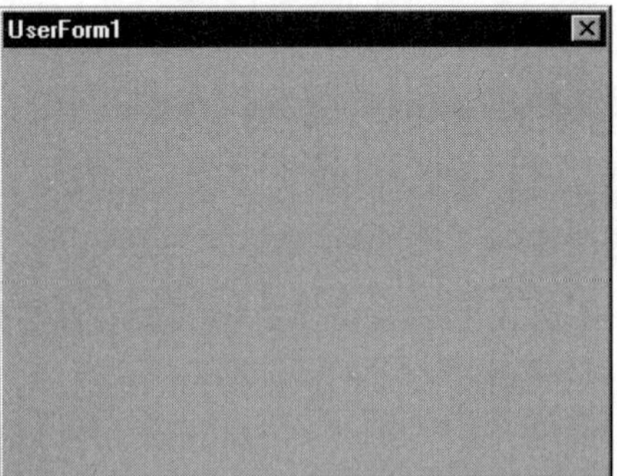

Figure 1.2 *A brand-new UserForm*

A UserForm is the only module that can be viewed from the IDE in two different ways:

- Graphically, by choosing View ➜ Object to open up the UserForm window (see Figure 1.2).
- With code, by choosing View ➜ Code to open up the Code window as shown here:

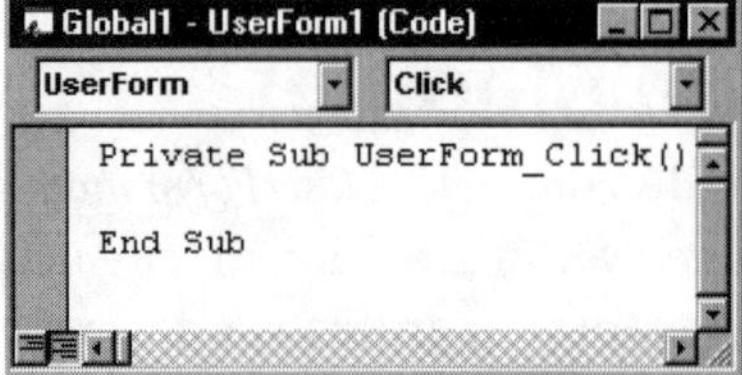

Opening the Code window displays the *event procedure* that will run if the UserForm is clicked. There are many events to choose from, but double-clicking any control automatically displays the primary event that you'll most likely want to respond to. You'll see how to access the other events later in this chapter, in the section "Coding Event Procedures."

Puttering Around in the Toolbox

VBA provides a set of common controls in a Toolbox window (see Figure 1.3). You can simply drag and drop individual controls onto a UserForm to develop GUI features for your application.

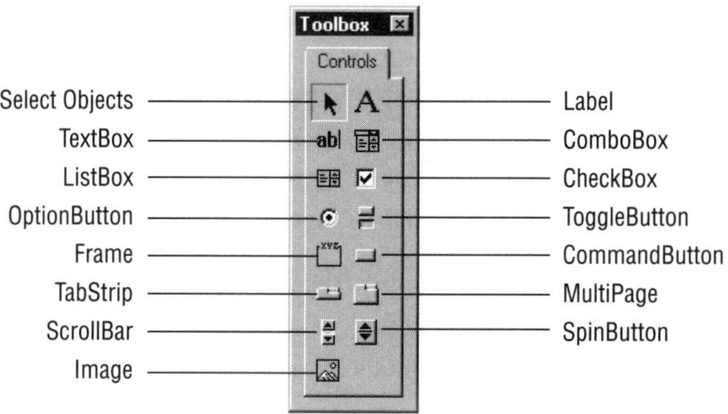

Figure 1.3 *Controls in the standard Toolbox*

If the Toolbox isn't on display, select the Toolbox command from the View menu or click the Toolbox icon (shown in the margin) at the end of the Standard toolbar. Both of these actions will be available for selection only when a UserForm has been added to a project and it is being viewed in its graphical form rather than as a Code window. To view a UserForm graphically, simply choose View ➜ Object.

These controls are all available for you to drag and drop onto your UserForm, making AutoCAD VBA a powerful visual programming system that's extremely efficient at quickly developing the GUI for a project—you can virtually design your whole GUI using only the mouse!

You will recognize most of the controls in the Toolbox because you have already experienced using them in other applications. Following are brief descriptions of what each control does:

Select Objects The Select Objects control is used to resize and move a control after it has been drawn on a UserForm. If you've double-clicked another control to insert multiple instances of it on the UserForm without returning to the Toolbox, you can click the Select Objects control to stop.

Label The Label control displays text that you've assigned to its Caption property at design time or in code. A Label control is often used to display information or indicate to a user what data should be entered into a TextBox control. The text displayed by the Label control is strictly read-only and cannot be changed by the user during run time.

TextBox The TextBox control allows users to input textual information during run time. It is common practice to assign the empty string ("") to this control's Text property to initialize it or to clear out any data that's no longer required.

ComboBox The ComboBox control combines the functionality of the TextBox control with that of the ListBox control to provide the user with the option of entering text into the TextBox, or clicking the down-arrow button and selecting an item from a drop-down list. When an item is selected from the list, it is automatically displayed in the text box at the top of the ComboBox. You can set the Style property of this control in order to restrict the user to selecting an item from the ListBox. This eliminates the need to test whether the user has entered a valid value.

ListBox The ListBox control enables the user to select one or more items from a list. If there are too many items to be displayed at once, a scroll bar will automatically appear. Even so, this control generally takes up more space than a ComboBox control, which needs only the same amount of space on the UserForm as a TextBox control.

CheckBox The CheckBox control enables the user to "check" (select) zero or more boxes from a group of CheckBoxes. This control is often used to indicate whether items are true or false, or to answer yes or no to questions. CheckBoxes are similar in function to OptionButtons, except that they allow more than one item to be selected at the same time.

OptionButton OptionButton controls are used in groups of options to allow selection of one option from the group. When only one group of OptionButtons is required, it can be placed directly onto the UserForm. When there is more than one group, Frame controls (described just below) are used to separate groups, to enable one OptionButton per group to be selected. You determine the OptionButton that will be the default selection. If the user selects another OptionButton from the same group, the old one is automatically deselected.

ToggleButton The ToggleButton control toggles between on or off, true or false, and yes or no. When clicked, its appearance changes to match its value; it toggles between a raised button appearance (off) to a pushed-in appearance (on). The Picture property of this control allows you to display a selection of options to the user in a graphical way.

Frame The Frame control allows a UserForm to be divided into areas where you can group other controls, such as OptionButtons and CheckBoxes. The Frame control and the controls inside it then behave collectively as a single entity. When you move the Frame, all the controls inside it move, too; when you disable the Frame, all its controls become disabled. Frames are typically used to create groups of OptionButtons on a UserForm, so that an option from each group can be selected rather than just a single option.

CommandButton The CommandButton control is used when you want something to happen as soon as the button is clicked. It is often used in dialog boxes with the caption "OK" for users to click when they've finished reading the message displayed to them. This control is useful for running macros by calling the macro in response to the control being clicked.

TabStrip The TabStrip control contains several pages, each displaying an identical set of controls. Adding a control to any page of the TabStrip control makes it appear on all pages. This control is used to enable viewing of several sets of data containing the same kind of information, one set per page. You provide the code to update the information in the controls according to the tab selected by the user. For example, you could display the name, address, and telephone number of your clients, one client per page.

MultiPage The MultiPage control is similar to the TabStrip control in that it has several pages that can be accessed by clicking their tabs. Each page from the MultiPage control has its own individual set of controls to enable the display of different kinds of information on each page, although the information would typically be related in some way. For example, you could display the name and address of a client on the first page, and information about the client's orders on other pages. In such a scheme, you would need to create a MultiPage control for each client.

ScrollBar The ScrollBar control allows you to place a scroll bar on a UserForm. The scroll bar can be either vertical or horizontal depending on its width and height. This control provides scrolling for controls that do not have scroll bars added automatically. Appropriate values are set for the control's Min and Max properties to define the limits for the Value property of the ScrollBar. The control's Value property will be set to a value dependent on the position of the slider bar in relation to each end of the scroll bar.

SpinButton The SpinButton control functions similarly to a ScrollBar control but doesn't have a slider bar. Up- or down-arrow buttons are displayed for the user to click in order to increment or decrement the number assigned to the control's Value property. The Value is typically displayed in another control, such as a TextBox or a Label.

Image The Image control is used to display graphics stored in the major graphical formats, such as bitmaps (`.bmp`), GIFs (`.gif`), JPEGs (`.jpg`), metafiles (`.wmf`), and icons (`.ico`). The image can be cropped, sized, or zoomed as required to fit the control's size. Image controls can be used as fancy command buttons or as toolbar buttons and can even display simple animations.

You can place as many instances of each control as you like onto the same UserForm. Visual Basic gives each instance a default name based on the name of the class it belongs to, appended to a sequential number—this enables each object to be uniquely identified. Visual Basic also assigns the properties of the control's position and dimensions on the UserForm based on where you've placed it and what size you've made it. All other properties are assigned a default setting.

Placing a Toolbox Control in a UserForm

This tutorial shows you how to drag and drop a TextBox control from the Toolbox onto a UserForm. The same technique is used to place any of the other controls onto a UserForm.

1. Click the TextBox icon (shown here) in the Toolbox and, without pressing the mouse button, move the mouse cursor over the UserForm.

   After you click the TextBox icon, the Toolbar button changes its appearance to look pressed in, as shown here:

   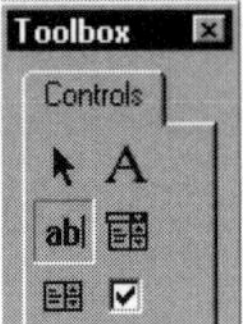

   And the mouse cursor changes, too, as it moves over the boundary of the UserForm. It becomes a cross alongside the TextBox control's icon.

2. Move the mouse cursor to the position where you want one of the corners of your text box to be, and press the left mouse button. While holding the mouse button down, move the cursor around and watch a rectangle with dashed lines follow the cursor, with one corner anchored at the position you've just selected. This rectangle indicates the size and position for the new text box that will be created when you release the mouse button.

   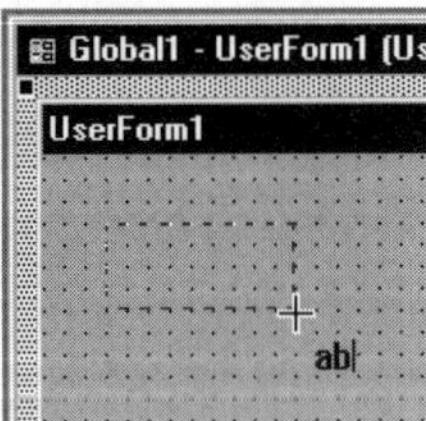

3. Still holding down the mouse button, move the cursor to the corner diagonal to the initial (anchored) one and release the mouse button. The new text box object replaces the dashed rectangle on the screen:

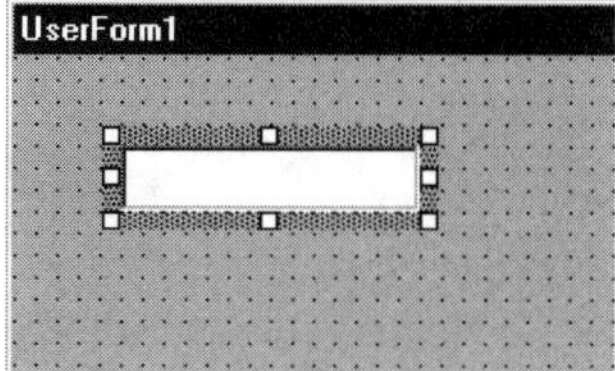

This becomes the new active control, as indicated by the handles and thick border that now appear around the rectangle. These can be used to make further adjustments to the size and position of the text box.

Changing the Dimensions and Position of a Toolbox Control

Click any control on a UserForm to make it the active control. Once active, the control is enclosed by a thick border with eight handles placed around it. You can click and drag these handles to change the position and dimensions of the control, as follows:

- If you move the cursor directly over the thick border but not on top of a handle, the cursor changes to a cross with two double-headed arrows (shown here) to allow you to reposition the whole control without changing its size. Simply click and hold down the mouse button and drag the control to its new position.

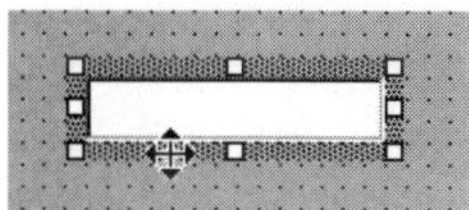

- If you move the cursor directly over any handle, the cursor changes to a double-headed arrow (shown here). This allows you to drag and drop the handle to change the size of the control while maintaining its position.

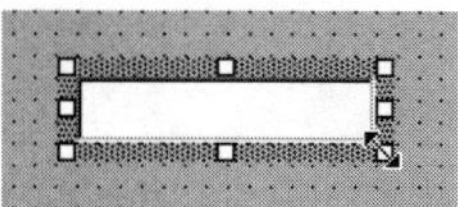

Now that you have an understanding of how to place components on your GUI, it's time to use these skills to develop your first simple application—I'm sure you're revved up ready to go.

Developing Your First Application

For your first application, we'll work with the Metric-Imperial Converter application, which converts metric measurements to imperial, and vice versa. This application uses two text boxes as shown in Figure 1.4. The interface allows the user to enter imperial measurements in yards into the first text box, then converts the measurement to metric and displays the results in the second text box. Alternatively, the user can enter metric measurements in meters into the second text box, and the application converts the value to imperial and displays it in the first text box.

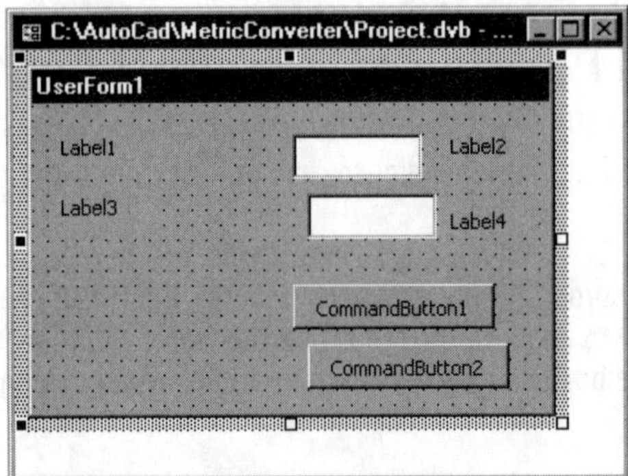

Figure 1.4 *GUI for the Metric-Imperial Converter application before any properties have been updated*

One command button is needed for the user to click in order to tell the application that the measurement has been entered. The second command button allows the user to stop the application.

Creating the GUI

Creating the GUI for the Metric-Imperial Converter application can be achieved using a single UserForm. Exercise 1.1 takes you through the steps required.

Exercise 1.1: Metric-Imperial Converter Application

1. Choose Tools → Macro → Visual Basic Editor to open the IDE.
2. Choose Insert → UserForm to create a UserForm. The graphical representation of the UserForm is displayed, along with the Toolbox.
3. Drag and drop a TextBox control from the Toolbox onto the UserForm and place it near the top right. In Figure 1.4, the two empty boxes are TextBox controls.

   The Name property of this text box is assigned as TextBox1 by default. The Name property of a control is the first item listed in the control's Properties window, which you'll see in the upcoming section "Setting Captions in the Properties Window." Default names all start with the type of control followed by a number to denote its place in the sequence of controls of the same type. So the next text box you add will be named TextBox2.
4. Drag and drop a Label control (shown here) and place it to the left of the TextBox control.

   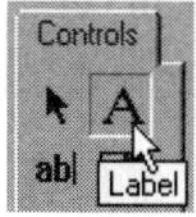

   The Name property of this Label control is Label1 by default, which is also the initial value assigned to its Caption property. The Label1 control is used to label the TextBox so that the user knows what its contents represent and can enter appropriate values.
5. Drag and drop a second label and position it to the right of the TextBox control. The Name property of this Label control is Label2 by default.
6. Drag and drop a second text box with two accompanying labels, and place them immediately below the first text box and labels. The default Name properties of these controls are TextBox2, Label3, and Label4.
7. Drag and drop a command button (shown here) from the Toolbox onto the UserForm, placing it below the second text box. The default Name and Caption properties of this command button are both CommandButton1.

8. Drag and drop a second command button and place it directly below the first. The Name and Caption properties of this command button are—you guessed it—CommandButton2.

9. Now that all the controls required by the GUI have been added to the UserForm, adjust the UserForm's dimensions by dragging and dropping its borders until it is a snug fit for all the controls you've placed inside it. The layout of controls should look similar to the one shown earlier in Figure 1.4.

How Default Settings Are Initiated

A lot of the default object settings, such as the color of the title bar and background, are retrieved from the *display scheme* set in the Microsoft Windows environment of the PC on which the application is running. In the examples throughout this book, the Windows Standard display scheme is used. If your PC is set to a different scheme, your GUI will have a similar appearance to some of the other Windows applications that run on your PC. Some default settings such as those specifying position and dimensions are determined as you drag and drop controls onto UserForms.

You can find out the display scheme setting for your PC by clicking the Display icon in Control Panel and selecting the Appearance tab in the Display Properties dialog box—the current setting is displayed in the Scheme list box, as shown here:

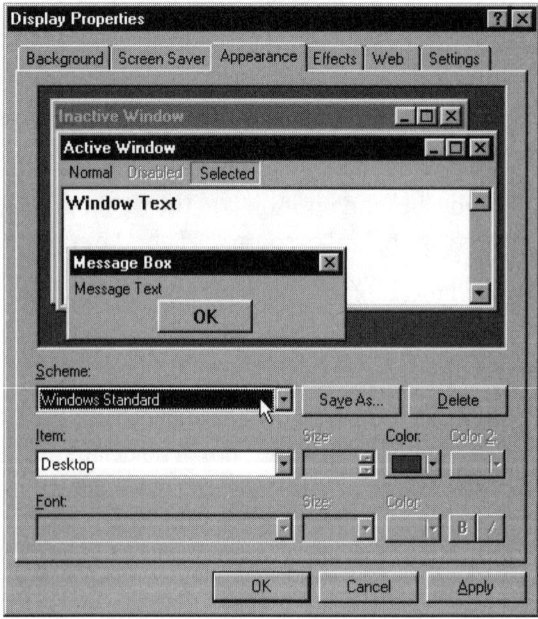

Setting Captions in the Properties Window

The following tutorial shows you how to set the Caption property of UserForm1 in the Metric-Imperial Converter application:

1. If the Properties window is not already on display, choose View ➜ Properties Window.
2. The Properties window appears, with property names listed in the left column and their settings listed in the right column. Select the appropriate tab to list the properties in this window alphabetically, as shown in Figure 1.5, or categorically, as shown in Figure 1.6. The list of properties belongs to the object named in the list box at the top (the active object), which is followed by the class the object belongs to.

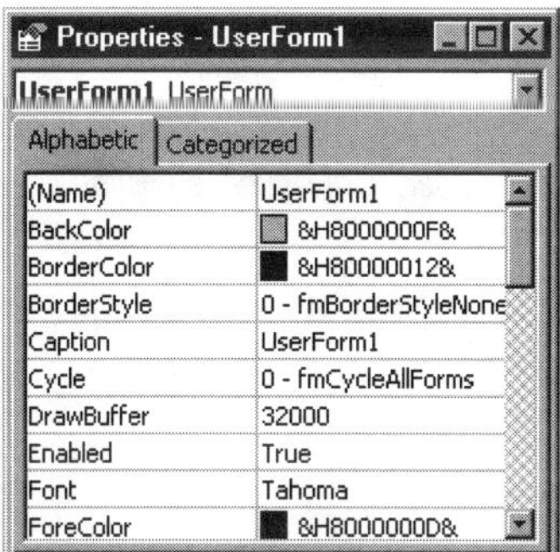

Figure 1.5 *Properties window Alphabetic tab*

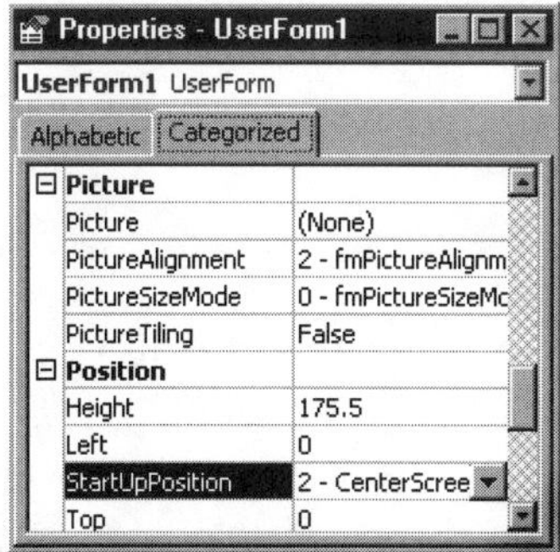

Figure 1.6 *Properties window Categorized tab*

3. If the object named at the top of the Properties window is not already UserForm1, click the down-arrow button at the right end of the Object box and select UserForm1 from the drop-down list.

   This drop-down list contains all the objects associated with the active UserForm. When UserForm1 is selected, all the properties listed in the window now belong to UserForm1. The graphical representation of UserForm1 becomes the active object and appears with a thick border and eight sizing handles.

4. Scroll the list of properties until the Caption property becomes visible in the left column and select it by double-clicking it. Both the Caption property and the setting "UserForm1" are highlighted, and the insertion point (I-beam mouse pointer) blinks at the end of the highlighted text in the settings column on the right.

5. Type **Metric-Imperial Converter**. This replaces the highlighted setting for the Caption property, and the text in the title bar of UserForm1 is updated as you enter each keystroke.

Although the Name and Caption properties start off with the same default setting, they are still two distinct properties, so the Name property still remains set to UserForm1 even after you change the Caption.

6. Repeat steps 2 through 5 to change the Caption properties of the labels and command buttons to those shown in Table 1.1.

Table 1.1 Controls and Their Caption Properties

CONTROL	CAPTION
Label1	Imperial Units
Label2	Yards
Label3	Metric Units
Label4	Meters
CommandButton1	Convert
CommandButton2	Close

The Properties window can be opened by selecting any graphical object and choosing View → Properties Window, or by right-clicking and selecting Properties from the shortcut menu, or by pressing the F4 function key.

The VBA Code Window

The *Code window* is where you enter the code that will interact with the user or manipulate AutoCAD objects. When you start a new AutoCAD project, a *drawing object* is automatically created and made the active document. You can refer to this object in code by its Name property, ThisDrawing. When you open the IDE and look in the Project Explorer window, the ThisDrawing object will be the only object listed (shown previously in Figure 1.1).

Every object listed in the Project Explorer window has its own Code window. One way to open the Code window for a particular object is to double-click it from the Project Explorer window. Here is the Code window for ThisDrawing:

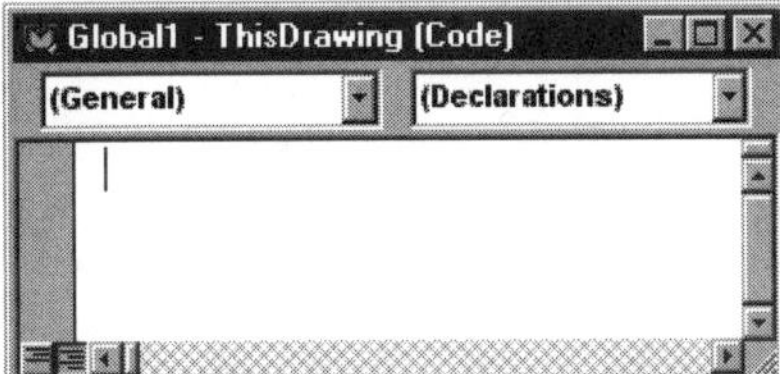

Displaying the Code Window

When double-clicked in the Project Explorer window, all the modules except UserForms will immediately display the Code window. When a UserForm is double-clicked, its graphical representation is displayed in the UserForm window. You must then double-click anywhere inside this UserForm window to display its Code window.

Every Code window has a drop-down list box of objects on the left, and a drop-down list box of procedures on the right. The Object list contains all the objects and controls attached to that module. In the example shown here, all the controls placed on UserForm1 are displayed.

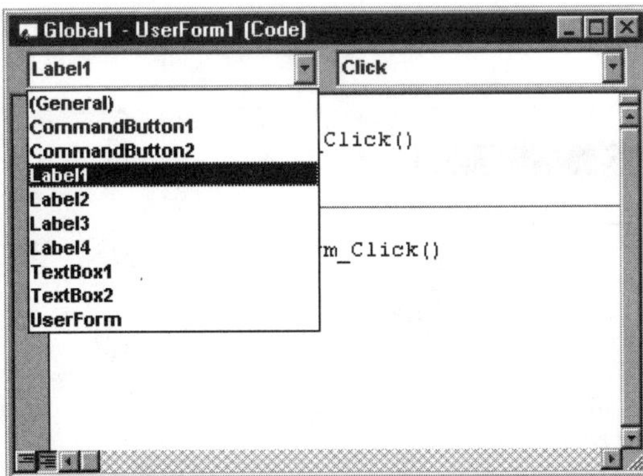

You can tell which UserForm the Code window belongs to by looking at the Caption on the title bar. Notice in the preceding example that there's an object named UserForm in the drop-down list. Because a UserForm has its own Code window, there is no need to append a distinguishing number after UserForm when you're referring to it in code in its own Code window. The Procedure list box on the right contains a list of all the procedures (including event procedures) associated with the object named in the Object box, as shown here:

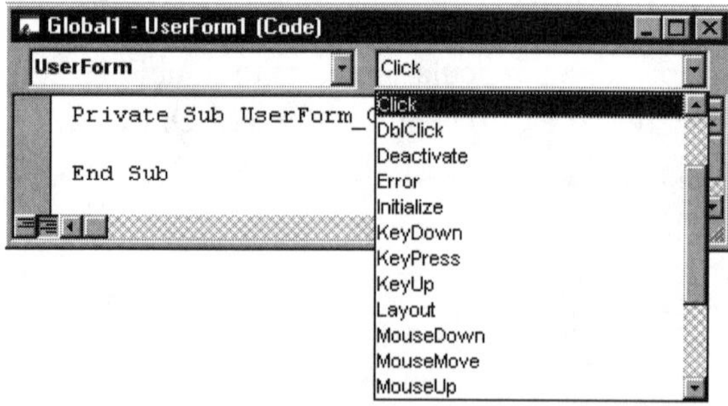

Coding Event Procedures

The following tutorial shows how to write the code to stop an application in response to the user's clicking the Close button:

1. If the Code window is displayed, choose View ➜ Object to display the graphical representation of UserForm1. Double-click CommandButton2. The Code window appears, containing the skeleton code for the CommandButton2_Click event procedure, with the I-beam cursor blinking in the blank line.
2. As shown in Figure 1.7, type

```
Unload Me
```

Figure 1.7 *The Code Window showing the CommandButton2_Click event procedure*

Now you're ready to start coding the response you want given to the user who's entering data into one of the text boxes. When the Metric-Imperial Converter application is run for the first time, both text boxes will be empty. The user enters a measurement into one text box and clicks CommandButton1 to convert the measurement and display the result in the other text box. When CommandButton1 is clicked, the application checks which text box contains the measurement so that it knows which conversion is required. If the user requires another, subsequent conversion and enters another measurement into a text box, the application must clear the other text box of data so that the correct conversion is used. The following steps show you how these actions are coded:

1. Open the Code window and select TextBox1 from the Object list.
2. Select KeyDown from the Procedure list, as shown in Figure 1.8.

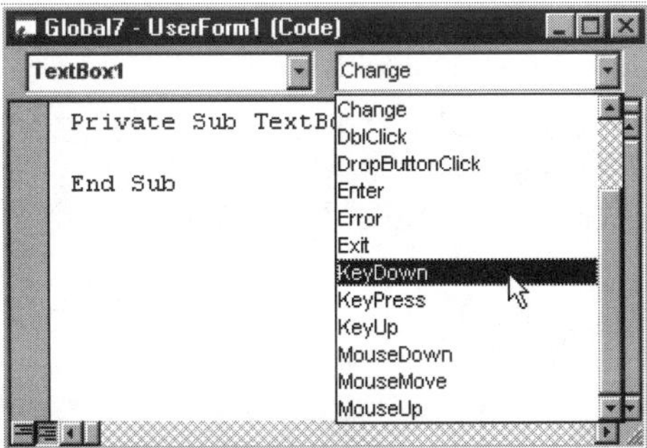

Figure 1.8 *Drop-down list of procedures (events) available for the TextBox class of object*

3. In the skeleton `TextBox1_KeyDown` event procedure, where the Entry cursor is blinking, type

```
TextBox2.Text = ""
```

4. Select TextBox2 from the Object list, and select KeyDown from the Procedure list.
5. In the skeleton `TextBox2_KeyDown` event procedure, type

```
TextBox1.Text = ""
```

6. Select CommandButton1 from the Object list, and the skeleton (first and last lines) of its Click event procedure will appear.

7. Type the following code inside the skeleton:

```
If TextBox1.Text = "" Then
    TextBox1.Text = TextBox2.Text * 1.0936
Else
    TextBox2.Text = TextBox1.Text * 0.9144
End If
```

That's all the coding necessary for this conversion application! Listing 1.1 provides a numbered listing of all the code, followed by an Analysis section that describes what each statement actually does. This application is available for use on the CD-ROM as Listing 1.1. You'll need to follow the instructions in the "Loading VBA Project Files" section in Chapter 2.

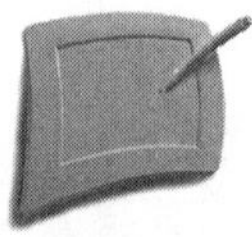

In the listings throughout the book, the numbers preceding each line of code are not part of the actual code. They are provided to help you follow the discussions in the Analysis sections.

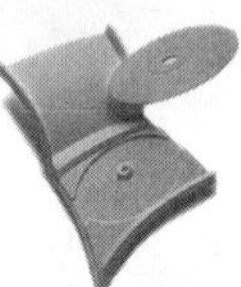

LISTING 1.1: METRIC-IMPERIAL CONVERSION MACRO

```
Private Sub CommandButton1_Click()
If TextBox1.Text = "" Then
    TextBox1.Text = TextBox2.Text * 1.0936
Else
    TextBox2.Text = TextBox1.Text * 0.9144
End If
End Sub
Private Sub CommandButton2_Click()
End
End Sub
Private Sub TextBox1_KeyDown(↵
   ByVal KeyCode As MSForms.ReturnInteger, ↵
   ByVal Shift As Integer)
TextBox2.Text = ""
End Sub
Private Sub TextBox2_KeyDown(↵
   ByVal KeyCode As MSForms.ReturnInteger, ↵
   ByVal Shift As Integer)
TextBox1.Text = ""
End Sub
```

ANALYSIS

You'll find the code shown in Listing 1.1 quite straightforward. This Analysis section has been included to take you through it line by line.

- Line 1 is the opening statement and declares the `CommandButton1_Click` event procedure. The code in this event procedure will be executed when the user clicks the Convert command button. This statement, along with the `End Sub` statement in Line 7, is provided as a skeleton procedure by the IDE.
- Line 2 checks to see if the `Text` property of `TextBox1` is empty, meaning that the user has entered meters into `TextBox2`; if so, the program executes the statement at Line 3. If `TextBox1` isn't empty, it contains yards, and the statement in Line 5 is executed. The section "Using Conditions to Control Code Execution" in Chapter 4 gives more information on `If` statements.
- Line 3 converts the meters entered into `TextBox2` to yards and assigns the results to the `Text` property of `TextBox1`. The value of the `Text` property is displayed in the text box.

`If` conditions and `Then`...`Else`...`End If`... conditional structures can be thought of as two separate parts—the `If` code block and the `Else` code block.

- Line 4 starts the `Else` part of the `If` statement. Execution jumps to this point if the condition in the `If` statement (Line 2) is False. Line 4 also serves as an end marker for the statements in the `If` code block when the condition is True, in which case execution jumps to the `End If` statement at Line 6.
- Line 5 converts the yards entered into `TextBox1` into meters and displays the results in `TextBox2`.
- Line 6 signifies the end of the `If` statement. Execution jumps to this point from the `Else` statement (Line 4) if the condition in Line 2 is True.
- Line 7 is the `End Sub` statement, which marks the end of the `CommandButton1_Click` event procedure.
- Line 8 is a blank line inserted to make it easier to see where one event procedure ends and another starts.
- Line 9 starts the `CommandButton2_Click` event procedure. This is the command button that has its Caption property set to Close (see step 6 of "Setting Captions in the Properties Window").

- Line 10 contains the End statement that stops executing your application by closing any open files and freeing any memory used by your application during run time.
- Line 13 is the opening statement for the TextBox1_KeyDown event procedure. Unlike the Click event procedures found in lines 1 and 9, the KeyDown event procedure gets passed the integer value representing the ASCII code for the character just entered. This is useful if you want to validate the character input, which is handled in the section "Validating Input" in Chapter 9.
- Line 14 assigns an empty string to the Text property of TextBox2. The empty string is denoted by two double quote characters (""). If a new conversion is starting, it doesn't make sense to have any values from the last conversion still displayed in the other text box.
- Line 18 clears the Text property of TextBox1 inside the TextBox2_KeyDown event procedure.

Running Your Application

To run your Metric-Imperial Converter application:

1. Ensure that UserForm1's window is open and selected.
2. Choose the Run ➜ Sub/UserForm menu command.
3. Test that your application is working by entering a value into one of the text boxes and clicking the Convert button. Verify that the results are what you expect. Repeat this verification for the other text box.
4. You may want to line up the controls on your UserForm to improve its appearance, as in Figure 1.9.

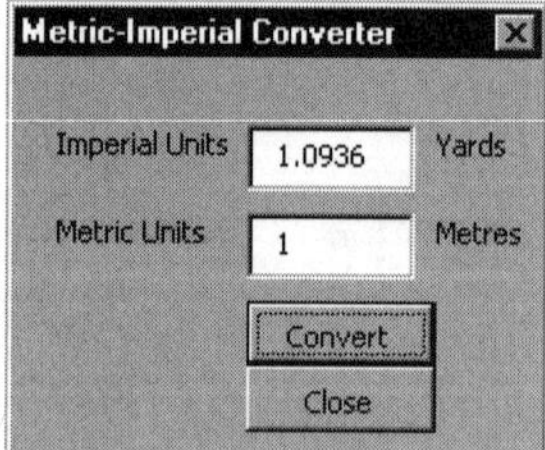

***Figure 1.9** The finished version of the Metric-Imperial Converter application's GUI with the captions set*

Saving Your Application

The IDE has one Save command on the File menu. The exact wording of this command depends on whether you have previously saved your project. Figure 1.10 shows the Save option on the File menu *before* the project has been saved to a file. Figure 1.11 shows how it appears afterward—with the full pathname of the project file.

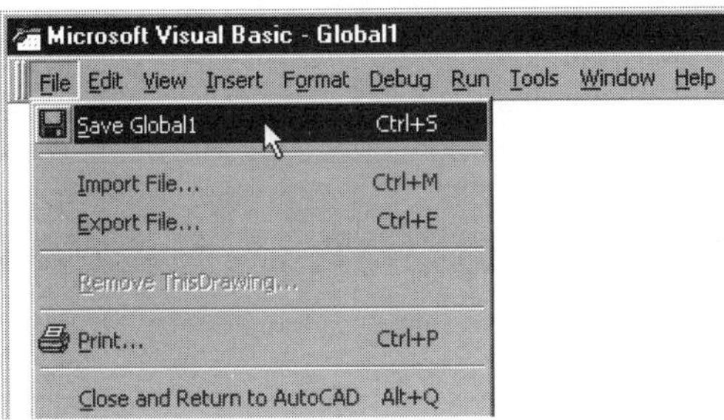

Figure 1.10 *The File menu option for saving a VBA project that has never before been saved*

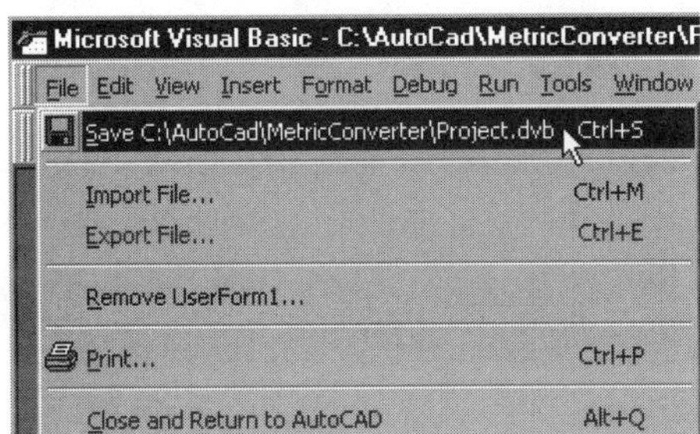

Figure 1.11 *The File menu option for saving a VBA project that's been saved previously*

To save your Metric-Imperial Converter project for the first time:

1. Choose File ➜ Save Global1. The Save As dialog box shown in Figure 1.12 appears. The controls in this dialog box will be familiar to you; they are much the same as those found in the Save As dialog boxes of other applications, including AutoCAD itself.

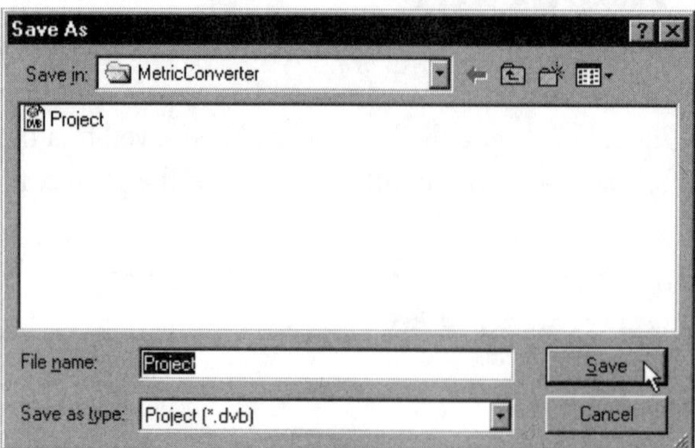

Figure 1.12 *The Save As dialog box, ready to save your project to the .DVB file of your choice*

2. Use the controls to create a new directory and click Save. Everything associated with the current Project will be saved in a single file with the extension `.dvb`.

3. Open the File menu. The Save command will now be followed by the full path of the .DVB file in which you've just saved your project.

Returning to AutoCAD

There are two menu commands that you can use to display the AutoCAD window, but they serve different purposes:

- Choose File ➜ Close and Return to AutoCAD, or use the shortcut Alt+Q. This command unloads the IDE completely before returning to AutoCAD.
- Click the View AutoCAD button.

  at the left of the Toolbar. This hides but does not close the IDE window and makes it accessible from the Taskbar. As you know from other Windows applications, you can much more quickly display a window that's already open by clicking its icon on the Taskbar rather than loading it in again from scratch.

Summary

After working through this chapter, you'll know how to

- Develop a simple VBA application.
- Open the VBA IDE.
- Drag and drop controls from the Toolbox onto a UserForm.
- Assign new values to Caption properties in the Properties window.
- Code event procedures to respond to the user's actions.
- Run your application.
- Save your application.
- Return to the AutoCAD window from the IDE.

Creating VBA Macros

AUTOCAD VBA

Chapter 2

In this chapter, you'll learn about macros. You'll see how to use them as stand-alone programs for completing simple tasks, as well as for running applications. You'll also gain experience using the editing features of the IDE to help you enter code and to do the typing of code elements for you.

This chapter covers the following topics:

- What is a macro?
- Creating a macro to add text to a drawing
- Using the VBA IDE's editing features to enter code
- Using VBA's Date and Time functions
- Loading VBA project files
- Creating a macro to start an application

What Is a Macro?

A *macro* is a block of code statements that perform a particular task. The task might be as simple as displaying a dialog box to remind users to update something on their drawing, or it might be starting up a VBA application. Macros are normally quite short and contain only a few lines of code.

Macros are great relief for those boring repetitive jobs we all have to do from time to time. By creating macros to do these jobs for you, you are left with time free to concentrate on the creative work that's more enjoyable. So macros will not only improve your workflow but also add to your job satisfaction!

Only macros placed inside the ThisDrawing object or a standard module are included in the list of macros available from the AutoCAD window. (Remember, a *module* is just a container for VBA code.) The next two sections describe these two important VBA elements and explain when to use one or the other for your macros.

ThisDrawing Object

The *ThisDrawing object* contains all the property settings to control the attributes for the active drawing, as well as all the methods and procedures to manipulate the active drawing. For example, the following statement sets the height of the active drawing to 12 units:

```
ThisDrawing.Height = 12
```

And this statement saves the changes to the active drawing:

```
ThisDrawing.Save
```

The drawing object has its own Code window in the IDE, with two items in the Object list—General and AcadDocument (see Figure 2.1).

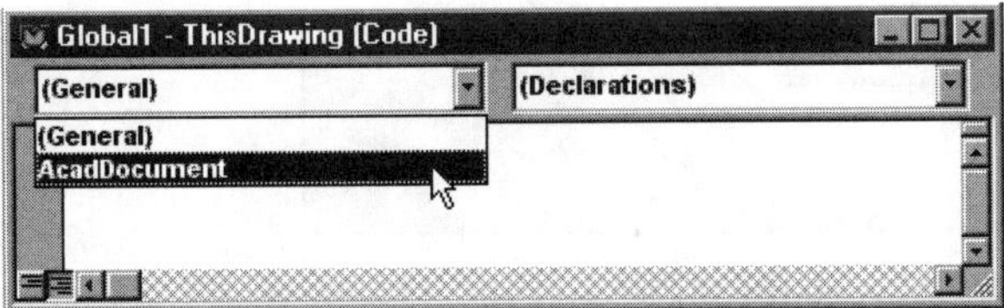

Figure 2.1 *Code window for the ThisDrawing object*

Macros that directly refer to specific objects in a one-off drawing should be placed in the ThisDrawing object, because these macros are dependent on the specific drawing objects' being available at run time.

Standard Modules

A *standard module* is where you put macros that aren't associated with any particular UserForm or with the drawing document. Then you can reuse the code from the standard module by including it in various other applications. This is also a good place to put macros that are called from several other modules within the same application, because this avoids any duplication of code.

To insert a standard module into your project from the IDE, you can choose Insert ➜ Module. You can also insert a standard module from the AutoCAD window by following these steps:

1. Choose Tools ➜ Macro ➜ Macros. Figure 2.2 shows the Macros dialog box.

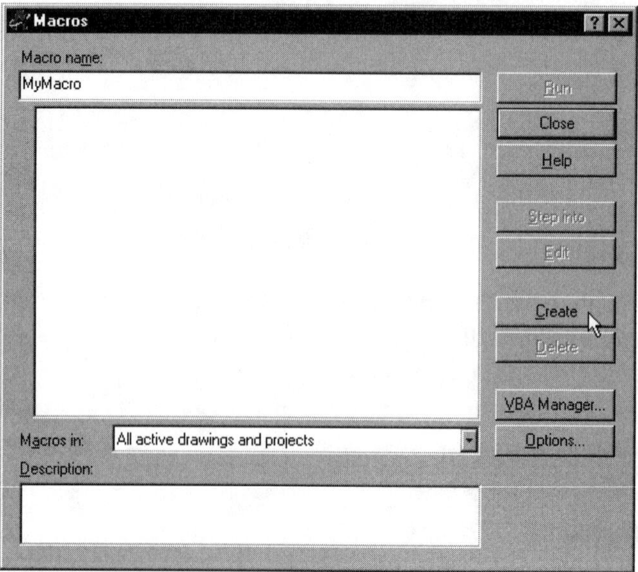

Figure 2.2 *Macros dialog box in AutoCAD*

2. Type the name of your macro into the Macro Name text box. The Create button becomes available for selection.
3. Click the Create button. The Select Project dialog box appears, with the macro's name displayed in the "Select..." instruction at the top of the dialog box. In the list of projects, `Drawing1.dwg` is the only item that appears:

4. Select `Drawing1.dwg` and click OK.

   A standard module is created and given the name Module1. The IDE opens, displaying Module1's Code window as shown in Figure 2.3. The macro appears in the Code window with the first and last lines already in place.

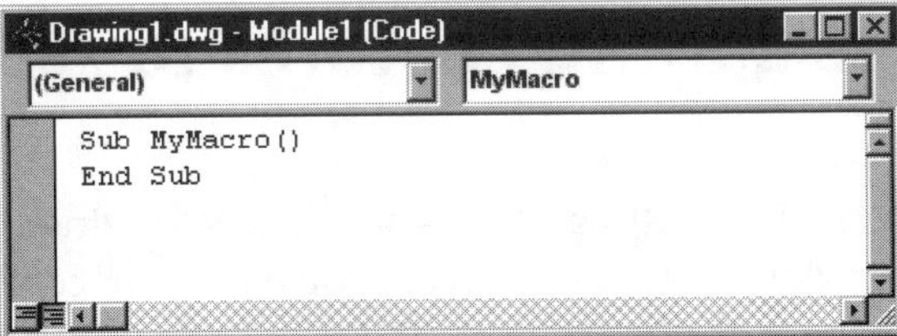

Figure 2.3 *Code window for Module1*

The Project Explorer now contains Module1 in its Modules list for the `Drawing1.dwg` project, and ThisDrawing in its AutoCAD Objects list, as shown here:

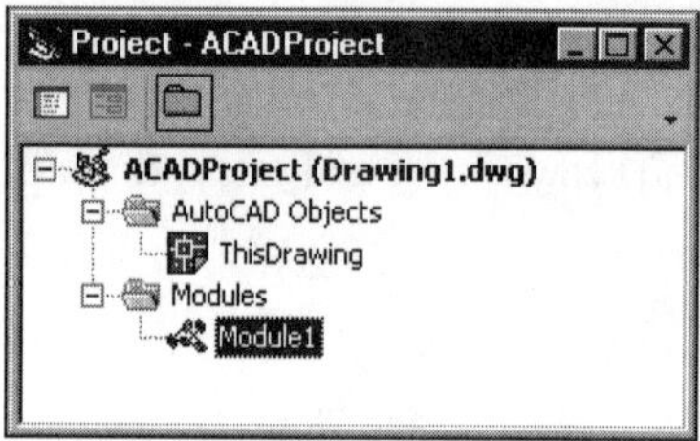

These lists can be expanded and contracted by clicking the little + and – symbols, just as you do files in Windows Explorer.

Creating a Macro to Add Text to a Drawing

One of the things you do most frequently when you create a drawing is to add some text for a title, a label, your name, or simply the date and time the drawing was created. You probably routinely add the same kind of information to every drawing you create, so it would be nice to create a simple macro that does this for you. Let's step through the code for such a macro, and see how to customize it to suit your specific needs.

The code for a macro is entered into a Code window in the IDE, which has some indispensable editing features that you'll find extremely user-friendly, such as the Auto List Members and the Complete Word features. You'll learn how to access and make full use of these features as you enter your macro's code.

Using the IDE's Editing Features to Enter Code

As you work through the steps of creating a macro to add text to a drawing, you'll get a lot of help from the drop-down lists that appear as you enter your code. These lists not only shorten your typing tasks, but they also, and more importantly, provide you with names and keywords appropriate to what you are typing. That means you don't have to memorize lots of programming details, and you're less dependent on the online Help facility.

Listing 2.1 later in this chapter gives the complete macro that you'll create here step by step. The Analysis section after the listing describes what each line of the code actually does. Exercise 2.1 starts at the very beginning and takes you through all the steps required in coding your DrawText macro, making full use of the editing features as you go.

EXERCISE 2.1: CREATING THE DRAWTEXT MACRO

1. Start AutoCAD and choose Tools ➜ Macro ➜ Visual Basic Editor. The VBA IDE appears, with one AutoCAD object named ThisDrawing listed in the Project Explorer window. If the Project Explorer window is not displayed, choose View ➜ Project Explorer to make it appear.
2. Double-click ThisDrawing. The Code window shown earlier in Figure 2.1 will open, with the Insertion cursor blinking and ready for you to start entering your code.
3. In the Code window, enter the text **`Sub DrawText`** and press Enter. The IDE appends a pair of parentheses to `DrawText` and adds an empty line followed by the `End Sub` statement, as shown here:

   `Sub` and `End Sub` are colored according to your foreground setting for keyword text. (You'll see how to change this color in the sidebar "Setting the Colors to Identify Keyword Text in the Code Window.") The Insertion cursor now blinks in the empty line to let you know that the IDE is waiting for you to enter code.
4. In the empty line, type the following, including the single quote (`'`) character at the beginning:

   ```
   'inserts the string "Hello" into the drawing area
   ```

   The single quote denotes that the line is a comment.
5. Press Enter. The comment text changes into the color specified as the foreground color for comment text.

Comments start with a single quote (') character. These lines are useful for jogging your memory if you ever need to revisit your code, or for clarification for someone else who is giving your code an update. Consider comments your opportunity to document what you've done.

Setting the Colors to Identify Keyword Text in the Code Window

The default color for keyword text in the IDE Code window is blue, but that can be changed to any color you want. Follow these steps:

1. Choose Tools → Options to open the Options dialog box (shown here) and select the Editor Format tab.

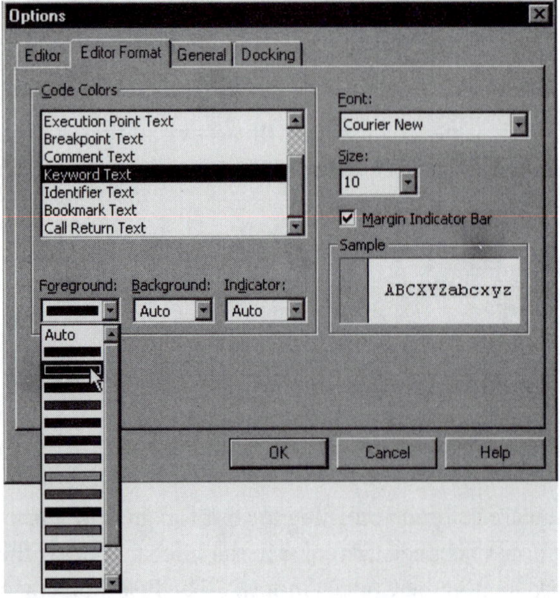

2. From the Code Colors list, select Keyword Text. The text in the Sample frame changes to the color specified in the Foreground color box. Select your desired color from the drop-down list, and the color of the sample text will be immediately updated.
3. Click OK to finish and return to the Code window.

6. Next, type the following statement. Be sure to capitalize the T and P in `TextPosition`, and to end the line with a space.

```
dim TextPosition(0 To 2) as
```

This statement is how you *declare* an array named `TextPosition` that can contain three elements. This array passes the position where you want to place the text, to the AddText method (see step 17). The capitalization of the array name in this *declaration* is maintained throughout the code, wherever this name is used.

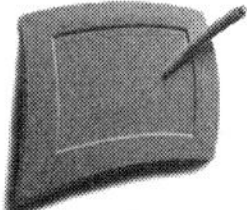

Capitalizing the first letter of individual words within a code element name not only enhances the readability of your code but also alerts you to any typing mistakes.

7. When you enter the space after the `as` in your `dim` statement, the Auto List Members feature of the editor displays the drop-down list of data types available for your array elements, as shown in Figure 2.4.

   If this drop-down list doesn't appear, you'll need to change the editor settings on your PC and try this step again (see "Changing the Editing Features Settings" sidebar later in this chapter if you need some help). Alternatively, you can leave the editor settings as they are and choose Edit ➜ Complete Word from the Code window; the same drop-down list will appear.

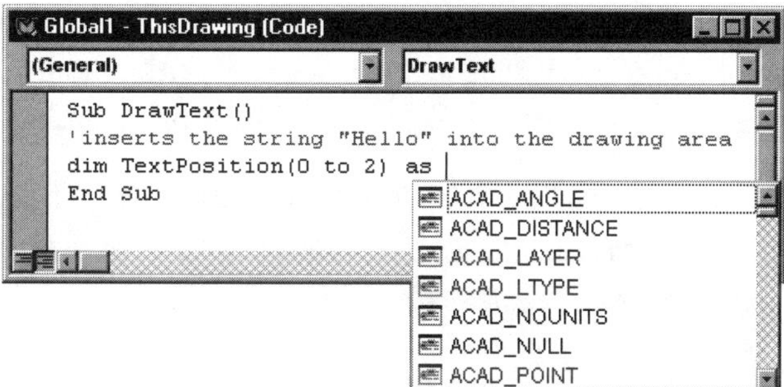

***Figure 2.4** The Auto List Members editor feature helps you complete the next part of a statement.*

8. Continue entering the statement by typing **do**. Watch the list of data types scroll as each character is entered.

9. When the `Double` entry is highlighted, press Enter. Your `do` is extended to `Double` in the Code window. The `dim` becomes `Dim`, and its color changes to the Keyword Text color setting, as do the `To` and `As Double`. The cursor jumps to the start of the next line, where the Insertion cursor blinks in readiness.

10. Type `t` and choose Edit ➜ Complete Word (or use the key-combination Ctrl+spacebar). A drop-down list of possible names, all beginning with *t*, is displayed as shown in Figure 2.5. The `TextPosition` array name you've just declared appears in this list.

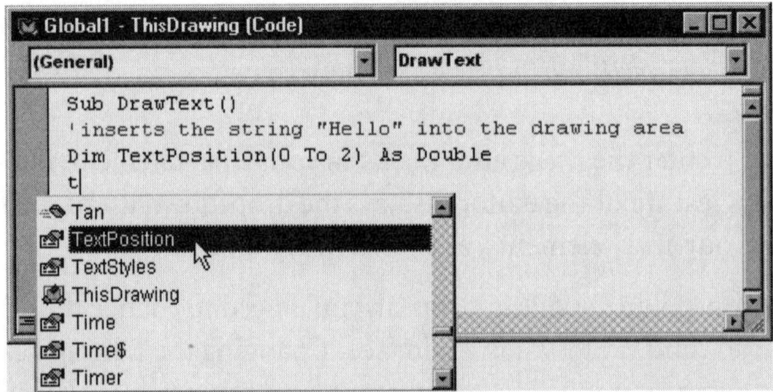

***Figure 2.5** Selecting TextPosition from the list of possible words displayed by the Complete Word editing feature*

11. Double-click `TextPosition` in the drop-down list. The **`t`** you entered is automatically expanded into **`TextPosition`**. As an alternative, you can enter **textposition** in its entirety; when you press Enter to move to the next line, the **t** and **p** will change to uppercase to match the array name declaration.

Use upper- and lowercase when entering names in declarations, but use lowercase when entering the rest of the code. The Visual Basic compiler will change the case of any names entered to match their declarations—that way you'll know if you've entered the name correctly.

12. Finish entering the line by typing **`(0)=1.5`** and press Enter. Notice that spaces are inserted at each side of the equals character (=). The insertion cursor is positioned at the start of the next line.

13. Repeat steps 8 through 11 to enter the next two lines of code. Complete each line by pressing Enter.

```
TextPosition(1) = 8.5
TextPosition(2) = 0.0
```

Notice that the `0.0` you entered in the second line automatically changes to `0#` when you press Enter, and the insertion cursor blinks patiently while it waits on the next line.

Figure 2.6 defines all the icons that represent the various objects, functions, properties, and methods provided by the Complete Word feature.

This Icon:	Represents a:
	Property
	Default Property
	Method
	Default Method
	Event
	Constant
	Module
	Class
	User Defined Type
	Global
	Library
	Project
	Built-in keywords and types
	Enum

Figure 2.6 *Meaning of icons next to items in the Complete Word list*

When you enter a decimal fraction with a zero after the decimal point, as in `0.0`*, the Visual Basic interpreter changes the zero into a hash character (#). This can be disconcerting to new users of Visual Basic. The # is a type-declaration character used to specify that the number is to be treated as a double precision floating-point number (Double type).*

14. In the Code window, type **`m`** and use the key-combination Ctrl+spacebar to display the drop-down list of all words starting with `m` that are possibilities for this statement.
15. Next, type **o.** `ModelSpace` appears highlighted in the drop-down list. (The ModelSpace collection of objects provides all the details needed to regenerate the Model Space. Later in this chapter, the Analysis section after Listing 2.1 describes the ModelSpace collection, so I'll skip the details for now.)

16. Type a period character (.). The `mo` is extended to `ModelSpace` followed by a period.

17. Finish the line of code by typing the following:

```
addtext "Hello",textposition,1.8
```

Press Enter. Spaces are inserted as needed and letters capitalized where appropriate. Your finished line of code becomes

```
ModelSpace.AddText "Hello", TextPosition, 1.8
```

That completes our text-insertion macro. Listing 2.1 shows the code in full, and the Analysis section that follows gives a line-by-line account of what is happening.

Listing 2.1: Text-Insertion Macro

```
1   Sub DrawText()
2       'inserts the string "Hello" into the drawing area
3       Dim TextPosition(0 To 2) As Double
4       TextPosition(0) = 1.5
5       TextPosition(1) = 8.5
6       TextPosition(2) = 0#
7       ModelSpace.AddText "Hello", TextPosition, 1.8
8   End Sub
```

Analysis

- Line 1 declares the name of the procedure as `DrawText`. This allows you to identify it later and run it as a macro (see next section).
- Line 2 contains comment text that is ignored by the Visual Basic interpreter; it is there simply to describe what the procedure does. Comment text always begins with a single quote character (`'`) so that it can be easily identified. Comments provide useful information to whoever is reading the code; I'm sure you'll find your own comments helpful if you ever need to update the code at a later date.
- Line 3 uses the `Dim` statement to declare an array containing three numbers as the double-precision floating-point type. These numbers will be used to specify the x-, y-, and z-coordinates to be used in positioning the text in 3D inside the Model Space window. Using an array has the advantage of being able to refer to all three numbers using the same name and an index value, as shown in lines 3 to 5.

- Lines 4 to 6 assign values to the three numbers in the `TextPosition` array. In line 6, the interpreter program automatically replaces the string `0.0` with `0#`, so don't think you've made a typo.
- Line 7 calls the `AddText` method of the ModelSpace collection to add a Text object to this collection, with the Text object's properties assigned to the values of the three arguments specified. The first argument is the text string to be displayed, followed by its position in the Model tab, and then by the height required for the text. If you want to experiment, try changing `"Hello"` into a string of your choice. (We'll go through an example together in the section "Updating Your DrawText Macro.")
- Line 8 ends the `DrawText` macro.

Now that you've gone to all the trouble of typing your code, it's always best to save your macro before you try to run it—just in case it causes AutoCAD to stop responding and you have to stop running it. You wouldn't want to start at the beginning again!

Saving a Macro

You already know that AutoCAD uses drawing files with the extension `.dwg` to save your drawings, and VBA uses project files with the extension `.dvb` to save all the components of your application from the IDE. These components include all your Visual Basic code, UserForms, and modules. Because the AutoCAD and VBA components are kept in separate files, you must remember to save both files individually. And when you come to open your project again, you must open them individually, too.

I'm sure you're already an expert at saving your drawings by choosing File ➜ Save in the AutoCAD window. To save your DrawText macro in a project file, choose File ➜ Save from the VBA IDE. Because you are saving your macro for the first time, `Global1` is appended to the Save menu command, as shown here:

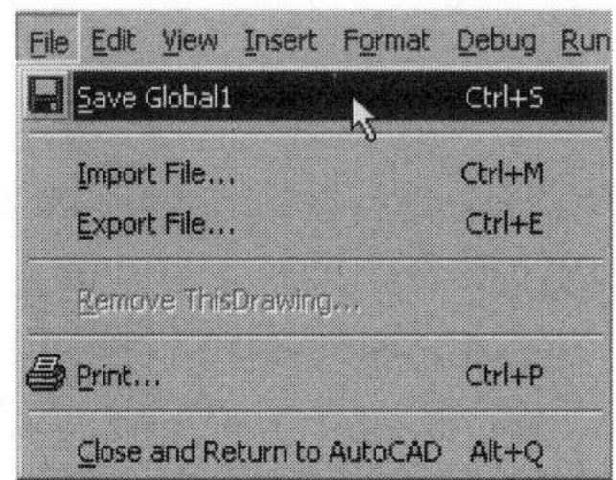

The Save As dialog box shown in Figure 2.7 appears next, with `Project` already in the File Name box, and `Project (*.dvb)` in the Save As Type box. You can maneuver your way around your directory system to the folder required, the same way you do in AutoCAD. You can also overtype the default filename `Project` with any name of your choice.

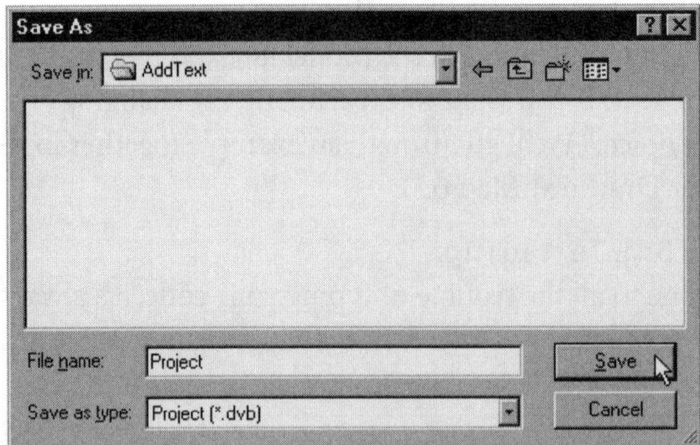

Figure 2.7 *Using the Save As dialog box to save your VBA macro*

In subsequent saves, the full pathname of the `Project.dvb` file will be appended to the Save menu command, as shown here:

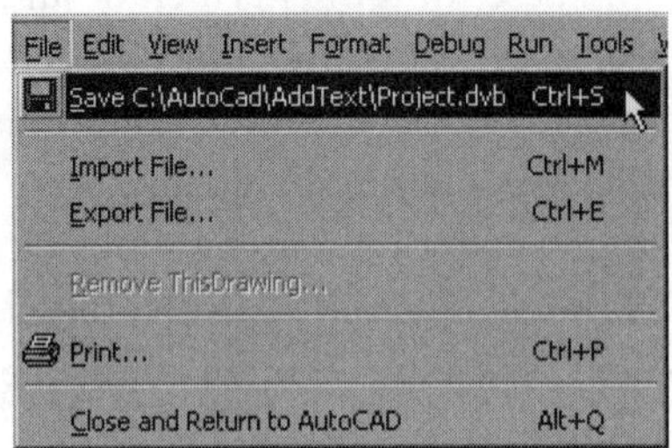

Running a Macro

Throughout the development stage of a project, it's much better to do trial runs from the IDE until you're satisfied that your macro is working the way you want it to. The IDE has many debugging features to help you during these tests, especially when your macros become longer and more complex. You'll learn how to use these debugging features later, in Chapter 10.

Once your macro is working exactly as planned, it's better to run it straight from AutoCAD without opening the IDE at all. Let's look now at both ways of running a macro.

Running a Macro from the IDE

To run your DrawText macro from the IDE, select the Run Sub/UserForm button from the toolbar:

Running a Macro from AutoCAD

When it is inconvenient to open the IDE just to run your macro, follow these steps to run it from the AutoCAD window:

1. From the AutoCAD menu, choose Tools ➜ Macro ➜ Macros. The Macros dialog box appears, containing a list of all the macros associated with the current ThisDrawing object, as shown in Figure 2.8.
2. Highlight your DrawText macro, and click Run to execute it.

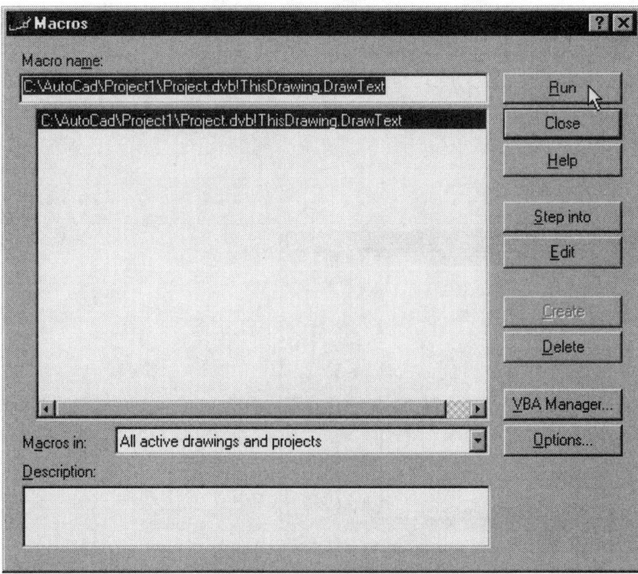

***Figure 2.8** Macros dialog box listing the macro associated with the current drawing object*

If your macro isn't listed in the Macro dialog box, make sure you have loaded the project file that contains it, and that it has been placed into either ThisDrawing or Module# (where # stands for any number). Procedures placed into UserForm modules are private and are not listed in the Macro dialog box. The section "Loading VBA Project Files" later in this chapter describes how a macro can be loaded manually or automatically.

Returning to AutoCAD

When you return to AutoCAD after running the DrawText macro, the text added by the macro is displayed in the Model Space, as shown in Figure 2.9. Your new text will also appear in the Layout1 (see Figure 2.10) and Layout2 tabs. Drawings are designed in the Model Space, and the two Layout tabs are used to plot your drawing to Paper Space.

Figure 2.9 *The text has been added to the Model Space by the AddText method.*

Figure 2.10 *The AddText method also updates the images in the Layout tabs for the current drawing.*

Using VBA's Date and Time Functions

Visual Basic provides numerous *functions* that you'll find easy to use. This section introduces two of them—Date and Time—that may be useful to include in your DrawText macro. The Date function returns a Variant type containing the string representing the current date, and the Time function returns a Variant type containing a string representing the current time; the content and format of both strings are dependent on your PC's settings.

Updating Your DrawText Macro

Because the Date and Time functions return strings, they can be used wherever any string is required in your code. Try replacing the `"Hello"` string in Line 7 of your `DrawText` macro with `Date`, as follows:

```
ModelSpace.AddText Date, TextPosition, 0.75
```

You don't need to enclose `Date` *in quotes because it is a function name. If you did use quotes, you would end up with the string "Date" in your drawing.*

Run your macro again and watch as the current date appears in the Model Space tab of your drawing object, as shown here:

You can add *both* the time and date to your drawing by expanding your code statement as follows:

```
ModelSpace.AddText Time & " " & Date, TextPosition, 0.75
```

The ampersand character (&) *concatenates* strings, so that the last character of one string is joined up with the first character of the next string. The string containing one blank character in the middle adds a space in order to visually separate the two strings when displayed. Here's how it looks:

Now that you have created a stand-alone macro, it's time to create a macro for starting up the Metric-Imperial Converter application developed in Chapter 1 (Listing 1.1). This macro can be called from the AutoCAD window. All you need to do is provide the code for showing the UserForm from the application. Before you can call the application, however, it has to be loaded. The next section shows how this is achieved.

Loading VBA Project Files

When you open a drawing file from the AutoCAD window, by default no VBA project file is loaded into memory. You'll need to load your project file manually before you can edit or run your macros. This section shows you how to change that.

If you prefer that your macros be loaded automatically, there are two options that you can set in the AutoCAD application so that specific files are loaded in one of two ways:

- Every time AutoCAD starts up.
- Whenever the current AutoCAD application is opened.

Loading a Project Manually

Manually loading the project file containing your macro is the best way to load macros that you don't need to run very often. The following steps explain how to do this:

1. From the AutoCAD window, choose Tools ➜ Macro ➜ Load Project. The Open VBA Project dialog box (see Figure 2.11) appears with a list of the project files contained in the current directory.

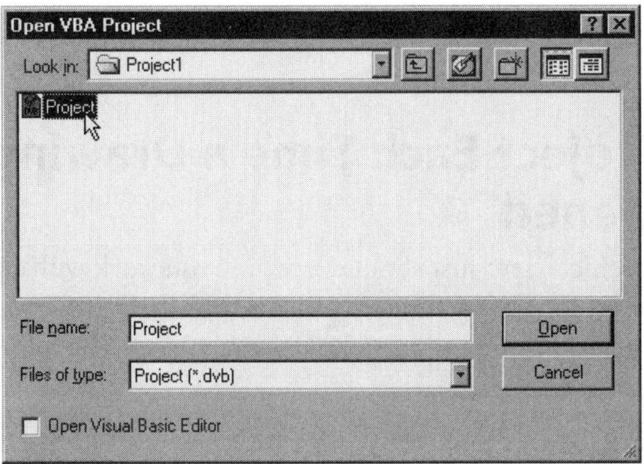

Figure 2.11 *Selecting a project from the Open VBA Project dialog box*

2. Ensure that the Open Visual Basic Editor check box (at the bottom of the dialog box) is marked, select the project containing the required macro, and click Open. If the AutoCAD message shown in Figure 2.12 appears, click Enable Macros to continue. The Code window for ThisDrawing appears, containing the DrawText macro.

This message box will always appear if its Always Ask Before Opening Projects With Macros check box is selected. If you don't want this warning message again, then simply uncheck the box. You can make the warning message show up again by clicking the Options button in the Macros dialog box (Figure 2.8) and selecting the Enable Macro Virus Protection option.

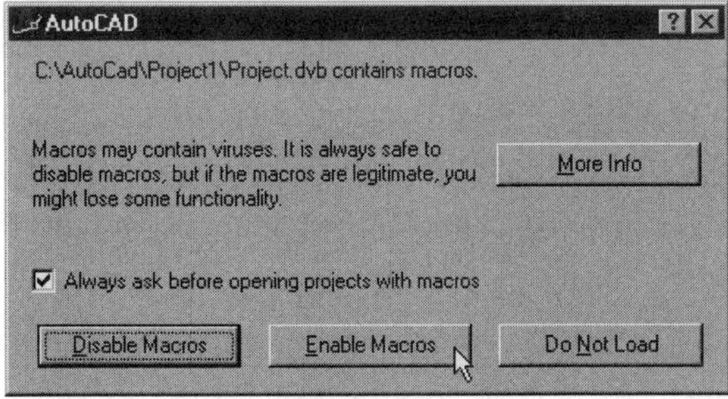

Figure 2.12 *Message box giving information about macros*

If you want the IDE to open so that you can edit the macro being loaded, make sure that the Open Visual Basic Editor check box is selected in the bottom-left corner of the Open VBA Project dialog box.

Loading a Project Each Time a Drawing Object Is Opened

If you need to run a specific macro just about every time you work with a particular AutoCAD drawing object, consider setting up AutoCAD so that it will automatically load this macro for you every time you open the drawing object. The following steps show you how this is achieved:

1. In AutoCAD, choose Tools ➜ Macro ➜ VBA Manager. The VBA Manager dialog box is displayed.
2. Select the project file to be loaded, and click the Embed button.
3. Close the dialog box and return to the AutoCAD window.

Loading a Project When AutoCAD Starts Up

If a macro is required by most of your AutoCAD drawings, consider setting up AutoCAD so that the project file containing the macro is loaded every time AutoCAD is opened. To load a project file every time AutoCAD starts up, follow these steps:

1. Choose Tools ➜ Load Application from the AutoCAD window. The Load/Unload Applications dialog box is displayed.
2. Click the Contents button in the Startup Suite frame. The Startup Suite dialog box (Figure 2.13) opens, listing all the project files that are automatically loaded when you start AutoCAD. (There were none on my PC.)
3. In the Startup Suite dialog box, Click Add. This opens the Add File To Startup Suite dialog box shown in Figure 2.14.
4. Select the project file containing the required macro and click Add. This returns you to the Startup Suite dialog box, which now contains the project file you've just added.
5. Close the Startup Suite dialog box. This returns you to the Load/Unload Applications dialog box, which now contains the text "Project.dvb was added to the Startup suite" in the frame along the bottom.

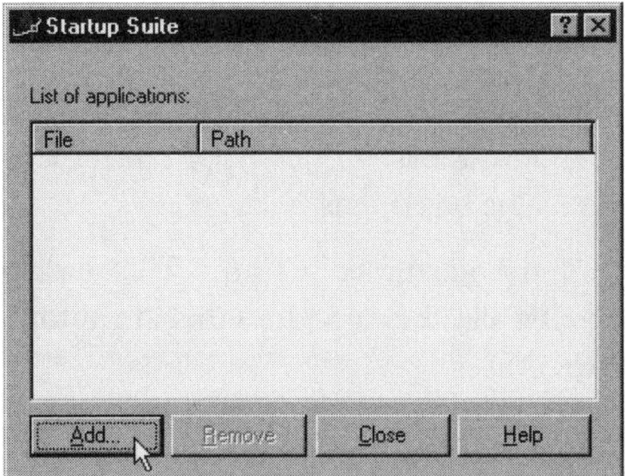

Figure 2.13 *Startup Suite dialog box*

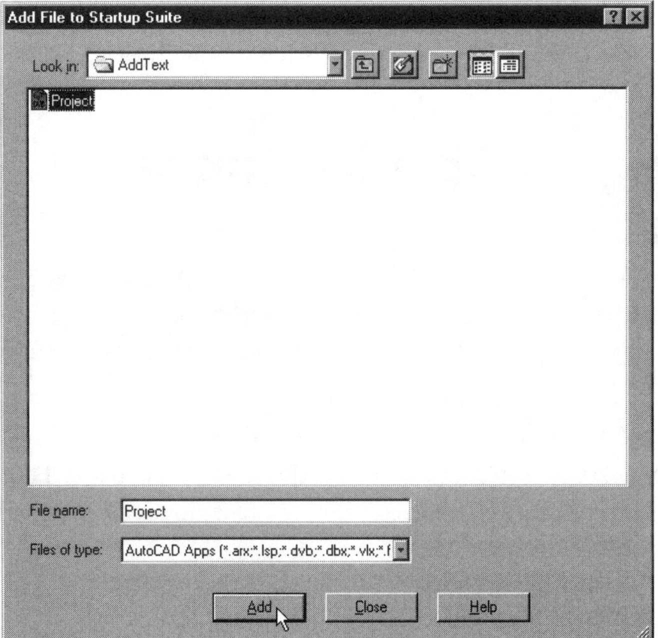

Figure 2.14 *Adding a file to the elements that run when AutoCAD starts up*

6. Click Close to return to the AutoCAD window. Your macro is now available for running at any time and will always appear in the list displayed in the Macros dialog box.

Canceling the Loading of a Project at Startup

If a project file always loads when AutoCAD is opened and you decide this is no longer necessary, follow these steps to remove it from the list in the Startup Suite dialog box:

1. In the AutoCAD window, choose Tools ➜ Load Application. The Load/Unload Applications dialog box opens.
2. Click the Contents button in the Startup Suite frame. The Startup Suite dialog box opens (Figure 2.14), listing all the project files that are automatically loaded when you start AutoCAD.
3. Select the project file you want to remove and click Remove. The name of the project file is no longer listed.
4. Click Close to return to the Load/Unload Applications dialog box.
5. Click Close to return to AutoCAD.

You can now open AutoCAD without the macro being loaded. If you occasionally need to use the macro again, you can always load it manually or add it back into the Startup list.

Starting an Application from a Macro

A VBA application can be run directly from the AutoCAD window without opening the IDE, if you write a macro that will open the UserForm. The following steps show you how to create such a macro to run the Metric-Imperial Converter application developed in Chapter 1.

1. If your Metric-Imperial Converter application isn't loaded, choose Tools ➜ Macro ➜ Load Project in the AutoCAD window. Then select the project file where the application is stored (see the preceding section "Loading VBA Project Files").
2. Open the IDE, and choose View ➜ Project Explorer if the Project Explorer window isn't already displayed. Click Module1. The Code window for Module1 opens.
3. Enter the following code:

```
Sub RunMetricToImperialConverter()
    UserForm1.Show
End Sub
```

Analysis of this code is given in Listing 2.2 at the end of this sequence of steps.

4. Choose File ➔ Close And Return To AutoCAD. The IDE closes, and you are returned to the AutoCAD window.
5. Choose Tools ➔ Macro ➔ Macros. The Macros dialog box appears, containing your macro.
6. Click Run. Your application starts up just as if you had run it from the IDE.
7. Click the command button with the Caption property set to Close. The application's window disappears, and it is unloaded from memory.

LISTING 2.2: APPLICATION STARTUP MACRO

```
1   Sub RunMetricToImperialConverter()
2       UserForm1.Show
3   End Sub
```

ANALYSIS

- Line 1 starts the procedure `RunMetricToImperialConverter`.
- Line 2 calls the `Show` method from `UserForm1` that displays this UserForm and runs the application until the user clicks the command button with the Close caption.
- Line 3 ends the procedure.

Summary

Now that you have worked your way through this chapter, you should

- Know what a macro is.
- Be able to develop macros to call VBA functions or to start an application.
- Know how to run a macro from the AutoCAD window or the IDE.
- Know how to call the Date and Time functions.
- Be able to load project files manually, to run each time a particular drawing is opened or each time AutoCAD starts up.

Quick Tour of the IDE

AUTOCAD VBA

Chapter 3

In this chapter, I'll take you on a quick tour of all the IDE components and some of the features they offer—that way you'll get an idea about how everything fits together.

This chapter covers the following topics:

- VBA IDE components
- Exploring the menu bar
- Printing UserForms
- Overview of the code commands
- Getting help

VBA IDE Components

The VBA IDE contains a collection of powerful commands and tools that you'll find extremely convenient and helpful for creating VBA macros and applications. In this chapter I've stuck to the components you'll find useful for creating your code. The whole of Chapter 10 is devoted to components for debugging (hunting down and fixing errors). Following are the components from the IDE covered in this chapter:

- Menu bar
- Toolbars
- Toolbox
- Project Explorer window
- Object Browser window
- Code window
- Properties window

Figure 3.1 illustrates a typical layout of these components in the IDE window. By default, the menu bar is positioned horizontally along the top of the window, immediately below the title bar. The menu bar contains a collection of items, each with its own drop-down list of commands. The standard toolbar typically sits snugly beneath the menu bar and provides fast access to some of the most-used menu commands. When the menu bar and standard toolbar are positioned as in Figure 3.1, they are said to be in their *docked* positions.

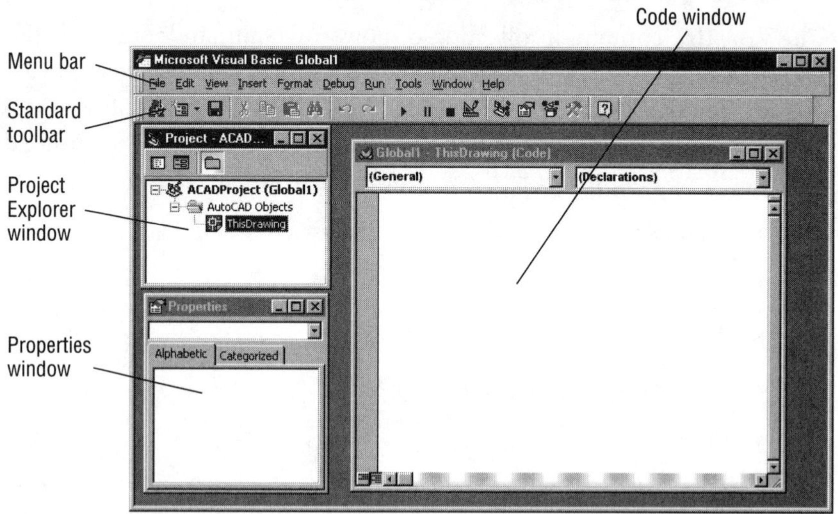

Figure 3.1 *VBA IDE menu bar and standard toolbar in their docked positions*

The menu bar and toolbars can be positioned anywhere on the screen using a drag-and-drop action. In fact, all the IDE windows can be moved by dragging and dropping their title bars, and they can be resized by adjusting their borders. However, when the menu bar and toolbar windows are docked, their title bars are sometimes hidden, so if you want them repositioned you'll need to drag them by the two parallel vertical bars on their left-hand sides.

Exploring the Menu Bar

The menu bar has 11 drop-down lists of menu commands. These provide access to all the commands available in the IDE. These Windows-style drop-down menus are what make VBA an easy-to-learn and easy-to-use powerful, visual system that saves you from having to memorize textual commands. Among other things, the commands available from the menu bar allow you to

- Save and print files
- Use the editing features
- Open and close windows in the IDE

- Insert forms and modules into your project
- Line up controls in forms
- Run and debug code
- Change settings that alter the appearance and behavior of the IDE
- Access the online Help facility

If you take a quick look at all the drop-down lists of menu commands, it won't take long to discover that quite a few of the commands are dimmed ("grayed") indicating that they are unavailable for selection. This is because they are considered inappropriate for selection in the current context. For example, most of the Edit commands will be dimmed unless there is something to edit, so you'll need to open a Code window to make them available.

The examples that follow use a few of the most common commands from each list to give you an idea of the power you have at your fingertips while working in the IDE.

Cascading Menus

Menu commands that sport an arrow at the far right are called *cascading menus.* Pausing the mouse cursor over these commands displays another drop-down list of related submenus. As shown here, several menu commands in the Format group have submenus:

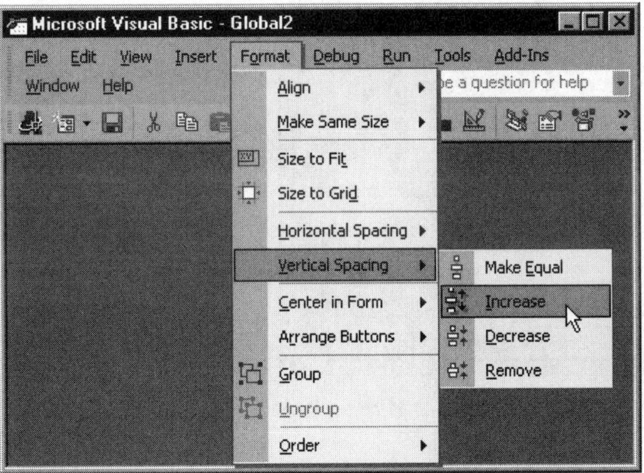

Setting Your IDE Options

The Tools menu commands allow you to access the Visual Basic Editor to create and run macros, set options to customize the features that are available, and set up your project's properties.

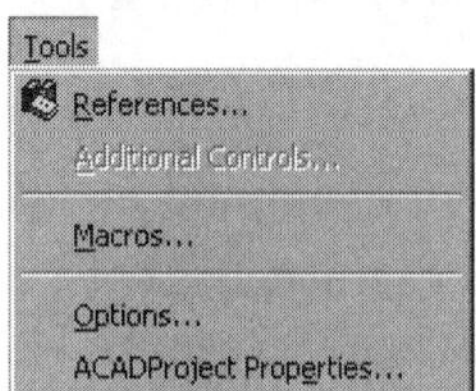

When you select Tools ➜ Options, the Options dialog box opens as shown in Figure 3.2. The options you can set from the Editor and General tabs of the Options dialog box are described in the next two sections. You have already seen how to set the color of the Keyword Text in the Editor Format tab (in the Chapter 2 sidebar "Setting the Colors to Identify Keyword Text in the Code window").

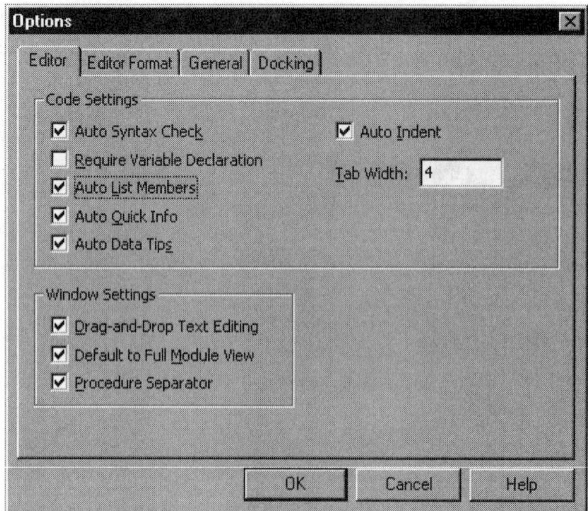

***Figure 3.2** Editor settings in the Options dialog box*

Editor Options

The Editor tab (Figure 3.2) contains the following settings that will help you as you enter your code:

Auto Syntax Check When this option is enabled (the check box is checked), the Visual Basic interpreter will examine the code for syntax errors line by line, as it is entered. If an error is found, the interpreter will change the color of the whole line to the color setting for the Syntax Error Text that has been set in the Editor Format tab. In the following example, you can see that the second line is different in appearance:

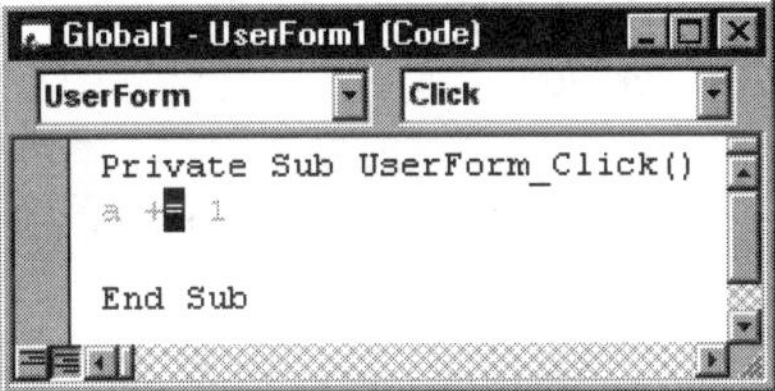

If any particular part of the line can be identified as causing the error, it is highlighted as shown just above, and a message box is displayed with a brief error message:

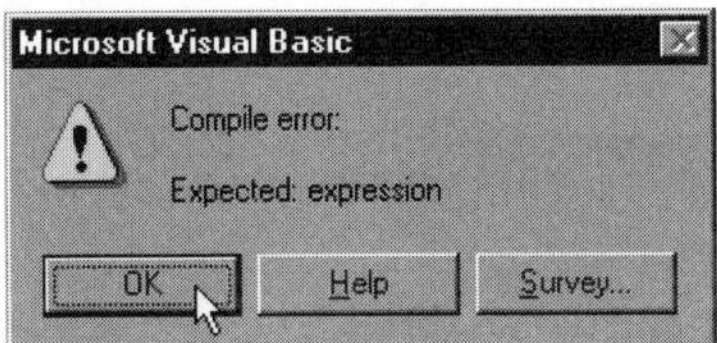

Clicking the Help button in this message box calls the VBA online Help facility to give a detailed explanation of the cause of the error:

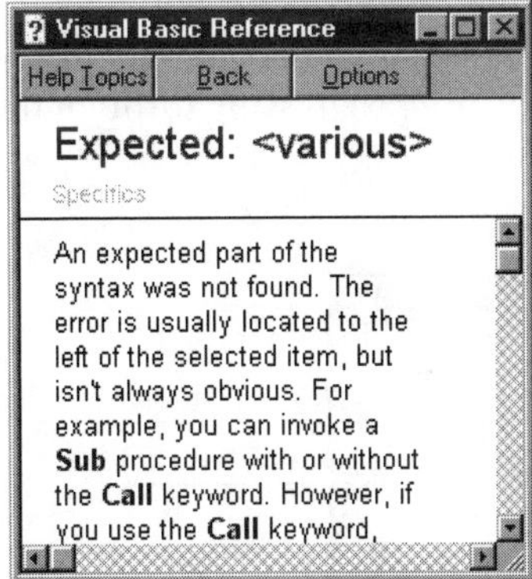

Chapter 2's sidebar "Setting the Colors to Identify Keyword Text in the Code Window" shows how to change the color of syntax error text.

Require Variable Declaration This option allows you to control whether or not variables must be declared before you can use them in code without getting an error message. You'll have an opportunity to study this option in Chapter 4, when you read about variables in detail and weigh up the pros and cons of enabling this control.

Auto List Members Enabling this option provides a drop-down list of valid items that can be used to complete the code you have entered so far. For example, Figure 3.3 shows the drop-down list that appears after you enter ThisDrawing followed by a full stop character (the period).

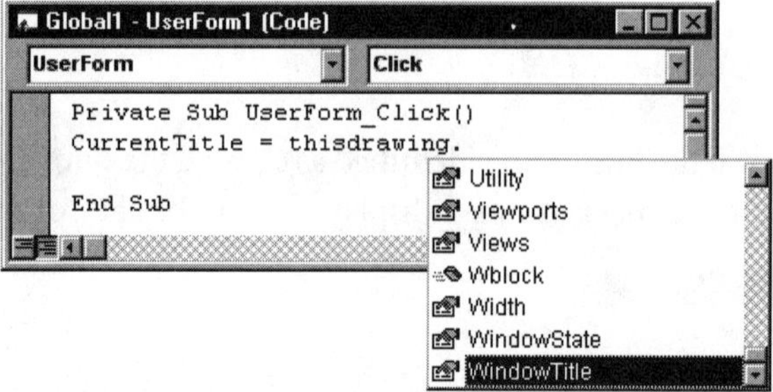

Figure 3.3 *List of valid code elements that can follow ThisDrawing*

Auto Quick Info When this option is turned on, a drop-down list will be displayed if you enter a function name followed by a parenthesis character, as shown in Figure 3.4. The list contains information about the parameters for which you are expected to provide values. The current parameter is always displayed in bold format to keep you informed of how you are progressing through the list.

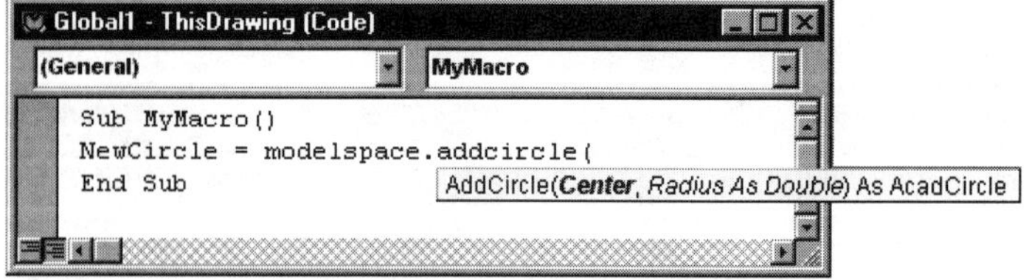

Figure 3.4 *List of parameters required by the AddCircle function*

Auto Data Tips Enabling this option tells the IDE to display the value of the variable currently under the mouse cursor when your application has stopped at a breakpoint or because of an error in the code:

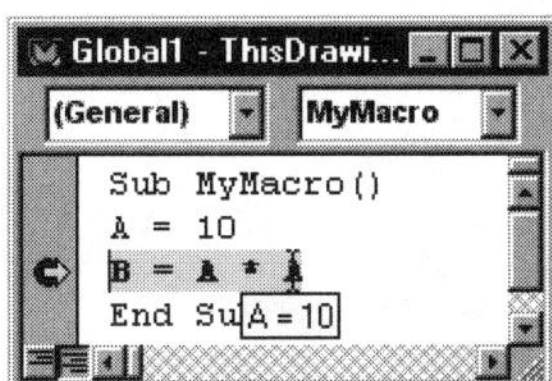

A breakpoint is a statement that you have chosen for the interpreter program to stop at, so that (for example) you can find the current values of variables. You'll find out how to use breakpoints in Chapter 10, "Debugging Your Code."

Auto Indent When this option is turned on and you indent a line of code using the Tab key, the subsequent lines of code will be lined up with the same indent, like this:

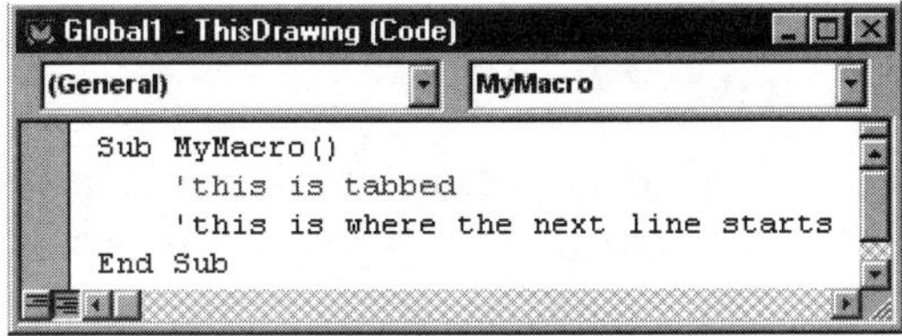

You can also control the number of spaces for the tab, by changing the number in the Editor tab's Tab Width text box (situated just below the Auto Indent check box).

General Options

The options on the General tab of the Options dialog box, shown in Figure 3.5, help you control the grid that is displayed as dots on the UserForm. You can make the grid dots visible or invisible, or adjust the spacing between them. You can also choose whether or not to display *ToolTips,* the little rectangles containing descriptive text that pop up when you pause the mouse cursor over a button or control. Also available here are settings that determine if and when your project is compiled into p-code if it is run from the IDE. When you start running your code with the Compile On Demand option turned on, only the coding statements visited during a particular run are compiled. When you run your code with Background Compile turned on, statements continue to be compiled while your application waits for you to perform the next interaction.

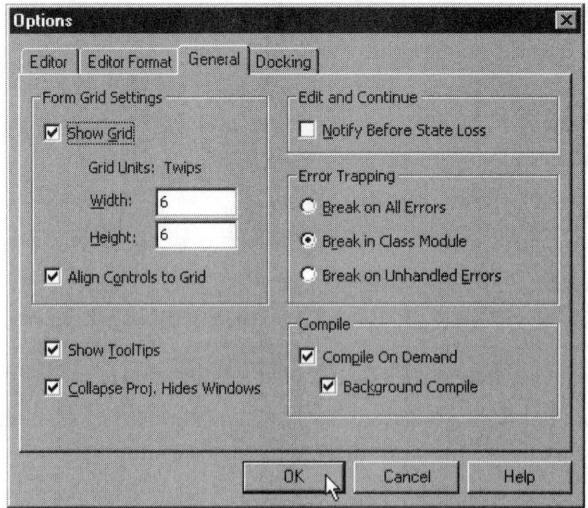

Figure 3.5 *General settings in the Options dialog box*

The IDE's Toolbars

The VBA IDE has four helpful toolbars. You can make them visible (or invisible) by choosing the View ➜ Toolbars command and selecting or deselecting them from the list (shown here):

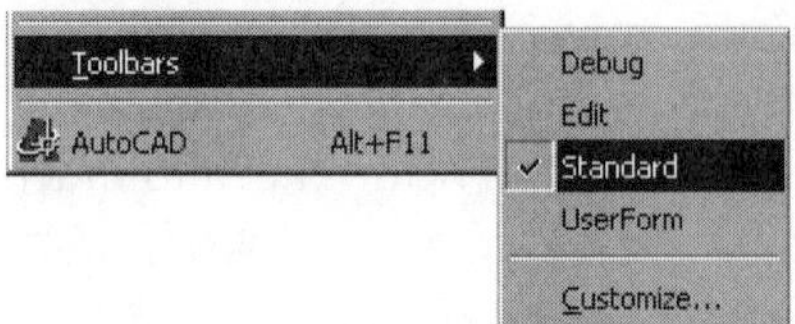

The toolbar buttons provide a fast path to some menu commands. You'll probably find them easier to use after you become accustomed to what menu commands are represented on each toolbar. The following sections briefly describe the buttons on the four toolbars.

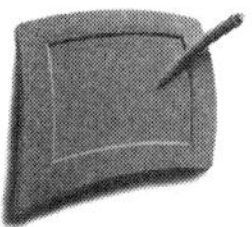

The Customize command on the Toolbars menu is covered in the sections "Customizing Menu Commands" and "Creating Your Own Toolbar" in Chapter 11. There I'll show you how to build toolbars for running commands from your applications, and how to customize existing toolbars to suit the needs of your applications.

Standard Toolbar

The standard toolbar, shown in Figure 3.6, is also the default toolbar. It is normally placed along the top of the window directly under the menu bar.

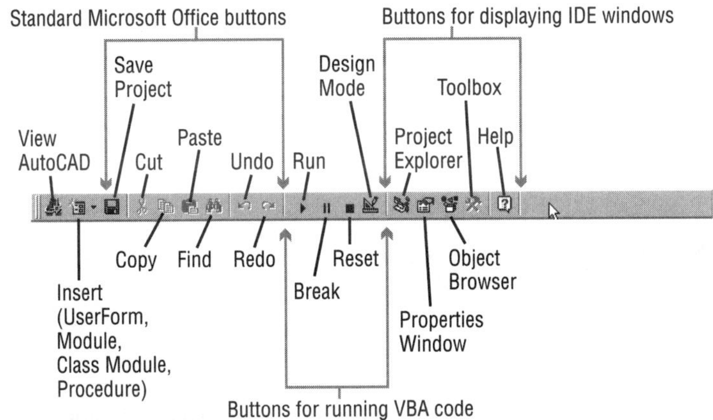

Figure 3.6 *The standard toolbar*

The Changing Face of the Insert Button

The Insert button has two parts—a button part and a drop-down list. This button is metamorphic, in that it changes its icon and function according to the last type of object inserted. So clicking the icon part of the button will insert the last inserted object type in your project.

Clicking the down-arrow on the button displays a drop-down list of all the objects that can be inserted using this button:

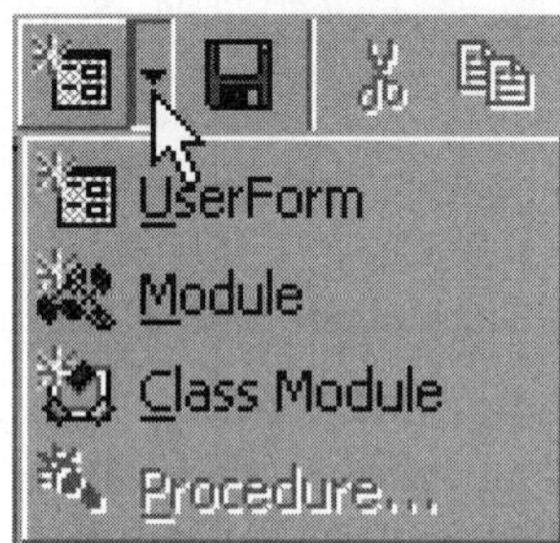

Selecting an item from this list inserts the object into your project, and updates the button's icon and function so that they reflect what you just selected.

In addition, the ToolTip text changes to match the button's new function. For example, after inserting a module into your project, the function of the Insert button changes to

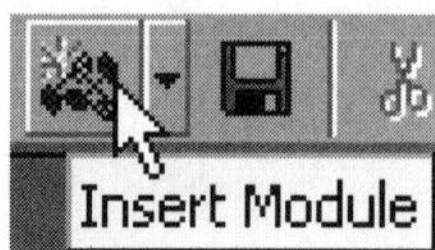

Until you get used to the icons representing each type of object, use the ToolTips to find out the type of object that will be inserted if you click the button. To see the ToolTip for any toolbar button, simply pause the mouse cursor over the top of it. If the ToolTip doesn't appear, choose Tools ➜ Options, click the General tab, and make sure that the Show ToolTips check box is selected.

Components in the Project Explorer Window

Any macros, programs, or applications you develop in the IDE are all considered a part of the current project and are all stored in a single file with the extension `.dvb`. You can view all the parts of a project in the Project Explorer window, which displays a hierarchical structure similar to the Microsoft Windows Explorer window (which I'm sure you're already familiar with). The Project Explorer window, shown here, can be viewed by selecting View ➜ Project Explorer or by pressing the Ctrl+R key-combination.

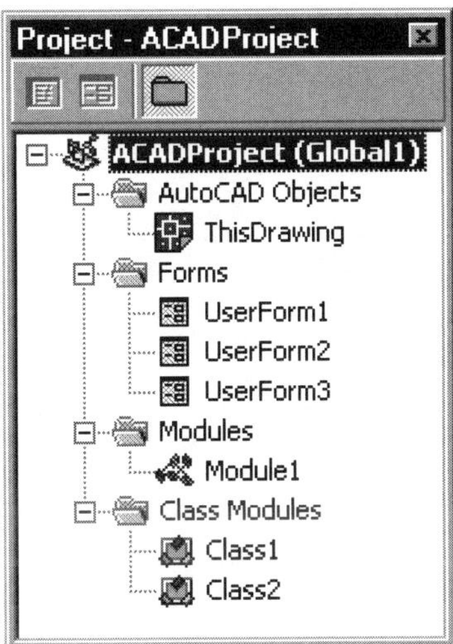

Notice the numbers appended to the end of the component names in the Project Explorer window (UserForm1, UserForm2, etc., Class1 and Class 2). These numbers uniquely identify the components. Since there is only one ThisDrawing component, it doesn't need a number.

Until a project has been saved for the first time, it is given the default filename `Global1`, which is just a temporary file. Once a file gets saved, `Global1` is replaced by the new filename.

Edit Toolbar Buttons

The Edit toolbar (Figure 3.7) provides direct access to some of the commands from the Visual Basic Editor's Edit menu and a couple of other commands for handling comments. The icons displayed on the buttons are identical to those shown beside the commands in the Edit menu's drop-down list.

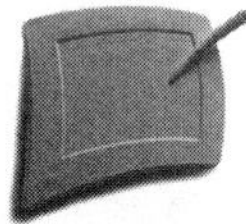

The Comment Block button is extremely useful during the debugging phase. It allows you to highlight adjacent lines of code and click to add the single quote character (') to the beginning of each selected line, which stops that code from being executed. If you want to execute these lines at any time after debugging, you can reverse the commenting by highlighting the lines again and clicking the Uncomment Block button.

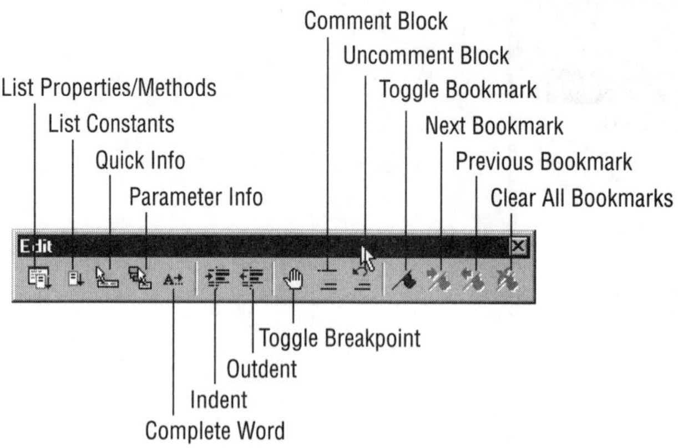

Figure 3.7 *The Edit toolbar*

Debug Toolbar Buttons

The Debug toolbar (Figure 3.8) provides fast access to the commands available from the Debug menu, as well as a few other commands. You'll find this toolbar extremely useful when your code doesn't work as you expected it to.

You'll learn later in Chapter 11 how to add existing functioning buttons, such as Toggle Breakpoint, to the toolbars you create for your applications.

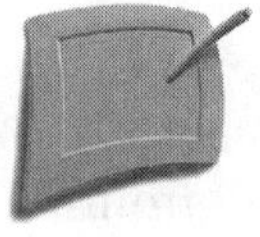

Notice that the Toggle Breakpoint button exists in both the Edit and Debug toolbars, giving you two points of quick access to this handy command.

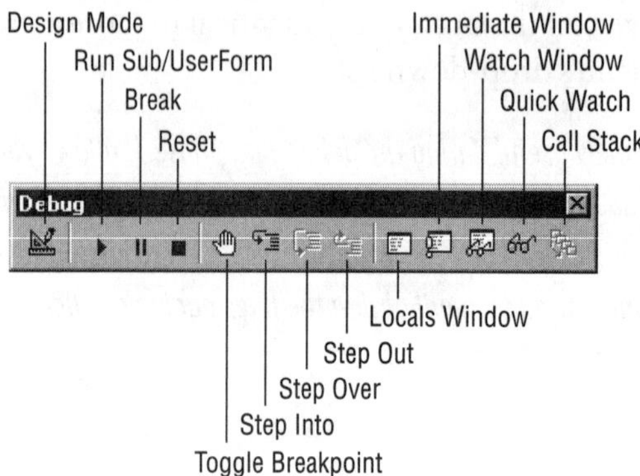

Figure 3.8 *The Debug toolbar*

UserForm Toolbar Buttons

Here on the UserForm toolbar (Figure 3.9) are buttons that give you an alternate means of accessing some of the commands available on the Format menu. These commands allow you to align, position, and size controls placed on UserForms.

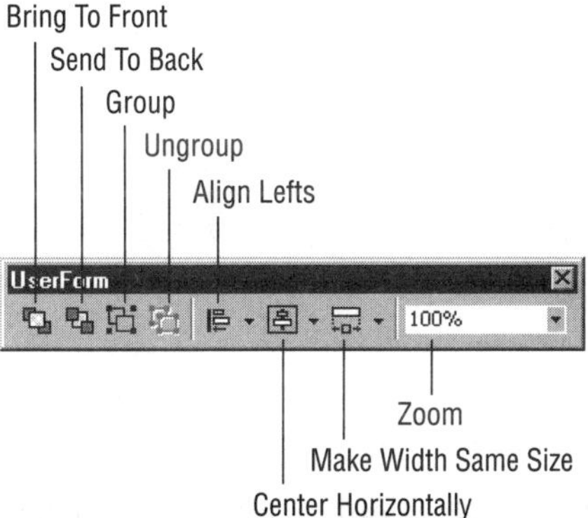

Figure 3.9 *The UserForm toolbar*

The following steps show you how to adjust the size and position of text boxes added to a UserForm:

1. Start a new project, add a UserForm, and place three text boxes on it.
2. Click the topmost text box; then hold down the Shift key while you click the other two text boxes. The handles of all the text boxes appear, indicating they are selected and active, as shown here:

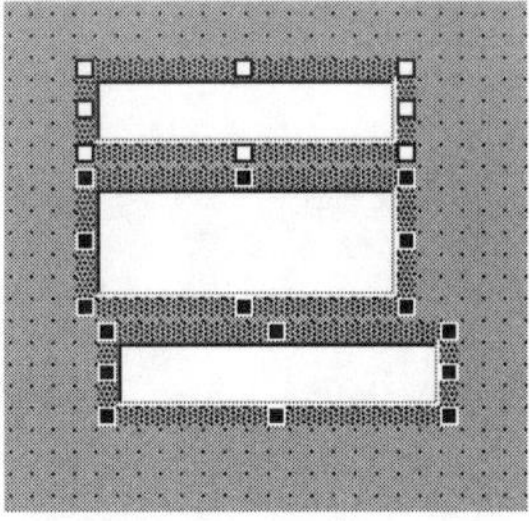

When several controls are active at the same time, the handles of the first control selected are filled with white to give the control a special status as the dominant control. The handles of the other selected controls are filled with black. The Format menu commands treat the dominant control as a guide for positioning or setting the dimensions of the others.

3. Choose Format ➜ Make Same Size ➜ Both. The size of the selected (black-handled) text boxes are adjusted to match the size of the dominant (white-handled) text box, as shown here:

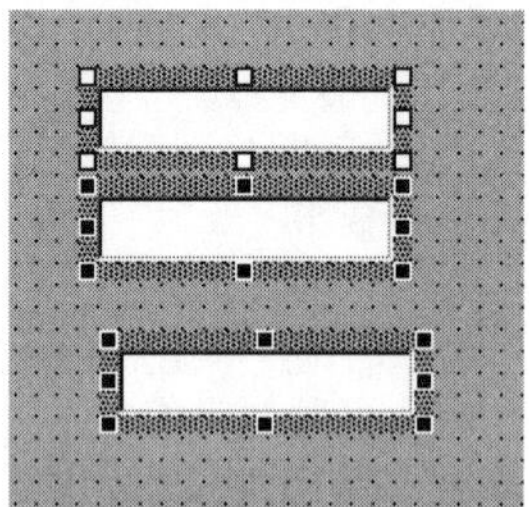

4. With all three text boxes still selected, choose Format ➜ Vertical Spacing ➜ Increase, and then choose this command again. The selected text boxes move down, to increase the space between adjacent pairs by one grid position each time you click the Increase command.
5. Choose Format ➜ Vertical Spacing ➜ Make Equal. The distance between the second and third text boxes is adjusted to be equal to the distance between the first and second boxes, as shown here:

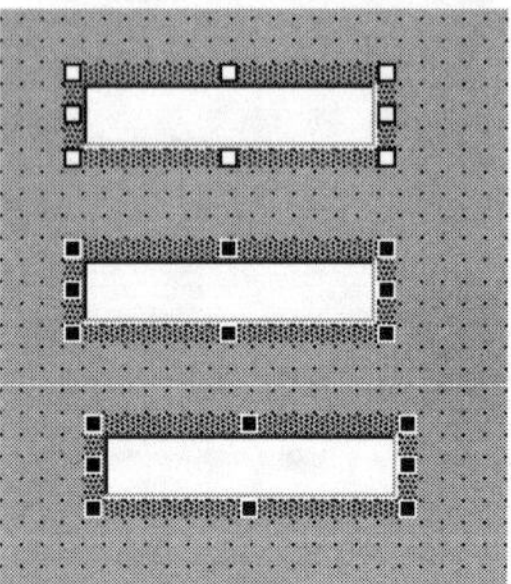

6. With all three text boxes still selected, choose Format ➜ Align ➜ Lefts, or click the Align Lefts toolbar button. The selected text boxes move horizontally so that their left borders line up with the left border of the dominant text box.

7. Position the cursor over the handle at the bottom-right corner of the top text box so that the cursor turns into a double-headed arrow. Hold down the mouse button and move the cursor until the dashed rectangle is the size required for the text box. Don't release the mouse button yet; notice that the dashed rectangle outline that follows the cursor is displayed at the same relative positions in all three text boxes, as shown here:

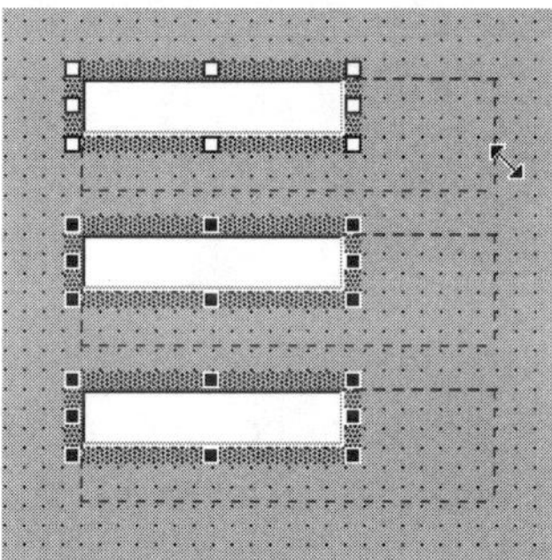

8. Now, release the mouse button. All the text boxes are resized to fit inside the dashed rectangles:

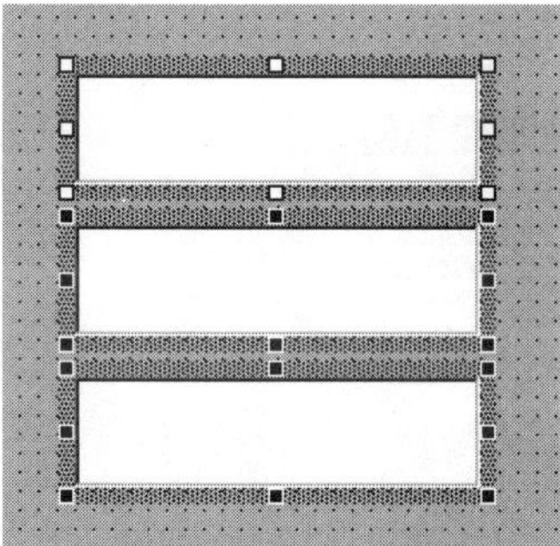

Printing UserForms

The IDE's Print command uses the default printer that has been designated in the operating system's Control Panel. To print the code from the module currently active in the Visual Basic Editor, follow these steps:

1. From the IDE, select a module and choose File ➜ Print. This displays the Print – ACADProject dialog box, shown here:

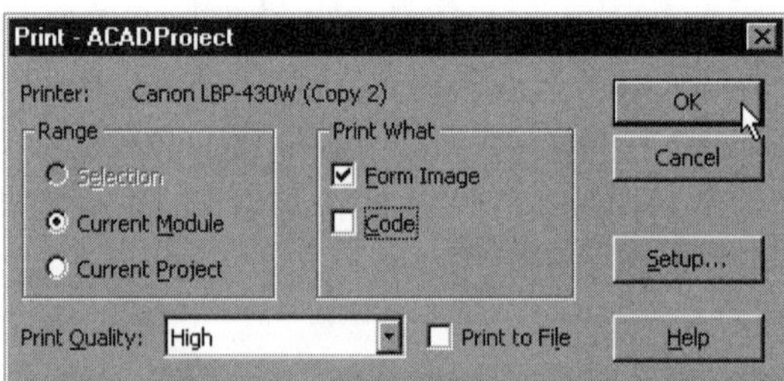

2. Click Setup to open the Print Setup dialog box (Figure 3.10). You'll see the familiar Print Setup dialog box that you've likely worked with in other Windows applications. These settings are set to values retrieved from the Microsoft Windows operating system environment.
3. Click OK to accept the current settings. The Print Setup dialog box closes, and you return to the Print – ACADProject dialog box.

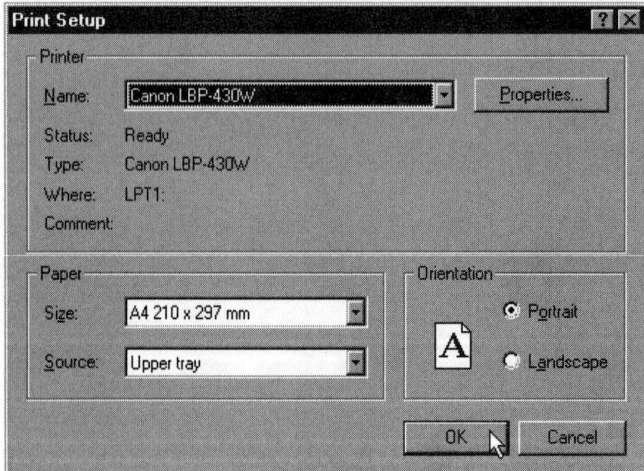

***Figure 3.10** The Print Setup dialog box displays the name of the default printer and other values retrieved from the Microsoft Windows environment.*

4. In the Range frame, the Current Module option button is selected by default. If necessary, select the Form Image check box under Print What and click OK. The code from the active module is sent to the default printer, the ACADProject dialog box closes, and you return to the IDE.

Menu Commands with an Ellipsis

Some menu commands end with an ellipsis (...) to let you know that a dialog box will appear when you select that command. An example is the Print... command in the File menu.

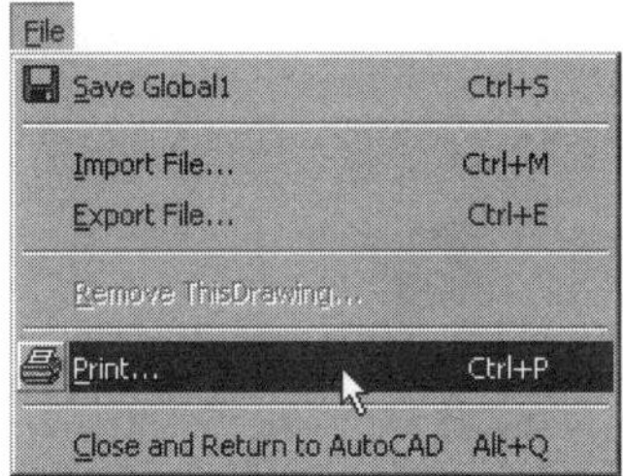

Some of these dialog boxes contain information taken straight from the Microsoft Windows environment—so you're ready to roll just with these default options.

Overview of the Code Commands

This section takes a quick look at some of the coding commands available from the Edit, Debug, and Run menus. You'll find that many of these commands are initially hidden. To make them available, a Code window must be open. Let's continue with the three-text-boxes project. Double-click anywhere on UserForm1 to open the Code window for UserForm1, displaying the first and last line for the `UserForm_Click` event procedure.

Commands for Editing Code

The commands in the Edit menu, shown just below, include indispensable editing tools, some of which you've already used. You experienced their convenience in Chapter 2, when they did your typing for you by completing words and popping up lists so you could choose what to enter next. Also included in the Edit menu are the Undo and Redo, Cut,

Copy and Paste, and Find and Replace commands, which are standard in many Windows applications—I'm sure you're familiar with these already. Notice also the Indent and Outdent commands, which allow you to quickly change the left-alignment position of your code lines.

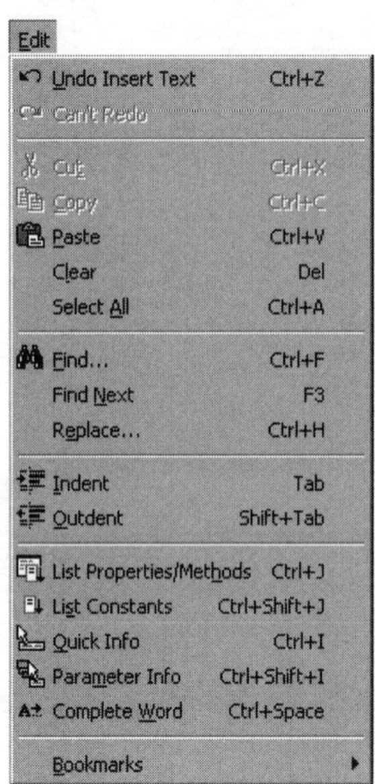

Commands for Debugging Code

The Debug menu commands, shown just below, allow you to run your code line-by-line while you watch the values of variables change. When you know that sections of your code are correct, then you can set breakpoints to allow your code to run as normal until it encounters a breakpoint, at which point execution stops and you can step through the untested sections of code one statement at a time. There is also a Compile ACADProject command that translates all of your code into a format that can be executed by your computer. This will make your application run faster, because Visual Basic normally translates the code into intermediate p-code one line at a time as it is required.

Chapter 10 discusses the various types of errors that can occur when you develop code, and how the Debug menu commands can help you hunt down the bugs that prevent your application from working properly.

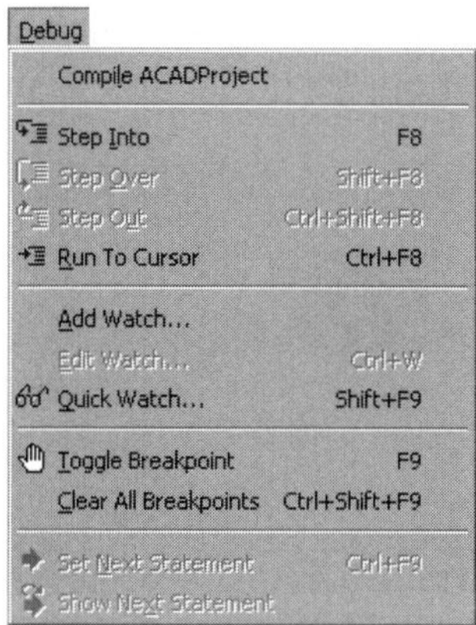

Commands for Running Code

The Run menu commands execute your code.

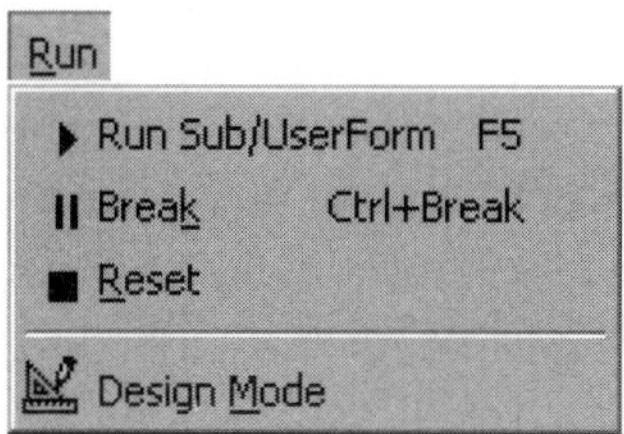

The Run commands evolve dynamically in several ways, according to whatever form or module is active, and whether or not the application is already in Run mode. For example, the Run Sub/UserForm command is only available when a UserForm is open; at other times, the command changes to Run Macro.

As indicated by the icons beside these menu commands, they all have a corresponding toolbar button. Each one also displays a ToolTip when you mouse over it. The ToolTip that pops up "evolves" in exactly the same way as the menu command:

If the application is running and stops at a breakpoint or at an error in your code, the Run command changes to let you continue from the breakpoint, as shown here:

The Reset command, when executed, causes the IDE to tidy up any memory usage, and prepares everything so that the application can run again without any interference from values stored during previous runs.

Getting Help

The online Help facility is another indispensable feature of the IDE—not only does it offer you a helpful explanation about many topics, but it often gives some sample code, too. You can copy this sample code and run it from the IDE. While you are building your expertise in Visual Basic, it is often useful to see how a method or property is actually put to work in coding statements. You may even be lucky enough to find a sample that you can use as the basis of a macro.

You're probably familiar with using the Help facility in AutoCAD. Well, the IDE's Help works exactly the same. The following steps show you how to copy and run the sample code for generating a random number from the IDE's Help facility:

1. Open the IDE and choose Help ➜ Microsoft Visual Basic Help. The Help window shown in Figure 3.12 appears.

2. As shown in Figure 3.12, enter the text **randomi** into the box labeled "Type the first few letters of the word you're looking for." As you type, watch the scrolling list of index entries in the large window. It rolls up to match the string you've entered so far.

   After you type the last letter (**i**), the Randomize Statement topic will be highlighted in the list box.

3. Click the Display button. The Visual Basic Reference window shown in Figure 3.13 appears, containing helpful information about the Randomize statement.

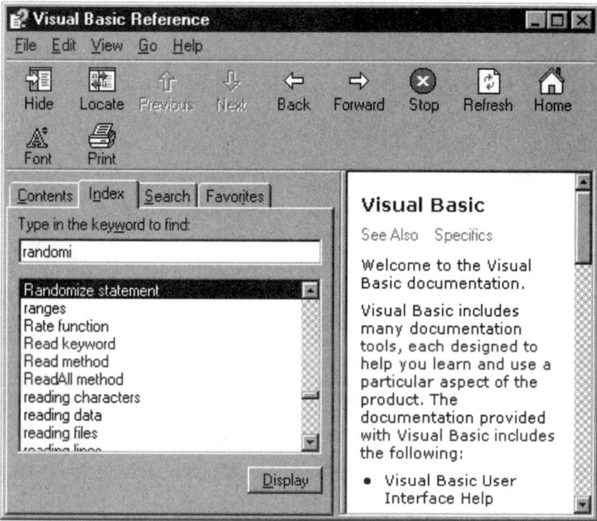

Figure 3.12 The Index tab from the IDE's online Help facility

Then click the `Example` link near the top-center of the reference window, and you'll see the sample code shown in the inset of Figure 3.13.

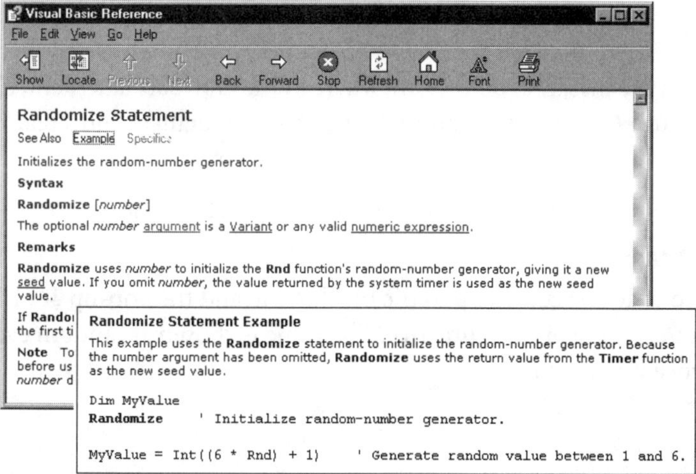

Figure 3.13 The inset shows a code example for Randomize statement after you click `Example` *link.*

4. Right-click anywhere in the Visual Basic Example window to display this pop-up menu:

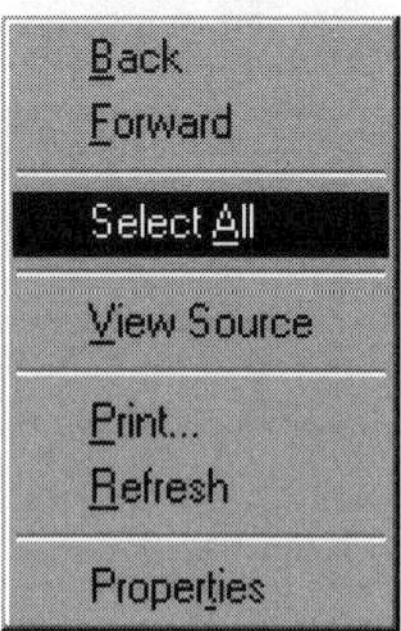

5. Choose Select All to highlight all the text. Right-click again and choose Copy from the pop-up menu. The content of the Example window is copied to the Clipboard.

6. Open the IDE, choose Insert ➜ Module, then choose Edit ➜ Paste. The Code window for Module1 opens, and all the text from the Example window is pasted into it.

7. Replace the text above the `Dim` statement with the name of your procedure; I've called mine RandomNumberGenerator, as shown in Figure 3.14. Notice I've also used the Edit ➜ Indent command to indent my code.

8. Add **`End Sub`** at the end, as shown in Figure 3.14.

9. With the insertion point somewhere in the `End Sub` statement, choose Debug ➜ Toggle Breakpoint. `End Sub` is highlighted, and a black circle with an arrowhead in it appears in the gray margin on the left.

10. Choose Run ➜ Run Sub/UserForm and pause the mouse cursor over `MyValue`.

    The code is executed up to the breakpoint, and the pop-up ToolTip displays a value, as shown in Figure 3.14. The value is chosen at random every time the procedure is run.

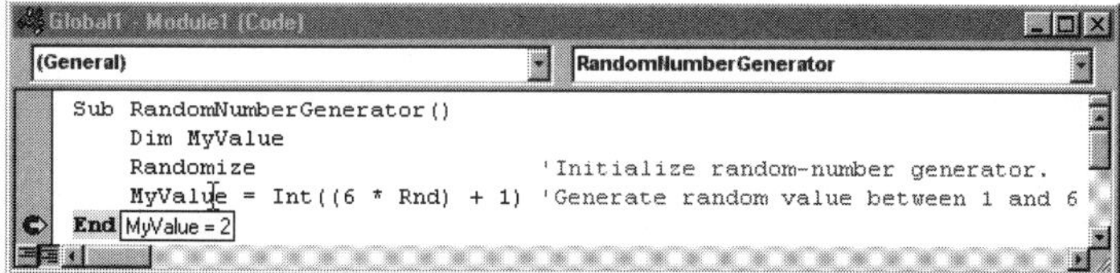

Figure 3.14 *Procedure name and* `End Sub` *statement have been added, shown here with the pop-up ToolTip giving the random value assigned to* `MyValue`.

Context-Sensitive Help

You can get immediate context-sensitive help by making an item in the IDE window active, and pressing the F1 function key. This opens the Help page for that topic if there is one. For example, highlight the Visual Basic word `Dim` and press F1 to open the Help window giving information about the `Dim` statement.

If you are a seasoned AutoCAD user, you'll know that the F1 key was originally used to view the full text window in AutoCAD. This was changed to F2 in AutoCAD 2000 and later versions, in order to conform to the Windows pseudo-standard of reserving F1 for viewing the Help facility.

Summary

After your quick tour of IDE in this chapter, you know how to use the IDE's features to do the following:

- Identify the components that make up the IDE.
- Display the Project Explorer window.
- Position and size Toolbox controls on a UserForm.
- Format several controls placed on a UserForm simultaneously.
- Print the graphical representation of a UserForm.
- Use the IDE's commands for running code.
- Set the options in the Editor tab of Tools ➜ Options.
- Access the online Help facility.
- Copy and run sample code on a specific topic from the online Help facility.

VBA Programming Concepts

AUTOCAD VBA

Chapter 4

This chapter explains the coding concepts and terminology of VBA. If you have previous experience in writing code, some of the material will be familiar to you, so you may want to make your first read a quick one. But I'm sure you'll find it a continuing handy reference as you gain experience. And for you uninitiated, the chapter provides invaluable instruction.

This chapter covers the following topics:

- How code instructs the computer
- Variables and constants
- Handling arrays of variables
- Defining your own types
- Using conditions to control code execution
- Repeating code
- An overview of objects, properties, methods, and events
- Setting the tab order for controls
- Comparing macros, functions, procedures, and applications

How Code Instructs the Computer

The *Visual Basic compiler* partially translates each line of code into p-code whenever you press Enter. It provides instant feedback when it discovers any obvious errors. This translated version of code is saved so that when you run your project, the compiler doesn't have to start from scratch, which saves time.

Using traditional compiled languages, you develop all the code before compiling it into machine language instructions for the PC to execute. Using Visual Basic, there are no longer two distinct steps because some compilation goes on in the background as you develop your code. Before beginning the final compilation step, most syntax errors will have been corrected, and the code will already be in a form that's part of the way there. It just has to undergo the finishing touches in order to become the machine-language instructions your PC can execute.

Statements and Expressions

All the code you write is made up of *statements* that may or may not contain *expressions*. Be sure you understand the difference between a statement and an expression. When the interpreter is translating a statement, any expression contained in the statement is reduced to a value before continuing.

Statements Any line of code in a VBA application is called a *program statement*. Because statements are partially compiled into p-code, they must be in a form that can be translated by the compiler program. Program statements can contain a mixture of keywords; names that identify variables; objects and their properties and methods; functions, macros, and procedures...and more. You'll find all these terms defined later in this chapter.

Expressions An expression is any combination of values and symbols that can be reduced to a single value. For example, the statement

```
txtMetricUnits.Text = txtImperialUnits.Text * 0.9144
```

contains an expression on the right of the equals sign (=). A value is retrieved from the TextBox control's Text property and multiplied by the conversion factor, to reduce the right-hand side of the equation to a single numerical value. This value is then assigned to the text box on the left-hand side.

In the statement

```
MetricToImperial = False
```

`False` is an expression that evaluates to a single numerical value representing False.

All about Variables

A *variable* is a name that's used to refer to a location in memory containing an item of data. Items of data can be anything from strings to whole numbers, from currency to decimal fractions. Figure 4.1 shows the Help window containing all types of data available and their memory requirements.

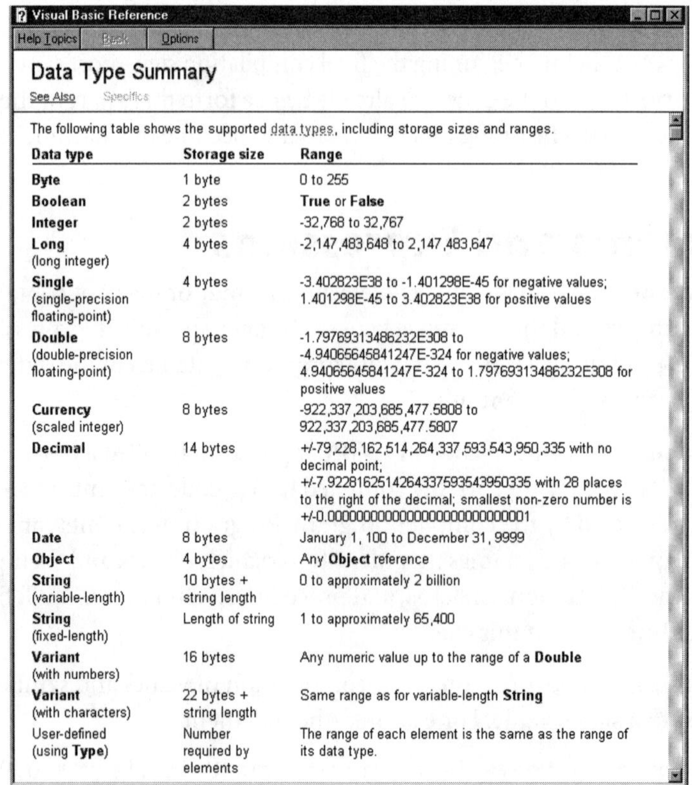

Visual Basic Reference

Help Topics | Back | Options

Data Type Summary

See Also   Specifics

The following table shows the supported data types, including storage sizes and ranges.

Data type	Storage size	Range
Byte	1 byte	0 to 255
Boolean	2 bytes	**True** or **False**
Integer	2 bytes	-32,768 to 32,767
Long (long integer)	4 bytes	-2,147,483,648 to 2,147,483,647
Single (single-precision floating-point)	4 bytes	-3.402823E38 to -1.401298E-45 for negative values; 1.401298E-45 to 3.402823E38 for positive values
Double (double-precision floating-point)	8 bytes	-1.79769313486232E308 to -4.94065645841247E-324 for negative values; 4.94065645841247E-324 to 1.79769313486232E308 for positive values
Currency (scaled integer)	8 bytes	-922,337,203,685,477.5808 to 922,337,203,685,477.5807
Decimal	14 bytes	+/-79,228,162,514,264,337,593,543,950,335 with no decimal point; +/-7.9228162514264337593543950335 with 28 places to the right of the decimal; smallest non-zero number is +/-0.0000000000000000000000000001
Date	8 bytes	January 1, 100 to December 31, 9999
Object	4 bytes	Any **Object** reference
String (variable-length)	10 bytes + string length	0 to approximately 2 billion
String (fixed-length)	Length of string	1 to approximately 65,400
Variant (with numbers)	16 bytes	Any numeric value up to the range of a **Double**
Variant (with characters)	22 bytes + string length	Same range as for variable-length **String**
User-defined (using **Type**)	Number required by elements	The range of each element is the same as the range of its data type.

Figure 4.1 *The Help window containing a summary of data types*

The Data Type Summary Help window is a useful one to keep on hand; you'll probably want to look it up a lot until you get used to all the different data types in VBA. The following steps show you how:

1. Open the IDE. Choose Help ➔ Microsoft Visual Basic Help if you are using AutoCAD 2000i, or choose Help ➔ Contents and Index if you are using earlier

versions of AutoCAD. The Visual Basic Reference dialog box appears (or the Help Topics: Visual Basic For Applications dialog for pre-2000i versions) with the I-beam cursor blinking in the text box. (If you want another look at this, see Figure 3.12 in Chapter 3.)

2. Type **data types** into the text box. The entries scroll by in the list box below, until the "data types" item appears highlighted.
3. Click Display. The Topics Found dialog box appears, as shown here:

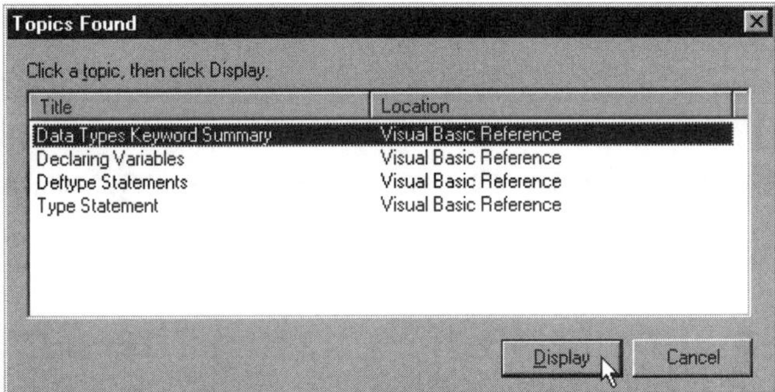

4. Select Data Types Keyword Summary and click Display. The Help window appears.

When a variable is declared, the interpreter allocates the exact amount of memory required by its type of data. For example, given the statement

```
Dim CurValue As Single
```

the interpreter would allocate a block of memory four bytes long and initialize it to 0.0. When this variable is assigned a value in a statement, such as `CurValue = 5.25`, the interpreter stores the 5.25 at this block of memory. When this variable is used in an expression such as

```
NewValue = CurValue * 1.25
```

the interpreter program retrieves the value 5.25 from memory.

Variables can be assigned as many different data values as your application requires while it is running, so variables make applications more adaptable than they would be if they used fixed values.

Memory Allocations for String Types

In the Help window for Data Type Summary, notice that the String type is allocated memory according to whether it's fixed-length or variable-length. Fixed-length strings are allocated 1 byte of memory for each character; variable-length strings are allocated 1 byte for each character, plus 10 bytes. Strings can be declared as fixed-length by specifying the number of characters; for example, the declaration `Dim Name As String * 30` ensures that `Name` is always exactly 30 characters long. If `Name` is assigned a string less than 30 characters, then trailing spaces are added to make it 30. If `Name` is assigned a string longer than 30 characters, the string is truncated to 30. Strings that are declared without a specified number of characters are by default variable-length strings.

When VBA encounters a string, it converts each character into a number according to its ASCII representation. (Appendix B lists ASCII codes.) The characters in the string "Hello" would be interpreted into five 1-byte numbers in the range 0 to 255. You can see how a string requires a lot more memory than a single integer number.

Declaring Variables Using the *Dim* Statement

A variable can be declared using the `Dim` statement with or without specifying its type:

```
Dim NewLength
Dim CurrentRadius as Single
```

If the type is omitted, then by default Visual Basic uses the Variant type and allocates the maximum amount of memory accordingly. The special Variant type has storage space allocated to it that's large enough to store data of any of the other types. Any variables that are not declared or that are declared without specifying their type are assumed to be Variant so that they can be assigned just about anything.

Several variables can be declared in the same `Dim` statement, separated by commas, even if their types are different. For example:

```
Dim CurrentWidth as Double, NewWidth as Long
```

For this reason, every variable that you don't want to end up as a Variant type must have its type specified in the `Dim` statement, even if it is declared on the same statement as other variables of the same type. In the following statement:

```
Dim ScalingFactorX, ScalingFactorY As Single
```

the variable `ScalingFactorX` would be interpreted as being a Variant type. This differs from some other languages, including C, in which the type is only specified once at the end of a list of variable names of the same type.

Important Reminder: Naming Conventions in VBA Code

Visual Basic has a few naming conventions that you *must* adhere to when you're naming macros, functions, variables, and constants in code:

- Names must always begin with a letter.
- Names cannot contain spaces, periods, or exclamation marks (!), or any of these characters: @ # $ &.
- Names cannot be greater than 255 characters in length.

To Declare or Not to Declare?

As explained, Visual Basic doesn't require variables to be explicitly declared. If you use this default convention, and if a name appears in code that hasn't been declared in the statements translated up to that point, a storage location large enough for a Variant type will be allocated to that name. And (whether you want it or not) a new variable is born—and no warning or error messages are given!

You may be tempted not to declare anything and just let Visual Basic do the work for you, but there are two good reasons why you should *not* automatically go down this road:

- Incorrectly spelled variable names are treated as new variables. That means expressions could be evaluated to an erroneous result. Or, if the new variable is a divisor, it could stop execution of your program with a Division By Zero error message box, as shown here:

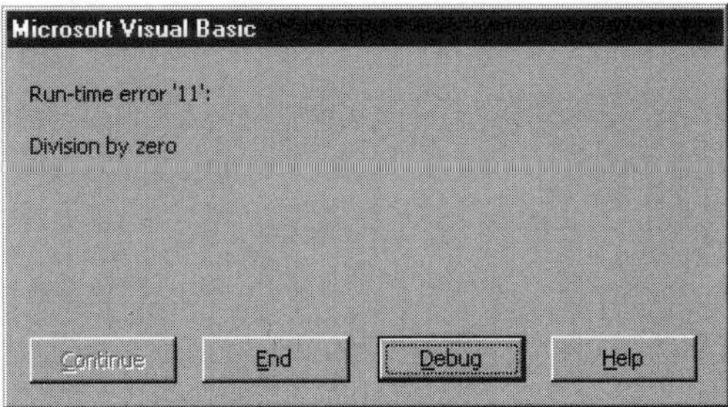

- Variables are allocated the *maximum* amount of memory; even an Integer type variable, which requires 2 bytes if declared, is allocated 16 bytes otherwise. Not only does this blow out the memory requirement of your application very quickly, especially if you are using untyped arrays, but it also increases run-time performance.

To avoid these situations, you can direct the interpreter program to verify that all the variables have been declared *before* they appear in the code, and if not, to give you an error message. This is done using a special `Option Explicit` statement.

Option Explicit *Statement*

The `Option Explicit` statement placed in a UserForm or module stipulates to the interpreter program that all variables contained in that UserForm or module must be declared; otherwise the interpreter must create an error and stop the application with the message shown here:

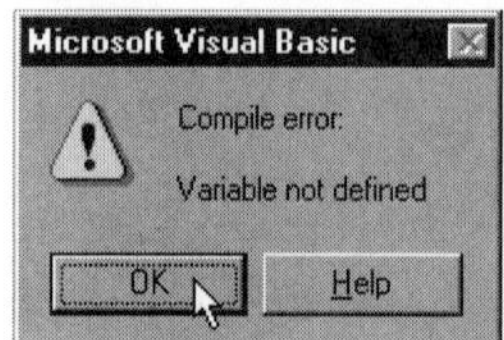

The `Option Explicit` statement is placed in the General Declarations section of the Code window for a UserForm or module. If you want these statements to be added automatically into the General Declarations section of all new UserForms and modules in future projects, you can arrange this by performing the following steps:

1. From the Visual Basic Editor choose Tools ➜ Options. The Options dialog box appears.
2. Select the Editor tab. In the list of Code Settings options, select the check box for Require Variable Declaration.
3. Click OK to return to the IDE. Now any new UserForm or modules you insert into any project in the future will open with the `Options Explicit` statement already in place in the General Declarations section of the Code window.

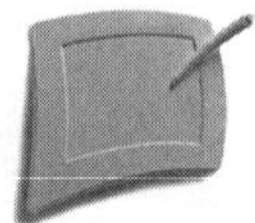

Any existing UserForms and modules are not affected when you enable the Require Variable Declaration setting.

Handling Arrays of Variables

Quite often your VBA code will contain lots of data items that all have the same type. An efficient way to handle these items is to declare a single entity called an *array* that allows you to refer to any item using the array's name and an index that identifies the item's position in the array.

Using an array makes the code much shorter because you don't need to have variable names for each item. For example, suppose you need to create 535 lines, all of type LineDetails. Using conventional variables, you would need to declare each item with a unique name, such as Line1, Line2... all the way up to Line535, to be able to refer to them in code. Your program would be extremely lengthy, with 535 declarations and 535 statements to access them. Using an array is the way around this kind of inefficiency.

Creating an Array

To create an array, you simply declare it, by providing its name followed by the number of elements required, less one, in parentheses. You need to subtract one because the first element starts at zero. You may also want to include its type (to avoid the assignment of the default Variant type). The interpreter allocates your specified number of consecutive memory locations with enough bytes to hold the values of all the array's elements. For example, in translating the following:

```
Dim AllLines(535) As LineDetails
```

the interpreter would multiply 536 by the number of bytes required to store a variable of the LineDetails type and allocate that memory to the array. Since an array is really just a group of variables all having the same type, arrays can be declared as any one of the types available for variables.

In terms of processing the array, you need only write the code to process one element and place it inside a loop structure. As described later in this chapter, the `For` loop is ideal for array processing.

Individual data items stored in an array are called elements.

Accessing Array Elements

Accessing individual elements in an array is achieved using an *index value.* The array name identifies the first memory location, and the index value represents the position in the list of the item required, so it's easy for the interpreter to retrieve the data for any element in the array. The first element in the array by default has an index value of zero, so that the interpreter simply multiplies the index of the array element required, by the amount of memory used to contain one element. The result is added to the starting memory location identified by the array's name.

Visual Basic arrays are different from the arraying of objects in AutoCAD, which duplicates objects and lays them out in some formation.

Visual Basic arrays can be declared using several different formats for the dimension. For example:

```
Dim StartPoint(2) as Single          'contains 3 elements
Dim EndPoint(0 to 3) as Single       'contains 4 elements
Dim AllLengths(1 to 5) as Integer    'contains 5 elements
```

In these array declarations, the first elements in `StartPoint` and `EndPoint` have an index of zero by default, but the first element in `AllLengths` has an index of 1 because it has been explicitly declared that way. When you specify a first element that is nonzero, the interpreter takes this into account every time it works out the memory location for the array element required.

Option Base *Statement*

Some people prefer to have the first element in all their arrays start from 1 rather than 0, since it is more logical to think of 1 as being the first element, 2 the second element, and so on. To ensure that this happens, you can always include the `1 to`... clause when you declare an array. Or you can place the `Option Base` statement in the General Declarations section of the Code window to specify a new starting value for the default index. The following statement ensures that all arrays declared in the same UserForm or module will automatically have their first element start at 1:

```
Option Base 1
```

Multidimensional Arrays

Most arrays represent a list of values and so have only one dimension, but two-dimensional arrays are also popular for representing things like tables and matrices. For example:

```
Dim AllPoints(10,3) as Single 'contains 11 x 4 elements
```

When this declaration is interpreted, the first dimension is considered to be the number of rows in the table; the second dimension is the number of columns.

Three-dimensional arrays are also quite common:

```
Dim AllData(0 to 4,5,1 to 6) as Double 'contains 5 x 6 x 6
elements
```

In fact, Visual Basic allows up to 60 dimensions.

All About Constants

A *constant* is the term given to a value that remains unchanged as long as the application is running. The values of some constants (such as pi) may never change. Others (such as TaxRates) may change from time to time. Such values should all be declared as constants and given names that can be used throughout the code. The names of constants follow the same naming conventions as variable names.

Replacing a constant value by a name not only makes the code easier to read and understand, but also easier to maintain. Any change to a constant's value need only be updated once, where the constant is declared and assigned its value. This saves you the time of looking for instances of a value that you want to change—and the errors possible in this process, because you could easily mistype the new value, miss an instance of the original value altogether, or update a value that has nothing to do with the constant.

Constants come in two flavors:

Symbolic Constants Also known as user-defined constants, *symbolic constants* are the ones you create with symbolic names and assigned values; they are declared in your code using the `Const` statement.

Intrinsic Constants Also known as built-in constants, *intrinsic constants* are an integral part of VBA and its controls for use with objects, methods, and properties.

Declaring Symbolic Constants

Symbolic (or user-defined) constants are declared in a `Const` statement. The definition of a constant resembles an equation starting with its name, followed by an equals sign, and then its value. The value can be a number, a string, an expression, or another constant. For example:

```
Counts MaximumHeight = 150
Counts DefaultDoorType = "Federation"
Counts MarkUpMultiplier = (100 + 25)/100
Counts BestHeight = MaximumHeight - 10
```

You can also specify a constant's type in the `Const` statement. For example:

```
Counts Epsilon as Double = 0.00001
```

If you don't specify the type, VBA uses the one that is the closest match to the constant's value.

Several constants can be declared on the same line separated by commas:

```
Counts MaximumSquares = 1000, MinimumSquares = 100
```

Constants with different types can also be declared on the same line, like this:

```
Counts MaxHeight as Single=2.5,MaxThickness as Integer=65
```

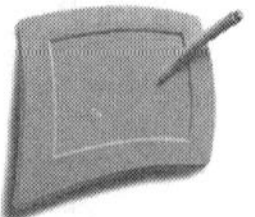

If you have a lot of constants to declare, sort them into small logical groups and declare them on consecutive lines, with a few on each line.

Viewing Built-in Constants in the Object Browser

VBA provides lots of built-in (intrinsic) constants that have been predeclared and assigned values ready for you to use without having to declare them. You can see these constants in the Object Browser window (shown in Figure 4.2).

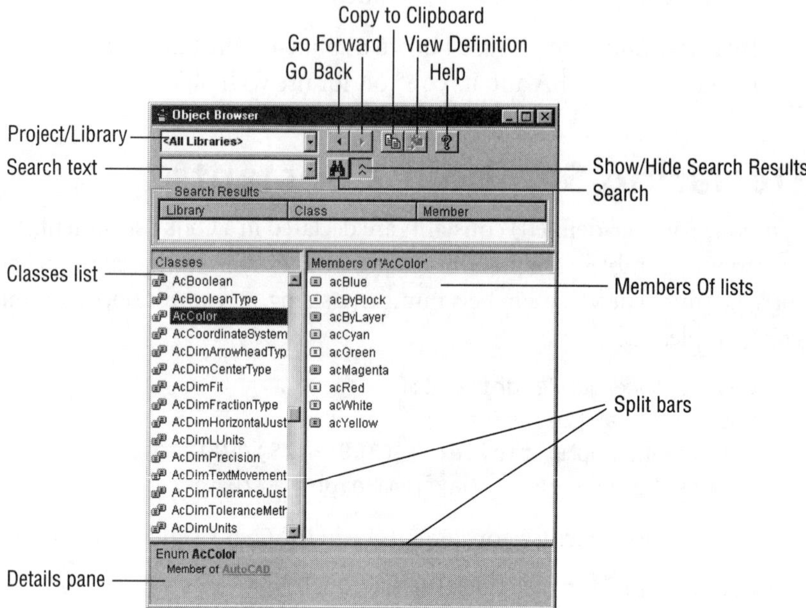

***Figure 4.2** Object Browser displaying the constants belonging to the enumerated type* `acColor`

All of the libraries listed in the Library box have their own set of constants, qualified by two-letter prefixes that identify the library they belong to. For example, constants from the AutoCAD library are prefixed with the letters `ac`, those from the MSForms library are prefixed `fm`, and those from the VBA library with `vb`. This enables you to install applications that have VBA capability and know that you won't get heaps of errors because of duplicate declarations of constants. Without this helpful prefix (if constants had only a name appropriate to their represented value), it would be impossible for you to confidently name your own constants without duplicating existing ones. In addition, there could be future problems when you update to new versions of software, should they duplicate one of your names.

The constants you yourself define are automatically placed in the ACADProject library and will not be listed with a prefix unless you declare them as such.

The following steps show you how to access the intrinsic constants listed in the Object Browser:

1. Open the Visual Basic Editor, and choose Insert ➜ Userform to add a UserForm to your project.
2. If the Object Browser window isn't already on display, choose View ➜ Object Browser.
3. Click the down-arrow button to open the Project/Library list box. A drop-down list of libraries appears, as shown here:

   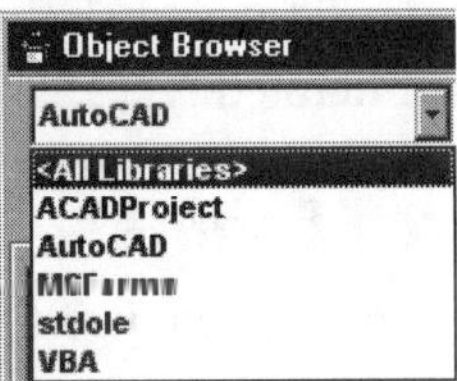

4. Select `<All Libraries>` from the list. The `<All Libraries>` item appears in the Project/Library box.
5. Scroll down the Classes list and select `fmBorders`. Information about the `fmBorders` item appears in the Details pane at the bottom of the Object Browser, and its members appear in the Members Of list, as shown in Figure 4.3. The `fmBorders` item is an Enumerated type, which means it can only be assigned one value from a set of predefined values, using either its name or its value.

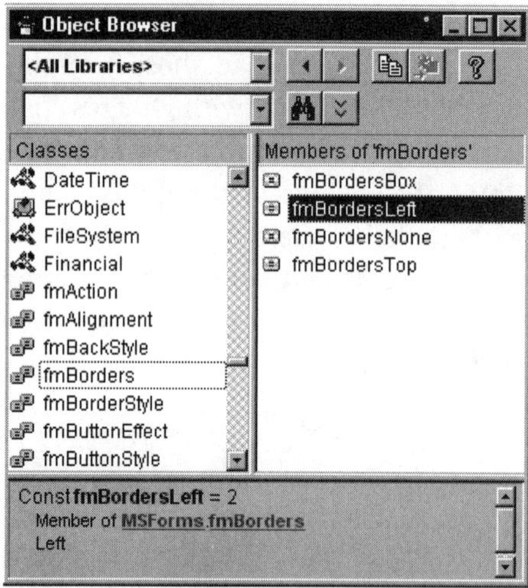

Figure 4.3 *Constant* `fmBordersLeft` *selected from the Members of fmBorders list*

6. Click the `fmBordersLeft` item from the Members Of list. The Details pane now contains information about this constant, including its value of 2 (see Figure 4.3).

7. One by one, click the other members of `fmBorders`. Notice how the values assigned to each member lie in the range 0 through 3; this sequential nature of values is also a characteristic of all Enumerated types.

Using the Object Browser's Search Engine

The Object Browser window offers a search facility to help you find strings within a library. You enter the string into the Search Text box directly under the Project/Library box. You can enter any string you like and even use VBA wildcards (see the accompanying sidebar).

The drop-down list from the Search text box contains up to five of the last strings you searched for since opening the IDE. When you click the Search button (the binoculars icon), the Object Browser searches the library for every occurrence of the string entered. You can also specify that you want to search for the whole word only, by right-clicking the Search button and selecting Find Whole Word Only from the shortcut menu, as shown here.

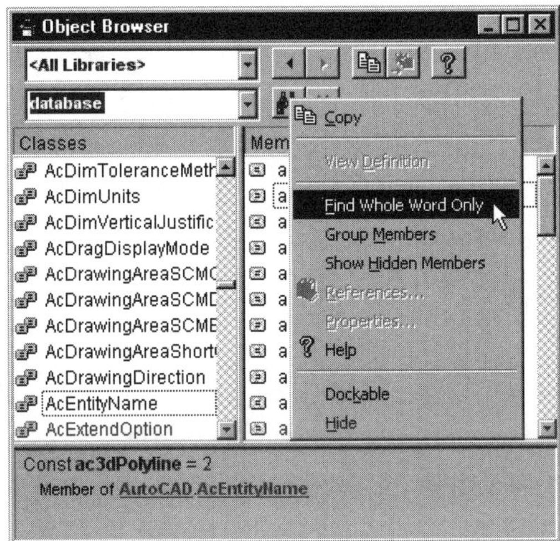

When the search is complete, the list of found items appears in the Search Results pane. It lists the library, class, and member names for each found item.

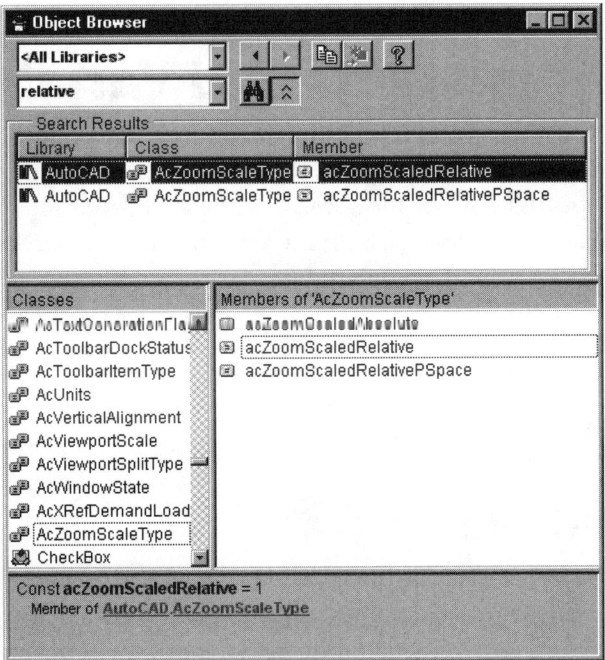

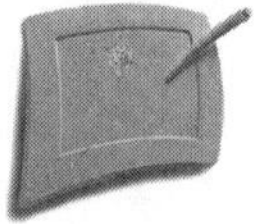

Constants vs. Variables for Efficiency: If a value will never change throughout the run time of the code, it is best to declare the value as a constant. This will make your code more efficient so it will run faster. When translated, any constant name is replaced by its actual value. That means during run time all the values are already in place; in contrast, the value of a variable has to be retrieved from memory each time its name is encountered.

VBA Wildcard Characters

You can include wildcard characters in your search string in the Object Browser. When it comes across these characters during the search, VBA tries to replace the wildcard with a character or a string of characters in an attempt to maximize the number of items it can find. These wildcard characters are available:

?	To replace any single character
*	To replace any number of characters
#	To replace any single digit

Scope of Constants and Variables

The *scope* of a constant or variable refers to whether or not it can be accessed from one procedure, from all procedures in a module, or from all procedures in the application. The level of scope depends on where the element has been declared and whether it has been declared as public or private. Variables and constants can have three levels of scope, as defined in the sections that follow:

- Procedure level
- Private-module (or UserForm) level
- Public-module level

Public vs. Private

All constants and variables are private by default. You can override the default by declaring them as public, provided that the declaration is inside a standard module rather than in a UserForm or procedure. From the point of view of maintaining the code, it is better to avoid declaring a constant or variable as public if it is only going to be used by procedures in the same module. This arrangement limits the amount of code that needs to be checked over if the value of that constant or variable ever needs to be updated.

Scope at the Procedure Level

A constant or variable declared *inside* a procedure using the `Const` or `Dim` statement is considered local and has a lifetime that lasts only while that procedure is running. This means that when the declaration statement is translated, the interpreter reserves the memory for variables or notes the values of constants. When the end of the procedure is encountered, the interpreter frees up the memory reserved for the local variables and no longer remembers the constants' values.

Although local variables and constants are restricted to being private, you can't declare them using the `Private` *keyword. If you try to do this, you'll get a run-time error message "Compile Error – Invalid attribute in Sub or Function."*

UserForm and Module-Level Scope

Any constant or variable declaration that is placed *outside* a procedure has UserForm or module-level scope. These declarations are placed in the General Declarations section of the Code window and are private by default.

Any constant or variable declared in a UserForm is restricted to being private. If the declaration is inside a module, the constant or variable is private by default but can be declared using the `Public` keyword to make it accessible from anywhere in the project.

Scope at the Private-Module Level

A module-level constant or variable can be declared as private, in order to limit its accessibility to procedures contained in the same module. For example:

```
Private Counts MaximumHeight = 1000
```

Limiting the scope in this way is useful when it comes to maintaining your code. In this example, if you ever want to change the value of the maximum height, you can quickly see where the constant is used in your code. Another benefit is that you can have another `MaximumHeight` constant declared as private in another module, and it can have a different value without causing any adverse effects on other modules.

Scope at the Public-Module Level

A module-based constant or variable can be declared as public, in order for it to be referenced from anywhere in the entire project. For example:

```
Public Counts NewRate = 3.5
```

In addition to scope, a variable also has a lifetime, which refers to the period of time that they hold onto their value. A variable declared inside a procedure can only be accessed within that procedure, so its lifetime will end when it loses its value between calls unless it is declared as a static variable (see the next section).

Static Statements and the Static Keyword

A variable declared using the `Static` statement is a local variable that retains its memory allocation for the whole time the application is running. When a procedure is revisited, the variable is still set to the same value that was last assigned to it.

At the procedure level, the `Static` keyword is used to preserve the memory values of all a procedure's variables between visits. Listing 4.1 shows the code for a small application that demonstrates the difference between *static procedures* and *static variables.* Exercise 4.1 demonstrates how the `TrueFlag` variable keeps its value between runs, while the `Incremental` variable does not.

EXERCISE 4.1: DEMONSTRATION OF *STATIC* KEYWORD'S EFFECTS ON THE LIFETIME OF VARIABLES

If you would like to try these procedures out, the following steps show you how to develop the GUI needed to run them:

1. Start AutoCAD, open the IDE, and choose Insert ➜ UserForm.
2. Drag and drop two text boxes and two command buttons onto the UserForm, starting from the top, as illustrated in Figure 4.4.
3. Change the Caption properties of the command buttons in the Properties window to **Switch It No 1** and **Switch It No 2**. (You may need to execute View ➜ Properties Window if the Properties Window is not already displayed.)
4. Enter the code shown in Listing 4.1 into the form's code window.
5. Select Run ‹ Run Sub/UserForm.

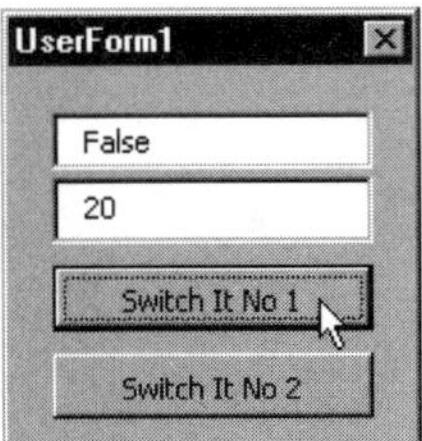

Figure 4.4 *The UserForm with two text boxes and two command buttons*

6. Repeatedly click the Switch It No 1 button. The static procedure runs with each click, and the top text-box switches between True and False, while the value in the second text-box increases by five each time.

7. Repeatedly click the Switch It No 2 button. The `SwitchIt2` procedure runs with each click, and the top text-box switches between True and False, because `TrueFlag` is declared as a static variable and so retains its previous value. The value in the second text-box remains at 5 because the `Incremental` variable is initialized to zero every time the `SwitchIt2` procedure runs (because the `Incremental` variable is allocated a fresh memory location each time).

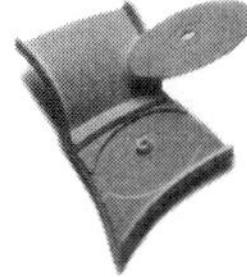

Listing 4.1: Application with *Static* Procedures and Variables

```
Private Static Sub SwitchIt1()
Dim TrueFlag As Boolean
Dim Incremental As Integer
TrueFlag = Not TrueFlag
TextBox1.Text = TrueFlag
Incremental = Incremental + 5
TextBox2.Text = Incremental
End Sub

Private Sub SwitchIt2()
Static TrueFlag As Boolean
Dim Incremental As Integer
TrueFlag = Not TrueFlag
TextBox1.Text = TrueFlag
Incremental = Incremental + 5
TextBox2.Text = Incremental
End Sub
```

```
18
19  Private Sub CommandButton1_Click()
20  SwitchIt1
21  End Sub
22
23  Private Sub CommandButton2_Click()
24  SwitchIt2
25  End Sub
```

ANALYSIS

- Line 1 declares procedure SwitchIt1 using the Static keyword, so that it holds onto all the memory allocated to its variables as long as UserForm1 stays loaded.
- Line 2 uses the Dim statement to declare the variable TrueFlag as a Boolean type. This will be assigned the default value False.
- Line 3 uses the Dim statement to declare the Incremental variable as an Integer type. This will be assigned the default value zero.
- Line 4 toggles the value of TrueFlag to False if it is True, or to True if it is False.
- Line 5 assigns the value of TrueFlag to the Text property of TextBox1, to display it to the user.
- Line 6 adds 5 to the value stored at the memory location referred to by the Incremental variable.
- Line 7 assigns the value referred to by Incremental to Textbox2's Text property to display it.
- Line 8 ends the static procedure SwitchIt1, but the storage locations allocated to the TrueFlag and Incremental variables are retained intact for the next call to SwitchIt1.
- Line 10 declares SwitchIt2 as a normal, run-of-the-mill procedure, so any variables it contains that are not declared as static variables themselves will actually lose their values when the procedure finishes executing.
- Line 11 declares the TrueFlag variable using the Static statement so that TrueFlag will hold onto its memory location and value for the whole time that UserForm is loaded.
- Line 12 uses the Dim statement to declare the Incremental variable as an Integer type and sets its value to zero.

- Line 13 toggles the value of `TrueFlag` from True to False and vice versa.
- Line 14 displays the value of `TrueFlag` in `TextBox1`.
- Line 15 adds five to the value of `Incremental`, which has just been set to zero—this has the same effect as assigning a 5 to `Incremental` each time.
- Line 16 displays the value of `Incremental` in `TextBox2`.
- Line 17 ends procedure `SwitchIt2` and frees the storage location allocated to `Incremental`.
- Line 19 starts the `Click Event` procedure of the command button with the caption "Switch It No 1."
- Line 20 calls `SwitchIt1` to perform the application's response to the click.
- Line 21 ends the `Click` event.
- Lines 23 through 25 are similar to lines 19 through 21 but call `SwitchIt2` in response to the Switch It No 2 button's being clicked.

When a UserForm is open, you can unload it by ending the application or by inserting the statement `Unload UserForm1` *when UserForm1 is its name, or more generically as Unload Me when it is the active UserForm. Exercise 1 in Chapter 5 discusses the Unload method in more detail.*

Defining Your Own Types

You may want to combine a few related items of data together into new types. These are called *user-defined types*. For example, suppose you want to create a type named LineDetails that combines all the details about a line. All you need to do is place the following type definition into the General Declarations section of a UserForm or module. You'll see this LineDetails type in action later when you get to Chapter 6.

```
Type LineDetails
    StartPosition(2) As Double
    EndPosition(2) As Double
    Thickness As Double
    Color As Integer
    Length As Double 'read-only
    Angle As Double 'read only
End Type
```

Notice how the declaration starts with `Type` and finishes with `End Type`, and that every element within the declaration has its type explicitly defined. These types need to be specified so that the interpreter can calculate the amount of memory required by a new type, by summing the memory requirements of each element. User-defined types can include other user-defined types, provided that they have been previously declared so that Visual Basic can do its memory calculations.

The benefits of having a user-defined type is that related items of data are grouped together in one named variable that can be passed as a procedure argument, rather than your having to pass each item individually. The scope rules that apply to constants and variables also apply to types. See the section "Scope of Constants and Variables" earlier in this chapter.

Using Conditions to Control Code Execution

`If` statements allow you to set conditions that determine whether or not a block of code gets executed. You have just seen the `If` statement in action in Listing 4.1. VBA offers a variety of `If` statement structures, which are all described in this section. Also included here is the `Select Case` statement, which allows the value of one variable or expression to determine which block of statements from a group to execute.

If...Then... Block

The `If` statement allows you to state conditions that must be met before a block of code statements can be executed. The conditional expression is usually some comparison, such as

```
A = 1
B > C
A + B <= C - D
A <> D
```

where > means greater than, <= means less than or equal to, and <> means not equal to. The "Comparison Operators" sidebar lists all the different combinations available. The block of code inside the `If` statement is executed only if the conditional expression evaluates to True; otherwise, execution jumps to the End If statement, or to the next line if the whole If statement block is contained in a single statement.

When an If statement block contains only one statement, the whole block can be written on a single line, as shown in the following FindMax function:

```
Function FindMax(Length1, Length2)
    If Length1 < Length2 Then Length1 = Length2
    FindMax = Length1
End Function
```

Alternatively, an If statement block with one statement can also be written over several lines, which requires an End If statement to indicate the end. For example, the same FindMax function can be written as

```
Function FindMax(Length1, Length2)
If Length1 < Length2 Then
    Length1 = Length2
End If
FindMax = Length1
End Function
```

Similarly, when there are several coding statements, these can be placed on separate lines, as in

```
If A = B then
    C = A + 1
    D = A * 2
    E = A - 3
End If
```

Or they can be placed on the same line separated by colons:

```
If A = B then
    C = A + 1: D = A * 2: E = A - 3
End If
```

Even the whole If statement can be placed on the same line:

```
If A = B then C = A + 1: D = A * 2: E = A - 3
```

Be aware, though, that code containing multiple statement lines is generally harder to read and maintain as compared with single statement lines.

You can have `If` statements nested inside other `If` statements, with each one terminated by an `End If`. For example:

```
If A = B then
    If  A = C then
        D = 3 * A
    End If
End If
```

Placing one `If` statement inside another `If` statement without any other coding statements is considered bad programming practice and can be avoided by combining the conditions, as follows:

```
If A = B and A = C then
    D = 3 * A
End if
```

Comparison Operators

Comparison operators are used to compare the values of two expressions and provide a True or False result. Here are the operators available in VBA:

=	Equals
>	Greater than
<	Less than
>=	Greater than or equal to
<=	Less than or equal to
<>	Not equal to

If...Then...Else...

The `If...Then...Else...` statement allows you to have two blocks of statements: one to be executed if the condition is True, and the other to be executed if the condition is False. For example:

```
If A = B then
    C = A
Else
    C = D
End If
```

The following example gives an `If...Then...Else...` statement that includes some nested `If` statements:

```
If Number = 1 Then
    Count1 = Count1 + 1
Else
    If Number = 2 Then
        Count2 = Count2 + 1
    Else
        If Number = 3 then
            Count3 = Count3 + 1
        Else
            CountX = CountX + 1
        End if
    End If
End If
```

VBA provides an `ElseIf` clause that is useful for combining an `Else` clause that's immediately followed by an `If` statement. For example, the `If...Then...Else...` block shown just above can be rewritten as follows:

```
If Number = 1 Then
    Count1 = Count1 + 1
ElseIf Number = 2 Then
    Count2 = Count2 + 1
ElseIf Number = 3 then
    Count3 = Count3 + 1
Else
    CountX = CountX + 1
End If
```

This rewrite avoids the need for so many `End If` statements and so much statement indenting. The statement in the last `Else` clause will be executed if the Number variable is not equal to 1, 2, or 3. This version is easier to read and maintain than the first version. However, where the same variable is being tested at every condition, a `Select Case` statement provides an even better alternative.

Select Case Statement

The `Select Case` statement provides a way of selecting a block of code to be executed according to the value of an expression given in the first line of this statement. The designated value can be just about anything; in the following statement, the expression is the name of the door style that's currently selected:

```
Select Case CurrentDoorStyle
Case "Tudor"
   Price = 125.00
Case "Victorian"
   Price = 115.00
Case "Federation"
   Price = 110.00
Case "Colonial"
   Price = 100.00
Case "Leadlight"
   Price = 210.00
Case "Interior2Panel"
   Price = 79.00
Case "Interior4Panel"
   Price = 89.00
Case Else
   Price = 0.00
End Select
```

The value of the variable `CurrentDoorStyle` is a string specifying the current door's style. When the `Select Case` statement is entered, this string is compared with the strings in each `Case` clause until either a match is found or the `Case Else` clause is encountered. The `Price` variable is then set to the price in the statement from the first `Case` clause that evaluates to True.

Using Loops to Repeat Code

This section shows you how to execute a block of code repeatedly, for a specified number of times using the `For` loop, or until a certain condition arises using the `While` loop. You'll find these two loops used in many of the coding exercises throughout this book. The `For` loop is especially useful when all the objects in a collection need to be accessed, and the `While` loop is especially useful for data input from either a file or the user.

Repeating Code a Set Number of Times

When you want to repeatedly execute a block of statements a specific number of times, use a For loop. The For loop has the following structure:

```
For Counter = Start to Finish [Step stepsize]
Statements
Next [Counter]
```

where Counter is the variable that keeps tabs on how many times the loop has been executed.

When the For loop is first entered, the Counter variable is initialized to Start. All the statements are then executed until the Next clause. If a step has been specified, it is added to the Counter; otherwise, Counter is incremented by one, which is the default. *Steps* specify how much the counter is incremented and can be positive or negative; negative steps are used when the value assigned to Start is greater than the value assigned to Finish.

When the Counter variable becomes greater than the Finish value (or less than, if you're using negative steps), code execution jumps to the statement after the Next clause.

The variable used for the loop counter should never be updated inside the loop. This may lead to a never-ending loop or the loop may be terminated prematurely.

The For loop is ideal for processing the data values in an array. With an array, the Start and Finish values are replaced by the index value for the first and last elements in the array. For example, to change the color of all the lines stored in the AllLines array to green, use the following code:

```
For Counter = 0 to 534
    AllLines(Counter).Color = acGreen
Next
```

For loops can be nested inside other For loops, which is ideal for processing multi-dimensional arrays. For example, consider the following three-dimensional array:

```
Dim AllData(0 to 4,5,1 to 6) as Double
```

To initialize all the elements in this array to zero, you'd use the following code:

```
For Index1 = 0 to 4
    For Index2 = 0 to 4
        For Index3 = 1 to 6
            AllData(Index1,Index2,Index3) = 0.0
        Next Index3
    Next Index2
 Next Index1
```

Although it's not a requirement, placing the loop counters after the `Next` clauses can improve the readability of your code, especially when several `For` loops are nested inside one another. The loop counters become even more important when there are lots of statements.

There is also a `For Each` loop that allows you to access each item from a collection of objects or an array. The syntax of the `For Each` loop is given in The Microsoft Forms Object Model section later in this chapter and you can see it in use in Listing 6.4 from Chapter 6.

Repeating Code an Unknown Number of Times

When you want to repeat a block of code while some condition evaluates to True (or False), but you don't know the number of times required, you need to include a `While` loop. The structure of the `While` loop is as follows:

```
While condition
statements
Wend
```

One of the most common uses of the `While` loop is to read data from a file when it is not always clear how many data items are actually in the file. You'll see how this is done in Chapter 11 where file input and output are described.

When the interpreter enters the `While` loop, it evaluates the condition. If the condition evaluates to True, the statements inside the `While` loop are executed until the `Wend` clause is encountered. Then the interpreter jumps back up to the start of the loop and evaluates the condition again. This looping is repeated until the condition becomes False, when execution jumps down to the statement after the `Wend` clause.

`While` *loops are the most likely cause of a program's failing to stop, so great care must be exercised to ensure that at least one of the variables in the condition actually changes inside the loop. The best place to update this variable is in the statement preceding the* `Wend` *clause.*

There is also a `Do` loop that lets you choose whether the condition is checked at the beginning or the end of the loop.

Overview of Objects, Properties, Methods, and Events

VBA is an object-oriented environment, containing many different classes of objects. Each class has its own set of properties to define the appearance of the objects, and methods to manipulate the objects that are instances of that class.

Some classes, such as Toolbox controls, also have their own set of event procedures that are coded with the application's response to user events. Don't let the substantial number of these objects, properties, methods, and events overwhelm you—a little goes a long way. You actually only need to know about a few of them to get started.

All about Objects

Everything relating to an object is defined in its class. There are two main groups of AutoCAD objects:

Drawing Objects Drawing objects represent anything that has been drawn in the Model Space tab of the AutoCAD window (for another look at this window, see Figure 2.9 in Chapter 2. Even when you draw a simple line, AutoCAD creates an object to store all the details needed to regenerate it.

VBA (UserForm) Objects UserForm objects represent anything that's included in the graphical user interface (GUI). So each time you drag and drop a control from the Toolbox, an object is created that is an instance of that class of control.

Classes of Objects

In the object-oriented paradigm, each type of object and all its properties, methods, and events are encapsulated in a single class that has the same name as the type of object it contains. *Classes* can be thought of as templates for creating as many objects as you need. A class contains the code required to create an instance of that class. For example, when a new object is created, its Name property is assigned the name of the class it is based on, followed by a sequential number to distinguish the new object from any other instances of the same class.

Objects are said to be instances of classes, and their properties, methods, and events are said to be members of that class.

Collections of Objects

Related objects are grouped together into collections. Collections of objects provide the same benefits as arrays, in that items in the collection can all be referenced using a single name and an index value. A collection differs from an array, however, in that it can contain different types of items. For example, AutoCAD has a ModelSpace collection containing all the objects associated with the Model Space tab. VBA has a Forms collection that contains all the UserForm objects associated with the GUI, UserForms contain objects such as text boxes and command buttons that the user interacts with.

AutoCAD maintains several collections of objects, including the ModelSpace, PaperSpace, Documents, Layers, LineTypes, TextStyles, and ViewPorts collections, as well as heaps more. When you insert a UserForm into a project, VBA creates a Controls collection, and any control objects you drag and drop from the Toolbox are automatically added to the Control collection as you place them on the UserForm.

As already mentioned, objects in a collection—called members—need not belong to the same class. You can reference members in several ways; one way is to use an exclamation mark character (`!`) to associate the object with the collection:

```
UserForm1.Controls!TextBox1.Text = ″Hello″
```

If you are an Excel user you will already be familiar with this notation.

An alternative referencing method is to use an index to identify the member's position within the collection. The "position" is the order in which it was placed on the UserForm:

```
UserForm1.Controls(0).Text = "Text box 1"
```

This statement sets the Text property of the first object placed on `UserForm1` to the string `″Text box 1″`. You can also replace the index number with the control's name if known:

```
UserForm1.Controls.("TextBox1").Text = "Hello"
```

Both examples of using indices make use of the fact that the Item method is the default method of any collection and so can be implied. The following statement explicitly uses the Item method and has a numerical index value (this is the format used throughout this book):

```
UserForm1.Controls.Item(0).Text = "Hello"
```

This statement is said to "fully qualify" the TextBox object. Because the Text property is the default property of a text box, and the Item method is the default method of a collection, and the Controls collection is the default collection of a UserForm, and UserForm1 is the active UserForm, the above statement can be entered in the Code window belonging to `UserForm1` as

```
TextBox1 = "Hello"
```

with the UserForm, the Controls collection, the Item method, and the Text property all being implied.

AutoCAD Drawing Objects

AutoCAD has its own set of drawing objects that help you add the various components needed to construct a drawing. Figure 4.5 shows the hierarchical structure of the AutoCAD object model.

Attaching the `Add` prefix to a drawing object's name is a common way to create drawing objects. For example, the following statement creates a Circle object:

```
Application.Documents.Item(0).ModelSpace.AddCircle Center, Radius
```

The Application Object

The AutoCAD *Application object* sits at the top of the model and represents the current session of the AutoCAD application. As you draw items, their details are stored in objects and added to this Application object. Because only one AutoCAD Application object is allowed per session, the application can be implied when accessing the objects it contains. So, the statement example from the preceding section can be rewritten as

```
Documents.Item(0).ModelSpace.AddCircle Center, Radius
```

The Documents Collection

The AutoCAD *Documents collection,* which is the next level down from the Application object, allows you to access any document that's currently open in the AutoCAD application. You use the `Item` method with an index value to denote the Document object's position in the collection.

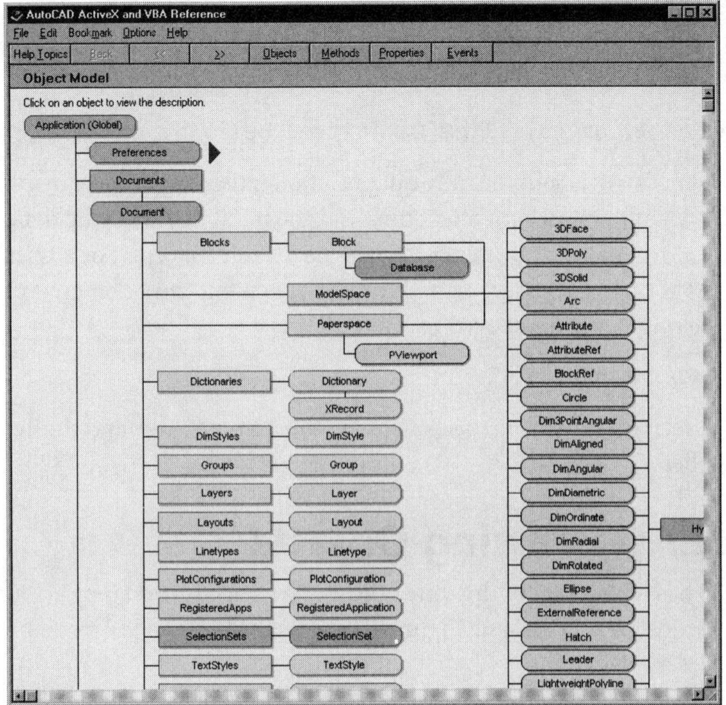

Figure 4.5 *The AutoCAD object model*

AutoCAD provides two ways to access the active (or current) document: via the ActiveDocument property (of the Application object), or by using the keyword `ThisDrawing`. These two methods are illustrated in the following two statements, which are equivalent:

```
ActiveDocument.ModelSpace.AddCircle MyCenter, MyRadius
ThisDrawing.ModelSpace.AddCircle MyCenter, MyRadius
```

You will need to use either of the above statements if you are entering code into a UserForm's Code window.

If you are using ThisDrawing's Code window, because only one document can be active at any point in time, the documents themselves can also be implied. So you can rewrite either of the preceding statements as follows:

```
ModelSpace.AddCircle MyCenter, MyRadius
```

The Documents collection includes the *ModelSpace collection*, which comprises all the objects from the Model Space tab, and the *Layouts collection*, which contains a Layout object for each Layout tab in the open AutoCAD application. Because the Document object can access any of the collections associated with drawing objects, and all the objects contained in these collections can be accessed individually, you can, in effect, access any drawing object in the currently open AutoCAD application. For example, the following For loop uses the Item method with Count as the index to access all the objects one by one from the ModelSpace collection, and assigns the value of the constant `acRed` to their Color properties:

```
Sub ChangeColor()
For Count = 0 To ModelSpace.Count
    ModelSpace.Item(Count).Color = acRed
Next
End Sub
```

The Microsoft Forms Object Model

AutoCAD's VBA is an object-oriented programming environment that contains a large collection of objects. Figure 4.6 shows the hierarchical structure of the Forms object model.

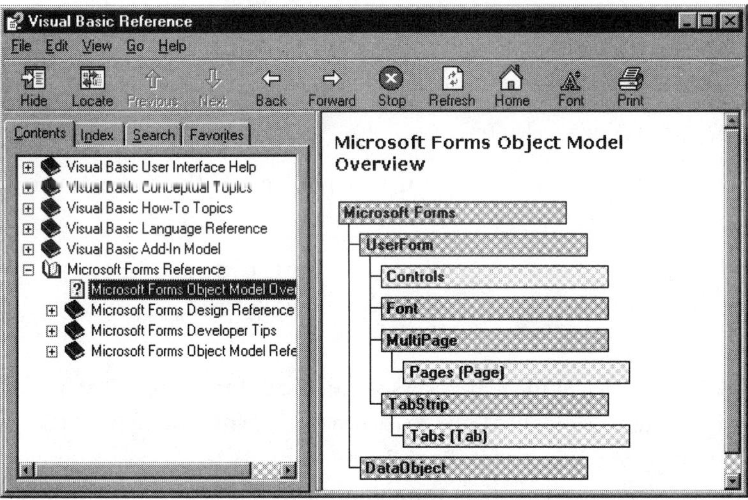

Figure 4.6 *Microsoft Forms object model*

To view the Microsoft Forms object model:

1. Choose Help ➜ Microsoft Visual Basic Help to display the Visual Basic References dialog box.
2. Select the Contents tab and click Microsoft Forms Reference to expand its list.
3. Double-click the Microsoft Forms Object Model Overview item. The Microsoft Forms object model appears in the right pane as shown in Figure 4.6.

Objects in the Forms object model have sets of properties, events, and methods that help you develop applications with which users can interact.

The Microsoft Forms Collection

The *Microsoft Forms collection* sits at the top of the model and contains all the UserForm objects from the next level down. A UserForm object, which can be a window or a dialog box, is the main part of the GUI; it acts like a container for the controls the user handles. Each UserForm has properties that are assigned values, allowing it to be maximized, minimized, or closed in the same way as any standard window. Other properties can be assigned text strings and colors to define how they will appear on the screen.

The Controls Collection

Each UserForm object has a *Controls collection* that contains all the Control objects that have been dragged from the Toolbox and positioned on the UserForm. A Control object from the Controls collection can be identified by a number representing the order in which it was placed on the UserForm. For example, a Label control that was the first object placed on UserForm1 can be accessed as

```
UserForm1.Controls(0)
```

This gives you the advantage of being able to access all the controls in a collection using a `For` loop, as follows:

```
For Each CurrentControl In Controls
    CurrentControl.BackColor = vbBlue
Next
```

The `For` statement initially accesses the first control from the Controls collection and assigns it to the `CurrentControl` variable. The next statement (`CurrentControl.BackColor = vbBlue`) sets its `BackColor` property to blue. At the `Next` statement, execution loops back to the beginning of the `For` statement, and the next control in the collection is assigned to the `CurrentControl` variable. The looping continues until all the controls in the collection have been set to blue.

The Label control that you used in the Metric Imperial Converter application in Chapter 1 can also be accessed using the following formats:

```
UserForm1.Controls!Label1
UserForm1.Controls("Label1")
UserForm1.Label1.
```

If you are accessing a control from code entered into the Code window that belongs to the same UserForm as the control, you can refer to the control by name and the UserForm portion can be implied, like this:

```
Label1
```

The format I've chosen for this book is to refer to controls by name only. The exception is when the control belongs to a different UserForm, when the name of the UserForm also needs to be included.

All about Properties

Each class of object has its own set of *properties*. These properties are initially set to default values when the object they belong to is first created. Properties define how an object appears on the screen, including things such as coloring, dimensions, and position—there is even a Visible property that can be set to False so that the object cannot be seen at all! Values can be assigned to properties at design time in the Properties window from the IDE. As well, properties can be assigned at run time by assigning values in code. For example, the Properties window for UserForms contains Height and Width entries, and the following statements show how these properties can also be assigned in code:

```
UserForm1.Height = 150
UserForm2.Width = 200
```

Design Time vs. Run Time

All the time you spend puttering around in the IDE developing a project is considered *design time* because you are still designing your project. Anything that happens while your code is actually executing is said to happen in *run time*. During design time, you will spend your time creating the GUI and developing the code to respond to a user's actions. While creating the GUI you will set properties such as Name, Caption, and Text in the Properties window.

Other kinds of items will require your attention in run time. For example, you may need to change a property while your application is running, such as making a control visible or invisible; or you may need to give a control such as a text box the focus, so that the Entry cursor appears inside it ready for the user's input.

Changing Properties with Preset Values

Many properties can only be set to one of a limited number of predefined values. These are the Enumerated types. Such properties can be set in the Properties window at design time, or by assigning them the values of predefined constants in code. When you select these properties from the Properties window, a down-arrow button appears in the settings column to indicate that a drop-down list of values is available for you to choose from.

The following steps show you how to change the StartUpPosition and BackColor properties of UserForm1:

1. Select UserForm1 from the Object list at the top of the Properties window. Select the StartUpPosition property. A down-arrow button appears to the right of the settings column to let you know that this property can only be set to one of the predefined values in the drop-down list that appears, as shown in Figure 4.7.

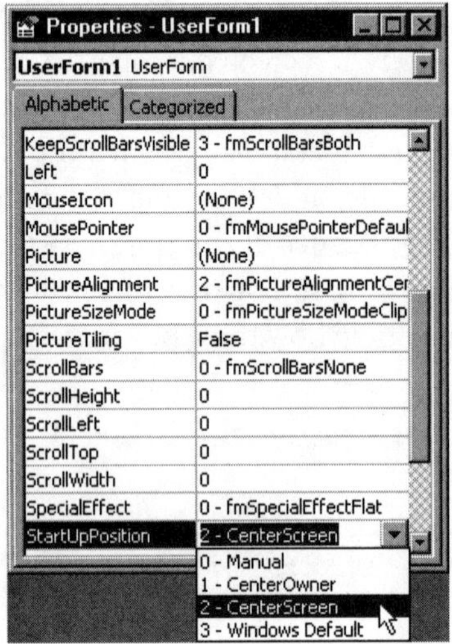

***Figure 4.7** The Drop-down list for the StartUpPosition property*

2. Select the CenterScreen setting. The setting appears in the settings column for the StartUpPosition property.

The StartUpPosition property is unique to the UserForm class of object and determines the position of the UserForm on the screen.

3. Continuing with UserForm1 still active, click the BackColor property in either tab (Alphabetic or Categorized) of the Properties Window, and click the down-arrow button that appears.
4. A drop-down list with two tabs appears. The System tab (Figure 4.8) contains all the color settings that have been assigned to Microsoft Windows components by the current Display Scheme in Control Panel. The Palette tab (Figure 4.9) contains the array of colors available in the default palette on your PC.

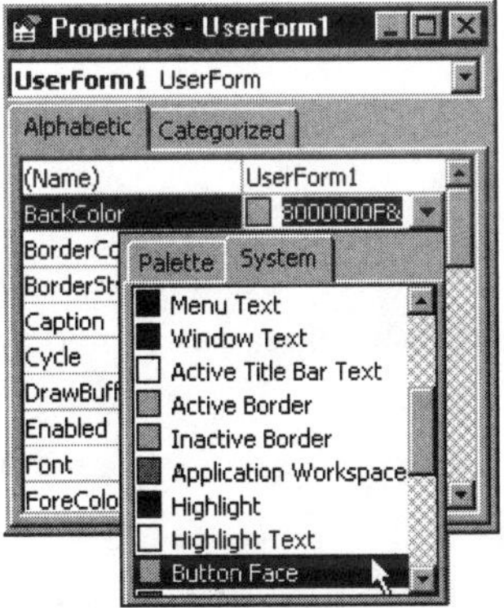

Figure 4.8 *System tab, containing colors assigned to Windows components according to the Display Scheme in use*

5. Open the Palette tab and click the top-left color square, which is white (Figure 4.9). The Palette disappears, and the background of the UserForm changes to the color selected.

Changing the background color of a UserForm does not automatically update the background color of any controls placed on that UserForm. These will need to have their background colors explicitly changed, too. For example, if the UserForm contains any Label controls, only their caption text should be visible now that you've changed the color in Step 4. If setting the background property has no effect, make sure the BackStyle property is set to `fmBackStyleOpaque`.

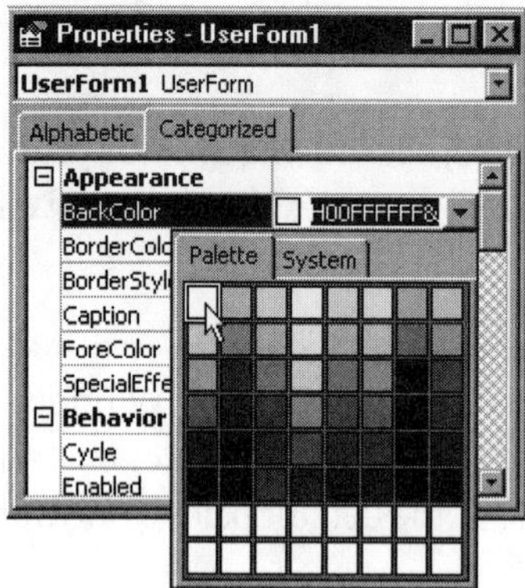

Figure 4.9 *Palette tab, containing the palette of colors available on your PC*

Changing Properties with Preset Values in Code

When assigning properties to the values of Enumerated types in code, a drop-down list containing all the constant names for these values will appear, as shown in Figure 4.10.

Figure 4.10 *A drop-down list of Enumerated types*

Changing Properties from Dialog Boxes

Some properties display an ellipsis button when selected. Clicking one of these buttons opens a dialog box that is often retrieved from the Microsoft Windows environment under which you're currently running. For example, the following steps show you how to change the Font property for UserForm1:

1. Start a new application, insert a UserForm, and add a Label control. From the Properties window, select Label1 from the Objects list and click the Font property. An ellipsis button appears at the right of the settings column, as shown in Figure 4.11.

***Figure 4.11** The ellipsis button beside the Font property indicates that a dialog box will be displayed when this is selected*

2. Click the ellipsis button. The Font dialog box appears (Figure 4.12).

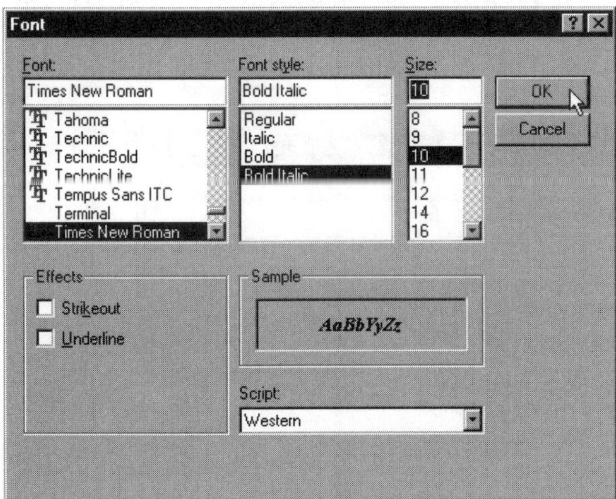

***Figure 4.12** The Font dialog box*

3. Select Times New Roman from the Font list, Bold Italic from the Font Style list, and 10 from the Size list. Click OK. The Font dialog box closes, and the Label1 text appears, written using the new Font property settings, as shown here:

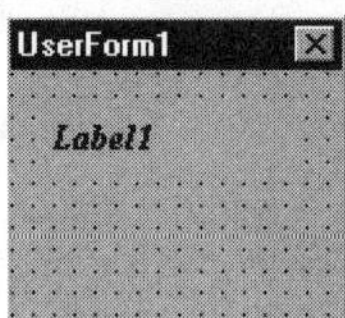

Now that you've read through the steps for changing properties in the Properties window at design time, let's see how to change them from code so that they are updated while your application is running.

Changing Properties from Dialog Boxes in Code

The following steps show you how to set the Font property in code so that the changes will occur at run time:

1. Double-click `CommandButton1`. The Code window opens, displaying the Click event procedure for the `CommandButton1` object.

2. Enter the following statement, finishing with a period character (`.`):

```
commandbutton1.font.
```

The pop-up list of properties belonging to the Font object appears. Compare this list with the items shown in the Font dialog box in Figure 4.12. You'll notice that many of the same options are available, such as strikethrough, etc.

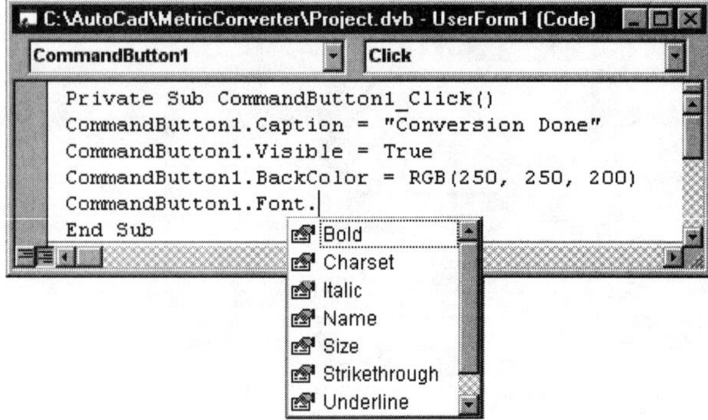

3. Type the remainder of the statement you started at Step 2 as follows:

```
commandbutton1.font.name="Arial Black"
```

Choose Run ➔ Run Sub/UserForm to run your program, and click the Convert button. The caption on the command button changes to the new settings.

When a property setting is adjusted in code, the new setting is only available while the application is running—the value assigned in the code will not be associated with that property in the Properties window when you return to Design mode.

All about Methods

A *method* is a procedure that performs some action on the object with which it is associated. Some examples of methods that belong to the AutoCAD drawing object are AddText, AddLine, GetAngle, and Rotate. When called, some methods have parameters to which you assign values by listing arguments in the same order as the parameters are declared. The pop-up text from the Parameter Info editing feature gives you the parameters in the order required. This order allows the interpreter to match up the parameters with the arguments.

The Rotate method has two parameters: the BasePoint which is the center of rotation, and the RotationAngle which is the angle to be rotated. These parameters are listed in a pop-up when you type **Rotate** into the Code window, followed by a space, as shown here:

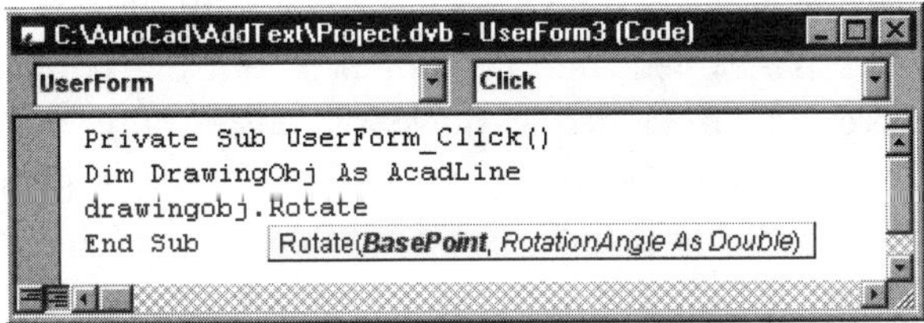

The method's parameters can be passed values using arguments, as follows:

```
DrawingObj.Rotate CenterOfRotation, RotationAngle
```

In this example, the variable `CenterOfRotation` argument is a three-element array to which you pass the x-, y-, and z-coordinates of a 3D point. The variable `RotationAngle` argument is passed an angle in radians as required by the Rotate method.

Other methods, such as GetAngle, return a value, so you need to assign the value returned to a variable, for example:

```
ReturnedAngle = ThisDrawing.Utility.GetAngle()
```

In an assignment statement, the interpreter still requires the parenthesis after the method's name even though there are no arguments to be passed.

When reading the properties and methods attached to an object, it is often less confusing to read from right to left. For example, the statement ReturnedAngle = ThisDrawing.Utility.GetAngle() can be read as "The variable ReturnedAngle is assigned the value returned by the GetAngle method of the Utility object, that is identified by the Utility property of the active document object named ThisDrawing."

All about Events

UserForms and the controls placed on them from the Toolbox all have their own sets of properties and methods that work in much the same way as those from the AutoCAD object model. Because these objects are part of the GUI, they are expected to respond to a user's actions, so they have their own predefined set of event procedures. For each control, it's up to you to decide what events your application is going to respond to and what the reaction will be.

The Microsoft Windows operating system continually monitors all the open windows on your PC for any sign of activity (events) from the user, from a program, or from a window. When an activity occurs, a message is sent to the operating system, which passes it around to all the open windows and their controls. Visual Basic automatically processes any relevant messages. If you've written code for a particular event happening to a specific control and the message comes in that the event has occurred, Visual Basic executes the code from that control's event procedure. This style of processing is called *event driven.*

Visual Basic's event-driven model can catch you up sometimes; you must remember that running code from one event can sometimes trigger another event procedure. For example, if you have coded the Change event procedure for a TextBox control and your code assigns a new text string to that text box, your Change event procedure will be invoked, which may cause your program to perform in some unexpected way that could even lead to an abnormal termination.

The set of executable events varies from control to control, but there is a lot of overlap, and often the same event is common to many controls. For example, the Click event is found in UserForms, text boxes, command buttons, option buttons, check boxes, and lots more.

The event procedures have names made up of the control's Name property, then an underscore character (_), followed by the name of the event. Here are a few examples:

```
CommandButton1_Click
OptionButton1_MouseDown
TextBox1_KeyPress
```

The IDE provides pairs of first and last statements for all event procedures—I refer to these throughout the book as skeleton procedures. *All you need to do is decide which user events you want to respond to, and code your response in the appropriate skeleton.*

Comparing VBA Programming Constructs

This section describes what is meant by each of the terms *macro*, *procedure*, *function*, *program*, and *application*, including the relationships and differences that exist among them.

Macros

A *macro* is a set of instructions that is executed each time its name or associated shortcut key is used. Macros can be one-liners or they can be quite lengthy and complex—they can even call other macros and run applications. Macros cannot have parameters, and they cannot return values, but they can be run from the AutoCAD window.

Macros are declared in the same way as normal procedures, using the Sub statement. For example:

```
Sub MyMacro( )
```

If you include any parameters inside the parentheses, for example,

```
Sub MyMacro(CurrentString As String)
```

Visual Basic will treat this block of code as a standard procedure, and it will not appear in the list in the Macros dialog box that's displayed from the AutoCAD window.

Procedures

A *procedure* contains a set of coding statements that perform a specific task. Visual Basic procedures are a series of statements enclosed between `Sub` and `End Sub` statements.

Procedures enable you to split a lengthy piece of code up into smaller more manageable parts, with each part becoming a procedure. It is good programming practice to use procedures when the same task needs to be performed from several different places—to avoid duplicate code.

For example, the Shelf Specification application shown in Figure 4.13 contains a procedure that examines the key pressed by the user to enter data into a text box, checking to see if it is a numeric character. If not, the application cancels the keystroke so that the non-numeric character is not appended to the string in the text box. The procedure is called by the KeyPress event procedures of all three text boxes.

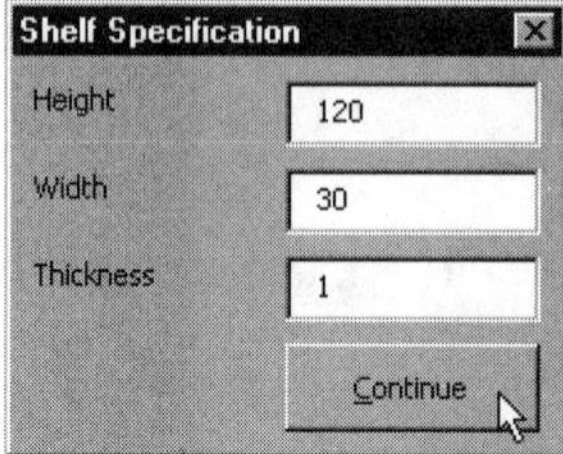

Figure 4.13 *Shelf Specification UserForm*

Exercise 4.2: The Shelf Specification Application for Dimensioning Shelves

The following steps show you how to develop the Shelf Specification application:

1. Start a new project and add a UserForm with three labels, three text boxes, and a command button.
2. Set the properties as shown in Table 4.1.
3. Type the CheckNumericKey procedure shown in Listing 4.2 into the General Declarations section of the UserForm. Enter the calls to it into the skeleton Keypress event procedures of the text boxes.

Table 4.1 Control Properties for Shelf Specification Application

OBJECT	CAPTION
UserForm1	Shelf Specification
Label1	Height
Label2	Width
Label3	Thickness
Command Button	Continue

4. Run your application from the Visual Basic Editor window and try entering some letters and numbers. The letters will be cancelled by the CheckNumericKey procedure and won't appear in any of the text boxes. Only when you type numeric characters will the numbers they represent be appended to the text box strings.

LISTING 4.2: CHECKNUMERICKEY PROCEDURE

```
Sub CheckNumericKey(ByRef Keyascii As MSForms.ReturnInteger)
    If Keyascii < 48 Or Keyascii > 57 Then
        Keyascii = 0
    End If
End Sub

Private Sub TextBox1_KeyPress(↵
   ByVal Keyascii As MSForms.ReturnInteger)
    CheckNumericKey Keyascii
End Sub

Private Sub TextBox2_KeyPress(↵
   ByVal Keyascii As MSForms.ReturnInteger)
    CheckNumericKey Keyascii
End Sub

Private Sub TextBox3_KeyPress(↵
   ByVal Keyascii As MSForms.ReturnInteger)
    CheckNumericKey Keyascii
End Sub
```

ANALYSIS

- Line 1 starts the `CheckNumericKey` procedure, which has one parameter that expects to be passed the character entered by the user. This procedure cancels any character entered that is outside the range 0 to 9.
- Line 2 verifies that the `Keyascii` character entered by the user is not in the range 48 through 57. The ASCII code for 0 is 48, and the ASCII code for 9 is 57, so the condition is True if a non-numeric key has been pressed. (Appendix B gives the ASCII codes for all keyboard characters.)
- Line 3 runs when a non-numeric key has been pressed; it sets the `Keyascii` variable to zero. When zero is passed back to the calling event procedure, the user input is cancelled.
- Line 4 ends the `If` statement.
- Line 5 ends the `CheckNumericKey` procedure.
- Line 6 is a blank line to make the code easier to read.
- Line 7 starts the `KeyPress` event procedure of `TextBox1`. The `KeyPress` event procedure has one parameter that is passed the ASCII code of the key pressed by the user while entering data into `TextBox1`.
- Line 8 calls the `CheckNumericKey` procedure with `Keyascii` as the argument. If a numeric key has been entered, the `Keyascii` value returned is appended to the end of the string displayed in the text box. If a non-numeric key has been entered, the `Keyascii` value returned is zero, and nothing is appended to the string.
- Line 9 ends the `KeyPress` event procedure of `TextBox1`.
- Line 10 is a blank line to make the code easier to read.
- Lines 11–13 and 15–17 contain the `Keypress` event procedures of the other two text boxes, which both call the `CheckNumericKey` procedure in exactly the same way as the `KeyPress` event procedure of TextBox1.
- Line 14 is a blank line to make the code easier to read.

Setting the Tab Order for Controls

When your application is running, you can tab from text box to text box. The tab order is the same as the order in which you added the controls. This section describes how you can change this order—especially if you want to add more controls as an afterthought.

If you have ever had a broken mouse, you may have resorted to pressing the Tab key to move around among controls. The following steps show you how to set the tabs in your application using the TabIndex property, so that users can tab through your controls in a logical order.

1. Start a new application and insert a UserForm containing two text boxes and a command button.
2. Choose Run ➜ Sub/UserForm. UserForm1 opens with the Enter cursor positioned inside the text box at the top.
3. Press the Tab key. The focus is moved to the next control in the Tab sequence, which is the second text box because it was placed on the UserForm after the first text box. By default, the Tab sequence follows the order in which the controls were placed on the UserForm.
4. Press Tab again. A dotted rectangle appears on the command button to show that it now has the focus. If you press Enter at this moment, the application will react as if you had clicked this command button and will execute the associated event.

Using the Shift+Tab key-combination allows you to go through the Tab sequence backwards.

5. Click the Close button to stop the application.

6. Press Tab again; this still works even though the application isn't running. This time, the control with the focus is displayed just like the active control is displayed—with a thick border and eight handles, as shown here:

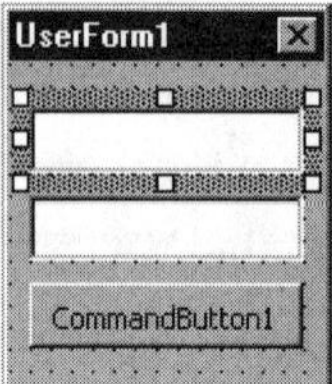

The order of the controls in the Tab sequence is initially determined by the chronological order in which controls were placed on the UserForm. If you are in Design mode, the Tab key visits all the controls in the sequence as you tab along. But when an application is actually running, only the controls with which the user interacts are visited by tabbing.

Suppose I need to add another text box between the two that are there already. By default, the Tab key will not visit this new, third text box until it has visited the command button. To change this arrangement, you set the TabIndex property in the Properties Window or in the code. The TabIndex property of each control is assigned a number that starts with zero, which represents the control's position in the Tab sequence. If you adjust the TabIndex number of one of the controls, it is slotted into that position in the sequence, and the TabIndex properties of all the other controls are automatically updated accordingly.

Functions

A *function* is a special kind of procedure that returns a single value, by assigning it to the function's name in the statement immediately before the `End Function` statement at the close of the function. You can append a type for this value to the end of the function's opening statement, as follows:

```
Function MyMacro(MyValue As Integer) As String
```

If the type is omitted, Visual Basic applies the Variant type.

Parameters and Arguments

A *parameter* is defined in the declaration of a function or procedure and is assigned a value by the calling statement, which is called an *argument*.

Parameters

Parameters make a procedure more generic, so it's quite common to have a list of parameters specified in parentheses as the first line (which is where the procedure is declared). Commas separate the parameters in the list, as shown here:

```
Sub ProcessTwoValues(Value1 As Integer, Value2 As Integer)
```

In the procedure call, arguments are used to pass values to these parameters, matching the values with parameters according to their order. For example, the procedure call for the `ProcessTwoValues` procedure could be as follows:

```
ProcessTwoValues 10, 6
```

where the first argument 10 is passed (or assigned) to the first parameter `Value1`, and the second argument 6 is passed (or assigned) to `Value2`.

Arguments

When you call a procedure that has parameters, you allocate values in the way of *arguments*. These arguments are matched up with the procedure's parameters, and the procedure executes. A procedure can be called in two ways:

```
ProcessTwoValues 4, 3
Call ProcessTwoValues (4, 3)
```

Both ways use the comma character (`,`) to separate the arguments. If you use the `Call` statement method, you must enclose the arguments in parentheses.

Programs

A *program* is a sequence of instructions that can be executed to perform some task. The term *program* is fairly generic and can encompass macros, procedures, and functions. The sequence of instructions can be in a high-level language such as Visual Basic, or in some other language that can be executed by a computer.

Applications

An *application* is a program developed to simplify a specific task such as word processing, spreadsheet analysis, or computer-aided drafting. The application is typically much larger than a single procedure, with plenty of facilities to perform various related things; the application seldom does just one particular thing.

An application normally has a GUI so that the user can interactively select the features to run. The act of selecting a feature causes one of the application's event procedures to run, which in turn might call a function, a macro, or a procedure that would carry out the user's requests.

Summary

After you've finished this chapter, you'll know the following about working with AutoCAD VBA:

- The difference between statements and expressions.
- How to declare variables.
- How to use the `Option Explicit` statement.
- How to handle arrays of variables.
- All about constants and how to view them in the Object Browser.
- Why you should use constants whenever possible.
- The different levels of scope for constants and variables.
- How to define your own types.
- The different flavors of `If` statements.
- How `Select Case` statements work.
- When to use `For` and `While` statements.
- The role of objects, properties, methods, and events.
- How to set the tab order for controls.
- The difference between macros, functions, and procedures.
- How to call procedures containing arguments.
- The difference between arguments and parameters.
- What programs and applications are.

Part 2

Drawing Lines and Solid Areas Using VBA Macros

In This Part

The AutoCAD Object Model

AUTOCAD VBA

Chapter 5

The *AutoCAD Object Model* defines the hierarchical structure for all objects that AutoCAD exposes to VBA. The AutoCAD Application object sits at the top and represents the entire AutoCAD application; at the next level down you'll find the AutoCAD Documents collection and the Document object, which include the drawing objects. Also at this level is the Preferences collection, which allows you to set your preferred AutoCAD options from your code.

In this chapter, you'll learn how to access the AutoCAD's various spaces and how to communicate with users from code using message boxes and the command line. At the end of the chapter you'll see demonstrations of some of the string-handling functions at work.

This chapter covers the following topics:

- The AutoCAD Application object
- Communicating with message boxes
- Working in the graphical object spaces
- The Preferences object
- Sending text to the AutoCAD command line
- Using the VB string-handling functions

This chapter marks the beginning of the part of this book that will be of most benefit to intermediate readers. As an AutoCAD developer, you must be able to find your way around the AutoCAD Object Model.

AutoCAD Application Object

The *AutoCAD Application object* sits at the top of the object model hierarchy and represents the whole AutoCAD application (see Figure 5.1). It contains all the details about the state of all components of the current AutoCAD session's environment, and everything the current session contains. To view the AutoCAD Object Model, choose Help ➜ Developer Help from the AutoCAD window, select the Contents tab, and click ActiveX and VBA Reference. The Object Model item is on top of the list.

In the object model hierarchy, objects are shown in boxes with rounded corners, and collections of objects are shown in boxes with squared corners.

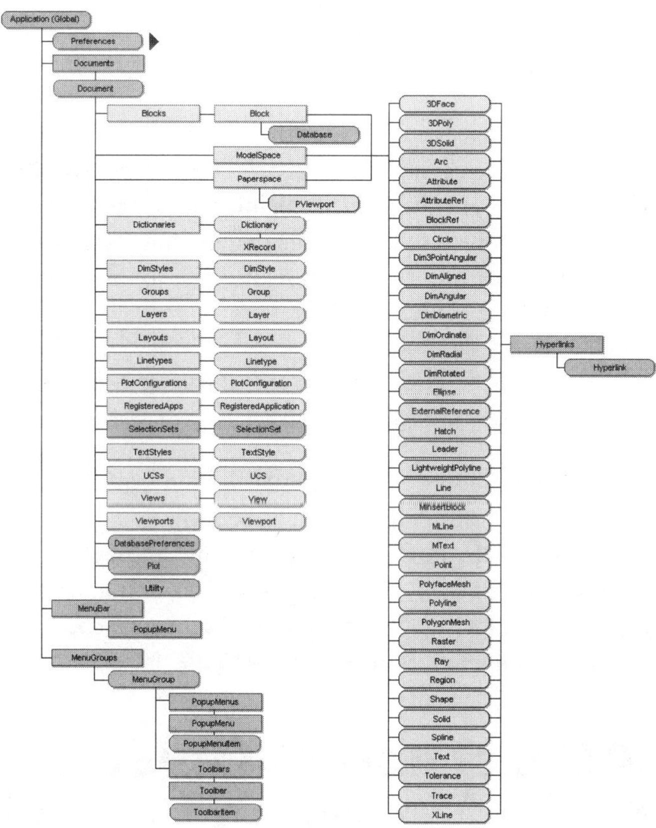

Figure 5.1 *The AutoCAD object model*

As you can see, the only way to access an AutoCAD object is through the Application object, which can be specified explicitly in a fully qualified statement, or implied by simply omitting the statement. For example, you can change the height of the active AutoCAD drawing from VBA code using the statement

```
Application.ActiveDocument.Height = 450
```

where the `ActiveDocument` is really the current AutoCAD drawing. Because there can only be one Application object ever, and one active document at any particular time, they can be omitted. Thus the preceding statement can be shortened to

```
Height = 450
```

and the interpreter automatically assumes that you mean the Height property of the current drawing.

The current drawing is automatically exposed to you from the IDE through its special `ThisDrawing` keyword to provide yet another way of referring to the same object:

```
ThisDrawing.Height = 450
```

This third statement performs exactly the same function as the other two; it's shorter than the first one and much clearer than the second one. Using `ThisDrawing`, it's easy to see (for example) that the Height property belongs to the active drawing rather than to the AutoCAD window or an active control. For conciseness and clarity, I use the `ThisDrawing` keyword throughout this book to refer to the current drawing.

The `ThisDrawing` *keyword is a good replacement for* `Application.ActiveDocument` *not only because it's more concise but also because it better reflects that the active drawing object is being referred to. Avoid writing code that's ambiguous, because it is harder to debug and update.*

In addition to providing access to documents, the Application object is your means to the MenuBar and MenuGroups collections; these allow you to control AutoCAD's menus and toolbars from code. You'll see how to do this in Chapter 11. Also available from the Application object is the Preferences object that, as mentioned, allows you to adjust the settings of the AutoCAD Options dialog box in your code. Later in this chapter, the section about the Preferences object gives you the details of how this is done.

AutoCAD Document Objects

A *Document object* represents an AutoCAD drawing and is positioned at the level immediately below the Application object in the object model hierarchy (see Figure 5.1).

Document objects contain graphical objects representing anything that's drawn on the active drawing (lines, circles, text, and so on).

Because AutoCAD allows you to have several drawings open inside the AutoCAD window, VBA provides the Documents collection to keep track of them all. You can access specific documents using the Item method from this collection. Follow the steps of Exercise 5.1 to develop the Finding Name application. This small application allows the user to enter a drawing object's position in the collection, and responds by displaying the drawing's name.

Exercise 5.1: The Finding Name Application

1. Open the IDE and insert a UserForm into a new project.
2. Drag and drop two text boxes, two labels, and a command button onto the UserForm, positioning them in a similar layout to that shown here. The user will enter the drawing number in the top text box.

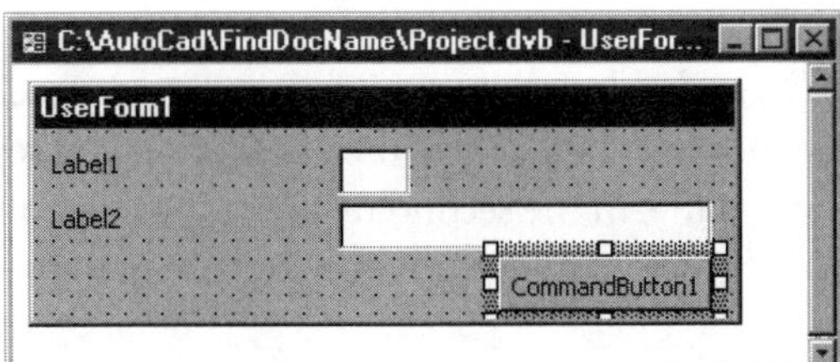

3. If the Properties window is not already displayed, choose View ➔ Properties Window. In the Properties window, change the Caption properties of the objects you entered in step 2, giving them the captions listed in Table 5.1.

Table 5.1 New Caption Property Settings for the GUI Objects in Finding Name

Object	Caption
UserForm1	Find Name of Drawing
Label1	Enter drawing number
Label2	The drawing's name is
CommandButton1	Exit

4. In the Properties window for CommandButton1, enter **x** for the Accelerator property.

   This makes the *x* in the Exit caption appear underlined, as shown just below. It lets users know that the Exit command button can also be "clicked" by pressing the Alt+x key-combination. This combination—x when pressed with Alt—is termed the *shortcut key.*

   Here is Userform1 after the captions have been updated and the Accelerator property has been set:

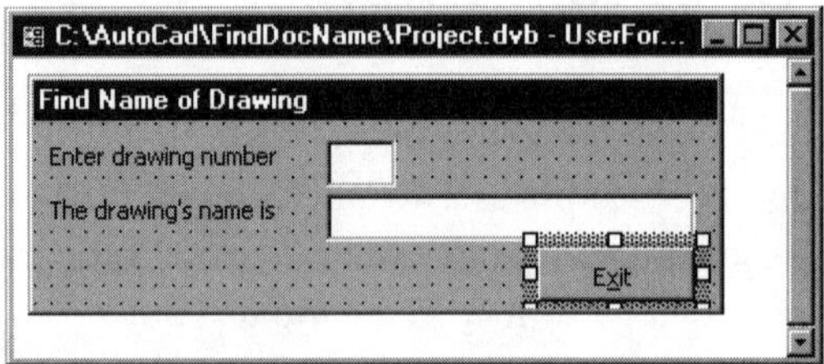

At this point you have developed the GUI for the First Name application. When the user enters a value into the top text box, the application will respond by displaying the appropriate document's name in the second text box. If no document is available at the index value entered by the user, a message will be displayed to the user.

Shortcut Keys

Shortcut keys allow users to interact with controls by pressing keys at the keyboard rather than clicking the mouse. In Windows applications, users expect to have alternatives to mouse-clicking command buttons and menu options. Some commands have a pseudo-standard or traditional shortcut key; for example, the shortcut for Exit is always x.

To create a shortcut key for a control, simply set its Accelerator property to the desired key. The only restriction is that the key must not be used as such by any other control in the same UserForm.

Coding the Finding Name Application

With the GUI in place, it is time to code the event procedures that will respond to the user's actions. You have to decide what actions you want your application to respond to. For this example, I have chosen responses for when the user changes the information in the text box and clicks on the command button. Enter the code from Listing 5.1 into the skeleton event procedures.

LISTING 5.1: THE FINDING NAME APPLICATION

```
1   Private Sub TextBox1_Change()
2       TextBox2.Text = ""
3       On Error Resume Next
4       TextBox2.Text = ↵
           Application.Documents.Item(CInt(TextBox1.Text)).Name
5       If TextBox1.Text <> "" And TextBox2.Text = "" Then
6           MsgBox "Document number " & TextBox1.Text & ↵
               " doesn't exist. Choose a smaller number!", ↵
               vbCritical, "Find Name Of Drawing - Error"
7           TextBox1.Text = ""
8       End If
9   End Sub
10
11  Private Sub CommandButton1_Click()
12      Unload UserForm1
13  End Sub
14
15  Private Sub UserForm_Terminate()
16      MsgBox "Have a Nice Day", vbOKOnly, "Find Name of ↵
           Drawing"
17  End Sub
```

ANALYSIS

- Line 1 starts the event procedure that will run if the contents of `TextBox1` are changed—for example, when the user presses any keyboard key while `TextBox1` has the focus.
- Line 2 sets the `Text` property of `TextBox2` to the empty string, to ensure that any previous document name is deleted.
- Line 3 contains the `On Error Resume Next` statement, which tests the value entered by the user to see if it will lead to a fatal error on line 4; if so, code execution jumps to the next statement (line 5).

  ***On Error Resume Next* Statement** This statement provides a way to test the water without jumping in. It allows your application to instruct the compiler to test whether executing the next statement would cause a run-time error; if so, the compiler skips it and jumps to the next statement. This allows an application to recover from what would have been a fatal error by ignoring the problematic statement altogether. Instead, the application continues to run as if nothing had happened. However—if your application is dependent on the skipped statement having run, you'll not be completely off the hook!

- Line 4 uses the `CInt` conversion function to convert the character string entered by the user to an integer value. The value returned by the `CInt` function replaces `CInt(TextBox1.Text)` in the statement and is passed as the argument in the call to the `Item` method of the `Documents` collection. The `Item` method returns the value of the `Name` property of the Document object, which is assigned to the `Text` property of `TextBox2` for displaying the result to the user.

  ***CInt* Function** The `CInt` function takes a number of any type and converts it to an integer value. The function takes the number passed to it and rounds it to the nearest integer value before returning it as the result. If the fractional part of the converted number is 0.5, this function rounds the number to the nearest even integer number. For example, if the result number is 1.5, the `CInt` function will return the value 2. If the number is 4.5, the `CInt` function will return 4.

  If the value used as the argument for `CInt` is not one of the types that can be converted to an integer (such as a string), an error is generated and your application will stop with a run-time error 13, "Type mismatch."

- Line 5 is the start of the `If` statement that checks whether the user has entered a number and whether the drawing's name is the empty string, which indicates that the document requested does not exist in the Documents collection.

- Line 6 calls the `MsgBox` function to display the dialog box shown in Figure 5.2 to warn the user about the critical error and to provide the information that the application cannot continue with the value entered. (The `MsgBox` function is explained at length in an upcoming section.) The message to be displayed is given as the first argument and is really three strings concatenated together using the Concatenation operator (&). The `vbCritical` constant used for the second argument displays the Critical (X) icon and an OK button inside the message box. The last argument is the caption that is to appear on the title bar of the message box.

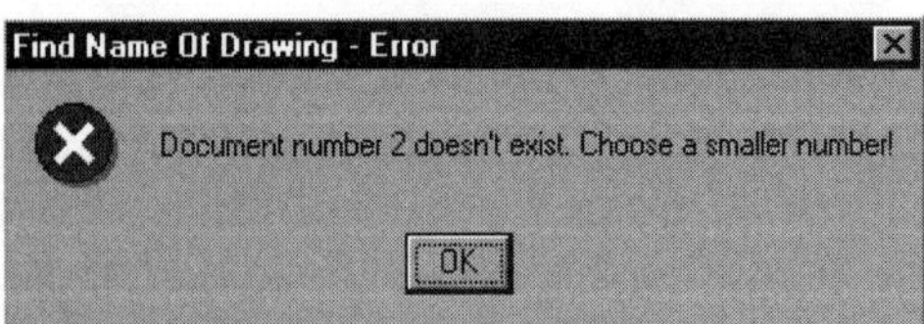

Figure 5.2 *Message box displayed when a document is not found*

- Line 7 clears the contents of `TextBox1` so that it's ready for the next user input.
- Line 8 marks the end of the `If` statement block.
- Line 9 is the end of the `Change` event procedure.
- Line 11 starts the Click event procedure for the command button.
- Line 12 uses the `Unload` statement with the argument `UserForm1`. This is used instead of the `End` statement so that the `Terminate` event procedure in Lines 15 through 17 is executed. This is in contrast to the `End` statement you have been using up until now, which just stops running the application then and there.

End Statement vs. *Unload* Statement

When the End statement is used to terminate an application, execution stops immediately and any memory used by the application is freed, and any open files are closed. When the Unload statement is used with a UserForm as the argument, the QueryClose and Terminate event procedures are triggered.

***QueryClose* Event Procedure** The `QueryClose` event procedure is used to query the user to see if they really do want to close the application. `QueryClose` has two parameters:

- `Cancel`, which can be set to True to cancel the user's action that started to terminate the application.
- `CloseMode`, which can be used to identify what caused the QueryClose event to be triggered. And if the application is to continue closing down, the memory it uses is freed and any open files are closed before execution is stopped.

***Terminate* Event Procedure** The Terminate event procedure is used to convey any last-minute information to the user, such as that the application has successfully closed down without any hitches. Terminate is triggered after a UserForm is unloaded—this procedure doesn't run if the application terminates abnormally or if an End statement has been used to stop the application in its tracks!

- Line 13 ends the `Click` event procedure.
- Line 15 starts the `Terminate` event procedure, which is triggered after `UserForm1` has been unloaded.
- Line 16 calls the `MsgBox` function and, as before (in Line 6), the first argument gives the message, the second one specifies the buttons and icons to be used, and the last one gives the caption for the title bar. This message box simply displays a

friendly gesture to the user (as shown in Figure 5.3) with an OK button that they can click when they've finished reading it.

- Line 17 ends the `Terminate` event procedure.

Figure 5.3 *Have a Nice Day message*

Now that you have coded your application, it's time to execute that code.

Running an Application from a Macro

To run your application from a macro, all you need to do is include a statement that opens the UserForm using the Show method. When you run the macro, the application will run just as if you had chosen Run ➜ Run Sub/UserForm from the VB Editor window.

EXERCISE 5.1: THE FINDING NAME APPLICATION (CONTINUED)

In the next series of steps, you'll set up your macro and run it.

1. Continuing in the VB Editor, select ThisDrawing from the Project Explorer window. (Choose View ➜ Project Explorer if it is not already displayed). The Code window for ThisDrawing appears.
2. Insert the following FindName macro into the Code window for ThisDrawing to enable your application to be run by a macro from the AutoCAD window:

   ```
   Sub FindName()
       UserForm1.Show
   End Sub
   ```

3. Open AutoCAD and choose File ➜ New to add a second drawing. It appears in the AutoCAD window with the title caption Drawing2.
4. Choose Tools ➜ Macro ➜ Macros. The Macros dialog box appears with the FindName macro listed.

5. Select FindName and click Run.
6. Enter **1** into the text box. `Drawing2.dwg` will appear in TextBox 2.

   Because the index for a collection begins at 0 rather than 1, the Item property number for the new drawing is 1.
7. Click the Exit command button to display the message box.
8. Click OK to close the message box and to close your application.

Running Your Application from the IDE

You can also run your application from the VB Editor. The following steps show you how:

Exercise 5.1: The Finding Name Application (continued)

1. Open the VB Editor and, with your application still loaded, choose Run ➜ Run Sub/UserForm.
2. Enter the number **0** into the top text box, as the drawing number. The filename `Drawing1.dwg` appears as the drawing name in the second text box because in any AutoCAD collection, the first item is in the zero position.

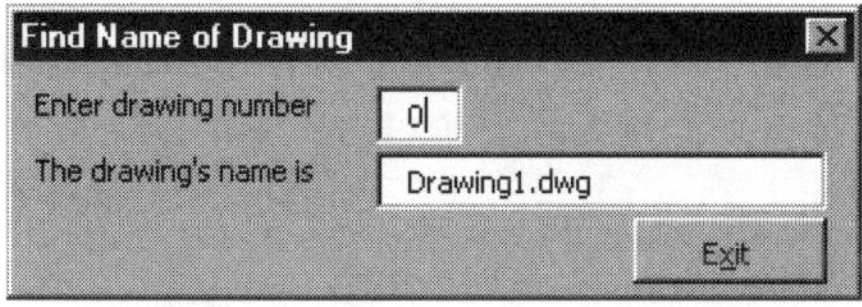

3. Click Exit to run the Terminate event procedure of the command button. The Have A Nice Day message box appears.
4. Click OK to close your application.

While you are developing code in the VB Editor, running your application from there is a quick way to see the results so far. After your code is fully implemented, you may find it more convenient to run your application from a macro without having to open the VB Editor. The next section shows you how.

Loading Your Application

Whether you run your application from the AutoCAD window or the VB Editor window, you will need to have your VBA project loaded. If you should close the AutoCAD window and reopen it again, your application will have vanished from the VB Editor window. The following steps show you how to access your code again if this should happen:

1. From the AutoCAD window, choose Tools ➔ Macro ➔ Load Project. The Open VBA Project dialog box appears.
2. Select the file containing your project and click Open. The Open VBA Project dialog box closes again, and your application is loaded into the VB Editor window.
3. From the Project Explorer window, select the module containing the code you want to access.

   If the module selected is a UserForm, the UserForm's graphical representation will appear; otherwise, the Code window for the selected module will appear. Double-click the graphical representation of the UserForm to open its Code window.

Communicating with Message Boxes

Message boxes are a special kind of dialog box that pop up while a Windows application runs, to provide brief messages to the user. The information is often an error message about something that has gone wrong, or a warning to let you know that you're trying to exit from an application without saving your work. It may also just be a piece of helpful information.

The MsgBox Function

The *MsgBox function* provides a quick-and-easy way to display message boxes to communicate with your users—only a single line of code is required. Following is the syntax for this function:

```
MsgBox prompt, buttons, title, helpfile, context
```

The `prompt` argument is the message that will appear in the message box and is the only argument that must be specified.

The *buttons* argument is optional and, if provided, must be one of the constants (or its integer value) that represents a button or an icon (see Table 5.2).

The *title* argument, also optional, specifies the caption displayed in the title bar. If this argument is omitted, the title text defaults to the string `"AutoCAD"`.

The *helpfile* and *context* arguments are also optional, but you can't have one without the other. The *helpfile* argument specifies the name of the Help file that contains context-sensitive Help text for the message box, and the *context* argument specifies the number allocated to the Help topic by the Help author.

Modal vs. Modeless Dialog Boxes

When a message box is displayed, it "seems" to take over your PC and you have to click one of its buttons to make it go away before you can continue working. This is because message boxes are usually displayed as *modal* rather than *modeless.*

Message boxes are usually modal dialog boxes, which means they must be closed by a user's response before the application will continue working. In comparison, forms are usually modeless and allow you to continue working while they are on display. Occasionally, you may want to make a UserForm modal, such as one that forces the user to give their name and password before continuing to run an application. The following statement shows how a Login UserForm can be opened as modal in code, by calling its `Show` method with the Visual Basic constant `vbModal` as the argument:

```
frmLogin.Show vbModal
```

Buttons in Message Boxes

Table 5.2 lists some of the constants with the buttons that appear in the message box when the constant is passed as the *buttons* argument in a call to the MsgBox function.

The first six constants in Table 5.2 display buttons, and the last four display icons. If only an icon constant is provided as the argument, the OK button is also included automatically. For example, this statement:

```
MsgBox "This message box contains the vbInformation icon!", ↵
   vbInformation
```

displays the message box shown in Figure 5.4.

Table 5.2 Constants and the Buttons They Represent

CONSTANT	BUTTON
vbOKOnly	OK button only
vbOKCancel	OK and Cancel buttons
vbAbortRetryIgnore	Abort, Retry, and Ignore buttons
vbYesNoCancel	Yes, No, and Cancel buttons
vbYesNo	Yes and No buttons
vbRetryCancel	Retry and Cancel buttons
vbCritical	Critical Message icon with OK button
vbQuestion	Warning Query icon
vbExclamation	Warning Message icon
vbInformation	Information Message icon

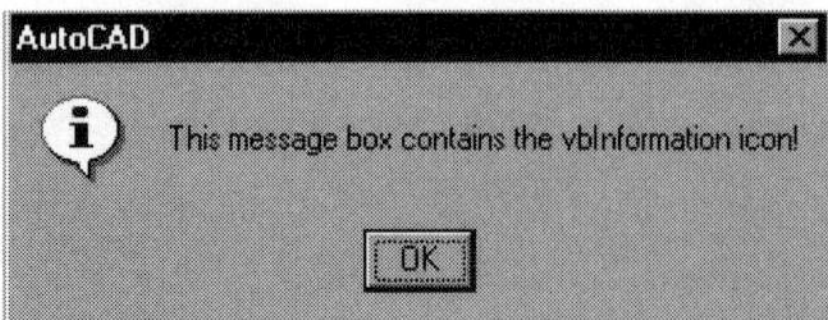

Figure 5.4 *Message box containing the Information icon*

This statement:

```
MsgBox "This message box contains the vbQuestion icon!", ↵
   vbQuestion
```

displays the message box shown in Figure 5.5.

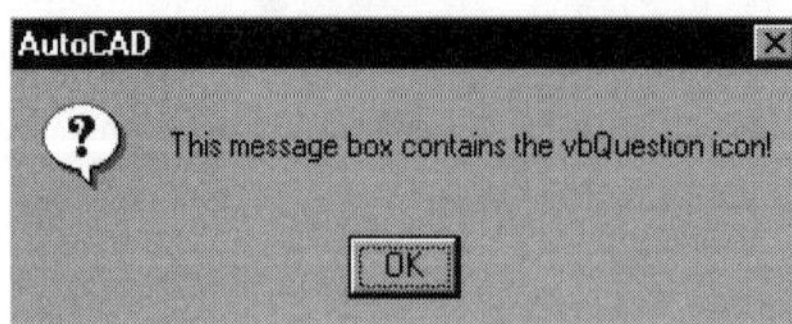

Figure 5.5 *Message box containing the Question icon*

As illustrated in Figure 5.6, you can add button and icon constants together using the plus sign character (+), as follows:

```
MsgBox ↵
   "This message box has vbInformation icon and ↵
   vbYesNo buttons!", vbYesNo + vbInformation
```

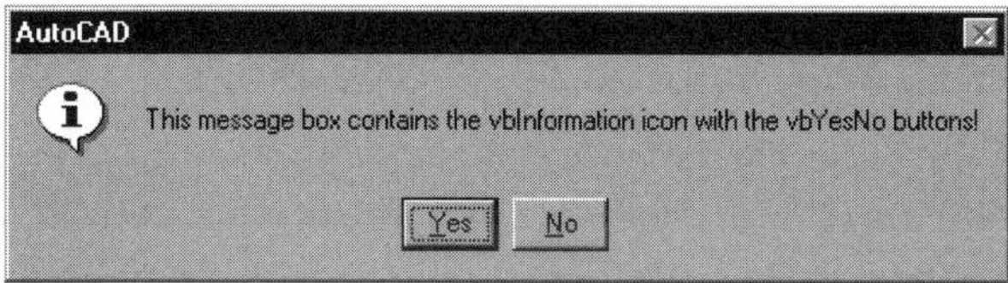

Figure 5.6 *Yes and No buttons in an Information message box*

The following code shows another example. This time we will add Abort, Retry, and Ignore buttons as shown in Figure 5.7:

```
MsgBox " This message box contains the vbQuestion icon and ↵
   the vbAbortRetryIgnore buttons!", ↵
   vbQuestion + vbAbortRetryIgnore
```

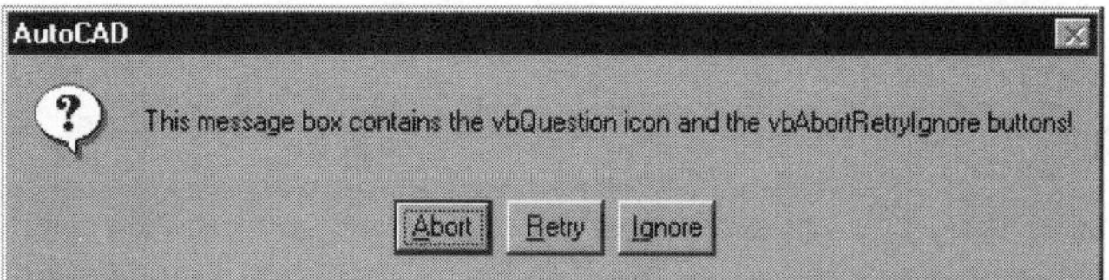

Figure 5.7 *Question icon with Abort, Retry, and Ignore buttons*

Be warned, though— if you go over the top and try to display more than one set of buttons at a time, you'll only get one set, which will be chosen by Visual Basic. If you try to choose more than one icon, you'll end up with none. For example, running the following statement:

```
MsgBox " This message box is supposed to contain the ↵
   vbQuestion and vbInformation icons and the ↵
   vbAbortRetryIgnore buttons!", ↵
   vbQuestion + vbAbortRetryIgnore + vbInformation
```

displays the message box shown here, with no icons and an OK button that was not requested:

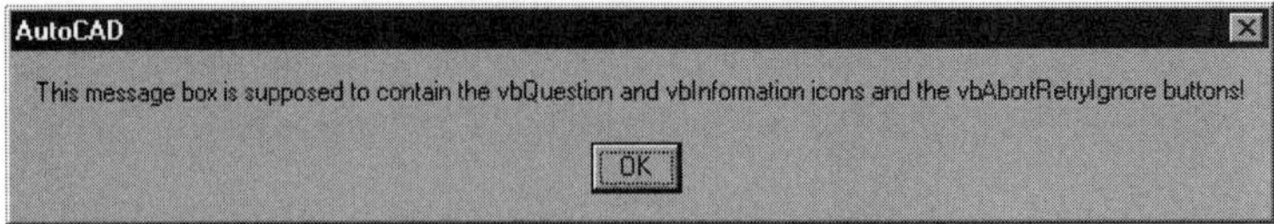

Responses to Button Clicks in Message Boxes

When the user clicks the button in a message box, the MsgBox function returns an integer value to indicate which button was clicked. These values can also be represented by the easier-to-remember built-in constants shown in Table 5.3.

Table 5.3 Constants for the Values Returned by the MsgBox Function

VALUE	CONSTANT
1	vbOK
2	vbCancel
3	vbAbort
4	vbRetry
5	vbIgnore
6	vbYes
7	vbNo

When the message box contains only one button, there's no point in assigning the returned value to a variable, and the MsgBox function can be called as shown in Lines 5 and 15 of Listing 5.1. When there is more than one button, you'll need to call this function from an assignment statement as follows:

```
Result = MsgBox("Are you sure you want to quit? ", vbYesNo, ↵
   "Find Name of Drawing"
```

The returned value is assigned to the variable Result, which has been declared as an integer. This enables your program to determine the button clicked by the user; the following two statements show you how. (Figure 5.8 illustrates the resulting dialog box.)

```
If Result = vbYes Then QuitNow = True
If Result = vbNo Then QuitNow = False
```

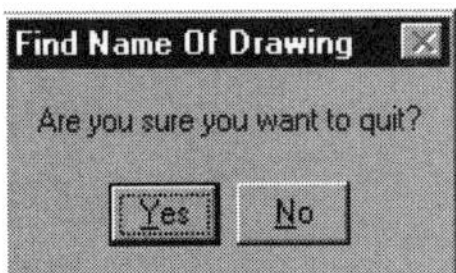

Figure 5.8 *Message box that gives the user the opportunity to continue running the application*

The MsgBox function is a useful way to communicate with the user if a simple decision is required. However, if you have a procedure that takes a while to run and you want to give the user a progress report as each stage is completed, but you don't need them to make any decisions or selections, you should use the Prompt method of the Utility object. It's discussed later in this chapter.

Next, we'll continue discussing objects by considering the ModelSpace and PaperSpace collections and the various kinds of graphical objects they can contain.

Graphical Object Spaces

All graphical objects belong to either the ModelSpace collection or the PaperSpace collection. These collections, in turn, belong to a Document object, which in turn belongs to a Documents collection. This arrangement is demonstrated in Figure 5.9.

In addition to the ModelSpace and PaperSpace collections, there is also a Blocks collection. Each Block object in the collection is capable of containing a group of graphical objects that can be inserted into drawings or can undergo transformations as if they were a single item.

ModelSpace Collection

The *Model Space* is the drawing area where you create your drawings—the Model tab from the AutoCAD window. There is only one Model tab, and any updates done to the model within this space are automatically reflected in any Paper Space pages that contain them. All the geometry that describes the model is stored in the *ModelSpace collection.*

PaperSpace Collection

The *Paper Space* is where you finalize the layout of specific views of your drawing ready for printing or plotting. Each Paper Space page is called a *Layout* and has a tab with

Layout1, Layout2, and so on in the AutoCAD window. You can have as many Layouts as you like, each representing a formatted page. All the information required for printing or plotting the Layouts is stored in the *PaperSpace collection*. The *PaperSpace property* of the Document object refers to the last Layout that was accessed.

Changing the ActiveSpace Property

The ActiveSpace property of the Document object is set to 1 (the built-in constant acModelSpace) if the model space is currently active, or 0 (the acPaperSpace constant) if the Paper Space is currently active. Let's write two macros that will toggle the active space from Model Space to Paper Space and vice-versa. Follow the steps of Exercise 5.2.

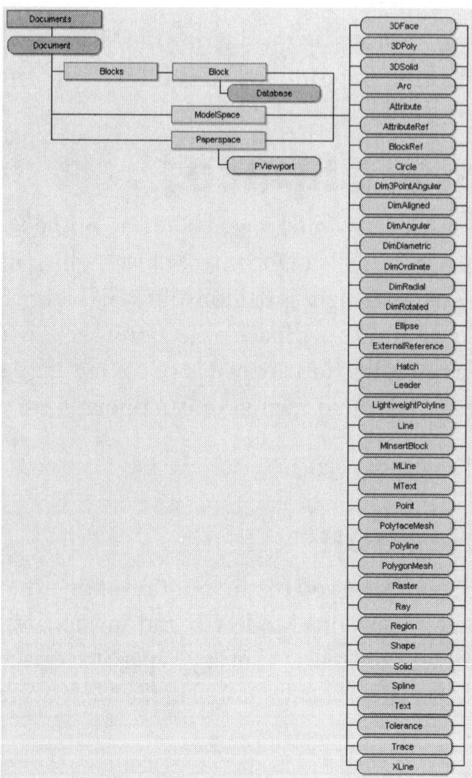

Figure 5.9 *Graphical objects in the object model*

Exercise 5.2: Changing from Model Space to Paper Space and Back Again

1. Start a new project in the IDE.
2. Choose Insert ➜ Module and enter the code for both macros given in Listing 5.2 into the Code window. The empty Code window for Module1 appears.
3. Return to the AutoCAD environment. Choose Tools ➜ Macro ➜ Macros and run the ModelSpaceToPaperSpace macro. The page with the Layout1 tab becomes the active page.
4. Choose Tools ➜ Macro ➜ Macros and run the PaperSpaceToModelSpace macro. The page with the Model tab becomes the active page.

Listing 5.2: ModelSpaceToPaperSpace Macro

```
1   Public Sub ModelSpaceToPaperSpace()
2       ThisDrawing.ActiveSpace = acPaperSpace
3   End Sub
4
5   Public Sub PaperSpaceToModelSpace()
6       ThisDrawing.ActiveSpace = acModelSpace
7   End Sub
```

Analysis

- Line 1 declares `ModelSpaceToPaperSpace` as a public macro so that it can be used by any module or UserForm in the same project.
- Line 2 uses the `ActiveSpace` property of `ThisDrawing` (the active document) to make the active space in the AutoCAD window the first Layout page from the PaperSpace collection.
- Line 3 ends the `ModelSpaceToPaperSpace` macro.
- Line 4 is a blank line to make the code easier to read.
- Line 5 opens the `PaperSpaceToModelSpace` macro as public.
- Line 6 makes the Model Space the active space, which opens the Model tab.
- Line 7 ends the `ModelSpaceToPaperSpace` macro.

Block Objects

A *Block object* contains one or more AutoCAD objects. As you add graphical objects to your drawing, you can add them to a specific Block object. All the objects in the same Block are considered to be a single entity when it comes to performing transformations or adding the Block to a drawing.

The ModelSpace, PaperSpace, and Blocks collections can be used interchangeably with any of the add-a-graphic methods, depending on which collection you're adding the graphical object to.

Adding Graphical Objects

Every graphical object that you can add from the AutoCAD window has a method, which allows you to add the same object with a VBA coding statement. AutoCAD also provides methods that you can use to create instances of these objects. Most of these methods have the word *Add* prefixed to the object's name—for example AddArc, AddCircle, and AddLine. In Exercise 5.3, you'll create a macro that adds a line to the Model tab.

Exercise 5.3: Creating a Line

1. Open a new project in the IDE, and choose Insert ➜ Module. Module1's Code window appears.
2. In the Code window, enter the CreateLine macro shown in Listing 5.3.
3. Return to the AutoCAD window and run the macro (choose Tools ➜ Macro ➜ Macros). A line will appear in the Model tab, as shown in Figure 5.10.

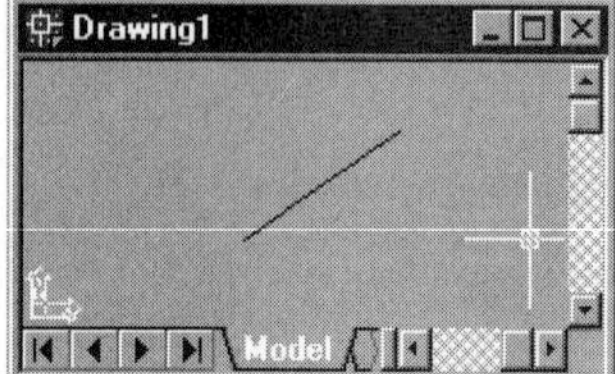

Figure 5.10 *Line generated by the CreateLine macro shown in Listing 5.3*

Listing 5.3: CreateLine Macro

```
1    Public Sub CreateLine()
2        Dim MyLineObject As AcadLine
3        Dim StartPoint(0 To 2) As Double, ↵
            EndPoint(0 To 2) As Double
4        StartPoint(0) = 1
5        StartPoint(1) = 3
6        StartPoint(2) = 2
7        EndPoint(0) = 4
8        EndPoint(1) = 5
9        EndPoint(2) = 4
10       Set MyLineObject = ThisDrawing.ModelSpace.AddLine↵
            (StartPoint, EndPoint)
11   End Sub
```

Analysis

- Line 1 opens the `CreateLine` macro.
- Line 2 declares the `MyLineObject` variable as being capable of referring to an `AcadLine` object.
- Line 3 declares the `StartPoint` and `EndPoint` as arrays with three elements of type Double.
- Lines 4 through 9 specify the x-, y-, and z-coordinates of the start and endpoints of the line in the World Coordinate System (WCS).
- Line 10 starts off by using the `AddLine` method to add the line defined by passing the two arguments specifying its endpoints to the ModelSpace object. It then uses the `Set` statement to assign to the variable `MyLineObject` a reference to the line being created. "Assigning a reference" means that there is never more than one definition of the line, so if it gets updated, all variables that reference it will automatically change, too.
- Line 11 ends the `CreateLine` macro.

Accessing Graphical Objects

Accessing a graphical object from the ModelSpace, PaperSpace, or Blocks collections is no different from retrieving an object from any collection. The Item method is used to return the object at the given position in the collection. For example, in the statement

```
Set MyLineObject = ThisDrawing.ModelSpace.Item(0)
```

the Item method returns the first object from the ModelSpace collection and assigns its reference to the variable MyLineObject—provided of course, that MyLineObject has been declared as an object of the correct type.

Drawing object types are generally given the name of the object (such as Line, Circle, and Ellipse) with the prefix *Acad*. For example, Line 2 of the AnimatedLine macro in Listing 5.4 shows the variable MyLineObject being declared as type AcadLine. This macro takes the line created by the CreateLine macro shown in Listing 5.3 and animates it by moving it around in the Model Space in 10 incremental steps.

LISTING 5.4: ANIMATEDLINE MACRO

```
1   Public Sub AnimatedLine()
2       Dim MyLineObject As AcadLine
3       Dim StartMoveVector(0 To 2) As Double
4       Dim EndMoveVector(0 To 2) As Double
5       Dim Count as Integer, Start as Single
6       Set MyLineObject = ThisDrawing.ModelSpace.Item(0)
7       For Count = 1 To 10
8           StartMoveVector(0) = Count
9           StartMoveVector(1) = Count
10          StartMoveVector(2) = Count
11          EndMoveVector(0) = Count + 1
12          EndMoveVector(1) = Count + 1
13          EndMoveVector(2) = Count + 1
14          MyLineObject.Move StartMoveVector, EndMoveVector
15          Start = Timer
16          While Timer < Start + 0.05
17          Wend
18          ZoomAll
19          MyLineObject.Update
20      Next
21  End Sub
```

Analysis

- Line 1 starts the `AnimatedLine` macro.
- Line 2 declares the variable `MyLineObject` as an `AcadLine` type.
- Lines 3 and 4 declare the variable arrays that will hold the 3D endpoints for the displacement vector that will be used by the `Move` method in Line 14.
- Line 5 declares the `Count` variable to be used in the `For` loop (Line 7) and the `Start` variable that will be used by the `While` loop (Line 16).
- Line 6 assigns a reference to the first item in the `ModelSpace` collection of the active drawing to the `MyLineObject` variable.
- Line 7 starts the `For` loop that will be repeated 10 times.
- Lines 8 through 13 assign values to the endpoints of the displacement vector to be used by the `Move` method (Line 14) based on the value of the loop counter `Count`. The displacement vector indicates the direction and distance that the line is to be moved.
- Line 14 calls the `Move` method of the line object referred to by `MyLineObject` using the two displacement vectors as arguments.
- Line 15 uses the `Timer` function to return a value representing the number of seconds elapsed since midnight and assigns it to the variable `Start`.
- Line 16 uses a `While` loop to pause the macro for $1/20$ second and slow down the animation. Because this number is very dependent on the speed of the hardware you're running, you'll probably need to adjust it to suit your PC.
- Line 17 marks the end of the `While` loop that didn't have any statements in its block because it was used simply as a timing device.
- Line 18 uses the `ZoomAll` method so that all the lines are displayed on the Model tab even if they extended outside the drawing area.
- Line 19 uses the `Update` method of the object referenced by `MyLineObject` to update it on the drawing screen.
- Line 20 ends the `For` statement block.
- Line 21 ends the `AnimatedLine` macro.

Accessing Generic Graphical Objects

All the drawing objects can be defined by a generic AcadEntity object, which exposes AcDbEntity functionality. All the ObjectName property settings start with AcDb followed by the class of object, such as Line, Point, or Polyline. If you are not sure what type of object will be returned from a collection, you can declare the referencing variable as an AcadEntity type and avoid any problems.

For example, the following `AddAnObject` macro declares the `NewObject` variable as being capable of referencing an `AcadEntity` object. After the declarations, the `NewObject` is set to the Line Object that's added to the ModelSpace collection. In the statement before it closes, the `NameOfObject` variable is assigned the value of the `ObjectName` property, which is `AcDbLine`.

```
Private Sub AddAnObject()
   Dim NewObject As AcadEntity
   Dim StartPoint(0 To 2) As Double
   Dim EndPoint(0 To 2) As Double
   Dim NameOfObject As String
   Set NewObject = ThisDrawing.ModelSpace.AddLine(StartPoint, ↵
      EndPoint)
   NameOfObject = NewObject.ObjectName
End Sub
```

Preferences Object

The Preferences object (Figure 5.11), contains all the settings from the pages of the AutoCAD Options dialog box (Figure 5.12).

The Preferences object contains nine properties that return objects, each representing the settings for the nine pages (tabs) in the Options dialog box. I've ordered the objects in Figure 5.11 to match the order of the pages shown in Figure 5.12. These objects allow you to control the way AutoCAD is customized from your code.

The following steps show you how to set the Source Content Units and Target Drawing Units text boxes to centimeters from the AutoCAD window, and then how to set them back to inches with VBA code. You'll see the strong similarities between both operations. To change inches to centimeters from the AutoCAD window, follow these steps:

1. From the AutoCAD window, choose Tools ➜ Options. The Options dialog box appears.

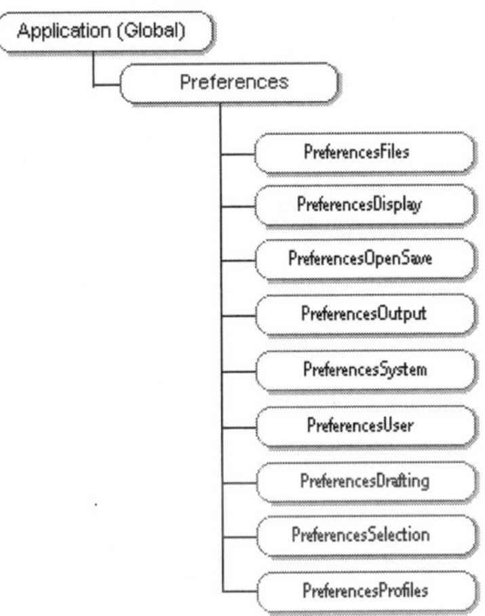

Figure 5.11 *The Preferences object's structure*

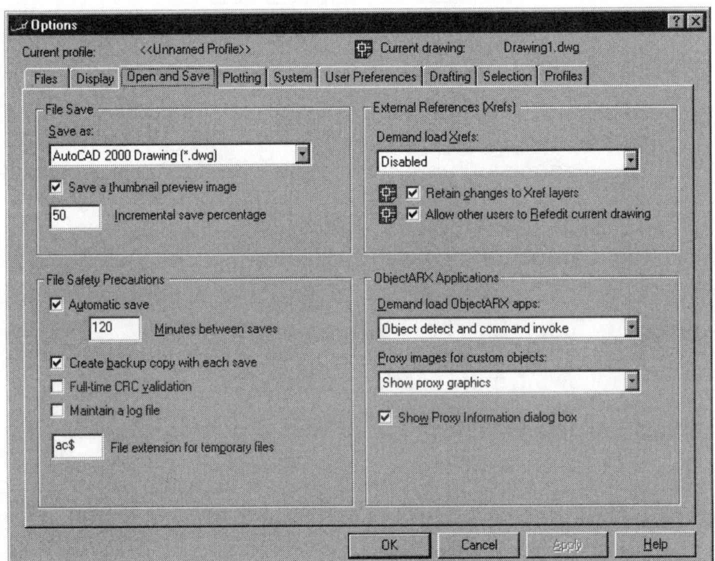

Figure 5.12 *AutoCAD's Options dialog box*

2. Click the User Preferences tab to open it (Figure 5.13). Choose Centimeters from the drop-down lists for both Source Content Units and Target Drawing Units.
3. Click OK to return to the AutoCAD window.

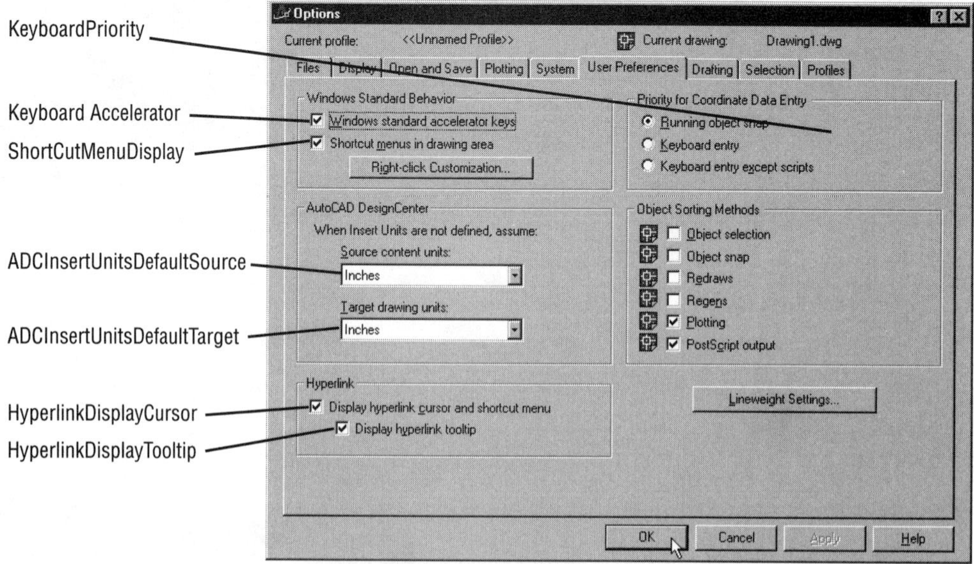

***Figure 5.13** The User Preferences page from the Options dialog box, and the VBA properties that correspond to its items*

Now I'm going to show you how to change the centimeters setting back to inches using VBA code, to demonstrate your interaction with the AutoCAD window as compared with creating code statements to execute your actions:

1. Open the IDE and double-click ThisDrawing from the Project Explorer window. (Choose View ➜ Project Explorer if this window is not already open.) The Code window for ThisDrawing opens.

2. Type the following macro declaration, and press Enter:

   ```
   Sub SetDrawingUnits
   ```

   When you press Enter, parentheses are automatically appended to the macro's name, a blinking cursor appears at the start of the next line, and the `End Sub` statement is added as a third line.

3. Type

   ```
   application.preferences.user.
   ```

   A drop-down list of properties and methods should appear as you enter each period character (`.`). If this doesn't happen, you'll need to go to Tools ➜ Options, open the Editor tab, and enable the Auto Quick Info option.

4. After you enter the last period character (after `user`), the drop-down list of properties shown in Figure 5.14 appears.

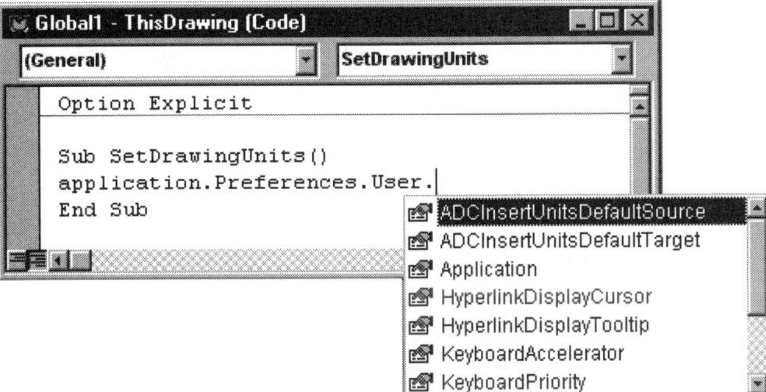

***Figure 5.14** Drop-down list of properties associated with User Preferences*

Notice how closely the names of these properties match the settings available in the User Preferences page shown earlier in Figure 5.13. I've labeled its boxes and frames with these property names to demonstrate the association between what you've been doing in the AutoCAD window versus how it's done in VBA code.

5. Select the ADCInsertUnitsDefaultSource property from the drop-down list and type an equals sign (=).

   The ADCInsertUnitsDefaultSource property is entered into the Code window, followed by the equals sign. You'll also get the drop-down list containing all the constants representing unit names, as shown here:

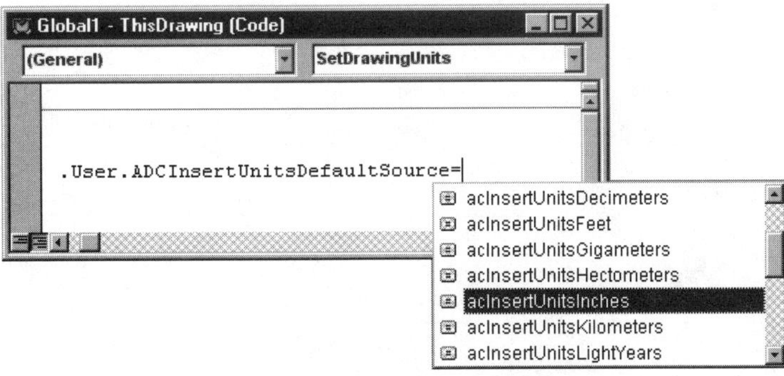

The ADC in ADCInsertUnitsDefaultSource *stands for AutoCAD Design Center, which is the caption of the frame that contains the text boxes displaying the settings for the ADCInsertUnitsDefaultSouce and ADCInsertUnitsDefaultTarget properties.*

6. Select the constant acInsertUnitsInches from the drop-down list and press Enter. The constant appears after the equals sign, and the blinking cursor is positioned at the start of the next line.
7. Repeat steps 3 through 6 again, but this time select ADCInsertUnitsDefault-Target at step 5.
8. Choose File ➜ Close And Return To AutoCAD, and then Tools ➜ Macro ➜ Macros. The Macros dialog box appears.
9. Make sure that the Global1!ThisDrawing.SetDrawingUnits macro appears in the Macro Name box, and click Run.
10. Choose Tools ➜ Options and select the User Preferences page. "Inches" should once again appear in the two boxes in the AutoCAD Design Center frame.

At step 5, you may have noticed three properties listed that all begin with *SCM,* and that haven't been identified in Figure 5.13. These are Short Cut Menu properties, which represent the settings for the menu that pops up when you right-click the drawing object in AutoCAD. Figure 5.15 shows the Right-Click Customization dialog box that opens when you click the Right-Click Customization button on the User Preferences page.

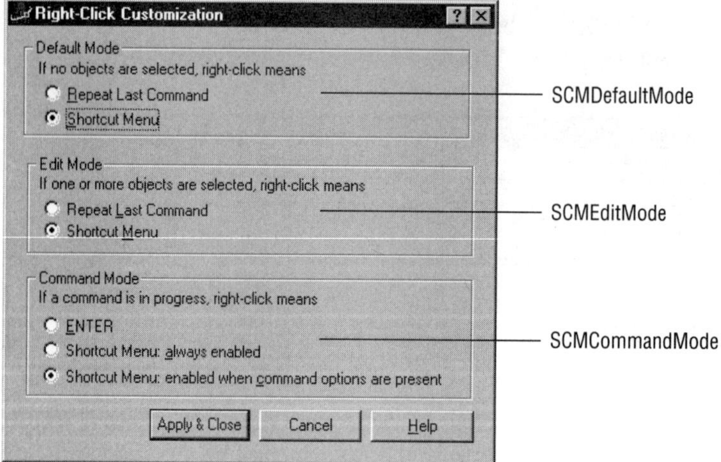

Figure 5.15 *Shortcut menu properties used in the Right-Click Customization dialog box*

Sending Text to the AutoCAD Command Line

Text strings can be sent from VBA code directly to the AutoCAD command line using the Prompt method of the *Utility object* (which you'll find in the object model at the end of the column of Document objects, just above the MenuBar collection). The Utility object enables your application to interact with the user via the command line, and by selecting points in the Model Space.

You'll see later in Chapter 17 how the Utility object can also be used to open and save drawings from the Web.

In Listing 5.5, the Prompt method is used to display messages on the command line, in order to indicate the application's progress as it reads the data from the file and creates all the drawing objects required. To try out this macro, start a new project and enter the Listing 5.5 code into ThisDrawing.

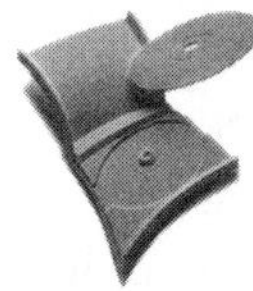

LISTING 5.5: DRAWVILLAPLANS MACRO

```
Sub DrawVillaPlans()
    CreateVillaPlans "Colonial"
End Sub

Sub CreateVillaPlans(VillaType As String)
    ThisDrawing.Utility.Prompt vbLf & ↵
       "Loading data for villa " & VillaType & vbLf
    ReadData VillaType
    ThisDrawing.Utility.Prompt vbLf & ↵
       "Drawing plans for " & VillaType & vbLf
    DrawPlans VillaType
    ThisDrawing.Utility.Prompt vbLf & ↵
       "Plans completed successfully!" & vbLf
End Sub

Sub ReadData(VType As String)
    'code goes here for reading the data required
End Sub

Sub DrawPlans(VType As String)
    'code goes here for drawing plans
End Sub
```

ANALYSIS

- Line 1 declares and starts the `DrawVillaPlans` macro.
- Line 2 calls the `CreateVillaPlans` procedure, designating the kind of villa required.
- Line 3 ends the `DrawVillaPlans` macro.
- Line 5 declares the `CreateVillaPlans` procedure with the `VillaType` parameter declared as a String type.
- Lines 6, 8, and 10 use the `Prompt` method of the Utility object to display the concatenated text strings.

When using the `Prompt` method to send commands to the AutoCAD command line, always place a carriage return (represented by `vbLf`) before and after the argument string, or else one prompt will be appended to the next.

- Lines 7 and 9 call the procedures `ReadData` (Line 13) and `DrawPlans` (Line 17).
- Lines 13 through 15 belong to the `ReadData` procedure that I've left empty in this example. This would normally contain the code for reading data from files. You'll see later in Chapter 12 how to input data from files for your application to use.
- Lines 17 through 19 make up the `DrawPlans` procedure, which also does nothing at this stage. It would normally contain code that uses the data in the `ReadData` macro at Line 13 to draw the villa's floor plan.

Run your code. When it's finished executing, the command-line area will display the three prompts from Lines 6, 8, and 10, as shown here:

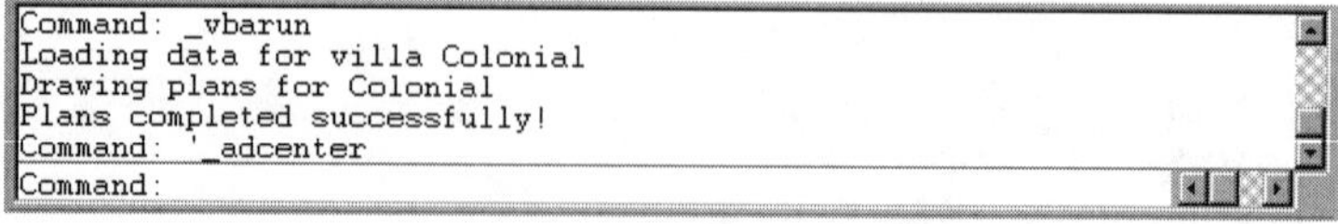

As you can see, the Prompt method is useful for providing feedback to the user while a procedure is running, provided that no decision is required from the user. If a simple decision is required, you'll have to use the MsgBox function instead (see the earlier section on MsgBox).

In fact, if you have a procedure like the one in Listing 5.5 (which takes a while to run), and you want to give the user a progress report as each stage is completed, you can use the Prompt method of the Utility object. Employing Message boxes in such cases would require the user to wait for the message to appear, and then click its OK button to move to the next stage. Doing this for a series of message boxes can be tedious and annoying. In contrast, the Prompt method allows the user to have a coffee break while the PC does all the work.

VB's String-Handling Functions

Visual Basic provides several functions dedicated solely to handling strings: Len, UCase, LCase, Left, Right, Mid, and Trim, to name just a few. Let's briefly define the role of some of the commonly used functions.

Len Function The Len function returns a Long type containing the number of characters in the string passed to it as an argument. If a variable is passed, Len will provide the number of bytes required to store the variable. If the variable represents a string, the result is exactly the same as the number of characters in the string, since each alphanumeric character is stored in a byte.

UCase and LCase Functions The UCase function changes to uppercase all the characters in the string passed to it. The LCase function changes them to lowercase characters. Both functions return a Variant containing the converted string.

Left and Right Functions The Left and Right functions return a specified number of characters from the left or right side of a string. The Left function has two required arguments: the string, followed by the number of characters you require for the leftmost substring that is returned as a Variant type. The Right function must be passed the string and the number of characters for the rightmost substring.

Mid Function The Mid function returns a specified number of characters from within a string. This function requires two arguments: the string itself, and the position within the string of the first character of the substring required. There is a third (optional) argument that lets you specify the length of the substring required. If this third argument is omitted, it is assumed you want to return all the characters from the first character to the end of the string.

Trim, LTrim, and RTrim Functions The Trim, LTrim, and RTrim functions all require a string passed to them as the argument. LTrim removes any leading blank spaces from the front of the string, RTrim removes any trailing blank spaces from the end of the string, and Trim removes any blank spaces from both ends of the string.

If the string passed to any of the string-handling functions contains NULL, they will return NULL.

In Exercise 5.4, you'll create a GUI in which you can enter a string and watch the effect of some of the string-handling functions.

Exercise 5.4: String Handling Functions Application

1. Start a new project. Add a UserForm with eight text box controls, seven command buttons, and a label, as shown here:

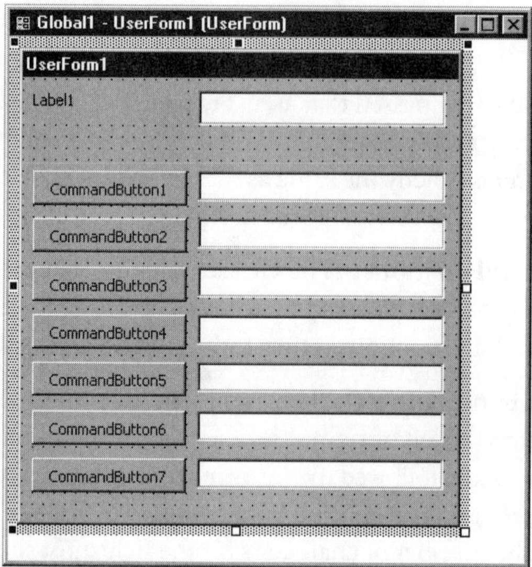

2. Update the Caption properties of these controls as shown in Table 5.4.
3. Enter the code for the skeleton event procedures for the command button controls as shown in Listing 5.6.
4. Run your application, enter a string, and try clicking all the command button controls. Figure 5.16 shows my attempt at this!

Table 5.4 Caption Property Settings for the GUI Objects

OBJECT	CAPTION
UserForm1	String Functions
Label1	Enter string
CommandButton1	Find length
CommandButton2	Uppercase
CommandButton3	Lowercase
CommandButton4	First four characters
CommandButton5	Last five characters
CommandButton6	Middle three
CommandButton7	Trim end spaces

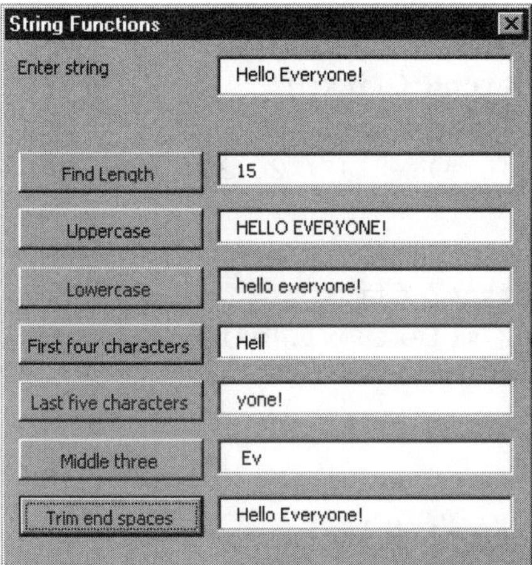

Figure 5.16 *Result of entering a text string and clicking all the command buttons*

Listing 5.6: Click Event Procedures for Command Buttons

```
1   Private Sub CommandButton1_Click()
2       TextBox2.Text = Len(TextBox1.Text)
3   End Sub
4
5   Private Sub CommandButton2_Click()
6       TextBox3.Text = UCase(TextBox1.Text)
7   End Sub
8
9   Private Sub CommandButton3_Click()
10       TextBox4.Text = LCase(TextBox1.Text)
11  End Sub
12
13  Private Sub CommandButton4_Click()
14      TextBox5.Text = Left(TextBox1.Text, 4)
15  End Sub
16
17  Private Sub CommandButton5_Click()
18      TextBox6.Text = Right(TextBox1.Text, 5)
19  End Sub
20
21  Private Sub CommandButton6_Click()
22      TextBox7.Text = Mid(TextBox1.Text, ↵
            (Len(TextBox1.Text) - 1) / 2, 3)
23  End Sub
24
25  Private Sub CommandButton7_Click()
26      TextBox8.Text = Trim(TextBox1.Text)
27  End Sub
```

Analysis

- Line 1 starts the `CommandButton1` click event procedure.
- Line 2 calls the `Len` function with the text entered into `TextBox1` as the argument and assigns the value returned to the Text property of `TextBox2`, which automatically displays the new text assigned to it in `TextBox2`.
- Line 3 ends the `CommandButton1` click event procedure.
- Line 5 starts the `CommandButton2` click event procedure.

- Line 6 calls the `UCase` function, which changes all the characters of the string entered into uppercase and displays them in `TextBox3`.
- Line 7 ends the `CommandButton2` click event procedure.
- Line 9 starts the `CommandButton3` click event procedure.
- Line 10 calls the `LCase` function, which converts the string entered in `TextBox1` into lowercase and displays the converted string in `TextBox4`.
- Line 11 ends the `CommandButton3` click event procedure.
- Line 13 starts the `CommandButton4` click event procedure.
- Line 14 calls the `Left` function with the text entered as the first argument and 4 as the second. The leftmost four characters are returned and displayed in `TextBox5`.
- Line 15 ends the `CommandButton4` click event procedure.
- Line 17 starts the `CommandButton5` click event procedure.
- Line 18 calls the `Right` function with the text entered and 5 as the arguments. This returns the last five characters and displays them in `TextBox6`.
- Line 19 ends the `CommandButton5` click event procedure.
- Line 21 starts the `CommandButton6` click event procedure.
- Line 22 calls the `Mid` function, which requires three arguments—a string, starting position, and the number of characters required. In Listing 5.6, the string entered is given as the first argument. The second argument is given as an expression containing a function call. The `Len` function returns the length of the string that is then halved and decremented to give the character before the middle of the string. The third argument is passed as the number 3 to determine the number of characters that will be displayed in `TextBox7`.
- Line 23 ends the `CommandButton6` click event procedure.
- Line 25 starts the `CommandButton7` click event procedure.
- Line 26 calls the `Trim` function to trim any leading or trailing spaces from the string entered into `TextBox1` and assigns the resultant string to `TextBox8`.
- Line 27 ends the `CommandButton7` click event procedure.

Summary

At the end of this chapter, you'll know the following about working with AutoCAD VBA:

- The role of the Application object.
- How the active document from the Application object can be represented by ThisDrawing.
- What the Documents collection contains.
- How to use the Item method to return an object from a collection.
- About the MsgBox function and when to use either it or the Prompt method to send messages to the user.
- How the `On Error Resume Next` statement can save your application from abnormal termination.
- About the CInt function and how it returns a value from the ASCII character set.
- Whether to use the `End` statement or the `Unload` statement.
- The function of the QueryClose and Terminate event procedures.
- The differences between the Model Space, the Paper Space, and the active space.
- How to create and add graphical objects to your ModelSpace, PaperSpace, or Blocks collections.
- How to access existing graphical objects.
- How to use the Preferences object to set the options of AutoCAD's Options dialog box.
- How to send messages for the user to the command line.
- How to use some of Visual Basic's string-handling functions.

Macro-izing Line Drawing

AUTOCAD VBA

Chapter 6

This chapter covers all you need to know about drawing lines in the AutoCAD window from VBA macros. You can draw continuous lines, dashed lines, or any other linetypes available in AutoCAD. You'll see how to draw your lines highlighted and colored, and even how to draw parallel lines—all from code.

You'll also learn how to develop an application one piece at a time by progressively adding some tried and tested UserForms and macros. Throughout this chapter the pieces will be developed individually, and after they're tested the application will be extended to incorporate them. Sometimes these macros will be used intact, and at other times the ideas they represent will be adapted slightly to suit.

This chapter covers the following topics:

- Drawing a line
- Setting linetypes
- Highlighting a line from a macro
- Highlighting and coloring all lines
- Identifying lines selected by the user
- Scales and weights for lines
- Scaling using a transformation matrix
- Multiple parallel lines

Drawing a Line

Drawing a line from code is achieved using the AddLine method, which creates a Line object based on the two endpoints passed to it as arguments in the call. Both endpoints are specified in the World Coordinate System (WCS). This new Line object is then added to the ModelSpace collection (or PaperSpace collection).

For the examples in this book, I've assumed all the drawing is done in the Model tab of the AutoCAD window, so the Model Space will be the preferred drawing space rather than the Paper Space.

Let's create an application that allows the user to input the coordinates for both endpoints of a line and then click a button to create and draw the line. This application, Exercise 6.1, will be adapted and extended in other sections throughout this chapter.

Exercise 6.1: Line Input Application

You'll begin by creating a new UserForm that allows the user to enter the coordinates of the endpoints defining a line.

1. Start a new project in the IDE and choose Insert ➜ UserForm. Double-click the Label icon in the Toolbox, and move the cursor to the top-left corner of the UserForm. The Label control's icon follows the cross cursor as it moves.

Double-clicking a Toolbox control allows you to place multiple instances of it on a UserForm without having to return to the Toolbox each time. Click anywhere inside the Toolbox to let Visual Basic know when you've finished.

2. With the cursor still in the top-left corner, click the mouse. A default-sized Label control appears with its top-left corner positioned at the center of the cross cursor, as shown here:

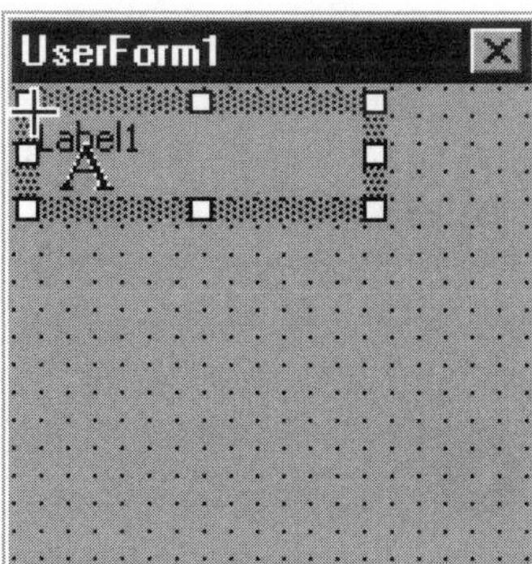

Notice how the cursor is still a cross and that the Label control's icon still follows it around after the click—this is because double-clicking Toolbox icons lets you add as many instances of a control as you like.

3. Move the cursor to roughly halfway down the UserForm, keeping it close to the left boundary. Click the mouse, and a second default-sized label appears.
4. Double-click the TextBox control icon in the Toolbox, and click the cursor roughly in the middle and near the top of the UserForm. The mouse pointer changes from a Label control icon to a TextBox control icon, and a default-sized TextBox control appears.

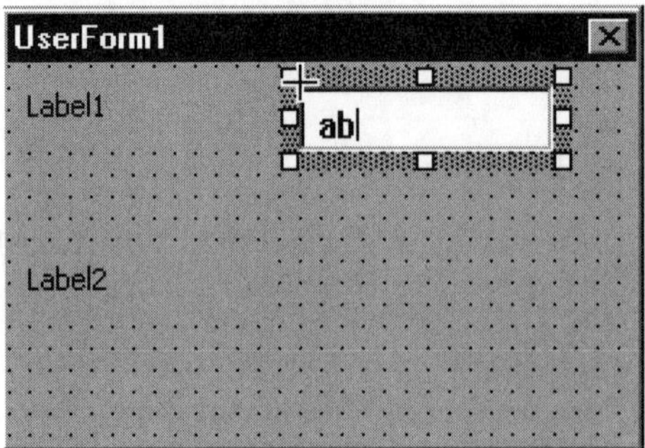

5. Position the cross cursor in the bottom-left corner of the TextBox control and click again. Repeat this until you have placed six text boxes on the UserForm, one below the other (see Figure 6.1). The six text boxes appear evenly spaced and perfectly aligned—if they're not, use the Format command to make any small adjustments required. In Chapter 3, the section "UserForm Toolbar Buttons" takes you through the steps involved in aligning and sizing groups of text boxes.
6. Double-click the CommandButton icon in the Toolbox, position the cross cursor in the bottom-left corner of the sixth text box, and click. The command button appears, aligned with the text boxes.
7. Position the cross cursor in the bottom-left corner of the first command button and click. A second command button appears, aligned with the first one.
8. Change the names of the UserForm and its text box and command button controls to those shown in Table 6.1, by overtyping the names in the Properties window. (Choose View ➜ Properties Window if this window is not already displayed.)

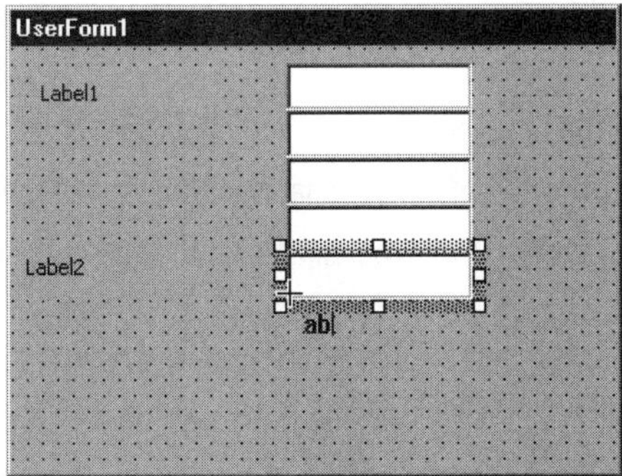

Figure 6.1 Placing TextBox controls in a UserForm so they are drawn aligned

Giving controls names that reflect their functions makes it easier to remember which control is which as the application is extended. Using the prefix naming conventions enables you to easily know the kind of control referred to by the name. In addition, it ensures that controls of the same type are listed together in the Object drop-down list in the Code window.

Table 6.1 Assigning Semantic Names to the Line Input UserForm and Its Controls

OLD NAME	NEW NAME
UserForm1	frmLineInput
TextBox1	txtStartPointX
TextBox2	txtStartPointY
TextBox3	txtStartPointZ
TextBox4	txtEndPointX
TextBox5	txtEndPointY
TextBox6	txtEndPointZ
CommandButton1	cmdDrawLine
CommandButton2	cmdExit

9. Change the Caption properties of the UserForm and its controls as shown in Table 6.2.

Table 6.2 Caption Properties for the Line Input UserForm

Control	New Caption
frmLineInput	Line Input
Label1	Enter the X, Y and Z coordinates for the start of the line.
Label2	Enter the X, Y and Z coordinates for the end of the line.
cmdDrawLine	Draw Line
cmdExit	Exit

10. Change the Accelerator property of the cmdDrawLine control to **D,** and to **x** for the cmdExit control. The D and x appear underlined on the command buttons (see Figure 6.2) to indicate they can be "clicked" using the Alt+D or Alt+x key-combinations.

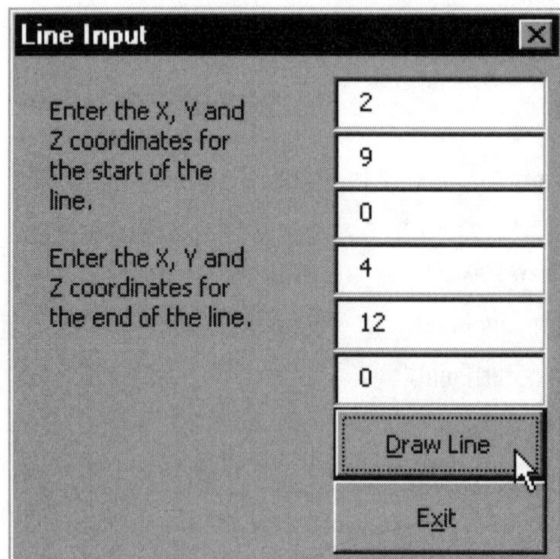

***Figure 6.2** The Line Input UserForm with new captions and accelerator keys*

The letter x is the pseudo-standard accelerator key for exiting from any Microsoft Windows application.

11. Enter the code shown in Listing 6.1. The CreateLine macro should be placed in the General Declarations section of the UserForm's Code window. This procedure transfers the values from the text boxes into two arrays, which are used as arguments in the call to the AddLine method.

LISTING 6.1: CREATELINE MACRO

```
1   Sub CreateLine()
2       Dim StartPoint(0 To 2) As Double
3       Dim EndPoint(0 To 2) As Double
4       StartPoint(0) = txtStartPointX
5       StartPoint(1) = txtStartPointY
6       StartPoint(2) = txtStartPointZ
7       EndPoint(0) = txtEndPointX
8       EndPoint(1) = txtEndPointY
9       EndPoint(2) = txtEndPointZ
10      With ThisDrawing.ModelSpace
11          .AddLine StartPoint, EndPoint
12          .Item(.Count - 1).Update
13      End With
14  End Sub
```

ANALYSIS

- Line 1 starts the `CreateLine` procedure.
- Lines 2 and 3 declare the two arrays that will hold the coordinates of the endpoints entered into the text boxes by the user. These must be arrays of the Double type so that they can be used as arguments when the `AddLine` method is called at Line 11.
- Lines 4 through 9 take the x-, y-, and z-coordinates input by the user into the six text box controls and assign them to the elements of the start and endpoint arrays. All the text box controls are accessed without fully qualifying them with the UserForm's name, and the Text property is implied for all the text boxes because it is the default property for this control.

The default property of the TextBox control is Text, so when the control's name appears in code on its own, VBA automatically assumes the Text property is required.

- Line 10 starts the `With ThisDrawing.ModelSpace` statement block, so that the ModelSpace collection will be used for unqualified items.
- Line 11 passes the `StartPoint` and `EndPoint` arrays as arguments to the `AddLine` method. This method creates a Line object defined by the coordinates passed to it and adds the object to the ModelSpace collection of objects.

- Line 12 uses the `Count` property to determine the number of objects currently in the ModelSpace collection. Since the index to the first object in the collection is zero, the last object is at `Count -1`. So the `Item` method is used to return the last object added to the collection (which is the line just added). The returned object's `Update` method is then called to redraw the object in the AutoCAD window—so your new line appears.
- Line 13 ends the `With ThisDrawing.ModelSpace` statement block.
- Line 14 ends the procedure.

EXERCISE 6.1: LINE INPUT APPLICATION (CONTINUED)

In the next set of steps, you're going to code the Click event procedures for the two command buttons, code the macro that runs this Line Input application, and run the application.

1. Continuing in the UserForm's Code window, select cmdDrawLine from the list of objects, and select Click from the list of procedures. In the skeleton Click event procedure that appears, insert the call to the CreateLine macro (Listing 6.1):

   ```
   CreateLine
   ```

   This Click event procedure of cmdDrawLine will run when the user clicks the Draw Line button or uses the Alt+D key-combination.

2. Place the `Unload Me` statement in the Click event procedure for the cmdExit command button. This event procedure runs when the user clicks the Exit button or uses the Alt+x key-combination. All the lines input by the user are already preserved in the ModelSpace collection, so there is nothing to be saved before quitting.

3. Choose Insert ➔ Module. Place the following DrawLine macro in Module1's Code window so that AutoCAD will include it in the list of macros (see step 4). The DrawLine macro uses the Show method to display the frmLineInput UserForm and thus start up the application.

   ```
   Sub DrawLine()
       frmLineInput.Show
   End Sub
   ```

4. To run the DrawLine macro, choose Tools ➜ Macro ➜ Macros, select DrawLine from the list (shown just below), and click Run. The Line Input UserForm appears. When the user clicks the Draw Line button, its Click event procedure is executed and calls the CreateLine procedure.

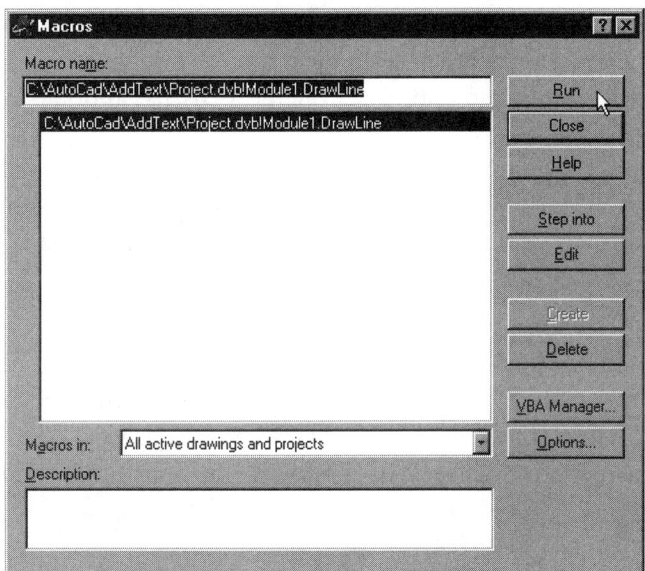

Every VBA project should have at least one macro so that you can kick-start the project from the Tools ➜ Macro ➜ Macros dialog box.

5. Enter the coordinates of a line. Use the Tab key or the Enter key to move from text box to text box in tab order. Then click the Draw Line button.

   This draws the line with the coordinates just entered in the Model tab of the AutoCAD window. In the background, VBA also creates a Line object and adds it to the ModelSpace collection.

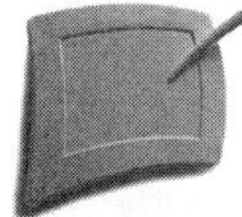

If you need information about tab order, read the next section. For even more help, read "Setting the Tab Order for Controls" in Chapter 4.

6. Save your project as **LineInput**.

A Control's TabIndex and TabStop Properties

The TabIndex property is assigned a numerical value that represents the order in which the object was added to the UserForm. When the UserForm is open, its controls can be given the focus in *tab order* by repeatedly pressing either the Tab or the Enter key. The appearance of a control when it's given the focus depends on the control's type. For example, when a text box is given the focus, the I-beam cursor appears inside the text box; when a command button is given the focus, its caption is enclosed in a dashed rectangle.

Although the TabIndex property of every control is allocated a number, VBA will automatically set to False the TabStop property of any controls that cannot be used for interacting with the user (such as Labels). The TabStop property determines whether or not a control is allowed to get the focus.

The *With* Statement

The `With` statement allows you to specify an item and then include it in a series of statements that use the item, without the need to qualify the item each time. Items can be an element from a user-defined type, an object, or a collection. For example:

```
With Object
    .Caption = "Click Here"
    .Accelerator = "C"
    .BackColor = acWhite
End With
```

Here, the three properties that start with a period character (`.`) are all assumed to belong to the object specified in the opening `With` statement.

VBA allows a `With` statement to be nested inside another `With` statement, with the unqualified object assumed to belong to the object or collection specified in the `With` statement block to which the unqualified object belongs. So you must qualify objects in the outer `With` block when they are used inside the inner `With` block. For example:

```
With Object1
    .Height = txtHeight
    .Color = txtColor
    With Object2
        .Height = Object1.Height
        .Color = Object1.Color
    End With
    .Width = Object2.Width + 3
End With
```

Here, the first Height and Color properties are inside the outer `With` block, so `Object1` is implied. The second Height and Color properties are inside the inner `With` block, so `Object2` is implied. The Width property in the second to last statement belongs to `Object1` because it lies inside the outer `With` block.

The advantages of using a `With` statement are that the code requires less typing, it is easier to read, and it will be more efficient to run, leading to improved performance.

Setting Linetypes

AutoCAD has a Linetypes collection that contains all the Linetype objects associated with the active drawing ThisDrawing. You can load as many Linetype objects as you like from the linetype library files. These files all have an extension `.lin` and are loaded by name into Linetype objects that become members of the Linetypes collection for your drawing.

After a linetype has been loaded, you can access it from the collection in the normal way—using the Item method with an index number. The index number must be *less than* the number of Linetype objects contained in the collection; otherwise, your program will grind to a halt.

Take care when accessing the Linetypes collection, to ensure that the Index value used is less than the number of Linetype objects. Trying to access a nonexistent Linetype will cause your program to terminate immediately.

Exercise 6.1: Line Input Application (continued)

Next, you'll add the AddNewLineType macro to the Line Input application.

From AutoCAD: The following steps show you how to load a linetype definition into a Linetype object from the AutoCAD window. This material may already be familiar to you, but I've included it here in order for you to compare this process with how it's done in VBA code.

1. Choose Format ➜ Linetype. The Linetype Manager dialog box appears (Figure 6.3).
2. Click the Load button. The Load or Reload Linetypes dialog box appears next, as shown in Figure 6.4. Notice that the filename `acad.lin` is displayed in the Filename box at the top—this is the default AutoCAD Linetypes file.

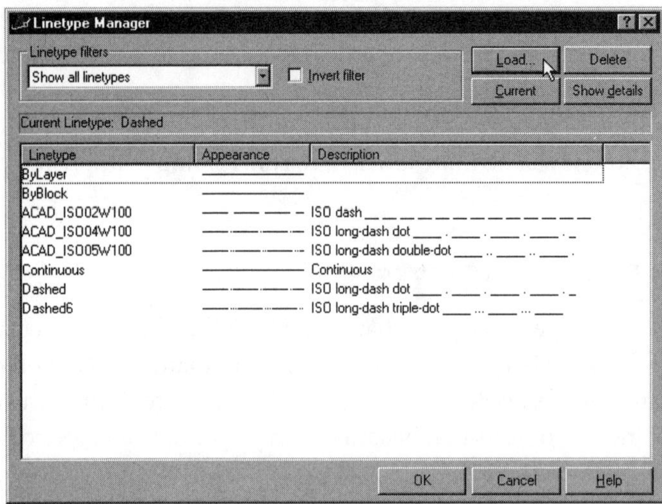

Figure 6.3 *Linetype Manager dialog box*

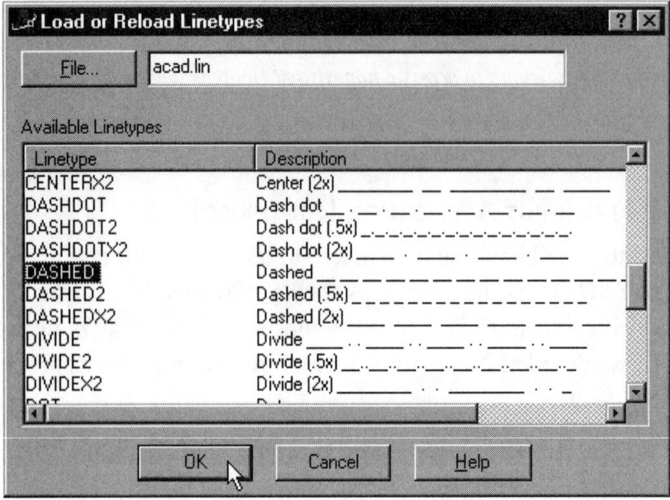

Figure 6.4 *Load or Reload Linetypes dialog box*

3. Select the DASHED linetype and click OK. When you return to the Linetype Manager dialog box, it now includes DASHED in the list of linetypes.

4. Select the DASHED linetype, click the Current button, and then click OK. The Linetype Manager dialog box closes and you return to the AutoCAD window, where the DASHED linetype is displayed in the Linetype box.

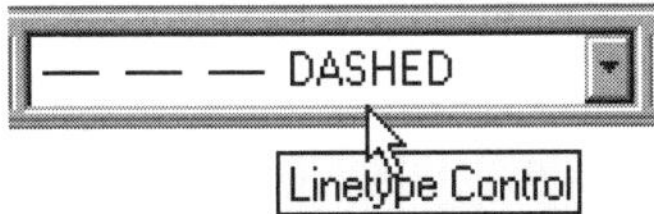

From VBA: Now let's take a look at how this same thing is achieved using VBA.

1. The AddNewLineType macro shown in Listing 6.2 loads the DASHED2 Linetype object and makes it the current linetype. Enter this macro into Module1 beside the DrawLine macro.
2. Run your macro from the Macros dialog box (AutoCAD window)—you'll only be able to do this once for each linetype; otherwise, line 2 will cause a run-time error when you try to load the same linetype twice.
3. If you want to run your macro again, you'll need to delete the DASHED2 linetype. However, since you cannot delete the current linetype, you'll need to make another linetype current before the deletion can take place. Here are the steps to do that:
   a. Choose Format ➔ Linetype to open the Linetype Manager dialog box (Figure 6.3).
   b. Select any Linetype from the list except DASHED2 and click Current. The selected linetype becomes the current linetype.
   c. Select DASHED2 from the Linetype list and click Delete. The DASHED2 linetype disappears from the list.
   d. Click OK to return to the AutoCAD window.

LISTING 6.2: ADDNEWLINETYPE MACRO

```
1   Sub AddNewLinetype()
2       Dim DashedLine As AcadLineType
3       ThisDrawing.Linetypes.Load "DASHED2", "acad.lin"
4       Set DashedLine = _ ThisDrawing.Linetypes.Item↵
           (ThisDrawing.Linetypes.Count - 1)
5       ThisDrawing.ActiveLinetype = DashedLine
6   End Sub
```

ANALYSIS

- Line 1 declares and starts the `AddNewLinetype` macro.
- Line 2 declares `DashedLine` as a variable that can refer to an `AcadLineType` object.
- Line 3 uses the `Load` method of the Linetypes collection to retrieve the linetype named DASHED2 from the file named `acad.lin`. When you compare this with the AutoCAD steps, in which the linetype was set manually from the AutoCAD window, the statement in Line 3 is equivalent to a combination of step 2, clicking Load, and step 3, selecting the linetype and clicking OK.
- Line 4 uses the `Item` method to retrieve the last Linetype object added to the Linetypes collection—the object named DASHED2 just loaded. The last object added has an index value equal to one less than the number of objects in the collection (`Count` property less one), since the first object starts at zero. The `Set` statement is used to assign a reference to this object to the variable `DashedLine`.
- Line 5 takes the Linetype object referenced by the `DashedLine` variable and assigns it to the `ActiveLinetype` property for the drawing. This is equivalent to step 4 in the AutoCAD procedure, where the DASHED linetype was selected and the Current button clicked.

The `AddNewLineType` procedure suffers from the fact that it can't be run more than once without updating the linetype's name in line 3.

Getting a Linetype from the User

Let's create a new UserForm containing a list box that displays a list of all the linetypes currently available and allows the user to select the one required. This Linetypes User-Form can then be used in conjunction with the LineInput UserForm developed as the first application in this chapter. The LineInput UserForm will get the coordinates from the user, and the Linetypes UserForm will get the line type; together they will be used to generate the new line.

EXERCISE 6.1: LINE INPUT APPLICATION (CONTINUED)

1. Start AutoCAD and choose Tools ➜ Macro ➜ Load Project. The Open VBA Project dialog box appears, for you to select the project you want to load (Figure 6.5).

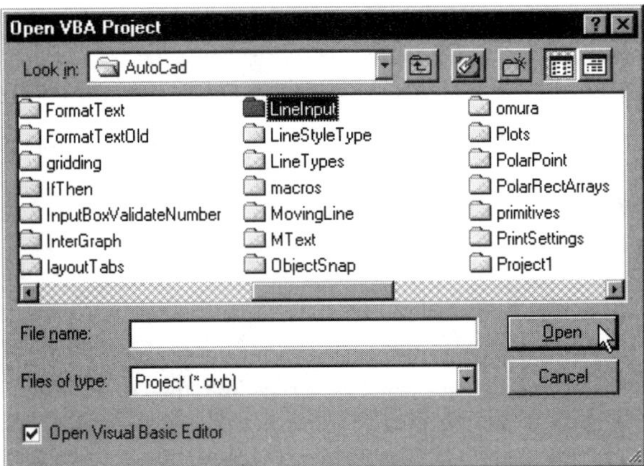

***Figure 6.5** The Open VBA Project displays a selection of folders and VBA projects.*

2. Select the project file containing your LineInput UserForm and click Open. The IDE opens with your UserForm.
3. Choose Insert ➜ UserForm to add a new UserForm. The Code window for UserForm1 appears. (Remember, the frmLineInput UserForm started life named UserForm1.)
4. Drag two command buttons and a label onto the UserForm. Click the List-Box icon

   in the Toolbox, and add a list box. The UserForm should look like this:

   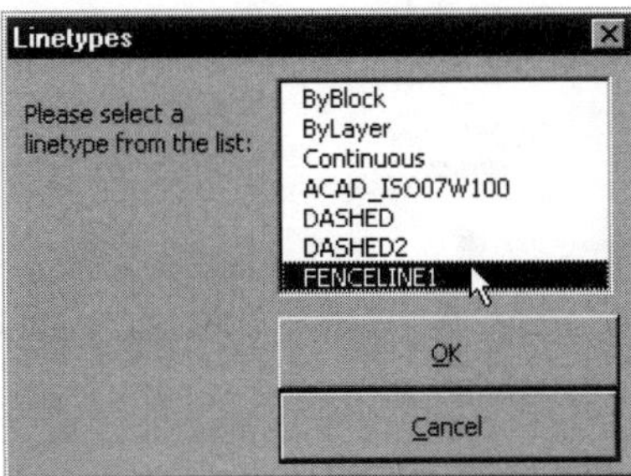

5. Change the Caption properties to those shown in Table 6.3.

Visual Basic assigns default names for UserForms and controls starting from UserForm1 on, rather than basing names on the number of UserForms or controls of the same type that already exist.

Table 6.3 Caption Properties for the Linetypes UserForm

CONTROL	NEW CAPTION
UserForm1	Linetypes
Label1	Please select a linetype from the list:
CommandButton1	OK
CommandButton2	Cancel

6. Change the Accelerator property of CommandButton1 to the letter **O**, and CommandButton2 to **C**. The familiar underscored characters will appear under these accelerator characters on the buttons.
7. Change the Cancel property of CommandButton2 to True, so that it will respond to the user's pressing of the Esc key—this is a Windows pseudo-standard.
8. Rename the UserForm and controls as shown in Table 6.4.

Table 6.4 Name Properties for the Linetypes UserForm

CONTROL	NEWNAME
UserForm1	frmLinetypes
CommandButton1	cmdOK
CommandButton2	cmdCancel
ListBox1	lstTypes

9. Type the code shown in Listing 6.3 into the skeleton for the Click event procedure of cmdOK.

The code in Listing 6.3 uses `While` loops rather than `For` statements. If `For` statements had been used, every item from the list box would need to be accessed, and the selected item compared with the Name property of every Linetype object in the Linetypes collection. Using the `While` statements allows us to stop searching as soon as we find what we are looking for—resulting in fewer accesses and faster results. This increase in efficiency becomes even more important when long lists or large collections are involved.

Listing 6.3: The OK Button's Click Event Procedure

```
1   Private Sub cmdOK_Click()
2   If lstTypes.ListIndex > -1 Then
3     ThisDrawing.ActiveLinetype = ↵
        ThisDrawing.Linetypes(lstTypes.List(lstTypes.ListIndex))
4   End If
5   Unload Me
6   End Sub
```

Analysis

- Line 1 starts `cmdOK`'s Click event procedure and is provided as a skeleton procedure when you select `cmdOK` from the Object list and `Click` from the Procedure list in the Code window.
- Line 2 tests to see if the `ListIndex` property of the list box is set to zero or more, which indicates that an item has been selected. `ListIndex` is `-1` if nothing is selected from a list box.
- Line 3 only runs if a list-box item has been selected; this line assigns the name of the selected item to the `ActiveLineType` property of `ThisDrawing.` Passing the `ListIndex` property of the `lstTypes` list box provides the index number of the selected item; the `List` method of the `lstTypes` provides the selected item's name.
- Line 5 unloads `Me`, which is the `frmLinetypes` UserForm, since it is no longer required.
- Line 6 ends the event procedure and is provided as part of the skeleton code.

Exercise 6.1: Line Input Application (continued)

In the next series of steps, you'll code the Cancel command button and the UserForm's Initialize event procedure.

1. Enter **Unload Me** into cmdCancel's Click event procedure. This allows users to cancel their request to select a new linetype.
2. Enter the code shown in Listing 6.4 into the UserForm's Initialize event procedure. This code adds all the linetypes to the list and makes the last item the selected one.

Listing 6.4: Initializing lstTypes to Contain All Lines from Linetypes Collection

```
1   Private Sub UserForm_Initialize()
2       Dim CurrentLinetype As AcadLineType
3       For Each CurrentLinetype In ThisDrawing.Linetypes
4           lstTypes.AddItem CurrentLinetype.Name
5           If CurrentLinetype.Name = ↵
               ThisDrawing.ActiveLinetype.Name Then
6               lstTypes.Selected(lstTypes.ListCount - 1) = True
7           End If
8       Next
9   End Sub
```

Analysis

- Line 1 starts the UserForm's `Initialize` event procedure that is instigated when the `frmLinetypes` UserForm is loaded. Notice how it is still called `UserForm` in the Object list of the `frmLinetypes` Code window.
- Line 2 declares `CurrentLinetype` as a variable that will refer to a Linetype object.
- Line 3 uses the `For Each` statement to assign a reference to the current Linetype objects as they are retrieved one by one from the Linetypes collection. The Linetypes collection contains all the linetypes that are listed in the Linetype Manager dialog box (see Figure 6.2).

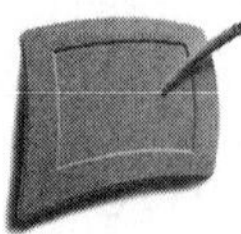

The `For Each...Next` version of the `For` loop can be used to process all the objects from a collection or all the elements from an array.

- Line 4 uses the `AddItem` method to add the name of the current linetype to the list box.
- Line 5 tests if the current linetype being added to the list is also the active linetype.

- Line 6 uses the `ListCount` property of the ListBox control to return the number of items currently in the list. Since the list starts at zero, then `Listcount -1` is the index to the last item added to the list box. The `Selected` property of the last item in the list is set to True, which will make it appear highlighted.
- Lines 7 and 8 end the `If` statement block and `For` loop, respectively.
- Line 9 ends the UserForm `Initialize` event procedure.

EXERCISE 6.1: LINE INPUT APPLICATION (CONTINUED)

In the next set of steps, you're going to include the Line Input UserForm shown in Figure 6.2, which will be used to input the coordinates of the line. Then the Linestyles UserForm will be called to set its style before drawing it in the AutoCAD window.

1. Display the Project Explorer window (choose View ➜ Project Explorer) and double-click `frmLineInput`.

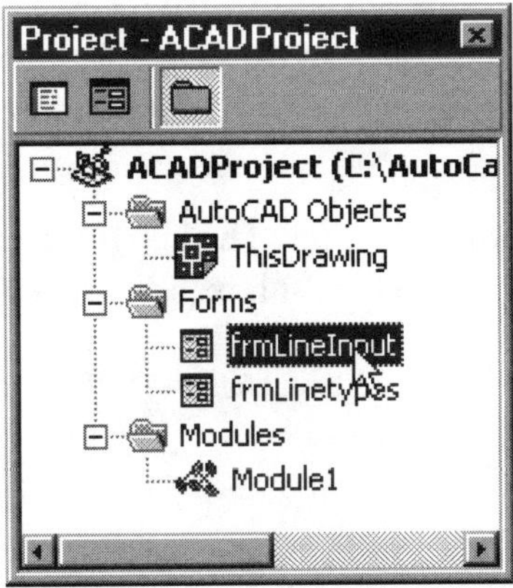

2. When the graphical representation of `frmLineInput` appears, choose View ➜ Code to open the Code window for `frmLineInput`.
3. Insert the `frmLinetypes.Show` statement to the `cmdDrawLine`'s Click event procedure as follows:

```
Private Sub cmdDrawLine_Click()
    frmLinetypes.Show
    CreateLine
End Sub
```

Now when the Draw Line command button is clicked to draw the line, this statement opens the Linetypes UserForm to let the user select a linetype. After the user makes a selection and clicks the OK button, the Linetypes UserForm will be unloaded again (see Line 5 of Listing 6.3). Execution will return to the cmdDrawLine_Click event procedure shown just above. This calls the CreateLine procedure to draw the line in the new linetype.

Running Your Line Drawing Application

The following steps show you how to add a few line types to your AutoCAD application before running the DrawLine macro. The Linetypes UserForm will display all the linetypes you add.

Exercise 6.1: Line Input Application (continued)

1. Follow the instructions given in the Setting Linetypes section earlier in this chapter to add a few different linetypes. Still in the AutoCAD window, choose the DrawLine macro from the Macros dialog box in the usual way. The Line Input UserForm appears, waiting for you to enter the six coordinates defining the next line.

2. Enter six numbers and click Draw Line. The Linetypes UserForm appears with all the loaded line styles listed in the list box (see Figure 6.6).

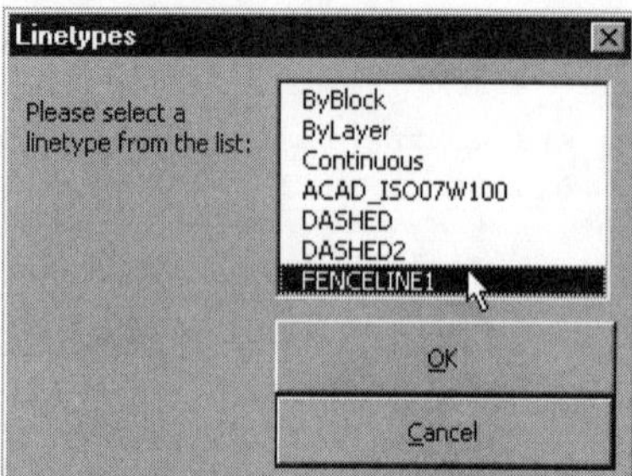

***Figure 6.6** Linetypes UserForm showing list of linetypes*

3. Select a linetype from the list and click OK. The Linetypes UserForm disappears, and the line is drawn in the Model Space. The Line Input UserForm remains open and waiting for your next input.

4. Repeat steps 2 and 3 to add a few more lines. Figure 6.7 shows my attempt at adding a few lines with different linetypes to the Model Space.

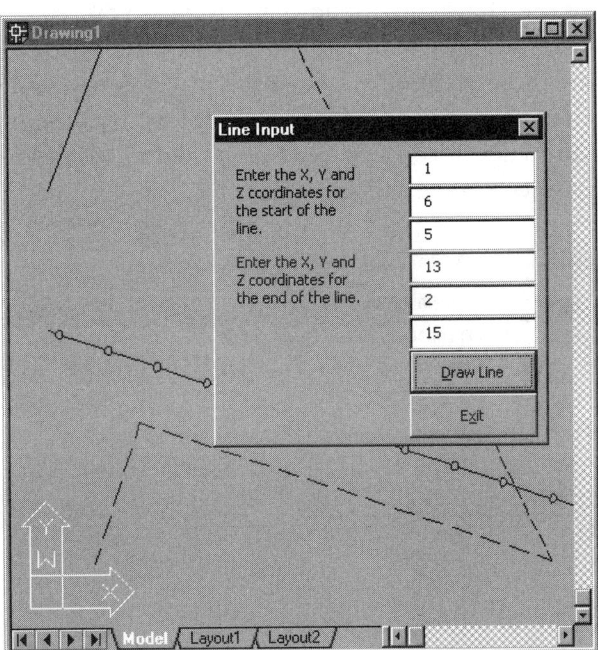

Figure 6.7 *Lines added to the Model Space using the Line Input and Linetypes UserForms*

Cancel and Default Properties and Buttons

Cancel Property Setting a command button's Cancel property to True designates it as the Cancel button, making it respond as if clicked when the user presses the Esc key.

Default Property Setting the Default property of a command button to True makes it the Default button, which responds as if clicked when the user presses the Enter key.

Cancel and Default Buttons Only one Cancel button and one Default button are allowed per UserForm. When you set the Cancel or Default property of one command button to True, then Visual Basic automatically sets it to False on the others. Both the Cancel and Default properties are unique to command buttons (or similar controls that behave like command buttons).

Highlighting a Line from a Macro

Using the Highlight method, you can specify whether or not a drawing object is to be drawn highlighted. When a line is highlighted, it is drawn using dashed lines.

The HighlightLastItemDrawn macro shown in Listing 6.5 takes the last drawing object that was added to the ModelSpace collection and highlights it by calling its Highlight method with the argument True. Enter this macro into Module1 of the Line Input project and try running it from the Macros dialog box. Try running it first without any lines in the Model tab to see the message box. Then add some lines and run it again to watch as your lines become dashed.

Listing 6.5: HighlightLastItemDrawn Macro

```
1   Sub HighlightLastItemDrawn()
2       If ThisDrawing.ModelSpace.Count = 0 Then
3           MsgBox "There is no line to highlight!"
4           Else
5           With ThisDrawing.ModelSpace
6               .Item(.Count - 1).Highlight True
7           End With
8       End If
9   End Sub
```

Analysis

- Line 1 starts the `HighlightLastItemDrawn` macro.
- Line 2 uses the `Count` property of the ModelSpace collection to return the number of drawing objects in the collection, and tests if the value returned is zero.
- Line 3 is executed only if the ModelSpace collection is empty. It calls the `MsgBox` function to let the user know that there are no lines to highlight.
- Line 4 starts the `Else` block that will only be executed if there is at least one object in the ModelSpace collection.
- Line 5 starts the `With` statement block, so that the properties and methods of the drawing object retrieved from the ModelSpace collection can be used without being fully qualified.
- Line 6 uses the `Count` property less one as the argument in the call to the `Item` method, to retrieve the last member object added to the ModelSpace collection—the last line drawn. Then the Boolean value `True` is passed as an

argument to the `Highlight` method so that the retrieved line will appear highlighted (dashed).

- Line 7 ends the `With` statement block.
- Line 8 ends the `If` statement block.
- Line 9 ends the `HighlightLastItemDrawn` macro.

Exercise 6.1: Line Input Application (continued)

Let's continue to extend our Line Input project by combining our newly created HighlightLastItemDrawn macro with another one that undoes the highlighting.

1. Insert another UserForm and add a CheckBox control in the top-left corner.
2. Change the Name and Caption properties of the UserForm and the check box control to those shown in Table 6.5. Here are the results:

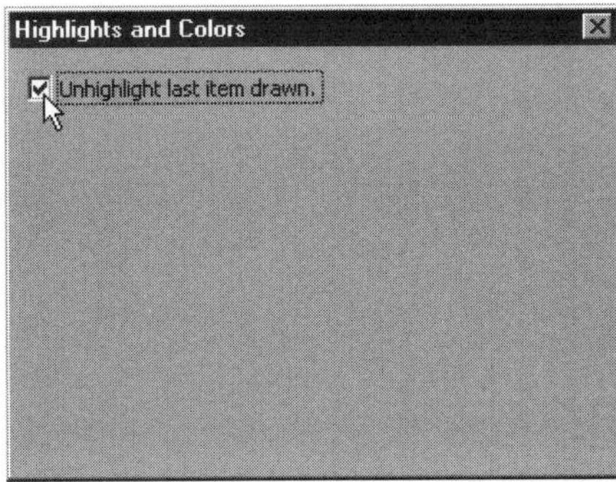

Table 6.5 Names and Captions for the Highlights and Colors UserForm

Control	New Name	New Caption
UserForm	frmHighlightAndColor	Highlights and Colors
CheckBox1	chkHighlightLast	Unhighlight last line drawn.

3. Enter the UnHighlightLastItemDrawn macro shown in Listing 6.6 into Module1 so that it can be run from the AutoCAD window as well as from the IDE. The chkHighlightLast_Click event procedure should be entered into the skeleton event procedure provided in frmHighlightAndColor's Code window.

I could take a different approach to this and combine the `HighlightLastItemDrawn` *and* `UnHighlightLastItemDrawn` *macros into one, but this would require testing the check box inside the macro. This arrangement would tie both macros to a control, rather than leaving them as general macros that can be called from anywhere in AutoCAD. Keeping the two macros separate and allowing the* `chkHighlightLast` *Click event procedure to decide between them means these macros can be reused again and again.*

4. Open the Line Input UserForm and add a new command button. Change the button's Name property to **cmdHighlight**, its Caption property to **Highlight and Color**, and its Accelerator property to **H** (see the results in Figure 6.8).

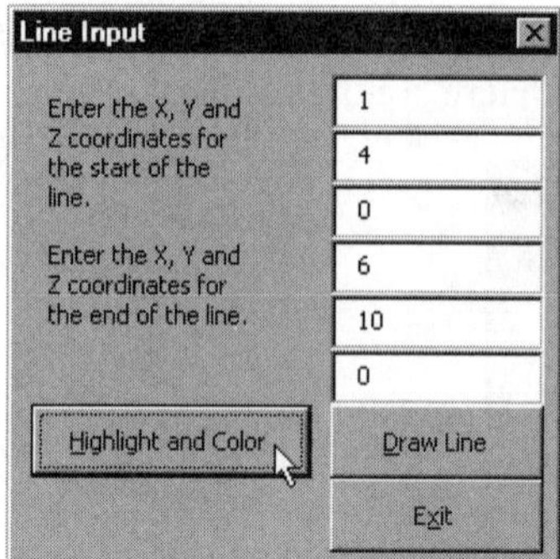

Figure 6.8 *Giving the order to highlight the line just generated*

5. Double-click the new command button to open the Code window containing the cmdHighlight_Click event procedure's skeleton. Enter this statement:

```
frmHighlightAndColor.Show
```

6. Return to the AutoCAD window, and make sure the TRACKS linetype has been loaded and appears in the Linetype Manager.
7. Run your project, and enter the coordinates of the line as shown in Figure 6.8.
8. Click the Draw Line button and select the TRACKS linetype from the Linetypes UserForm.
9. Click the Highlight and Color button. When the HighlightAndColor UserForm appears, check the Highlight Last Line Drawn check box and click OK to return to the Line Input UserForm.

10. Click Exit to return to the AutoCAD window, where your new TRACKS line will be on display (Figure 6.9).

Figure 6.9 *My TRACKS line after highlighting*

Listing 6.6: UnHighlightLastItemDrawn Macro with the Event Procedure That Runs It

```
Sub UnHighlightLastItemDrawn()
    If ThisDrawing.ModelSpace.Count = 0 Then
        MsgBox "There is no line to unhighlight!"
    Else
        With ThisDrawing.ModelSpace
            .Item(.Count - 1).Highlight False
            .Item(.Count - 1).Update
        End With
    End If
End Sub

Private Sub chkHighlightLast_Click()
    If chkHighlightLast Then
        HighlightLastItemDrawn
    Else
        UnHighlightLastItemDrawn
    End If
End Sub
```

ANALYSIS

- Lines 1 through 10 contain the statements for the `UnHighlightLastItemDrawn` that are much the same as for the `HighlightLastItemDrawn` from Listing 6.5, except for the message and the argument passed to `Highlight` being False instead of True.
- Line 12 starts the Click event procedure of the check box control `chkHighlightLast`. This runs if the user clicks on the check box, regardless of whether it's already checked or not. The user's click action updates the check box before the Click event procedure is instigated.
- Line 13 starts the `If` statement by testing if the Highlight Last Line Drawn check box is checked.
- Lines 14 and 16 call the `HighlightLastItemDrawn` and `UnhighlightLastItemDrawn` macros.
- Line 17 ends the `If` statement.
- Line 18 ends the `chkHighlightLast_Click` event procedure.

Now that you can highlight one line, why not highlight them all—the next section shows you how.

Highlighting and Coloring All Lines

The macros in this section highlight or unhighlight all the lines (or drawing objects) in the ModelSpace collection in one hit. Listing 6.7 shows the HighlightAllItems and UnHighlightAllItems macros. This code should be placed into Module1 of the Line Input project beside the HighlightLastItemDrawn macro; then they will be listed in the Macros dialog box.

Place a few lines in the drawing area of the Model tab and run the highlighting macro from the AutoCAD window—watch all your lines become dashed to indicate they have been highlighted. Undo the highlighting by selecting the UnHighlightAllItems macro from the Macros dialog box, and watch all your lines return to normal.

LISTING 6.7: HIGHLIGHTALLITEMS AND UNHIGHLIGHTALLITEMS MACROS

```
Sub HighlightAllItems()
    Dim LineObject As AcadEntity
    For Each LineObject In ThisDrawing.ModelSpace
        LineObject.Highlight True
```

```
5       Next
6   End Sub
7
8   Sub UnHighlightAllItems()
9       Dim LineObject As AcadEntity
10      For Each LineObject In ThisDrawing.ModelSpace
11          LineObject.Highlight False
12      Next
13  End Sub
```

Analysis

- Line 1 is the start of the `HighlightAllItems` macro.
- Line 2 declares the `LineObject` as a variable that refers to an `AcadEntity` object.
- Line 3 uses the `For Each...Next` statement to process all the member objects of the ModelSpace collection one by one. Remember, this collection can contain objects of different types.
- Line 4 calls the `Highlight` method for the current drawing object, with `True` as the argument.
- Line 5 uses the `Next` keyword to end the `For Each` statement.
- Line 6 ends the `HighlightAllItems` macro.
- Lines 8 through 13 are much the same as the statements in Lines 1 through 6, except that `Highlight` is set to `False`.

Because the HighlightAllItems and UnHighlightAllItems macros are almost identical, I could have incorporated them both into a single procedure. This procedure would need a True or False value passed to it as an argument. Such an arrangement, however, would mean that the new procedure would lose its macro status and would not be listed in the Macros dialog box. If these macros were larger and more complex, it would be better to combine them into one procedure and introduce two new macros to call the combined procedure with a Boolean value. That way there would still be two highlighting macros listed in the Macros dialog box.

Exercise 6.1: Line Input Application (continued)

Now you're ready to expand the Line Input project again by allowing for a color to apply to all the lines in the drawing space.

1. Open the frmHighlightAndColor UserForm in the IDE using the Object Browser.
2. Drag and drop two more check box controls onto the UserForm and place them below the first ones. Add a list box control and two command buttons, arrange them as shown just below, and change the Name and Caption properties for the controls to those listed in Table 6.6.

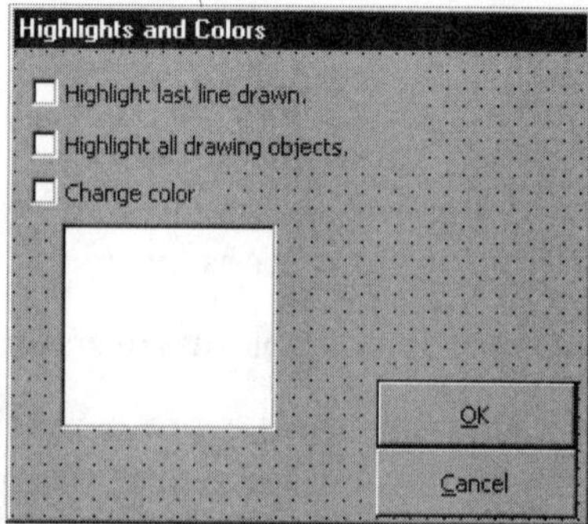

Table 6.6 Name and Caption Properties for Highlights and Colors UserForm

Old Name	New Name	New Caption
CheckBox1	chkHighlightLast	Highlight last line drawn.
CheckBox2	chkHighlightAll	Highlight all drawing objects.
CheckBox3	chkNewColor	Change color
ListBox1	lstColors	—
CommandButton1	cmdOK	OK
CommandButton2	cmdCancel	Cancel

3. Set the Accelerator property of cmdOK to the letter **O,** and to **C** for cmdCancel. Make cmdOK the Default button by setting its Default property to True, and make cmdCancel the Cancel button by setting its Cancel property to True.
4. Enter the code shown in Listing 6.8, placing the `Dim` declaration statement and the `GetColorSelected` procedure into the General Declarations section of frmHighlightAndColor UserForm.

LISTING 6.8: GETCOLORSELECTED PROCEDURE

```
1   Dim CurrentDrawingColor As Integer
2
3   Sub GetColorSelected()
4       Select Case lstColors.ListIndex
5           Case 0
6               CurrentDrawingColor = vbBlack
7           Case 1
8               CurrentDrawingColor = acRed
9           Case 2
10              CurrentDrawingColor = acYellow
11          Case 3
12              CurrentDrawingColor = acGreen
13          Case 4
14              CurrentDrawingColor = acCyan
15          Case 5
16              CurrentDrawingColor = acBlue
17          Case 6
18              CurrentDrawingColor = acMagenta
19          Case Else
20              CurrentDrawingColor = acWhite
21      End Select
22  End Sub
```

ANALYSIS

- Line 1 declares the `CurrentDrawingColor` variable in the General Declarations section so that it can be accessed by both the `GetColorSelected` procedure and the `lstColors_Click` event procedure.
- Line 3 starts the `GetColorSelected` procedure.
- Lines 4 through 21 contain the `Select Case` block of statements and use the `ListIndex` property of the `lstColors` list box as the test expression. The `ListIndex` property is set to the index of the selected color, or to –1 if no color is selected. If `ListIndex` is –1, the statement in `Case Else` will be executed. At the end of the block, `CurrentDrawingColor` will be set to the value of one of the color constants. (The `Select Case` statement was introduced in Chapter 4.)
- Line 22 ends the `GetColorSelected` procedure.

You can run any of these macros from the Macros dialog box, but it will be easier for a user if you incorporate them all into a project and allow the user to call them from a UserForm window. Listing 6.9 shows the event procedures that call these macros. Enter the statements into the skeleton event procedures provided in the Code window for frmHighlightAndColor.

LISTING 6.9: THE CHKHIGHLIGHTALL CHECK BOX CLICK EVENT PROCEDURE

```
Private Sub chkHighlightAll_Click()
   If chkHighlightAll Then
       HighlightAllItems
   Else
       UnHighlightAllItems
   End If
End Sub

Private Sub chkNewColor_Click()
    lstColors.Visible = True
End Sub

Private Sub cmdCancel_Click()
    Unload Me
End Sub

Private Sub cmdOK_Click()
    Unload Me
End Sub

Private Sub lstColors_Click()
    Dim CurrentObject As AcadLine
    GetColorSelected
    For Each CurrentObject In ThisDrawing.ModelSpace
        CurrentObject.Color = CurrentDrawingColor
        CurrentObject.Update
    Next
End Sub

Private Sub UserForm_Initialize()
    lstColors.Visible = False
    lstColors.AddItem "Black"
```

```
33      lstColors.AddItem "Red"
34      lstColors.AddItem "Yellow"
35      lstColors.AddItem "Green"
36      lstColors.AddItem "Cyan"
37      lstColors.AddItem "Blue"
38      lstColors.AddItem "Magenta"
39      lstColors.AddItem "White"
40  End Sub
```

ANALYSIS

- Lines 1 through 7 contain the `chkHighlightAll_Click` event procedure. If the check box is checked, `HighlightAllItems` is called to display all the drawing objects with dashed lines; otherwise, `UnHighlightAllItems` is called to display all the objects with solid lines.
- Lines 9 through 11 execute if the Change Color check box is clicked. A list box containing the list of colors is displayed.
- Lines 13 through 15 are executed if the user clicks the Cancel button. The `frmHighlightAndColor` UserForm is unloaded.
- Lines 17 through 19 execute when the user clicks the OK button and unloads the `frmHighlightAndColor` UserForm.
- Line 21 starts the `lstColors_Click` event procedure.
- Line 22 declares `CurrentObject` as a variable that can refer to an `AcadLine` object.
- Line 23 calls the `GetColorSelected` procedure that sets the `CurrentDrawing-Color` variable to the value of a color constant.
- Lines 24 through 27 contain a `For Each` loop statement block that sets the `CurrentObject` variable to each drawing object in the ModelSpace collection, and sets its color to the `CurrentDrawingColor` before redrawing it to update it on the screen.
- Lines 30 through 40 contain the `UserForm_Initialize` event procedure that is executed when the `frmHighlightAndColor` UserForm is first loaded. This event procedure makes the list box invisible and assigns the list colors it will contain.

Identifying Lines Selected by the User

AutoCAD allows users to select a set of drawing objects and then makes these objects into a temporary collection—the SelectionSet collection that belongs to the ThisDrawing object. This set only exists as long as the drawing remains open. This collection can be referenced by a variable declared as being capable of referring to an AcadSelectionSet object. Each member object can be referenced by a variable that is declared as referring to an AcadEntity object. An AcadEntity class of object can contain any AutoCAD object. In this section it will be used to reference individual objects from the SelectionSet collection.

EXERCISE 6.1: LINE INPUT APPLICATION (CONTINUED)

The GetUsersSelection macro shown in Listing 6.10 lets the user select lines (or other drawing objects) and then changes the color of all the selected items to green. Enter this macro into Module1 of your Line Input project.

LISTING 6.10: GETUSERSSELECTION MACRO

```
1   Sub GetUsersSelection()
2       Dim UsersSelection As AcadSelectionSet
3       Dim DrawingSelected As AcadEntity
4       'delete the selection set if it already exists
5       With ThisDrawing
6           On Error Resume Next
7           .SelectionSets("CurrentSelection").Delete
8           'get selection from user
9           MsgBox "Select objects! Hit Enter to finish!"
10          Set UsersSelection = ↵
              .SelectionSets.Add("CurrentSelection")
11          UsersSelection.SelectOnScreen
12          For Each DrawingSelected In UsersSelection
13              DrawingSelected.Color = acGreen
14          Next
15      End With
16  End Sub
```

ANALYSIS

- Line 1 starts the `GetUsersSelection` macro.

- Line 2 declares `UsersSelection` as being a variable that refers to an `AcadSelectionSet` class of object. The `AcadSelectionSet` object contains the set of drawing objects currently selected from the screen.
- Line 3 declares `DrawingSelected` as being a variable that refers to an `AcadEntity` object. An `AcadEntity` class of object can be any AutoCAD object. This variable will be set up to reference each drawing object in the selection set, as it is processed in the `For` loop.
- Line 5 uses the `With ThisDrawing` statement so that its SelectionSets collection can be used without fully qualifying it.
- Line 6 uses the `On Error` statement to handle any error that may occur in line 7.
- Line 7 deletes the `SelectionSet` object named `CurrentSelection` from the SelectionSets collection. If this macro is being run for the first time since the Line Input application was last opened, the named object won't actually exist. If it weren't for the `On Error` statement at line 6, the application would go into error mode now and stop functioning.
- Line 9 uses the `MsgBox` function to give helpful information to users about what the application expects them to do next (Figure 6.10). The command line doesn't give any idea about how to stop the selection process, and this could cause problems if the user isn't familiar with commands in the AutoCAD command line.

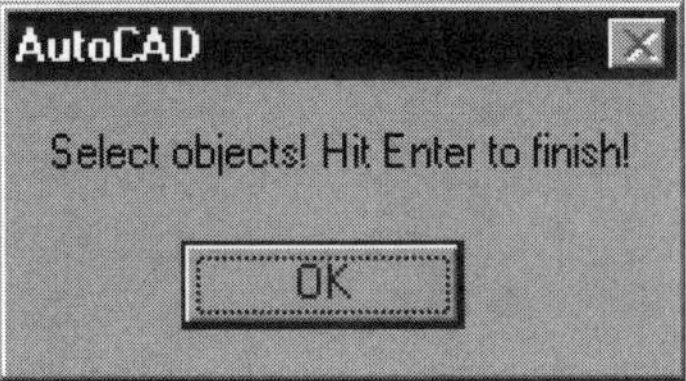

Figure 6.10 *Message box giving the user instructions of for what to do next*

- Line 10 uses the `Add` method to create a new SelectionSet object and add it to the SelectionSet collection of ThisDrawing. The `Set` statement is used to create a reference to the object named `CurrentSelection` in the SelectionSet collection, and set up the `UsersSelection` object to refer to it.

- You can add as many SelectionSet objects as you wish to a drawing, but only one SelectionSets collection is allowed.
- Line 11 uses the `SelectOnScreen` method of the UsersSelection set of objects to prompt the user from the command line to "Select objects." Then it waits while the user selects all the required drawing objects and finishes with the Enter key.

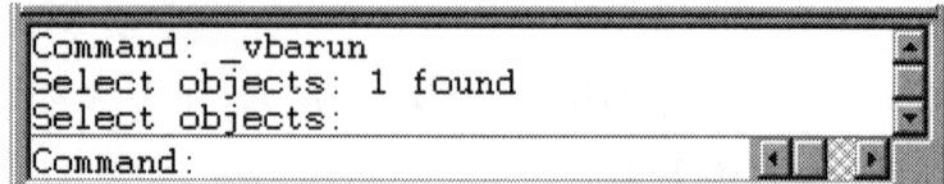

- Line 12 starts the `For` loop, which sets up the `DrawingSelected` variable as a reference to each object in the `UsersSelection` set. If the user didn't select any objects, execution jumps to the statement after the loop (line 15).
- Line 13 sets the `Color` property of the selected drawing object, currently referred to by the `DrawingSelected` variable, to green.
- Line 14 contains the `Next` keyword that marks the end of the `For` loop.
- Line 15 ends the `With` block of statements.
- Line 16 ends the macro.

To run your new macro from the AutoCAD window:

1. Choose Tools ➜ Macro ➜ Macros and select GetUsersSelection from the list of macros. The message shown in Figure 6.10 appears.
2. Click OK. The message box closes.
3. Click on lines to select them. As you do, the lines change from solid to dashed.
4. Press Enter. The selected lines change to solid green lines.

Scales and Weights for Lines

So far you've seen how to write code for an application that allows the user to select lines, change their type and color, and make them appear highlighted. There are a couple of other things you may want to do in this application; these include scaling the linetype or the line itself, and specifying a weight to control the thickness of a line.

Exercise 6.1: Line Input Application (continued)

Let's add another UserForm to our Line Input project to allow the user to enter the scaling factors or the weights—just follow these steps:

1. Choose Insert ➜ UserForm to add a new UserForm.
2. Place three label controls, three text box controls, and three command buttons and arrange them as shown in Figure 6.11. Then change the property settings as listed in Table 6.7.

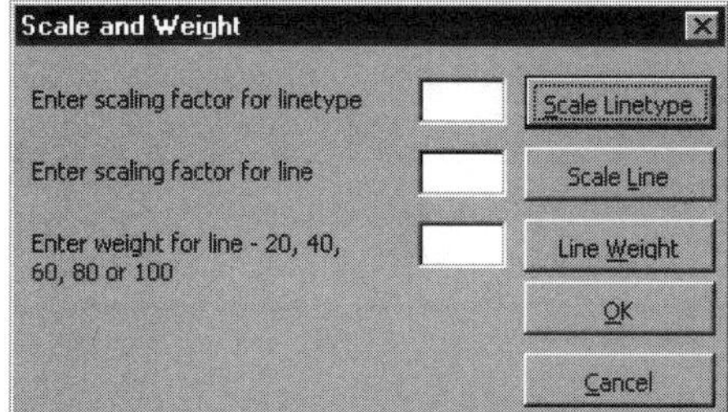

***Figure 6.11** Scale and Weight UserForm*

Table 6.7 Names and Captions for the Scale and Weight UserForm

Old Name	New Name	Caption
UserForm1	frmScaleAndWeight	Scale and Weight
Label1	—	Enter scaling factor for linetype
TextBox1	txtScaleLineType	—
CommandButton1	cmdScaleLinetype	Scale Linetype
Label2	—	Enter scaling factor for line
TextBox2	txtScaleLine	—
CommandButton2	cmdScaleLine	Scale Line
Label3	—	Enter weight for line = 20, 40, 60, 80 or 100
TextBox3	txtLineWeight	—
CommandButton3	cmdLineWeight	Line Weight
CommandButton4	cmdOK	OK
CommandButton5	cmdCancel	Cancel

3. Update the Accelerator property of the cmdScaleLinetype button to **S**, the cmdScaleLine button to **L**, the cmdLineWeight button to **W**, the cmdOK button to **O**, and the cmdCancel button to **C**. These characters will then appear underlined on their respective command buttons.

4. Enter the Scale Line command button Click event procedures (Listing 6.11) into the skeleton code.

The scale of a linetype determines how many times its pattern is repeated for each unit of the line. When the scale is small, the pattern is finer.

LISTING 6.11: THE SCALE LINE COMMAND BUTTON'S CLICK EVENT PROCEDURE

```
1   Private Sub cmdScaleLine_Click()
2       'scales a line with respect to the origin
3       Dim BasePoint(0 To 2) As Double
4       BasePoint(0) = 0#
5       BasePoint(1) = 0#
6       BasePoint(2) = 0#
7       With ThisDrawing.ModelSpace
8           .Item(.Count - 1).Color = acGreen
9           .Item(.Count - 1).ScaleEntity BasePoint, ↵
                CDbl(txtScaleLine)
10          .Item(.Count - 1).Update
11      End With
12  End Sub
```

ANALYSIS

- Line 1 starts the `cmdScaleLine_Click` event procedure that scales the last line drawn (with respect to the origin).
- Line 3 declares the `BasePoint` variable array for storing the three coordinates of the position to be used as the basis for the scaling.
- Lines 4 through 6 assign the origin to the `BasePoint` array.
- Line 7 starts the `With` statement block so that unqualified items will be assumed to belong to the ModelSpace collection.
- Line 8 sets the `Color` property of the last line added to the ModelSpace collection to green.

- Line 9 uses the `ScaleEntity` method that scales a line (or drawing object) equally in all x, y, and z directions. The method requires a 3D point specified in the WCS to use as the basis for the scaling. It also needs a scaling factor, which is used to multiply the differences between the endpoint coordinates and the base point coordinates to compute the new endpoint positions. Scaling with respect to the origin can be thought of as simply multiplying the coordinates of the two endpoints without the need to consider the base point, which has all zero coordinates.

EXERCISE 6.1: LINE INPUT APPLICATION (CONTINUED)

Now code the Scale Line Type command button's Click event procedure. Enter the `cmdScaleLinetype` Click event procedure (Listing 6.12) into the skeleton code in the Scale and Weight UserForm.

LISTING 6.12: THE SCALE LINETYPE COMMAND BUTTON'S CLICK EVENT PROCEDURE

```
1   Private Sub cmdScaleLinetype_Click()
2       'scales a linetype
3       ThisDrawing.SetVariable "LTSCALE", ↵
           CDbl(txtScaleLinetype)
4       With ThisDrawing.ModelSpace
5           .Item(.Count - 1).Color = acYellow
6           .Item(.Count - 1).Update
7       End With
8   End Sub
```

ANALYSIS

- Line 1 starts the `cmdScaleLinetype` event procedure that scales the linetype according to the scale entered by the user. (The smaller the scale, the finer the pattern.)
- Line 3 uses the `SetVariable` method to set the value of the AutoCAD system variable for scaling linetypes. The first argument, `"LTSCALE"`, specifies that the Linetype system variable is to be scaled; the second argument passes the value entered in the text box by the user. The default scaling factor is 1.0, meaning one unit of linetype per unit of line. The function `CDbl` is used to ensure that the text from the text box is converted to `Double`, which is the type required by the `LineWeight` property.

- Lines 4 and 5 are similar to Lines 7 and 8 in Listing 6.11, except that the line is colored yellow instead of green.
- Lines 6 through 8 are identical to Lines 10 through 12 in Listing 6.11 and serve the same purpose.

Exercise 6.1: Line Input Application (continued)

Next you'll code Click event procedures for the Line Weight, OK, and Cancel command buttons. Enter the `cmdLineWeight` Click event procedure (Listing 6.13) into the skeleton code in the Scale and Weight UserForm.

Listing 6.13: The Line Weight, OK, and Cancel Click Event Procedures

```
1   Private Sub cmdLineWeight_Click()
2       'sets the lineweight to 20, 40, 60, 80 or 100
3       'the lineweight must be one of this set
4       'if the number entered is not in the set
5       'this procedure crashes (terminates abnormally)
6       With ThisDrawing.ModelSpace
7           On Error Resume Next
8           .Item(.Count - 1).Lineweight = CDbl(txtLineWeight)
9           .Item(.Count - 1).Color = acCyan
10          .Item(.Count - 1).Update
11      End With
12  End Sub
13
14  Private Sub cmdCancel_Click()
15      Unload Me
16  End Sub
17
18  Private Sub cmdOK_Click()
19      Unload Me
20  End Sub
```

Analysis

- Line 1 starts the `cmdLineWeight_Click` event procedure that updates the line weight for the last line drawn, to the weight entered into the third text box by the user.
- Line 6 starts the `With` statement block, so that items belonging to the Model-Space collection can be used without being fully qualified.

- Line 7 contains the `On Error` statement. I have included this statement because of the high probability that the user will enter a number that AutoCAD will find invalid.
- Line 8 sets the `LineWeight` property to the value entered by the user. If this value is not a valid line weight, this statement produces an error—but the `On Error Resume Next` statement on line 6 saves the day!
- Line 9 assigns the value of the AutoCAD constant `acCyan` to the `Color` property of the last line added to the ModelSpace.
- Line 10 calls the `Update` method to display the last line with its new attributes.
- Line 11 ends the `With` statement block.
- Line 12 ends the `cmdLineWeight_Click` event procedure.
- Lines 14 through 16 contain the Cancel command button's Click event procedure that unloads the Scale and Weight UserForm.
- Lines 18 through 20 contain the OK command button's Click event procedure that unloads the UserForm and returns to the Line Input UserForm.

Follow these steps to incorporate the Scale and Weight UserForm into the Line Input application:

1. Open `frmLineInput` and add a command button. Change its Caption property to **Scale and Weight**, its Name to **cmdScaleAndWeight**, and its Accelerator to **S.** Here is the code to enter into the command button's Click event procedure's skeleton, so that the following new UserForm is displayed:

```
Private Sub cmdScaleAndWeight_Click()
    frmScaleAndWeight.Show
End Sub
```

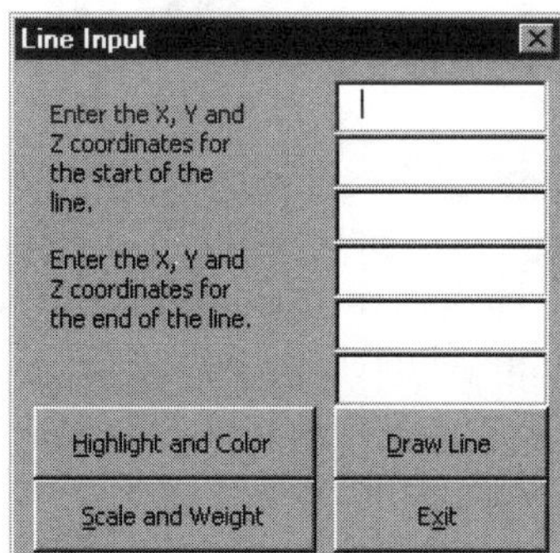

2. Return to the AutoCAD window and draw a dashed line in the Model Space. Choose Tools ➜ Macro ➜ Macros and run the DrawLine macro. The Line Input UserForm appears.
3. Click Scale and Weight. Try entering a scaling factor such as 0.5, 1.5, or 2 into the top text box, clicking Scale Linetype each time to see the effect. The Scale and Weight version of the UserForm appears. The length of the dashes from the last line entered change, and the line turns yellow.
4. Enter a scale factor for a line into the second text box. Make it a small number, close to 1. Since the line is scaled with respect to the origin, it has a tendency to go off the screen with larger numbers. For example, a scaling factor of 2 will double the distance of the endpoints from the origin of the Model Space. Click Scale Line. The line jumps away from the origin and changes in size, as well as turning green.
5. AutoCAD line weights have a limited number of AutoCAD constants that all have the prefix `acltwt` followed by a number. The value of these constants do not run in sequential order, so many numbers have no line weight equivalent and will give an error if entered by the user. For this reason a choice of five numbers is provided, and an `On Error Resume Next` statement is included to pick up the pieces when an unacceptable number is entered.
6. Enter **200** as the line weight value into the bottom text box and click Line Weight. Click the Close button of the Scale and Weight UserForm to return to the Line Input UserForm. Click Exit to return to the AutoCAD window.
7. Choose File ➜ Plot Preview from the AutoCAD window and the last line drawn will appear thicker than normal.

Scaling Using a Transformation Matrix

In this section you'll learn how scaling can be achieved by calling the TransformBy method with a transformation matrix that includes the scaling factors passed to it as an argument. The scaling factors are the values that determine how large an object grows in the x, y, and z directions; these values can be different.

I've started a completely new project in this section, to demonstrate the TransformBy method. The project starts by developing an application that allows the user to enter a scaling factor and then click a button to scale the last line added to the ModelSpace collection. The line's endpoints are multiplied by the scaling factor. This kind of scaling is said to be *with respect to the origin.* Not only does the length of the line change but also its distance from the origin.

The project continues by introducing scaling *with respect to a fixed point.* The fixed point is commonly the center of the object; then, when it is scaled, it simply gets bigger but maintains its relative distance from the origin.

The next two sections take you through the steps required to develop this scaling application.

Scaling a Line with Respect to the Origin

In this section you'll see how to set up a transformation matrix to scale the last line added to the Model tab with respect to the origin. This has the same effect as calling the ScaleEntity method with a base point at position (0, 0, 0).

Exercise 6.1: Line Input Application (continued)

1. Start a new project and add a UserForm.
2. Add a label, text box, and command button control to the UserForm, arranged as shown here. Then change the Name and Caption properties to those listed in Table 6.8.

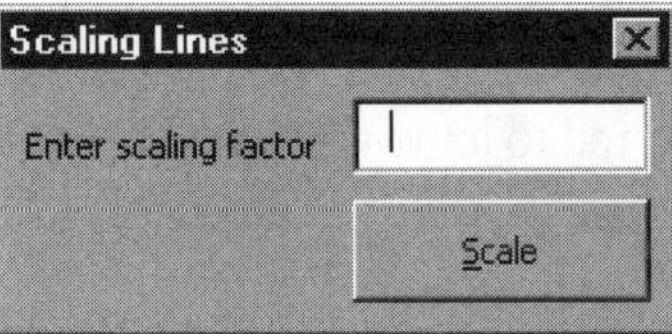

Table 6.8 Property Settings for the Scaling Lines Project

Old Name	New Name	Caption
UserForm1	frmTransformations	Transformations
Label1	—	Enter scaling factor
TextBox1	txtScaleFactor	—
CommandButton1	cmdScale	Scale

3. Set the Accelerator property of cmdScale to **S**, so that it can be accessed from the keyboard.

4. Enter the code shown in Listing 6.14 into the cmdScale_Click event procedure. This procedure takes the last drawing object added to the ModelSpace collection and scales it with respect to the origin. You'll see how to handle scaling with respect to a fixed point (base point) in the next section.

5. Choose Insert ➜ Module to add a module to your project and enter the following macro. By placing it in a module rather than the UserForm itself, you enable it to be run from the AutoCAD Macros dialog box:

```
Sub ScalingTransformation()
frmTransformations.show
End Sub
```

6. Return to the AutoCAD window and draw a line close to the origin.

7. Run the ScalingTransformation macro. The Scaling Line UserForm appears.

8. Enter **1.25** as the scaling factor.

Always keep your scaling factor close to 1, so that there's less chance of your line disappearing off the screen.

Both endpoints of the line will increase their distance from the origin by one-quarter, so your line will appear to move, as well as grow longer by one-quarter. After the transformation, your line will be colored red to let you know that the transformation has in fact taken place (just in case the change isn't very obvious).

Listing 6.14: Code for the Scale Command Button's Click Event Procedure

```
Private Sub cmdScale_Click()
    'scales last line entered using the scaling factor ↵
       input by user
    Dim TransMatrix(0 To 3, 0 To 3) As Double
    Dim Index1 As Integer, Index2 As Integer
    'initialize transformation matrix
    For Index1 = 0 To 3
        For Index2 = 0 To 3
             TransMatrix(Index1, Index2) = 0#
        Next
    Next
```

```
11      'place user's scale factors into matrix
12      TransMatrix(0, 0) = CDbl(txtScaleFactor)
13      TransMatrix(1, 1) = CDbl(txtScaleFactor)
14      TransMatrix(2, 2) = CDbl(txtScaleFactor)
15      TransMatrix(3, 3) = 1#
16      'update last line drawn
17      With ThisDrawing.ModelSpace
18          .Item(.Count - 1).TransformBy (TransMatrix)
19          .Item(.Count - 1).Color = acRed
20          .Item(.Count - 1).Update
21      End With
22      Unload Me
23  End Sub
```

Analysis

- Line 1 starts the `cmdScale_Click` event procedure that executes when the user clicks the command button.
- Line 3 declares the two-dimensional array that will hold the 4×4 scaling transformation matrix.
- Line 4 declares the two variables that are used to access the rows and columns of the 4×4 transformation matrix.
- Line 6 starts the outer `For` loop that initializes `Index1` to zero and increments it until, at the start of each loop, it reaches 4. The `Index1` variable is used to represent the row number of the `TransMatrix` array.
- Line 7 starts the inner `For` loop that initializes `Index2` to zero and increments it until it reaches 4. `Index2` is incremented at the start of each loop and is used to represent the column number of the `TransMatrix` array.
- Line 8 initializes the current element (given by `Index1,Index2`) in the transformation matrix to zero, in readiness for beginning a new scaling transformation.
- Lines 12 through 15 set the diagonal elements of the scaling matrix to perform the scaling transformation required. The first three elements are all set to the values entered by the user. The transformation matrix to scale about the origin is:

$$\begin{bmatrix} S_x & 0 & 0 & 0 \\ 0 & S_y & 0 & 0 \\ 0 & 0 & S_z & 0 \\ 0 & 0 & 0 & 1 \end{bmatrix}$$

- Line 17 starts the `With` statement block.
- Line 18 calls the `TransformBy` method of the last line drawn, passing the scaling transformation as the argument.
- Line 19 updates the `Color` property of the last line drawn with red to show that the transformation has taken place, in case it's not obvious.
- Line 20 uses the `Update` method to redraw the last line so that it is displayed as scaled.
- Line 21 ends the `With` statement block.
- Line 22 unloads the Transformations UserForm, leaving the user to continue with the AutoCAD session.

Scaling with Respect to a Fixed Point

When an object is scaled with respect to a fixed point, that fixed point is more often than not the object's center. This allows the object to grow in size from the center outward without changing its center's position. The scaling example done in this section calculates the center of the line being scaled and uses that as the basis for the scaling.

Before starting the project, let's take a look at the underlying math that makes the result of this transformation so different from the result of scaling with respect to the origin.

To scale about a fixed point really requires three different transformations that can be combined into one for efficiency. The first matrix translates the fixed point so that it lies at the origin. The second matrix scales the object. If the fixed point is the object's center point, then this matrix will cause the object to grow bigger or smaller without its center moving around the screen. The third transformation translates the fixed point back to its starting position. Following are the three transformations in matrix form:

$$\begin{bmatrix} 1 & 0 & 0 & 0 \\ 0 & 1 & 0 & 0 \\ 0 & 0 & 1 & 0 \\ -x_f & -y_f & -z_f & 1 \end{bmatrix} \begin{bmatrix} S_x & 0 & 0 & 0 \\ 0 & S_y & 0 & 0 \\ 0 & 0 & S_z & 0 \\ 0 & 0 & 0 & 1 \end{bmatrix} \begin{bmatrix} 1 & 0 & 0 & 0 \\ 0 & 1 & 0 & 0 \\ 0 & 0 & 1 & 0 \\ x_f & y_f & z_f & 1 \end{bmatrix}$$

It is more efficient to multiply these matrices together into one composite matrix before applying them to the vertices of the object:

$$\begin{bmatrix} S_x & 0 & 0 & 0 \\ 0 & S_y & 0 & 0 \\ 0 & 0 & S_z & 0 \\ (1 - S_x)x_f & (1 - S_y)y_f & (1 - S_z)z_f & 1 \end{bmatrix}$$

EXERCISE 6.1: LINE INPUT APPLICATION (CONTINUED)

Now that you know the three matrices involved in scaling with respect to a fixed point, you are ready to assign values to the transformation matrix that represents all three matrices in code. Let's continue expanding the Scaling Lines project:

1. To the Scaling Lines project, add a second command button immediately below the Scale command button. Change the new button's Name property to **cmdScaleToCenter,** its Caption property to **Scale to Center,** and its Accelerator property to **C** for keyboard access.
2. Enter the cmdScaleToCenter_Click event procedure given in Listing 6.15 into the skeleton event procedure provided in the frmTransformations UserForm.
3. Add the GetCenter macro (Listing 6.16) into Module1, and add the following declaration at the top of Module1 to enable it to be accessed by both the GetCenter macro and the cmdScaleToCenter_Click event procedure:

   ```
   Global CenterPoint(0 To 2) As Double
   ```
4. Draw a line and run the ScalingTransformation macro. Try entering a scaling factor and click the Scale to Center button. The last line drawn will be scaled and colored blue.

Because the TransformBy method works in three dimensions, your line may not appear to be scaled by the correct amount.

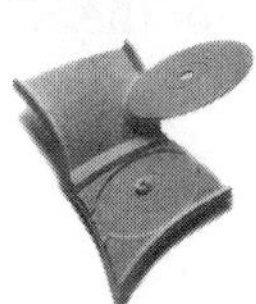

LISTING 6.15: SCALE TO CENTER COMMAND BUTTON'S CLICK EVENT PROCEDURE

```
Private Sub cmdScaleToCenter_Click()
    'scales wrt center using the scaling factor ↵
       input by user
    GetCenter
    Dim TransMatrix(0 To 3, 0 To 3) As Double
    Dim Index1 As Integer, Index2 As Integer
    'initialize transformation matrix
    For Index1 = 0 To 3
        For Index2 = 0 To 3
            TransMatrix(Index1, Index2) = 0#
        Next
    Next
    'place user's scale factors into matrix
```

```
13      Dim ScaleFactor As Double
14      ScaleFactor = frmTransformations.txtScaleFactor
15          TransMatrix(0, 0) = CDbl(ScaleFactor)
16          TransMatrix(1, 1) = CDbl(ScaleFactor)
17          TransMatrix(2, 2) = CDbl(ScaleFactor)
18          TransMatrix(3, 0) = CDbl((1 - ScaleFactor) * ↵
               CenterPoint(0))
19          TransMatrix(3, 1) = CDbl((1 - ScaleFactor) * ↵
               CenterPoint(1))
20          TransMatrix(3, 2) = CDbl((1 - ScaleFactor) * ↵
               CenterPoint(2))
21          TransMatrix(3, 3) = 1#
22      'update last line drawn
23      With ThisDrawing.ModelSpace
24          .Item(.Count - 1).TransformBy (TransMatrix)
25          .Item(.Count - 1).Color = acBlue
26          .Item(.Count - 1).Update
27      End With
28      Unload Me
29  End Sub
```

ANALYSIS

- Line 1 starts the `cmdScaleToCenter_Click` event procedure that will run when the Scale to Center command button is clicked. This procedure calls `GetCenter` to compute the center point and uses it as the fixed point for the scaling rather than the origin. It scales the last line drawn in the Model Space.
- Line 3 calls the `GetCenter` macro that calculates the center of the last line added to the Model Space and assigns it to the global array `CenterPoint`.
- Line 4 declares the two-dimensional array that will be assigned the transformation matrix.
- Lines 7 through 11 initialize the elements of the matrix to zero.
- Lines 13 and 14 declare the `ScaleFactor` variable and assign it the scale factor input by the user.
- Lines 15 through 21 assign values to the nonzero elements of the composite matrix given at the beginning of this section.

- Line 24 calls the `TransformBy` method with the composite matrix to transform the last line object that was added to the ModelSpace collection.
- Lines 25 and 26 assigns the Color property of the last line to blue and calls the update method to update the drawing space.
- Line 27 ends the `With` statement.
- Line 28 unloads the `frmTransformations` UserForm.
- Line 29 ends the `cmdScaleToCenter_Click` event procedure.

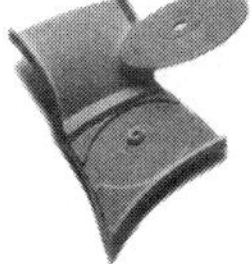

Listing 6.16 The GetCenter Macro

```
1   Sub GetCenter()
2       Dim LineObj As AcadLine
3       With ThisDrawing.ModelSpace
4           Set LineObj = .Item(.Count - 1)
5       End With
6       CenterPoint(0) = (LineObj.StartPoint(0) + ↵
           LineObj.EndPoint(0)) / 2#
7       CenterPoint(1) = (LineObj.StartPoint(1) + ↵
           LineObj.EndPoint(1)) / 2#
8       CenterPoint(2) = (LineObj.StartPoint(2) + ↵
           LineObj.EndPoint(2)) / 2#
9   End Sub
```

Analysis

- Line 1 starts the `GetCenter` macro.
- Line 2 declares the `LineObj` as being a variable capable of referring to an `AcadLine` type of object.
- Line 4, the variable `LineObj`, is set up as the reference for the last Line object added to the ModelSpace collection.
- Lines 6 through 8 use the `StartPoint` and `EndPoint` properties of the Line object to calculate the x-, y-, and z-coordinates of the center point.

The center point of any object is the average of all the x-, y-, and z-coordinates of the vertices that define it.

Multiple Parallel Lines

As you probably already know, *multilines* come in various styles and are typically used for drawing walls or anything else that requires parallel lines. As you draw a line using the Standard style of multiline, it is accompanied by a second line that is a set distance apart.

Exercise 6.1: Line Input Application (continued)

Listing 6.17 shows how multilines are drawn from a macro. Enter the DrawMultipleLines macro into Module1.

Listing 6.17: The DrawMultipleLines Macro

```
1   Sub DrawMultipleLines()
2       Dim MultiLineObj As AcadMLine
3       Dim Vertices(0 To 17) As Double
4       Vertices(0) = 3: Vertices(1) = 3: Vertices(2) = 0
5       Vertices(3) = 5: Vertices(4) = 6: Vertices(5) = 0
6       Vertices(6) = 3: Vertices(7) = 7: Vertices(8) = 0
7       Vertices(9) = 7: Vertices(10) = 5: Vertices(11) = 0
8       Vertices(12) = 5: Vertices(13) = 6: Vertices(14) = 0
9       Vertices(15) = 3: Vertices(16) = 3: Vertices(17) = 0
10      Set MultiLineObj = ↵
           ThisDrawing.ModelSpace.AddMLine(Vertices)
11  End Sub
```

Analysis

- Line 1 starts the `DrawMultipleLines` macro.
- Line 2 declares `MultiLineObj` as a variable that can contain a reference to an `AcadMLine` object.
- Line 3 declares the array of vertices to be used to store the coordinates for the points required by the `AddMLine` method in line 10.
- Lines 4 through 9 assign the values of the x-, y-, and z-coordinates to specify one point per line.
- Line 10 uses the `AddMLine` method to create multiple lines passing through the array of points passed to it as an argument. These lines are stored in an `MLine` object that the variable `MultiLineObj` is set up to reference.

This is the end of the Line Input application that's been running since the beginning of this chapter.

Using Arc Objects

In VBA the Arc object is created using the AddArc method that requires four arguments to draw the arc. These arguments are the center and radius of the circle on which the arc is based, and the start and end angles that determine the arc's position and length. This time, let's prompt the user and allow them to respond by entering input in the command line or clicking the mouse in the drawing space. Listing 6.18 shows how this is achieved using the Utility object.

Exercise 6.2: Drawing Arcs Application

Start a new project and enter the DrawArc macro into ThisDrawing's Code window.

Listing 6.18: DrawArc Macro

```
1   Public Sub DrawArc()
2       Dim NewArcObj As AcadArc
3       Dim Center As Variant
4       Dim Radius As Double
5       Dim StartAngle As Double, EndAngle As Double
6       With ThisDrawing.Utility
7           Center = .GetPoint↵
               (, vbCr & "Click on center point.")
8           Radius = .GetDistance↵
               (Center, vbCr & "Enter the radius")
9           StartAngle = .GetAngle↵
               (Center, vbCr & "Enter the start angle")
10          EndAngle = .GetAngle↵
               (Center, vbCr & "Enter the end angle")
11      End With
12      Set NewArcObj = ThisDrawing.ModelSpace.AddArc↵
           (Center, Radius, StartAngle, EndAngle)
13      NewArcObj.Update
14  End Sub
```

Analysis

- Line 1 starts the `DrawArc` macro that prompts the user from the command line to enter the data required to specify the arc. Then it creates an Arc object and calls the `Update` method to draw it.
- Line 2 declares the `NewArcObj` variable as being capable of referencing an `AcadArc` type of object.

- Lines 3 through 5 declare the variables that will be used to store the values input by the user before being passed as arguments in the call to the `AddArc` method.
- Line 6 starts the `With` statement so that the properties and methods of the `Utility` object of the `ThisDrawing` document can be used without being fully qualified.
- Line 7 uses the `GetPoint` method to get the point selected from the Model tab by the user.
- Line 8 uses the `GetDistance` method to get the radius from the user, who can either enter it in the command line using the keyboard, or click the screen (as shown).

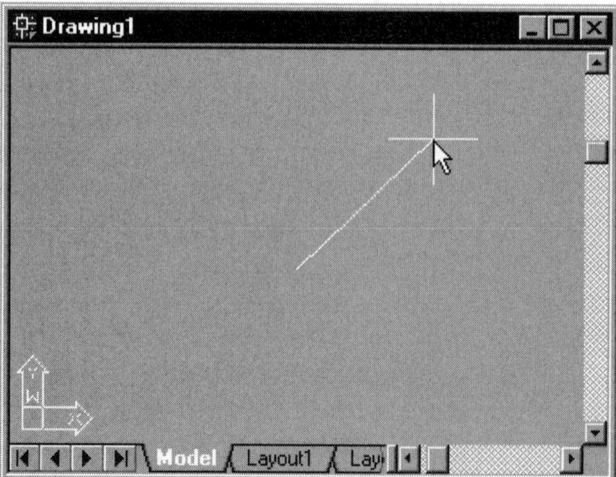

- Lines 9 and 10 use the `GetAngle` method to get the start and end angles from the user, who can enter them using the keyboard or the mouse. The command line keeps the user up-to-date on what is required next.

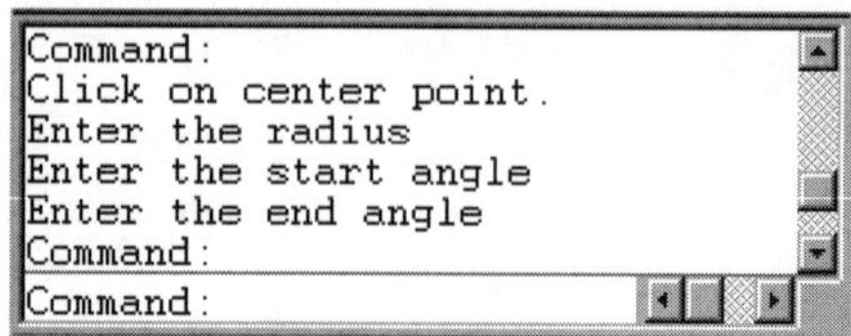

- Line 12 makes the `NewArcObj` variable into a reference to the `Arc` object created using the `AddArc` method that is called with the four data items entered by the user.

- Line 13 uses the `Update` method to draw the arc on the screen.

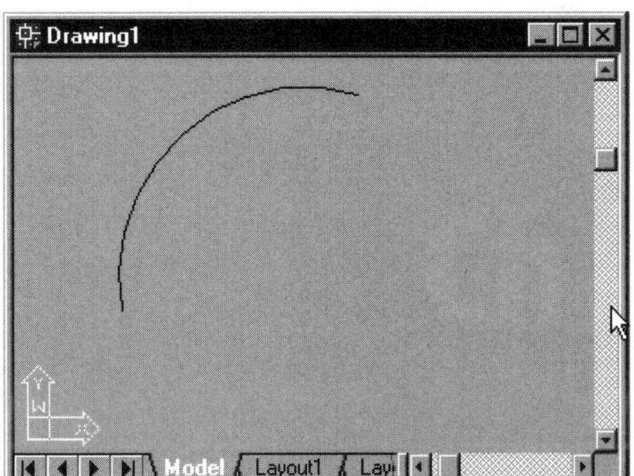

- Line 14 ends the `DrawArc` macro.

Lots of Arcs

In this example, let's call the AddArc method inside a `For` loop and create lots of arcs, one inside the other. Listing 6.19 shows how this is achieved, and Figure 6.12 shows the result.

Exercise 6.3: Creating a Collection of Adjacent Arcs

Start a new project and enter the LotsOfArcs macro into ThisDrawing's Code window.

Listing 6.19: LotsOfArcs Macro

```
Sub LotsOfArcs()
Dim NewArcObj As AcadArc
Dim Center As Variant
Dim Radius As Double
Dim StartAngle As Double, EndAngle As Double
Dim Counter As Integer
With ThisDrawing.Utility
    Center = .GetPoint(, vbCr & "Click on center point.")
End With
For Counter = 1 To 5
    Radius = Counter / 2#
```

```
12      StartAngle = 0
13      EndAngle = 180
14      Set NewArcObj = ThisDrawing.ModelSpace.AddArc↵
           (Center, Radius, StartAngle, EndAngle)
15      NewArcObj.Update
16  Next
17  End Sub
```

Analysis

- Line 1 starts the `LotsOfArcs` macro.
- Line 2 declares the `NewArcObj` variable as being capable of referencing an `AcadArc` type of object.
- Lines 3 through 5 declare the variables that will be used to store the values input by the user before being passed as arguments in the call to the `AddArc` method.
- Line 6 declares the `Counter` variable that will be used to set the radii for the arcs, and as an array index for the Arc object's array.
- Line 7 starts the `With` statement so that the properties and methods of the `Utility` object of the `ThisDrawing` document can be used without being fully qualified.
- Line 8 uses the `GetPoint` method to get the point selected from the Model tab by the user.
- Line 10 starts the `For` loop.
- Line 11 assigns the `Radius` variable half the value of the `Counter` variable. Varying this changes the distance between adjacent arcs.
- Lines 12 and 13 assign values for the start and end angles; these are identical for all the arcs.
- Lines 14 and 15 are the same as Lines 12 and 13 from Listing 6.18.
- Line 16 ends the `For` loop.
- Line 17 ends the `LotsOfArcs` macro.

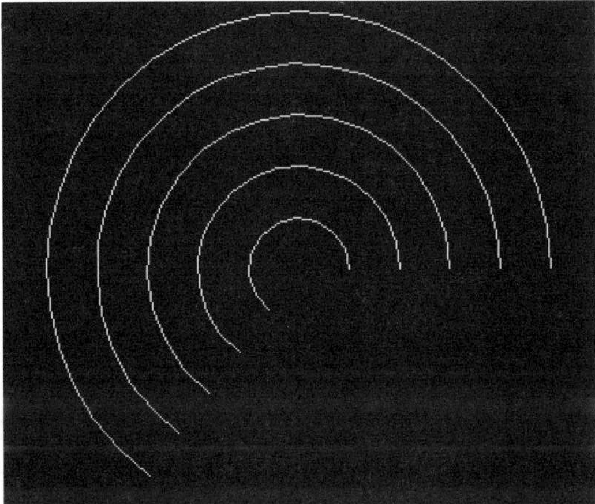

Figure 6.12 Adjacent arcs drawn with the LotsOfArcs macro (Listing 6.19)

Summary

At the end of your work in this chapter, you'll know how to do the following tasks and understand the related concepts in VBA code:

- Draw a line based on user's input.
- Highlight and color a line from a macro.
- Load a linetype and assign it to a line.
- Assign a weight to a line to control its thickness.
- Identify one or more lines selected by the user.
- Draw multiple parallel lines on your drawing space from a macro.
- Scale a line using the ScaleEntity method.
- Scale a line using the TransformBy method.
- Understand the math behind scaling.

- Know the difference between scaling with respect to the origin, and scaling with respect to a fixed point.
- Draw an arc, allowing the user to enter data using the keyboard or clicking in the Model tab.
- Draw a series of arcs automatically in a `For` loop.
- Add items to a list box control.
- Determine the selected item from the list in a list box.
- Make a command button the default or the cancel button for a UserForm.
- Use the `With` statement to condense your code statements.
- Grow a project in small stages.

Macro-izing Solid Areas

AUTOCAD VBA

Chapter 7

This chapter introduces VBA techniques for working with solid areas. You'll learn how to add a circle to your drawing and fill it with color. Also covered are freeform shapes: how to draw them and calculate the area they cover from a VBA macro. The ComboBox control is introduced, and you'll see how to format points displayed in the drawing space. Island Detection styles are discussed. Input boxes are used to communicate and retrieve input from the user. The final project in this chapter creates a drawing of a range top by prompting the user for its outside dimensions and number of burners. Then the project calculates the size and positions for the burners and draws them, all from a macro.

This chapter covers the following topics:

- Drawing circles
- Drawing freeform shapes
- Calculating areas of shapes
- Filling objects using inner and outer loops
- Working with input boxes
- Drawing a range top from a macro

Drawing Circles

Drawing a circle requires calling the AddCircle method with two arguments—an array containing the coordinates defining its center, and a radius to define the circle's size. The AddCircle method creates a Circle object and adds it to the specified ModelSpace, PaperSpace, or Blocks collection. The Circle object is accessed by a variable that's set up to contain a reference to it.

You can specify the values required for the center and radius in the following three ways:

- Assign values in code, which has the disadvantage of producing identical circles each time it is run (although sometimes this is exactly what is required). This is achieved in the same way that the endpoints of a line were assigned in the CreateLine macro from Listing 5.3 in Chapter 5.
- Create a UserForm and ask the user to enter values into text box controls. This requires the user to enter the three coordinates defining the center into text boxes in much the same way as for the Line Input UserForm from Chapter 6, except the three textboxes for the second endpoint are replaced by one text box to contain the radius.
- Use methods from the Utility object to prompt the user to enter values into the AutoCAD command line, or to mouse-click points in the Model Space. This technique is demonstrated in Exercise 7.1.

You can also use combinations of these methods.

Exercise 7.1: The DrawCircle Macro

Listing 7.1 uses the third technique mentioned above: putting the Utility object to work. It shows how a circle can be generated from a macro using the Utility object's methods to interact with the user. We prompt them to provide the center and radius in much the same way as for adding an Arc object in Chapter 6.

For this exercise, start a new project and place the macro into the ThisDrawing module so that it will appear in the Macros dialog box on your computer.

Listing 7.1: DrawCircle Macro

```
Public Sub DrawCircle()
    Dim CircleObject As AcadCircle
    Dim Center As Variant
    Dim Radius As Double
    'give instructions to user in the command line
```

```
6       With ThisDrawing.Utility
7           Center = .GetPoint(, "Click the position ↵
               for the center.")
8           Radius = .GetDistance(Center, "Enter the radius.")
9       End With
10   'create a Circle object and draw it in red
11       Set CircleObject = ThisDrawing.ModelSpace.AddCircle↵
            (Center, Radius)
12       CircleObject.Color = acRed
13       CircleObject.Update
14   End Sub
```

ANALYSIS

- Line 1 starts the `DrawCircle` macro that prompts the user to input the center and radius of a circle, and then draws a red circle to the user specifications.
- Line 2 declares `CircleObject` as a variable that can be set up to refer to a `Circle` object.
- Line 3 declares `Center` as a Variant type. This is an excellent way of getting around the fact that normally the values of an array's elements must be assigned individually. The `Center` variable is assigned the value returned from the `GetPoint` method (line 7), which is a Variant type containing a three-element array of doubles that contain the x-, y-, and z-coordinates of the point clicked by the user. After this assignment, you can retrieve each coordinate's value separately from the `Center` variable just as if you had declared it as an array; for example, `X = Center(0)`.
- Line 4 declares the `Radius` variable, which is assigned the value returned by the `GetDistance` method of the Utility object (returned by the Utility property of ThisDrawing).
- Line 6 starts the `With` statement block and uses the Utility property to retrieve the Utility object from the ThisDrawing collection. The Utility object is used to set up the automatic qualifier for the items starting with a period character (`.`) inside the `With` statement block.
- Line 7 calls the `GetPoint` method of the Utility object to prompt the user to click on the position for the circle's center. The text passed as the second argument appears in the AutoCAD command line. This method returns the three coordinates of the point clicked, which are assigned to the `Center` variable.

- Line 8 calls the `GetDistance` method to prompt the user to enter the circle's radius. The `Center` is passed as the first argument to act as the base point. A rubber-band line anchored at this base point appears to follow the mouse cursor around as the user moves it.
- Line 9 ends the `With` statement block.
- Line 11 uses the `AddCircle` method to create a Circle object with the user's specifications and adds it to the ModelSpace collection. A reference to this new Circle object is assigned to the variable `CircleObject` that was declared in line 2 as an `AcadCircle` type.
- Line 12 assigns the value of the AutoCAD constant `acRed` to the `Color` property, which will be the color of the boundary of the Circle object.
- Line 13 uses the `Update` method to refresh the drawing space to draw the circle.

Figure 7.1 shows a circle generated using this macro. Notice how the Circle object's color property refers only to the color of its circumference and that no color fill has been performed.

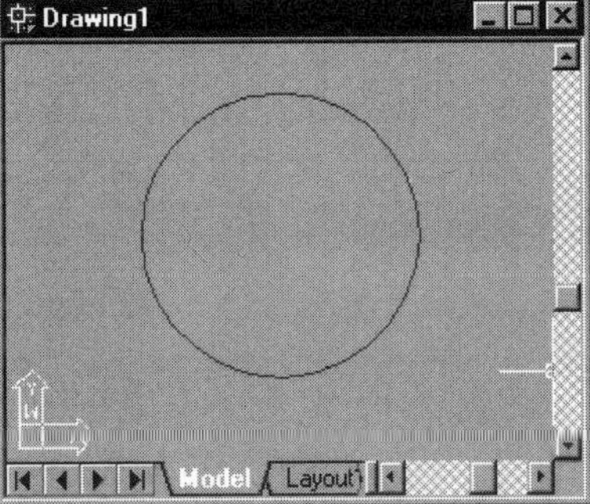

Figure 7.1 *Circle produced by the DrawCircle macro in Listing 7.1*

Drawing Filled Circles

In this section you'll learn how to fill a circle with color by employing a Hatch object that can fill any area with a solid fill or one of the industry-standard hatch patterns available. AutoCAD gives you a choice of over 50 such patterns. You can also use patterns from external libraries or define your own patterns based on the current linetype.

The AddHatch Method

A Hatch object is created and added to the ModelSpace collection using the AddHatch method. This method has three parameters:

PatternType The PatternType parameter specifies one of three AutoCAD constants:

- acHatchPatternTypePredefined, which uses the PatternName string to search for the pattern in AutoCAD's default pattern file `acad.pat`
- acHatchPatternTypeUserDefined, which uses the current linetype to define a new pattern
- acHatchPatternTypeCustomDefined, which uses the PatternName string to search for the pattern in `.pat` library files rather than the default `acad.pat` file

PatternName The PatternName argument is a string containing the name of the hatch pattern to be used. AutoCAD uses the PatternType setting to determine whether to look in the default `acad.pat` file for the named pattern, or to look in one of the other `.pat` files that contain custom-defined patterns.

Associativity The Associativity argument is set to True if the hatch is to be associated with the boundary that contains it, and False otherwise. When set to True, an associative hatch will change when its boundary is modified. On the other hand, a nonassociative hatch is independent of its boundary, so the hatch pattern will remain in place even after the original boundary is modified or removed.

Like all objects in VBA, the AddHatch method should always be in an assignment statement, using the `Set` statement to set to a variable the reference to the Hatch object being created.

Remember, the first statement after creating your Hatch object should be a call to the AppendOuterLoop method, to ensure that the outer boundary for the hatch pattern is closed. If any other operation is attempted, then AutoCAD cannot predict what will happen next.

Exercise 7.2: Drawing a Filled Circle

For this exercise, start a new project and place the macro into ThisDrawing's Code window. That way it will appear in the Macros dialog box on your PC so that it can be run from the AutoCAD window.

Listing 7.2: DrawFilledCircle Macro

```
1   Sub DrawFilledCircle()
2       'HatchObject will reference the new Hatch object
3       Dim HatchObject As AcadHatch
4       'OuterCircle becomes the circle defining the outer ↲
           loop boundary
5       Dim OuterCircle(0) As AcadCircle
6       Dim Center As Variant
7       Dim Radius As Double
8       'get Center position and radius from the user
9       With ThisDrawing.Utility
10          Center = .GetPoint(, "Click the position ↲
               for the center.")
11          Radius = .GetDistance(Center, "Enter the radius.")
12      End With
13      'create Circle object and assign reference ↲
           to OuterCircle
14      Set OuterCircle(0) = ThisDrawing.ModelSpace.AddCircle↲
           (Center, Radius)
15      OuterCircle(0).Color = acYellow
16      OuterCircle(0).Update
17      'create Hatch object and assign reference to HatchObject
18      Set HatchObject = ThisDrawing.ModelSpace.AddHatch↲
           (acHatchPatternTypePredefined, "SOLID", True)
19      'add the outer loop boundary to the Hatch object
20      HatchObject.AppendOuterLoop (OuterCircle)
21      HatchObject.Evaluate
22      HatchObject.Update
23  End Sub
```

Analysis

- Line 1 starts the `DrawFilledCircle` macro, which prompts the user in the command line to input the center and radius of a circle. These values are used to create the circle that forms the outer loop boundary when the circle is filled with solid color.
- Line 3 declares `HatchObject` as a variable capable of referencing a Hatch object.
- Line 5 declares `OuterCircle` as being a single-element array capable of containing a reference to a Circle object. Notice how it is declared with a dimension of

zero; this can also be written as `0 to 0`, and is interpreted as containing one element. `OuterCircle` needs to be an array because it is passed as an argument to the `AppendOuterLoop` method (line 20) that expects an array of one or more objects collectively defining the closed boundary that can be used for doing the filling.

- Line 6 declares `Center` as a Variant type so that it can be assigned the x-, y-, and z-coordinates returned by the `GetPoint` method in a single assignment statement, and thereafter can be treated like an array with an index value to access each coordinate separately.
- Lines 9 through 12 contain the `With` statement block that uses methods from the Utility object to prompt the user to enter the center and radius of the circle to be filled. The user can respond by entering values into the command-line window, or by checking points in the Model tab.
- Line 14 uses the `AddCircle` method to add a Circle object to the user's specifications to the ModelSpace collection, and assigns a reference to this new object to the first and only element in the `OuterCircle` array.
- Line 15 changes the color of the circle to yellow.
- Line 16 updates the screen to show the yellow circle.
- Line 18 calls the `AddHatch` method to create a Hatch object, and adds it to the ModelSpace collection. The first argument passed to this method is the AutoCAD constant `acHatchPatternTypePredefined`, to instruct the interpreter to search the default `acad.pat` file for the definition of the pattern named in the second argument as `SOLID`. The third argument passes the value `True` to the `Associativity` parameter so that the pattern is associated with the circular boundary.
- Line 20 uses the `AppendOuterLoop` method to set the outer-loop boundary for the fill. The one-element array `OuterCircle` that references the Circle object is passed as the argument to provide the boundary. Lines 18 and 20 should always be treated as an inseparable pair, because if line 20 were omitted, AutoCAD would enter an unpredictable state.
- Line 21 calls the `Evaluate` method that finds the point where the pattern definition lines intersect with the hatch boundary. When solid-fill hatch patterns have been requested, as is the case here, the `Evaluate` method divides the hatch area into triangles and fills each one with the fill color. If the boundary passed

to the AppendOuterLoop method (line 20) is not a single closed loop, this fact will be picked up by Evaluate, and the application will simply stop and give an error message.

- Line 22 calls the Update method of the Hatch object to draw the filled circle in the Model tab.
- Line 23 ends the DrawFilledCircle macro.

Figure 7.2 shows the result of running the DrawFilledCircle macro.

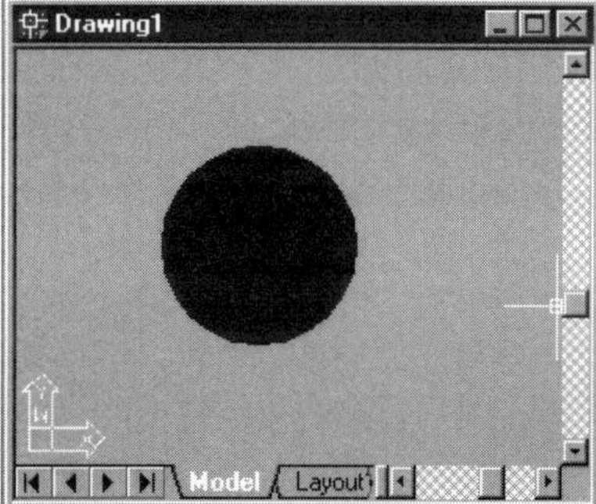

Figure 7.2 *Circle created and filled by the DrawFilledCircle macro (Listing 7.2)*

Circle of Bricks Application

When you have a specific effect in mind, filling a circle with a Hatch pattern may not give you the look you want. Suppose you want a circle of brick pavers, for example. Figure 7.3 shows the result of changing SOLID to BRICK at Line 18 of Listing 7.2.

Exercise 7.3: Draw Circular Pavers Application

Let's create an application that provides a much better visual solution than the circle filled with a BRICK hatch pattern. The following steps show you how it's done:

1. Start a new project and add a UserForm. Place a TextBox and accompanying Label, a Frame containing two OptionButtons, and two command buttons, as shown in Figure 7.4.
2. Change the object values in the Properties window to those shown in Table 7.1.

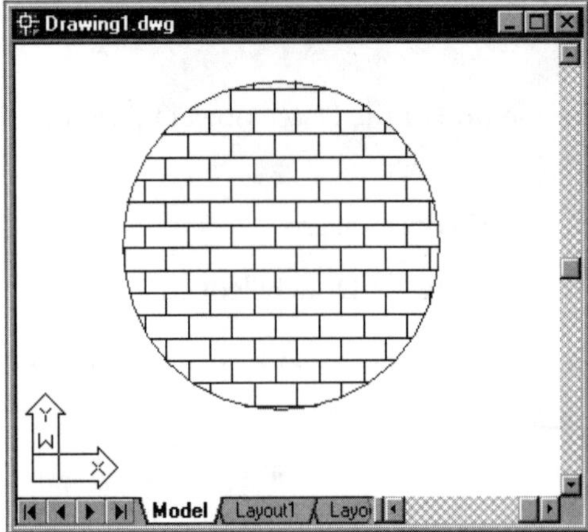

Figure 7.3 *Circle filled with BRICK hatch pattern instead of SOLID.*

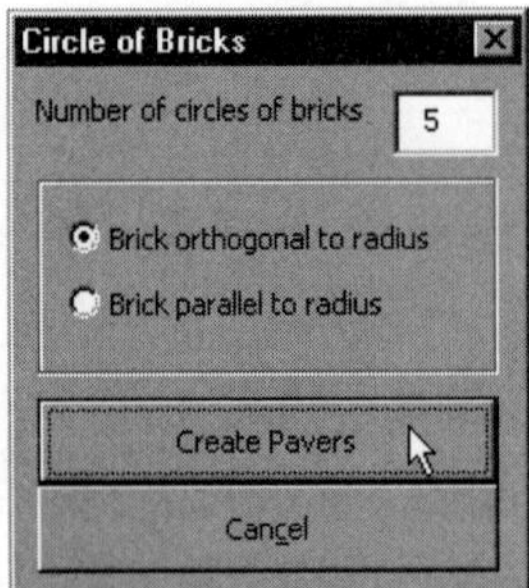

Figure 7.4 *GUI for the Circle of Bricks application*

3. Enter the code shown in Listing 7.3 into the UserForm's Code window.

   The DrawCircularPavers procedure draws all the red circles and calls the DrawMortar procedure to draw the lines between bricks. Both procedures are private by default, so they won't be listed in the AutoCAD Macros dialog box.

Table 7.1 Property Values for Controls in Circle of Bricks Application

Old Name	New Name	Caption
UserForm1	frmCircleOfBricks	Circle of Bricks
Label1		Number of circles of bricks
TextBox1	txtNumberOfCircles	
Frame1	—	Select the middle for drawing points
OptionButton1	optBrickOrthogonal	Brick orthogonal to radius
OptionButton2	optBrickParallel	Brick parallel to radius
CommandButton1	cmdCreatePavers	Create Pavers
CommandButton2	cmdCancel	Cancel

Listing 7.3: DrawCircularPavers Procedure

```
Sub DrawCircularPavers()
Dim BrickCircles() As AcadCircle
Dim Center As Variant, Radius As Double
Dim Counter As Integer
ReDim BrickCircles(txtNumberOfCircles)
'get Center position and radius from the user
With ThisDrawing.Utility
    Center = .GetPoint( ↵
        , "Click the position for the center.")
    Radius = .GetDistance(Center, "Enter the radius.")
End With
    'create Brick circle objects
For Counter = 0 To txtNumberOfCircles - 1
    Set BrickCircles(Counter) = ↵
       ThisDrawing.ModelSpace.AddCircle(Center, ↵
       Radius - Counter * Radius / txtNumberOfCircles)
    BrickCircles(Counter).Color = acRed
    BrickCircles(Counter).Update
    DrawMortar Center, Counter, Radius
Next
End Sub

Sub DrawMortar(Center As Variant, Counter As Integer, ↵
   Radius As Double)
    'declare variables for end points for line
```

```
22  Dim StartPoint(0 To 2) As Double, EndPoint(0 To 2) As Double
23  Dim Theta As Double, StepSize As Double
24  Static Adjust As Double
25  If frmCircleOfBricks.optBrickParallel = True Then
26      StepSize = 15 * Pi / 180
27  Else 'place brick orthogonal to radius
28      StepSize = 30 * Pi / 180
29      If Adjust = 0# Then
30          Adjust = 15 * Pi / 180
31      Else
32          Adjust = 0#
33      End If
34  End If
35  For Theta = 0 To 360 * Pi / 180 Step StepSize
36      StartPoint(0) = (Radius - Counter * Radius / ↵
           txtNumberOfCircles) * Cos(Theta + Adjust) + Center(0)
37      StartPoint(1) = (Radius - Counter * Radius / ↵
           txtNumberOfCircles) * Sin(Theta + Adjust) + Center(1)
38      EndPoint(0) = (Radius - (Counter + 1) * Radius / ↵
           txtNumberOfCircles) * Cos(Theta + Adjust) + Center(0)
39      EndPoint(1) = (Radius - (Counter + 1) * Radius / ↵
           txtNumberOfCircles) * Sin(Theta + Adjust) + Center(1)
40      StartPoint(2) = 0#: EndPoint(2) = 0#
41      With ThisDrawing.ModelSpace
42          .AddLine StartPoint, EndPoint
43          .Item(ModelSpace.Count - 1).Update
44      End With
45  Next
46  End Sub
```

Analysis

- Line 1 starts the `DrawCircularPavers()` procedure from the frmCircleOf-Bricks UserForm.
- Line 2 declares the `BrickCircles` as a dynamic array—you can tell from the empty parentheses. This array will contain the references to the circle objects.
- Line 3 declares the `Center` and `Radius` variables that are assigned values entered by the user in the AutoCAD window.
- Line 4 declares the `Counter` variable that is used as the loop counter in the `For` loop.

- Line 5 redimensions the `BrickCircles` dynamic array to make it large enough to contain the number of circles requested by the user.
- Lines 7 through 10 get the central point and radius of the circle from the user.
- Line 12 starts the `For` loop that uses `Counter` to access each circle on the `BrickCircle` array.
- Line 13 creates a Circle object. The `Counter` variable is used both as an index to the `BrickCircles` array and also as an ordinary variable to calculate the radius for the current circle. The circles are generated from largest to smallest, and references to them are stored in the array.
- Lines 14 and 15 set the color of the new circle and draw it on the screen.
- Line 16 calls the `DrawMortar` procedure (Line 20) to draw the lines between the bricks forming the current circle.
- Line 17 ends the `For` loop.
- Line 18 ends the `DrawCircularPavers` procedure.
- Line 20 starts the `DrawMortar` procedure.
- Line 22 declares the `StartPoint` and `EndPoint` arrays that are used to store the coordinates of the current line-between-bricks being drawn.
- Line 23 declares `Theta`, which is the angle at which the line-between-bricks will be drawn, and `StepSize`, which determines the number of bricks that make up the circle.
- Line 24 declares the `Adjust` variable to rotate the bricks by half a brick every second row. This variable is declared as `Static` so that it keeps its value between circles.
- Line 25 starts the outer `If` statement by testing to see if the "Brick parallel to radius" option button is selected.
- Line 26 sets the `StepSize` to 15 degrees multiplied by pi / 180, to ensure that `StepSize` is assigned radians. This accommodates bricks that are placed so that their length is parallel to the radius at that point.
- Line 27 starts the `Else` part of the `If` statement.
- Line 28 sets the `StepSize` variable to 30 degrees converted to radians. This accommodates bricks that are placed at right angles to the radius at that point.

- Lines 29 through 33 contain the inner `If` statement block that toggles the value of the `Adjust` variable between zero and half a brick length, to give the staggered effect shown in Figure 7.5.
- Line 34 ends the outer `If` statement block.
- Line 35 starts the `For` loop that uses `Theta` as the angle in radians between successive lines-between-bricks.
- Lines 36 through 40 assign values of coordinates to the start and endpoints of the current brick line. They use the `Sin` and `Cos` functions to calculate the x- and y-coordinates.
- Lines 41 through 44 contain the `With` statement block that creates a line and displays it on the screen.
- Lines 45 and 46 end the `For` loop and `DrawMortar` procedure, respectively.

In these next two steps, you will see how to write a macro to start your Circle of Bricks application, and how to code the Click event procedures for the two command buttons.

1. Choose Insert ➜ Module, and enter the following global constant declaration into Module1 with the DrawCircleOfBricks macro:

```
Global Const Pi = 3.14159

Sub DrawCircleOfBricks()
    frmCircleOfBricks.Show
End Sub
```

   The DrawCircleOfBricks macro opens the Circle of Bricks UserForm and is the only procedure from the project listed in the AutoCAD Macros dialog box.

2. Now all you have left to do is add the code to the event procedures for the two command buttons. Enter the code shown in Listing 7.4 into the Circle of Bricks UserForm's Code window. There will be two skeleton Click event procedures for the two command buttons already waiting.

LISTING 7.4: THE COMMAND BUTTON EVENT PROCEDURES

```
Private Sub cmdCancel_Click()
    Unload Me
End Sub

Private Sub cmdCreatePavers_Click()
```

```
6         Unload Me
7         DrawCircularPavers
8     End Sub
```

Analysis

- Line 1 opens the `cmdCancel` Click event procedure.
- Line 2 unloads the Circle of Bricks UserForm and return to the AutoCAD window without making any changes.
- Line 5 starts the event procedure that runs when the user clicks the Create Pavers command button.
- Line 6 unloads the Circle of Bricks UserForm.
- Line 7 calls the `DrawCircularPavers` procedure to draw the lines between the bricks in the current circle.
- Line 8 ends the event procedure.

Now run your Circle of Bricks application from the AutoCAD Macros dialog box. Figure 7.5 shows the result of running the application with the default settings shown in Figure 7.4. Figure 7.6 shows the result of running the application with "7" entered as the number of circles of bricks, and with the "Brick parallel to radius" option selected.

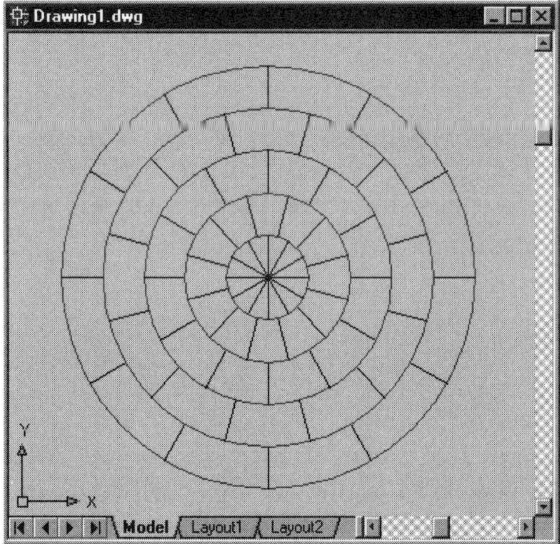

***Figure 7.5** Result of Circle of Bricks application with the settings from Figure 7.4*

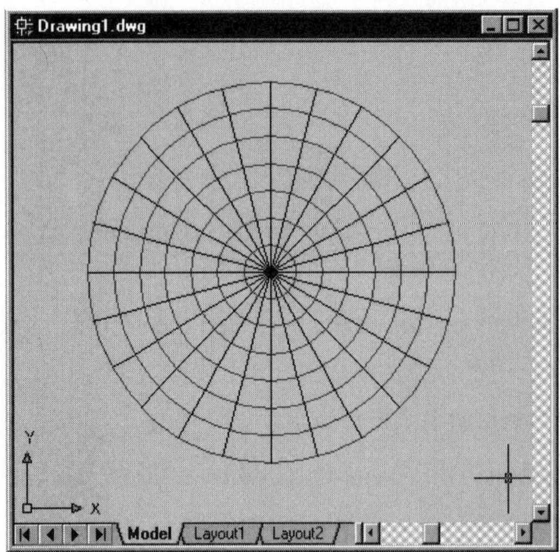

Figure 7.6 *Result of Circle of Bricks application with 7 circles and the "Brick parallel to radius" option*

Drawing Freeform Shapes

In this section you'll see how to develop an application that allows the user to select points defining a shape from the Model Space and fill it with a fill pattern. The user will be allowed to choose the fill pattern, as well as the representation of the selected points in the drawing.

EXERCISE 7.4: DRAWING FREEFORM SHAPES

1. Start a new project, and choose Insert ➜ UserForm to add a new UserForm. Place two ComboBox controls

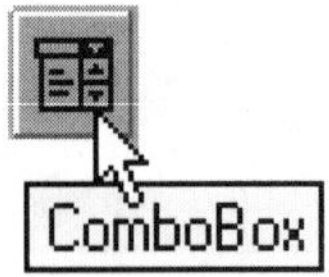

dragged from the Toolbox, with accompanying Labels. Make the ComboBoxes roughly the same height as a text box control. Figure 7.7 gives a good arrangement for these controls. The drop-down lists of the Combo Box controls will display the available point middles and fill patterns for the user to select, to be used in the Hatch object.

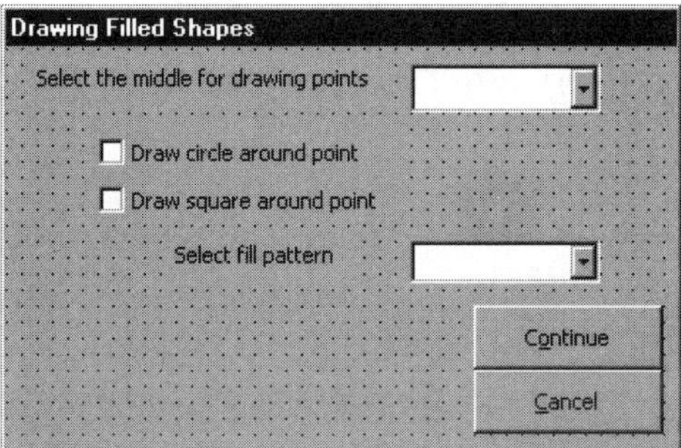

Figure 7.7 *GUI for specifying how points will be drawn, and the fill pattern*

2. Add two CheckBox controls that will be used to designate whether a circle, a square, or both surround the middle that is drawn to represent a point.
3. Add two command buttons, one for continuing the drawing and one for canceling the whole thing and returning to AutoCAD.
4. Change the properties of the UserForm and its controls to those listed in Table 7.2.

Table 7.2 Properties for the GUI Controls for Drawing Filled Shapes

Old Name	New Name	Caption
UserForm1	frmDrawFilledShape	Drawing Filled Shapes
ComboBox1	cboPointMiddle	—
ComboBox2	cboFillPattern	—
CheckBox1	chkCircleAroundPoint	Draw circle around point
CheckBox2	chkSquareAroundPoint	Draw square around point
CommandButton1	cmdContinue	Continue
CommandButton2	cmdCancel	Cancel
Label1	—	Select the middle for drawing points
Label2	—	Select fill pattern

5. Listing 7.5 adds the list of middles and fill patterns to the combo boxes in the UserForm's Initialize event procedure. It also sets their Text properties to the default middle and fill values. Enter this code into the UserForm_Initialize skeleton.

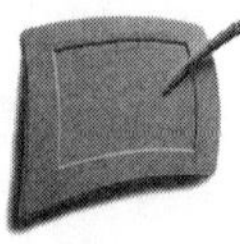

The CheckBox control has the capability to display text and so does not require an accompanying Label control.

LISTING 7.5: INITIALIZE PROCEDURE

```
1   Private Sub UserForm_Initialize()
2       'add items to the middle combo box
3       With cboPointMiddle
4           .AddItem "dot"
5           .AddItem "empty"
6           .AddItem "plus"
7           .AddItem "cross"
8           .AddItem "line"
9           'set the default item
10          .Text = "empty"
11      End With
12      'add items to the fill combo box
13      With cboFillPattern
14          .AddItem "SOLID"
15          .AddItem "BRICK"
16          .AddItem "DOLMIT"
17          .AddItem "ZIGZAG"
18          .AddItem "LINE"
19          .AddItem "BOX"
20          .AddItem "DOTS"
21          .AddItem "EARTH"
22          .AddItem "HONEY"
23          'set the default item
24          .Text = "SOLID"
25      End With
26  End Sub
```

ANALYSIS

- Line 1 starts the `Initialize` event procedure that automatically runs when the UserForm is first loaded.

- Line 3 opens the `With` block so that items can be added to the `cboPointMiddle` combo box without the `AddItem` method being fully qualified.
- Lines 4 through 8 use the `AddItem` method to add to the first combo box all the items available for the point middle. These items will be included in the drop-down list that appears when the user clicks on the down-arrow button to the right of the combo box.
- Line 10 sets the `Text` property of the combo box to `"empty"`, which becomes the default and will appear in the combo box when the UserForm opens.
- Line 11 ends the `With` statement block.
- Line 13 opens the `With` statement block so that items can be added to the drop-down list in the `cboFillPattern` combo box without the `AddItem` method being fully qualified.
- Lines 14 through 22 add fill patterns to the `cboFillPattern` combo box.
- Line 24 sets the `Text` property of the Fill Pattern combo box to `"SOLID"`, which will appear in the combo box as the default.
- Line 25 ends the `With` statement block.
- Line 26 ends the `Initialize` event procedure.

Now you need a macro that first obtains the user's requirements for drawing points and filling shapes, then prompts the user to click on the required points in the Model tab, and finally makes sure the shape is closed before filling it with the pattern requested. The macro shown in Listing 7.6 does all these things. Enter this code into a standard module (choose Insert ➤ Module).

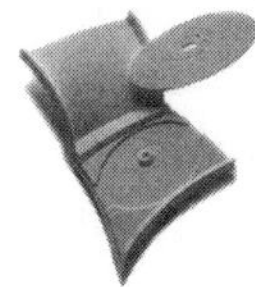

Listing 7.6: DrawGenericShape Macro

```
1   Sub DrawGenericShape()
2       frmDrawFilledShape.Show
3       GetShape 'get points defining shape from user
4       CloseShape
5       DrawFilledShape
6       Unload frmDrawFilledShape
7   End Sub
```

Analysis

- Line 1 starts the `DrawGenericShape` procedure, which is the main macro for this application.

- Line 2 starts the GUI by loading and displaying the UserForm, to allow the user to designate the requirements for visually representing the points clicked and the pattern for filling polygons. When the UserForm is loaded, its `UserForm_Initialize` event procedure is executed (Listing 7.5). When the user has finished selecting options for the points and the fill for the shape, the UserForm is closed and execution returns to line 3 in this macro.
- Line 3 calls the `GetShape` procedure (Listing 7.7) that prompts the user to enter the points specifying the required shape into the AutoCAD window.
- Line 4 calls the `CloseShape` procedure that creates a last point for the shape and assigns the same coordinates as the first point, so that the shape is guaranteed to be closed when the `DrawFilledShape` procedure is called in the next statement. The shape will be correctly filled even if it is convex, as shown here:

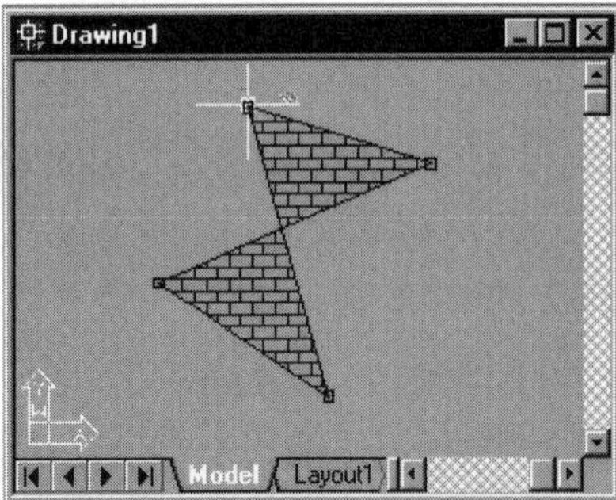

- Line 5 calls the `DrawFilledShape` procedure that fills the shape with the fill pattern selected by the user.
- Line 6 unloads the `frmDrawFilledShape` UserForm.
- Line 7 ends the `DrawGenericShape` procedure.

Listing 7.7 shows the `GetShape` procedure that prompts the user to enter the points defining the shape. Your next step is to enter this code into Module1.

LISTING 7.7: GETSHAPE PROCEDURE

```
Public Sub GetShape()
Dim OuterCircle(0) As AcadCircle
Dim NewPoint As AcadPoint 'reference to current Point object
Dim Point3D As Variant 'last point input
Dim Center(0 To 2) As Double, CircleRadius As Double
Dim Finished As Boolean
```

```
7   Finished = False
8   NumberOfElements = -1
9   'draw a red circle for user to click when finished
10  CircleRadius = 0.25
11  Set OuterCircle(0) = ThisDrawing.ModelSpace.AddCircle↵
       (Center, CircleRadius)
12  OuterCircle(0).Color = acRed
13  OuterCircle(0).Update
14  ZoomAll
15  While Not Finished
16      'continue receiving user input until the red circle ↵
           is clicked
17      Point3D = ThisDrawing.Utility.GetPoint(, "Click on ↵
           next point or red circle to finish!")
18      If Sqr(Point3D(0) ^ 2 + Point3D(1) ^ ↵
           2 + Point3D(2) ^ 2) < CircleRadius Then
19        'red circle has been clicked
20        Finished = True
21        OuterCircle(0).Delete 'removes red circle
22        ThisDrawing.Regen acActiveViewport
23      Else 'update number of array elements and ↵
           redimension the array
24        NumberOfElements = NumberOfElements + 3
25        ReDim Preserve PolyArray(0 To NumberOfElements)
26        'add the last three coordinates input by the ↵
             user to the array
27        PolyArray(NumberOfElements - 2) = Point3D(0)
28        PolyArray(NumberOfElements - 1) = Point3D(1)
29        PolyArray(NumberOfElements) = Point3D(2)
30        Set NewPoint = ↵
             ThisDrawing.ModelSpace.AddPoint(Point3D)
31        'draw line if required
32        If NumberOfElements > 2 Then RedrawPolyline
33      End If
34  Wend
35  End Sub
```

Analysis

- Line 1 starts the `GetShape` procedure that stores the points entered by the user in a dynamically expanding array that is extended as each point is selected, to ensure that it contains all the points clicked so far. A polyline based on this array is redrawn each time it's updated, so that the user always sees the points they have already entered.

- Line 2 declares the `OuterCircle` variable that is capable of referencing a circle object. The user will click inside this circle when they have finished entering their shape points.
- Line 3 declares `NewPoint` as a variable capable of holding a reference to a point object.
- Line 4 declares `Point3D` as a Variant, so that it can be assigned a three-dimensional array by the GetPoint method of the Utility object. As previously stated, the only way an array can be assigned as a whole rather than element by element is by declaring it as a Variant.
- Line 5 declares the array holding the x-, y-, and z-coordinates of the circle's center, and the circle's radius.
- Line 6 declares the `Finished` variable as Boolean. This variable is set to False until the user clicks inside the red circle. The `While` loop block (Lines 15 through 34) continues to be executed until `Finished` becomes False.
- Line 7 sets `Finished` to False so that the `While` loop block of statements will be run at least once.
- Line 8 sets the `NumberOfElements` variable to `-1` so that it reflects the highest index value of the `PolyArray` array—this value will become zero after the first point has been entered. For example, at line 24 you'll see that this variable is incremented by 3 so that the first point's coordinates will be stored at positions 0 through 2 in the array (lines 27 through 29), and the second point's coordinates will be stored at 3 through 5, and so on.
- Line 10 assigns 0.25 to the `CircleRadius` variable. This can be set to any value you choose, but it should be made large enough that the user can easily click it.
- Line 11 calls the `AddCircle` method to add a circle to the ModelSpace collection, and assigns a reference to it to the `OuterCircle` variable.
- Line 12 sets the color of the circle to red.
- Line 13 calls the `Update` method of the circle object to ensure that it appears in the Model Space.
- Line 14 calls the `ZoomAll` method to ensure that the entire drawing (including the red circle) appears on the screen.

- Line 15 starts the `While` loop block.
- Line 17 calls the `GetPoint` method to prompt the user to click a point in the Model tab and assigns the coordinates of the point to the `Point3D` variable.
- Line 18 tests to see if the last point entered falls inside the circle, indicating that the user has finished.
- Line 20 runs if the user clicked inside the circle; it sets the `Finished` variable to True to stop the `While` loop looping.
- Line 21 deletes the red circle object from the ModelSpace collection.
- Line 22 calls the `Regen` method to update the active viewport, which makes the circle disappear from the screen.
- Line 23 starts the `Else` part of the `While` statement block, which runs when the user has clicked a point in the Model tab.
- Line 24 adds 3 to the `NumberOfElements` variable; this is because storing the x-, y-, and z-coordinates of the point clicked requires that three more elements are added to the array size.
- Line 25 redimensions the array to accommodate the new point. The `Preserve` word is used here to instruct the interpreter not to throw away the existing contents, but rather to extend the array by appending the three new elements.
- Lines 27 through 29 assign the coordinates of the point clicked to the `Point3D` array.
- Line 30 creates a new `Point` object and assigns a reference to it to the `New-Point` variable.
- Line 32 tests if the user is clicking their second point and, if so, calls the `RedrawPolyline` procedure (Listing 7.8). This procedure deletes the last polyline from the screen and generates a new one containing the point just clicked by the user.
- Lines 33, 34, and 35 end the `If` statement, `While` loop, and `GetShape` macro, respectively.

Now, with the Drawing Filled Freeform Shapes application in place, you need to add the global procedures that draw the filled shape. Redraw the polyline, defining the freeform shape after an additional boundary point has been added, and close the application.

1. Enter the CloseShape, DrawFilledShape, and RedrawPolyline procedures (Listing 7.8) into Module1.
2. Place the `Dim` statements in Lines 1 through 6 into the General Declarations section of Module1's Code window.

LISTING 7.8: ENTERING GLOBAL VARIABLES AND PROCEDURES INTO MODULE1

```
1       'PolygonObject will reference the Polyline object
2       Dim PolygonObject(0) As AcadPolyline
3       'PolyArray will contain all points clicked by user
4       Dim PolyArray() As Double
5       'NumberOfElements set to number of elements in the array
6       Dim NumberOfElements As Integer
7
8   Public Sub CloseShape()
9       'add the last point to the array and make it
10      'the same coordinates as the first one to ensure closure
11      NumberOfElements = NumberOfElements + 3
12      ReDim Preserve PolyArray(0 To NumberOfElements)
13      PolyArray(NumberOfElements - 2) = PolyArray(0)
14      PolyArray(NumberOfElements - 1) = PolyArray(1)
15      PolyArray(NumberOfElements) = PolyArray(2)
16      RedrawPolyline
17  End Sub
18
19  Public Sub DrawFilledShape()
20      'HatchObject will reference the Hatch object
21      Dim HatchObject As AcadHatch
22      'create Hatch object and assign reference to HatchObject
23      Set HatchObject = ThisDrawing.ModelSpace.AddHatch↵
           (acHatchPatternTypePreDefined, ↵
           frmDrawFilledShape.cboFillPattern.Text, True)
24      'add the outer loop boundary to the Hatch object
25      HatchObject.AppendOuterLoop (PolygonObject)
26      HatchObject.Color = 180
27      HatchObject.Evaluate
28      HatchObject.Update
29  End Sub
30
31  Public Sub RedrawPolyline()
32      'delete last Polyline, create nextand draw it
```

```
33      With ThisDrawing.ModelSpace
34          If NumberOfElements > 5 Then PolygonObject(0).Delete
35          Set PolygonObject(0) = .AddPolyline(PolyArray)
36          PolygonObject(0).Color = acBlue
37          PolygonObject(0).Update
38      End With
39  End Sub
```

ANALYSIS

- Lines 1 through 6 declare the variables that will be used in various places throughout the code in this module.
- Lines 8 through 17 contain the `CloseShape` procedure that is called after the user presses the Enter key. This procedure places one last point identical to the first point into the `PolyArray` array, and calls the `RedrawPolyLine` procedure to redraw the shape.

The first and last points of a shape to be filled must be equivalent to ensure that the polyline is closed; otherwise the color will bleed through any gaps in the bounding polyline and cover the drawing area. You cannot put the onus on the user, because the mouse isn't accurate enough to select a specific screen pixel.

- Line 19 starts the `DrawFilledShape` procedure that uses a Hatch object to fill the shape entered by the user.
- Line 21 declares the `HatchObject` variable as being capable of referencing a Hatch object.
- Line 23 calls the `AddHatch` method to create a Hatch object and add it to the ModelSpace collection. The `AddHatch` method is called with the AutoCAD constant `acHatchPatternTypePredefined` so that the interpreter searches the `acad.pat` file for the definition of the pattern. The second argument, `frmDrawFilledShape.cboFillPattern.Text`, uses the Text property setting from the Fill Pattern combo box containing the pattern's name. Lastly, the `True` value is passed to the `Associativity` parameter so that the pattern changes with the boundary.
- Line 25 calls the `AppendOuterLoop` method with the single-element `PolygonObject` array that is set up to reference a `PolyLine` object in the assignment statement in line 35.

- Lines 26 through 28 all use the reference to the Hatch object to change its color, to calculate how it will appear inside the boundary, and to redraw it in the Model Space. Line 26 sets the `Color` property to 180—up until now I've always used one of AutoCAD's color constants, but you can also use a number in the range 0 through 256.

The Color property of an object can be assigned AutoCAD color constants or a number in the range 0 to 256.

- Line 31 starts the `RedrawPolyline` procedure, which deletes the old Polyline object and creates a new one that includes the point just entered by the user. It draws the new polyline to give the user feedback on how their shape is progressing.
- Line 34 tests to see how many coordinates have been added to the array so far, because the Polyline object isn't created until the user has entered the second point. If `NumberOfElements` is greater than 5, then the Polyline object exists and needs to be deleted using the `Delete` method as shown. This test is necessary because any attempt to delete an object before it has been created will cause your application to terminate abnormally.
- Line 35 creates a new Polyline object containing all the points entered so far.
- Lines 36 and 37 assign blue to the `Color` property and redraw the polyline in the ModelSpace, so that the user can view all the points they have entered to date.
- Line 38 ends the `With` statement block.
- Line 39 ends the `RedrawPolyline` procedure.

Listing 7.9 shows the code that responds to the user's click of the Continue button. This button's Click event procedure calculates a number that determines how a point will appear when it's passed with the PDMODE system variable that determines how points are drawn. When this is done, the UserForm is closed and returns the user to the AutoCAD window. Enter the code given in Listing 7.9 into the Cancel command button's Click event procedure.

Listing 7.9: The Cancel Command Button's Click Event Procedure

```
Private Sub cmdCancel_Click()
    frmDrawFilledShape.Hide
End Sub
```

```
5   Private Sub cmdContinue_Click()
6       'calculate PointDisplay based on user selections
7       Dim PointDisplay As Integer
8       Select Case cboPointMiddle.Text
9           Case "dot"
10              PointDisplay = 0
11          Case "empty"
12              PointDisplay = 1
13          Case "plus"
14              PointDisplay = 2
15          Case "cross"
16              PointDisplay = 3
17          Case "line"
18              PointDisplay = 4
19      End Select
20      If chkCircleAroundPoint.Value = True ↵
           Then PointDisplay = PointDisplay + 32
21      If chkSquareAroundPoint.Value = True ↵
           Then PointDisplay = PointDisplay + 64
22      'use the system variable PDMODE to draw points to ↵
           the user's specification
23      ThisDrawing.SetVariable "PDMODE", PointDisplay
24      Unload Me
25  End Sub
```

Analysis

- Lines 1 through 3 contain the `cmdCancel_Click` event procedure that closes the UserForm and returns the user to the AutoCAD window.
- Line 5 starts the `cmdContinue_Click` event procedure that calculates the setting required by the system variable to draw the points in the format required by the user, and to fill the shape with the pattern selected.
- Lines 7 through 23 calculate the `PointDisplay` variable and pass it as the argument to the system variable `PDMODE`. This variable is given a value in the range 0 to 4 according to the middle required. If a circle is required around the point, then 32 is added; if a square is required, then 64 is added.
- Line 24 unloads the Draw Filled Shape UserForm.
- Line 25 ends the `cmdCancel_Click` event procedure.

To run your application, open the Macros dialog box from the AutoCAD window and select DrawGenericShape. Figure 7.8 shows the Model tab with the following settings: Cross has been selected as the middle; the Draw Circle Around Point check box has been selected; and the ZigZag fill pattern has been chosen from the Select Fill Pattern combo box. Figure 7.9 shows the Model tab after the red circle was clicked, which caused the CloseShape procedure to take the last point entered by the user and join it up with the first one entered.

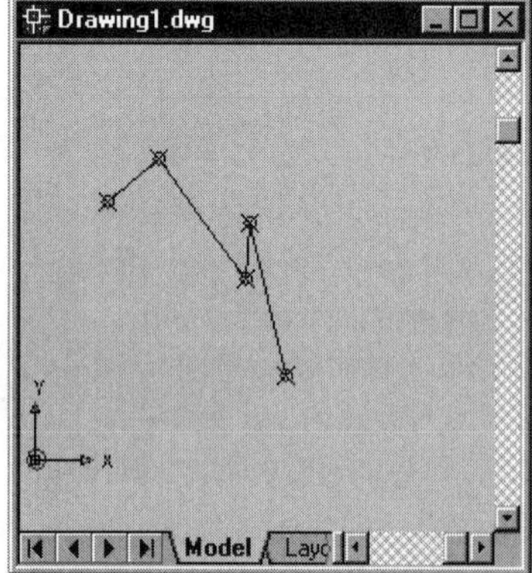

***Figure 7.8** The Model tab after the user has entered points defining a shape*

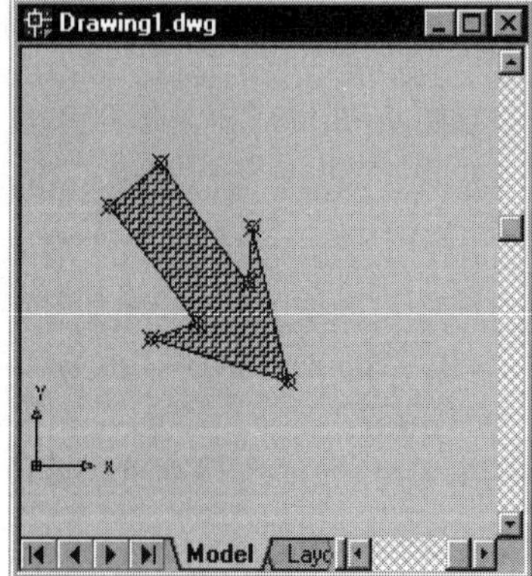

***Figure 7.9** Shape filled with ZIGZAG pattern*

Calculating Areas of Shapes

AutoCAD has an Area property that holds the calculated area of any closed shape such as an arc, circle, ellipse, or polyline. Let's extend the Drawing Filled Shapes project to incorporate a display of the shape's area after the user has pressed Enter to draw it. The results are displayed in a message box (Figure 7.10).

The CalculateAreaOfShape procedure shown in Listing 7.10 shows how simple this is to do. This procedure is not stand-alone, in that it must be called from within the DrawGenericShape macro, so that the PolygonObject variable refers to a Polyline object and is available so that we can access its Area method. Call CalculateAreaOfShape from the DrawGenericShape macro given in Listing 7.6, just after the call to the DrawFilled-Shape macro.

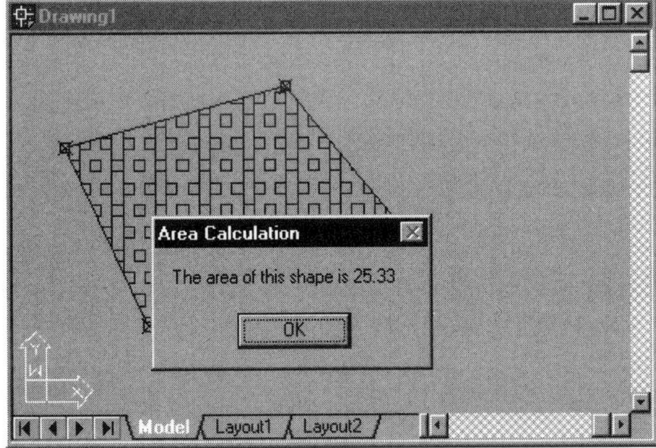

Figure 7.10 *Message box displaying the area calculated for the shape just entered*

Listing 7.10: CalculateAreaOfShape Macro

```
1   Public Sub CalculateAreaOfShape()
2       MsgBox "The area of this shape is " ↵
           & Format(PolygonObject(0).Area, "###0.00"), , ↵
           "Area Calculation"
3   End Sub
```

Analysis

- Line 1 starts the `CalculateAreaOfShape` procedure that displays the value of the Polyline object's Area property in a message box.

- Line 2 uses the `MsgBox` function to display the area to the user. (This function is discussed in the section "Communicating with Message Boxes" in Chapter 5.) The message argument uses the `Format` function, which returns a variant containing a string formatted as specified by a format string. In this statement, the function is passed the Area property's value and returns a number with two decimal places after the point.

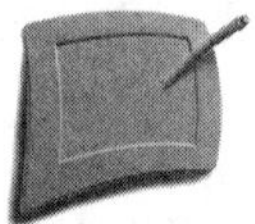

You'll find out more about formatting text in Chapter 9.

- Line 3 ends the `CalculateAreaOfShape` procedure.

Filling with Inner and Outer Loops

In this project you'll see how to fill areas that are nested inside other areas, and the various results that can be achieved using the Island Detection styles. To see the styles available from the AutoCAD window, choose Draw ➜ Hatch to open the Boundary Hatch dialog box, and select the Advanced tab (see Figure 7.11).

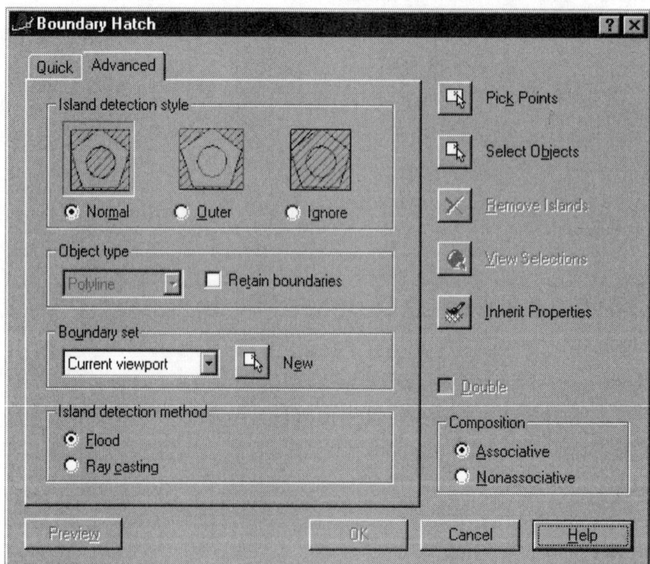

Figure 7.11 *Advanced tab of the Boundary Hatch dialog box*

The Island Detection style defines how objects that are nested inside the outermost hatch boundary are filled. There are three settings available:

Normal Hatching starts at the outermost boundary and moves inward. When the next nested boundary is encountered, the hatching is toggled on or off. The result is that inner objects are alternately shaded and unshaded. Figure 7.12 shows a door drawn using the Normal Island Detection style.

Outer Hatching starts from the outermost boundary and moves inward, stopping as soon as the first nested boundary is encountered.

Ignore Everything inside the outermost boundary is hatched; any nested boundaries are ignored.

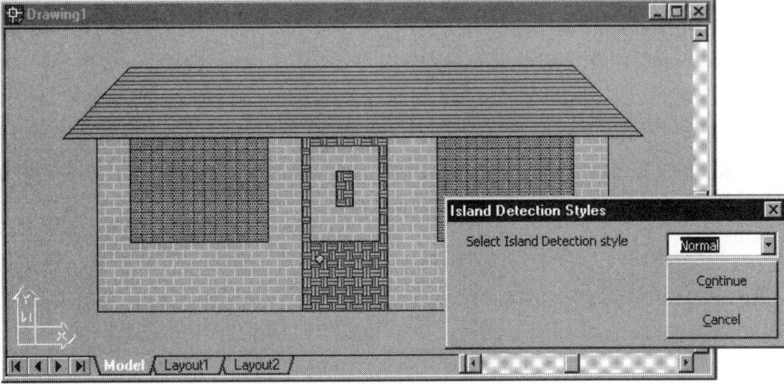

Figure 7.12 *Door drawn using the Normal Island Detection hatch style*

If there are no nested objects, the Island Detection setting has no effect on the drawing.

Let's develop a small GUI that allows the user to select one of the three Island Detection styles. Each time they click on a new style, the drawing in the Model tab is updated to show the effect of the selected style.

Exercise 7.5: Island Detection Styles Application

1. Start a new project. Add a Label, a ComboBox control, and two command buttons to the UserForm (see the dialog box shown in Figure 7.12).
2. Change the Name and Caption properties to those shown in Table 7.3.

Table 7.3 Name and Caption Properties for Island Detection Styles UserForm

OLD NAME	NEW NAME	CAPTION
UserForm1	frmIslandStyles	Island Detection Styles
ComboBox1	cboIslandStyle	—
Label1	—-	Select Island Detection style
CommandButton1	cmdContinue	Continue
CommandButton2	cmdCancel	Cancel

3. Change the Accelerator property of the Continue command button to **o,** and the Cancel button to **C.**
4. Enter the code from Listing 7.11 into the skeleton event procedures provided in the UserForm's Code window.

The Initialize event procedure is long and repetitive, and I apologize for this. The code is available to copy/paste from the CD. Normally when a procedure needs lots of data, it reads it from a data file; you'll see how this is done when you get to Chapter 12.

5. Run your project from the VBA IDE, and watch the drawing in the Model tab change as you make new selections from the combo box.

LISTING 7.11: EVENT PROCEDURES FOR THE ISLAND DETECTION STYLES USERFORM

```
Dim HatchObject As AcadHatch

Private Sub cboIslandStyle_Change()
    Select Case cboIslandStyle.Text
        Case "Normal"
        HatchObject.HatchStyle = acHatchStyleNormal
        Case "Outer"
        HatchObject.HatchStyle = acHatchStyleOuter
        Case "Ignore"
        HatchObject.HatchStyle = acHatchStyleIgnore
    End Select
    HatchObject.Evaluate
    HatchObject.Update
```

```
End Sub

Private Sub cmdCancel_Click()
    HatchObject.HatchStyle = acHatchStyleNormal
    HatchObject.Evaluate
    HatchObject.Update
    Unload Me
End Sub

Private Sub cmdContinue_Click()
    Unload Me
End Sub

Private Sub UserForm_Initialize()
    'declare all AcadEntity reference variables ↵
       for hatch loops
    Dim RoofLoop(0) As AcadEntity
    Dim WallLoop(0) As AcadEntity
    Dim Window1Loop(0) As AcadEntity
    Dim Window2Loop(0) As AcadEntity
    Dim DoorLoop(0) As AcadEntity
    Dim DoorWindow1Loop(0) As AcadEntity
    Dim DoorWindow2Loop(0) As AcadEntity
    Dim DoorHandleLoop(0) As AcadEntity
    'declare arrays to hold the points defining the house
    Dim Roof(0 To 14) As Double
    Dim Wall(0 To 14) As Double
    Dim Window1(0 To 14) As Double
    Dim Window2(0 To 14) As Double
    Dim Door(0 To 14) As Double
    Dim DoorWindow1(0 To 14) As Double
    Dim DoorWindow2(0 To 14) As Double
    Dim CircleCenter(0 To 2) As Double
    'define the roof
    Roof(0) = 2#: Roof(1) = 8#: Roof(2) = 0#
    Roof(3) = 15#: Roof(4) = 8#: Roof(5) = 0#
    Roof(6) = 17#: Roof(7) = 6#: Roof(8) = 0#
    Roof(9) = 0#: Roof(10) = 6#: Roof(11) = 0#
   Roof(12) = 2#: Roof(13) = 8#: Roof(14) = 0#
    Set HatchObject = ThisDrawing.ModelSpace.AddHatch ↵
       (acHatchPatternTypePreDefined, "LINE", True)
```

```
Set RoofLoop(0) = ↵
   ThisDrawing.ModelSpace.AddPolyline(Roof)
HatchObject.AppendOuterLoop (RoofLoop)
HatchObject.Color = acRed
HatchObject.Evaluate
HatchObject.Update
'define the wall
Wall(0) = 1#: Wall(1) = 6#: Wall(2) = 0#
Wall(3) = 16#: Wall(4) = 6#: Wall(5) = 0#
Wall(6) = 16#: Wall(7) = 1#: Wall(8) = 0#
Wall(9) = 1#: Wall(10) = 1#: Wall(11) = 0#
Wall(12) = 1#: Wall(13) = 6#: Wall(14) = 0#
Set HatchObject = ThisDrawing.ModelSpace.AddHatch ↵
   (acHatchPatternTypePreDefined, "BRICK", True)
Set WallLoop(0) = ↵
   ThisDrawing.ModelSpace.AddPolyline(Wall)
HatchObject.AppendOuterLoop (WallLoop)
HatchObject.Color = acYellow
HatchObject.Evaluate
HatchObject.Update
'define the left window
Window1(0) = 2#: Window1(1) = 6#: Window1(2) = 0#
Window1(3) = 6#: Window1(4) = 6#: Window1(5) = 0#
Window1(6) = 6#: Window1(7) = 3#: Window1(8) = 0#
Window1(9) = 2#: Window1(10) = 3#: Window1(11) = 0#
Window1(12) = 2#: Window1(13) = 6#: Window1(14) = 0#
Set HatchObject = ThisDrawing.ModelSpace.AddHatch ↵
   (acHatchPatternTypePreDefined, "dots", True)
Set Window1Loop(0) = ↵
   ThisDrawing.ModelSpace.AddPolyline(Window1)
HatchObject.AppendOuterLoop (Window1Loop)
HatchObject.Color = acBlue
HatchObject.Evaluate
HatchObject.Update
'define the right window
Window2(0) = 11#: Window2(1) = 6#: Window2(2) = 0#
Window2(3) = 15#: Window2(4) = 6#: Window2(5) = 0#
Window2(6) = 15#: Window2(7) = 3#: Window2(8) = 0#
Window2(9) = 11#: Window2(10) = 3#: Window2(11) = 0#
Window2(12) = 11#: Window2(13) = 6#: Window2(14) = 0#
Set HatchObject = ThisDrawing.ModelSpace.AddHatch ↵
```

```
        (acHatchPatternTypePreDefined, "dots", True)
    Set Window2Loop(0) = ↵
        ThisDrawing.ModelSpace.AddPolyline(Window2)
    HatchObject.AppendOuterLoop (Window2Loop)
    HatchObject.Color = acBlue
    HatchObject.Evaluate
    HatchObject.Update
    'define the door
    Door(0) = 7#: Door(1) = 6#: Door(2) = 0#
    Door(3) = 9.5: Door(4) = 6#: Door(5) = 0#
    Door(6) = 9.5: Door(7) = 1#: Door(8) = 0#
    Door(9) = 7#: Door(10) = 1#: Door(11) = 0#
    Door(12) = 7#: Door(13) = 6#: Door(14) = 0#
    Set HatchObject = ThisDrawing.ModelSpace.AddHatch ↵
        (acHatchPatternTypePreDefined, "earth", True)
    Set DoorLoop(0) = ↵
        ThisDrawing.ModelSpace.AddPolyline(Door)
    HatchObject.AppendOuterLoop (DoorLoop)
    HatchObject.Color = acGreen
    HatchObject.Evaluate
    HatchObject.Update
    'define the window in the door
    DoorWindow1(0) = 7.25: DoorWindow1(1) = 5.75: ↵
        DoorWindow1(2) = 0#
    DoorWindow1(3) = 9.25: DoorWindow1(4) = 5.75: ↵
        DoorWindow1(5) = 0#
    DoorWindow1(6) = 9.25: DoorWindow1(7) = 3#: ↵
        DoorWindow1(8) = 0#
    DoorWindow1(9) = 7.25: DoorWindow1(10) = 3#: ↵
        DoorWindow1(11) = 0#
    DoorWindow1(12) = 7.25: DoorWindow1(13) = 5.75: ↵
        DoorWindow1(14) = 0#
    Set DoorWindow1Loop(0) = ↵
        ThisDrawing.ModelSpace.AddPolyline(DoorWindow1)
    HatchObject.AppendInnerLoop (DoorWindow1Loop)
    HatchObject.Color = acBlue
    HatchObject.Evaluate
    HatchObject.Update

    DoorWindow2(0) = 8#: DoorWindow2(1) = 5#: ↵
        DoorWindow2(2) = 0#
```

```
119       DoorWindow2(3) = 8.5: DoorWindow2(4) = 5#: ↵
             DoorWindow2(5) = 0#
120       DoorWindow2(6) = 8.5: DoorWindow2(7) = 4#: ↵
             DoorWindow2(8) = 0#
121       DoorWindow2(9) = 8#: DoorWindow2(10) = 4#: ↵
             DoorWindow2(11) = 0#
122       DoorWindow2(12) = 8#: DoorWindow2(13) = 5#: ↵
             DoorWindow2(14) = 0#
123       Set DoorWindow2Loop(0) = ↵
             ThisDrawing.ModelSpace.AddPolyline(DoorWindow2)
124       HatchObject.AppendInnerLoop (DoorWindow2Loop)
125       HatchObject.Color = acBlue
126       HatchObject.Evaluate
127       HatchObject.Update
128       'define the door handle
129       CircleCenter(0) = 7.5: CircleCenter(1) = 2.5: ↵
             CircleCenter(2) = 0#
130       Set DoorHandleLoop(0) = ThisDrawing.ModelSpace.AddCircle ↵
             (CircleCenter, 0.125)
131       HatchObject.AppendInnerLoop (DoorHandleLoop)
132       HatchObject.Color = acRed
133       HatchObject.Evaluate
134       HatchObject.Update
135       'add items to the combo box
136       cboIslandStyle.AddItem "Normal"
137       cboIslandStyle.AddItem "Outer"
138       cboIslandStyle.AddItem "Ignore"
139       'set default combo box island style
140       cboIslandStyle.Text = "Normal"
141 End Sub
```

Analysis

- Line 1 declares `HatchObject` as a variable capable of referencing a Hatch object. This declaration is made in the General Declarations section of the UserForm's Code window so that it can be accessed by any procedure from this UserForm.
- Lines 3 through 14 contain the `Change` event procedure of the `Island` combo box. These statements run in the event that the user selects a different style; the `HatchStyle` property is set to one of the AutoCAD constants, depending on the user's latest choice. The `Evaluate` method is called to recompute where the

hatch pattern intersects with the boundary using the new style, before the Update method redraws it on the Model Space.

Notice how `cbo` is used as the prefix for the combo box, as per Windows object-naming conventions.

- Lines 16 through 21 contain the Click event procedure for the Cancel command button. This reinitializes the `HatchStyle` to Normal before evaluating the pattern-boundary intersections and redrawing the shape. The last statement unloads the UserForm and returns the user to the AutoCAD window.
- Lines 23 through 25 unload the UserForm, leaving the `HatchStyle` set at the last one selected by the user, and then return to the AutoCAD window.
- Lines 27 through 141 contain all the statements from the `Initialize` event procedure that runs when the UserForm is first loaded.
- Lines 29 through 36 declare one-element arrays that are all capable of referencing an AutoCAD object. An array is required as the argument by the `AppendOuterLoop` method, rather than a single value variable.
- Lines 38 through 44 declare arrays that will contain the doors and windows definitions.
- Lines 47 through 51 assign the coordinates defining the roof to the `Roof` array.
- Line 52 calls the `AddHatch` method to create a Hatch object and sets up the `HatchObject` variable to refer to it.
- Line 53 calls the `AddPolyLine` method to create a PolyLine object that defines the roof. The `RoofTop` array is set up as a reference to the PolyLine object.
- Line 54 calls the `AppendOuterLoop` method of the Hatch object to specify the boundary of the outer loop. This method must be called before any inner loops can be defined.
- Line 55 assigns the color red to the Hatch object.
- Line 56 calls the `Evaluate` method to evaluate the lines or fill color to be used for the Hatch pattern.
- Line 57 updates the Hatch object.
- Lines 58 through 69 perform the same operations on the wall definition as Lines 46 through 57 did on the roof.

- Lines 70 through 105 perform the same operations for the windows and door as Lines 46 through 57 did for the roof.
- Line 113 calls the `AppendInnerLoop` method to add the `DoorWindowLoop` array to the current `HatchObject` that already contains an outer loop.

The AppendOuterLoop method must be called as soon as the AddHatch method has been executed to create a new Hatch object. The AppendInnerLoop method should not be called before the AppendOuter-Loop has set up the outer boundary.

Working with Input Boxes

Input boxes are the special dialog boxes that pop up and ask the user to enter some piece of information that the application needs to continue. This function shares some similarities with the MsgBox function, but the dialog box displayed to the user in this case has a TextBox control in which the user enters their input. Figure 7.13 shows the list of parameters for the InputBox function.

The Prompt parameter is the only one that VBA requires be entered, and it expects a string that gives the user instructions about what data should be entered into the text box.

Listing 7.12 is the GetUserInput macro that calls the InputBox function with the two arguments listed to display the Input Box shown in Figure 7.14.

LISTING 7.12: GETUSERINPUT MACRO

```
1   Sub GetUserInput()
2       Dim MyName As String
3       MyName = InputBox↵
            ("Please enter your name", "Login Details")
4   End Sub
```

ANALYSIS

Line 3 calls the `InputBox` function, with the prompt and title parameters being passed the string values shown. The `InputBox` function then puts everything into modal mode while it waits for the user to enter their name or click one of the command buttons.

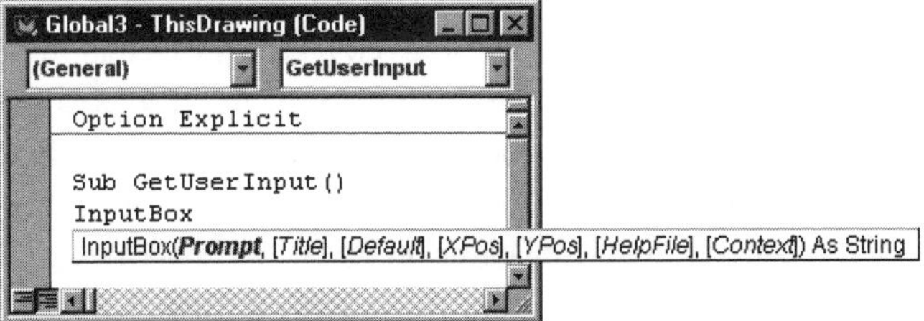

Figure 7.13 *Parameter list for the InputBox function*

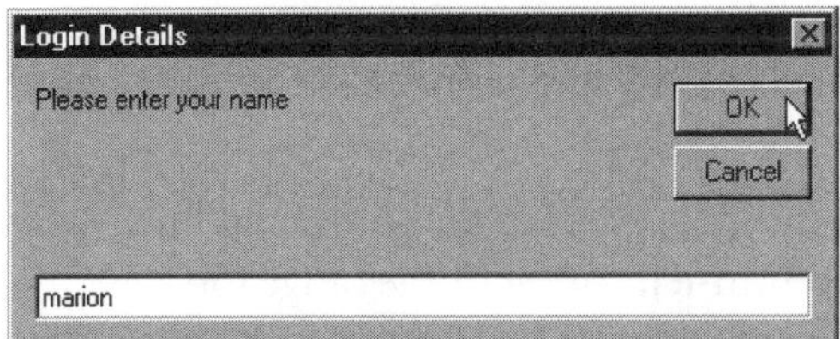

Figure 7.14 *Input box receiving name data*

Multiple-Line Prompts

If the instructions in the Prompt argument for an input box require more than one line, you can insert carriage returns using the Visual Basic constant vbCr at the point where you want to start the next line. For example, the statement

```
MyName = InputBox("Please enter your name" & vbCr ↵
   & "followed by your telephone number", "Login Details")
```

creates the prompt shown in Figure 7.15.

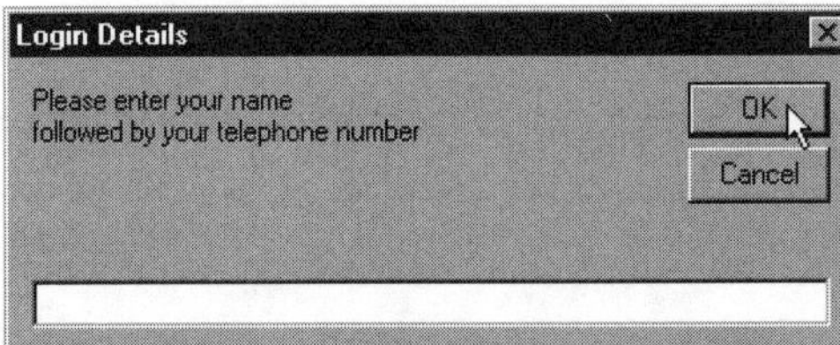

Figure 7.15 *Input box with two-line prompt*

Drawing a Range Top from a Macro

This next project combines several of the topics covered in this chapter. It uses the Utility object to prompt the user to click the points defining the position and dimensions of the range top, and then draws the range top. Then the InputBox function is used to prompt the user to enter the number of burners required—this is the only GUI employed by the project. It takes yet another approach to drawing circles—the ones that represent the range-top's burners—calculating their size and position in the macro itself before drawing them on the range top.

Exercise 7.6: The Draw Range Top Application

1. Start a new project and enter the code shown in Listing 7.13 into the ThisDrawing Code window.
2. Run your project. A prompt appears in the command line, asking you to click the position for the bottom-left corner of the range top.
3. Click at the point required for the corner. The command line now asks you to specify the opposite corner.
4. Click the opposite corner. The input box appears, prompting for the number of hot plates required and telling you what sort of input is expected.

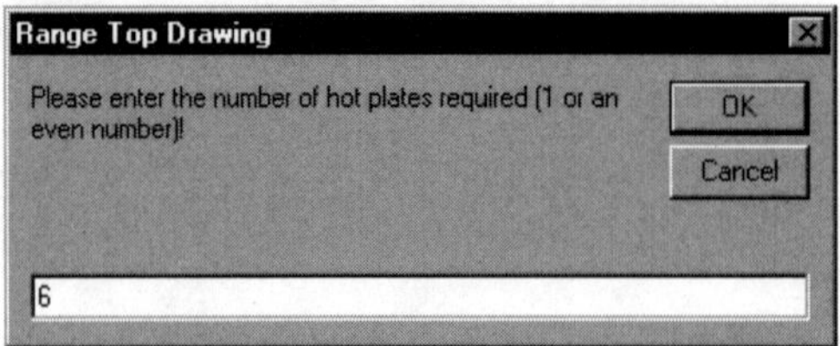

5. Enter a number and click OK. The range top appears in the Model Space, with the number of burners you specified.

Figure 7.16 shows a selection of range tops created using this macro.

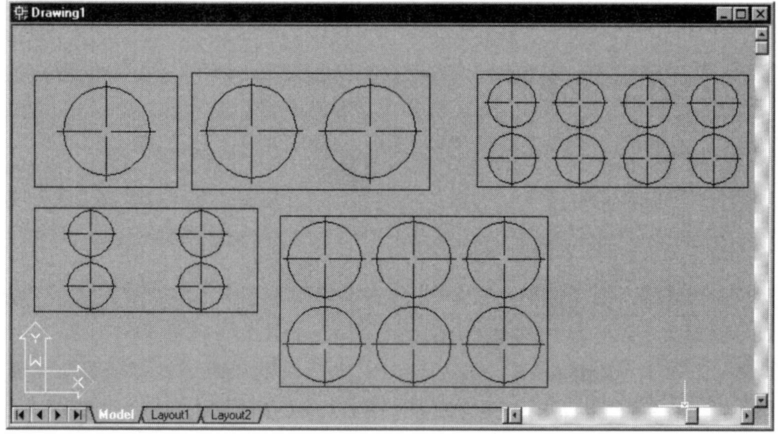

Figure 7.16 *Variety of range tops produced by the DrawRangeTop macro*

Listing 7.13: DrawRangeTop Macro

```
Sub DrawRangeTop()
    'range top related declarations
    Dim RangeObject As AcadPolyline
    Dim Depth As Variant, Width As Variant
    Dim Corner1 As Variant, Corner2 As Variant
    Dim Range(0 To 14) As Double
    Dim LineObject As AcadLine
    'circle related declarations
    Dim HotPlateObject As AcadCircle
    Dim Center(0 To 2) As Double
    Dim Radius As Double
    'Burner related declarations
    Dim NumberOfHotPlates As Integer
    Dim PlatesInARow As Integer, PlatesInACol As Integer
    Dim Count1 As Integer, Count2 As Integer
    Dim StartPoint(0 To 2) As Double, ↵
       EndPoint(0 To 2) As Double
    'prompt user for dimensions
    With ThisDrawing.Utility
```

```
        Corner1 = .GetPoint(, ↵
           "Click position for ↵
           bottom-left corner of range top.")
        Corner2 = .GetPoint(, "Specify opposite corner.")
    End With
    Range(0) = Corner1(0): Range(1) = Corner1(1): ↵
       Range(2) = Corner1(2)
    Range(3) = Corner1(0): ↵
       Range(4) = Corner2(1) + Depth: Range(5) = Corner1(2)
    Range(6) = Corner2(0) + Width: ↵
       Range(7) = Corner2(1) + Depth: Range(8) = Corner2(2)
    Range(9) = Corner2(0) + Width: ↵
       Range(10) = Corner1(1): Range(11) = Corner1(2)
    Range(12) = Corner1(0): Range(13) = Corner1(1): ↵
       Range(14) = Corner1(2)
    Set RangeObject = ↵
       ThisDrawing.ModelSpace.AddPolyline(Range)
    RangeObject.Update
    Width = Range(9) - Range(0)
    Depth = Range(4) - Range(1)
    'prompt user for number of hot plates
    NumberOfHotPlates = InputBox("Please enter the ↵
       number of hot plates required (1 or an even ↵
       number)!", "Range Top Drawing")
    'calculate layout of hot plates
    If NumberOfHotPlates > 2 Then
        PlatesInARow = NumberOfHotPlates / 2#
        PlatesInACol = 2
    Else
        PlatesInARow = NumberOfHotPlates
        PlatesInACol = 1
    End If
    'calculate position for each hot plate
    For Count2 = 1 To PlatesInACol
        Center(1) = ↵
           Range(1) + (Depth / (2# * PlatesInACol)) ↵
           + (Count2 - 1) * (Depth / 2#)
        For Count1 = 1 To PlatesInARow
```

```
        Center(0) = ↵
           Range(0) + (Width / (2# * PlatesInARow)) ↵
           + (Count1 - 1) * (Width / PlatesInARow)
        If (Width / PlatesInARow) < ↵
           (Depth / PlatesInACol) Then
            Radius = Width / (2 * PlatesInARow + 2#)
        Else
            Radius = Depth / (2 * PlatesInACol + 0.5)
        End If
        Dim Adjustment As Double
        Adjustment = Radius / 8#
        'create and draw circle representing hot plate
        With ThisDrawing.ModelSpace
            Set HotPlateObject = ↵
               .AddCircle(Center, Radius)
            HotPlateObject.Update
            'draw four lines on top of hot plate for gas
            StartPoint(0) = Center(0): StartPoint(1) = ↵
               Center(1) + Adjustment: StartPoint(2) = ↵
               Center(2)
            EndPoint(0) = Center(0): EndPoint(1) = ↵
               Center(1) + Radius + Adjustment: ↵
               EndPoint(2) = Center(2)
            Set LineObject = ↵
               .AddLine(StartPoint, EndPoint)
            LineObject.Update
            StartPoint(0) = ↵
               Center(0) + Adjustment: StartPoint(1) = ↵
               Center(1): StartPoint(2) = Center(2)
            EndPoint(0) = ↵
               Center(0) + Radius + Adjustment: ↵
               EndPoint(1) = Center(1): EndPoint(2) = ↵
               Center(2)
            Set LineObject = ↵
               .AddLine(StartPoint, EndPoint)
            LineObject.Update
            StartPoint(0) = Center(0): StartPoint(1) = ↵
               Center(1) - Adjustment: StartPoint(2) = ↵
               Center(2)
```

```
67                      EndPoint(0) = Center(0): EndPoint(1) = ↵
                           Center(1) - Radius - Adjustment: ↵
                           EndPoint(2) = Center(2)
68                      Set LineObject = ↵
                           .AddLine(StartPoint, EndPoint)
69                      LineObject.Update
70                      StartPoint(0) = ↵
                           Center(0) - Adjustment: StartPoint(1) = ↵
                           Center(1): StartPoint(2) = Center(2)
71                      EndPoint(0) = ↵
                           Center(0) - Radius - Adjustment: ↵
                           EndPoint(1) = Center(1): EndPoint(2) = ↵
                           Center(2)
72                      Set LineObject = ↵
                           .AddLine(StartPoint, EndPoint)
73                      LineObject.Update
74                  End With
75              Next
76          Next
77  End Sub
```

ANALYSIS

- Line 1 starts the `DrawRangeTop` macro, which interacts with the user to obtain the information needed to draw the outline of the range top, and then calculates the size and position of each of the burners.
- Lines 19 and 20 prompt the user for the position of two diagonally opposite corners for drawing the range top.
- Lines 22 through 26 assign the values of the x-, y-, and z-coordinates that make up the four corners of the range top, plus a fifth corner that is a duplicate of the first so that all four edges are drawn.
- Lines 29 and 30 calculate the width based on the x-coordinates from the `Range` array, and the depth based on the y-coordinates.
- Line 32 calls the `InputBox` function to get input from the user. The first argument is the prompt; the second argument is the caption for the title bar of the input box.

- Lines 33 through 40 determine how many rows and columns will be used when the hot plates are placed on the range top.
- Line 42 starts the outer `For` loop that executes once for each column of hot plates.
- Line 43 calculates the y-coordinate for the center.
- Line 44 starts the inner `For` loop that is repeated for each row of hot plates.
- Line 45 calculates the x-coordinate for the center.
- Lines 46 through 50 calculate the largest radius for the hot plates, based on the range top's dimensions and the number of burners required.
- Line 51 declares the `Adjustment` variable that determines how far the four radial lines will be translated from the hot plates' centers.
- Line 52 assigns a value to the `Adjustment` variable. This makes it easy to update the adjustment value, since it only needs to be done in this statement.
- Line 55 draws the circle representing the hot plate.
- Lines 57 through 73 create four Line objects and add them to the drawing.
- Line 74 ends the `With` statement block.
- Lines 75 and 76 end the two `For` loops.
- Line 77 ends the `DrawRangeTop` macro.

Summary

After reading this chapter, you'll know how to do the following tasks and understand the related concepts in VBA code:

- Draw circles.
- Access points and distances specified in the AutoCAD window from a macro.
- Fill a circle with color.
- Draw a circle of bricks from an application.
- Set the boundaries for hatching outer loops and inner loops.

- Fill nested shapes using the Island Detection style.
- Use the Associativity argument of the AddHatch method to determine whether or not the hatch pattern gets updated with the boundary.
- Draw any shape, fill it with a hatch pattern, and find out its area.
- Add Hatch objects to the ModelSpace collection.
- Use the Variant type as a means of passing a three-element array in one assignment statement.
- Add items to a combo box and determine the one selected by the user at run time.
- Use the Input Box function to receive input from the user.
- Place an array of objects into a rectangular area in the Model Space, using a macro to calculate the size and positions.

Part 3

Reusability and Customization

In This Part

Templates and Reusability

AUTOCAD VBA

Chapter 8

This is the first chapter of Part 3 on "Reusability and Customization"—and templates are one of the simplest ways to provide just that. Templates don't tend to get misplaced in the way macros sometimes do. (By the way, you'll see in Chapter 11 how to create permanent menu commands and toolbars to integrate your macros into the AutoCAD application, so you don't have to remember where they are.) If you are an intermediate user of VBA, you probably already know how to create your own templates—but did you know that macros, too, can be included in those templates? This chapter offers a few useful ones.

AutoCAD has lots of different techniques for duplicating and reusing drawing items, helping you reduce the repetition associated with setting up drawing options and duplicating drawing objects. You'll learn how to create a template to set up the drawing environment for a floor plan, and a macro that does the same thing. You'll also see how to duplicate existing objects and set up a new user coordinate system.

This chapter covers the following topics:

- Templates for reusability
- Setting the drawing units
- All about grids and snapping
- Changing the environment settings from a macro
- Creating the floor plan from a macro
- Creating a template
- Macros vs. templates
- User coordinate systems (UCS)
- Copying objects from a macro

Templates for Reusability

Templates are blueprints for reproducing drawings with identical drawing objects and environment settings. You already use a template, perhaps without realizing it, every time you open AutoCAD and a Model Space and display at least two Layout pages containing a blank drawing. Templates allow you to create new drawings automatically, just like photocopying a layout that you want to reproduce with some identical features. After you've opened a drawing based on the template, you need only concentrate on entering the parts that differ from drawing to drawing.

A template is a special type of file that contains all the settings needed to re-create a drawing, including environmental settings, as well as the drawing objects you'll want to include in all the drawings you create based on that template. For example, a template can contain settings such as measurement units, objects such as lines and circles, specific user coordinate systems (UCSs), grid points, and viewports.

If you repeatedly make new drawings and set them up with the same UCS and the same drawing environment settings, or you often need to duplicate parts of drawings, then you should consider creating templates containing only these settings and parts. The next time you need to create one of these drawings, you can do so simply and efficiently based on the template. All the settings and parts saved in the template will be included automatically. Then you just need to draw the additional parts and make any other adjustments required.

In this chapter, we'll customize the drawing environment to make it suitable for drawing a simple floor plan of a small apartment in a building with several stories. The whole drawing can be saved as a template usable for reproducing the floor plans for other apartments, with adjustments made to meet buyers' specifications. As we adjust each setting, I'll show you how to do the same thing from a macro. The various stages involved in creation of this template are as follows:

1. Changing the drawing units to feet and inches
2. Switching grid points inside a specified area
3. Setting the spacing for grid points and viewing the whole grid
4. Setting the snap spacing and snapping clicked points to grid points, to make drawings more accurate and to ensure that all lines connect
5. Drawing the floor plan

When the floor plan is complete, a main macro will be created to call the macros involved in each of these stages. Then you'll learn how to create a template that will reproduce the same floor plan at the touch of a button. The next time you need to create a floor plan, you'll be able to choose between running the macro to make the plan, or basing your drawing on the settings from the template.

Setting the Drawing Units

AutoCAD provides several different units of measurement for use in your drawings. These units range from microinches to miles in imperial units, and from millimeters to kilometers in metric. Let's start by taking a look at the list of unit formats available.

1. From the AutoCAD window choose Format ➜ Units. The Drawing Units dialog box appears (Figure 8.1).

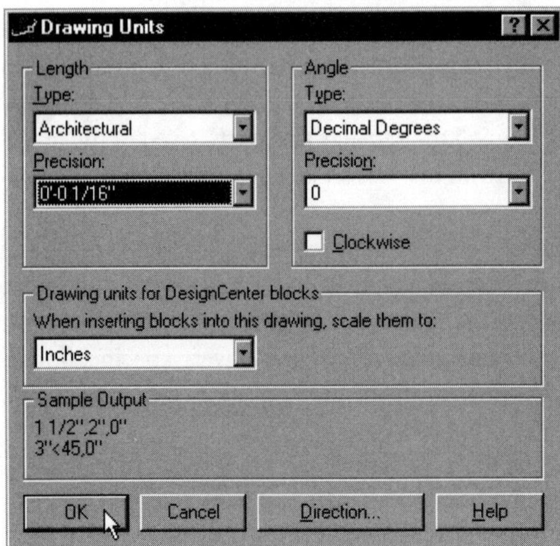

Figure 8.1 Drawing Units dialog box

2. In the Length section of the dialog box, click the down-arrow button to open the Type drop-down list. Choose Architectural.

3. Open the Precision drop-down list and choose 0"-0 1/16". Click OK. In the status bar, the units displayed on the left are now displayed in feet and inches. As

you move the cursor, the coordinates are updated in increments of 1/16" according to the selected Precision setting.

Following are before-and-after pictures of the status bar. The coordinates in the status bar here are in inches as a decimal fraction:

2.5646, 2.5627, 0.0000

And here is the status bar showing the same point after the unit and precision settings were changed:

0'-2 9/16", 0'-2 9/16", 0'-0"

Both the Engineering and Architectural unit formats are in feet and inches and assume that each unit represents an inch. The other formats can be in any unit of measurement.

Setting Drawing Units from VBA Code

Setting the drawing units from a macro involves setting the UnitsFormat property of one of the Dimension objects to the unit required. The formats available can be represented by an AutoCAD constant such as acDimLDecimal (the default), acDimLEngineering, or acDimLArchitectural. Figure 8.2 shows the complete list of constants available.

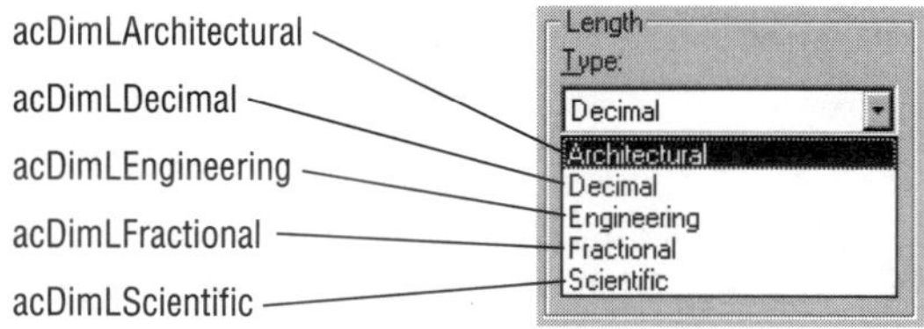

Figure 8.2 *AutoCAD constants representing the Length types available in the Drawing Units dialog box*

The UnitsFormat property setting of a linear Dimension object, such as the aligned Dimension (DimAligned) object, determines the unit format that is used for any dimension text displayed in your drawing.

Let's create a set of macros (Listing 8.1) that allow you to input a line, set the unit required, position the dimension text, and display it aligned with the drawing object. The SetUnitsFormat macro uses the DimensionObject variable that was set up as a reference to the DimAligned Dimension object, which was added to the ModelSpace collection in the DrawAlignedDimension macro. The SetUnitsFormat procedure ensures the Architectural format is used. The Update method called at the end of the procedure causes any change to be immediately reflected on the screen.

Listing 8.1 shows the five macros from the set. These can all be placed in ThisDrawing module's Code window.

LISTING 8.1: FIVE MACROS FOR AUTOMATING DIMENSIONS

```
Dim TextPosition(0 To 2) As Double
Dim DimensionObject As AcadDimAligned
Dim StartPoint (0 To 2) As Double, ↵
   EndPoint(0 To 2) As Double4
Sub SetUnitsFormat()
    'Sets the UnitsFormat for a linear Dimension object
    DimensionObject.UnitsFormat = acDimLArchitectural
    DimensionObject.Update
End Sub

Sub SetTextPosition()
    'sets the position for the text for the linear dimension
    TextPosition(0) = (StartPoint(0) + EndPoint(0)) / 2 - 2
    TextPosition(1) = (StartPoint(1) + EndPoint(1)) / 2
    TextPosition(2) = 0
End Sub

Sub DrawAlignedDimension()
    'Draw an aligned dimension
    ' Create an aligned Dimension object in model space
    Set DimensionObject = ↵
                 ThisDrawing.ModelSpace.AddDimAligned(↵
                      StartPoint, EndPoint, TextPosition)
    DimensionObject.Update
End Sub

Sub DrawALine()
    'Draws the line to be dimensioned
```

```
27        Dim LineObject As AcadLine
28        Dim StartVariant As Variant, EndVariant As Variant
29        With ThisDrawing.Utility
30            StartVariant = .GetPoint(, "Click on position for ↵
                 start of line.")
31            EndVariant = .GetPoint(, "Click on position for ↵
                 end of line.")
32        End With
33        StartPoint(0) = StartVariant(0)
34        StartPoint(1) = StartVariant(1)
35        StartPoint(2) = StartVariant(2)
36        EndPoint(0) = EndVariant(0)
37        EndPoint(1) = EndVariant(1)
38        EndPoint(2) = EndVariant(2)
39        Set LineObject = ↵
             ModelSpace.AddLine(StartPoint, EndPoint)
40        LineObject.Update
41    End Sub
42
43    Sub CreateDimensionedLine()
44        'calls four macros to create and display ↵
             dimensioned line
45        DrawALine
46        SetTextPosition
47        DrawAlignedDimension
48        SetUnitsFormat
49    End Sub
```

ANALYSIS

- Line 1 declares the global variable `TextPosition` that will be set to the coordinates of the halfway mark of the line in the `SetTextPosition` macro. The `TextPosition` variable is then used by the `DrawAlignedDimension` macro to position the dimension text.
- Line 2 declares the `DimensionObject` as a variable capable of referencing an AutoCAD Dimension object.
- Line 3 declares the `StartPoint` and `EndPoint` variables as the Variant type, so that the three-element arrays containing the 3D points defining the line can be assigned to these variables from the `GetPoint` method in a single statement.

- Line 5 starts the `SetUnitsFormat` macro, which sets the format for the units to Architectural. Figure 8.3 shows the dimension text using this format.

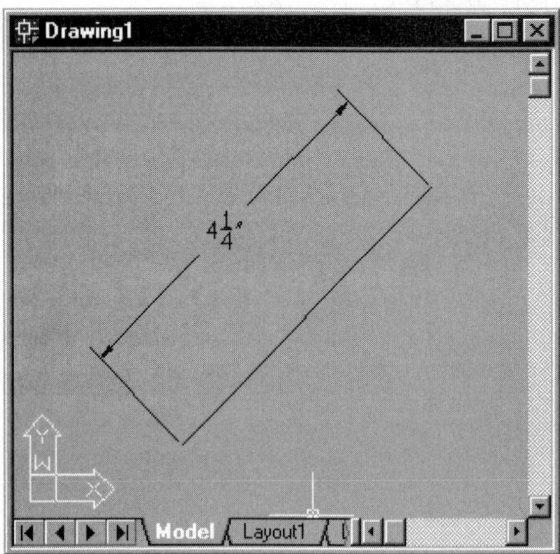

Figure 8.3 *Drawing aligned dimensions using architectural units*

- Line 7 assigns the value of the AutoCAD constant `acDimLArchitectural` to the `UnitsFormat` property of the Dimension object.
- Line 8 calls the `Update` method of the Dimension object to ensure that its dimension text is displayed in the Architectural format.
- Line 9 ends the `SetUnitsFormat` macro.
- Line 11 starts the `SetTextPosition` macro that calculates the halfway points for each coordinate and assigns them to the `TextPosition` array.
- Lines 13 through 15 assign to each coordinate the point halfway along the line being dimensioned. This code deducts 2 from the x-coordinate, to display the dimension text just to the left of the extension line.
- Line 16 finishes the `SetTextPosition` macro.

- Line 18 starts the `DrawAlignedDimension` macro, which creates a Dimension object and draws the dimension text in the drawing.
- Line 21 calls the `AddDimAligned` method to create a Dimension object containing the definition of an aligned dimension that's drawn parallel to the original line. The extension line is defined by the coordinates of its start and endpoints, which are passed to the `AddDimAligned` method as arguments. The dimension text is displayed at the `TextPosition` passed as the third argument. The `DimensionObject` variable is set up to reference this new Dimension object.
- Line 22 updates the screen so that the new dimension will appear.
- Line 23 ends the `DrawAlignedDimension` macro.
- Line 25 starts the `DrawALine` macro that calls the others to provide the complete service.
- Line 27 declares the `LineObject` variable as being capable of referring to the `AcadLine` object.
- Line 28 declares the `StartVariant` and `EndVariant` variables of variant type so they can be passed the value returned by the `GetPoint` method.
- Line 29 starts the `With` statement block.
- Lines 30 and 31 call the `GetPoint` method of the `Utility` object to prompt the user to click on the start and endpoints defining a line.
- Line 32 ends the `With` statement.
- Lines 33 through 38 assign the coordinates of the points selected by the user from the `StartVariant` and `EndVariant` to the `StartPoint` and `EndPoint` arrays.
- Line 39 creates a Line object based on the points just entered and assigns a reference to the object to the `LineObject` variable.
- Line 40 calls the `Update` method of the Line object to ensure that it is displayed on the screen.
- Line 41 ends the `DrawALine` macro.
- Line 43 starts the `CreateDimensionedLine` macro that calls the other macros, to create a line and draw it with Architectural format dimensions.

- Line 45 calls the `DrawALine` macro that interacts with the user to create and display a line.
- Line 46 calls the `SetTextPosition` macro to calculate the position for the dimension text.
- Line 47 calls the `DrawAlignedDimension` macro to draw the dimension text.
- Line 48 calls the `SetUnitsFormat` macro to ensure that the Architectural format is used.
- Line 49 ends the `CreateDimensionedLine` macro.

Try running your macros from the AutoCAD window. Choose the DrawALine macro from the Macros dialog box and click Run.

In addition to DimAligned used here, there are other linear Dimension objects available: DimDiametric, DimOrdinate, DimRadial, and DimRotated. These objects can be added to the ModelSpace collection in the normal way, by their Add... methods. There are also two angular Dimension objects: Dim3PointAngular and DimAngular. You'll see how these are drawn later in Chapter 11.

All about Grids

A *grid* is a net of regularly spaced dots that together provide a visual cue in the drawing area, making it easier to position points defining lines or other drawing components in the Model Space (see Figure 8.4). You can define boundary limits for the grid, as well as control the horizontal and vertical distances between points on the grid.

Displaying Grid Points

To display the grid from the AutoCAD window, simply click the GRID button in the status bar found along the bottom boundary of the AutoCAD window. A pattern of dots should appear in the drawing area to represent grid points.

If this doesn't happen, you'll probably get an error message in the command line. You'll see how to overcome this in the next few sections, but sometimes repeatedly executing the View ➜ Zoom ➜ In command will eventually display the grid points.

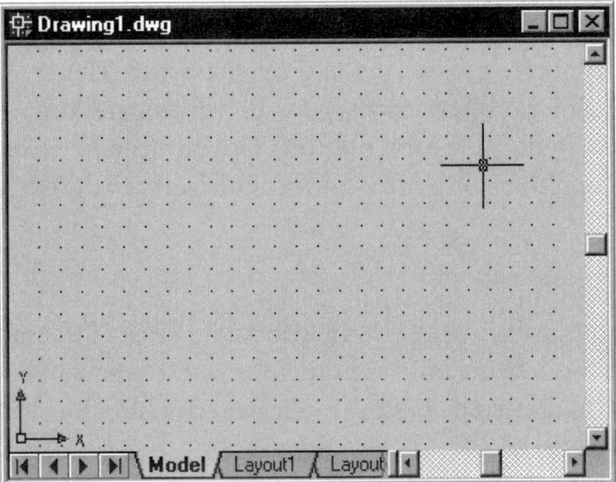

Figure 8.4 Grid points in the drawing area

Displaying Grid Points from a Macro

The GridOn property of the Viewport object controls whether or not grid points are displayed. When GridOn is set to True, the points are displayed at intervals dictated by the current Grid Spacing setting—just as if you'd clicked the GRID button. The following ShowGrid macro demonstrates how this property is set in code to display grid points from a macro. I've started a new project and placed the ShowGrid macro into the ThisDrawing Code window.

```
Sub ShowGrid()
    Dim NewViewport as AcadViewport
    Set NewViewport = ThisDrawing.ActiveViewport
    NewViewport.GridOn = True
    ThisDrawing.ActiveViewport = NewViewport
End Sub
```

Notice how the ActiveViewport property has to be reassigned to NewViewport, which is a reference to itself, in order to toggle the grid on or off. Using the Regen method (see next section) doesn't have any effect because it doesn't reset the active viewport.

The Active Viewport

A *viewport* is a rectangular area that displays all or part of a drawing from the Model Space. The viewport definition is stored in the Viewport object. The Viewports collection contains all the Viewport objects associated with a drawing. Although several viewports can be visible at the same time, only one viewport can be designated as the active one—this is referenced by the ActiveViewport property of the current drawing document:

```
ThisDrawing.ActiveViewport
```

If you update any of the properties in a viewport, you must regenerate it using the Regen method of the ThisDrawing object in order for your changes to be reflected in the Model Space. This is achieved by passing to the Regen method the viewports that have changed:

```
ThisDrawing.Regen acActiveViewport
```

Two AutoCAD constants can be used for the argument: acActiveViewport to regenerate only the objects associated with the active viewport, and acAllViewports to regenerate the entire drawing. Regenerating a viewport involves recalculating the screen coordinates and view resolution of all objects associated with that viewport.

Setting Grid Limits

You can set the boundaries that enclose the grid in the drawing area, which can serve as a useful guide while you are drawing. The following steps show you how this is done from the AutoCAD window:

1. Choose Format ➜ Drawing Limits. The command line will prompt you to specify the coordinates of the lower-left corner of the grid and gives their current setting as 0, 0.
2. Press Enter to accept the current setting. The command line changes to a prompt for the upper-right corner limit.
3. Type **25, 25** and press Enter. The grid expands to the edge of the drawing area. (If these values are too large for your drawing, go ahead and make them smaller.)

Setting Grid Limits from a Macro

Grid limits can be set from a macro using the Limits property of the current drawing document, as shown in the following SetGridLimits macro. The Limits property is set to a four-element array containing the positions of two diagonally opposite corner points of the rectangular area that will contain the grid. In the macro, the two corners defining the grid limits are (0, 0) and (25, 25). The first two elements define the x- and y-coordinates of the bottom-left corner of the boundary, and the last two elements define the top-right corner. To try it out, add the SetGridLimits macro to the same project that contains ShowGrid.

```
Sub SetGridLimits()
    'sets grid limits
    Dim GridLimits(0 To 3) As Double
    GridLimits(0) = 0: GridLimits(1) = 0: ↵
       GridLimits(2) = 25#: GridLimits(3) = 25#
    ThisDrawing.Limits = GridLimits
    ThisDrawing.Regen acActiveViewport
End Sub
```

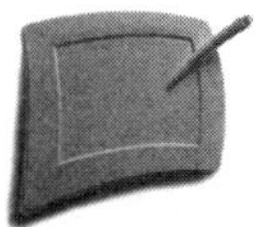

The `Limits` property not only determines the area that the grid will cover but also what will be displayed when the `ZoomAll` method is called.

You can also find out what the grid limits are by setting up a Variant-type variable and assigning to it the value returned by the Limits property. For example:

```
Dim CurrentLimits As Variant
CurrentLimits = ThisDrawing.Limits
```

The coordinates defining the corners can then be accessed as if CurrentLimits variable were a four-element array.

Displaying the Whole Grid

The Zoom All command on the View menu displays the entire area defined by the Limits property settings. Simply choose View ➜ Zoom ➜ All from the AutoCAD window, and the whole grid will be displayed fitting snugly inside the Model Space area.

In Figure 8.5, the status bar reflects the position of the crosshairs cursor at the top-right grid point after running the SetGridLimits macro. The cursor's x- and y-coordinates are shown in the status bar as roughly (25', 25').

The View ➜ Zoom ➜ All command preserves the shape of a grid rather than extending it over the whole Model Space.

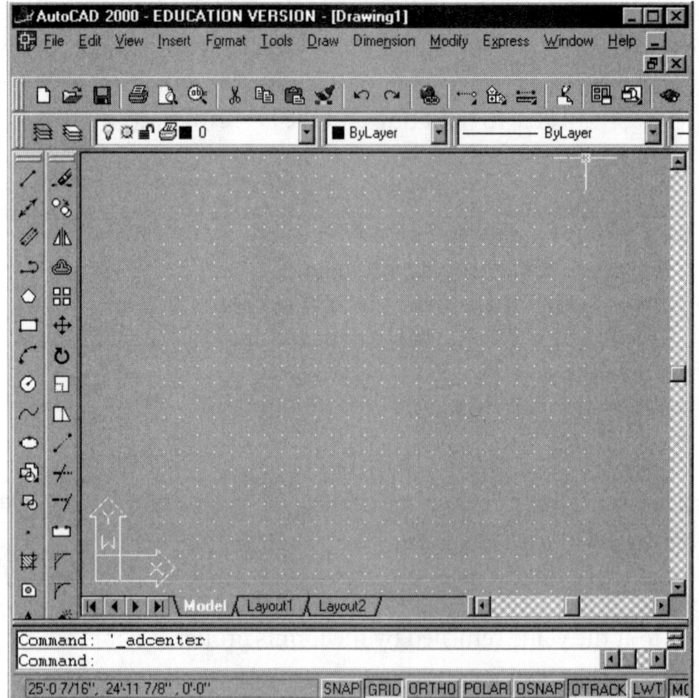

***Figure 8.5** Grid after using View → Zoom → All*

Zoom Toolbar

VBA has an entire toolbar dedicated to zooming.

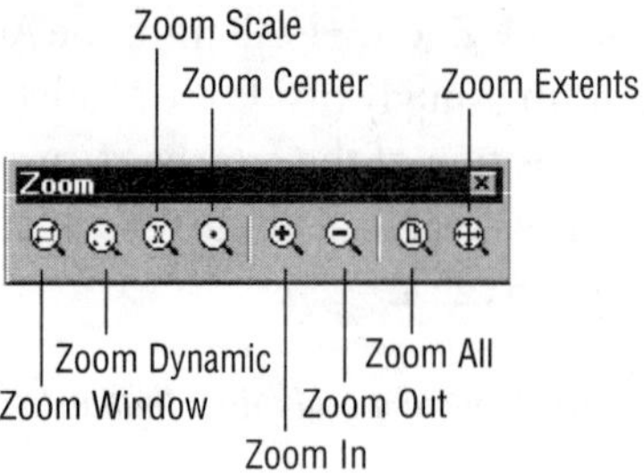

Displaying the Whole Grid from a Macro

The ZoomAll method allows you to see the entire grid in the Model Space—why not add it to your ShowGrid project, too?

```
Sub ZoomAllGrid()
    ZoomAll
End Sub
```

If the message "Grid too dense to display" appears in the command line when you run the ZoomAll macro, the grid points are too close together to display them all. You can solve this problem by repeatedly executing View → Zoom → In. Eventually you will be able to see part of the grid. If you need to view the whole grid area, change the spacing settings so that fewer grid points are required (see next section).

Setting the Spacing for Grid Points

The default spacing between grid points for Architectural drawing units is 1/2". If your drawing grows to, say, 25 feet square (like our floor plan), that means 600×600 grid points—approximately one point per screen pixel. If all these points were drawn, the grid would end up as a rectangle filled with solid color. When grid points are displayed too close together, it defeats the purpose of having them in the first place; it becomes virtually impossible to select one point without also selecting its neighbors. For this reason, AutoCAD won't display grid points unless they are spaced at a reasonable distance.

If the spacing between grid points is too small, AutoCAD displays the error message "Grid Too Dense To Display," and no grid points are displayed.

When you set the distance between grid points, consider the amount of accuracy you need for your drawing. In the floor plan you're about to develop, accuracy to one foot is probably more than adequate—this gives you a grid of 25×25 points.

To adjust the spacing between grid points:

1. Choose Tools → Drafting Settings. The Drafting Settings dialog box appears (Figure 8.6).
2. Type **12** to replace the default 6 in the GridX Spacing text box; do the same for the GridY Spacing value. (You don't need to type the " symbol for inches because this is the default.) The drawing space now contains a grid of 25×25 dots.

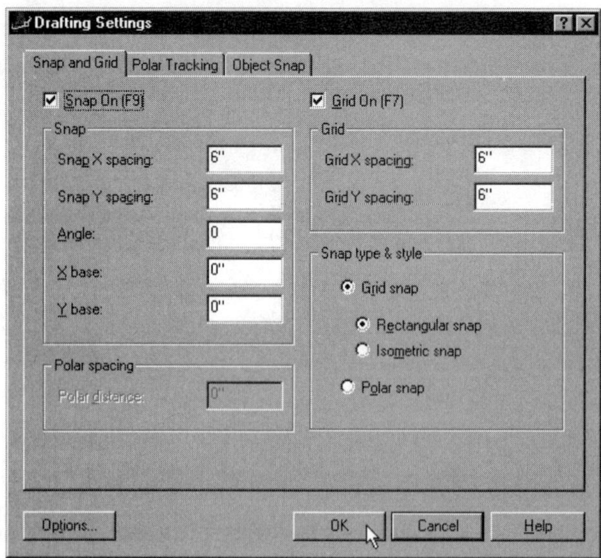

Figure 8.6 *Use the Drafting Settings dialog box to set grid-point spacing*

The inch symbol (") is not required when entering a value for GridX Spacing and GridY Spacing in the Drafting Settings dialog box; inches is the default unit. However, for settings in feet, you always have to enter the foot symbol (').

Setting the Spacing for Grid Points from a Macro

The SetGridSpacing method sets the grid spacing in the active viewport. This method requires two arguments—the horizontal and vertical spacing increments. The AdjustGridSpacing macro given here sets the spacing to 12" in both directions before reactivating the viewport to display the grid points with their new spacing. To try the AdjustGridSpacng macro, add it to your ShowGrid macro project.

```
Sub AdjustGridSpacing()
    Dim NewViewport as AcadViewport
    Set NewViewport = ThisDrawing.ActiveViewport
    NewViewport. SetGridSpacing 12#, 12#
    ThisDrawing.ActiveViewport = NewViewport
End Sub
```

All about Snapping

The *snap mode* makes the crosshairs cursor jump from snap point to snap point as you move the cursor around the screen. This is an excellent tool for ensuring that any lines that need to join up will actually meet, because snap mode snaps any point clicked to the nearest snap point.

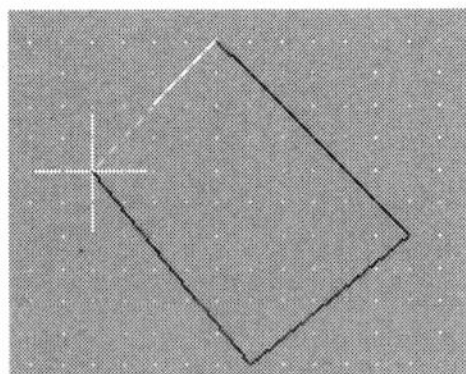

To turn the snap mode on from the AutoCAD window, simply click the SNAP button located on the status bar next to the GRID button.

Even when snap mode is turned on, the snap points are invisible. In order to see where the snap points are located, you'll need to display a grid with the same space settings.

Enabling snap mode from a macro is quite straightforward—you set the SnapOn property to True or False. The following SnapToGrid macro shows how easy it is to activate the snap-to-grid points in the active viewport. This is another macro for your ShowGrid project.

```
Sub SnapToGrid()
    Dim NewViewport as AcadViewport
    Set NewViewport = ThisDrawing.ActiveViewport
    NewViewport. SnapOn = True
    ThisDrawing.ActiveViewport = NewViewport
End Sub
```

Setting the Snap Spacing

The setting for snap spacing determines the level of accuracy for positioning the points selected from the Model Space. To set the snap spacing from the AutoCAD window, follow these steps:

1. Choose Tools ➜ Drafting Settings to open the Drafting Settings dialog box (shown earlier in Figure 8.6).

2. Enter **12** into the Snap X Spacing and Snap Y Spacing boxes and click OK. You return to the AutoCAD window. Now, as you move the crosshairs cursor around, it appears to jump from grid point to grid point.

The snap point spacing need not be the same as the grid point spacing. Figures 8.7 through 8.10 provide examples of some of the various configurations possible.

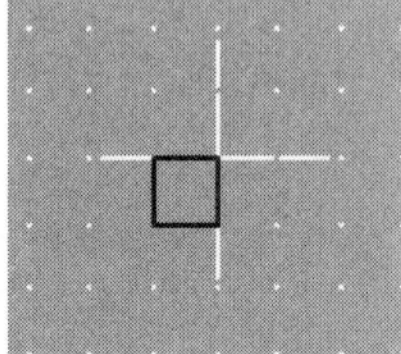

Figure 8.7 *The smallest square that can be drawn when the grid spacing and the snap spacing are the same*

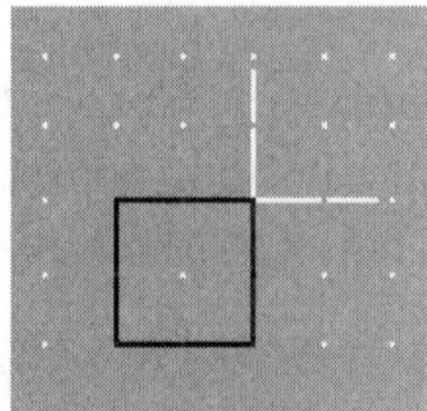

Figure 8.8 *The smallest square that can be drawn when the snap spacing is twice the grid spacing in both directions*

Setting the Snap Spacing from a Macro

The SetSnapSpacing method allows you to specify the horizontal and vertical snap spacing for the active viewport by passing their values as arguments. The AdjustSnapSpacing macro shows you how; add it to your ShowGrid project and try it out.

```
Sub AdjustSnapSpacing()
    Dim NewViewport as AcadViewport
    Set NewViewport = ThisDrawing.ActiveViewport
    NewViewport.SetSnapSpacing 12#, 12#
    ThisDrawing.ActiveViewport = NewViewport
End Sub
```

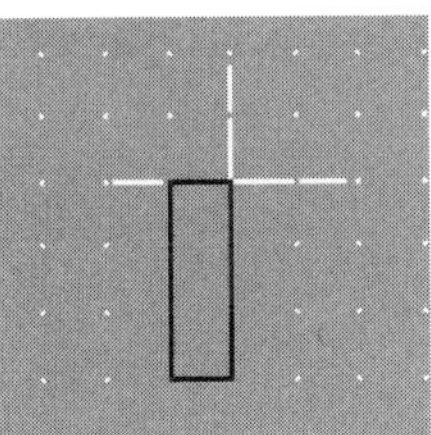

Figure 8.9 *The smallest rectangle that can be drawn when the snap spacing is set to 1 in the horizontal direction and 3 in the vertical direction*

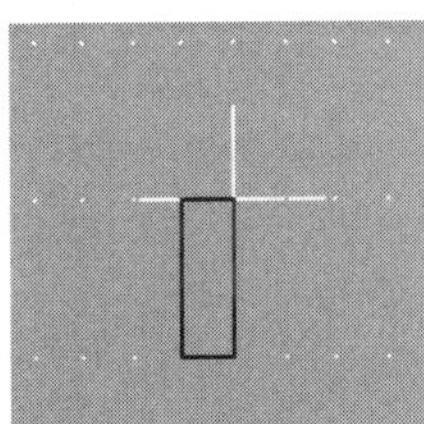

Figure 8.10 *The smallest rectangle that can be drawn when the snap and grid spacing are set to 1 in the horizontal direction and 3 in the vertical direction*

Changing All the Environment Settings from a Macro

Listing 8.2 shows the declarations from the General Declarations section of the Code window, and the SetUpEnvironment macro that calls all the macros for the various stages of establishing the drawing environment. This sets up the dimension items for a single line defined by the StartPoint and EndPoint arrays. This macro should be placed in ThisDrawing alongside ShowGrid and called from the Macros dialog box.

Listing 8.2: Setting Up Environment and Declaring Global Variables

```
Dim DimensionObject As AcadDimAligned
Dim StartPoint(0 To 2) As Double, EndPoint(0 To 2) As Double
Dim TextPosition(0 To 2) As Double
```

```
5   Sub SetUpEnvironment()
6       'call all macros required to set up environment
7       CreateDimensionedLine
8      ShowGrid
9      SetGridLimits
10      AdjustGridSpacing
11      AdjustSnapSpacing
12      SnapToGrid
13      ZoomAllGrid
14  End Sub
```

ANALYSIS

- Line 1 declares the `DimensionObject` variable as being capable of containing a reference to a `DimAligned` object. This variable must be declared here to make it accessible to all the macros in ThisDrawing. It is set in the `DrawAligned-Dimension` macro to refer to the newly created `DimAligned` object and is used by the `SetUnitsFormat` macro to ensure that units of this object are set to Architectural.
- Lines 2 and 3 declare the start and endpoints for the extension of the aligned dimension object and the position for its text.
- Line 5 starts the `SetUpEnvironment` macro that calls all the other macros developed so far in this chapter.
- Lines 7 through 9 assign values to the start and endpoints and the text position used by the `DimAligned` object.
- Lines 7 through 13 call the various macros used throughout this section for setting up the environment to make it suitable for drawing the floor plan in our example.
- Line 14 ends the `SetUpEnvironment` macro.

Creating the Floor Plan from a Macro

As you've probably already gathered, you can develop macros that will create complete drawings, without your needing to hardly lift a finger. Figure 8.11 contains a simple floor plan of an apartment block, drawn by the DrawFloorPlan macro in Listing 8.3. This macro uses multilines for the outside walls, and normal run-of-the-mill lines for the inside walls. The code assigns actual numbers to the different components; these numbers are said to be *hard-wired* into the code. This makes the code totally inflexible, which is exactly what we want in this case.

Multilines are generated by the MLine object and can comprise up to 16 parallel lines.

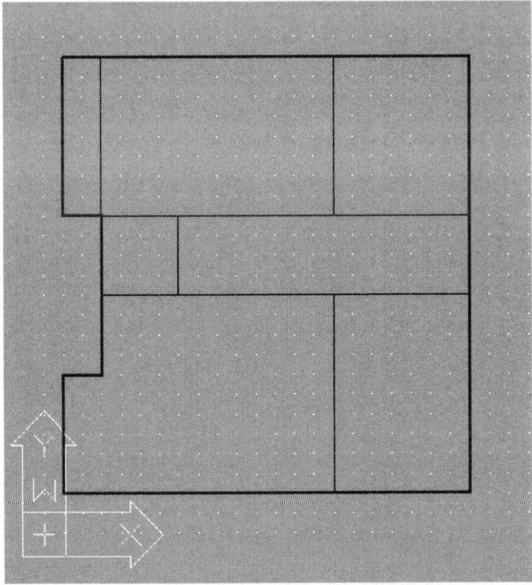

Figure 8.11 *A floor plan drawn by running the DrawFloorPlan macro in Listing 8.3*

Listing 8.3: DrawFloorPlan Macro

```
Sub DrawFloorPlan()
    'draw the floor plan of one apartment
    Dim CurrentLineObject As AcadLine
    Dim OuterWall(0 To 26) As Double
    Dim InsideWall1(0 To 2) As Double
    Dim InsideWall2(0 To 2) As Double
```

```
Dim InsideWall3(0 To 2) As Double
Dim InsideWall4(0 To 2) As Double
Dim InsideWall5(0 To 2) As Double
Dim InsideWall6(0 To 2) As Double
Dim InsideWall7(0 To 2) As Double
Dim InsideWall8(0 To 2) As Double
Dim InsideWall9(0 To 2) As Double
Dim InsideWall10(0 To 2) As Double
Dim InsideWall11(0 To 2) As Double
Dim InsideWall12(0 To 2) As Double
'draw outside wall as multiline
OuterWall(0) = 12#: OuterWall(1) = 288#: ↵
   OuterWall(2) = 0#
OuterWall(3) = 264#: OuterWall(4) = 288#: ↵
   OuterWall(5) = 0#
OuterWall(6) = 264#: OuterWall(7) = 24#: ↵
   OuterWall(8) = 0#
OuterWall(9) = 12#: OuterWall(10) = 24#: ↵
   OuterWall(11) = 0#
OuterWall(12) = 12#: OuterWall(13) = 96#: ↵
   OuterWall(14) = 0#
OuterWall(15) = 36#: OuterWall(16) = 96#: ↵
   OuterWall(17) = 0#
OuterWall(18) = 36#: OuterWall(19) = 192#: ↵
   OuterWall(20) = 0#
OuterWall(21) = 12#: OuterWall(22) = 192#: ↵
   OuterWall(23) = 0#
OuterWall(24) = 12#: OuterWall(25) = 288#: ↵
   OuterWall(26) = 0#
ThisDrawing.ModelSpace.AddMLine (OuterWall)
'draw all inside walls
InsideWall1(0) = 36#: InsideWall1(1) = 288#: ↵
   InsideWall1(2) = 0#
InsideWall2(0) = 36#: InsideWall2(1) = 192#: ↵
   InsideWall2(2) = 0#
Set CurrentLineObject = ThisDrawing.ModelSpace.AddLine(↵
   InsideWall1, InsideWall2)
InsideWall3(0) = 180#: InsideWall3(1) = 288#: ↵
   InsideWall3(2) = 0#
InsideWall4(0) = 180#: InsideWall4(1) = 192#: ↵
   InsideWall4(2) = 0#
```

```
34      Set CurrentLineObject = ThisDrawing.ModelSpace.AddLine(↵
           InsideWall3, InsideWall4)
35      InsideWall5(0) = 36#:  InsideWall5(1) = 192#: ↵
           InsideWall5(2) = 0#
36      InsideWall6(0) = 264#: InsideWall6(1) = 192#: ↵
           InsideWall6(2) = 0#
37      Set CurrentLineObject = ThisDrawing.ModelSpace.AddLine(↵
           InsideWall5, InsideWall6)
38      InsideWall7(0) = 84#: InsideWall7(1) = 192#: ↵
           InsideWall7(2) = 0#
39      InsideWall8(0) = 84#: InsideWall8(1) = 144#: ↵
           InsideWall8(2) = 0#
40      Set CurrentLineObject = ThisDrawing.ModelSpace.AddLine(↵
           InsideWall7, InsideWall8)
41      InsideWall9(0) = 36#:   InsideWall9(1) = 144#: ↵
           InsideWall9(2) = 0#
42      InsideWall10(0) = 264#: InsideWall10(1) = 144#: ↵
           InsideWall10(2) = 0#
43      Set CurrentLineObject = ThisDrawing.ModelSpace.AddLine(↵
           InsideWall9, InsideWall10)
44      InsideWall11(0) = 180#: InsideWall11(1) = 144#: ↵
           InsideWall11(2) = 0#
45      InsideWall12(0) = 180#: InsideWall12(1) = 24#: ↵
           InsideWall12(2) = 0#
46      Set CurrentLineObject = ThisDrawing.ModelSpace.AddLine(↵
           InsideWall11, InsideWall12)
47  End Sub
```

Analysis

- Line 1 starts the `DrawFloorPlan` macro; it draws the outside walls using multilines, and the inside walls using normal lines.
- Line 3 declares the `CurrentLineObject` variable as being capable of containing a reference to a Line object.
- Line 4 declares an array with 27 elements that will be assigned the nine three-dimensional points that define the outside wall, with the first point being assigned to the last point to ensure closure.
- Lines 5 through 16 declare a three-element array for each of the 12 interior walls. *Note:* If you're tempted to turn this into a two-dimensional array, keep in

mind that the AddLine method requires a one-dimensional array containing the three coordinate values defining a point.

- Lines 18 through 26 assign values in inches to the OuterWall array.
- Line 27 uses the AddMLine method to draw the polyline stored in the OuterWall array with multiple parallel lines. To see a close-up of these lines, follow the steps in the sidebar "Zooming In on an Area."
- Lines 29 through 46 assign values to the six interior walls and use the AddLine method to create a Line object for each one.
- Line 47 ends the DrawFloorPlan macro.

Zooming In on an Area

The following steps show you how to select an area from the Model Space and magnify its contents:

1. Choose View ➜ Zoom ➜ Window.
2. Click on one corner of the area you want to magnify.
3. Move the mouse cursor to the corner diagonally opposite, and click the mouse. Move the mouse; as you do, a rectangle moves with it, anchored at the first corner.
4. Click the mouse on the second corner, and the defined area appears magnified.

Creating a Template

The easiest way to create a template is to make a drawing that contains parts you would like to duplicate in other drawings using the template. You can create this template drawing from scratch, or you can take the easy approach: Open a drawing near to what you want to achieve, and then edit out the bits you don't want. Either way, all you need to do is save it as a template. A new file is created with the filename extension .dwt, and your original drawing is left intact in its drawing (.dwg) file.

Let's create a template for the floor plan:

1. Open your drawing containing the floor plan.
2. Choose File ➜ Save As. The Save Drawing As dialog box appears, with the default AutoCAD drawings folder displayed in the Save In box, and *.dwg selected in the Save Type box.

3. Select AutoCAD Drawing Template File (`*.dwt`) from the Save As Type drop-down list. The folder where you keep your AutoCAD templates appears in the Save In box (at the top), and the selected `*.dwt` appears in the Save As Type box.

4. In the File Name box, enter **FPApartment1** and click Save. The Template Description dialog box appears with a default description of your template.

*Do not name your template **acad** or **acadiso** unless you want it to become one of the two AutoCAD default template files for English or metric-unit templates.*

5. Enter a brief description about your template in the Description box. This description will be displayed in the Create New Drawing dialog box, which you'll use in the next section.

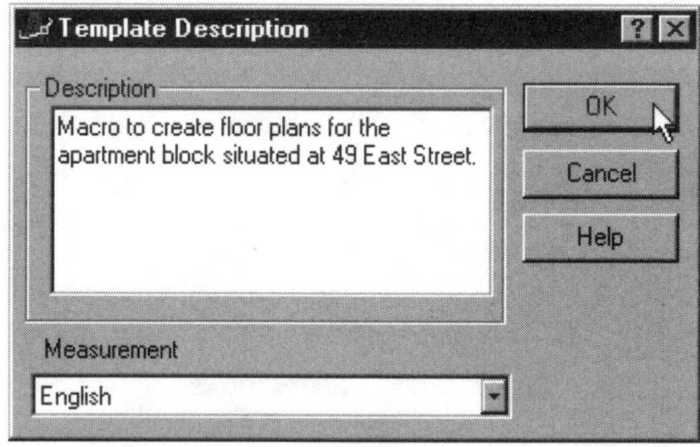

6. Click OK. Your template is saved in a file with the extension `.dwt` and placed in the AutoCAD Template folder on your PC with the other AutoCAD template files.

Creating a New Drawing from a Template

Creating a new drawing document based on a template is done using the Create New Drawing dialog box, which displays the list of templates available on your PC. AutoCAD displays this dialog box automatically whenever you start AutoCAD or when you create a new drawing file. (If this doesn't happen, you'll need to go to Tools ➜ Options and enable the Show Startup Dialog option. The following procedure includes this step.)

1. Choose Tools ➜ Options. The Options dialog box appears.

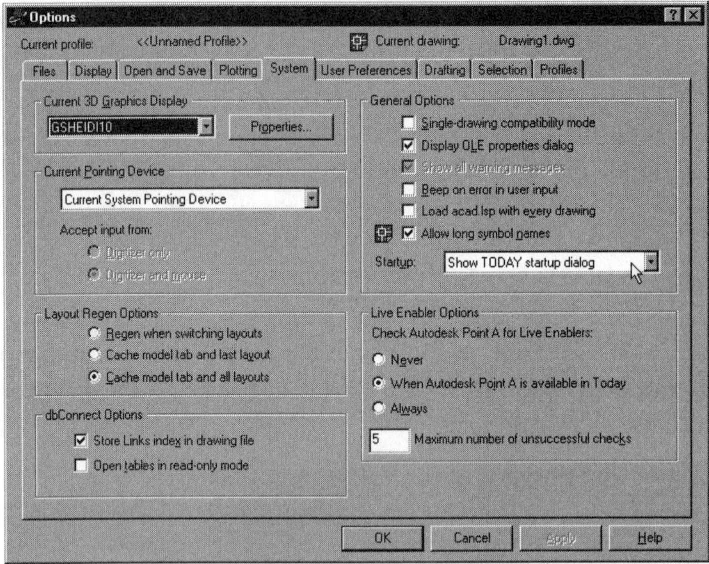

Figure 8.12 Enabling the Startup Dialog option

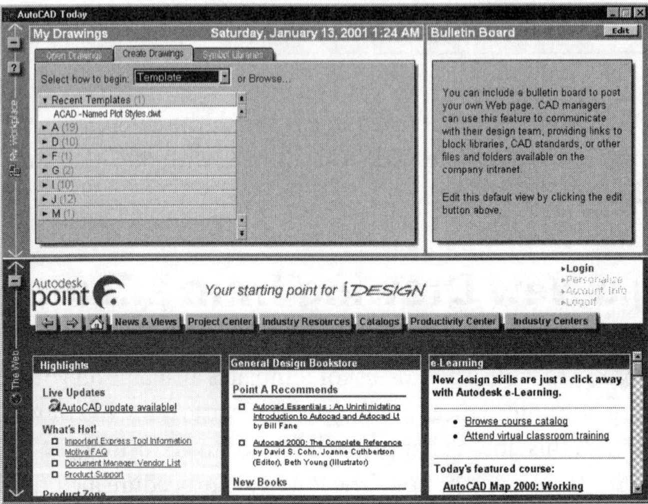

Figure 8.13 Selecting a template from the AutoCAD Today dialog box

2. Open the Systems tab, and select the Show TODAY Startup Dialog in the General Options frame (Figure 8.12). This setting makes the Create New Drawing dialog box appear, and you can proceed to create a new drawing based on a template.
3. Open AutoCAD if necessary. Choose File ➜ New from the AutoCAD window. The AutoCAD Today dialog box appears (Figure 8.13).
4. Click the Create Drawings tab (see Figure 8.13). Select the `FPApartment1.dwt` template, and click OK. The drawing document opens, with the floor plan already drawn and all the macros loaded and ready for you to use.

Macros vs. Templates

Now that you can draw the floor plan and set all the environment settings from a macro or from a template, you'll need to decide which one you're going to use.

The template can only be used when the drawing document is being created, but the macro can be used anytime after the drawing document has been created. In addition, one of the benefits of the macro is that it can become part of a larger integrated system of projects just by calling it from another macro or procedure.

Working with a User Coordinate System

The *UCS* (*user coordinate system*) is defined as a coordinate system that's tailor made for a particular drawing or part of a drawing, by specifying its position and orientation in 3D space. You can define as many UCSs as you want, and each definition is stored in its own UCS object. Each drawing has only one UCSs collection, which contains all the UCS objects associated with that drawing.

A UCS object contains all the information required to reproduce a user-defined coordinate system, such as the origin and the directions of the x-, y-, and z-axes in 3D space. The origin can be positioned anywhere, and the axes can point in any direction as long as they remain perpendicular. This information is all contained in a *transformation matrix* that can be used to transform drawing objects from their UCS to ones defined in the WCS.

In a document where no UCS is defined, the World Coordinate System (WCS) can be thought of as the default UCS.

Creating a UCS from a Macro

Creating a new UCS object is achieved using the Add method of the UCSs collection. This method requires three distinct points: the origin, a point along the x-axis, and a point along the y-axis. The UserCoordinateSystems property returns the UCSs collection of the current drawing document.

The SetUpNewUCS macro given in Listing 8.4 shows how to create a new UCS object and add it to the UCSs collection of ThisDrawing. The origin is positioned at (2, 3, 1) in 3D space. Lines starting at the origin and passing through points (3, 3, 1) and (2, 4, 1) define the new directions for the x- and y-axes. The two axes must be perpendicular—AutoCAD applies the right-hand rule to these axes in order to compute the direction for the z-axis. When the macro is run, the UCS Icon repositions itself at the position of the new origin.

The Add method that creates the UCS requires four arguments: the origin, a point on the x-axis, a point on the y-axis, and the name you want to give to your new UCS object. Place the SetUpNewUCS macro in your ShowGrid project, and add the following line to declarations in the General Declarations section:

```
Dim UCSObject As AcadUCS
```

Listing 8.4: SetUpNewUCS Macro

```
Sub SetUpNewUCS()
    'Creates a new UCS named "MyUCS" in current drawing
    Dim Origin(0 To 2) As Double
    Dim PointOnXAxis(0 To 2) As Double
    Dim PointOnYAxis(0 To 2) As Double
    'Define the origin and the x, y-axes for the new UCS
    Origin(0) = 2#: Origin(1) = 3#: Origin(2) = 1#
    PointOnXAxis(0) = 3#: PointOnXAxis(1) = 3#:↵
       PointOnXAxis(2) = 1#
    PointOnYAxis(0) = 2#: PointOnYAxis(1) = 4#:↵
       PointOnYAxis(2) = 1#
    ' Add the UCS to the UCSs collection
    Set UCSObject = ThisDrawing.UserCoordinateSystems.Add↵
       (Origin, PointOnXAxis, PointOnYAxis, "MyUCS")
    ThisDrawing.ActiveUCS = UCSObject
End Sub
```

ANALYSIS

- Line 1 starts the `SetUpNewUCS` macro that defines the origin and the orientation of the axes for a new UCS, and creates it.
- Lines 3 through 5 declare the arrays in which to store the x-, y-, and z-coordinates for the origin, and the points on the x- and y-axes that provide the orientation.
- Line 7 assigns the values of the coordinates of the point that will become the origin of the new UCS.
- Lines 8 and 9 assign the values of the coordinates of the points along the x- and y-axes.
- Line 11 calls the Add method of the UCSs collection returned by the `UserCoordinateSystems` property, to create a new UCS object and add it to the collection. The first argument passes the three-dimensional point defining the origin; the next two arguments pass points lying along the x-axis and y-axis; and the last argument passes the name for the new UCS.

The Add method tests to see if the points passed to its parameters define perpendicular axes. If they don't, a run-time error is displayed in a dialog box and your program terminates abnormally.

- Line 12 uses the `ActiveUCS` property of the current Document object to make the new UCS object the active one. A UCS object must be made active before any changes appear on the screen.
- Line 13 ends the `SetUpNewUCS` macro.

Viewing the UCS Matrix

The GetUCSMatrix method returns the 4×4 transformation matrix that defines the UCS coordinate system—this matrix is known as the *UCS matrix.*

Let's add a UserForm to our ShowGrid macro project—that way you'll have somewhere to display the transformation matrix returned by the GetUCSMatrix.

1. Select Insert ➜ UserForm; then add a large label and a command button.
2. Change the Name and Caption properties to those shown in Table 8.1.
3. Change the Accelerator property of cmdContinue to **C**.

Table 8.1 New Properties for the UCS Transformation Matrix Project

OLD NAME	NEW NAME	CAPTION
UserForm1	frmTransformationMatrix	UCS Transformation Matrix
Label1	lblTransMatrix	—
CommandButton1	cmdContinue	Continue

4. Add the following statement to the skeleton event procedure of the cmdContinue control.

```
Private Sub cmdContinue_Click()
frmTransformationMatrix.hide
End Sub
```

5. Enter the GetTransformationMatrix code shown in Listing 8.5 into the ThisDrawing Code window.

6. Run your code; the 4×4 matrix values will appear in the label. Figure 8.14 shows the transformation matrix.

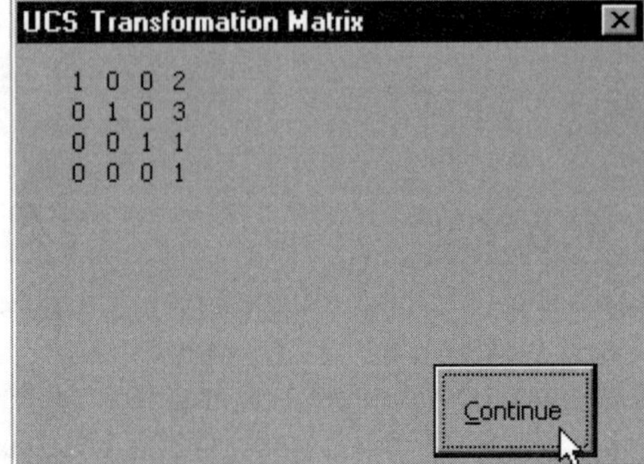

Figure 8.14 *The transformation matrix retrieved by the GetUCSMatrix method*

Listing 8.5: GetTransformationMatrix

```
1    Sub GetTransformationMatrix()
2        Dim UCSMatrix As Variant
3        Dim Count1 As Integer, Count2 As Integer
4        UCSMatrix = UCSObject.GetUCSMatrix
5        With frmTransformationMatrix
6        .lblTransMatrix.Caption = ""
7        For Count1 = 0 To 3
8            For Count2 = 0 To 3
9                .lblTransMatrix.Caption = ↵
                    .lblTransMatrix.Caption & UCSMatrix↵
                    (Count1, Count2) & "    "
10           Next
11           .lblTransMatrix.Caption = ↵
                .lblTransMatrix.Caption & vbCr
12       Next
13       .Show
14       End With
15   End Sub
```

Analysis

- Line 1 starts the `GetTransformationMatrix` macro that retrieves the UCS matrix and displays it in a UserForm (Figure 8.14).
- Line 2 declares the variable `UCSMatrix` as type Variant so that it can be assigned all 16 elements of the transformation matrix in one statement. After the assignment, the elements can be accessed from this variable in the same way as a two-dimensional array.
- Line 3 declares the two indices that will be used to access the data contained in the `UCSMatrix` variable.
- Line 4 calls the `GetUCSMatrix` method to return the UCS transformation matrix and assign it to the variable `UCSMatrix`.
- Line 5 uses the `With` statement so that the Label controls in the `frmTransformationMatrix` UserForm can be used without qualifying them. These are used to display the UCS matrix.

- Line 6 assigns an empty string to the `Caption` property of the Label control that will be used to display the UCS matrix.
- Line 7 starts the outer `For` loop that will handle the rows of matrix elements.
- Line 8 starts the inner `For` loop that will handle each column of matrix elements.
- Line 9 appends the value from the current column (`Count2`) of the current row (`Count1`) to the Label control's Caption property followed by a string containing three spaces.

VBA strings are delimited using quote characters (").

- Line 10 ends the inner `For` loop.
- Line 11 appends a carriage return to the end of the Label's `Caption` property, because all the columns in the current row have just been processed.
- Line 12 ends the outer `For` loop.
- Line 13 uses the `Show` method to display the UserForm that now contains the UCS matrix.
- Line 14 ends the `With` statement.
- Line 15 ends the `GetTransformationMatrix` macro.

Toggling the USC Icon On and Off

The UCS icon (see Figure 8.15) represents the axes displayed in the Model Space. This icon can be toggled on and off by choosing View ➜ Display ➜ UCS Icon and selecting On or Off in the flyout menu:

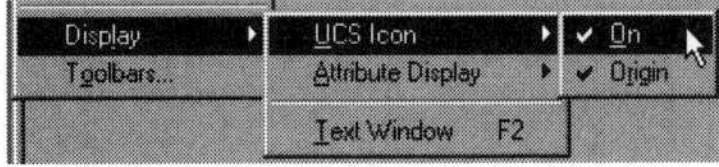

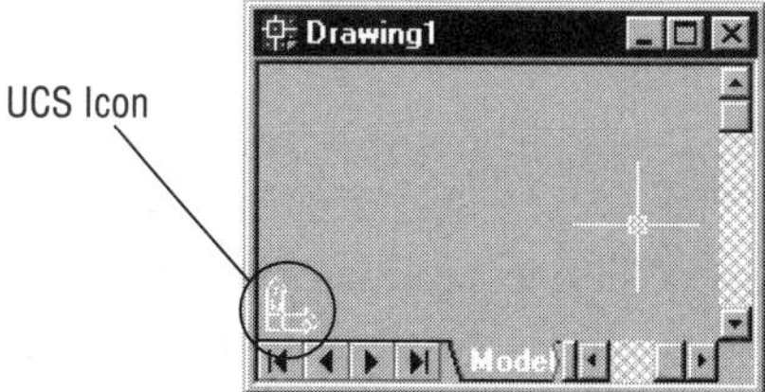

Figure 8.15 *UCS Icon's default position is in the bottom-left corner of the drawing space.*

Toggling the UCS Icon from a Macro

Displaying or not displaying the UCS Icon can be controlled from a macro, as well, by setting the UCSIconOn property to True or False as shown in Listing 8.6. Add the ToggleUCSIcon macro to your ShowGrid macro project.

Listing 8.6: ToggleUCSIcon Macro

```
1    Sub ToggleUCSIcon()
2        'Toggles the UCSIcon On/Off
3        ThisDrawing.ActiveViewport.UCSIconOn = ↵
            Not (ViewportObject.UCSIconOn)
4    End Sub
```

Analysis

- Line 1 starts the `ToggleUCSIcon` macro, which displays the UCS Icon if it isn't already displayed and hides it if it is.
- Line 3 uses the `Not` operator to negate the current setting of the `UCSIconOn` property of the active viewport and assign the value to the `UCSIconOn` property. This avoids the need for an `If...Then...Else...` statement block.
- Line 4 ends the `ToggleUCSIcon` macro.

Copying Objects Using a Macro

This section shows you how to copy the data contained in an existing object to a new object of the same type. This is achieved using the CopyObject method of the ModelSpace object, with which you can duplicate objects and add them to the collection. Listing 8.7 shows how a Circle object can be copied to produce four more that are then adjusted to make them smaller. Figure 8.16 shows the result. This is another macro for your ShowGrid group.

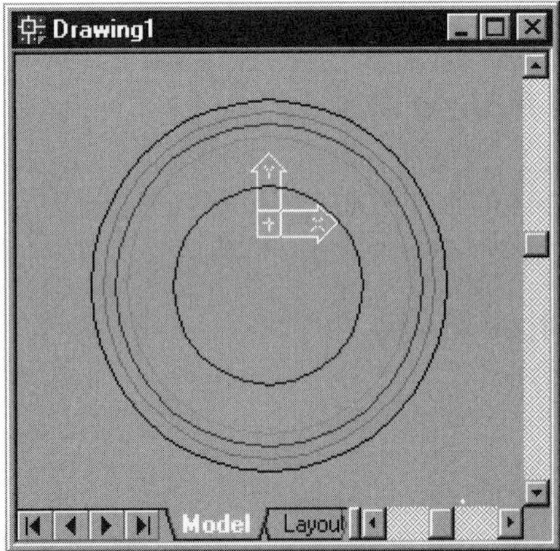

Figure 8.16 Original circle (largest) and four copies with adjusted radii.

Listing 8.7: ReplicateObjects Macro

```
Sub ReplicateObjects()
    'Create a Circle object and copy it four times
Dim CircleObject As AcadCircle
Dim AcadColor(3) As Integer
Dim CircleCenter(2) As Double
Dim CurrentCopy As Integer
AcadColor(0) = acGreen
AcadColor(1) = acRed
AcadColor(2) = acCyan
AcadColor(3) = acBlue
```

```
11  CircleCenter(0) = 2
12  CircleCenter(1) = 2
13  CircleCenter(2) = 0
14  Set CircleObject = ThisDrawing.ModelSpace.AddCircle(↵
       CircleCenter, 3)
15  For CurrentCopy = 0 To 3
16      Set CircleObject = CircleObject.Copy
17      CircleObject.Radius = ↵
                        CircleObject.Radius - 0.2 * CurrentCopy
18      CircleObject.Color = AcadColor(CurrentCopy)
19  Next
20  End Sub
```

Analysis

- Line 1 starts the ReplicateObjects macro, which creates a Circle object and then copies it to make four more Circle objects. Then the copies' color and radii are set to different values.
- Line 3 declares the CircleObject as an AcadObject object.
- Lines 4 and 5 declare the AcadCircle and CircleCenter arrays that will define the four copies of the circle, which have a common center.
- Line 6 declares the CurrentCopy variable that will be used in the creation of the circle copies.
- Lines 7 through 10 assign the color values to the AcadColor array.
- Lines 11 through 13 assign the coordinates of the center of the circle to be added.
- Line 14 sets the CircleObject up as a reference to the new Circle object returned from the AddCircle method.
- Line 15 contains the For loop that repeats itself four times to make the four copies of the circle.
- Line 16 sets up the variable CircleObject as a reference to a copy of the circle returned by the Circle object's Copy method.
- Lines 17 and 18 set the Radius property to a smaller value for each new circle and also sets the Color property.
- Lines 19 and 20 end the For loop and the ReplicateObjects macro, respectively.

Summary

After working your way through this chapter, you'll know how to do all of the following in AutoCAD VBA:

- Create a template from a drawing document and create a drawing document from a template.
- Change the drawing units from a macro.
- Display the grid points from a macro, adjust the grid-point spacing, and specify the limits of the drawing area to be covered by the grid points.
- Set spacing for grid points.
- Use the Zoom All to view the whole grid area inside the Model Space.
- Zoom in on a selected area.
- Control snap points and associate them with grid points; adjust the spacing for snap points.
- Draw multilines.
- Create a user coordinate system (UCS).
- Retrieve the UCS matrix.
- Toggle the UCS Icon on and off from a macro.
- Copy objects from the current document, using a macro.

Creating Drawings with Text

AUTOCAD VBA

Chapter 9

In this chapter you'll learn how to use macros to create new drawing documents and duplicate objects in rectangular and polar formations. You'll also see how to annotate arrows to provide information about items in your drawing.

This chapter covers the following topics:

- Creating new drawing documents from a macro
- Creating arrays of objects
- Setting text attributes
- Formatting numbers, times, and dates
- Validating input
- Adding text to arrows

Creating New Drawing Documents from a Macro

This section shows you how to use the Add method to create a new drawing document and add it to the Documents collection. The Add method has one optional parameter that allows you to stipulate the template on which you want to base your new drawing. If no argument is passed in the call, the default template is used.

Exercise 9.1 shows how to develop the Select Drawing Template application that includes the code in Listing 9.1. This application displays all the templates available in the AutoCAD default template directory, and creates a drawing document based on the template selected by the user. Figure 9.1 shows the selection of the FPApartment1 template we developed in Chapter 8. The new document automatically becomes the active document and so can be accessed as ThisDrawing.

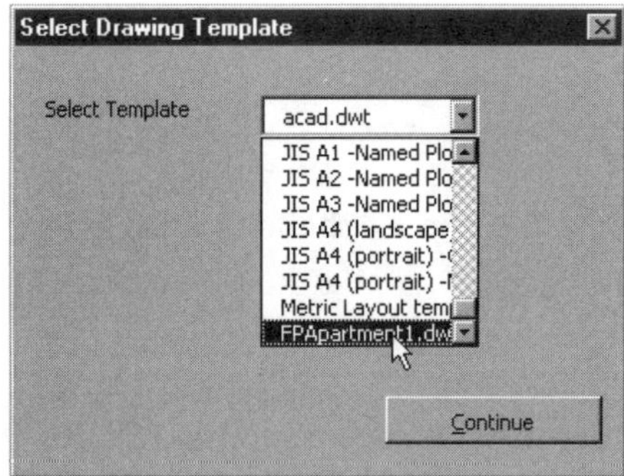

Figure 9.1 Select Drawing Template application

EXERCISE 9.1: SELECT DRAWING TEMPLATE APPLICATION

To develop this template-selection application for yourself, follow these steps:

1. Create a new project and add a UserForm.
2. Drag in a label, combo box, and command button from the Toolbox, arranging them as shown in Figure 9.1.
3. Change the Caption properties of the UserForm, the label, and the command button as shown in Figure 9.1. Items will be added to the combo box in the code.

4. Enter the code for the responses to opening the UserForm and for clicking the Continue button (Listing 9.1).

5. Run your application, select a template from the combo box, and click Continue. AutoCAD opens a new drawing document based on the selected template.

Listing 9.1

```
1   Private Sub CommandButton1_Click()
2   Dim NewDocument As AcadDocument
3   Set NewDocument = Documents.Add(ComboBox1.Text)
4   Unload Me
5   End Sub
6
7   Private Sub UserForm_Initialize()
8   Dim MyPath As String, MyFileName As String
9   MyPath = Preferences.Files.TemplateDwgPath & "\*.dwt"
10  MyFileName = Dir(MyPath, vbNormal) 'get first template file
11  Do While MyFileName <> ""
12      ComboBox1.AddItem MyFileName
13      MyFileName = Dir 'get next template
14  Loop
15  If ComboBox1.ListCount > 0 Then ComboBox1.ListIndex = 0
16  End Sub
```

Analysis

- Line 1 starts the command button's Click event procedure.
- Line 2 declares the `NewDocument` variable as being capable of storing a reference to a Document object.
- Line 3 uses the `Add` method of the Documents collection to create a new drawing document based on the template selected from the combo box, and adds the document to the collection. The `NewDocument` variable is set up as a reference to this new object, which can also be referred to as the active drawing ThisDrawing.
- Line 4 unloads the UserForm because it is no longer required.
- Line 5 ends the Click event procedure of the command button.
- Line 7 starts the `Initialize` event procedure of the UserForm that is executed when the UserForm is displayed for the first time during the current session.

- Line 8 declares the `MyPath` and `MyFilename` variables as strings.
- Line 9 assigns to `MyPath` the string returned by the `TemplateDwgPath`, concatenated (joined) with `\*.dwt`. The Preferences object holds the options from the Options dialog box, and the `PreferencesFiles` object returned by the `File` property holds all the options from the Files tab of the Options dialog box (see Figure 9.2).

`TemplateDwgPath` contains the path for the template files used by the start-up wizards; this path is listed in the Files tab of the Options dialog box.

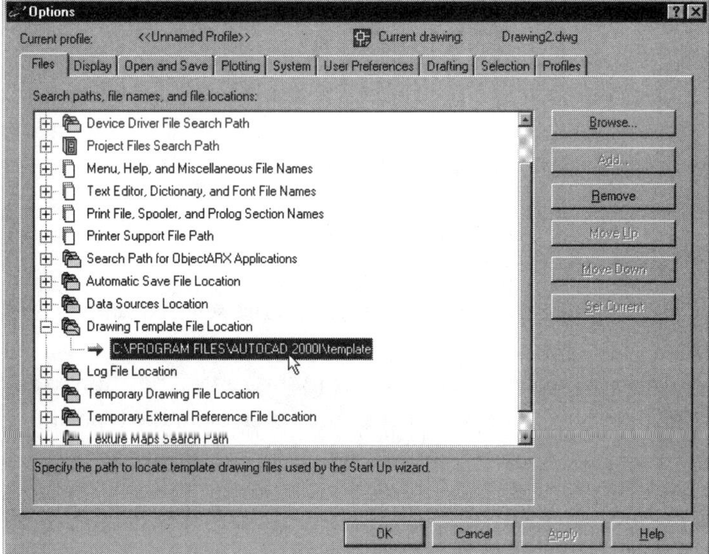

***Figure 9.2** Files tab of the Options dialog box*

- Line 10 calls the `Dir` function to return the string representing the pathname of the first file from the template directory that matches the `\*.dwt` pattern.
- Line 11 starts the `Do While` loop that will loop through the current directory and add all the template filenames to the Select Template combo box's drop-down list.
- Line 12 adds the template filename to the Select Template list.

- Line 13 calls the `Dir` function to return the filename containing the next template from the directory.
- Line 14 ends the `While` loop.
- Line 15 uses the `ListCount` property to test if there are any items in the combo box, and if so it sets the `ListIndex` property of the combo box to zero so that the first item from the Select Template drop-down list will appear in its text box.
- Line 16 ends the initializations for the combo-box items.

Creating Arrays of Objects

AutoCAD can create an array of objects all based on the same specified object. The duplicate objects can be placed in a formation by rotating them around a specified point (*polar array*), or placed in a regular grid pattern (*rectangular array*). The next two sections describe how this is achieved manually in AutoCAD and by using VBA code. You'll easily see the strong connection between the data requested by command-line prompts and the settings made in code statements.

Polar Arrays

AutoCAD creates a polar array based on one or more selected objects being rotated a given number of times around a selected central position within a specified number of degrees. AutoCAD calculates the distance from this central position to a reference point on the last object selected. The reference point depends on the type of object selected. Table 9.1 provides several types of objects and their reference points.

Table 9.1 Objects and Their Reference Points

Object	Reference Point
Line	Endpoint
Ellipse, circle, arc	Center
Block, shape	Insertion base point
Text	Starting position

The following steps show how to create a polar array containing 20 shapes.

1. Start a new project and draw an ellipse in the Model Space.

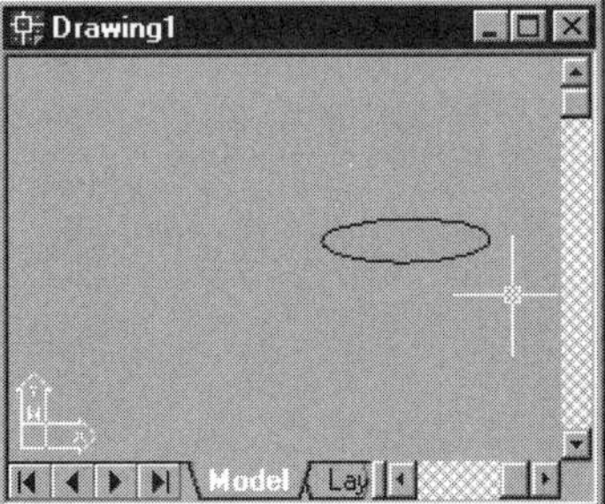

2. Still in the AutoCAD window, select the ellipse and choose Modify ➜ Array or select the Array icon from the Modify toolbar. The Array dialog box shown in Figure 9.3 appears.

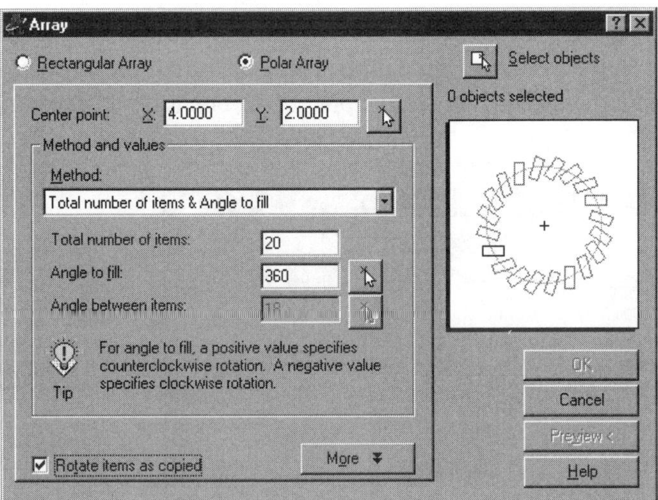

Figure 9.3 *Array dialog box*

3. Select the Polar Array option button.
4. Enter **4** and **2**, the coordinates of the center of rotation, into the X and Y boxes.
5. Enter **20** as the number of items required in the Total Number Of Items box. The original object is the first item, so you'll always need to enter at least 2.

6. Type 360 into the Angle To Fill box so that the array is a full circle. Positive angles rotate in a counterclockwise direction, and negative angles rotate in a clockwise direction.

   Click OK. The original ellipse is duplicated 19 times as it is rotated around the center of rotation, as shown here:

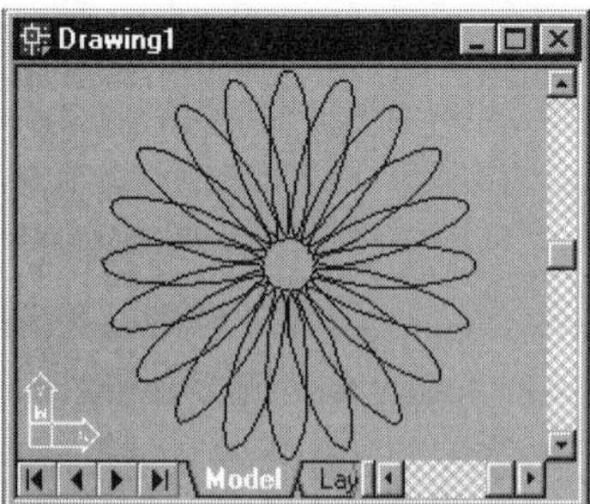

The Array dialog box provided with AutoCAD 2000i displays a basic preview of what you can expect for the options checked and the information entered. In Figure 9.4 you can see what happens if the total number of items is reduced to 10, the angle to fill is 180 degrees, and the Rotate Items As Copied check box is not checked.

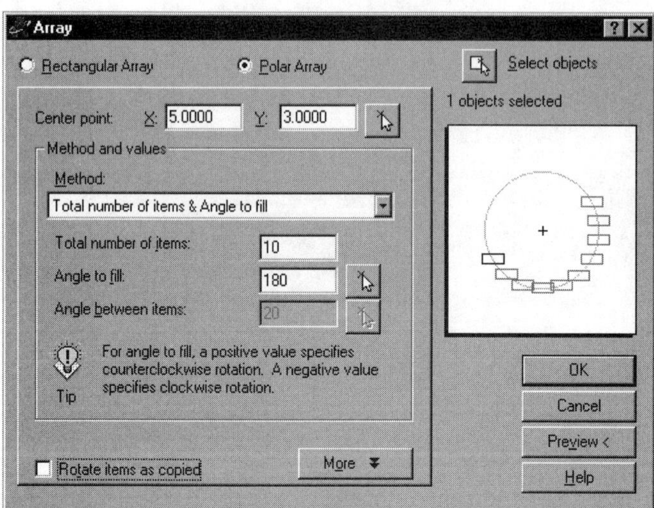

Figure 9.4 *Array dialog box with the angle to fill set to 180° and with the Rotate Items As Copied check box left turned off*

Setting the Angle To Fill to 180° produces a half circle of objects. AutoCAD calculates the start and end angle for filling based on the position of the object being copied in relation to the origin. Disabling the Rotate Items As Copied setting means that the rectangle being rotated retains the same orientation to the axes.

Creating Polar Arrays from a Macro

When called in a macro, the ArrayPolar method creates a polar array of objects and assigns it to a variable that's been declared as a Variant type. The following three parameters are all required by ArrayPolar; these parameters replace the data you entered at steps 4, 5, and 6, respectively in the preceding section.

NumberOfObjects Defines the number of objects required. The value must be 2 or more, since the original object is counted as one.

AngleToFill Specifies the angle (in radians) to be used for the rotation. A positive value rotates in a counterclockwise direction, and a negative value rotates in a clockwise direction.

CenterPoint Specifies the center of rotation.

Exercise 9.2: Rotating User-Defined Shapes

The project created in this exercise prompts the user to select the points defining a shape and rotates them about the origin by 360° degrees, creating 12 objects on the way. These steps show you how to develop the project using some of the code you created in Chapter 7.

1. Start a new project. Into the ThisDrawing module, copy the GetShape macro from Listing 7.7 in Chapter 7, and the CloseShape and RedrawPolyline macros from Listing 7.8.

2. Update the GetShape macro by adding the following declaration statement after the NewPoint variable's declaration:

```
Dim LastPoint (0 to 2) as Double
```

3. Replace the statement in Line 17 (Listing 7.7) with the following `If...Then...Else...` statement block:

```
If NumberOfElements = -1 Then 'first point being entered
    Point3D = ThisDrawing.Utility.GetPoint(, ↵
       "Click on next point or inside the red ↵
       circle to finish.")
```

```
Else 'use LastPoint for rubber-banding
    Point3D = ThisDrawing.Utility.GetPoint(Lastpoint, ↵
       "Click on next point or inside the red ↵
       circle to finish.")
End
```

4. Add the declarations and macros shown in Listing 9.2 into the ThisDrawing module.

5. Run the RotateGenericShape macro from the AutoCAD window. Create a polyline shape close to the origin, since that has been specified as the center of rotation. (I created a triangle, as shown here.)

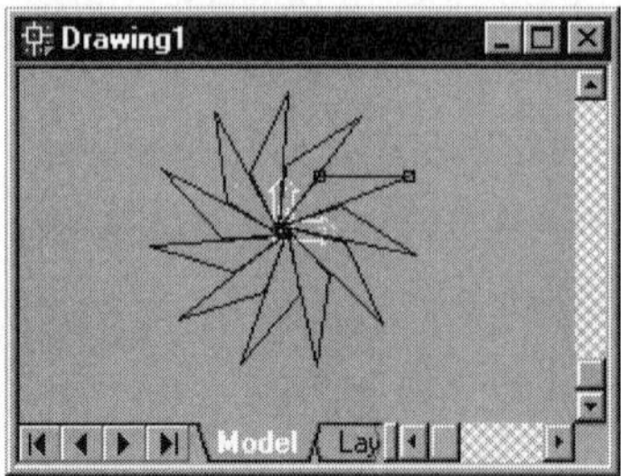

LISTING 9.2

```
Dim PolygonObject(0) As AcadPolyline
'PolyArray contains points clicked by the user
Dim PolyArray() As Double
'NumberOfElements is current number of elements in the array
Dim NumberOfElements As Integer

Public Sub RotateGenericShape()
    'Prompts user for shape and creates a polar array
    GetShape
    RotateShape
End Sub

Public Sub RotateShape()
    Dim PolarArray As Variant
    Dim Center(0 To 2) As Double
    Dim Angle As Double
    Center(0) = 0#: Center(1) = 0#: Center(2) = 0#
```

```
18      Angle = (3.14159265 / 180) * 360 '360 degrees in radians
19      PolarArray = PolygonObject.ArrayPolar(12, Angle, Center)
20  End Sub
```

Analysis

- Lines 1 through 5 are declaration statements for variables that are used by more than one macro or procedure from ThisDrawing.
- Line 7 starts the `RotateGenericShape` macro to get the shape from the user and to create the polar array.
- Line 9 calls the `GetShape` macro to interact with the user and get the polyline points. When the points have all been selected and the Enter key pressed, the `GetShape` macro finishes and Line 10 is executed.
- Line 10 calls the `RotateShape` macro.
- Line 11 ends the `RotateGenericShape` macro.
- Line 13 starts the `RotateShape` macro that rotates the shape around the point stored in the `Center` array, to produce the shapes in the polar array.
- Line 14 declares the `PolarArray` variable as type Variant so that it can be assigned the contents of all the elements in the array in one statement.
- Line 15 declares the `array` that will be assigned the coordinates of the center of rotation.
- Line 16 declares the angle that will determine when the rotation will stop. For example, Figure 9.5 shows the result of calling the `ArrayPolar` method with an angle of 135° converted to radians.
- Line 17 assigns zeros to the `Center` array for the x-, y-, and z-coordinates of the center of rotation.
- Line 18 converts 360° to radians and assigns the result to the `Angle` variable.
- Line 19 calls the `ArrayPolar` method with 12 as the number of objects to be defined, an angle of 360° converted to radians so that objects will be evenly distributed in a complete circle, and the origin as the center of rotation.
- Line 20 ends the `RotateShape` macro.

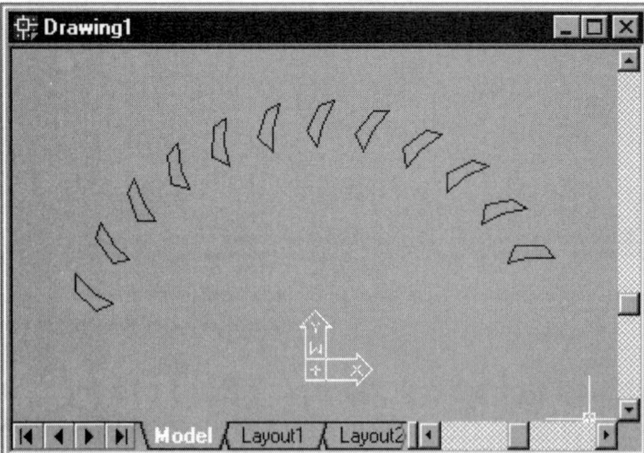

Figure 9.5 *Result of ArrayPolar with angle of 135 degrees converted to radians*

Rectangular Arrays

The *rectangular array* feature in AutoCAD makes copies of a selected object and positions them lined up in a specified number of rows and columns. The following steps show how this is done from the AutoCAD window:

1. Start a new project and draw the shape that you want to duplicate. Here, I've drawn an arc and a line:

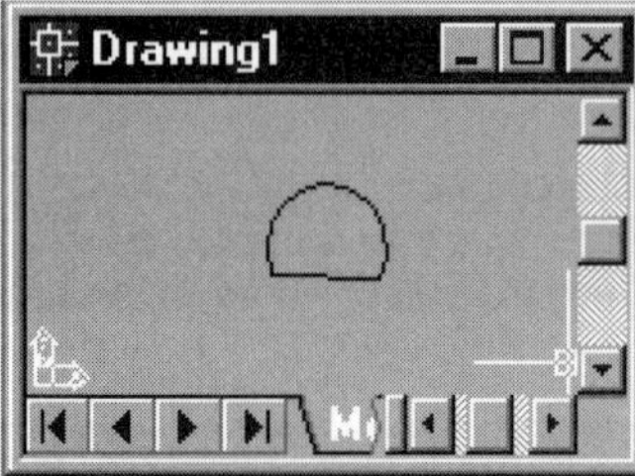

2. Select the arc and the line and choose Modify ➜ Array. The Array dialog box appears.
3. Select the Rectangular Array option button. The controls in the Array dialog box change to prompt you for the information required to draw a rectangular array (Figure 9.6).

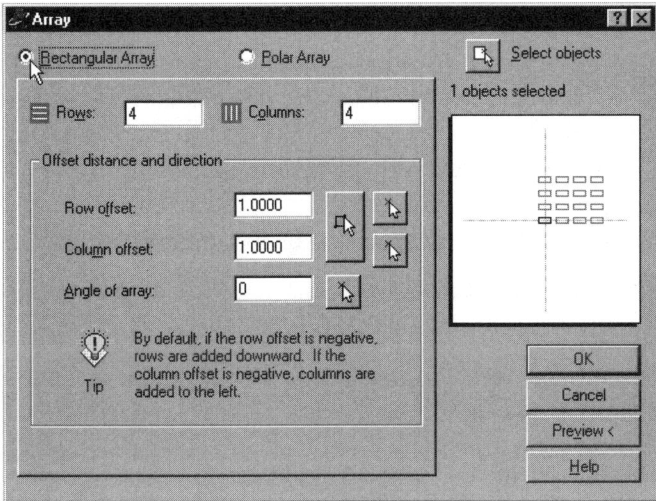

Figure 9.6 *Array dialog box set up to produce a rectangular array*

4. Enter **3** and **4** into the Rows and Columns boxes**.** The space on the right displays a preview of the formation of objects that will be drawn with the number of rows and columns entered.
5. Enter **2.5** in the Row Offset and Column Offset boxes. These represent the vertical and horizontal distances between the centers of objects from adjacent rows and columns.
6. Click OK and the original shape is duplicated 11 times in the Model space, providing the number of rows and columns requested.

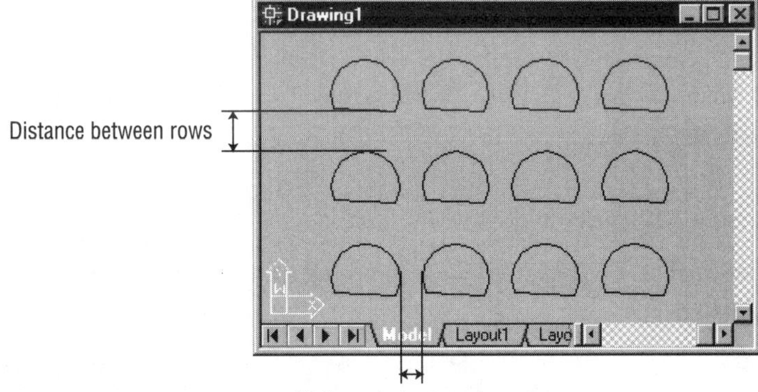

Creating Rectangular Arrays from a Macro

Rectangular arrays can also be created from a macro using the ArrayRectangular method, which requires arguments containing the same information that is entered in the Array dialog box. The ArrayRectangular method creates a rectangular array based on currently selected objects. This method works in 2D or 3D, so it has additional parameters to allow creation of several formations of objects in an array with three dimensions.

The parameters required by the ArrayRectangular method are as follows:

NumberOfRows Specifies the number of rows of objects to be created. Cannot be zero or negative.

NumberOfColumns Specifies the number of columns required for the formation of objects. Cannot be zero or negative.

NumberOfLevels Defines the number of formations required for 3D rectangular arrays. Cannot be zero or negative. This is set to 1 in the CreateRectangularArray macro to create a 2D formation.

DistanceBetweenRows Gives the distance between adjacent rows of objects. If this distance is positive, the rows are added upward from the selected objects; if negative, the rows are added downward.

DistanceBetweenColumns The distance between adjacent columns of objects. If this distance is positive, columns are added to the right of the selected objects; if negative, they are added to the left.

DistanceBetweenLevels Specifies the distance between each formation of objects. If this distance is positive, the levels are added in a positive direction; if negative, they are added in a negative direction.

The values assigned to the NumberOfRows, NumberOfColumns and NumberOfLevels arguments cannot be zero or negative.

If the values passed to NumberOfRows and NumberOfColumns are both 1, there is no reason to call the ArrayRectangular method.

Exercise 9.2: Rotating User-Defined Shapes (continued)

Listing 9.3 lists the CreateRectangularArray macro, which prompts the user for the shape to be used as a basis before calling the ArrayRectangular method to create a formation of identical objects. Add this new macro to the ThisDrawing module.

Figure 9.7 shows the results of running this macro with a square-type shape. To see your shape reproduced in three dimensions, click the 3D Orbit icon

in the toolbar. Then drag and drop on the circular handles that appear in the Model Space until you view your formation at the angle required.

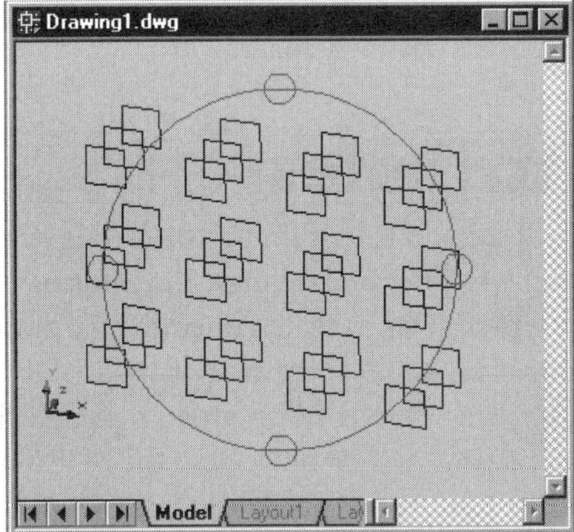

Figure 9.7 *Result of running CreateRectangular Array macro (Listing 9.3)*

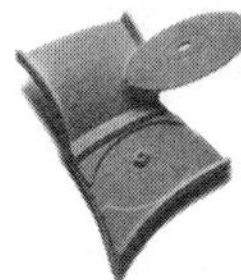

Listing 9.3

```
Public Sub CreateRectangleArray()
    Dim RectangleArray As Variant
    GetShape
    RectangleArray = PolygonObject(0) .ArrayRectangular ↲
       (3, 4, 3, 2.5, 2.5, 1.25)
End Sub
```

ANALYSIS

- Line 1 starts the `CreateRectangleArray`, which prompts the user to enter the shape to be used as the basis for creating a rectangular formation of objects.
- Line 2 declares the `RectangleArray` variable as type Variant, so that the whole rectangular array can be assigned to it in the same statement.
- Line 3 calls the `GetShape` method to get the polyline for use as the basis for the formation.
- Line 4 calls the `ArrayRectangular` method to create a formation of objects based on the `Polyline` object referenced by `PolygonObject`. The arguments specify that a formation containing three rows and four columns, three deep, is required. The distance between each row and column is 2.5, and the depthwise distance between is 1.25. The array returned is assigned to the `RectangleArray` variable.
- Line 5 ends the `CreateRectangularArray` macro.

Setting Text Attributes

Almost every drawing you create will contain text of some sort. In this section we'll consider text for providing such things as titles of drawings, and informative notes providing, for example, the name of the person who created or edited the drawing, the date created or updated, and the drawing's scale. There are two types of text objects; the one used depends on whether the text string is to be displayed on a single line or over multiple lines. These two objects are called the Text object and the MText object, and are created by calling the AddText (see Chapter 1) and AddMText methods.

The Text object is created by calling the AddText method, which has three parameters—text to be drawn, the position for the bottom-left corner of the first character, and the height of the text. The MText object is created by calling the AddMText method; it, too, has three parameters—the position for the first character, the width of the bounding box, and the text string itself. The bounding box not only defines the height of the text but also limits the amount of text placed on each line. Word-wrap is used to break the text into lines when the boundary is reached.

Setting Text Attributes in AutoCAD

Whether you're creating a Text or an MText object, often you will want to specify the font that will define how text characters are shaped. AutoCAD has several compiled

SHX fonts as well as TrueType fonts. (SHX fonts are AutoCAD-compiled shape fonts. TrueType fonts are drawn by the Windows operating system unless the text has been transformed in some way when they are drawn by AutoCAD.) You can see the list of fonts available on your PC by displaying the Text Style dialog box from AutoCAD's Format menu.

The following steps show you how to specify a font from the AutoCAD window.

1. Start a new project and choose Format ➜ Text Style. The Text Style dialog box (Figure 9.8) appears with Standard already entered in the Style Name box.

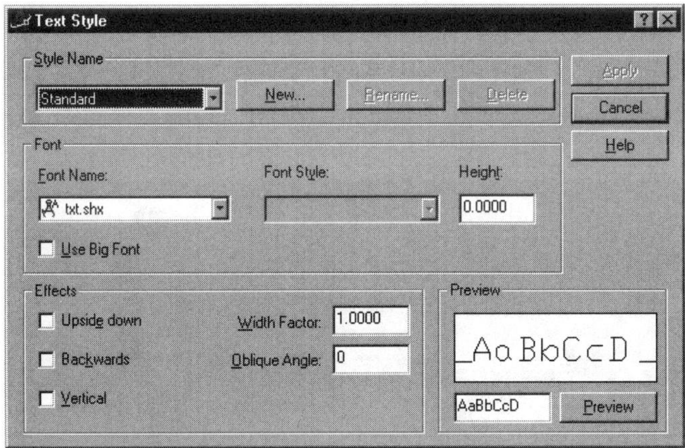

***Figure 9.8** The default text style in AutoCAD is Standard*

2. Click New. The New Text Style dialog box appears, with Style1 displayed in the Style Name box.
3. Replace Style1 with the style name of your choice—I've entered MyStyle.

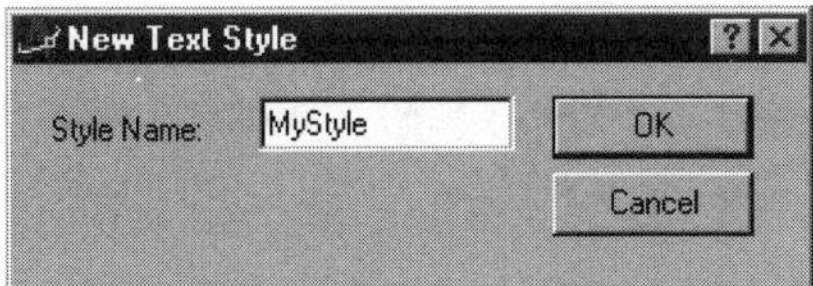

Click OK, and the New Text Style dialog box closes. You return to the Text Style dialog box, which now displays the new style name in its Style Name box.

4. In the Font frame of the dialog box, open the Font Name drop-down list containing all the fonts available on your PC. Select Times New Roman, and watch as the Preview box in the bottom right-hand corner is updated to display text in the new font.

5. Still in the Font frame, change the Height to **1.0** and click Apply, then click Close. The Text Style dialog box closes and you return to the AutoCAD window.

6. Select the spot where you want to place your text in the Model space, and choose the Multiline Text icon

   from the end of the Draw toolbar. The Multiline Text Editor dialog box appears, containing the name of the font just selected and the new text height.

7. Enter the text string required. Your entry appears inside the text area of the dialog box, drawn with the new font and height. Because you're in the Multiline Text Editor, your text will be spread over several lines.

   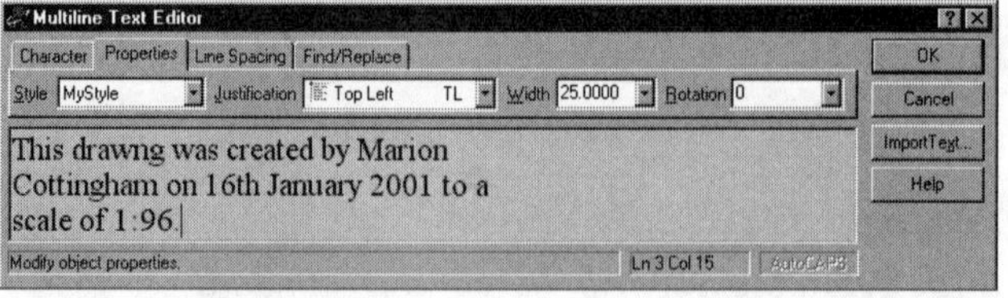

8. Click OK. The Multiline Text Editor dialog box closes, and the text is displayed in the Model Space.

Setting Text Attributes from a Macro

The AddMText method allows you to draw your text from a macro in much the same way as in the steps of the preceding exercise. The AddMText method has three parameters:

InsertionPoint Specifies the position where the text will be placed. This parameter uses the notion of a bounding box around the text and the position specified is actually the point where the top-left corner of this box will be placed.

Width The width of the bounding box in screen units that determines the number of characters that will be displayed for each line.

TextString The text to be displayed. Can also include format codes to specify attributes, such as the font to be used (*filename*), the color (*Cvalue*), the width (*Wvalue*), and the height (*Hvalue*).

The DrawMultilineText macro shown in Listing 9.4 shows this method being called from code, and Figure 9.9 shows the results.

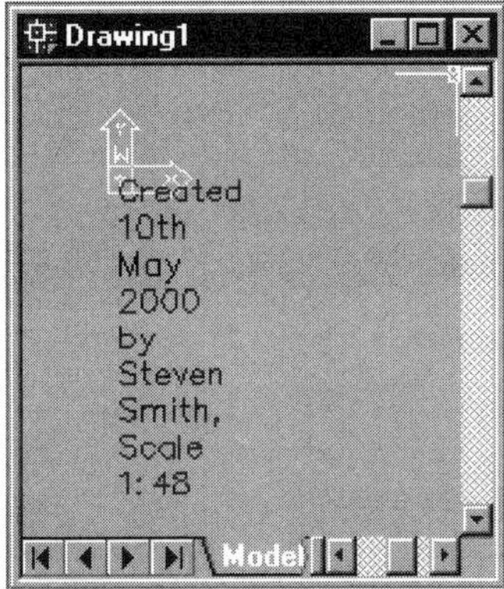

Figure 9.9 *Text drawn in the Model Space as a result of running the DrawMultilineText macro (Listing 9.4)*

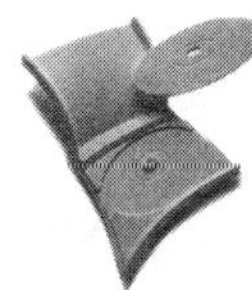

Listing 9.4: DrawMultilineText Macro

```
1   Public Sub DrawMultilineText()
2       Dim MTextObject As AcadMText
3       Dim Position(0 To 2) As Double
4       Position(0) = 0#: Position(1) = 0#: Position(2) = 0#
5       Set MTextObject = ThisDrawing.ModelSpace.AddMText( ↵
           Position, 4, "\fromanc.shx;\H1.0;" & ↵
           "Created 10th May 2000 by Steven Smith, Scale 1:48")
6       ThisDrawing.Regen acActiveViewport
7   End Sub
```

Analysis

- Line 1 starts the `DrawMultilineText` macro.
- Line 2 declares the variable `MTextObject` as being capable of referring to an MText object.

- Lines 3 and 4 declare the `Position` array and assign values to its elements that provide the x-, y-, and z-coordinates defining the text's position in the Model Space.
- Line 5 calls the `AddMText` method that not only draws the text string over multiple lines but also changes its font and height in the same call (see Figure 9.9).

  The third argument to `AddMText` contains the format codes to specify the font and the height for the text, as well as the text itself. If you are unsure of the font files on your PC, chances are the SHX font files will be found in `C:\Program Files\ACAD2000\FONTS`. Otherwise, you'll need to use the Windows Find command to search for them. SHX files are easily identified because their icon contains the letters SHX:

- Line 6 redraws the active document ThisDrawing in the active view.
- Line 7 ends the `DrawMultilineText` macro.

Formatting Text from a Macro

The macro in Listing 9.4 specifies the font and height of text strings, and their position in the drawing. Let's go a step further and see how to display text with the boldface or italic attribute, and how to control the orientation.

Various methods and properties are used to format and manipulate text inserted in AutoCAD drawings. These include making text bold or italicized, displaying it upside down or backwards, and controlling its height, width, and slant. This section shows you how to implement these attributes in a VBA application that comprises one UserForm containing several frames with option buttons and text boxes. The text in the Model Space is updated immediately in response to any selection made by the user.

Using Frames and Option Buttons

Frames help you to group related items together in the same area of a UserForm. They are often used as containers for OptionButton controls, where only one option button from a group can be selected at any particular time. To accomplish this, several frames can be placed on the same UserForm and the user can select one option button per frame. In contrast, placing all the option buttons directly onto a UserForm would mean having to set their GroupName properties to allow one option button per group to be selected.

Figure 9.10 shows the UserForm you'll create in this exercise, which allows the user to choose various text formatting options. Each frame contains a logical group of items and has been given appropriate caption text. Exercise 9.3 shows you how to create the GUI for this application.

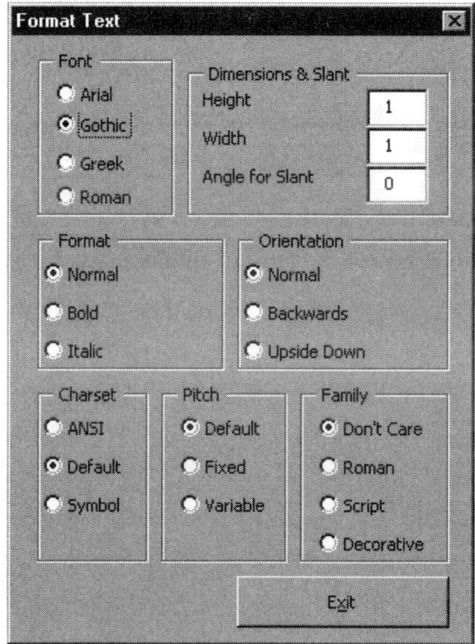

Figure 9.10 *Format Text application's GUI, with lots of frames and option buttons to help users select their choices*

EXERCISE 9.3: FORMAT TEXT APPLICATION

1. Start a new project and insert a UserForm. Place seven frames in a layout similar to that shown in Figure 9.10. Start from the top left with the Font frame, then Dimensions & Slant, Format, and so on, placing the Family frame last. Put the option buttons, text boxes, and labels into each frame, moving from top to bottom. (The order is important in this case, so that all the names of your controls will match the names from the Old Names column in Table 9.2 coming up.)

2. Add a command button at the bottom of the UserForm, and you're ready to update the properties of all the controls to the values given in Table 9.2.

Table 9.2 Properties of the Elements in the Format Text Application GUI

Old Name	New Name	Caption
UserForm1	frmFormatText	Format Text
Frame1	—	Font
Frame2	—	Dimensions & Slant
Frame3	—	Format
Frame4	—	Orientation
Frame5	—	Charset
Frame6	—	Pitch
Frame7	—	Family
OptionButton1	optArial	Arial
OptionButton2	optGothic	Gothic
OptionButton3	optGreek	Greek
OptionButton4	optRoman	Roman
OptionButton5	optNormalFormat	Normal
OptionButton6	optBold	Bold
OptionButton7	optItalic	Italic
OptionButton8	optNormalOrientation	Normal
OptionButton9	optBackwards	Backwards
OptionButton10	optUpsideDown	Upside Down
OptionButton11	optANSI	ANSI
OptionButton12	optCharsetDefault	Default
OptionButton13	optSymbol	Symbol
OptionButton14	optPitchDefault	Default
OptionButton15	optFixed	Fixed
OptionButton16	optVariable	Variable
OptionButton17	optDontCare	Don't Care
OptionButton18	optFamilyRoman	Roman
OptionButton19	optScript	Script
OptionButton20	optDecorative	Decorative

Table 9.2 Properties of the Elements in the Format Text Application GUI (*continued*)

CommandButton1	cmdExit	Exit
TextBox1	txtHeight	—
TextBox2	txtWidth	—
Textbox3	txtSlant	—
Label1	—	Height
Label2	—	Width
Label3	—	Angle for Slant

3. Insert the End statement into the Click event procedure of the cmdExit command button, as follows:

   ```
   Private Sub cmdExit_Click()
       Unload Me
   End Sub
   ```

4. Enter the code in Listing 9.5 into the General Declarations section of the UserForm's Code window.

Listing 9.5 contains the initializations that are made when the UserForm is first loaded, along with all the global declarations required. For convenience, I've placed the event procedures for each group of option buttons into separate listings.

LISTING 9.5: DECLARATIONS AND INITIALIZATIONS FOR THE FORMAT TEXT APPLICATION

```
'charset constants
Const ANSI_CHARSET = 0
Const DEFAULT_CHARSET = 1
Const SYMBOL_CHARSET = 2
'pitch constants
Const DEFAULT_PITCH = 0
Const FIXED_PITCH = 1
Const VARIABLE_PITCH = 2
'family constants
Const FF_DONTCARE = 0
Const FF_ROMAN = 16
```

```
    Const FF_SCRIPT = 64
    Const FF_DECORATIVE = 80
    'global declaration
    Dim MTextObject As AcadMText
    Dim TextObject As AcadText
    Dim TextStyleObject As AcadTextStyle
    Dim Position(0 To 2) As Double
    Dim Initializing As Boolean
    Dim CurString As String
    Dim CurFont As String
    Dim CurCharset As Long
    Dim CurPitch As Long, CurFamily As Long
    Dim BoldRequired As Boolean, ItalicsRequired As Boolean
    Dim BackwardsRequired As Boolean
    Dim UpsideDownRequired As Boolean

Private Sub UserForm_Initialize()
    Initializing = True
    Position(0) = 0#: Position(1) = 0#: Position(2) = 0#
    CurString = InputBox( ↵
     "Please enter string to be formatted.", "Format String")
    Set MTextObject = ThisDrawing.ModelSpace.AddMText( ↵
       Position, 1#, CurString)
    Set TextStyleObject = ThisDrawing.TextStyles.Add( ↵
       "MyStyle")
    'Font frame
    optGothic.Value = True
    'Dimensions & Slant frame
    txtHeight.Text = 1#
    txtWidth.Text = 1#
    txtSlant.Text = 0#
    'Format frame
    BoldRequired = False
    ItalicsRequired = False
    optNormalFormat.Value = True
    'Orientation frame
    BackwardsRequired = False
    UpsideDownRequired = False
    optNormalOrientation.Value = True
    'Charset frame
```

```
49       optCharsetDefault.Value = True
50       'Pitch frame
51       optPitchDefault.Value = True
52       'Family frame
53       optDontCare.Value = True
54       TextStyleObject.Height = CDbl(txtHeight.Text)
55       TextStyleObject.Width = CDbl(txtWidth.Text)
56       TextStyleObject.ObliqueAngle = CDbl(txtSlant.Text)
57       MTextObject.Update
58       Initializing = False
59   End Sub
```

Analysis

- Lines 1 through 13 use the `Const` statement to declare the constants that are used to represent the options in the Charset, Pitch, and Family frames (see Figure 9.10).
- Lines 15 through 17 declare the form-level variables that are set up as references to objects created using the `Add###` method. Both the MText and Text types of objects are employed in this project, because some of the options only affect one of the types and some affect both. For example, the options available in the Orientation frame only work with Text objects.
- Line 18 declares the array to store the three coordinates defining the position for the bottom-left corner of the first character in the string when it's viewed in its normal upright position.
- Line 19 declares the `Initializing` variable as Boolean. This prevents the statements of the `UpdateText` procedure from executing when the code from `UserForm_Initialize` triggers events that execute the event procedures that call the `UpdateText` procedure.
- Lines 20 through 23 declare the variables that reflect the current options selected from each frame.
- Lines 24 through 26 declare the Boolean variables that reflect the current settings from the Format and Orientation frames.
- Line 28 starts the `UserForm_Initialize` event procedure, which runs whenever the UserForm is loaded and initializes all the variables used by the event procedures.

- Line 29 sets the `Initializing` variable to True to prevent the statements inside the `UpdateText` procedure from being executed while all these initializations are taking place. This `Initializing` variable is set to False again in Line 58, at the end of this event procedure.
- Line 31 calls the `InputBox` function to display an input box in which the user will enter their string (shown later in Figure 9.11).
- Line 32 creates an MText object containing the user's string.
- Line 33 adds a new TextStyle object named `MyStyle` to the TextStyles collection.
- Line 35 sets the Gothic option button's Value property to True. This displays the button during run-time as the button selected from the group, until another button is selected instead.
- Lines 37 through 39 assign values to the Text properties of the three text boxes from the Dimensions & Slant frame. These values appear in the text boxes when the user starts up the application.
- Lines 41 through 43 set the two Boolean variables associated with the Format frame to False and make the Normal option button the one that's selected.
- Lines 45 through 47 set the orientation variables to False and make the Normal option button the selected one.
- Lines 49, 51, and 53 make one option button each from the Charset, Pitch, and Family frames the selected buttons.
- Lines 54 through 56 assign the default values from the text boxes to the `Height`, `Width` and `ObliqueAngle` properties of the `TextStyleObject`.
- Line 57 calls the `Update` method of the `MText` object so that the user's text appears in the Model Space.
- Line 58 sets the `Initializing` variable back to False so that the statements inside the `UpdateText` procedure will be executed as required.
- Line 59 ends the `UserForm_Initialize` event procedure.

Your next step is to enter the UpdateText procedure given in Listing 9.6 into the General Declarations section at the beginning of the code. This procedure is called by several other procedures to update the UserForm and display the text in the best possible way; it even ensures that all the text is visible in the Model Space.

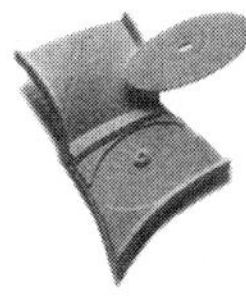

LISTING 9.6: UPDATETEXT PROCEDURE

```
1   Public Sub UpdateText()
2   If Not Initializing Then
3       ThisDrawing.ActiveTextStyle = TextStyleObject
4       ThisDrawing.Regen acActiveViewport
5       On Error Resume Next
6       MTextObject.Delete
7           TextObject.Delete
8           If BackwardsRequired = True Or ↵
               UpsideDownRequired = True Then
9                Set TextObject = ↵
                    ThisDrawing.ModelSpace.AddText( ↵
                    CurString, Position, CDbl(txtHeight.Text))
10          Else
11               Set MTextObject = ↵
                    ThisDrawing.ModelSpace.AddMText( ↵
                    Position, CDbl(txtWidth.Text), CurString)
12          End If
13          ZoomAll
14      End If
15  End Sub
```

ANALYSIS

- Line 1 starts the `UpdateText` procedure that's called throughout the UserForm's event procedures to update the text in the Model Space. This procedure resets the `ActiveTextStyle` property to the current `TextStyleObject` that has just been updated by an event procedure, and regenerates the active viewport. These statements are both required to update the text in the Model Space. The procedure continues by creating a new Text or MText object to replace the old one, using the orientation options to decide what type of object is required.

- Line 2 starts the `If` statement block that encloses all the statements in the procedure and ends at Line 14. The condition uses the `Not` operator with the `Initializing` variable to prevent the statements in the `If` block from executing until the `UserForm_Initialize` event procedure has finished.

- Line 3 makes the TextStyle object referenced by the variable `TextStyleObject` the `ActiveTextStyle` object.

- Line 4 regenerates the active viewport so that the new active text style takes effect.
- Line 5 catches any error that may occur in the same procedure, such as trying to delete an `MTextObject` that doesn't exist.
- Line 6 deletes the object reference by the `MTextObject` variable if it exists. Otherwise, an error is created; Line 5 causes the error to be ignored and Line 7 to be executed.
- Line 7 deletes the `TextObject` if it exists. Otherwise, Line 5 causes the generated error to be ignored and Line 8 to be executed.
- Line 8 checks to see if either the `BackwardsRequired` or the `UpsideDownRequired` variable is set to True, which means that a Text object must be created to cope with this.
- Line 9 creates a new Text object and assigns a reference to it in the `TextObject` variable.
- Line 10 starts the `Else` block that handles the `MTextObject`.
- Line 11 is executed whenever the `BackwardsRequired` and `UpsideDownRequired` variables are both set to False. This statement creates a new MText object and sets up a reference to it in the `MTextObject`.
- Line 12 ends the `If` statement.
- Line 13 calls the `ZoomAll` method to zoom the active viewport and display the entire drawing.
- Line 14 ends the outer `If` statement.
- Line 15 ends the `UpdateText` macro.

In these next steps, you will begin the process of entering all the event procedures responsible for displaying the various frames in the Format Text application.

1. Type the following macro into the ThisDrawing's Code window to open the Format Text UserForm from a macro:

```
Public Sub FormatText()
frmFormatText.Show
End Sub
```

2. Enter the code from Listing 9.7 into the UserForm Code window. This code provides all the event procedures that are associated with the Font frame.

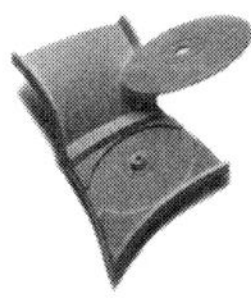

Listing 9.7: UpdateFont Procedure

```
1    Sub UpdateFont()
2        TextStyleObject.SetFont CurFont, BoldRequired, ↵
            ItalicsRequired, CurCharset, CurPitch Or CurFamily
3        UpdateText
4    End Sub5
6    Private Sub optArial_Click()
7        CurFont = "Arial"
8        UpdateFont
9    End Sub
10
11    Private Sub optGothic_Click()
12       CurFont = "gothicg"
13       UpdateFont
14   End Sub
15
16   Private Sub optGreek_Click()
17       CurFont = "greekc"
18       UpdateFont
19   End Sub
20
21   Private Sub optRoman_Click()
22       CurFont = "romanc"
23       UpdateFont
24   End Sub
```

Analysis

- Lines 1 through 4 contain the `Update` procedure that passes the `CurFont` variable to the `SetFont` method of the active `TextStyle` object. The `UpdateText` procedure is then called to display the effect in the Model Space.
- Lines 6 through 24 contain the Click event procedures for the four option buttons in the Font frame. Each event procedure assigns the name of a font to the `CurFont` variable.

Next, enter the code from Listing 9.8, which contains all the event procedures associated with the text boxes in the Dimensions & Slant frame.

Listing 9.8: Event Procedures for Dimensions & Slant Frame

```
1    Private Sub txtHeight_Exit↵
       (ByVal Cancel As MSForms.ReturnBoolean)
2        TextStyleObject.Height = CDbl(txtHeight.Text)
3        UpdateText
4    End Sub
5
6    Private Sub txtWidth_Exit↵
       (ByVal Cancel As MSForms.ReturnBoolean)
7        TextStyleObject.Width = CDbl(txtWidth.Text)
8        UpdateText
9    End Sub
10
11   Private Sub txtSlant_Exit↵
       (ByVal Cancel As MSForms.ReturnBoolean)
12       TextStyleObject.ObliqueAngle = CDbl(txtSlant.Text)
13       UpdateText
14   End Sub
15
16   Private Sub Frame2_Exit↵
       (ByVal Cancel As MSForms.ReturnBoolean)
17       UpdateText
18   End Sub 16  Private Sub Frame2_Exit
```

Analysis

- Lines 1 through 14 list the three `Exit` event procedures that run whenever another control gets the focus. These procedures set the `Height`, `Width`, and `ObliqueAngle` properties of the active `TextStyle` object before calling the `UpdateText` procedure to display the effect in the Model Space.
- Lines 16 through 18 contain the `Exit` event procedure for the frame, with Caption property as Dimensions & Slant.

A control's Exit event procedure runs when the control loses the focus.

Next, enter the code from Listing 9.9, which contains all the event procedures for the option buttons of the Format frame.

LISTING 9.9: EVENT PROCEDURES FOR FORMAT FRAME

```
1   Private Sub optNormalFormat_Click()
2       BoldRequired = False
3       ItalicsRequired = False
4       UpdateFont
5   End Sub
6
7   Private Sub optBold_Click()
8       BoldRequired = True
9       ItalicsRequired = False
10      UpdateFont
11  End Sub
12
13  Private Sub optItalic_Click()
14      ItalicsRequired = True
15      BoldRequired = False
16      UpdateFont
17  End Sub
```

ANALYSIS

Lines 1 through 17 contain the Click event procedures for the option buttons of the Format frame. These procedures set the `BoldRequired` and `ItalicsRequired` Boolean variables to appropriate values before calling `UpdateFont` from Listing 9.7. This procedure uses them as arguments in the call to the `SetFont` method before calling the `UpdateText` procedure to update the text in the Model Space.

Next, enter the code from Listing 9.10, which lists the event procedures from the option buttons of the Orientation frame.

LISTING 9.10: EVENT PROCEDURES FOR ORIENTATION FRAME

```
Private Sub optNormalOrientation_Click()
    UpsideDownRequired = False
    BackwardsRequired = False
    TextStyleObject.TextGenerationFlag = 0
    UpdateText
End Sub

Private Sub optBackwards_Click()
```

```
9       BackwardsRequired = True
10      TextStyleObject.TextGenerationFlag = acTextFlagBackward
11      UpdateText
12  End Sub
13
14  Private Sub optUpsideDown_Click()
15      UpsideDownRequired = True
16      TextStyleObject.TextGenerationFlag = acTextFlagUpsideDown
17      UpdateText
18  End Sub
```

ANALYSIS

Lines 1 through 18 list the three Click event procedures for the option buttons of the Orientation frame. These procedures set the `UpsideDownRequired` and `BackwardsRequired` Boolean variables to appropriate values, as well as assign the value of an AutoCAD constant to the `TextGenerationFlag` property of the `TextStyle` object. The `UpdateText` procedure is then called to redraw the text.

Next, enter the code from Listing 9.11, which gives the procedures for the option buttons of the Charset frame.

LISTING 9.11: EVENT PROCEDURES FOR CHARSET FRAME

```
1   Private Sub optANSI_Click()
2       CurCharset = ANSI_CHARSET
3       UpdateFont
4   End Sub
5
6   Private Sub optCharsetDefault_Click()
7       CurCharset = DEFAULT_CHARSET
8       UpdateFont
9   End Sub
10
11  Private Sub optSymbol_Click()
12      CurCharset = SYMBOL_CHARSET
13      UpdateFont
14  End Sub
```

ANALYSIS

Lines 1 through 14 contain the three event procedures for the Charset frame. These procedures assign global constants to the `CurCharset` variable before calling the

`UpdateFont` procedure from Listing 9.7. This procedure uses the `CurCharSet` variable as an argument to the `SetFont` method, before calling `UpdateText` to show the effect.

Next, enter the code from Listing 9.12, which contains the event procedures for the option buttons of the Pitch frame.

Listing 9.12: Event Procedures for Pitch Frame

```
1   Private Sub optPitchDefault_Click()
2       CurPitch = DEFAULT_PITCH
3       UpdateFont
4   End Sub
5
6   Private Sub optFixed_Click()
7       CurPitch = FIXED_PITCH
8       UpdateFont
9   End Sub
10
11  Private Sub optVariable_Click()
12      CurPitch = VARIABLE_PITCH
13      UpdateFont
14  End Sub
```

Analysis

Lines 1 through 14 list the three Click event procedures of the option buttons for the Pitch frame. These procedures set the `CurPitch` variable to the appropriate global constant before calling the UpdateFont procedure from Listing 9.7. This procedure uses the `CurPitch` variable as an argument to the `SetFont` procedure before calling the `UpdateText` procedure to redraw the text in the Model Space.

Finally, enter the code from Listing 9.13, which gives the event procedures for the option buttons in the Family frame.

Listing 9.13: Event Procedures for Family Frame

```
Private Sub optDontCare_Click()
    CurFamily = FF_DONTCARE
    UpdateFont
End Sub

```

```
6   Private Sub optFamilyRoman_Click()
7       CurFamily = FF_ROMAN
8       UpdateFont
9   End Sub
10
11  Private Sub optScript_Click()
12      CurFamily = FF_SCRIPT
13      UpdateFont
14  End Sub
15
16  Private Sub optDecorative_Click()
17      CurFamily = FF_DECORATIVE
18      UpdateFont
19  End Sub
```

Analysis

Lines 1 through 19 contain the Click event procedures for the four option buttons of the Family frame. These procedures set the `CurFamily` variable to the values of global constants. This variable is used by the `UpdateFont` procedure as an argument in the call to the `SetFont` method. As usual, `UpdateText` is then called to redraw the text in the Model Space.

Now run your completed Format Text application, and enter some text when the Format String input box appears (Figure 9.11). Try selecting various option buttons and watch their effect on your text in the Model Space. Some settings rely on others; for example, the Normal option from the Font frame must be selected before the Symbol option from the Charset has any effect. Figures 9.12 through 9.15 illustrate a few of the effects available.

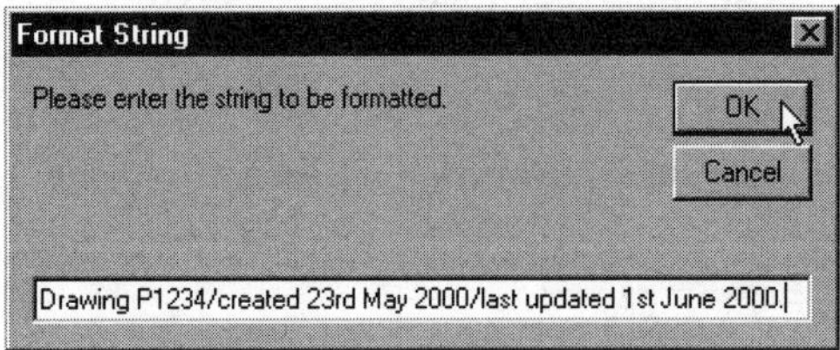

***Figure 9.11** Entering text in the Format String input box*

Figure 9.12 *Result when the Backwards option button is selected*

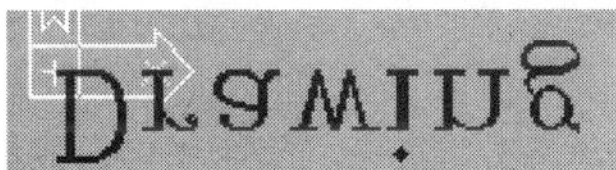

Figure 9.13 *Result when the Upside Down option button is clicked*

Figure 9.14 *Result when Symbol is selected from the Charset frame*

Figure 9.15 *Result when 10 is entered into the Angle For Slant text box*

Formatting Numbers, Times, and Dates

VBA provides a Format function that allows you to specify how you want a number, time, or date displayed in your drawing. This function converts the value passed to it as an argument into a text string, according to the format string passed to it as the second argument. The format string contains a collection of symbols with which you designate how the number will appear.

The syntax of the Format function is as follows:

```
Format(expression, format, firstdayofweek, firstdayofyear)
```

Only the first parameter requires a value; the others are optional.

Formatting Numbers

Let's start with formatting numbers. Table 9.3 shows the list of symbols available for the argument, and a description of the effect they have in the formatted string.

Table 9.3 Symbols for Format Function Argument to Format a Number

Symbol	Description
0	Digit placeholder that's replaced by a leading or trailing zero if no digit occurs at this position
#	Digit placeholder that's never replaced by a zero
.	Decimal placeholder
,	Thousands separator
$ – + ( ) space	Literal characters that are displayed as themselves

Table 9.4 shows you some formatted numbers along with the format strings used to produce them. There are also a few named formats that you can pass to the format parameter. These include Percent, which multiplies the value by 100 and adds a percent sign; Currency, which adds a thousands separator if required, and always shows two digits after the point; Fixed, which displays at least one digit before the point and two digits after.

Table 9.4 Results after Formatting Numbers Using the Format Strings

ORIGINAL NUMBER	FORMAT STRING	FORMATTED RESULT
1234.5	"00000.000"	01234.500
1234.5	"#####.###"	1234.5
1234	"##,##0.0#"	1,234.0
1234.50	"$#,##0.00"	$1,234.50
11011101	"#### ####"	1101 1101

Formatting Times and Dates

The Format function can format time and date values in much the same way as it formats numbers.

The following statement shows how the Now function can be used as the first argument in the Format function call. I have used the named format Short Date as the second argument.

```
CurDate = Format(Now, "Short Date")
```

The Now function returns, for example, the string `1/17/01 2 52 32 PM`. The above statement reformats this to `1/17/01`.

You can use the Now function to retrieve the current date value from your computer's system. The Now function returns a Variant containing both the date and time in a format based on your computer system's date and time setup. This is the setup in the Regional Settings Properties dialog box available from Windows Control Panel. The settings used here are English – United States; an example of the time and date returned by the Now function is as follows:

```
4/21/2000 10:45:03 PM
```

The Format function has its own set of symbols for formatting dates and times. Table 9.5 shows some of these, along with the result of passing the date returned by Now to the Format function.

VBA has predefined named formats for dates and times, such as vbShortDate, vbLongDate, vbShortTime, and vbLongTime, that all use the format specified in your PC's regional settings.

Table 9.5 Result of Formatting Times and Dates

FORMAT STRING	RESULT
"hh:mm am/pm"	10:40 pm
"m/d/yyyy"	4/21/2000
"mmm dd yy"	Apr 21 00
"mmmm dd yy"	April 21 00
"hh:mm am/pm dddd, mmmm dd, yyyy"	10:41 pm Monday, April 21, 2000

Validating Input

The text entered by the user into an input box or any other control that can accept text should normally be *validated* to prevent it from causing abnormal termination of the application. In the example given in Listing 9.14, this TextBox control

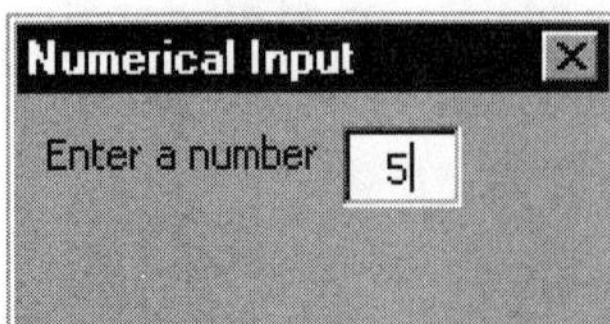

expects a numerical character to be entered by the user. If the user presses a number key, the number is appended to the `TextBox` string; otherwise, the key being pressed is ignored.

You can extend this example so that it will also accept non-numeric characters such as a period or a comma. Just replace Line 2 of Listing 9.14 with the following:

```
If (KeyAscii < Asc("0") Or KeyAscii > Asc("9")) ↵
   And KeyAscii <> Asc(".") And KeyAscii <> Asc(",") Then
```

You could also change the < and > to > and < if you wanted to accept only non-numeric characters.

LISTING 9.14

```
1    Private Sub TextBox1_KeyPress(ByVal KeyAscii As ↵
       MSForms.ReturnInteger)
2         If KeyAscii < Asc("0") Or KeyAscii > Asc("9") Then
```

```
3          KeyAscii = 0 'cancel the character
4          Beep
5       End If
6   End Sub
```

Analysis

- Line 1 starts the `TextBox1_KeyPress` event procedure that's executed each time the user presses a keyboard key. This event procedure has one parameter that is passed the numeric ASCII code for the character associated with the key just pressed. (Appendix B gives a table of all the ASCII codes and the characters they represent.)
- Line 2 uses the `Asc` function to return the integer ASCII code for the one-character string passed to `Asc` as an argument. Since the characters 0 through 9 have ASCII codes 48 through 57, it checks to see if the `KeyAscii` character is less than 48 or greater than 57; if so, then the character is not a number.
- Line 3 sets `KeyAscii` to zero, which represents the Null character. This has the effect of canceling the key pressed, and nothing is appended to the end of the string in the `Text` property.
- In Line 4, the `Beep` statement sounds a noise to let the user know that something is wrong with their entry. The sound made depends on the hardware and control settings of the PC.
- Line 5 ends the `If` statement.
- Line 6 ends the `TextBox1_KeyPress` event procedure.

Adding Text to Arrows

It is common practice to include annotated arrows in a drawing; the arrow points at a particular item to give some information about it. This can also be done from code using the Leader object, which combines text with an arrow that points to a drawing object. The arrow's head can be one of several types, and its tail can be made up of one or more straight lines or spline segments. (Splines are curved lines and are discussed later in Chapter 13.) A Leader object is added to the ModelSpace collection using the AddLeader method.

The following exercise shows you how to include annotated arrows in your drawings.

Exercise 9.4: Draw Arrow Application

1. Start a new project and add a UserForm.
2. Place a combo box and label, and a Frame containing two option button controls as shown in Figure 9.16.

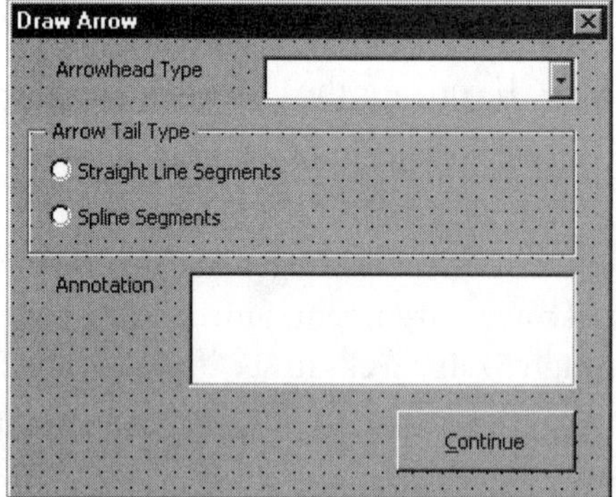

Figure 9.16 *GUI for the Draw Arrow application*

3. Add a text box with an accompanying label, and a command button.
4. Set the two properties given in Table 9.6.
5. I have opted not to rename the option buttons because their Click events all contain one line of code and it is easy to see what the code does. Set the captions of these buttons as shown in Figure 9.16.
6. In the Properties window, set the Multiline property of the text box to True, and the Accelerator property of the command button to **C.**

Table 9.6 Properties of the Draw Arrow Controls

Old Name	New Name	Caption
UserForm	frmArrows	Draw Arrow
ComboBox1	cboArrowhead	—
TextBox1	txtArrowText	—
CommandButton1	cmdContinue	Continue

7. Copy the GetShape macro from the earlier section "Creating Polar Arrays From A Macro" into the ThisDrawing Code window, and change its name as follows:

```
Public Sub GetTail()
    'Prompt the user to select points to define the ↵
      arrow's tail
```

8. Enter the code shown in Listing 9.15 into the ThisDrawing module Code window. This listing contains the DrawArrow macro that is used to open the application from the Macros dialog box, and the RedrawPolyline macro that re-creates a new polyline, which includes the last point clicked.

Listing 9.15: Declarations and Macro for Running the Application

```
1       Dim PolygonObject(0) As AcadPolyline
2       'Points defining arrow tail input by the user
3       Dim PolyArray() As Double
4       'NumberOfElements is current number of elements in array
5       Dim NumberOfElements As Integer
6
7   Public Sub DrawArrow()
8       frmArrows.Show
9       Unload frmArrows
10    End Sub
11
12  Public Sub RedrawPolyline()
13      'Display the arrow tail input so far
14      With ThisDrawing.ModelSpace
15          If NumberOfElements > 5 Then PolygonObject(0).Delete
16          Set PolygonObject(0) = .AddPolyline(PolyArray)
17          PolygonObject(0).Color = acBlue
18          PolygonObject(0).Update
19      End With
20  End Sub
```

Analysis

- Lines 1 through 5 declare the module level variables that are used by various procedures.
- Line 7 starts the `DrawArrow` macro that opens the `frmArrow` UserForm.

- Line 8 calls the `Show` method of the `frmArrows` UserForm to display it on the screen.
- Line 9 unloads the Draw Arrow UserForm.
- Line 10 ends the `DrawArrow` macro.
- Line 12 starts the `RedrawPolyline` procedure that deletes the last polyline and creates a new one containing the point just entered by the user.
- Line 14 starts the `With` statement block so that the properties and methods from the Model Space tab of the active drawing can be used without being fully qualified.
- Line 15 deletes the Polyline object named `PolygonObject`.
- Line 16 creates a new Polyline object based on the latest `PolyArray`, including the last point selected, and assigns it to the `PolygonObject` array.
- Line 17 sets the color of the Polyline object to blue.
- Line 18 calls the `Update` method of the `PolygonObject` to redraw it in the Model Space so that the last point is included.
- Line 19 ends the `With` statement.
- Line 20 ends the `RedrawPolyline` macro.

Exercise 9.4: Draw Arrow Application (continued)

Now enter the code from Listing 9.16 into the ThisDrawing's Code window. This code contains the `CreateArrow` macro that creates an arrow to the user's specifications.

Listing 9.16: CreateArrow Macro

```
Public Sub CreateArrow()
    'create an arrow with user's selections
    Dim LeaderObject As AcadLeader
    Dim TextObject As AcadMText
    Dim EndTail(0 To 2) As Double
    GetTail
    'set EndTail to last point input by user
    EndTail(0) = PolyArray(NumberOfElements - 2) - 1
    EndTail(1) = PolyArray(NumberOfElements - 1)
    EndTail(2) = PolyArray(NumberOfElements)
    'add the text and Leader objects to ModelSpace collection
```

```
12      With ThisDrawing.ModelSpace
13          Set TextObject = .AddMText( ↵
               EndTail, 2#, frmArrows.txtArrowText.Text)
14          Set LeaderObject = .AddLeader( ↵
               PolyArray, TextObject, ArrowTailType)
15      End With
16      'assign arrowhead selected by the user to Leader object
17      LeaderObject.ArrowheadType = ArrowheadType
18  End Sub
```

Analysis

- Line 1 starts the `CreateArrow` macro, which creates an arrow according to the user's specifications.
- Line 3 declares the `LeaderObject` variable as being capable of referring to an `AcadLeader` object. This object comprises an arrowhead, a tail, and an object containing the annotation.

In this example, the annotation is provided using an MText object, but a Tolerance or a BlockRef object can also be used.

- Line 4 declares the `TextObject` variable to refer to the MText object that will be associated with the Leader object.
- Line 5 declares `EndTail` as an array of doubles so that it can be used as an argument in the call to the `AddMText` method at Line 13.
- Line 6 calls the `GetTail` procedure that prompts the user to input the arrow's tail.
- Lines 8 through 10 set the elements of the `EndTail` array to the coordinates of the last point selected by the user.
- Line 12 uses the `With` statement, so that methods from the ModelSpace object can be used without being fully qualified.
- Line 13 creates a new `MText` object based on the position stored in `EndTail`, which is the last point selected for the arrow's tail.
- Line 14 creates a new Leader object by passing its parameters: the points selected by the user, a reference to the `MText` object, and the type of tail required for the arrow.

- Line 15 ends the `With` statement block.
- Line 17 assigns the `ArrowHeadType` set in an event procedure to the `ArrowHeadType` property of the Leader object.
- Line 18 ends the `CreateArrow` macro.

EXERCISE 9.4: DRAW ARROW APPLICATION (CONTINUED)

In the next set of steps, you will finish off your application and run it to try it out.

1. Insert a standard Module and add the following two declarations:

```
Public ArrowheadType As Integer
Public ArrowTailType As Integer
```

2. Type the event procedures given in Listing 9.17 into the skeleton event procedures provided in the frmArrows Code window.

LISTING 9.17: EVENT PROCEDURES FOR DRAW ARROW APPLICATION

```
Private Sub cmdContinue_Click()
    If txtArrowText = "" Then
        MsgBox "Please enter text for your arrow.", ,↵
           "Arrow Text"
    Else
        frmArrows.hide
        ThisDrawing.CreateArrow
    End If
End Sub

Private Sub cboArrowhead_Change()
    Select Case cboArrowhead.Text
    Case "Dot"
        ArrowheadType = acArrowDot
    Case "Dot Small"
        ArrowheadType = acArrowDotSmall
    Case "Dot Blank"
        ArrowheadType = acArrowDotBlank
    Case "Origin"
        ArrowheadType = acArrowOrigin
    Case "Open"
        ArrowheadType = acArrowOpen
    Case "Open 90"
```

```
            ArrowheadType = acArrowOpen90
        Case "Open 30"
            ArrowheadType = acArrowOpen30
        Case "Closed"
            ArrowheadType = acArrowClosed
        Case "None"
            ArrowheadType = acArrowNone
        Case "Oblique"
            ArrowheadType = acArrowOblique
        Case "Box Filled"
            ArrowheadType = acArrowBoxFilled
        Case "Box Blank"
            ArrowheadType = acArrowBoxBlank
        Case "Closed Blank"
            ArrowheadType = acArrowClosedBlank
        Case "Datum Filled"
            ArrowheadType = acArrowDatumFilled
        Case "Datum Blank"
            ArrowheadType = acArrowDatumBlank
        Case "Integral"
            ArrowheadType = acArrowIntegral
        End Select
    End Sub

    Private Sub OptionButton1_Click()
        ArrowTailType = acLineWithArrow
    End Sub

    Private Sub OptionButton2_Click()
        ArrowTailType = acSplineWithArrow
    End Sub

    Private Sub UserForm_Initialize()
        With cboArrowhead
            .AddItem "Dot"
            .AddItem "Dot Small"
            .AddItem "Dot Blank"
            .AddItem "Origin"
            .AddItem "Open"
            .AddItem "Open 90"
```

```
63          .AddItem "Open 30"
64          .AddItem "Closed"
65          .AddItem "None"
66          .AddItem "Oblique"
67          .AddItem "Box Filled"
68          .AddItem "Box Blank"
69          .AddItem "Closed Blank"
70          .AddItem "Datum Filled"
71          .AddItem "Datum Blank"
72          .AddItem "Integral"
73          .Text = "None" 'set default item
74      End With
75  End Sub
```

Analysis

- Line 1 starts the `cmdContinue` Click event procedure.
- Line 2 starts the `If` statement and determines whether the text box is empty.
- Line 3 calls the `MsgBox` function to let the user know the text for the arrow hasn't been entered.
- Line 4 starts the `Else` part of the `If` statement.
- Line 5 hides the `frmArrows` UserForm so that the user can gain full access to the Model Space in the AutoCAD window.
- Line 6 calls the `CreateArrow` macro from the ThisDrawing module.
- Lines 7 and 8 end the `If` statement and the Click event procedure, respectively.
- Line 10 starts the `Change` event procedure of the combo box. This procedure is responsible for assigning the arrowhead selected by the user to the `ArrowheadType` variable.
- Lines 11 through 44 contain the `Select Case` statement block that assigns the value of an AutoCAD constant to the `ArrowheadType` variable according to the item selected by the user from the combo box.
- Line 45 ends the `Change` event procedure of the combo box.
- Lines 47 through 49 and Lines 51 through 53 contain the Click event procedures of the two option buttons that set the `ArrowTailType` variable to the appropriate AutoCAD constant.

- Line 55 starts the `Initialize` event procedure of the `frmArrows` UserForm.
- Lines 56 through 74 contain the `With` statement block that enables the `AddItem` method to create the arrowhead type items in the combo box.
- Line 75 ends the `Initialize` event procedure of the `frmArrows` UserForm.

Exercise 9.4: Draw Arrow Application (continued)

Now all the coding is finished. All you have left to do is run the application to test it and see if it performs as you want it to.

1. Run the `DrawArrow` macro from the Macros dialog box in AutoCAD. Select an arrowhead type from among the 16 options provided, and an arrow tail type.
2. Enter the text to be displayed at the end of your arrow into the Annotation box and click Continue.

   Figure 9.17 shows the text I entered, and Figure 9.18 shows the results.

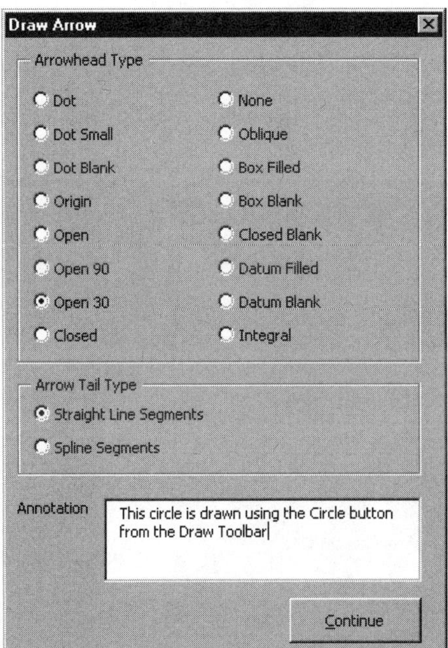

Figure 9.17 *Selecting the Open 30 arrowhead type and the Straight Line Segments arrow tail*

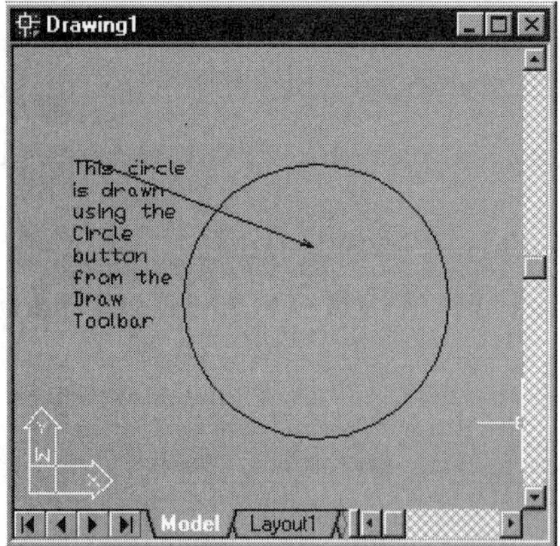

Figure 9.18 *Results of selections shown in Figure 9.17*

3. Try drawing a zigzag arrow tail, using straight-line segments and using spline segments, and compare the difference. Figure 9.19 shows a polyline through the points I selected for my arrow's tail, and Figure 9.20 shows the spline curve that used these points as control points.

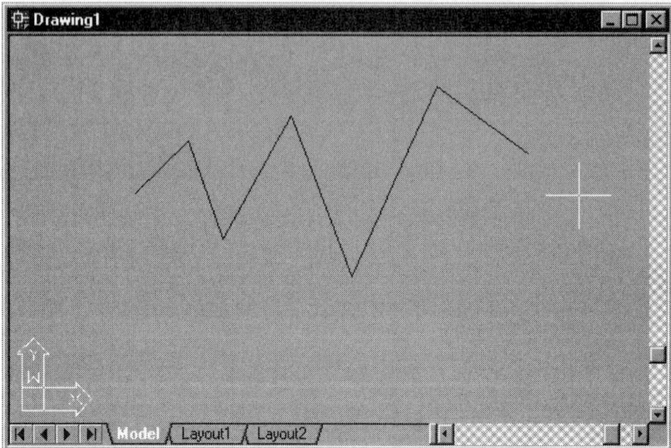

Figure 9.19 *Polyline through the points selected for the spline segments shown in Figure 9.20*

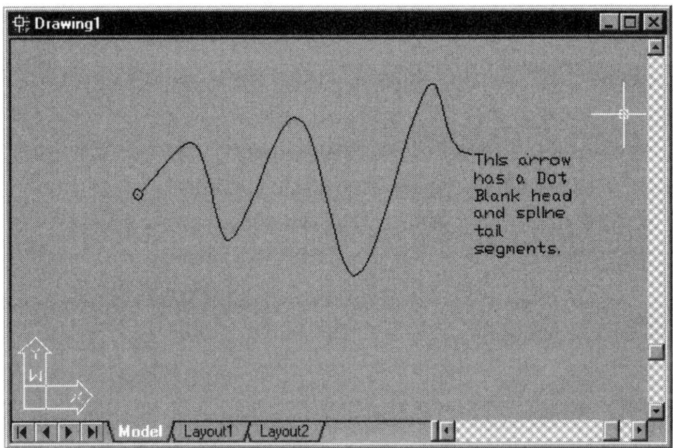

Figure 9.20 *Arrow drawn with spline tail segments*

Summary

After reading this chapter, you should be able to do all of the following:

- Create a new drawing document from a macro.
- Create a rectangular array based on a freeform shape from a macro.
- Create a polar array based on a freeform shape from a macro.
- Format text from a macro.
- Use frames and option buttons.
- Format numbers, dates, and times using the VBA Format function.
- Validate numerical input from a macro.
- Develop an application to add annotated arrows to your drawing.

Debugging Your Code

AUTOCAD VBA

Chapter 10

If your application doesn't react the way you intended, or if it produces unexpected results or simply stops working for no apparent reason, then your program probably has what's known as a bug. The process of hunting down and correcting bugs is called *debugging*. This chapter describes various types of errors you may accidentally introduce into your code. It also discusses the extremely useful features that are available from the VBA IDE to help you identify and fix your problems when things go wrong.

This chapter covers the following topics:

- Types of errors you may encounter
- Commands on the Debug menu
- Using breakpoints
- Using watches
- The IDE's debugging windows
- Viewing the Call stack
- Choosing a debugging tool

Types of Errors

You may encounter the following types of errors in the VBA code you work with:

- *Logic errors* are made during the development phase as you write the code.
- *Compiler errors* are sometimes discovered by the VBA interpreter immediately after you enter a statement. Sometimes they are discovered by the compiler program when it tries to translate the code into an executable form.
- *Run-time* errors occur during execution time.

The VBA IDE doesn't attempt to fix any of these errors for you, but it does provide useful features to help you when things go wrong. You'll be able to do as much as possible to ensure that the code you enter is syntactically correct so that the interpreter program can understand it. Other features assist in debugging your code when it doesn't quite work in the way it's supposed to.

The next three sections describe these three classifications of errors in more detail.

Logic Errors

Logic errors, introduced as you develop the VBA code, only become obvious when your application doesn't perform as expected. For example, suppose your application requires the user to enter a telephone number into a text box and, as each key is pressed, validates the corresponding character to ensure that it's a number. If not, the application rejects it and sounds a beep.

The text box control in your application has a KeyPress event procedure that is passed the numeric ASCII code of the last key pressed as its KeyAscii parameter. The KeyPress event procedure for the telephone number entry in Listing 10.1, for example, is syntactically correct, runs like a dream without giving any error messages, doesn't fall over—and yet, when you enter a *letter* into the text box instead of a number, your letter is accepted and appended to the Text property string. Which was not the original idea and isn't supposed to happen.

The error here is in the condition of the `If` statement. As written, the condition will always be False because there is no key you can press that produces a character that is both less that the ASCII code for zero and greater than the ASCII code for 9. For this condition to be True, the character input would have to be represented by two different ASCII codes.

To rectify this event procedure, the `And` from the `If` statement on Line 2 must be changed to an `Or`. That way, only numbers will get displayed in the text box and the others will be discarded.

If you want to run this event procedure and examine it as you work through this chapter, you'll need to set up a GUI with a UserForm containing a label and a command button control as shown in Figure 10.1. Change the Caption properties to those shown in the figure, and update the Name property of your text box to txtTelephone.

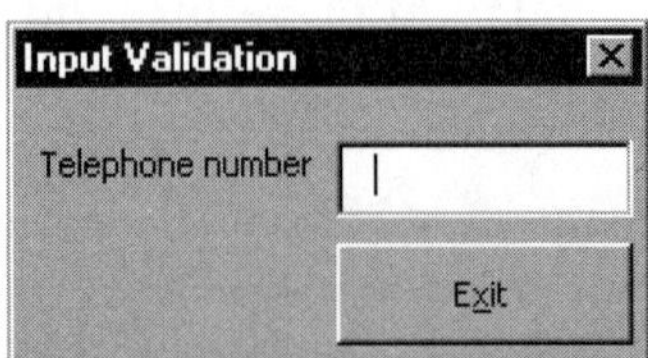

Figure 10.1 *Input Validation GUI for prompting the user to enter a telephone number*

Listing 10.1: KeyPress Event Procedure

```
1   Private Sub txtTelephone_KeyPress( ↵
      ByVal KeyAscii As MSForms.ReturnInteger)
2   If KeyAscii < Asc("0") And KeyAscii > Asc("9") Then
3       KeyAscii = 0
4       Beep
5   End If
6   End Sub
```

Analysis

- Line 1 starts the `KeyPress` event procedure of the `txtTelephone` text box. This has a `ByVal` parameter, `KeyAscii`, that's assigned the ASCII code value of the character associated with the key just entered. The `KeyAscii` parameter is passed a reference to the Microsoft Form's ReturnInteger object, which allows you to reject any invalid characters.
- Line 2 uses the `If` statement with a condition that attempts to verify that the `KeyAscii` character is not in the range 0 through 9. It mistakenly uses the `And` operator, however, instead of the `Or` operator. The result is that any character entered gets accepted and appended to the text in the text box.

- Line 3 cancels the keypress and is only executed if the condition in the `If` statement evaluates to True.
- Line 4 sounds a beep to alert the user that the last character input has been rejected.
- Line 4 ends the `If` statement block.
- Line 5 ends the `KeyPress` event procedure.

Compiler Errors

Compiler errors occur because you have entered code incorrectly. Some compiler errors are picked up right away when you enter a statement that doesn't meet the syntax requirements of the Visual Basic language. Other compiler errors are detected during compile time, while your source code is being translated into executable code ready for running by the Compile ACADProject command under the Debug menu.

Getting Feedback as You're Entering Code

The VBA IDE can be set up to provide immediate feedback as soon as you enter a statement containing a syntax error. For example, if you enter the following statement and press Enter:

```
If A = B
```

you'll see the following message box containing the error message about an expected Then:

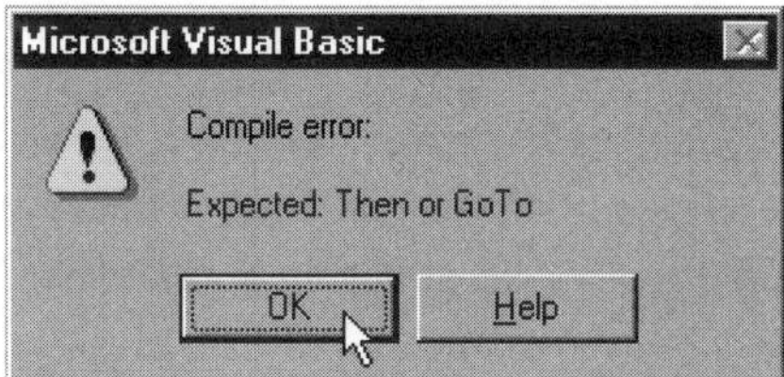

If you try this and no message appears, you'll need to make sure that you have enabled the Auto Syntax Check option in the IDE Options dialog box (Figure 10.2):

1. Choose Tools ➔ Options and select the Editor tab.
2. If the Auto Syntax Check option isn't on, select the check box to enable it.
3. Click OK to return to the VBA IDE.

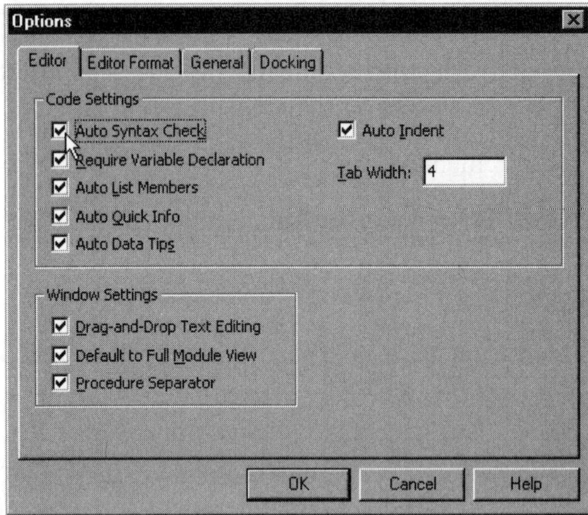

***Figure 10.2** The Editor tab from Tools → Options contains the Auto Syntax Check option.*

ByVal Parameters vs. *ByRef* Parameters

A `ByVal` parameter is passed a copy of a variable, so if the procedure changes the value of the parameter, only the copy is changed. This means the variable still keeps its original value.

A `ByRef` parameter is passed a reference to a variable that enables access to the contents in its memory address allocation. Updating a `ByRef` parameter updates the memory address contents, so the variable will still be set to the new value after the procedure has finished executing.

A `ByVal` parameter can also be passed a reference to a `ReturnBoolean`, `ReturnEffect`, `ReturnInteger`, or `ReturnString` object. As such, `ByVal` acts more like a `ByRef` parameter, in that you can update the named parameter, and the `Value` property of the object will retain the new value even after the procedure has finished.

Errors during the Compilation Stage

Following are a couple of examples of errors that often occur as you compile the entire application into executable code. (This is the last step you'll do prior to running the code.)

- Variables that are not defined even although the `Option Explicit` statement is included at the start of the module. When the compiler comes across such variables, it displays the message "Compiler error: Variable not defined."

- Missing arguments from calls to a method or function. When a method or function call does not include all the required arguments, the message "Compiler error: Argument not optional" appears.

Run-Time Errors

A run-time error occurs while the code is being executed and usually means that a statement has attempted to perform some invalid operation.

One common run-time error is when your code tries to divide a number by a variable that's set to zero.

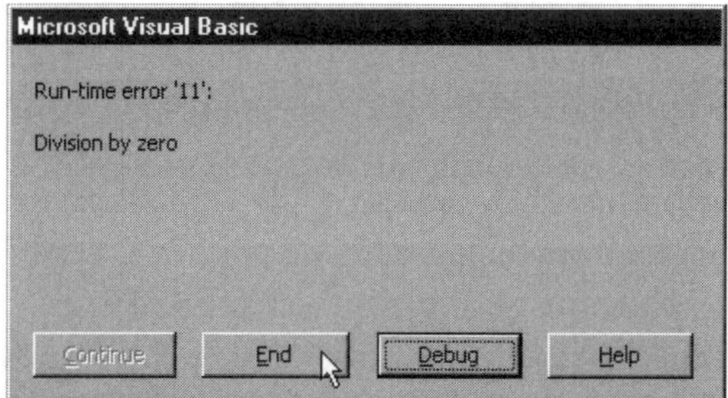

When you're working with variables that are supposed to be set up as references to objects, another common run-time error you might make is to forget to include the `Set` in the assignment statement. For example, the following statement

```
NewDocument = Documents.Add("Template1")
```

produces a message box containing the error message "Run-time error '91': Object variable or With block variable not set." This statement should have been written as follows:

```
Set NewDocument = Documents.Add("Template1")
```

Err Object

The properties of the Err object are assigned the details of a run-time error. They uniquely identify the error, give its source, and provide a description including (if possible) how to handle the error. The following table lists and describes the Err object's properties. The Err object's properties are initially set to zero or to empty strings. When an error occurs, they are reset to values and strings that provide useful information about the error.

Number Numerical value in the range 0 to 65,535 that, in combination with the Name property, uniquely identifies the error. This property is used as the argument passed to the `Error` statement.

Source Returns the name of the object or the application that caused the error.

Description Contains an error message from the application or an object.

HelpFile Pathname for the Visual Basic Help file.

HelpContext The Help file's context ID for the error associated with the Number property.

LastDLLError Contains the system error code for the last call to a Dynamic Link Library (DLL).

Debug Menu Commands

The aim of the game is to find out where your application went wrong and why. Because bugs can be introduced to an application in a variety of ways, there are no steadfast, tried-and-tested techniques that you can apply when hunting down the bug. VBA's debugging features are nonetheless a big help.

The Visual Basic Editor's Debug menu commands (Figure 10.3) enable the code to be compiled into p-code and checked for syntax errors. Other commands allow you to step through your code statement-by-statement, or to stop execution temporarily at a designated statement (*breakpoint*). You can even watch the value of variables change as you execute each statement.

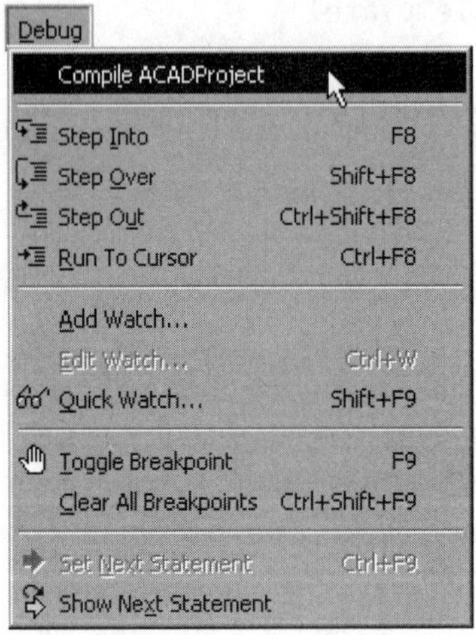

Figure 10.3 *Debug menu commands*

Using Breakpoints

When your application doesn't quite perform up to scratch, you'll more than likely be able to narrow the problem down to a few statements or a single procedure. In the process of debugging, you can set a breakpoint at the start of the problem area, so that when you run your application it will temporarily stop at the breakpoint with all the variable and property values still intact.

The following steps show you how to set a breakpoint at the problematical `If` statement from Listing 10.1:

1. Display the `txtTelephone_KeyPress` event procedure in the Code window.
2. In the Margin Indicator bar that runs down the left border of the Code window, click next to the `If` statement. The line is highlighted, and a dot appears in the Margin Indicator bar.

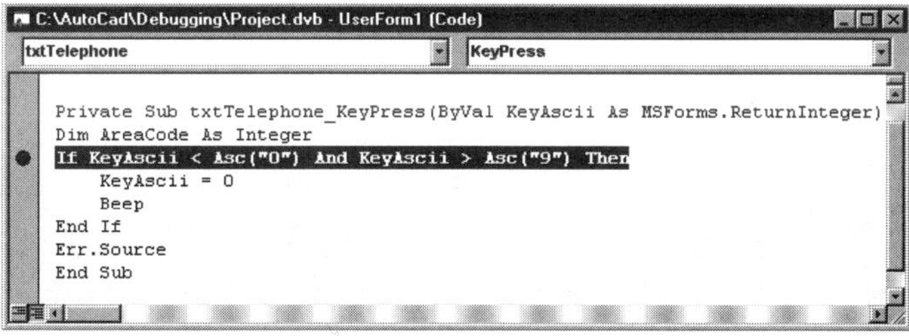

3. Run the Input Validation application you set up earlier, and enter the letter **a** in the text box when prompted. The Code Window appears with the breakpoint statement highlighted and an arrow in the Margin Indicator bar.

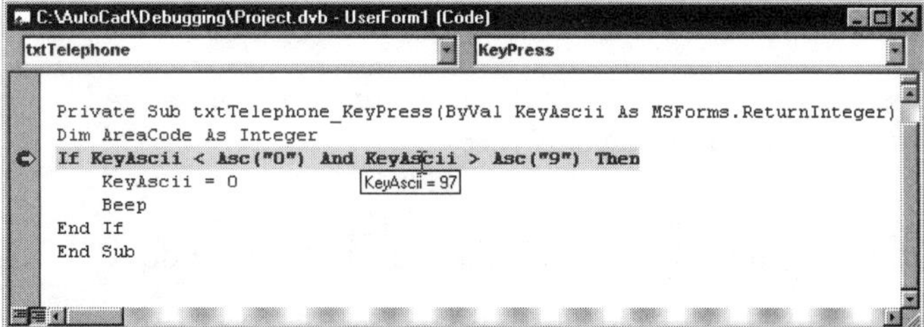

4. Pause the mouse cursor over any of the variables, and a ToolTip box appears with their values.

When you've stopped at a breakpoint, you can drag the little yellow arrow forward or backward to skip or repeat code in the same procedure.

Using Quick Watch

The Quick Watch command displays the values of highlighted sections of code. This is useful for evaluating whole expressions. Let's continue with the `If` statement in the Input Validation example:

1. Highlight the `If` condition as shown in Figure 10.4, and choose Debug ➜ Quick Watch.

   As you can see in the figure, the Quick Watch dialog box appears, with the Context frame indicating the project, the UserForm, and event procedure. The Expression frame contains the segment you have highlighted, and the Value frame contains the result of evaluating the expression. (Of course, you need to have an idea of the value you are expecting in order to know whether the result is correct or not.)

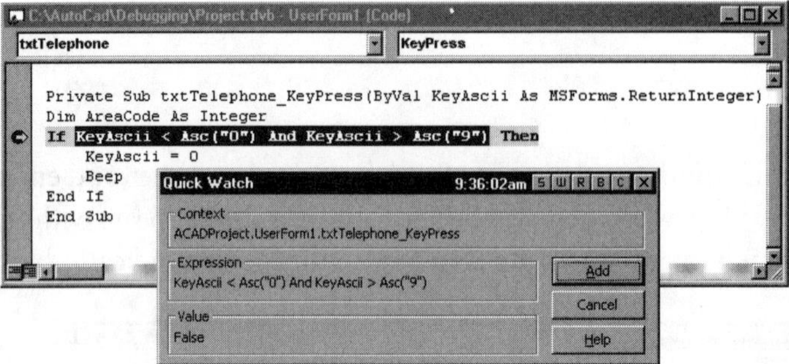

***Figure 10.4** Using the Quick Watch feature to evaluate the condition in the* `If` *statement*

2. Click the Add button in the Quick Watch window.

   You'll see the Watches window (Figure 10.5), containing the information from the Quick Watch dialog box. This window will remain open and allow you to continue watching the selected expression as you work. (The Watches window is described more thoroughly in the upcoming section "Using the IDE's Debugging Windows.")

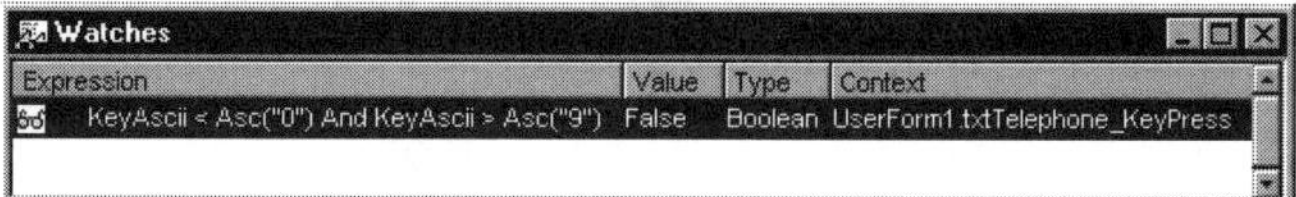

Figure 10.5 *Watches window*

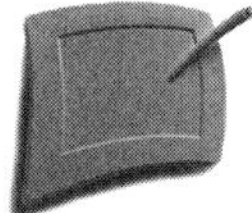

In the Quick Watch window, the value of a variable or a property is shown in a ToolTip if you pause the mouse over that element. An expression can be evaluated in much the same way by highlighting it before positioning the mouse.

Stepping Through Code

When execution has stopped at a breakpoint, there are four commands available in the Debug menu to help you step through the code. Each command works in a slightly different way.

Step Into This command allows you to step through the code statement by statement. It puts your application into run mode, executes the current statement, moves to the next statement, and reverts to break mode. The next statement can be in another procedure.

Step Over With this command you can step over the procedure or function called by the current statement. The procedure or function is completely executed "en block" *before* breaking at the next statement, which is the one after the statement making the call.

Step Out This command steps out of the current procedure by executing any remaining statements, returning to the calling procedure, and breaking at the statement after the call.

Run to Cursor This command runs all the statements, from the current one all the way to the statement containing the insertion cursor, and then enters break mode again.

If you want to watch the value of a variable, property, or expression as it changes over a block of code rather than at a particular breakpoint, you will benefit from making use of the debugging windows that are described in the next section.

Using the IDE's Debugging Windows

The debugging interface allows you to monitor variables and expressions as they change values from statement to statement as you step through your code. The VBA IDE contains three debugging windows that you'll find useful for this purpose: the Immediate window, the Watch window, and the Locals window. In this section you will learn how to interact with these windows and obtain the information you need to complete your debugging process.

The Immediate Window

The Immediate Window allows you to execute specific procedures, change values of variables or properties, and evaluate expressions. You can work inside the Immediate Window while your application is in break mode, or you can add debug statements into your code that will appear in the Immediate Window even while the code is running.

Typing Commands into the Immediate Window

The only command available from inside the Immediate window is the Print method. This displays the values of variables and expressions inside the Immediate window. Because there is only one method belonging to the Debug object, the wildcard character **?** can be used as a quick alternative.

Here are the steps for viewing information from inside the Immediate window using the Print method. We'll demonstrate this by continuing to work with the code in Listing 10.1.

1. Follow the instructions given earlier in the "Using Breakpoints" section, and set a breakpoint at the `If` statement.
2. Choose View ➜ Immediate Window. The Immediate Window appears.
3. Run the Listing 10.1 code and enter a number into the text box. The code stops at the breakpoint, and the Immediate Window appears.
4. Type **`Print KeyAscii`** into the Immediate Window and press Enter. The information requested is displayed as shown in Figure 10.6.

```
Immediate
print keyascii
 49
print asc("9")
 57
print asc("0")
 48
print KeyAscii < Asc("0") Or KeyAscii > Asc("9")
False
```

Figure 10.6 *Using the Print method in the Immediate window*

If you want to see the value of an expression without having to type it, all you need to do is type **Print** (or **?**) into the Immediate Window, cut and paste a copy of the expression, and press the Enter key (see Figure 10.6). The values of properties of any currently accessible UserForm or control can be displayed using the same technique. Here's how the wildcard character can be used to display the values of several variables at once:

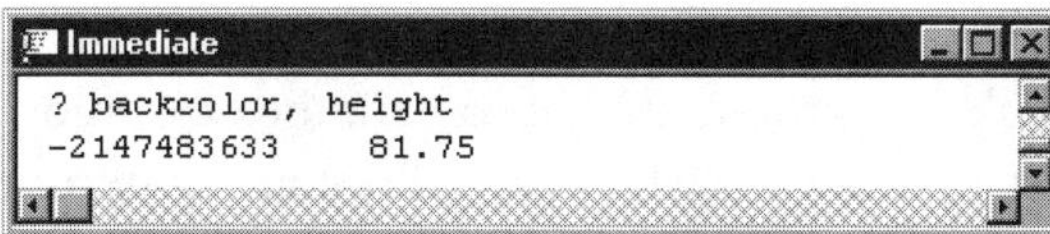

Controlling the Immediate Window from Code

The Print method from the Debug object provides a way of printing information to the Immediate window from your code. The syntax of the `Debug.Print` statement is

```
Debug.Print <outputlist>
```

where the *`outputlist`* is a mixture of strings and variables you want displayed.

You can concatenate as many strings and variables as you like for the *`outputlist`* you pass to the Print method. For example, the following statement

```
Debug.Print number1 & " + " & number2; " = "; answer
```

displays this in the Immediate window:

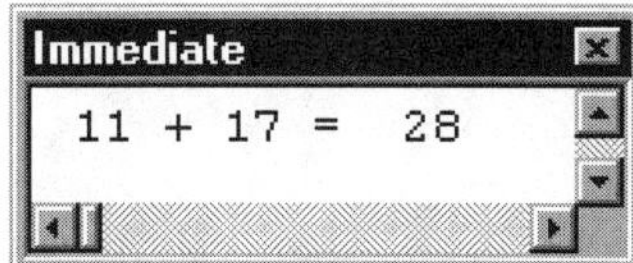

The Watches Window

The Watches Window is used to watch the value of expressions as they change during run time. There are three menu commands available to control this window:

- Add Watch
- Edit Watch
- Quick Watch

The Add and Edit commands allow you to add expressions to be watched and to adjust expressions that are already being watched; these are discussed in the following two sections. The Quick Watch command was described earlier in "Using Breakpoints."

Adding an Expression to the Watches Window

To add an expression to the Watches Window:

1. Highlight the expression in the Code window.
2. Choose Debug ➜ Add Watch. The Add Watch dialog box appears, with the highlighted expression in the Expression box. The Context frame contains the names of the module and procedure that contain the expression. Figure 10.7 shows the Add Watch dialog box when the faulty condition from our example `If` statement is selected.

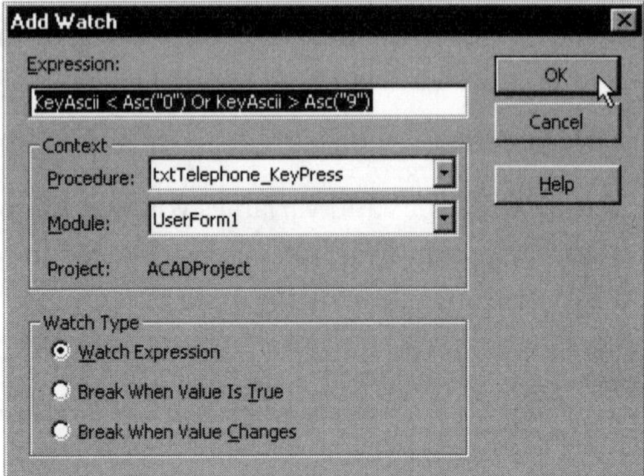

***Figure 10.7** The Immediate window containing the result of the Debug statement*

3. Click OK in the Add Watch dialog box. The Watches Window appears, containing the expression, its value and type, and the UserForm and procedure that contain it.

Editing an Expression in the Watches Window

To edit an expression from within the Watches window:

1. In the Watches window, select the expression to be updated.
2. Choose Debug → Edit Watch. The Edit Watch dialog box opens, with the selected expression highlighted in the Expression box, ready for you to edit (see Figure 10.8). This dialog box is the same as the Add Watch dialog, except that it has an additional button that allows you to delete a watched expression.

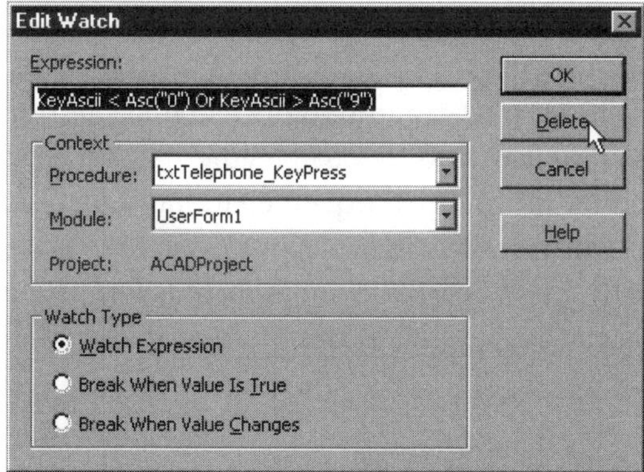

Figure 10.8 *Add Watch dialog box*

The Locals Window

The Locals window displays a list of the properties and variables that can be accessed locally within the current procedure. What you see depends on the module or UserForm to which the procedure belongs. For example, it displays

- The properties of the current UserForm if the procedure is an event procedure
- The global variables from the General Declarations section of the UserForm
- Variables declared locally in the procedure itself

An expression added to the Watches window can be deleted from the Edit Watch dialog box, but it's much simpler just to select it from the Watches window and press the Delete key.

Figure 10.9 shows the Locals window when execution has stopped at a breakpoint inside the cmdContinue_Click event procedure from Listing 7.9 in Chapter 7.

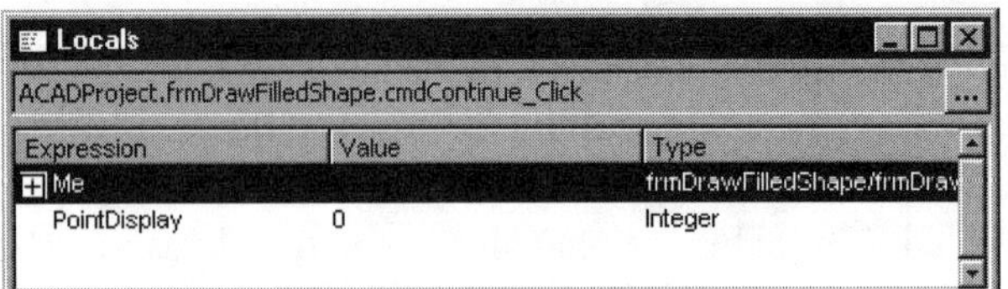

***Figure 10.9** Locals window displaying details about the variables and property values accessible from the event procedure shown at the top of the window*

You'll have no trouble finding your way around the hierarchical structure in the Locals window. Just click the Plus icon next to Me in Figure 10.9, for example. The Plus changes to a Minus icon, and the list for Me is expanded to show all the values of its properties (see Figure 10.10, which shows cmdContinue expanded, as well). The Me keyword refers to the currently active UserForm and is included in the Locals window for the Click event because it can be accessed by this event procedure.

Locals

ACADProject.frmDrawFilledShape.cmdContinue_Click

Expression	Value	Type
Me		frmDrawFilledShape/frmDraw
_Default	"???¶?¶□□□□ □□□??□□□	String
BackColor	-2147483633	OLE_COLOR
BorderColor	-2147483630	OLE_COLOR
BorderStyle	fmBorderStyleNone	fmBorderStyle
Caption	"Drawing Filled Shapes"	String
cboFillPattern		ComboBox/ComboBox
cboPointMiddle		ComboBox/ComboBox
chkCircleAroundPoint		CheckBox/CheckBox
chkSquareAroundPoint		CheckBox/CheckBox
cmdCancel		CommandButton/CommandBu
CmdContinue		CommandButton/CommandBu
Accelerator	"o"	String
AutoSize	False	Boolean
BackColor	-2147483633	OLE_COLOR
BackStyle	fmBackStyleOpaque	fmBackStyle
BoundValue	False	Variant/Boolean
Cancel	False	Boolean
Caption	"Continue"	String
ControlSource	<Could not set the ControlSo	String
ControlTipText	""	String
Default	False	Boolean

***Figure 10.10** Expanded lists show the values for all properties*

The `Me` *keyword provides a way to refer to the form associated with the code that's currently running.*

The Locals window for a macro placed in a module contains any global declarations made at the start of the module, and any local variables from the macro (Figure 10.11).

Locals

ACADProject.Module1.GetShape

Expression	Value	Type
Module1		Module1/Module1
NumberOfElements	0	Integer
PolyArray		Double()
PolygonObject		AcadPolyline(0 to 0)
PolygonObject(0)	Nothing	AcadPolyline
NewPoint	Nothing	AcadPoint
Point3D	Empty	Variant/Empty
Finished	False	Boolean

Figure 10.11 *Locals window for a macro from a standard module*

The Locals window for a drawing document is shown in Figure 10.12. In this case, Me is used to refer to the current drawing document and contains things such as `ActiveUCS` and `ActiveViewport`, which are related to the Model Space.

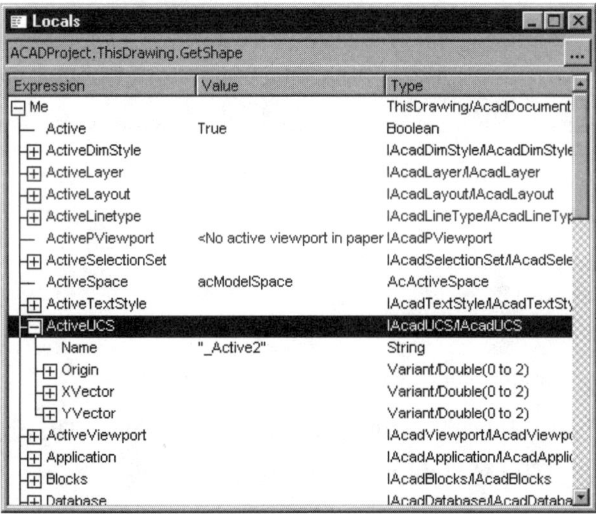

Figure 10.12 *Locals window for a drawing document*

Which Debugging Aid to Use?

Following are some suggestions for getting the most out of the IDE's debugging windows:

Immediate Window When you need to follow a variable's value changes as your program runs, use a `Debug.Print` statement in your code to print a variable's value to the Immediate window. That way you have a record of the changes as a reference and for analysis after your program has finished running. You'll find this much easier than stepping through line-by-line and trying to remember what happened.

Locals Window Use the Locals window when you need to examine a large number of variables at once. For this task, Locals is easier to use than Watches.

Watches Window Use the Watches window when you want to evaluate more complex expressions. (Alternatively, you can assign the results of an expression to a single variable and use a `Debug.Print` statement.) Or use the Watches window if you just want to break when the variable reaches some value.

The Call Stack

The View menu contains a Call Stack command that is only available when you're in break mode during run time. The Call stack contains the sequence of calls that have been made to get to the current procedure. The following steps show you how to view the Call Stack dialog box.

1. Start a new project and add a UserForm containing a text box.
2. Type the code given in Listing 10.2 into the Code window for ThisDrawing.
3. Add the following into the skeleton event procedure in UserForm1's Code window. This code calls procedure B from ThisDrawing's Code window.

```
Private Sub TextBox1_Change()
ThisDrawing.B
End Sub
```

4. Set a breakpoint at the `End Sub` statement of procedure C.
5. Click anywhere inside procedure A and run your project. The project will start running at procedure A and so will display UserForm1.

6. Enter a character into the text box to execute its Change event procedure. Procedure B of ThisDrawing is executed, which calls procedure C. Procedure C sets variable A to the character entered in the text box and unloads the UserForm before stopping at the breakpoint.
7. Choose View → Call Stack. Figure 10.13 shows the Call Stack dialog box.

Remember that the Call Stack menu command is only available when running in break mode.

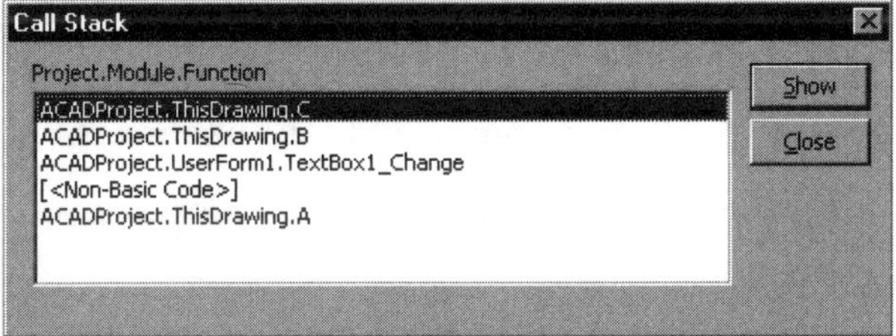

Figure 10.13 *The Call stack*

LISTING 10.2

```
Sub A()
    UserForm1.show
    B
End Sub

Sub B()
    C
End Sub

Sub C()
    Dim A As String
    A = UserForm1.TextBox1.Text
    Unload UserForm1
End Sub
```

Analysis

- Lines 1 through 4 contain procedure A, which displays `UserForm1` and calls procedure B.
- Lines 6 through 8 contain procedure B, which calls procedure C.
- Line 10 through 14 contain procedure C, which assigns the contents of the text box to variable A and unloads `UserForm1`.

Summary

After reading this chapter, you will know the following about debugging your AutoCAD VBA code:

- Distinguishing between logic, compiler, and run-time errors.
- How to set the Auto Syntax Check option to get feedback as you enter code.
- The function of the Err object.
- How to set breakpoints.
- Using the Quick Watch menu command.
- How to step through your code line by line.
- How to step over all the code in a procedure called from the code you are testing.
- How to step out of the procedure you are in and return to the statement after the one that called it.
- How to enter a Print command in the Immediate Window.
- How to display details in the Immediate Window from code.
- Adding expressions to the Watch Window.
- Editing expressions from the Watch Window.
- Using the Locals Window.

Dimensioning Drawings from Your Own Menus and Toolbars

AUTOCAD VBA

Chapter 11

This chapter shows you how you can add measurements to your drawings using various dimensioning styles, by selecting options within a VBA application. Most of these are the same styles represented on AutoCAD's Dimension menu and Dimensions toolbar, but you can also create your own custom dimension styles.

Up until now in this book, you've run macros from the Macros dialog box or from controls placed on a UserForm. Here in this chapter you'll learn how to add your own menus and toolbars from which to select and run your macros. Obviously, you don't want to add too many menu items, but macros used on a regular basis are prime candidates for such customization. In exploring customization, you'll code macros to customize a new group of menu commands in the AutoCAD window. These custom commands will apply the dimensioning styles by instigating the same event procedures as the original VBA application—without the user's ever needing to click a button. You'll then create a toolbar with buttons for quick access to the custom dimensioning commands.

This chapter covers the following topics:

- AutoCAD's dimensioning styles
- Dimensioning drawings from an application
- Customizing menu commands
- Creating a menu to run macros
- Creating your own toolbar
- Adding toolbar buttons

AutoCAD's Dimensioning Styles

AutoCAD provides six different dimensioning styles for including measurements in your drawings, to provide the lengths of lines and sizes of angles that make up the separate parts. To add a measurement from the AutoCAD window, you first select the drawing object to be dimensioned. Then you're prompted to designate any other information, such as positions for the various parts, needed for achieving the dimension style. AutoCAD does the rest and then displays the measurement.

The six dimensioning styles are available from the commands of the pull-down Dimension menu group—three commands for dimensioning lines, and three for dimensioning arcs and circles. The commands are shown in Figure 11.1.

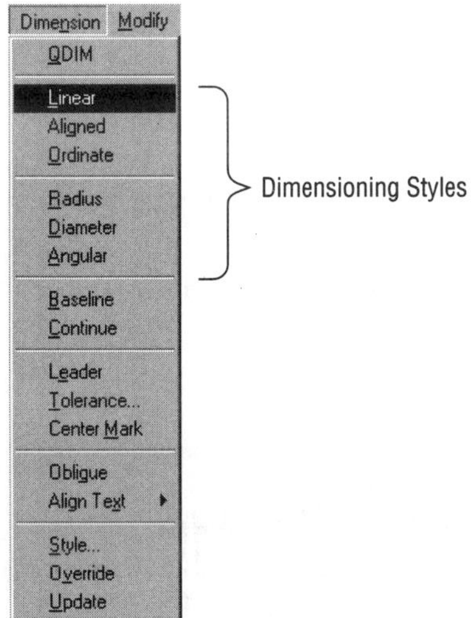

Figure 11.1 *Dimensioning styles available from the Dimension menu*

You are very likely familiar with AutoCAD's Dimension toolbar (Figure 11.2). The buttons on this toolbar not only provide a quick way of running Dimension menu commands but also give a graphical representation of the function that will be performed if that button is clicked.

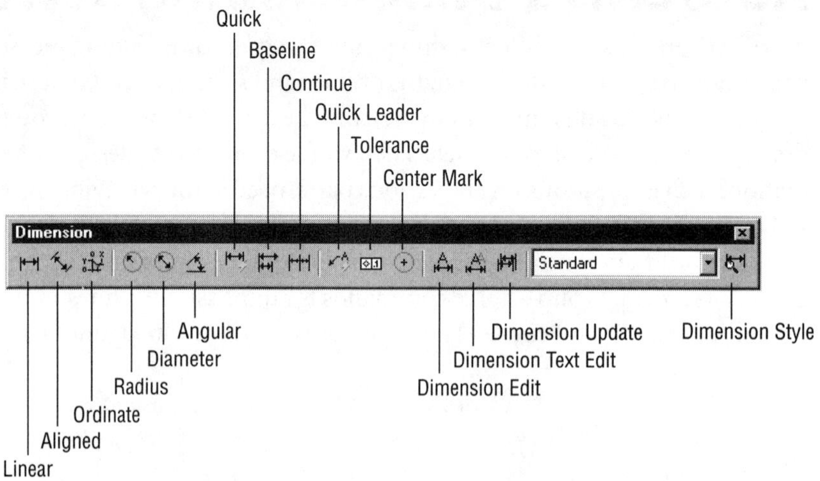

Figure 11.2 *AutoCAD's Dimension toolbar*

Of course, measurements can also be added from VBA code. We'll explore this process in the sections coming up.

Figure 11.3 demonstrates how the styles affect the dimensions added to a drawing.

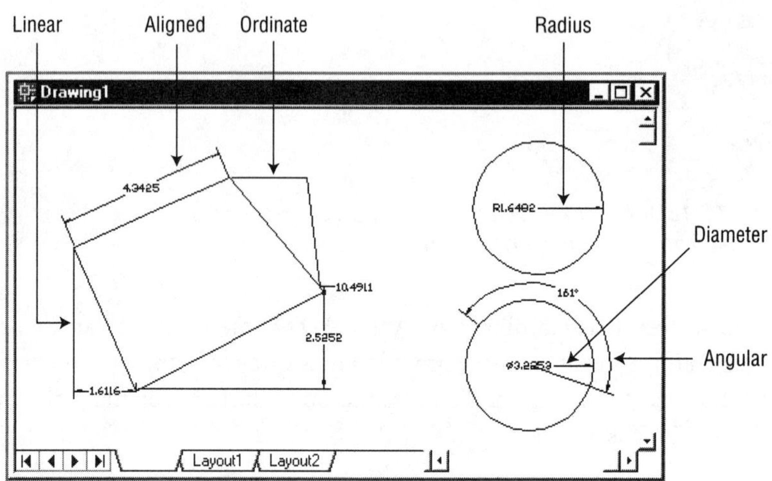

Figure 11.3 *Effects of dimension styles*

Dimensioning Drawings from an Application

The AutoCAD object model has seven objects to represent the dimension styles—Aligned, Angular, Diametric, Ordinate, Radial, Rotated, and 3 Point Angular (see Figure 11.4). As you can see, these are almost equivalent to what's available from the AutoCAD window. The differences are that the Dimension menu's Linear style is missing from the object model, and the model has two others that don't have equivalents on the Dimension menu: Rotated and 3 Point Angular.

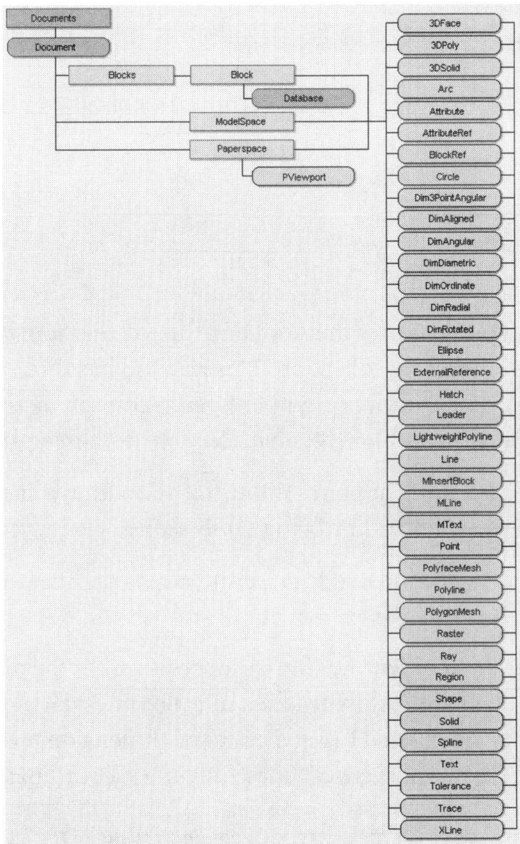

Figure 11.4 *Dimension objects in the AutoCAD object model*

In the sections that follow, each dimension style is described briefly. Then we'll go on to creating a small application that demonstrates how an object for each dimension style can be created in code.

The Aligned Dimensioning Style

The Aligned dimensioning style draws a linear dimension. The measurement text is positioned halfway along the line being dimensioned, accompanied by two arrows pointing outward from the text toward the two line extensions (see Figure 11.5).

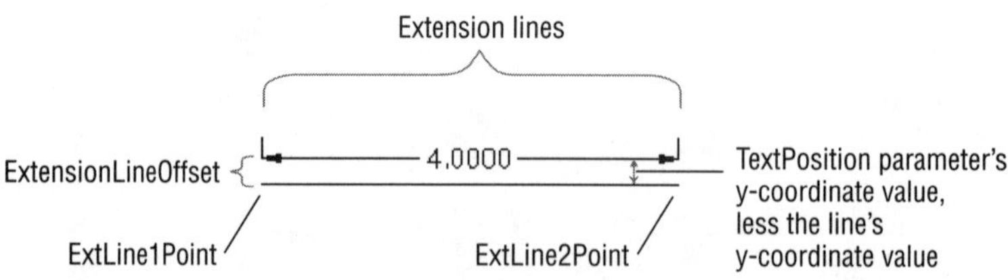

Figure 11.5 *Line with Aligned dimensioning*

The Aligned dimensioning style uses the AddDimAligned method to add a DimAligned object to the ModelSpace collection. This method has three parameters, of Variant type, that expect to be passed three arguments, each containing the x-, y-, and z-coordinates of a point in an array of type Double. Here are the three parameters:

ExtLine1Point This is the first endpoint of the extension line, which is often at the same position as the start of the line being dimensioned.

ExtLine2Point This is the second endpoint of the extension line, which is usually at the endpoint of the line being dimensioned.

TextPosition This parameter identifies the offset position for the dimension text, which is always centered along the dimensioned line. For lines that are mainly horizontal, only the y-coordinate is used to determine the dimension text's distance from the line; similarly, for mainly vertical lines, only the x-coordinate is used.

For dimension objects, VBA only utilizes either the x- or the y-coordinate value of the TextPosition, depending on whether the line being dimensioned is closer to being horizontal or closer to being vertical.

These three parameters aren't quite enough to define all the attributes of the dimension style shown in Figure 11.3, however. You also need to set the ExtensionLine-Offset property to control the distance between the extension line and the line being dimensioned.

The DimAligned object also has numerous properties you can set to your liking. Figure 11.6 shows the effect of setting the properties that define the color, line weight, arrowhead size, and extension line offset attributes.

Figure 11.6 *The aligned dimension produced by setting the properties for color, line weight, arrowhead size, and extension line offset*

The Angular Dimensioning Style

The Angular dimensioning style displays an angular dimension for a circle (or an arc), given the circle's center and the two points on the circumference that are intersected by the extension lines (see Figure 11.7).

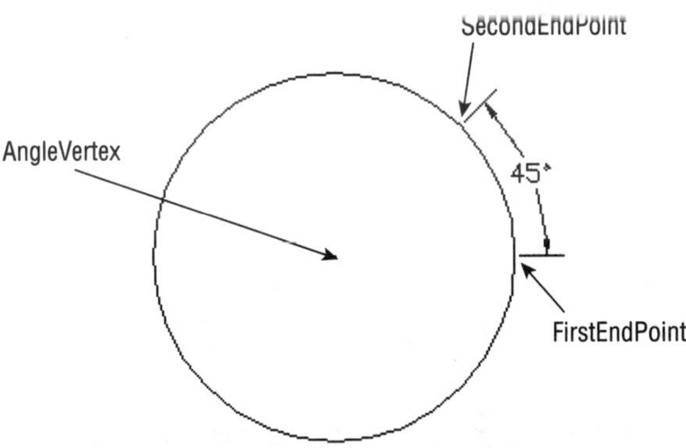

Figure 11.7 *The Angular dimensioning style*

The AddDimAngular method creates a DimAngular object and adds it to the ModelSpace collection. This method has four Variant parameters that all expect to be passed the x-, y-, and z-coordinates of points as an array of Doubles. Here are the parameters:

AngleVertex The center of the circle or the arc, or the point where the two dimensioned lines meet.

FirstEndPoint The point where the first extension line intersects with the circle or arc.

SecondEndPoint The point where the second extension line intersects with the circle or arc.

TextPoint The position for the dimension text.

The Diametric Dimensioning Style

The Diametric dimensioning style displays the length of the diameter of a circle or an arc (see Figure 11.8). It requires the two endpoints that define the diameter and the length of the leader line. The AddDimDiametric method has three parameters:

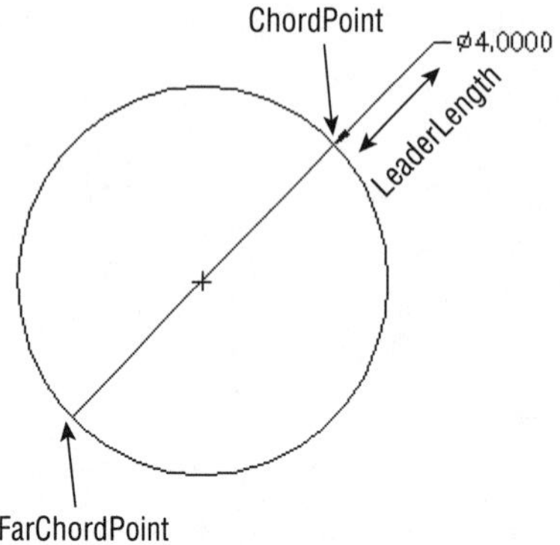

Figure 11.8 *The Diametric dimensioning style*

ChordPoint This parameter is a Variant type containing the x-, y-, and z-coordinates of the diameter point on the circle nearest to where the dimensioning text will appear.

FarChordPoint This is a Variant containing the coordinates of the diameter point on the circle farthest from where the dimensioning text will appear. If this point is at a 180° rotation from the ChordPoint, then the diametric dimension will pass through the center of the circle and will equal the length of the diameter (see Figure 11.8). If this point is *not* at a 180° rotation, the diametric dimension measurement will be less than the diameter (see Figure 11.9).

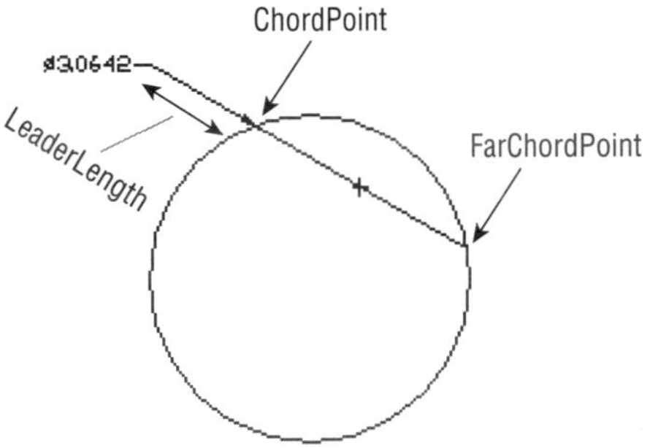

Figure 11.9 *The diametric dimension when the ChordPoint is 110° around the circle's circumference and the FarChordPoint is 10°*

LeaderLength This parameter is a Double type and is passed the distance between the first diameter point and the dimension text.

The Ordinate Dimensioning Style

The Ordinate dimensioning style displays the x- or y-coordinate value of the definition point. It has an arrow from a leader endpoint to the specified definition point (see Figure 11.10). If the arrow is more horizontal than it is vertical, the dimension text will display the x-coordinate; otherwise it will display the y-coordinate. For example, in Figure 11.10 the definition points in the two bottom circles have their y-coordinates displayed, and the upper two dimensions have their x-coordinates displayed.

The Ordinate dimensioning style is based on the origin, which is often repositioned somewhere on the object. In Figure 11.10, I chose Tools ➜ Move UCS and moved the UCS icon to the bottom-left corner of the rectangle to make it the new position for the origin.

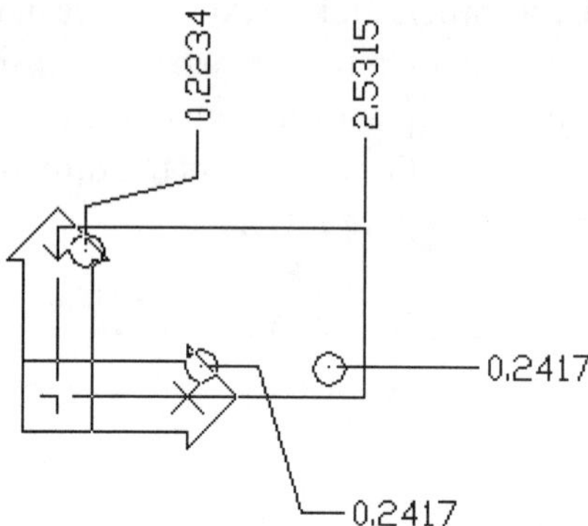

Figure 11.10 *Ordinate dimensioning style*

When creating an ordinate dimension from the AutoCAD window, you will be prompted to select the definition point and then the leader endpoint. As you move the mouse to specify the leader endpoint, the arrow will sometimes zigzag its way to the position of the DefinitionPoint if it can't draw a horizontal or vertical line directly there.

The AddDimOrdinate method creates a DimOrdinate object and adds it to the ModelSpace collection. This method has three parameters:

DefinitionPoint This is the point to be dimensioned that's declared as a Variant type but expects to be passed a three-element array of Double types.

LeaderEndPoint This is the endpoint for the leader line and the point where the dimension text will be displayed. This is a Variant that expects to be passed a three-element array of Doubles.

UseXAxis This Boolean parameter, when set to True, displays the x-coordinate value of the definition point as the dimension text; otherwise, the y-coordinate value is displayed.

The Radial Dimensioning Style

The Radial dimensioning style displays the length of the radius of a circle or an arc (see Figure 11.11).

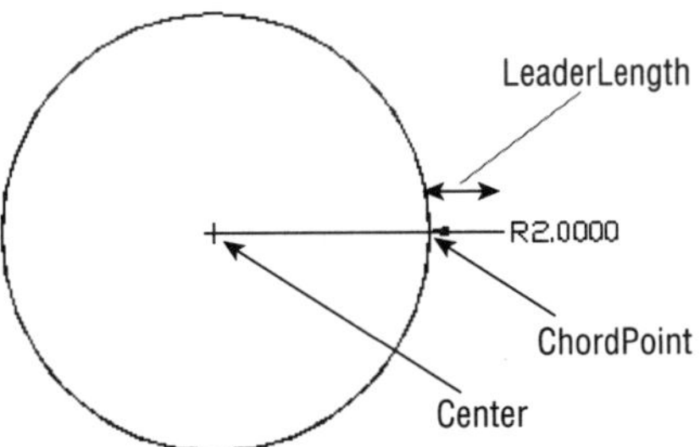

Figure 11.11 *Radial dimensioning type*

If the gradient of the dimension line is greater than 15° and the dimension text is outside the circle or arc, then AutoCAD will draw a hook line that is one arrowhead in length, as shown here:

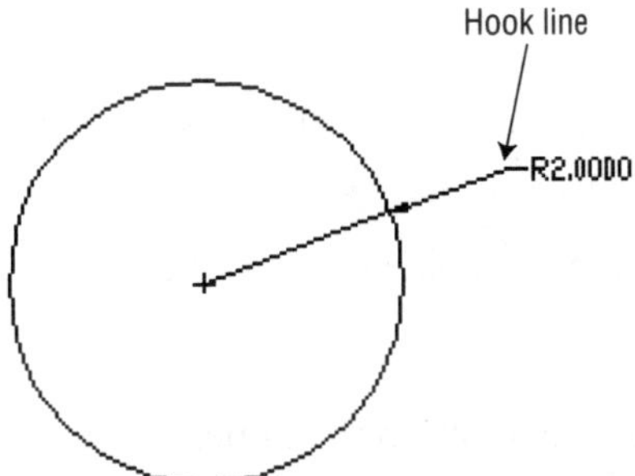

The AddDimRadial method is called to create a new DimRadial object and add it to the ModelSpace collection. This method has three parameters:

Center This parameter is declared as a Variant and is passed the coordinates of the center point of the circle or arc as an array.

ChordPoint This parameter is a Variant and is passed the coordinates defining the point where the leader line is attached to the circle or arc.

LeaderLength This Double-type parameter represents the length between the dimension text and the point defined by ChordPoint.

The Rotated Dimensioning Style

The Rotated style is similar to the Aligned style, but instead of the dimension text and leader lines being parallel to the line being dimensioned, they are rotated by a specified number of degrees. The extension lines are adjusted so that the leader lines (if extended) pass through a specified point (see Figure 11.12).

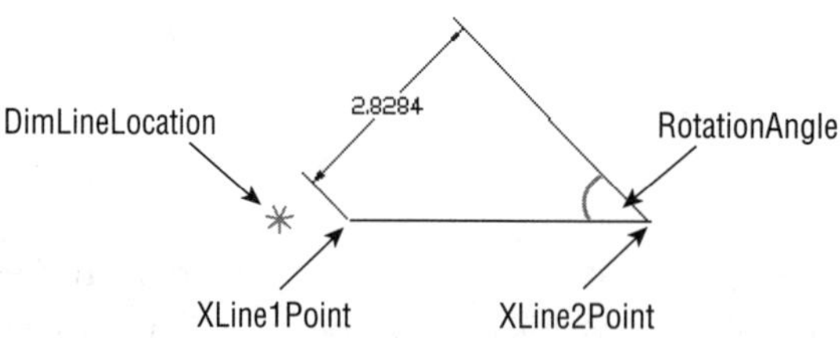

Figure 11.12 *Rotated dimensioning style*

The AddDimRotated method has four parameters. The first three are Variant types that expect to be passed three-element arrays of type Double.

XLine1Point This is the start of the line being dimensioned.

XLine2Point This is the end of the line being dimensioned.

DimLineLocation This identifies the point on the dimension line.

RotationAngle This specifies the angle of rotation in radians for displaying the dimension text.

The 3 Point Angular Dimensioning Style

The 3 Point Angular dimensioning style measures the angle between three points (see Figure 11.13).

The AddDimAngular method creates an angular dimension for a circle, an arc, or the angle between two lines. This method has four parameters; all are declared as Variant types but expect to be passed three-element arrays of type Double.

AngleVertex This parameter contains the coordinates of the vertex of the angle being measured. This is often the center of a circle or an arc but can also be the common vertex of two lines.

FirstEndPoint This is the point of intersection between the drawing object and the first extension line.

SecondEndPoint This is the point where the extension line intersects with the drawing object.

TextPoint This is the position in the drawing document where the dimension text will be displayed.

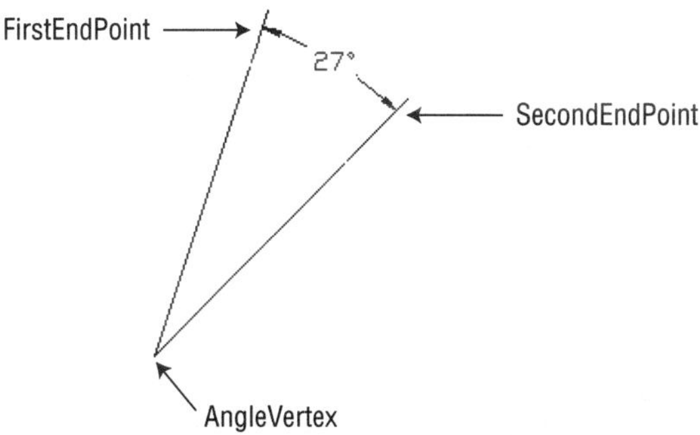

***Figure 11.13** 3 Point Angular dimensioning style*

A Dimensioning Application

Let's create a simple application that contains a single UserForm with a frame containing an option button for each style. This application (Exercise 11.1) is illustrated in Figure 11.14.

Exercise 11.1: Creating a Dimensioning Application

1. Start a new project and insert a UserForm.
2. Add a frame and a command button.
3. Place seven option button controls inside the frame—one for each Dimension object.
4. Change the properties of the UserForm and controls to those shown in Table 11.1.

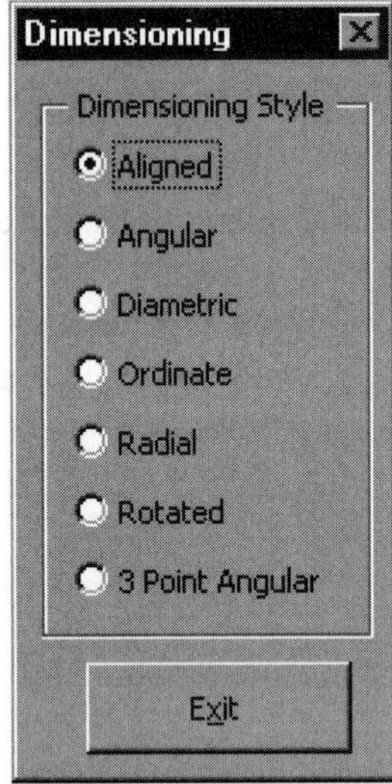

Figure 11.14 *GUI for selecting a dimensioning style*

Table 11.1 Properties for the Dimensioning UserForm

OLD NAME	NEW NAME	CAPTION
UserForm1	frmDimensionStyles	Dimensioning
Frame1	—	Dimensioning Style
OptionButton1	optAligned	Aligned
OptionButton2	optAngular	Angular
OptionButton3	optDiametric	Diametric
OptionButton4	optOrdinate	Ordinate
OptionButton5	optRadial	Radial
OptionButton6	optRotated	Rotated
OptionButton7	opt3PointAngular	3 Point Angular
CommandButton1	cmdExit	Exit

Now you can begin entering the code to draw each of the seven styles of dimension. All these listings, 11.1 through 11.8, are on the book's CD.

First up is the Aligned dimension. Enter the code from Listing 11.1 into the event procedure in the UserForm Code window. This will draw an Aligned dimension when the user clicks the optAligned option button.

Listing 11.1: Adding an Aligned Dimension Object

```
1   Private Sub optAligned_Click()
2      Dim DimensionObject As AcadDimAligned
3      Dim LineObject As AcadLine
4      Set LineObject = ThisDrawing.ModelSpace.AddLine( ↵
          Point1, Point2)
5      LineObject.Update
6      Set DimensionObject = ↵
          ThisDrawing.ModelSpace.AddDimAligned( ↵
          Point1, Point2, TextPosition)
7      DimensionObject.ExtensionLineOffset = Offset
8   DimensionObject.ArrowheadSize = 0.5
9   DimensionObject.Color = acCyan
10  ThisDrawing.Preferences.LineWeightDisplay = True
11  DimensionObject.DimensionLineWeight = acLnWt030
12     DimensionObject.Update
13     ZoomAll
14  End Sub
```

Analysis

- Line 1 starts the event procedure that will run when the Aligned option button is clicked.
- Line 2 declares the `DimensionObject` variable that will be set up to refer to a `DimAligned` object.
- Lines 3 through 5 declare the `LineObject` variable, set it to refer to the new Line object being added, and update the drawing in Model Space to display the line. The variables `Point1` and `Point2`, used as arguments, are declared in the General Declarations section in Line 3 of Listing 11.8 and assigned values in Lines 13 and 14 of that listing.

- Line 6 creates a new `DimAligned` object and sets up the variable `DimensionObject` to refer to it. `Point1` and `Point2` of the actual line are used to define the extension line. The `TextPosition` argument is global to the UserForm; it is declared at Line 4 of Listing 11.8 and assigned values in Lines 16 through 18 of that listing.
- Line 7 sets the `ExtensionLineOffset` property to the distance required between the start of the extension lines and the line being dimensioned (see Figure 11.3). The default value of this property is 0.0625.
- Lines 8 and 9 increase the arrowhead size and the color for the text, arrows, and extension lines.
- Line 10 sets the `LineWeightDisplay` property of the `Preferences` object to True so that the adjustment made to the line's weight at Line 11 will take effect when the dimensioning elements are drawn by the `Update` method at Line 12.
- Line 11 sets the `DimensionLineWeight` property to an AutoCAD constant to define the thickness of leader lines.
- Line 12 redraws the `DimensionObject` in the Model Space.
- Line 13 ensures that all drawing objects are displayed on the screen.
- Line 14 ends the Click event procedure for drawing Aligned dimensions.

Next, enter the code shown in Listing 11.2. This draws an Angular dimension in response to the user's clicking the `optAngular` option button.

LISTING 11.2: ADDING AN ANGULAR DIMENSION OBJECT

```
Private Sub optAngular_Click()
    Dim DimensionObject As AcadDimAngular
    Dim CircleObject As AcadCircle
    Dim FirstEndPoint(0 To 2) As Double
    Dim SecondEndPoint(0 To 2) As Double
    Set CircleObject = ThisDrawing.ModelSpace.AddCircle( ↵
       Center, Radius)
    CircleObject.Update
    FirstEndPoint(0) = Center(0) + Radius
    FirstEndPoint(1) = Center(1)
    FirstEndPoint(2) = Center(2)
    SecondEndPoint(0) = Center(0) + ↵
```

```
           Radius * Cos(45 * Pi / 180)
12      SecondEndPoint(1) = Center(1) + ↵
           Radius * Sin(45 * Pi / 180)
13      SecondEndPoint(2) = Center(2)
14      Set DimensionObject = ↵
           ThisDrawing.ModelSpace.AddDimAngular( ↵
           Center, FirstEndPoint, SecondEndPoint, TextPosition)
15      DimensionObject.AngleFormat = acDegrees
16      DimensionObject.Update
17      ZoomAll
18  End Sub
```

Analysis

- Line 1 starts the event procedure that runs whenever the Angular option button is clicked.
- Lines 2 and 3 declare the variables for referring to the `DimAngular` and `Circle` objects.
- Lines 4 and 5 declare the two arrays to hold the coordinates for the two endpoints of the arc.
- Line 6 creates a Circle object and sets up the `CircleObject` variable to reference it.
- Line 7 draws the new Circle object in the Model Space.
- Lines 8 through 10 assign the coordinates of the starting point for the arc.
- Line 11 through 13 assign the coordinates of the endpoint for the arc. These coordinates are assigned the values of the point where a line drawn at 45° to the *x*-axis would intersect with the circle. The 45° are converted to radians in the calls to the `Cos` and `Sin` functions.
- Line 14 uses the `AddDimAngular` method to create a `DimAngular` object and adds it to the ModelSpace collection. This line also sets up the `DimensionObject` variable as a reference to the object.
- Line 15 sets the `AngleFormat` property to the AutoCAD enumerated type `acDegrees` (the default). Other formats available for this property are `acAngleUnits`, `acDegreeMinuteSeconds`, `acGrads`, and `acRadians`.
- Line 16 draws the Dimension object in the Model Space.

- Line 17 calls the `ZoomAll` method to display all the drawing objects in the active viewport.
- Line 18 ends the Click event procedure of the Angular option button.

Next up is the Diametric dimension. Enter the code shown in Listing 11.3, which contains the Click event procedure for the Diametric option button.

Listing 11.3: Adding a Diametric Dimension Object

```
1    Private Sub optDiametric_Click()
2        Dim DimensionObject As AcadDimDiametric
3        Dim LineObject As AcadLine
4        Dim CircleObject As AcadCircle
5        Dim ChordPoint(0 To 2) As Double, ↵
            FarChordPoint(0 To 2) As Double
6        Set CircleObject = ThisDrawing.ModelSpace.AddCircle( ↵
            Center, Radius)
7        CircleObject.Update
8        ChordPoint(0) = Center(0) + Radius * Cos(45 * Pi / 180)
9        ChordPoint(1) = Center(1) + Radius * Sin(45 * Pi / 180)
10       ChordPoint(2) = Center(2)
11       FarChordPoint(0) = Center(0) + ↵
            Radius * Cos(225 * Pi / 180)
12       FarChordPoint(1) = Center(1) + ↵
            Radius * Sin(225 * Pi / 180)
13       FarChordPoint(2) = Center(2)
14       Set LineObject = ThisDrawing.ModelSpace.AddLine( ↵
            ChordPoint, FarChordPoint)
15       LineObject.Update
16       Set DimensionObject = ↵
            ThisDrawing.ModelSpace.AddDimDiametric(ChordPoint, ↵
            FarChordPoint, 1.5)
17       DimensionObject.Update
18       ZoomAll
19   End Sub
```

Analysis

- Line 1 starts the Click event procedure of `optDiametric`, which runs whenever the Diametric option button is clicked.

- Line 2 declares the `DimensionObject` variable as being capable of referring to a `DimDiametric` type of object.
- Line 3 declares the `LineObject` variable as being capable of referring to a Line object. This variable will be set to the line that's created for displaying the diameter.
- Line 4 declares the Circle object that will be diametrically dimensioned.
- Line 5 declares `ChordPoint` and `FarChordPoint` as three-element arrays of Double types.
- Line 6 creates a Circle object and adds it to the ModelSpace collection.
- Line 7 draws the circle in the Model Space.
- Lines 8 through 10 assign the values to the `ChordPoint` array using the `Cos` and `Sin` functions to calculate the x- and y-coordinates at 45° around the circle's circumference.

The `Cos` and `Sin` functions expect the angle passed to their parameters to be specified in radians rather than degrees. To convert from degrees to radians, multiply the number of degrees by pi/180, where pi is declared as a constant and given the value 3.14159 (see Listing 11.9).

- Lines 11 through 13 use the `Cos` and `Sin` functions to calculate the point on the circumference at 225° and assign its coordinates to the elements of the `FarChordPoint` array.
- Lines 14 and 15 create a Line object containing the `ChordPoint` and `FarChordPoint` as the two endpoints specifying the line, and draw the line in the Model Space.
- Line 16 calls the `AddDimDiametric` method to add a dimension for the line just drawn. The third argument passes 1.5 to the `LeaderLength` parameter that determines the distance of the leader drawn between the dimension text and the `ChordPoint`.
- Line 17 calls the `Update` method to draw the dimension text and leader line.
- Line 18 calls the `ZoomAll` method to adjust the current viewport so that all the drawing objects are visible.
- Line 19 ends the Click event procedure of the `optDiametric` option button.

Next, enter the event procedure shown in Listing 11.4, which displays an ordinate dimension.

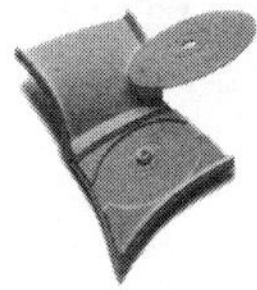

Listing 11.4: Adding an Ordinate Dimension Object

```
1   Private Sub optOrdinate_Click()
2      Dim DimensionObject As AcadDimOrdinate
3      Dim LineObject As AcadLine
4      Dim DefinitionPoint(0 To 2) As Double
5      Dim LeaderEndPoint(0 To 2) As Double
6      Set LineObject = ThisDrawing.ModelSpace.AddLine( ↵
          Point1, Point2)
7      LineObject.Update
8      DefinitionPoint(0) = (Point1(0) + Point2(0)) / 2#
9      DefinitionPoint(1) = (Point1(1) + Point2(1)) / 2#
10     DefinitionPoint(2) = (Point1(2) + Point2(2)) / 2#
11     LeaderEndPoint(0) = DefinitionPoint(0)
12     LeaderEndPoint(1) = DefinitionPoint(1) + 2#
13     LeaderEndPoint(2) = DefinitionPoint(2)
14     Set DimensionObject = ↵
          ThisDrawing.ModelSpace.AddDimOrdinate( ↵
          DefinitionPoint, LeaderEndPoint, True)
15     DimensionObject.ExtensionLineOffset = Offset
16     DimensionObject.Update
17     ZoomAll
18  End Sub
```

Analysis

- Line 1 starts the Click event procedure of the `optOrdinate` option button.
- Line 2 declares the `DimensionObject` variable as being capable of referencing a `DimOrdinate` object.
- Line 3 declares the `LineObject` variable as being capable of referencing a Line object.
- Lines 4 and 5 declare the `DefinitionPoint` and `LeaderEndPoint` arrays that are passed as arguments in the call to the `AddDimOrdinate` method.
- Line 6 creates a Line object containing the line defined by the two endpoints `Point1` and `Point2` that are assigned x-, y-, and z-coordinate values in the `UserForm_Initialize` event procedure of Listing 11.8.

- Line 7 redraws the line in the Model Space.
- Lines 8 through 10 assign the coordinates of the midpoint of the line created at Line 6 to the `DefinitionPoint` array.
- Lines 11 through 13 assign to the `LeaderEndPoint` array the coordinates of a point that is two units directly above the `DefinitionPoint`.
- Line 14 calls the `AddDimOrdinate` method to create a new `DimOrdinate` object and add it to the ModelSpace collection. This method is passed a point on the line and the leader's endpoint, with the `UseXAxis` parameter passing `True` to display the x-axis value.
- Line 15 uses the `ExtensionLineOffset` to specify the distance between the extension lines and the origin points. The `Offset` variable is set to 0.25 in the `UserForm_Initialize` event procedure given in Listing 11.8; the default value for this property is 0.625.
- Line 16 redraws the Dimension object in the Model Space.
- Line 17 calls the `ZoomAll` method to display all the drawing objects in the Model Space.
- Line 18 ends the `optOrdinate` Click event procedure.

Next up is the Radial dimension. To add this to the application, enter the code for the `optRadial_Click` event procedure given in Listing 11.5.

LISTING 11.5: ADD A RADIAL DIMENSION OBJECT

```
Private Sub optRadial_Click()
    Dim DimensionObject As AcadDimRadial
    Dim CircleObject As AcadCircle
    Dim LineObject As AcadLine
    Dim ChordPoint(0 To 2) As Double
    Set CircleObject = ThisDrawing.ModelSpace.AddCircle( ↵
       Center, Radius)
    CircleObject.Update
    ChordPoint(0) = Center(0) + Radius
    ChordPoint(1) = Center(1)
    ChordPoint(2) = Center(2)
    Set LineObject = ThisDrawing.ModelSpace.AddLine( ↵
       Center, ChordPoint)
```

```
12        LineObject.Update
13        Set DimensionObject = ↵
             ThisDrawing.ModelSpace.AddDimRadial( ↵
             Center, ChordPoint, 1.25)
14        DimensionObject.Update
15        ZoomAll
16    End Sub
```

Analysis

- Line 1 starts the Click event procedure for the Radial option button.
- Line 2 declares the `DimensionObject` variable as being capable of referencing a `DimRadial` object.
- Line 3 declares the `CircleObject` variable as being capable of referencing a Circle object.
- Line 4 declares the `LineObject` variable as being capable of referring to a Line object. The Line object is used to display the radius being dimensioned.
- Line 5 declares the `ChordPoint` array with three elements.
- Lines 6 and 7 create the Circle object and draw it in the Model Space.
- Lines 8 through 10 assign values to the `ChordPoint` array to specify the coordinates of the point to which the leader will be attached.
- Line 11 draws a line representing the radius from the center to the point for the leader.
- Line 12 draws the radius in the Model Space.
- Line 13 calls the `AddDimRadial` method to create a `DimRadial` object that will display the radius as the measurement in the dimension text.
- Lines 14 and 15 redraw the Dimension object and ensure that all drawing objects appear in the Model Space.
- Line 16 ends the Click event procedure of the Radial option button.

Next, enter the Click event procedure for the `optRotated` option button (Listing 11.6).

Listing 11.6: Adding a Rotated Dimension Object

```
1   Private Sub optRotated_Click()
2       Dim DimensionObject As AcadDimRotated
3       Dim LineObject As AcadLine
4       Dim DimLineLocation(0 To 2) As Double
5       DimLineLocation(0) = Point1(0) - 1#
6       DimLineLocation(1) = Point1(1)
7       DimLineLocation(2) = Point1(2)
8       Set LineObject = ThisDrawing.ModelSpace.AddLine( ↵
           Point1, Point2)
9       LineObject.Update
10      Set DimensionObject = ↵
           ThisDrawing.ModelSpace.AddDimRotated( ↵
           Point1, Point2, DimLineLocation, (45 * Pi / 180))
11      DimensionObject.Update
12      ZoomAll
13  End Sub
```

Analysis

- Line 1 starts the Click event procedure for the Rotated option button.
- Line 2 declares the `DimensionObject` variable as being capable of referring to a `DimRotated` object.
- Line 3 declares the `LineObject` variable as being capable of referencing a Line object.
- Lines 4 through 7 declare the `DimLineLocation` array and assign its elements the coordinates of a point that is one unit to the left of Point1, in the x-axis direction.
- Lines 8 and 9 create a line, add it to the ModelSpace collection, and then draw it in the Model Space.
- Line 10 creates a `DimRotated` object and adds it to the ModelSpace collection. The first two arguments define the line drawn at Line 9 of the macro. The next argument passes the point stored in `DimLineLocation`, and the last argument converts 45° to radians and passes the result.
- Line 11 draws the new Dimension object.
- Line 12 zooms the viewport to display all the drawing objects.
- Line 13 ends the Click event procedure of the `optRotated` option button.

The last object is the 3 Point Angular dimension. Enter the code shown in Listing 11.7, which runs in response to a click on the `opt3PointAngular` option button.

Listing 11.7: Adding a 3 Point Angular Dimension Object

```
1   Private Sub opt3PointAngular_Click()
2       Dim DimensionObject As AcadDim3PointAngular
3       Dim CircleObject As AcadCircle
4       Dim FirstEndPoint(0 To 2) As Double
5       Dim SecondEndPoint(0 To 2) As Double
6       Set CircleObject = ThisDrawing.ModelSpace.AddCircle( ↵
           Center, Radius)
7       CircleObject.Update
8       FirstEndPoint(0) = Center(0) + Radius
9       FirstEndPoint(1) = Center(1)
10      FirstEndPoint(2) = Center(2)
11      SecondEndPoint(0) = Center(0) + ↵
           Radius * Cos(45 * Pi / 180)
12      SecondEndPoint(1) = Center(1) + ↵
           Radius * Sin(45 * Pi / 180)
13      SecondEndPoint(2) = Center(2)
14      Set DimensionObject = ↵
           ThisDrawing.ModelSpace.AddDim3PointAngular( ↵
           Center, FirstEndPoint, SecondEndPoint, TextPosition)
15      DimensionObject.AngleFormat = acDegrees
16      DimensionObject.Update
17      ZoomAll
18  End Sub
```

Analysis

- Line 1 starts the Click event procedure of the 3 Point Angular option button.
- Line 2 declares the `DimensionObject` as being capable of storing a reference to a `Dim3PointAngular` dimension object.
- Line 3 declares the `CircleObject` variable as being capable of referencing a Circle object.
- Lines 4 and 5 declare the arrays to hold the coordinates of the two endpoints that define the position where the extension lines intersect with the object being dimensioned.

- Lines 6 and 7 create a new Circle object and draw it in the Model Space.
- Lines 8 through 10 assign the values for the coordinates of the point where the first extension line intersects with the circle's circumference to the `FirstEndPoint` array.
- Lines 11 through 13 assign the coordinates of the point where the second extension line intersects with the circle. The `Cos` and `Sin` functions are called to make this point 45° around the circumference from the first point.
- Line 14 calls the `AddDim3PointAngular` method to create a `Dim3PointAngular` object and add it to the ModelSpace collection. The `DimensionObject` is set up to reference this new object.
- Line 15 assigns the `AngleFormat` property of the Dimension object to the AutoCAD constant `acDegrees`. The `AngleFormat` property allows you to specify the unit format for angular dimensions. The other constants available are `acDegreeMinuteSeconds`, `acGrads`, and `acRadians`.
- Line 16 draws the Dimension object in the Model Space.
- Line 17 calls the `ZoomAll` method to ensure that all the drawing objects are visible in the Model Space.
- Line 18 ends the `opt3PointAngular_Click` event procedure.

Finally, to complete the application, enter the declarations of the global variables and the Pi constant, the Click event procedure for the Exit command button, and the Initialize event procedure for the UserForm.

Listing 11.8: Global Declarations and Remaining Event Procedures

```
Option Explicit
Const Pi = 3.14159
Dim Point1(0 To 2) As Double, Point2(0 To 2) As Double
Dim TextPosition(0 To 2) As Double
Dim Center(0 To 2) As Double, Radius As Double
Dim Offset As Double

Private Sub cmdExit_Click()
    Unload Me
End Sub

```

```
12  Private Sub UserForm_Initialize()
13      Point1(0) = 1#: Point1(1) = 1#: Point1(2) = 0#
14      Point2(0) = 5#: Point2(1) = 1#: Point2(2) = 0#
15      Offset = 0.25
16      TextPosition(0) = 2#
17      TextPosition(1) = 1# + Offset
18      TextPosition(2) = 0#
19      Center(0) = 0#: Center(1) = 0#: Center(2) = 0#
20      Radius = 2#
21  End Sub
```

ANALYSIS

- Line 1 contains the `Option Explicit` statement to ensure that all variables used throughout the code from the UserForm Code window have been declared before use.
- Line 2 declares the constant `Pi` and assigns it a value.
- Lines 3 through 6 declare the variables and arrays that are used by several of the application's event procedures.
- Lines 8 through 10 contain the Click event procedure that is executed when the user clicks the Exit command button. This procedure unloads the UserForm to stop the application.
- Line 12 starts the initialization event procedure of the UserForm object. This runs when the UserForm is loaded in response to the user's actions.
- Lines 13 through 20 assign initial values to the global arrays and variables. These are really the default values that are required so that the application can run without the user's having to supply values for everything.
- Line 21 ends the `UserForm_Initialize` event procedure.

Saving Your Dimension Styles

When you've devoted a lot of time to creating a new style with all the required property settings, you'll want to be able to use it again. All these attributes can be saved in a DimStyle object from the DimStyles collection for later use. The Add method of the DimStyles collection creates a new DimStyle object based on the settings from the currently active DimStyle object of the active document ThisDrawing; a variable is set up as a reference to this new object (see Line 3 of Listing 11.9).

To set up your new DimStyle object with the attributes required, you'll need to assign values to the system variables to get the effect you want; then you call the `CopyFrom` method of `DimStyleObject`. This method is capable of copying the dimension styles from any of the dimension objects, as well as from another DimStyle object. Exercise 11.2 shows you how to create a new dimension style from a macro.

Exercise 11.2: Create Dimension Macro

1. Enter the CreateDimensionStyle macro (Listing 11.9) into the ThisDrawing module of a new drawing object.
2. Run the macro from the AutoCAD window and try adding a few dimensioning measurements. The leader line will be displayed colored blue, the extension lines will be colored cyan, and the dimension text will be colored green.
3. Choose Dimension ➜ Style. The DimensionStyle Manager dialog box appears, with the new style MyDimStyle included in the Styles list (see Figure 11.15).

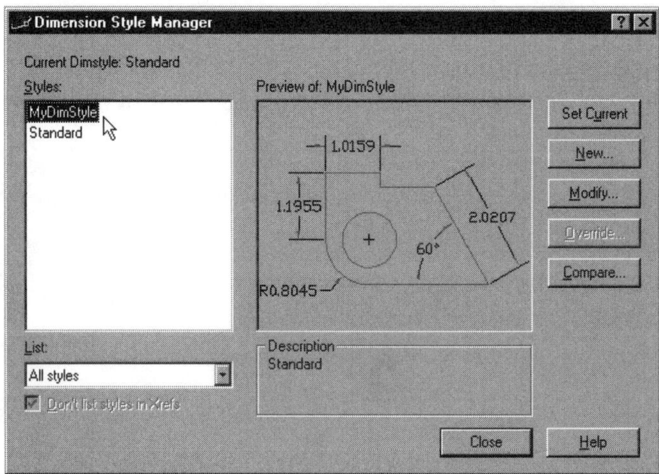

***Figure 11.15** Dimension Style Manager including the new style MyDimStyle created by the CreateDimensionStyle macro (Listing 11.9)*

4. Select MyDimStyle from the Styles list and watch the drawing change color in the Preview box.

LISTING 11.9: CREATEDIMENSIONSTYLE MACRO

```
1   Public Sub CreateDimensionStyle()
2       Dim DimStyleObject As AcadDimStyle
3       Set DimStyleObject = ThisDrawing.DimStyles.Add( ↵
           "MyDimStyle")
4       SetVariable "DIMCLRD", acBlue
5       SetVariable "DIMCLRE", acCyan
6       SetVariable "DIMCLRT", acGreen
7       DimStyleObject.CopyFrom ThisDrawing
8   End Sub
```

ANALYSIS

- Line 1 starts the `CreateDimensionStyle` macro.
- Line 2 declares the `DimStyleObject` as being capable of storing a reference to a DimStyle object.
- Line 3 uses the Add method of the `DimStyles` collection to create a new DimStyle and add it to the collection. This method has only one parameter that allows you to specify a name for your style.
- Lines 4 through 6 use the `SetVariable` method to set the value of AutoCAD system variables. Table 11.2 lists and describes some of the system variables that are available.

Table 11.2 Useful Dimension System Variables

SYSTEM VARIABLE	ELEMENTS CONTROLLED
DIMCLRD	Color of the dimension line, arrowhead, and leader line
DIMCLRE	Extension line color
DIMCLRT	Dimension text color
DIMGAP	Gap between extension line and text
DIMJUST	Dimension line text justification
DIMTXT	Text height
DIMTXSTY	Text style

- Line 7 uses the `CopyFrom` method to copy the settings from the current dimension style used by ThisDrawing to the new `DimStyle` object referred to by `DimStyleObject`.
- Line 8 ends the `CreateDimensionStyle` macro.

Using Your Own Dimension Style

Any style listed in the Dimension Style Manager dialog box can be designated as the active Dimension style. Listing 11.10 gives you a macro that makes the style named MyDimStyle the active style.

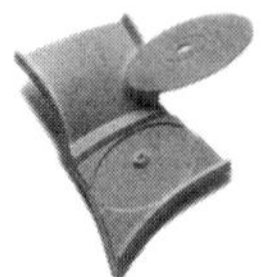

Listing 11.10: UseMyDimStyle Macro

```
1   Public Sub UseMyDimStyle()
2       Dim DimStyleObject As AcadDimStyle
3       Set DimStyleObject = ThisDrawing.DimStyles.Item( ↵
           "MyDimStyle")
4       ThisDrawing.ActiveDimStyle = DimStyleObject
5   End Sub
```

Analysis

- Line 1 starts the `UseMyDimStyle` macro.
- Line 2 declares the `DimStyleObject` variable as being capable of referencing a DimStyle object.
- Line 3 uses the `Item` method of the `DimStyles` collection to retrieve the DimStyle object named `MyDimStyle` and sets up a reference to it in the `DimstyleObject` variable.
- Line 4 sets the `ActiveDimStyle` property of the ThisDrawing document to the `DimStyleObject`. This has the effect of making `MyDimStyle` the active DimStyle in the active drawing.
- Line 5 ends the `UseMyDimStyle` macro.

Now that you know how to add dimension styles to your drawings, you may occasionally want to deviate from the exact geometry of the drawing. The next section shows you how to add information about the deviation to your drawings using the Tolerance object.

Incorporating the Tolerance Object

The Tolerance object represents a geometric tolerance—a deviation away from the geometric style used throughout the drawing. To highlight this deviation, the tolerance is displayed inside a feature control frame; this frame is a rectangle drawn around the text in much the same style as for a ToolTip.

A Tolerance object is added to the ModelSpace collection using the AddTolerance method, which has three parameters:

Text This parameter holds the string to be displayed in the feature control frame.

InsertionPoint This is the position for the tolerance text to be displayed.

Direction This identifies the direction for the tolerance text.

Listing 11.11 shows how to create a Tolerance object from a macro. Running this macro produces the feature control frame shown here:

There is zero tolerance at this point!

LISTING 11.11: CREATETOLERANCEOBJECT MACRO

```
1   Public Sub CreateToleranceObject()
2       Dim ToleranceObject As AcadTolerance
3       Dim InsertionPoint(0 To 2) As Double
4       Dim Direction(0 To 2) As Double
5       Dim MyText As String
6       InsertionPoint(0) = 1#
7       InsertionPoint(1) = 1#
8       InsertionPoint(2) = 0#
9       Direction(0) = 1#: Direction(1) = 0#: Direction(2) = 0#
10      MyText = "There is zero tolerance at this point!"
11      Set ToleranceObject = ↵
          ThisDrawing.ModelSpace.AddTolerance( ↵
          MyText, InsertionPoint, Direction)
12      ZoomAll
13  End Sub
```

ANALYSIS

- Line 1 starts the `CreateToleranceObject` macro.

- Line 2 declares the `ToleranceObject` variable as being capable of referring to a Tolerance object.
- Lines 3 and 4 declare the three-element arrays used to store the tolerance position and direction.
- Line 5 declares the `MyText` variable as being a string type.
- Lines 6 through 8 assign the coordinate values for the insertion point where the tolerance text will be positioned.
- Line 9 assigns the direction for the text: 1 in the x-axis direction and 0 in the y and z directions. This produces a horizontal feature control frame. To make it vertical, simply set the y-axis direction to 1 and the others to 0.
- Line 10 assigns a text string to the `MyText` variable. In VBA, strings are always enclosed in parentheses.
- Line 11 calls the `AddTolerance` method to create a Tolerance object and add it to the ModelSpace collection. The `ToleranceObject` variable is set up to refer to this new object.
- Line 12 ensures that the viewport is adjusted so that all drawing objects appear in the Model Space.
- Line 13 ends the `CreateToleranceObject` macro.

Customizing Menu Commands

Windows menu systems are hierarchical—you can select a menu group from the menu bar, and a drop-down list appears to give you access to the menu commands from that group. In this section you'll learn how to create your own menu group and how to access its items from code.

In VBA code, the items from a menu group are accessed using an index value that represents their positions in the menu. The commands in drop-down menus are normally already related in some way and can be collected into further subgroups using separators within the drop-down menu. These separators are given index values in the same way as the menu items themselves.

The Windows environment ensures that if there isn't enough room to display all of a group's commands on the screen simultaneously, an arrow will be displayed at the top or bottom of the drop-down menu. The arrow indicates that there are additional items available and to enable all items in the menu to be accessed.

Creating a New Menu to Run Macros

In the object model's PopupMenus collection, each PopupMenu object contains a drop-down menu. To create a new drop-down menu, you simply use the Add method to create another PopupMenu object and add it to the collection. To create a submenu, you use the AddSubMenu method; and the AddMenuItem method to add items to that submenu. This arrangement will become clearer to you when you run the CreateMenu macro (Listing 11.12) and see the results.

In this next exercise, you'll add a new menu group containing the commands for controlling the dimensioning features. Listing 11.12 gives the CreateMenu macro that creates all the items and commands for the menu. The macro then lists all the macros for each menu command, which update the value of the option buttons from the Dimensions application, instigating their Change event procedures.

Exercise 11.3: Create Menu Group Macro

To try out the CreateMenu macro:

1. Enter the code from Listing 11.12 into the ThisDrawing module of the same project as your Dimension application.
2. Run the CreateMenu macro from the AutoCAD window or from the IDE and select a few menu commands from the group. Watch as measurements are added to the Model Space.

Listing 11.12: CreateMenu Macro

```
Public Sub CreateMenu()
    'create new menu group for the AutoCAD menubar
    Dim MenuGroupObject As AcadMenuGroup
    Dim MenuObject As AcadPopupMenu
    Dim SubMenuObject1 As AcadPopupMenu
    Dim SubMenuObject2 As AcadPopupMenu
    Dim MenuItemObject As AcadPopupMenuItem
    'create group of menu items and give them a menubar name
    Set MenuGroupObject = ↵
       ThisDrawing.Application.MenuGroups.Item(0)
    Set MenuObject = MenuGroupObject.Menus.Add(↵
       "NewDimensions")
    'create two sub menu items
    Set SubMenuObject1 = MenuObject.AddSubMenu(0, "Linear")
    Set SubMenuObject2 = MenuObject.AddSubMenu(1, "Angular")
```

```
    'add commands to the sub menu items
    Set MenuItemObject = SubMenuObject1.AddMenuItem( ↵
        MenuObject.Count + 1, "Aligned", ↵
        "-vbarun ThisDrawing.AlignedDimension" & vbCr)
    Set MenuItemObject = SubMenuObject1.AddMenuItem( ↵
        MenuObject.Count + 1, "Ordinate", ↵
        "-vbarun ThisDrawing.OrdinateDimension" & vbCr)
    Set MenuItemObject = SubMenuObject1.AddMenuItem( ↵
        MenuObject.Count + 1, "Rotated", ↵
        "-vbarun ThisDrawing.RotatedDimension" & vbCr)
    Set MenuItemObject = SubMenuObject2.AddMenuItem( ↵
        MenuObject.Count + 1, "Angular", ↵
        "-vbarun ThisDrawing.AngularDimension" & vbCr)
    Set MenuItemObject = SubMenuObject2.AddMenuItem( ↵
        MenuObject.Count + 1, "Diametric", ↵
        "-vbarun ThisDrawing.DiametricDimension" & vbCr)
    Set MenuItemObject = SubMenuObject2.AddMenuItem( ↵
        MenuObject.Count + 1, "Radial", ↵
        "-vbarun ThisDrawing.RadialDimension" & vbCr)
    ' Display the menu on the menu bar
    MenuObject.InsertInMenuBar ↵
      (ThisDrawing.Application.MenuBar.Count + 1)
End Sub

Public Sub AlignedDimension()
    frmDimensionStyles.optAligned.Value = True
End Sub

Public Sub AngularDimension()
    frmDimensionStyles.optAngular.Value = True
End Sub

Public Sub DiametricDimension()
    frmDimensionStyles.optDiametric.Value = True
End Sub

Public Sub RadialDimension()
    frmDimensionStyles.optRadial.Value = True
End Sub
```

```
41  Public Sub OrdinateDimension()
42      frmDimensionStyles.optOrdinate.Value = True
43  End Sub
44
45  Public Sub RotatedDimension()
46      frmDimensionStyles.optRotated.Value = True
47  End Sub
```

ANALYSIS

- Line 1 starts the `CreateMenu` macro.
- Line 3 declares the `MenuGroupObject` variable as being capable of referencing a MenuGroup object. This object is at the top of the pecking order for menus.
- Line 4 declares the `MenuObject` variable as being capable of referencing a PopupMenu object. The PopupMenu object is second in line in the hierarchical menu structure and has its name displayed in the menu bar:

- Lines 5 and 6 declare the `SubMenuObject1` and `SubMenuObject2` as being capable of referencing PopupMenu objects. These objects are used to create the two submenus that are used to split the dimensioning styles into linear and angular categories, as shown in Figures 11.16 through 11.18.
- Line 7 declares the `MenuItemObject` as being capable of referencing a Popup-MenuItem object. This object is at the end of the line and will carry out the command if selected by the user.
- Line 9 sets up the `MenuGroupObject` variable to reference the first item in the MenuGroups collection—this is the menu group displayed in the AutoCAD window.
- Line 10 uses the Add method of the Menus collection to create a new pop-up menu with the name `NewDimensions`—this name will be displayed in the menu bar the next time you return to the AutoCAD window.
- Line 12 uses the `AddSubMenu` method to add a `PopupMenu` object. The first argument is an index value that determines its position in the pop-up list. The second argument is the string that will appear in the pop-up menu.

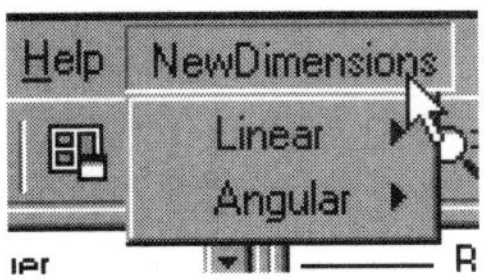

Figure 11.16 Two submenu items defined in two PopupMenu objects

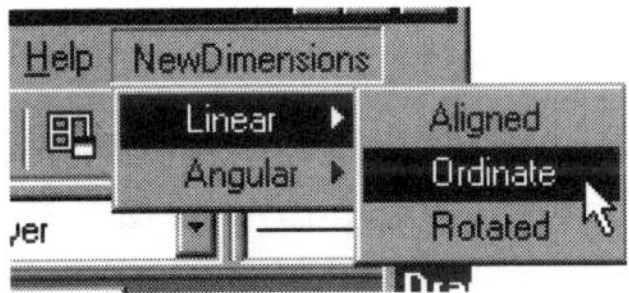

Figure 11.17 Three menu commands accessible from the Linear submenu item and defined in a PopupMenuItem object

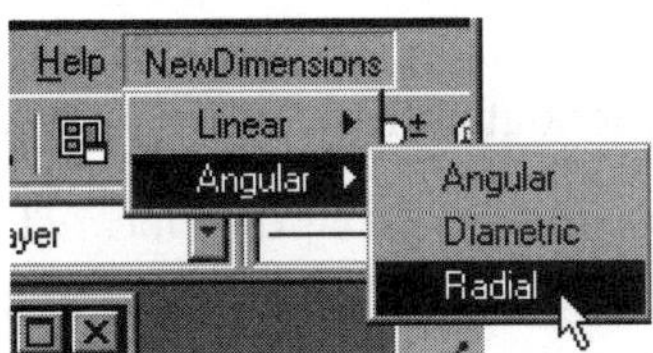

Figure 11.18 Three menu commands accessible from the Angular submenu item and defined in a PopupMenuItem object

- Line 13 adds another `PopupMenu` object.
- Lines 15 through 20 call the `AddMenuItem` method to add a `PopupMenuItem` object that represents a menu command. The first argument provides its index, defining the position in the pop-up menu where the item is to be added. The second argument is the string that's to appear in the pop-up menu. The third argument is the macro to be run from the command line in the AutoCAD window if this menu item is selected. The `-vbarun` at the start of the command alerts AutoCAD to the fact that you are going to run a VBA macro. The macro

itself must be qualified by the module it belongs to, and the whole thing must be followed by a carriage return to start executing the macro.

- Line 22 inserts the pop-up menu into the AutoCAD menu bar at the location specified in the argument. This statement adds the menu to the end after the Help group.
- Lines 25 through 47 are the macros called from the six menu commands. Each macro changes its associated option button control's value to execute the Change event procedure from the original Dimensions application.

To Remove a Menu Group

After you create a menu group, it will automatically be included every time you start AutoCAD until you remove it. The following steps show you how to take the menu group you've just added out of the menu bar but allow it to remain available for redisplay.

1. From the AutoCAD window, choose Tools ➔ Customize ➔ Menus. The Menu Customization dialog box appears (Figure 11.19).
2. In the Menu Bar tab, select NewDimensions from the Menu Bar list and click Remove. The item disappears from the Menu Bar list.
3. Click Close. The Menu Customization dialog box closes and you return to the AutoCAD window, from which the menu item has disappeared.

Although the instance of the NewDimensions menu has disappeared from the menu, the NewDimensions menu item is still present and available to be added again. Running the macro given in Listing 11.13 will consequently give a run-time error. You can remove all the custom menu items in one hit by returning to the AutoCAD default menu group, as described in the next section.

To Restore the AutoCAD Menu Group

You can restore the AutoCAD default menu group, which removes any custom menu items you have added and adds any default menu items you have deleted. The following instructions show you how:

1. Type **Menu** on the AutoCAD command line. The Select Menu File dialog box appears.
2. Click Menu Template (*.mnu) in the Files Of Type drop-down list and select acad: AutoCAD Menu Template.

3. Click Open. Figure 11.20 shows the warning that appears, telling you that if you proceed all your customization changes will be lost.

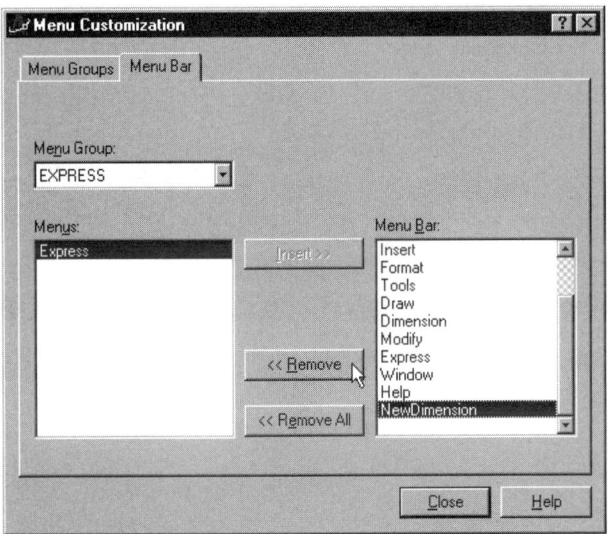

Figure 11.19 *Menu Customization dialog box*

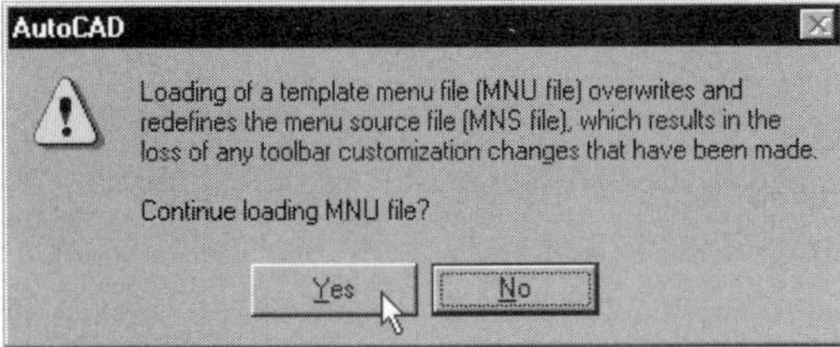

Figure 11.20 *Message box that lets you know that you will lose your customized changes if you proceed.*

Creating Your Own Toolbar

Toolbar buttons are added to a toolbar in much the same way as menu items are added to the menu bar, as you did in the preceding section. To create a new toolbar, you call the Add method to create another Toolbar object and add it to the Toolbars collection.

To add a button to your new toolbar, you call the AddToolbarButton method of a Toolbar object. This method requires four arguments to be passed in the call:

Index This parameter specifies the position of the button in the toolbar.

Name This is the name of the toolbar button to be displayed as the ToolTip if the user pauses the mouse over the button.

HelpString This parameter contains the string that appears in the status line in the bottom-left corner of the AutoCAD window.

Macro This is the macro associated with the button. The macro string appears in the command line, so it must start with `-vbarun` and finish with a carriage return in order for the macro to run.

Listing 11.13 is the CreateToolbar macro, which creates a toolbar containing six buttons shown here:

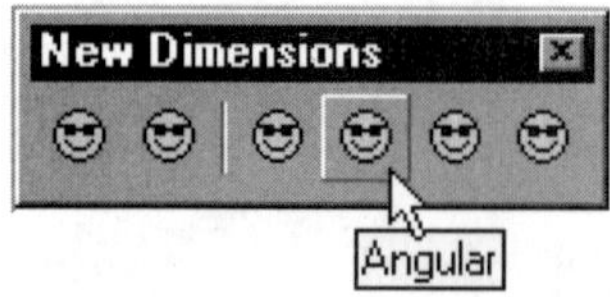

LISTING 11.13: CREATETOOLBAR MACRO

```
Public Sub CreateToolbar()
    Dim MenuGroupObject As AcadMenuGroup
    Dim ToolbarObject As AcadToolbar
    Dim ToolbarItemObject As AcadToolbarItem
    Dim ButtonObject As AcadToolbarItem
    Set MenuGroupObject = ↵
       ThisDrawing.Application.MenuGroups.Item(0)
    Set ToolbarObject = MenuGroupObject.Toolbars.Add( ↵
       "New Dimensions")
    Set ButtonObject = ToolbarObject.AddToolbarButton( ↵
       0, "Align", "alignment dimension", ↵
       "-vbarun ThisDrawing.AlignedDimension" & vbCr)
    Set ButtonObject = ToolbarObject.AddToolbarButton( ↵
       1, "Ordinate", "ordinate dimension", ↵
       "-vbarun ThisDrawing.OrdinateDimension" & vbCr)
    Set ButtonObject = ToolbarObject.AddToolbarButton( ↵
       2, "Rotate", "rotate dimension", ↵
       "-vbarun ThisDrawing.RotateDimension" & vbCr)
```

```
11      Set ButtonObject = ToolbarObject.AddSeparator(2)
12      Set ButtonObject = ToolbarObject.AddToolbarButton( ↵
           4, "Angular", "angular dimension", ↵
           "-vbarun ThisDrawing.AngularDimension" & vbCr)
13      Set ButtonObject = ToolbarObject.AddToolbarButton( ↵
           5, "Diametric", "diametric dimension", ↵
           "-vbarun ThisDrawing.DiametricDimension" & vbCr)
14      Set ButtonObject = ToolbarObject.AddToolbarButton( ↵
           6, "Radial", "radial dimension", ↵
           "-vbarun ThisDrawing.RadialDimension" & vbCr)
15      ToolbarObject.Visible = True
16   End Sub
```

ANALYSIS

- Line 1 starts the `CreateToolbar` macro.
- Lines 2 through 5 declare all the variables that will reference the objects associated with toolbars.
- Line 6 sets up the `MenuGroupObject` to refer to a `MenuGroup` from the MenuGroups collection of the current application (AutoCAD).
- Line 7 adds a new Toolbar object named New Dimensions to the first item of the MenuGroups collection of the current application—this is the New Dimensions menu group.
- Lines 8 through 14 (except Line 11) call the `AddToolbarButton` to create new `ToolbarButton` objects.
- Line 11 calls the `AddSeparator` method to add a separator bar.
- Line 15 sets the `Visible` property of the Toolbar object to `True`. This has the same effect on toolbar buttons as calling the Update method to display Drawing objects.
- Line 16 ends the `CreateToolbar` macro.

What makes toolbars so user-friendly is the icons on their buttons that provide a visual cue to the commands represented. When you add a toolbar button, the smiley face is the default button—which you'll of course change to something else that helps the user choose a button on the toolbar. The following steps show you how to redesign the icon for our Align dimensioning style.

1. In the AutoCAD window, choose View ➜ Toolbars to open the dialog box shown in Figure 11.21. This dialog box must be open before you can progress to step 2.

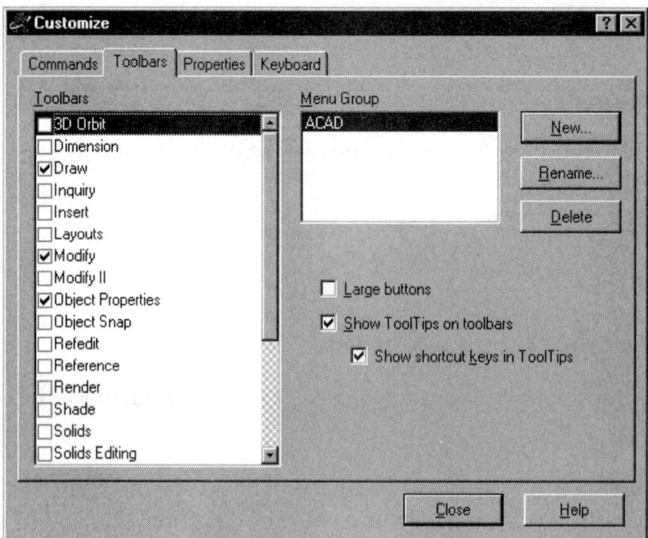

Figure 11.21 *Customizing a toolbar*

2. Click New. In the New Toolbar dialog box that appears, type **New Dimensions** into the Toolbar Name box. Click OK to return to the Customize dialog box.
3. Open the Commands tab of the Customize dialog box and select User Defined from the list in the Categories frame on the left. Drag and drop the User Defined button from the Commands frame on the right onto your toolbar.

   The toolbar will expand horizontally but will still look empty. If you pause the mouse over the toolbar, the text "User Defined Button" will appear as a ToolTip.
4. With the Customize dialog box still open, right-click the User Defined button in the new toolbar and choose Properties from the pop-up menu. The Properties tab from the Customize dialog box changes to a Button Properties tab (Figure 11.22).
5. Click the Edit button. The Button Editor dialog box appears (Figure 11.23).

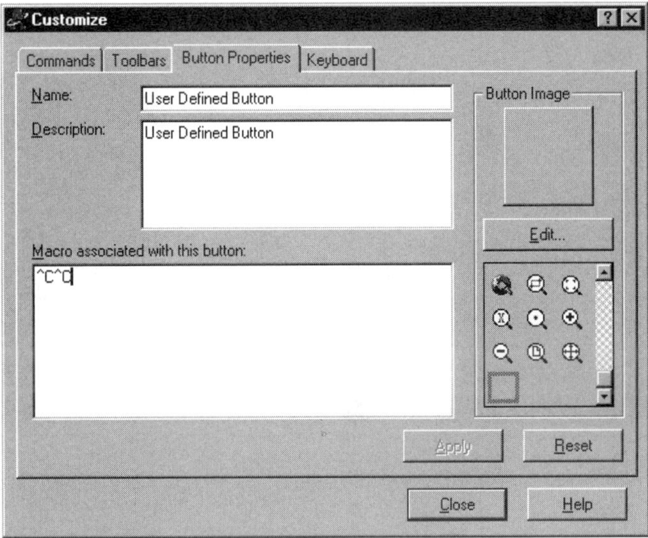

Figure 11.22 *Setting button properties*

Figure 11.23 *Editing the new button*

6. Check the Grid box to display a grid on the button, and then draw the icon you want displayed. See Figure 11.24.

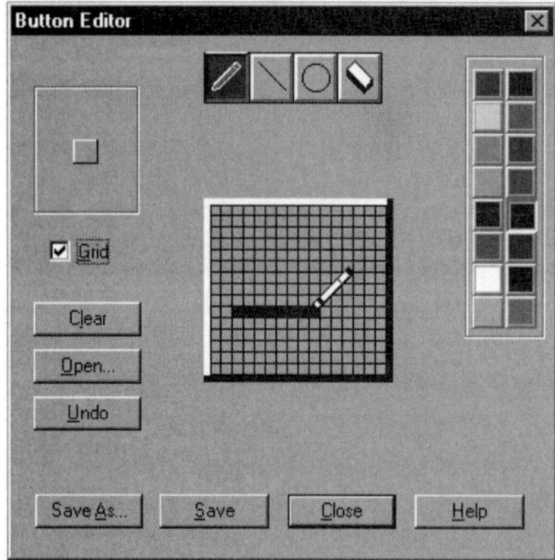

Figure 11.24 *Drawing in the Button Editor*

7. Click Save and save your icon to a file.
8. Click Close in the Button Editor to return to the Button Properties dialog box—the new icon is ready now to be placed on the toolbar button.
9. Click Apply. The icon in the toolbar changes to the new icon:

Now that you've seen how it's done, I'll leave it up to you to redesign the icons for the other buttons in the new toolbar.

Adding Preprogrammed Toolbar Buttons

You can add buttons from any other toolbars that AutoCAD provides. These are preprogrammed to work in their normal way if clicked from your custom toolbar. The following steps show you how to add a functional toolbar button to the New Dimensions toolbar you created in the preceding exercise:

1. If the Customize dialog box is not already open, right-click any button on the toolbar and choose Customize.

2. From the Commands tab, choose Dimension from the Categories frame. The dimensioning commands and their icons appear in the Commands frame, as shown in Figure 11.25.

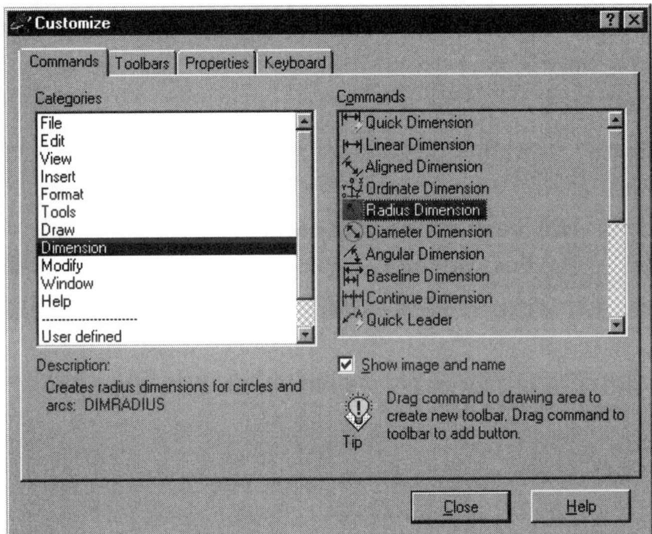

Figure 11.25 *Choose Dimension in the Commands tab*

3. Drag and drop the commands you require into your toolbar.

   The mouse icon changes as you drag each command to the toolbar. When your cursor reaches the toolbar, a vertical line appears to indicate where the new button will be positioned.

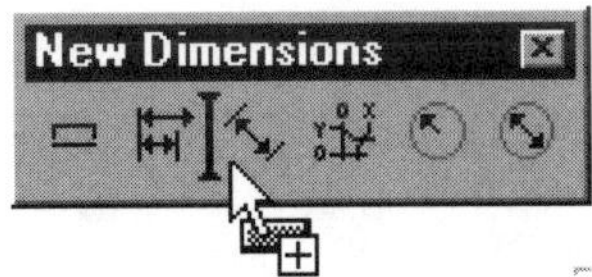

Summary

After reading this chapter, you'll be able to

- Add measurements to your drawings using the dimensioning styles available from the AutoCAD window.
- From a VBA application, use the seven dimensioning styles for adding measurements.
- Save a custom dimensioning style and use it again later.
- Use the Tolerance object to display geometric deviation.
- Create your own hierarchical menu group.
- Create your own toolbar.
- Design your own toolbar button icons.
- Add toolbar buttons for existing functions.

File Input and Output

AUTOCAD VBA

Chapter 12

Files are useful for saving drawings and other pieces of data that are needed by a procedure or application to perform some function. This makes the procedure or application more powerful because it can use various sets of data simply by changing the file. AutoCAD already does this using different drawing files. Here in Chapter 12 you'll see how to control files from macros. This includes saving drawings to files, copying files, and testing to see if a file exists. You'll also see how to perform data input and output, and process data files.

This chapter covers the following topics:

- Handling drawing files in your VBA code
- Displaying the Open and SaveAs dialog boxes
- Writing data to a file from code
- Opening files in Input and Output modes

Handling Drawing Files in Your Code

This section describes elements of VBA that allow you to perform fundamental file-control tasks from your code, including creating a drawing and saving it to a file. You'll see how to copy the contents from one drawing file to another, as well as how to verify whether a specified file actually exists.

Creating a New Drawing from a Macro

You're probably already quite familiar with AutoCAD's File ➜ New command for creating a new drawing, and the Insert ➜ Layout ➜ New Layout command to add a new Layout tab. When you want to create a new drawing from a macro, you call the Add method of the Documents collection. To add a new Layout tab, you use the Add method of the Layouts collection.

Exercise 12.1: Drawings and Layouts Application

Let's create a new application that shows new documents and layouts being created from code. The application will allow the user to enter the number of layouts required and specify whether or not to use the existing drawing document or create a new one. The following steps take you through this whole process:

1. Create a new project, open the VB Editor window, and insert a UserForm.
2. Insert a label-and-text-box pair, a check box, and a command button as shown here:

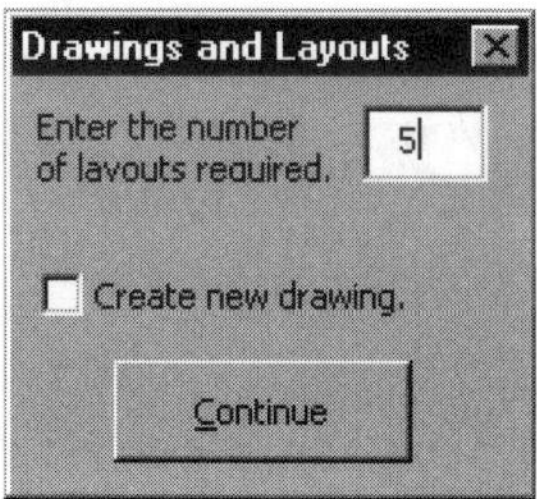

3. Change the Caption properties to those shown in Table 12.1. Make sure the WordWrap property of Label1 is set to True so that all the text is displayed over two lines. Make the Accelerator property of the command button **C**.

Table 12.1 Caption Properties for the Drawings and Layouts UserForm

CONTROL NAME	NEW CAPTION
UserForm1	Drawings and Layouts
Label1	Enter the number of layouts required.
CheckBox1	Create new drawing
CommandButton1	Continue

4. Now you're ready to enter the code given in Listing 12.1. It contains the DoDrawingSetup macro that generates a new drawing if required, and adjusts the number of Layout tabs to the number requested by the user.

LISTING 12.1: DODRAWINGSETUP MACRO

```
Private Sub DoDrawingSetup()
    Dim NumberLayouts As Integer, NumberRequired As Integer
    Dim Count As Integer
    NumberRequired = UserForm1.TextBox1.Text
    If UserForm1.CheckBox1.Value Then Documents.Add
    ThisDrawing.Regen acActiveViewport
    NumberLayouts = ThisDrawing.Layouts.Count
    If NumberLayouts - 1 < NumberRequired Then
        For Count = NumberLayouts To NumberRequired
            ThisDrawing.Layouts.Add ("Layout" & Count)
        Next
    Else
        For Count = ↵
           NumberLayouts To NumberRequired + 2 Step -1
             ThisDrawing.Layouts.Item ↵
                ("Layout" & Count - 1).Delete
        Next
    End If
    ThisDrawing.Regen acActiveViewport
End Sub

Private Sub CommandButton1_Click()
    DoDrawingSetup
    Unload Me
End Sub
```

Analysis

- Line 1 starts the `DoDrawingSetup` procedure that adjusts the number of Layout tabs in the active drawing or in a new drawing, to the number of Layout tabs requested by the user.
- Line 2 declares the variables that are assigned the number of Layouts in the current drawing document (`NumberLayouts`) and the number of Layouts now required by the user (`NumberRequired`).
- Line 3 declares `Count`, which will act as the index to objects in the Layouts collection.
- Line 4 assigns the number of Layout tabs entered into the text box, to the `NumberRequired` variable.
- Line 5 tests to see if the Create New Drawing checkbox has been checked; if so, the Add method is used to add a new drawing document to the Documents collection.
- Line 6 uses the `Regen` method to redraw everything in the active viewport displaying the new drawing document. It also makes the new document the active one, so that it can be referred to as ThisDrawing from this statement on.
- Line 7 assigns the value of the `Count` property of the Layouts collection to the `NumberLayouts` variable. The `Count` property represents the number of layouts in the active document, but since it also includes the Model tab, it has a value of 3 when ThisDrawing contains a Model and two Layout tabs.
- Line 8 starts the `If...Then...Else...` block by determining whether the number of actual layout tabs, excluding the Model tab, is less than the number of Layout tabs required.
- Line 9 runs only if more Layout tabs are required. This statement starts the `For` loop block that adds Layout tabs. It initializes `Count` to the value of `NumberLayouts`, and increments it each time through the loop until the value of `NumberRequired` is reached. When both `NumberLayouts` and `NumberRequired` are the same, the loop is executed for the last time, so entering the number 3 in the Input Box will still execute the loop and add a Layout tab.
- Line 10 uses the `Add` method to create a new Layout object and add it to the Layouts collection. The `Add` method has one argument: a string containing the caption that will appear on the tab. (The name I've given all my tabs is `Layout`

followed by a number, in keeping with the original tab-naming system that AutoCAD uses by default.

- Line 11 contains the `Next` statement that ends the `For` loop block.
- Line 12 starts the `Else` part of `the If...Then...Else...` block that is executed if the condition at Line 8 is False, which means that fewer Layout tabs are required.
- Line 13 starts the `For` loop that deletes Layout tabs. `Count` is initialized to `NumberLayouts` and is decremented by the negative step until it is less than `NumberRequired` plus 2. So if you have three Layout tabs in your drawing and you enter 2 in the Input box, then `Count` will be initialized to 4 and compared with `NumberRequired` plus 2—which is also 4, and the statement at Line 14 will be executed only once to delete one tab.
- Line 14 calls the `Delete` method to delete the rightmost Layout tab in the drawing. This is at the `Count -1` position since the first Layout tab is at position zero.
- Line 15 ends the `For` loop block.
- Line 16 ends the `If...Then...Else...` block of statements.
- Line 17 calls the `Regen` method, passing the AutoCAD constant `acActive-Viewport` as the argument, to display the updates just made to the drawing document.
- Line 18 ends the `DoDrawingSetup` procedure.
- Line 20 starts the Click event procedure of the command button.
- Line 21 calls the `DoDrawingSetup` procedure.
- Line 22 uses the `Unload` statement with the `Me` keyword to stop the application and return the user to the AutoCAD window, which will now contain the drawing document setup specified by the user.
- Line 23 ends the Click event procedure for the command button.

With the DoDrawingSetup macro in place, enter the following macro into the Code window for ThisDrawing. This is the name that will appear in the list of macros:

```
Public Sub DrawingAndLayouts()
   UserForm1.Show
End Sub
```

Then run your application and enter a value into the text box. Watch as the drawing setup changes.

Long names that reflect the entire function of a macro make it easier to identify the macro you want to run, especially when you have developed a long list of macros. VBA allows names of up to 255 characters, so you should never run out of names to identify your macros and functions.

Now that you know how to create a drawing and control the number of Layout tabs, the next step is to save your newly created drawing to a file.

Saving a Drawing to a File

You have a choice of two methods for saving a drawing—Save and SaveAs.

- The Save method is used when you want to save changes to a drawing that's been read from an open file. This method saves the latest version of your drawing by overwriting the original version using the same file.
- The SaveAs method is used to save a drawing for the first time. This method will prompt you for the name of the file where the drawing's details are to be placed.

If you call the Save method to save a new drawing, Visual Basic automatically converts this into a call to the SaveAs method.

Saving a New Drawing

The SaveAs method serves two purposes:

- To save a drawing that's never been saved before
- To save an existing drawing to a different file

This method has one parameter that is passed the pathname of the file. For example, the following statement saves the active drawing document:

```
ThisDrawing.SaveAs ("c:\AutoCAD\MyProject.dvb")
```

When you call the SaveAs method, it doesn't matter if the file passed as the argument exists or not. If it already exists, the file's contents are deleted and the current version is written to the file. If it doesn't already exist, a new file is created and the current version is placed there.

Saving an Existing Drawing

If a drawing has already been saved to a file, then it only needs to be saved again if any changes have occurred since it was last opened. The Saved property of the current document allows you to test for whether the file has changed. This property returns a value of True if the contents of a file have changed since it was last saved, or False otherwise. Listing 12.2 gives the SaveDrawing macro that calls the Saved method, and then only calls the Save method if changes have occurred.

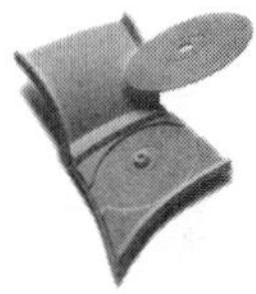

LISTING 12.2: SAVEDRAWING MACRO

```
1   Public Sub SaveDrawing
2   If Not ThisDrawing.Saved Then ThisDrawing.Save
3   End Sub
```

ANALYSIS

- Line 1 starts the `SaveDrawing` macro, which determines whether the contents of a file have changed since the file was last saved and, if so, saves the latest version.
- Line 2 checks to see if ThisDrawing has been saved since the last edit, and if not, calls the Save method to save the drawing to the same file from which the drawing was read. Notice how the condition has shortened the expression

  ```
  ThisDrawing.Saved = True
  ```

  to just

  ```
  ThisDrawing.Saved
  ```

  These produce the same result, because for Boolean variables False is represented as zero and True is represented by –1.When Visual Basic converts numeric values to Boolean, zero represents False and all other values represent True. The expression `ContentsChanged` would be evaluated to –1, which in turn would be evaluated to True.

When information is saved to a file that doesn't already exist, Visual Basic creates an empty file and places the information into it. When information is saved to a file that already exists, Visual Basic deletes any information in the file before placing the new information into it. Before allowing users to save information to an existing file from your application, it is helpful to warn them that the file already exists and allow them to backtrack in order to avoid destroying important information. Listing 12.3 in the next section shows you how to verify whether or not a file currently exists.

Verifying That a File Exists

You'll get a run-time error if you try to open a file that doesn't actually exist, or if your application calls a procedure that requires a file to exist—such as the FileCopy statement given in the next section. If there is any doubt about a file's existence, it's better to search for the file before you try to open it. The macro in Listing 12.3 prompts the user to enter the name of a file, then calls the FileExists function to check whether or not the file is stored on the system. If it isn't, a message box informs the user that the filename entered is a nonexistent file, and no attempt is made to open it.

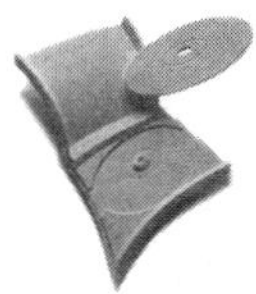

Listing 12.3: GetNewFile Macro and FileExists Function

```
1   Public Sub GetNewFile()
2       Dim DataFileEntered As String
3       DataFileEntered = InputBox( ↵
   "Enter the pathname of your drawing file:", "Data File")
4       If Not FileExists(DataFileEntered) Then
5           MsgBox "Error - the file " & DataFileEntered & ↵
               " doesn't exist!", , "Error"
6       End If
7   End Sub
8
9   Public Function FileExists(DataFileEntered As String) ↵
       As Boolean
10      Dim MatchingFileName As String
11      MatchingFileName = Dir(DataFileEntered)
12      If Len(MatchingFileName) = 0 Then
13         FileExists = False
14      Else
15         FileExists = True
16      End If
17  End Function
```

Analysis

- Line 1 starts the `GetNewFile` macro that prompts the user for the filename and then validates whether or not the name entered is that of an existing file.
- Line 2 declares the string variable that will be assigned the filename entered by the user.

- Line 3 calls the `InputBox` function (shown here) to prompt the user to enter the name of the file they want to copy, and assigns the input string to the `DataFileEntered` variable.

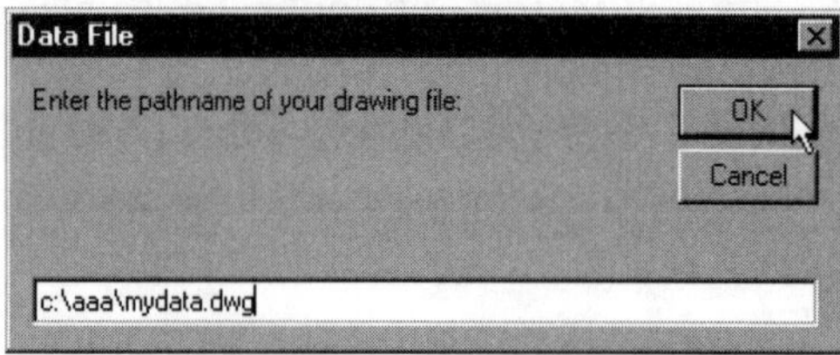

- Line 4 calls the `FileExists` function, passing the `DatFileEntered` string as an argument.
- Line 5: If no matching file exists, this line displays a message box to let the user know that there is no existing file matching the user-entered pathname.
- Line 6 ends the `If` statement block.
- Line 7 ends the `GetNewFile` macro.
- Line 9 starts the `FileExists` function that returns True or False, depending on whether a file exists with the same pathname as the string passed to its parameter.
- Line 10 declares the `MatchingFileName` variable as a string.
- Line 11 passes the string entered by the user to the `Dir` function, which returns a string containing the first filename it finds that matches the user's string. This string is assigned to the `MatchingFileName` variable.
- Line 12 uses the `Len` function to provide the number of characters in the filename string returned by `Dir`. If the length of the string in `MatchingFilename` is zero, then there are no filenames that match the string entered by the user. To see other functions for processing strings, see the section on string handling at the end of Chapter 5.

- Line 13 runs if the file doesn't exist and assigns `False` to the function's name, so that the function returns `False` to the calling statement.
- Line 14 contains the `Else` statement.
- Line 15 runs if the file exists and assigns `True` to the function's name, so that `True` is returned to the calling statement.
- Line 16 ends the `If...Then...Else...` statement block.
- Line 17 ends the `FileExists` function.

Copying Files

Copies of files can be made from a macro using the FileCopy statement. This statement is called with two arguments—the file's Source and the file's Destination. Both of these are strings containing pathnames. The Source provides the name of the file you want to copy, and Destination specifies where the contents of the Source are to be copied. Listing 12.4 gives the CopyFile macro that calls the FileCopy statement with the names of two files.

The FileCopy statement requires both the Source and Destination files to be closed. If either is open, an error occurs and execution stops. FileCopy also requires that the Source file exist.

Listing 12.4

```
1   Public Sub CopyFile()
2       FileCopy "C:\AutoCad\MyProject.dwg", ↵
           "C:\AutoCAD\CopyProject.dwg"
3   End Sub
```

Analysis

- Line 1 starts the `CopyFile` macro.
- Line 2 uses the `FileCopy` statement with the `Source` and `Destination` hard-wired into the code.
- Line 3 ends the `CopyFile` macro.

To make the FileCopy macro more general, you can allow the user to enter the names of the Source and Destination files. Listing 12.3 from the preceding section shows how to prompt the user for a filename and then find out if it exists.

Displaying Open and Save As Dialog Boxes

The Open and Save As dialog boxes are commonly used for opening and saving files in most Windows applications. VBA makes these readily available for use in your applications, via the Microsoft Common Dialog Control. All you need do is add the control to the Toolbox in the VB Editor.

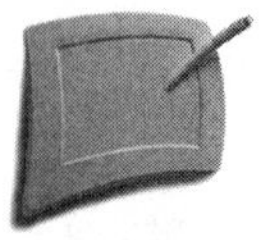

VBA is extremely powerful and can use many of the controls supplied with the Windows applications you have installed on your computer. A complete list of the controls available on your PC can be viewed from the Additional Controls dialog box. You can add any of these controls into your Toolbox, from which you can then drag and drop them onto UserForms in the normal way. These controls retain their full functionality, making them extremely reusable.

If you have to distribute your application, it's best to stick with the plain-vanilla controls provided by default. Just because a control is present on your PC doesn't mean it will be on others—unless the user has previously installed an application that uses this control.

Here are the steps for adding the Common Dialog Control (or any other controls listed on your PC) to the Toolbox. (I hope you have this control on your PC; otherwise, you'll need to use a macro like GetNewFile to open a file and write a macro for saving a file.)

1. Start a new project, open the VB Editor, and add a UserForm.
2. Right-click any control from the Toolbox and choose Additional Controls from the shortcut menu. The dialog box shown in Figure 12.1 appears, containing its long list of all the controls available on your PC that can be added to the Toolbox.
3. Scroll down the Available Controls list and select Microsoft Common Dialog Control version 6.0, as shown in Figure 12.1. The location of the file containing this control is displayed in the frame at the bottom. (The Caption property for this frame has changed to the selected item.)

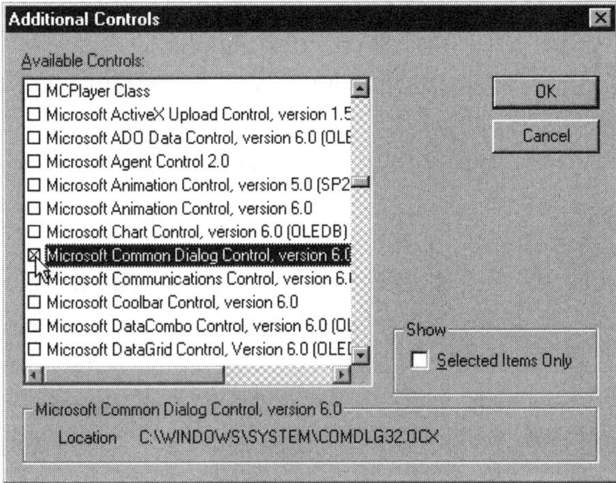

Figure 12.1 *Additional Controls dialog box*

4. Click OK. The CommonDialog control's icon appears at the bottom of the Toolbox:

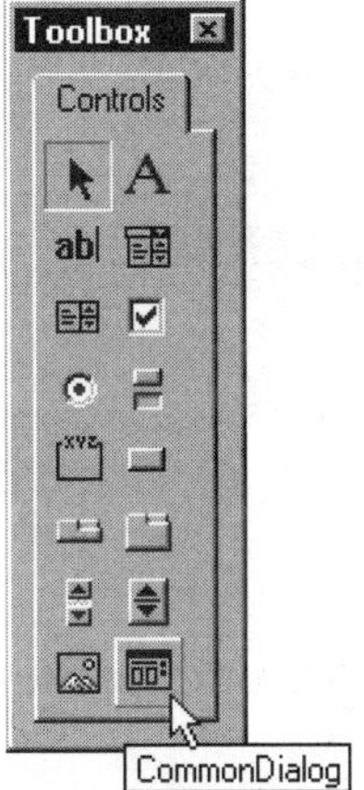

If you want to remove the CommonDialog control from your Toolbox, simply right-click its Toolbox button and select Delete CommonDialog from the pop-up menu.

Using the CommonDialog Control

The CommonDialog control provides a set of common dialog boxes with appropriate controls already set up. These predefined dialog boxes are used throughout most Windows applications and will be familiar to you. In this section you'll see how to utilize the Open and SaveAs dialog boxes contained in properties of this control.

Open Dialog Box

The Open dialog box (Figure 12.2) displays the list of files and folders available from your PC, or on a disk or CD in one of the PC's drives.

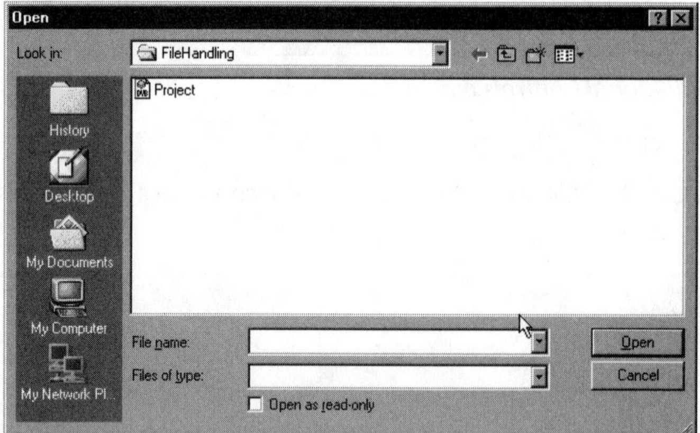

Figure 12.2 *Predefined Open dialog box*

The CommonDialog control has its own set of properties and methods. For example, the ShowOpen method is used to display the Open dialog box, and the Filter property can be set to restrict the types of files that will be included in the list of files. Setting the Filter property in the Properties Window to that shown in Figure 12.3 will display "All Files (*.*)" in the Files of Type box.

The Filter property can also be set in code, as follows:

```
CommonDialog1.Filter = "All Files (*.*)"
```

Exercise 12.2 shows the effect of setting the Filter property on the File Types list in the Open dialog box.

Exercise 12.2: Showing the Open Dialog Box

Listing 12.5 shows how to set up a more complex filtering system that contains a list of filters, and how to designate one of them to be displayed in the Files of Type box when the dialog box opens.

Here are the steps for using the CommonDialog control in an application:

1. If you haven't already done so, follow the steps given at the start of the section "Displaying Open and Save As Dialog Boxes" so that you have a project with a UserForm and the CommonDialog control in the Toolbox.
2. Drag and drop a CommonDialog control onto the UserForm. You can place it anywhere you like, because the control is never visible while the application is running.

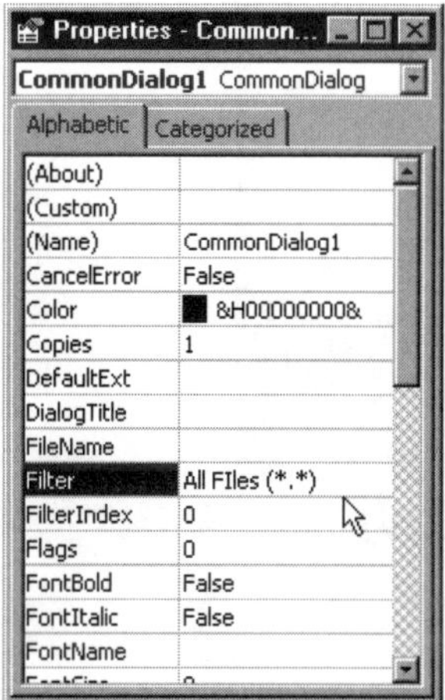

***Figure 12.3** Properties window for CommonDialog1*

You'll find it impossible to resize the CommonDialog control; VBA won't let you. When this control is placed on a UserForm during design time, it appears as a square button with its own little icon. When the UserForm is displayed to the user during run time, this control becomes invisible.

3. Add a command button to the UserForm, make its Caption property Open, and make its Accelerator property **O**.

4. Type the following statements into the command button's Click event procedure:

```
GetDefaultFile
Unload Me
```

5. Enter the GetDefaultFile procedure (Listing 12.5) into the General Declarations section of the UserForm's Code window.

6. Run the application and click Open. The Open dialog box shown in Figure 12.4 appears, with the new property values. Figure 12.5 shows the list of types specified in Line 2 of the GetDefaultFile procedure.

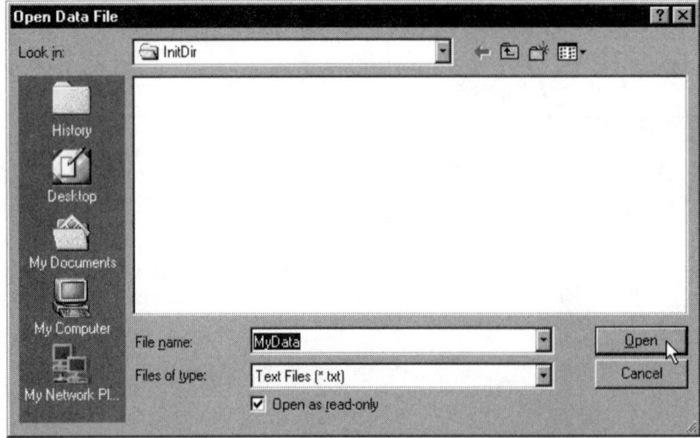

Figure 12.4 *Open dialog box with the new property settings from Listing 12.5*

Figure 12.5 *List of file types produced by Filter property setting from Listing 12.1*

Listing 12.5: GetDefaultFile Procedure

```
1    Sub GetDefaultFile()
2        CommonDialog1.Filter = "All Files (*.*) |*.*|" ↵
            & "Text Files (*.txt) |*.txt|" ↵
            & "Drawing Files (*.dwg) |*.dwg|" ↵
            & "Bitmaps (*.bmp) |*.bmp|"
3        CommonDialog1.FilterIndex = 2
4        CommonDialog1.DialogTitle = "Open Data File"
5        CommonDialog1.InitDir = "c:\InitDir"
6        CommonDialog1.FileName = "MyData.txt"
7        CommonDialog1.ShowOpen
8        NewFileName = CommonDialog1.FileName
9    End Sub
```

Analysis

- Line 1 starts the `GetDefaultFile` macro.
- Line 2 assigns a string defining the filter to the `Filter` property of `CommonDialog1`:
    - The asterisk character is a wildcard character. Thus `*.*` means "list all filenames with all extensions."
    - The pipe symbol (|), ASCII code 124, shares a key on most keyboards with the backward slash symbol (\ ). The pipe is used to split the filter text into sections.
    - The text *before* the first pipe determines what appears in the Files of Type box. The text *after* the first pipe is a directive to Windows about what types of files to display.
    - The second pipe separates the current Files of Type entry from the next one.
    - The concatenation characters (&) join all the substrings together.

Do not include spaces in the directive to Windows containing the types of files to be displayed. If you do, these spaces will be included in the search, resulting in no files being displayed.

- Line 3 assigns 2 to the `FilterIndex` property to indicate that the second item from the list of filters is to be displayed in the Files of Type box by default.

- Line 4 assigns the `DialogTitle` property the caption that's to appear in the Title bar of the Open dialog box.
- Line 5 specifies the initial folder (or directory) to be displayed in the Look In box at the top of the Open dialog box.
- Line 6 specifies the filename that's to appear in the File Name box when the Open dialog box first opens.
- Line 7 calls the `ShowOpen` method to display the Open dialog box.
- Line 8 assigns the pathname represented by the `FileName` property of `CommonDialog1` to the `NewFileName` variable.
- Line 9 ends the `GetDefaultFile` macro.

If a default data file is associated with an application, it is helpful to the user to display this file's details in the boxes provided. Then when the Open dialog box is displayed, all the user has to do is click Open unless they want to open another file.

Save As Dialog Box

The Save As dialog box (Figure 12.6) is very similar to the Open dialog box and has the same Filter and FilterIndex properties to restrict the types of files that appear in the File Name drop-down list. This dialog box uses the ShowSave method to display the Save As dialog box from code.

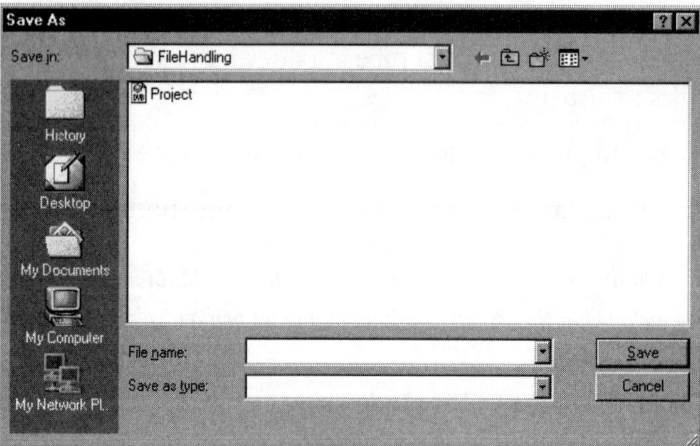

***Figure 12.6** Save As dialog box*

If a file is currently open, Microsoft Windows will automatically display its details in the Save As dialog box; this is typically what the user requires. You can override this, however, by assigning the name of another folder to the InitDir property, and the name of a file to the FileName property. Then these names will appear in the Save As box. Listing 12.5 in the preceding section demonstrated how these properties were set in code.

You can also force the user to select a file by displaying the Save As dialog box without anything preselected. Do this by setting the InitDir and the FileName properties to the empty string:

```
CommonDialog1.FileName = ""
CommonDialog1.InitDir = ""
```

Now that you know how to open and save files containing the information needed by your application, you are now ready to learn how to read and write information from and to files.

When data is being read from a file, the data is considered input; when it is being written to a file, data is considered output.

Writing Data to a File from Code

Writing data to a file (output) is done using the Write statement or the Print statement—but before you can write to a file, you must open it using the Open method. The Write and Print statements write data to a sequential file; both statements have two parameters—the file number and an output list. As demonstrated in the following Click event procedure, items in the outputlist of the Write statement are separated by commas. Items in the outputlist of the Print statement are separated by semicolons or spaces.

```
Private Sub UserForm_Click()
Open "c:/test/temp.txt" For Append As 1
Dim a As Integer, b As Integer, c As Integer, d As String
a = 1: b = 2: c = 3: d = "Hello"
Write #1, a, b, c, d, "world"
Write #1, 1, 2 * b
Print #1, a; b; c; d; "world"
Print #1, 1; 2 * b
Close 1
End Sub
```

When the Write statement sends data to a file, quotation marks (") are placed around strings, and commas are used to separate items in the file. After the last item in the list has been sent, a carriage return and linefeed character are automatically written to the file so that the next data item sent will be placed at the start of a new line.

When the Print statement sends data to a file, there are no quotation marks delimiting strings. Any semicolons or spaces from the *`outputlist`* are replaced character for character by spaces. Figure 12.7 shows the result of running the code shown just above.

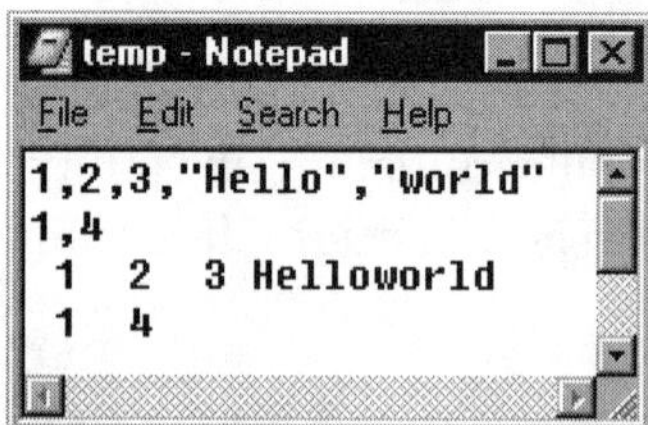

Figure 12.7 *Difference between the data written to a file using the Write statement (top) and the Print statement (bottom)*

The Write statement is normally used when items need to be retrieved from the file individually. Print, on the other hand, is normally used when data is read back from the file line-by-line.

EXERCISE 12.3: DRAWING DETAILS APPLICATION

Let's develop a small application that displays text boxes where the user can enter a description of a drawing and a number that identifies it. The application then appends these items to a file. We'll start by developing the GUI:

1. Start a new project, add a UserForm, with two label controls, two text boxes, and two command buttons. Aim for something like this:

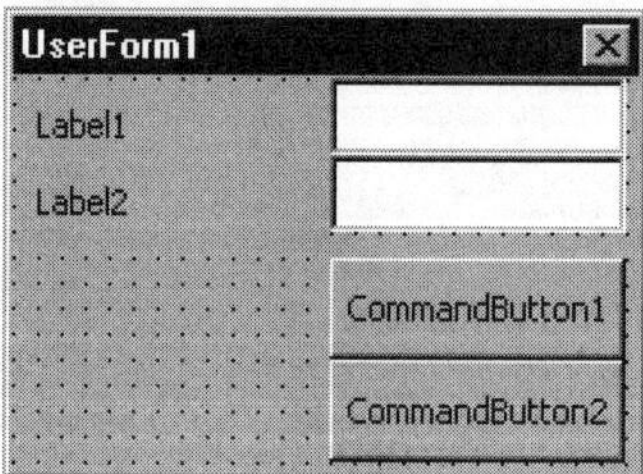

2. Update the properties for these controls to those shown in Table 12.2.
3. Enter the code for the Click event procedures, shown in Listing 12.6. *Note:* For Line 5 to run without error, the folder name must already exist, so if you want to use the same code per se, you'll have to create a new folder of the same name on your C drive.

Table 12.2 Properties for the GUI of Drawing Details UserForm

OLD NAME	NEW NAME	CAPTION
UserForm1	frmDrawingDetails	Drawing Details
Label1	—	Description
Label2	—	Number
TextBox1	txtDescription	—
TextBox2	txtNumber	—
CommandButton1	cmdSaveToFile	Save to File
CommandButton2	cmdExit	Exit

4. Run the code and enter strings into the two text boxes. Then click the Save To File button.

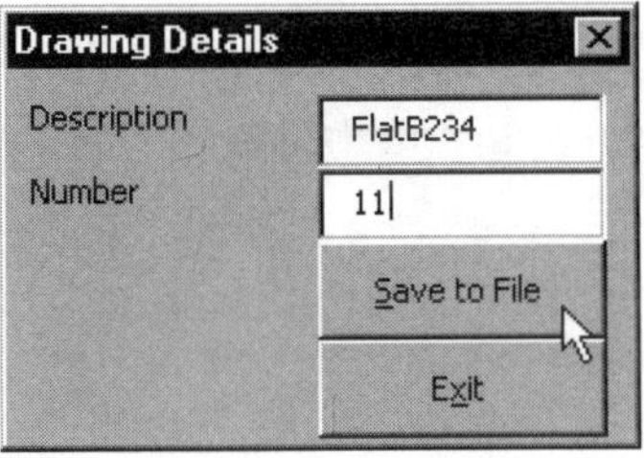

5. Use Microsoft WordPad, Notepad, or Word to view the contents of your data file. The three sets of data I entered were saved as follows:

```
"FlatB234","11332"
"Unit20S","10106"
"Flat10A","10032"
```

Listing 12.6: Click Event Procedures for the Two Command Buttons

```
1   Private Sub cmdSaveToFile_Click()
2       If txtDescription = "" And txtNumber = "" Then
3           MsgBox "No drawing details have been entered!", , ↵
               "Drawing Details"
4       Else
5           Open "C:\AcadFiles\DataFile1.dat" For Append As 1
6           Write #1, txtDescription, txtNumber
7           Close #1
8       End If
9   End Sub
10
11  Private Sub cmdExit_Click()
12      Unload Me
13  End Sub
```

Analysis

- Line 1 starts the Click event procedure of the `CMDSaveToFile` command button.
- Lines 2 and 3 verify that something has in fact been entered in at least one of the text boxes; if not, a message is sent to the user.
- Line 4 contains the `Else` statement.
- Line 5 opens the data file to be appended so that each entry is added to the end of the file, leaving any previous entries intact. Without the `For Append` included in this statement, the `Open` would delete any information contained in the file.
- Line 6 uses the `Write` statement to add the latest text box entries to the end of the data file.
- Line 7 uses the `Close` statement with the file number `#1` as the argument to close the file.
- Line 8 ends the `If` statement block.
- Line 9 ends the Click event procedure of the `CmdSaveToFile` command button.
- Line 11 starts the Click event procedure of the `CmdExit` command button.
- Line 12 contains `Unload Me` to stop the application and closes any files that may still be open.
- Line 13 ends the Click event procedure of the `CmdExit` command button.

Now that you know how to append data to a file, let's take a look at the other modes that can be used for opening files.

Input and Output Modes for Opening Files

This section describes how to open files for input (reading the data) and output (writing the data). A file must be open before you can read any data from it or write any data to it.

As you have already seen, VBA provides the Open statement for this purpose. Here is the syntax of the Open statement:

```
Open pathname For mode As Filenumber
```

pathname This argument uniquely identifies a file.

mode The *mode* can be Input, Output, Append, Binary, or Random.

- Input: The application reads data from a file.
- Output: The application writes data to the file. Any existing data in the file are deleted when the file is opened.
- Append: The application writes data to the end of the file. Any data in the file when it is opened remains intact.
- Binary: The data in the file can be read and written in bytes. Using bytes means that the data can be any type.
- Random: This is the default mode. Data are read from the file by assigning them to variables.

Opening a file in Output mode deletes all the data from the file, whereas opening a file in Append mode preserves any data already in the file.

Filenumber The `Filenumber` is also called *file handle* and can range from 1 to 511 inclusive. This enables hundreds of different files to be open at the same time, all with unique identification numbers. File handles can be specified explicitly, like this:

```
Open MyDataFile For Input As 5
```

or they can be assigned to a variable. If you have a few files in a large application, then declaring variable names for each handle makes your code easier to understand, debug, and maintain over time. Listing 12.7 gives an example of variable names being used to identify two files.

LISTING 12.7: VARIABLE NAMES USED TO IDENTIFY FILES

```
1   Dim DimensionData As Integer
2   Dim GridData As Integer
3   DimensionData = FreeFile
4   Open DimensionFile For Input As DimensionData
5   GridData = FreeFile
6   Open GridFile For Input As GridData
7   Input #DimensionData, Name, Length, Height
8   Input #GridData, Xspacing, YSpacing
```

ANALYSIS

- Lines 1 and 2 declare the two variables that will be used to represent the file handles for the two input files.
- Line 3 calls the `FreeFile` function, which returns the next free file number.
- Line 4 uses the variable `DimensionData` as the file handle when the `DimensionFile` is opened.
- Line 5 calls the `FreeFile` function again, which returns the next free file number.
- Line 6 opens the `GridFile` using the `GridData` file handle.
- Lines 7 and 8 use the `Input` statement with the two variables representing the file handles, to read in data from the two files.

The Application Path Property

You will often want to take the default folder for a data file and make it a subfolder in the same folder as the application. VBA provides the Application object, a global object that is initialized to the pathname of the active application. This object has a Path property that is set to the drive and folder where the application is running. For example, while AutoCAD is running, the Path property is set to `C:\AutoCAD 2000i` (or whatever directory is home to AutoCAD on your PC). This path property string can be extended to include the name of the folder where the data files will be stored. I've stored my string in a variable called ApplicPath:

```
Dim ApplicPath As String
ApplicPath = Application.Path & "\DataFiles\"
```

The Open statement can then extend ApplicPath to include the name of the file required from that folder; for example:

```
Open ApplicPath & "DrawingData1.txt" For Input As 1
```

Using the Input Statement to Read Data from a File

The Input statement retrieves data from a file item by item, or several items at a time, or as an entire line. (Files must be open before you can read from them, as stated earlier.) VBA expects data items sharing the same line in the data file to be separated by commas.

Listing 12.8 contains three macros that use the Input statement to read individual data items, read a whole line at a time, or read a whole file. For illustration purposes, each statement that reads in data is followed by a Debug.Print statement that displays the input in the Immediate window.

LISTING 12.8: PROCEDURES FOR COPYING DATA FROM A FILE

```
Public Sub CopyVariables()
    Dim Description As String, Number As Integer
    Open "C:\AcadFiles\DataFile1.dat" For Input As 1
    While Not EOF(1)
        Input #1, Description, Number
        Debug.Print Description, Number
    Wend
    Close 1
End Sub

Public Sub CopyWholeLine()
    Dim CurrentLine As String
    Open "C:\AcadFiles\DataFile1.dat" For Input As 1
    While Not EOF(1)
        Line Input #1, CurrentLine
```

```
16              Debug.Print CurrentLine
17          Wend
18          Close 1
19      End Sub
20
21      Public Sub CopyWholeFile()
22          Dim Currentlines As String
23          Open "C:\AcadFiles\DataFile1.dat" For Input As 1
24          Currentlines = Input(LOF(1), 1)
25           Debug.Print Currentlines
26          Close 1
27      End Sub
```

ANALYSIS

- Line 1 starts the `CopyVariables` macro, which reads individual data items and assigns them to variables.
- Line 2 declares the variables that are assigned the data read from the file.
- Line 3 opens the file in Input mode.
- Line 4 uses the `EOF` (End Of File) function, which returns True when the end of a file is reached or False otherwise. This function has one parameter, the file number, which must be the file handle of an open file.
- Line 5 reads two items from the current line of the data file and assigns them to the `Description` and `Number` variables.
- Line 6 calls the `Print` method of the `Debug` object that appends the file data assigned to the `Description` and `Number` to the Immediate window.
- Line 7 contains the end of the `While` loop.
- Line 8 closes the input file, making any further input impossible.
- Line 9 ends the `CopyVariables` macro.
- Line 11 starts the `CopyWholeLine` macro that reads items from the data file one line at a time.
- Line 12 declares the `CurrentLine` variable as a string.

- Line 13 opens the data file for input.
- Line 14 starts the `While` loop that will continue looping until all the data has been input from the file.
- Line 15 uses the `Line Input` statement to read a whole line from the input file and assign it to the `CurrentLine` variable.
- Line 16 calls the `Print` method of the `Debug` object to display the value of the `CurrentLine` variable in the Immediate window.
- Line 17 ends the `While` loop.
- Line 18 closes the input file.
- Line 19 ends the `CopyWholeLine` macro.
- Line 21 starts the `CopyWholeFile` macro.
- Line 22 declares the `CurrentLines` as a String type.
- Line 23 opens the data file for input.
- Line 24 calls the `Input` function with two arguments: the number of characters to return, and the file number. For the first argument, the `LOF` function is called with the file number to return the number of bytes in the file—this is the same as the number of characters. This results in the `CurrentLines` variable's being assigned all the characters in the file.
- Line 25 calls the `Print` method of the `Debug` object to display the value of the `CurrentLines` variable in the Immediate window.
- Line 26 closes the file.
- Line 27 ends the `CopyWholeFile` macro.

Closing Files

The Close statement is used to close files that were opened by the Open statement while an application was running. Closing a file stops data being read from or written to the file. It is often called with a file number to close a single file, but it can be called without a file number to close *all* open files. When you close a file, all the buffer space that was assigned to it is released, and the file number no longer accesses that file.

Summary

After working your way through this chapter, you will be able to do all of the following from VBA macros:

- Create new drawings with a specified number of Layout tabs.
- Save a new or an existing drawing to a file.
- Write code to copy files, and test to see if a file exists.
- Add the CommonDialog control to your Toolbox and use it to display the Open and Save As dialog boxes.
- Add any control available on your PC to the Toolbox.
- Open and close files.
- Write data to a file.
- Input single items of data, whole lines of data, and complete files of data.

Part 4
2D Drawing Techniques

In This Part

Working with 2D Drawing Techniques

AUTOCAD VBA

Chapter 13

This chapter looks first at the drawing features provided by AutoCAD that help you draw with precision—features such as grid patterns and snap points that help your lines join up exactly, and polar tracking to help you position lines at the correct angle. You'll also learn how to draw spline curves and create shapes from your VBA code, and to move them around in the drawing area.

- Improving drawing precision by changing grid and snap angles
- Controlling polar tracking
- Drawing splines
- Adding shapes to drawings
- Moving objects with the Move method in your code

Interactive Drawing Techniques for Precision

The accuracy of a drawing depends on how precisely the points defining it have been positioned in the drawing area. Because of the miniscule size of a pixel and the inaccuracy of the mouse, it's difficult to click on any particular pixel. This has repercussions when you want to draw precisely horizontal or vertical lines or if you need two lines to meet exactly. AutoCAD has several features to overcome this problem and increase the precision capability as you construct your drawings.

You have already met up with grid patterns and snap points in Chapter 8. In this section you'll learn how to set the grid points at an angle, and how to control polar tracking.

Changing Grid and Snap Angles

You know that the grid is a net of regularly spaced dots that provide a visual cue for users while moving the mouse cursor around the drawing area. The Snap feature restricts the cursor to snap positions in order to ensure that any points selected using the mouse are at a snap point. Since snap points are invisible to the user, they are commonly represented using grid points.

As you learned in Chapter 8, snap points are an excellent tool, as well, for ensuring that lines drawn independently will actually join up.

Listing 13.1 shows how to set up the spacing between grid dots and snap points. Both features are switched on from the macro. To try out this macro, place it in ThisDrawing's Code window and add the following declaration statement to the General Declarations section:

```
Const Pi = 3.14
```

Figure 13.1 shows the grid dots rotated 30° as a result of running the SnapToGrid macro.

LISTING 13.1: SNAPTOGRID MACRO

```
Public Sub SnapToGrid()
    With ThisDrawing.ActiveViewport
        ' Turn on Snapping and reset the viewport.
        .SetGridSpacing 2#, 2#
        .SetSnapSpacing 1#, 1#
```

```
6           .SnapRotationAngle = 30 * pi / 180
7           .SnapOn = True
8           .GridOn = True
9       End With
10      ThisDrawing.ActiveViewport = ThisDrawing.ActiveViewport
11      ZoomAll
12  End Sub
```

ANALYSIS

- Line 1 starts the `SnapToGrid` macro that sets the grid as well as the snap spacing and angle, and turns both features on.
- Line 2 uses the `With` statement so that the methods and properties set for the snap and grid features can be used without needing to fully qualify them. These features are all contained in the Viewport object.
- Lines 4 and 5 call the `SetGridSpacing` and `SetSnapSpacing` methods with arguments defining the horizontal and vertical spacing. These arguments have been set to 1 for both directions of snap points, and to 2 for both directions of grid dots.
- Line 6 sets the `SnapRotationAngle` property to 30°. This changes the angle of the snap points and the grid points, as well as rotating the cursor.
- Lines 7 and 8 set the `GridOn` and `SnapOn` properties to `True` so that the grid dots will be visible, and the crosshair cursor will snap to the snap points as it is moved around the Model Space. When running this macro, the crosshair cursor will snap to the grid points, and also to halfway between adjacent grid points because of the different values passed as arguments in Lines 4 and 5.
- Line 9 ends the `With` statement.
- Line 10 assigns the active viewport to itself so that the entire drawing is regenerated. This updates the active viewport to display the grid dots and turns on the snap mode.
- Line 11 calls the `ZoomAll` method to display the entire drawing.
- Line 12 ends the `SnapToGrid` macro.

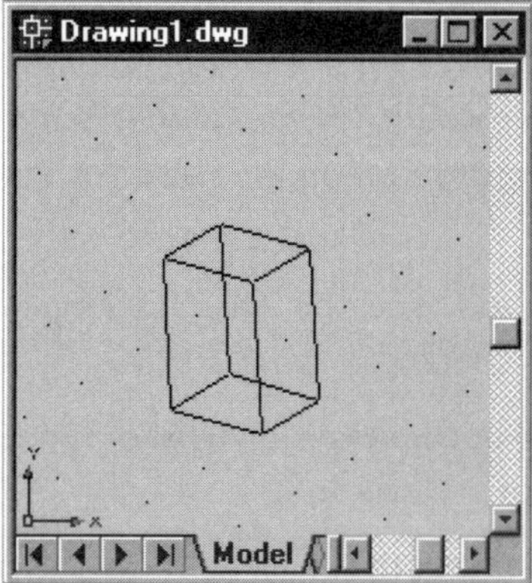

Figure 13.1 *Grid dots rotated at a 30° angle by the SnapToGrid macro (Listing 13.1)*

Controlling Polar Tracking

AutoCAD's Polar Tracking feature gives you the option of drawing exactly horizontal and exactly vertical lines, or drawing lines using any of the polar angles given in Figure 13.2 (which are converted to radians). This allows you to draw lines at common polar angles with complete precision.

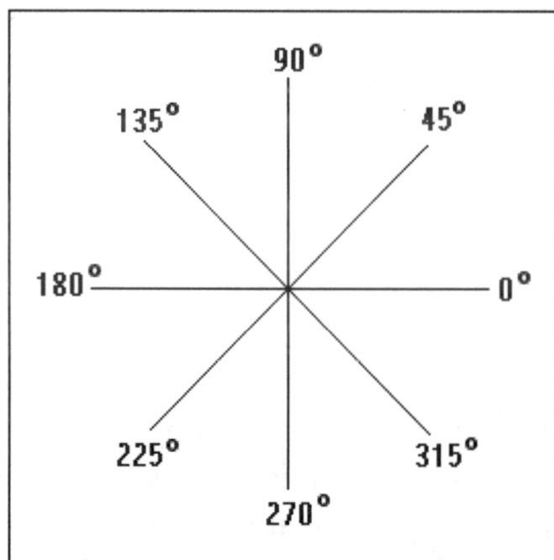

Figure 13.2 *AutoCAD's default system for specifying the angles for polar coordinates*

If you already are familiar with the advantages of the Polar Tracking feature, you may want to skip to the next section and see how the same precision can be achieved in code. If you've never used Polar Tracking, try doing it from the AutoCAD window first. Then you'll see clearly the difference between doing it from AutoCAD and doing it from code. The following steps show you how to turn on the Polar Tracking feature from the AutoCAD window:

1. Choose Tools ➜ Drafting Settings and select the Polar Tracking tab. Make sure the Polar Tracking On check box is checked.
2. For the incremental angle, select 30 in the drop-down list or type **30** in the box. Click OK to return to the AutoCAD window.
3. Click to select the position for the start of the line, and move the cursor to the position for the second point. A rubber-band line based at the start position follows the crosshair cursor as you move it around in the Model Space.
4. Move the cursor until the line is almost horizontal. A dashed horizontal line is displayed, emanating from the start position, and a ToolTip appears as shown in Figure 13.3.

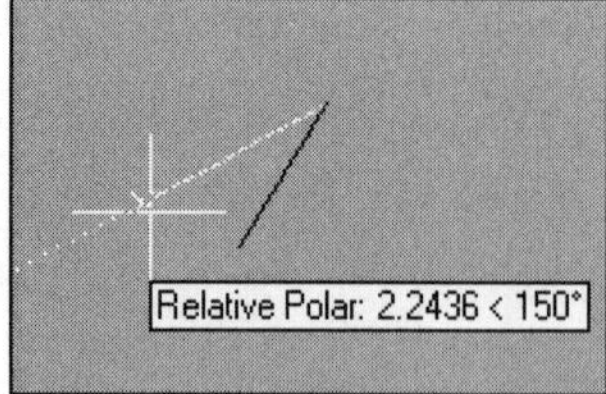

***Figure 13.3** Polar Tracking with an incremental angle of 30°*

5. Move the cursor around in a circular motion and watch a dashed line appear every 30° (Figure 13.3).

Macro for Creating a Polar Point

A polar point can be achieved from a macro by prompting the user to select a base point, an angle, and a distance, and then calling the PolarPoint method with these three things as arguments. Listing 13.2 shows the CreatePolarPoint macro. It prompts the user to enter the details of the polar coordinates for the new point. The following steps show you how to develop and run this project.

Exercise 13.1: Creating a Polar Point

1. Enter the CreatePolarPoint macro (Listing 13.2) in the ThisDrawing Code window.
2. Run the macro from the Macros dialog box in the AutoCAD window. `Select base point` appears in the command line.
3. Select the point that you want to use as your base point. `Enter angle` appears in the command line, and a rubber-band line starting from the base point now follows the crosshair cursor as you move it around in the Model Space. The x- and y-coordinate values in the status bar change to distance and angle values, as shown here:

   3.4203< 34 , 0.0000

4. When the required angle is displayed, click the mouse button. The command in the command window changes to `Enter distance`, and the rubber-band line continues to follow the crosshair cursor.
5. Stretch or shrink the rubber-band line to the length required, and click the mouse. (The angle doesn't matter at this stage because it will not affect the angle already entered.) When you click the mouse, the macro draws a line between the base point and the new point you've just specified.

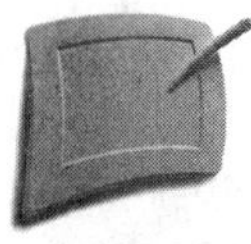

The length of the line is the first number displayed in the coordinates section of the status bar—you'll find this useful as a drawing guide.

Listing 13.2: CreatePolarPoint Macro

```
Public Sub CreatePolarPoint()
    Dim LineObject As AcadLine
    Dim BasePoint As Variant
    Dim NewPoint As Variant
    Dim AngleInRadians As Double
    Dim Distance As Double
    BasePoint = ThisDrawing.Utility.GetPoint ↵
       (, "Select base point")
    AngleInRadians = ThisDrawing.Utility.GetAngle ↵
       (BasePoint, "Enter angle")
```

```
9       Distance = ThisDrawing.Utility.GetDistance ↵
           (BasePoint, "Enter distance")
10      NewPoint = ThisDrawing.Utility.PolarPoint ↵
           (BasePoint, AngleInRadians, Distance)
11      Set LineObject = ThisDrawing.ModelSpace.AddLine ↵
           (BasePoint, NewPoint)
12      LineObject.Update
13  End Sub
```

ANALYSIS

- Line 1 starts the `CreatePolarPoint` macro, which prompts the user for the base point, then the angle, and finally the distance.
- Lines 2 through 6 declare the variables used in the macro.
- Line 7 calls the `GetPoint` method to prompt the user to select the base point, and assigns the coordinates of the point clicked to the `BasePoint` variable.
- Line 8 calls the `GetAngle` method that prompts the user to enter an angle. As the user moves the cursor around the screen, the angle in degrees is displayed in the coordinates section of the status bar. The angle is measured as being between the x-axis and the direction of the line. When the user clicks the mouse, this angle is converted to radians before being returned by the `GetAngle` method.
- Line 9 calls the `GetDistance` method that prompts the user to enter the distance from the new point to the base point. The distance and angle values continue to be displayed in the status bar.
- Line 10 calls the `PolarPoint` method with the base point, angle in radians, and distance. This method calculates the coordinates of the new point as being the specified distance along the line drawn from the base point at the specified angle.
- Lines 11 and 12 create a Line object containing the line defined by the base point and the new point, and draw it in the Model Space.
- Line 13 ends the `CreatePolarPoint` macro.

Drawing Splines

A spline is a smooth curve defined by a set of points. Rather than having straight lines between adjacent points, the spline has curves. The set of points are called control points because they control the shape of the curve. AutoCAD uses the non-uniform rational B-spline (NURBS) quadratic or cubic curve.

In VBA code, splines are created using the AddSpline method. It has three parameters: a set of control points, and the tangents at the two end control points of the spline. The DrawSpline macro given in Listing 13.3 calls the GetControlPoints macro, creates the two tangents, and creates the spline. To try this out, follow these steps:

Exercise 13.2: Drawing a Spline

1. Create a new project and enter the code given in Listing 13.3 into the Code window of the ThisDrawing module.
2. Run the Draw Spline application and try drawing a few splines. Figure 13.4 shows some that were created by this macro.

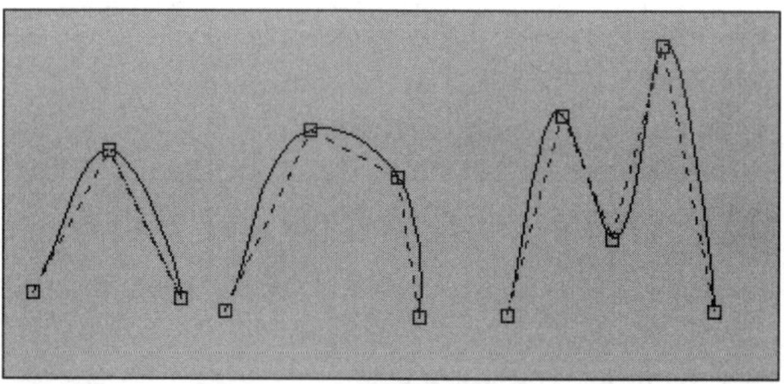

Figure 13.4 *Splines created by the DrawSpline macro*

3. Next, try selecting the same position for the first and last points to make your spline into a closed shape. Figure 13.5 shows three closed splines.

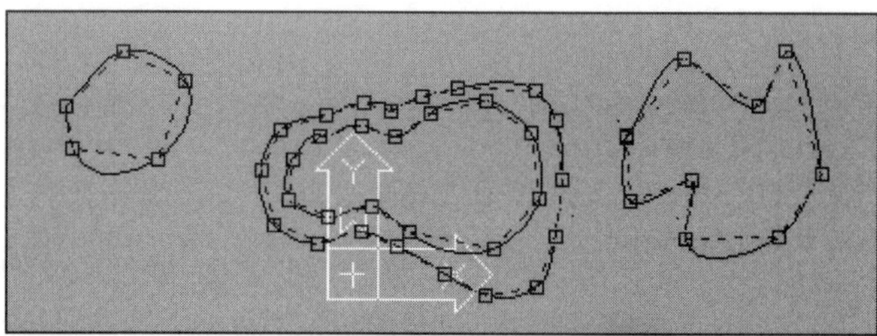

Figure 13.5 *Closed spline curves created by selecting the first points again after all the other points were entered*

LISTING 13.3: MACRO FOR DRAWING A SPLINE

```
Dim PolygonObject As AcadPolyline
Dim ControlPoints() As Double
Dim MaxArrayIndex As Integer

Public Sub DrawSpline()
Dim SplineObject As AcadSpline
Dim StartTangent(0 To 2) As Double, ↵
   EndTangent(0 To 2) As Double
    GetControlPoints
    StartTangent(0) = ControlPoints(3) - ControlPoints(0)
    StartTangent(1) = ControlPoints(4) - ControlPoints(1)
    StartTangent(2) = ControlPoints(5) - ControlPoints(2)
    EndTangent(0) = ControlPoints(MaxArrayIndex - 6) ↵
       - ControlPoints(MaxArrayIndex - 3)
    EndTangent(1) = ControlPoints(MaxArrayIndex - 5) ↵
       - ControlPoints(MaxArrayIndex - 2)
    EndTangent(2) = ControlPoints(MaxArrayIndex - 4) ↵
       - ControlPoints(MaxArrayIndex - 1)
    Set SplineObject = ThisDrawing.ModelSpace.AddSpline↵
       (ControlPoints, StartTangent, EndTangent)
    SplineObject.Update
End Sub

Public Sub GetControlPoints()
    Dim CurrentPoint As Variant
    Dim Finished As Boolean
    Finished = False
    MaxArrayIndex = -1
    While Not Finished
        'keep looping until the Enter key is pressed
        On Error Resume Next
        CurrentPoint = ThisDrawing.Utility.GetPoint↵
           (, "Click on next control point or hit Enter ↵
           to finish!")
        If Err.Number <> 0 Then 'Enter key pressed
            Finished = True
        Else
            MaxArrayIndex = MaxArrayIndex + 3
            ReDim Preserve ControlPoints(0 To MaxArrayIndex)
            'add new point to the array
```

```
34                ControlPoints(MaxArrayIndex - 2) = ↵
                     CurrentPoint(0)
35                ControlPoints(MaxArrayIndex - 1) = ↵
                     CurrentPoint(1)
36                ControlPoints(MaxArrayIndex) = CurrentPoint(2)
37                If MaxArrayIndex > 2 Then
38                    With ThisDrawing.ModelSpace
39                        If MaxArrayIndex > 5 ↵
                           Then PolygonObject.Delete
40                        Set PolygonObject = ↵
                           .AddPolyline(ControlPoints)
41                        PolygonObject.Color = acBlue
42                        PolygonObject.Update
43                    End With
44                End If
45            End If
46        Wend
47    End Sub
```

Analysis

- Line 1 declares the `PolygonObject` variable as being capable of referencing a Polyline object.
- Line 2 declares the `ControlPoints` array as a dynamic array by not dimensioning it.
- Line 3 declares the `MaxArrayIndex` variable that is used to keep tabs on the number of coordinates values stored in the `ControlPoints` array.
- Line 5 starts the `DrawSpline` macro that calls `GetControlPoints` and then uses the points as the basis for creating and drawing a spline curve.
- Line 6 declares the `SplineObject` variable that will be set up to reference the Spline object.
- Line 7 declares the two arrays that will be assigned the direction vectors of the start and end tangents.
- Line 8 calls the `GetControlPoints` macro that fills the `ControlPoints` array with points selected by the user.
- Lines 9 through 11 take the three components of the direction vector for the line between the first two control points and assign them to the `StartTangent` array.

- Lines 12 through 14 assign to the `EndTangent` the direction vector components for the line between the last two control points.
- Line 15 calls the `AddSpline` method to create a Spline object and adds it to the ModelSpace collection.
- Line 16 calls the `Update` method to draw the spline curve in the Model Space.
- Line 17 ends the `DrawSpline` macro.
- Line 19 starts the `GetControlPoints` macro that prompts the user to enter points, and appends them onto the `ControlPoints` array.
- Line 20 declares the `CurrentPoint` variable as a Variant so that it can be assigned a three-element array containing the coordinates.
- Line 21 declares `Finished` as Boolean. This variable is used to determine when the user has finished entering control points.
- Line 22 sets `Finished` to `False` so that the `While` loop block statements will be executed at least once.
- Line 23 sets the `MaxArrayIndex` value to a negative value, to indicate that the first three coordinates have not yet been allocated to the array.
- Lines 24 through 46 form the `While` statement block, which continually prompts the user for control points until the Enter key is pressed.
- Line 47 ends the `GetControlPoints` macro.

Because the macro stores the points selected in a Polyline object (Line 40) and stores the spline curve in a Spline object (Line 15), each object can be selected individually. You may find it useful to select the polyline and delete it, leaving the spline curve as shown in Figure 13.6.

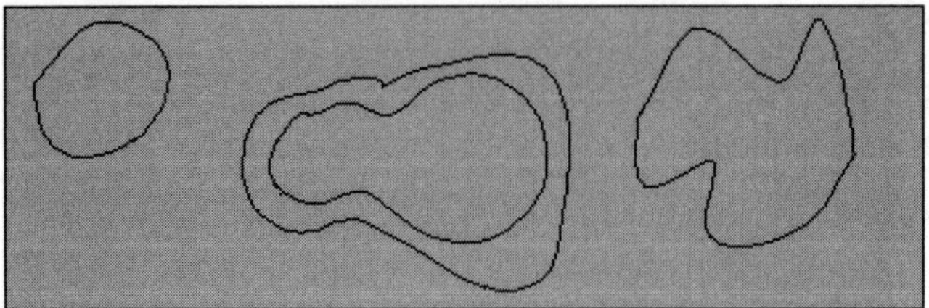

Figure 13.6 *Spline curves with the polylines deleted*

You can adjust any of the control points of the spline: Click the spline to highlight it and then select one of the highlighted points. The point selected will become highlighted in red, and you'll be able to drag it around the screen with the curve following the mouse cursor (see Figure 13.7). When the curve has the shape you want, simply let go of the mouse button.

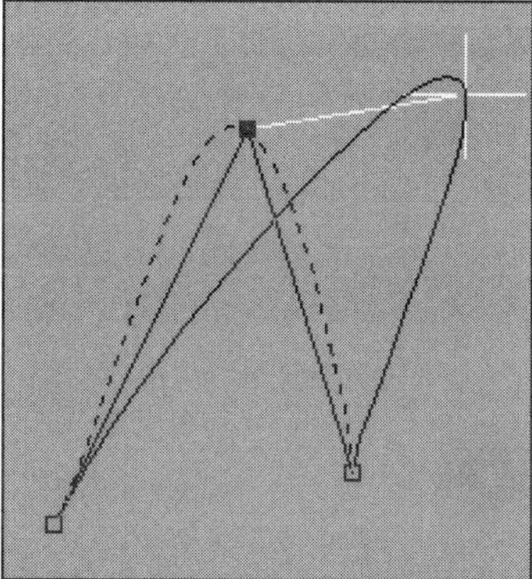

***Figure 13.7** Making adjustments to a control point from a Spline curve*

Adding and Loading Shapes

A Shape object can contain a mixture of lines, arcs, and circles that collectively define a shape. The AddShape method is used to create a Shape object based on a template shape, which is identified by its name in an SHX file. AddShape has four parameters: the shape's name, its position in the drawing area, the scaling factor, and the rotation angle.

Before you can add a shape to your drawing, it must be loaded into AutoCAD. The LoadShapeFile method is used to load a shape file and to make the various shapes it contains available for use in the current drawing. (Shape files can contain more than one shape.) Here are the steps to view a shape file and the shapes it contains:

1. From the AutoCAD window, type **`load`** in the command line and press Enter. The Select Shape File dialog box appears.

2. Double-click the Support folder in the list and select the `ltypeshp` file. Click Open. The Select Shape File dialog box closes and you return to the AutoCAD window.

3. Type **shape** in the command line and press Enter. AutoCAD responds with the prompt `Enter shape name or [?]:`.

4. Enter **?**, and you're prompted to `Enter shape name(s) to list <*>:`.

5. Press Enter without typing anything. The Available Shapes list appears, as shown in Figure 13.8.

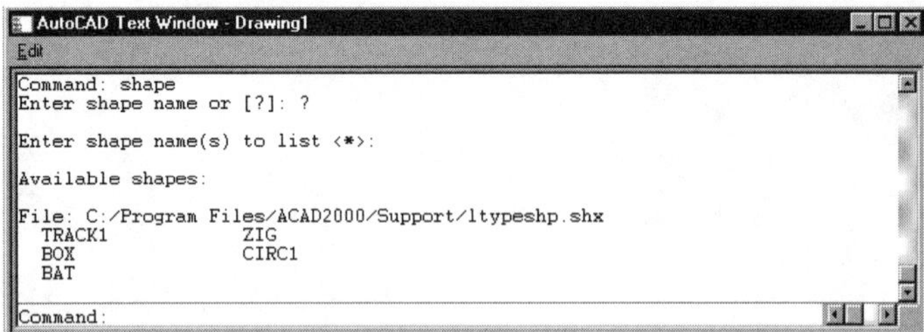

Figure 13.8 *The sequence of prompts and responses required to see the shapes available*

Loading and Adding Shapes from a Macro

If you know the name of the shape file you want to use, you can load this file and use it to add a shape to the active drawing document. Listing 13.4 gives the code for the GetShapeFromFile macro, which names the box shape as being the one required. Figure 13.9 shows this box drawn in the Model Space as a result of running the macro.

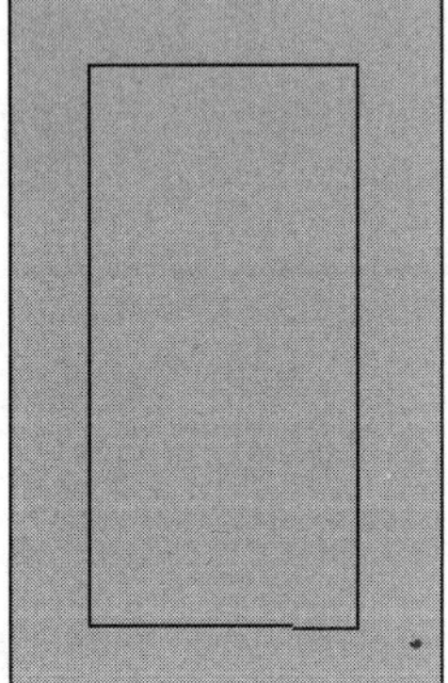

Figure 13.9 *The box shape drawn by running the GetShapeFromFile macro (Listing 13.4)*

If you would like to try this macro, enter it into ThisDrawing's Code window and add the following declaration statement to the General Declarations section:

```
Const Pi = 3.14
```

You may need to update the filename in Line 4 as required by your installation.

Listing 13.4: GetShapeFromFile Macro

```
1   Public Sub GetShapeFromFile()
2       Dim ShapeObject As AcadShape
3       Dim InsertionPoint(0 To 2) As Double
4       ThisDrawing.LoadShapeFile ↵
           ("C:/Program Files/ACAD2000i/Support/ltypeshp.shx")
5       InsertionPoint(0) = 1#
6       InsertionPoint(1) = 1#
7       InsertionPoint(2) = 0#
8       Set ShapeObject = ThisDrawing.ModelSpace.AddShape ↵
           ("box", InsertionPoint, 2#, pi / 2#)
9       ShapeObject.Update
10      ZoomAll
11  End Sub
```

Analysis

- Line 1 starts the `GetShapeFromFile` macro, which retrieves the shape named `"box"` from the shape file and displays it in the Model Space.
- Line 2 declares the `ShapeObject` variable as being capable of referencing a Shape object.
- Line 3 declares the `InsertionPoint` array that will be assigned the coordinates of the position where the shape will be placed.
- Line 4 uses the `LoadShapeFile` method to load the shape file into AutoCAD so that shapes can be retrieved from it to add to the current drawing.
- Lines 5 through 7 assign values to the `InsertionPoint` to specify where the shape's single point is placed. The single point appears when the shape is selected. The single point for the box shape is shown later in Figure 13.11.
- Line 8 calls the `AddShape` method to create a Shape object, with the `box` shape being passed as the first argument. The `InsertionPoint` variable is passed as the second argument to specify where the positioning point is to be placed (see

Figure 13.11). The third argument is the scaling factor, passed explicitly as `2` so that the shape doubles in size when drawn. The last argument is the rotation angle if the shape is to be rotated—in this case it's `pi / 2`, which will rotate the shape by 90°.

- Line 9 redraws the shape in the Model Space.
- Line 10 calls the `ZoomAll` method to ensure that all the shapes are visible in the Model Space.
- Line 11 ends the `GetShapeFromFile` macro.

Shape objects have the advantage that only one positioning point is needed, rather than a collection of points to define their outlines. This becomes an advantage if you ever need to select a Shape object. For example, Figure 13.10 appears to contain two rectangles. The one on the left was drawn using the Rectangle icon from the Draw toolbar, and the one on the right is the Shape object, `box`. When these rectangles are selected, four points are highlighted on the one to the left, while only one point is highlighted on the right one.

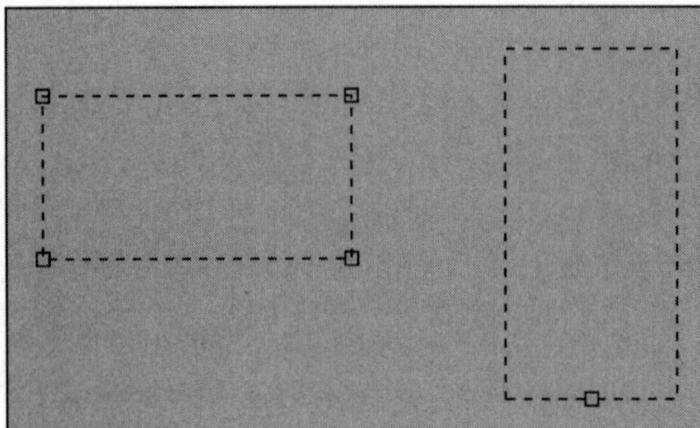

***Figure 13.10** The rectangle on the left drawn using the Draw Toolbar is defined by four points, whereas the* `box` *shape on the right is defined by only one point.*

The single point that is highlighted in a shape generated from a Shape object represents its position on the screen. If you want to move the shape to a new position, you may find it helpful to drag it to its new position using the positioning point as the basis, as shown in Figure 13.11.

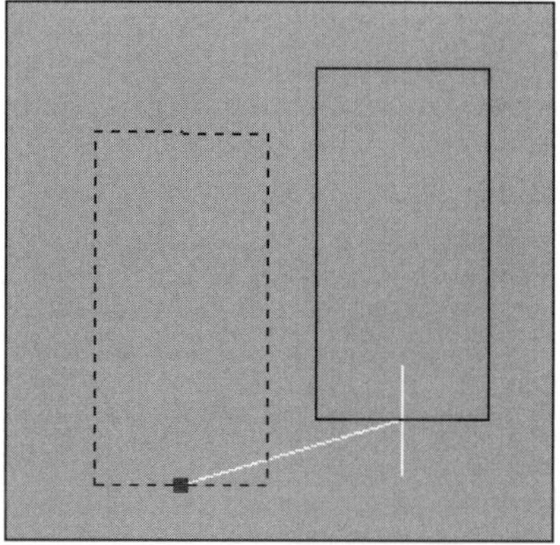

Figure 13.11 *Dragging the* box *shape around the screen by its positioning point*

Moving a Drawing Object from within Code

Drawing objects can be moved around the Model Space using their Move method, which has two parameters that define a direction vector for the move. The direction vector determines not only the direction but also how far the object will move. The MoveShape macro given in Listing 13.5 demonstrates the use of the Move method to move a Shape object around the Model Space in small steps. Exactly the same technique is used for any of the Circle, Line, and Ellipse, and other drawing objects.

To try this macro, place it into the Code window for ThisDrawing. Then copy into the Code window the GetShapeFromFile macro given in Listing 13.4, making adjustments to this macro as described in the Analysis section following Listing 13.5. You'll likely need to adjust the value assigned to the NumberOfMoves constant, because specific hardware configurations will influence the speed of the object.

Listing 13.5: GetShapeFromFile Macro

```
Const pi = 3.14
Const NumberOfMoves = 200
Dim ShapeObject As AcadShape

```

```
Public Sub GetShapeFromFile()
    Dim InsertionPoint(0 To 2) As Double
    ThisDrawing.LoadShapeFile ↵
       ("C:/Program Files/ACAD2000/Support/ltypeshp.shx")
    InsertionPoint(0) = 1#
    InsertionPoint(1) = 1#
    InsertionPoint(2) = 0#
    Set ShapeObject = ThisDrawing.ModelSpace.AddShape ↵
       ("box", InsertionPoint, 2#, pi / 2#)
    ShapeObject.Update
    ZoomAll
    MoveShape
End Sub

Public Sub MoveShape()
    'moves a shape from a to b in one or more steps
    Dim StartPoint As Variant, EndPoint As Variant
    Dim CurrentPosition(0 To 2) As Double
    Dim LastPosition As Variant
    Dim IncX As Double, IncY As Double
    Dim Count As Integer, ButtonClicked As Integer
    StartPoint = ThisDrawing.Utility.GetPoint (, ↵
      "Enter the starting position for the direction of ↵
      the move.")
    EndPoint = ThisDrawing.Utility.GetPoint (StartPoint, ↵
      "Enter the finish position for the direction of ↵
      the move.")
    ButtonClicked = MsgBox ↵
     ("Do you want to animate the move?", vbYesNo, ↵
     "Moving Shapes")
    If ButtonClicked = vbYes Then
        IncX = (EndPoint(0) - StartPoint(0)) / NumberOfMoves
        IncY = (EndPoint(1) - StartPoint(1)) / NumberOfMoves
        LastPosition = StartPoint
        CurrentPosition(0) = StartPoint(0)
        CurrentPosition(1) = StartPoint(1)
        For Count = 1 To NumberOfMoves
            CurrentPosition(0) = CurrentPosition(0) + IncX
            CurrentPosition(1) = CurrentPosition(1) + IncY
            ShapeObject.Move LastPosition, CurrentPosition
```

```
37              LastPosition = CurrentPosition
38              ShapeObject.Update
39          Next
40      Else
41          ShapeObject.Move StartPoint, EndPoint
42          ShapeObject.Update
43      End If
44  End Sub
```

ANALYSIS

- Line 1 declares `pi` as a constant value.
- Line 2 declares the constant `NumberOfMoves` and sets its value to `200`. This is the number of moves a shape will undergo if the user clicks Yes to animate the move. You may want to change this value according to your hardware configuration. Increasing the value will slow down the animation, and decreasing the value will speed it up.
- Line 3 declares the `ShapeObject` variable as being able to refer to a Shape object. In Listing 13.4 this was declared inside the `GetShapeFromFile` macro, but here it has been moved to the General Declarations section so that it can also be used inside the `MoveShape` macro.
- Lines 5 through 15 contain the `GetShapeFromFile` macro. It is much the same as the macro of the same name shown in Listing 13.4, except that the `ShapeObject` declaration is now in the General Declarations section, and the macro now calls the `MoveShape` macro (Line 14).
- Line 17 starts the `MoveShape` macro that moves a shape from one position to another in a single step, or as an animated sequence over several steps.
- Line 19 declares `StartPoint` and `EndPoint`, which will be used to define the endpoints of the line that represents the direction in which the shape will move and the length of the move.
- Line 20 declares `CurrentPosition` as an array rather than a Variant type, since the elements need to be accessed individually to increment the x- and y-coordinates separately.
- Line 21 declares the `LastPosition` as a Variant rather than an array, because this element needs to be assigned the contents of the `CurrentPosition` array.

Making `LastPosition` a Variant allows this assignment to happen in a single statement.

- Line 22 declares the increment in the x direction to be `IncX`, and the increment in the y direction to be `IncY`. These are needed so that the shape ends up at the position specified by `EndPoint` after the number of moves determined by the setting of the `NumberOfMoves` constant.
- Line 23 declares the `Count` variable that will be used by the `For` loop, and the `ButtonClicked` variable that will be used by the `MsgBox` function to assign the value representing the user's response.
- Lines 24 and 25 prompt the user to enter the direction vector for the move.
- Line 26 calls the `MsgBox` function to prompt the user to click a button to indicate whether or not they want an animated move.
- Line 27 starts the `If...Then...Else...` statement block by checking to see if the user clicked the Yes button.
- Lines 28 and 29 calculate values for the increments in the x and y directions, so that the `EndPoint` position is reached after the shape has moved by the value of `NumberOfMoves`.
- Line 30 initializes the `LastPosition` variable to the `StartPoint` before entering the `For` loop.
- Lines 31 and 32 assign the `CurrentPosition` the coordinates from the `StartPoint`.
- Line 33 starts the `For` loop that will be executed until `Count` is equal to the value of `NumberOfMoves`.
- Lines 34 and 35 add the x and y increments onto the `CurrentPosition` variable's coordinates, to get the next position to which the shape will be moved.
- Line 36 calls the `Move` method of the Shape object, with the `LastPosition` and `CurrentPosition` variables as the arguments. The `Move` method moves the line along the direction vector defined by these two variables.
- Line 37 sets the `LastPosition` coordinates to the `CurrentPosition` coordinates in readiness for the next move.
- Line 38 draws the Shape object at its new position in the Model Space.

- Line 39 ends the `For` loop.
- Line 40 starts the `Else` part of the `If...Then...Else...` statement, which will be executed if the user clicks the No button at Line 26.
- Line 41 calls the `Move` method with the `StartPoint` and `EndPoint` variables so that the move is accomplished in a single step.
- Line 42 calls the `Update` method to draw the shape at its new position in the Model Space.
- Line 43 ends the `If...Then...Else...` statement block.
- Line 44 ends the `MoveShape` macro.

Summary

After working through this chapter, you'll be able to do all of the following from a macro:

- Control the grid and snap angles.
- Create a polar point from a macro.
- Create and manipulate Spline objects.
- Load a shape from an SHX file.
- Move a drawing object around the Model Space in a single step or as an animated sequence.

Grouping Objects

AUTOCAD VBA

Chapter 14

This chapter discusses several different methods for grouping drawing objects into a single entity so that you can operate on them "en block," allowing you to work more efficiently. The entities demonstrated here are layers, blocks, Xref blocks, selection sets, and groups.

This chapter covers the following topics:

- Grouping objects into layers
- The On, Freeze, and Lock options
- Grouping objects into blocks
- Using selection sets
- Using groups

Collecting Objects into Layers

Layers are something that you use all the time in AutoCAD, although you may not always be aware of it—every drawing object that you add to a drawing is associated with a layer. Whenever you start a new drawing, AutoCAD creates a default layer named Layer0 and makes it the active layer. All of the objects you add to your drawing are added to the active layer. If you want to draw on a different layer, you have to create that layer and make it the active one.

You'll find layers extremely useful for collecting the various entities that make up a drawing into logical groups. Each group can be drawn in a different color so that it can be easily distinguished. All of the layers associated with a particular drawing are stored in its `.dwg` file, so you can quickly display the entities belonging to a particular layer simply by setting its LayerOn property to True (see "Accessing All Layers from a Macro" later in this chapter). Similarly, you can make all the elements invisible by setting the LayerOn property to False. This gives you the advantage of being able to display just the elements you need to see, on the layers you need to see, as you're adding drawing objects to another layer. For example, when you create the floor plan for the villa in Chapter 8, you may want to add dimensions on a separate layer. That way you can easily display the dimensions whenever they're required, and turn them off again at other times.

Creating Layers from the AutoCAD Window

In AutoCAD, a new layer is created from the Layer Properties Manager dialog box (Figure 14.1). A newborn layer is given the default name of Layer#, where # is a sequential number.

If you want your new layer to inherit the same properties as an existing layer, you need only select the existing layer before clicking the New button in the Layer Properties Manager.

The following steps show you how to create a new layer from within AutoCAD:

1. Choose Format ➜ Layer. The Layer Properties Manager dialog box appears, with a list of all the layers associated with the active drawing.
2. Click the New button in the upper right of the dialog box. A new layer named Layer1 is created and added to the list, immediately below the layer selected before you clicked New. Automatically, Layer1 inherits the same property values as the layer that was selected when you clicked New.

3. Select the new layer in the list, and change any of its attributes. You can do this in either the list or the Details frame. For example, try changing Layer1 to MyLayer in the Details frame. The new details immediately appear in the layers list, and vice versa.

4. Click OK to return to the AutoCAD window.

You'll see later in this chapter how to make layers visible/invisible and how to designate a layer as the active one.

Creating layers from a macro is straightforward—you simply add a Layer object to the Layers collection. The next section shows you how.

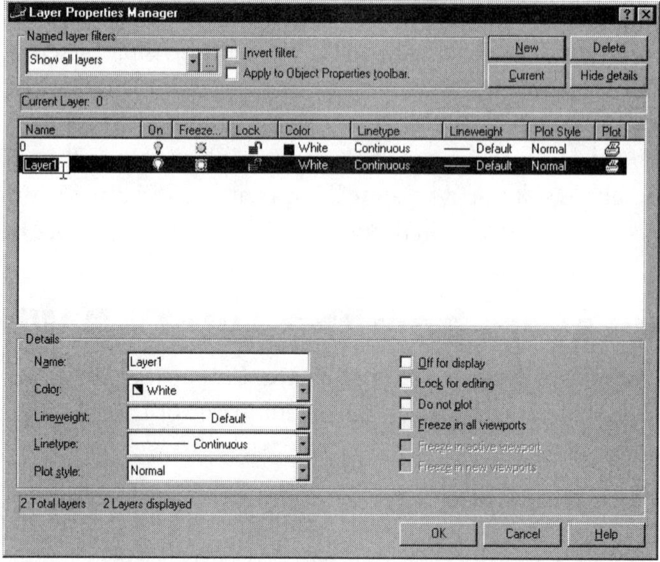

Figure 14.1 *Inserting a new layer from the Layer Properties Manager*

Creating Layers from a Macro

AutoCAD VBA has a Layers collection that contains Layer objects for every layer listed in the Layer Properties Manager (Figure 14.1). As usual, you create new Layer objects using the collection's Add method, and you access a Layer object using the Item method with an index or the layer's name as the argument. Also as usual, the Count property represents the number of Layer objects in the collection.

In this section you'll see how to re-create the villa floor plan from Chapter 8 on two layers, one for the inside walls and the layer for external walls. Then you'll create a third layer and add dimension objects to it.

When you've achieved this enhancement to the floor plan, you'll see how quick and easy it is to show a drawing's dimensions or make them invisible simply by setting the LayerOn property to True or False. In addition, we'll set the Color property of a layer so that you can easily distinguish the entities from the various layers on display.

The DrawFloorPlanWithDimensions macro given in Listing 14.1 calls three other procedures. First, it calls an adapted version of the DrawFloorPlan macro (Listing 8.3 in Chapter 8) to create two layers containing the inside and outside walls of the floor plan. Then it calls the CreateDimensionStyle macro (Listing 14.2) to make a new DimStyle object named MyDimStyle. Lastly, the AddDimensions procedure (Listing 14.3) is called to create a new Layer object and add a group of dimension objects to it. This is all covered in the following exercise, in which you'll enter the code and then update the reused code from Listing 8.3.

EXERCISE 14.1: DRAW FLOOR PLAN WITH DIMENSIONS

1. Open a new drawing and copy the DrawFloorPlan macro from Listing 8.3 (Chapter 8) into the Code window for the current project's ThisDrawing. Make it Public by changing the first statement to

```
Public Sub DrawFloorPlan()
```

I have explicitly declared this macro as Public, even though that is the default, because this project comprises other procedures that I am declaring as Private. The explicit declaration prevents confusion for anyone who revisits the code in the future. I have chosen to make procedures Public if they can be run on their own, and Private otherwise.

2. With the Code window for ThisDrawing still open, enter the following statements after Line 26 of the DrawFloorPlan macro, which assigns values to elements 24–26 of the OuterWall array. These new statements add a new layer named OutsideWalls and make it the active layer:

```
Dim OutsideLayer As AcadLayer
Set OutsideLayer = ThisDrawing.Layers.Add("OutsideWalls")
ThisDrawing.ActiveLayer = ↵
   ThisDrawing.Layers("OutsideWalls")
```

3. Enter the following statements after Line 28, which contains the comment `'draw all inside walls`. These new statements add a new layer named InsideWalls and make it the active layer.

```
Dim InsideLayer As AcadLayer
Set InsideLayer = ThisDrawing.Layers.Add("InsideWalls")
ThisDrawing.ActiveLayer = ThisDrawing.Layers("InsideWalls")
```

4. Next, enter the DrawFloorPlanWithDimensions macro (Listing 14.1) into the Code window for ThisDrawing. This will draw the floor plan and the dimensions of its external walls on three separate layers.

LISTING 14.1: DRAWFLOORPLANWITHDIMENSIONS MACRO

```
1   Public Sub DrawFloorPlanWithDimensions()
2       DrawFloorPlan
3       CreateDimensionStyle
4       AddDimensions
5   End Sub
```

ANALYSIS

- Line 1 opens the `DrawFloorPlanWithDimensions` macro, which calls three other procedures to create three layers containing the inside walls, the external walls, and the external walls' dimensions.
- Line 2 calls the `DrawFloorPlan` macro to draw the internal walls on one layer and the outside walls on another layer.
- Line 3 calls the `CreateDimensionStyle` macro (Listing 14.2) that creates a new style for dimensioning objects and makes it the active style.
- Line 4 calls the `AddDimensions` macro (Listing 14.3) that creates a new layer with dimension objects for the external walls.
- Line 5 ends the `DrawFloorPlanWithDimensions` macro.

Your next step is to enter the `CreateDimensionStyle` macro given in Listing 14.2 into the Code window for ThisDrawing. This macro creates a new DimStyle object, assigns values to its properties, and makes it the active style. I have declared this macro as Public because it can be run in isolation from the other procedures.

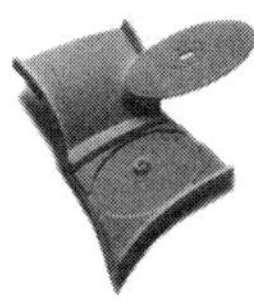

LISTING 14.2: CREATEDIMENSIONSTYLE MACRO

```
1   Public Sub CreateDimensionStyle()
2       Dim DimStyleObject As AcadDimStyle
3       Set DimStyleObject = ↵
           ThisDrawing.DimStyles.Add("MyDimStyle")
4       SetVariable "DIMCLRD", acGreen
5       SetVariable "DIMCLRE", acGreen
6       SetVariable "DIMCLRT", acGreen
7       SetVariable "DIMDEC", 0
8       ThisDrawing.ActiveDimStyle = DimStyleObject
9   End Sub
```

ANALYSIS

- Line 1 starts the `CreateDimensionStyle` macro. It creates a new style for dimension objects and makes it the active style, so that the dimension objects added by the `AddDimension` macro (Listing 14.3) will adopt this style.
- Line 2 declares the `DimStyleObject` variable as being capable of referring to a DimStyle object.
- Line 3 sets up the `DimStyleObject` variable as a reference to a new DimStyle object named `MyDimStyle`.
- Lines 4 through 6 use the `SetVariable` method to assign color values to system variables. The `DIM` stands for dimension, the `CLR` stands for color, and `D`, `E`, and `T` stand for dimension line, extension line, and text, respectively.
- Line 7 uses the `SetVariable` method to assign zero to the system variable `DIMDEC` that controls the number of places shown after the decimal point in the dimension text.

The `SetVariable` method serves the same purpose as entering the `SETVAR` command into the AutoCAD command line.

- Line 8 makes the `DimStyleObject` just created into the active dimension style so that any new dimension objects added are based on this style.
- Line 9 ends the `CreateDimensionStyle` macro.

Next, enter the AddDimensions procedure from Listing 14.3 into the Code window for ThisDrawing. This macro creates a new Layer object named DimensionsLayer and adds dimension objects to it. I have declared this procedure as Private so that it won't appear in the Macros dialog box, since it depends on the existence of the floor plan.

LISTING 14.3: ADDDIMENSIONS MACRO

```
Private Sub AddDimensions()
'add a DimAligned object to lines from the ModelSpace ↵
    collection
Dim DimensionObject As AcadDimAligned
Dim LayerObject As AcadLayer
Dim TextPosition(0 To 2) As Double
Dim Startpoint(0 To 2) As Double, EndPoint(0 To 2) As Double
Dim WallPoints As Variant
Set LayerObject = ThisDrawing.Layers.Add("DimensionsLayer")
ThisDrawing.ActiveLayer = LayerObject
LayerObject.LayerOn = True
ThisDrawing.Layers("OutsideWalls").LayerOn = True
ThisDrawing.Layers("InsideWalls").Lock = True
ThisDrawing.Layers("InsideWalls").LayerOn = True
Dim Count As Integer
Dim Entry As AcadEntity
For Each Entry In ThisDrawing.ModelSpace
    If Entry.ObjectName = "AcDbMline" Then
        WallPoints = Entry.Coordinates
        For Count = 0 To 21 Step 3
            Startpoint(0) = WallPoints(Count)
            Startpoint(1) = WallPoints(Count + 1)
            Startpoint(2) = WallPoints(Count + 2)
            EndPoint(0) = WallPoints(Count + 3)
            EndPoint(1) = WallPoints(Count + 4)
            EndPoint(2) = WallPoints(Count + 5)
            If Count = 0 Then
                TextPosition(1) = 0.5 'top
                ElseIf Count = 3 Then 'right
                    TextPosition(0) = ↵
                       WallPoints(3) - WallPoints(0)
                ElseIf Count = 6 Then
                    TextPosition(1) = -0.5 'bottom
```

```
32                  Else: TextPosition(0) = -0.5 'left
33              End If
34              Set DimensionObject = ↵
                   ThisDrawing.ModelSpace.AddDimAligned↵
                      (Startpoint, EndPoint, TextPosition)
35              DimensionObject.ExtensionLineOffset = 0.0625
36              DimensionObject.PrimaryUnitsPrecision = ↵
                   acDimPrecisionZero
37              DimensionObject.ArrowheadSize = 0.5
38              DimensionObject.Color = acGreen
39              DimensionObject.TextHeight = 10#
40              DimensionObject.UnitsFormat = acDimArchitectural
41              ThisDrawing.Preferences.LineWeightDisplay = True
42              DimensionObject.DimensionLineWeight = acLnWt030
43              DimensionObject.Update
44          Next
45          ZoomAll
46      End If
47  Next
48  ThisDrawing.Layers("InsideWalls").LayerOn = True
49  ThisDrawing.Layers("InsideWalls").Lock = False
50  End Sub
```

ANALYSIS

- Line 1 starts the `AddDimensions` procedure.
- Line 3 declares the `DimensionObject` variable as being capable of referring to a DimAligned object.
- Line 4 declares the `LayerObject` variable as being capable of referring to a Layer object.
- Line 5 declares the `TextPosition` array that will be assigned the x-, y-, and z-coordinates of the position for the dimension text.
- Line 6 declares the arrays to hold the start and end positions for the extension lines of the `DimensionObject`.
- Line 7 declares the `WallPoints` array as a Variant so that it can be passed the points defining the external walls in a single statement.

- Line 8 creates a new Layer object named `DimensionsLayer` and adds it to the Layers collection, setting up the `LayerObject` variable to refer to the new layer.
- Line 9 makes the new layer the active layer.
- Line 10 sets the `LayerOn` property of the new layer to `True` to display it.
- Line 11 sets the `LayerOn` property of the `OutsideWalls` layer to `True` to display it.
- Line 12 sets the `Lock` property of the `InsideWalls` layer to `True` so that it can't be updated.
- Line 13 sets the `LayerOn` property of the `InsideWalls` layer to `True` to display it.
- Line 14 declares the `Count` variable that will be used in the `For` loop.
- Line 15 declares the `Entry` variable as an `AcadEntity` type, which means that it can refer to any object.
- Line 16 starts the `For Each` loop. At each iteration, this statement will set up `Entry` as a reference to the next object in the ModelSpace collection.
- Line 17 determines whether the `ObjectName` property of the object currently assigned to `Entry` is the name of an Mline object, since the points defining the external walls are contained in an Mline object.
- Line 18 assigns the coordinates contained in the Mline object, referenced by the `Entry` variable, to the Variant type `WallPoints`. After the assignment, the points in `WallPoints` can be accessed as if `WallPoints` had been declared as an array.
- Line 19 starts the `For` loop that adds dimension objects to the external walls defined by `WallPoints`.
- Lines 20 through 25 assign the next six coordinates from `WallPoints` to the x-, y-, and z-coordinates of the `Startpoint` and `EndPoint` arrays.
- Line 26 starts the `If...Then...Else...` statement block that determines the x- or y-coordinate for the `TextPosition`. For the left and right walls, only the x-coordinate is required; for the top and bottom walls, only the y-coordinate is required.
- Line 27 is executed if `Count` is zero, to set the y-coordinate for the `TextPosition`.

- Lines 28 and 29 are executed if `Count` equals 3, which means the wall on the right is being dimensioned (and the text position depends on the difference between the x-coordinates of the two points defining the top wall).
- Lines 30 and 31 are executed if `Count` equals 6, which means that the bottom wall is being dimensioned.
- Line 32 contains the `Else` statement that is executed when `Count` is greater than 6, which means that a wall down the left side is being dimensioned.
- Line 33 ends the `If...Then...Else...` statement block.
- Line 34 creates a new `DimAligned` object and adds it to the ModelSpace collection. The `AddDimAligned` method has three parameters: the start and endpoints for the extension lines, and the position for the dimension text. The extension lines' start and endpoints are often the same as the start and endpoints for the line being dimensioned.
- Line 35 assigns a value to the `ExtensionLineOffset` that specifies the distance to be used as the offset from the original points.
- Line 36 sets the `PrimaryUnitsPrecision` property to the AutoCAD constant `acDimPrecisionZero`. This specifies that no decimal places are required for displaying the dimension.
- Lines 37 through 40 assign values to properties of the dimension object.
- Line 41 makes sure that lines are displayed at their associated line weights, by setting the `LineWeightDisplay` property of the Preferences collection to `True`. This property is often switched off, because AutoCAD takes longer to regenerate a drawing that contains lines more than one pixel wide.
- Line 42 assigns the value of the AutoCAD constant `acLnWt030` to the `DimensionLineWeight` property of the dimension object.
- Line 43 updates the dimension object to ensure that it appears in the Model Space.
- Line 44 ends the `For` loop that creates all the dimension objects.
- Line 45 calls the `ZoomAll` method to ensure that all the objects in the Model Space are visible.
- Line 46 ends the `If...Then...Else...` statement block that started at Line 17.

- Line 47 ends the `For` loop that started at Line 16.
- Lines 48 and 49 set the `LayerOn` property `InsideWalls` to `True`, and the `Lock` property to `False`. Without these two lines, you cannot run the `DrawFloor-PlanWithDimensions` macro more than once, because the code to add the inside walls causes an error if the layer is set up so that it can't be edited.
- Line 50 ends the `AddDimensions` macro.

Now let's try generating the three layers.

1. Run the DrawFloorPlanWithDimensions macro to generate the three layer groups.
2. In the AutoCAD window, click the down-arrow button in the Layers box at the top. The names of the three new layers appear in the drop-down list, as shown in Figure 14.2. Figure 14.3 shows the floor plan created with the dimensions adjusted to suit.

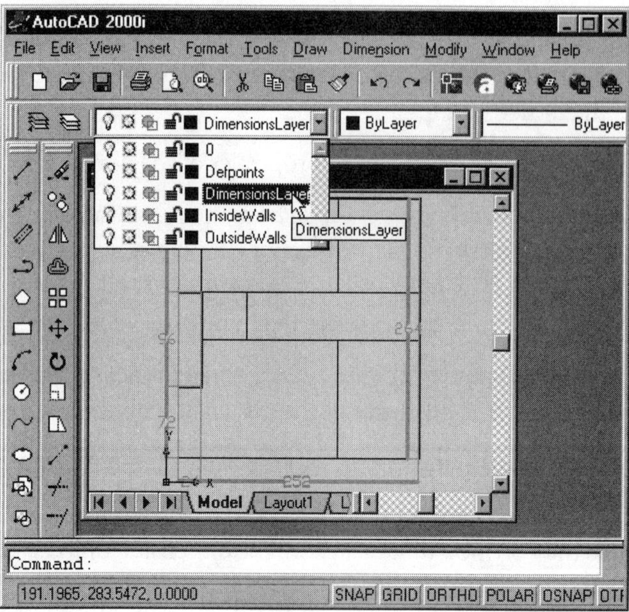

Figure 14.2: *AutoCAD with the new list of layers after running the application for dimensions*

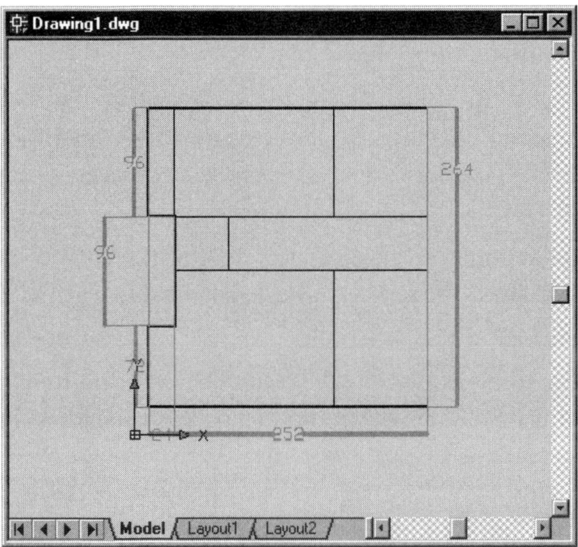

Figure 14.3: *Floor plan showing the objects from all three layers*

3. In the DimensionsLayer layer, click the light-bulb icon; its ToolTip says "Turn a layer On or Off."

The light bulb will change from yellow to dark gray to denote that the layer has been turned off, and its drawing objects won't be visible. The new drawing will revert to displaying the floor plan—the dimensions will have completely disappeared.

Changing Settings in the Layer Properties Manager

You can change the visual properties of a layer from the Layer Properties Manager. (This dialog box is shown earlier in Figure 14.1; to open it, choose Format ➜ Layer.)

Reopen this dialog box now, and you'll see that it displays five layers, including the original layers 0 and Defpoints.

Following are the steps to change the settings of any layer in the Layer Properties Manager:

1. In the Name column, select the DimensionsLayer layer, the InsideWalls layer, or the OutsideWalls layer. The details for the selected layer appear in the boxes from the Details frame.
2. Let's change the settings for color and line weight (thickness) on the drawing objects associated with the selected layer. Click the down arrow to open the Color list.

   If you are using AutoCAD 2000i, select Other from the bottom of the list; otherwise, select any item. The Select Color dialog box appears (Figure 14.4).

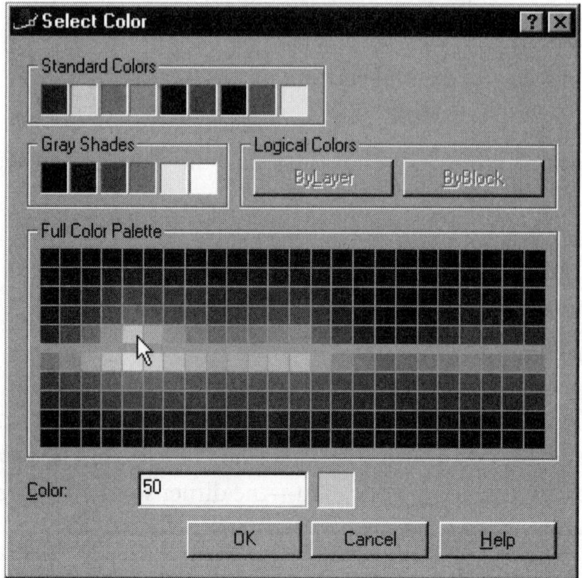

***Figure 14.4** Selecting a color for a layer's objects*

3. Select a color and click OK. You return to the Layer Properties Manager, where the new color is now displayed in the Color box.
4. Click the down arrow to open the Lineweights list and select an item. If you are running AutoCAD 2000i, the item selected is the line weight. If you are using

an earlier version of AutoCAD, however, the Lineweight dialog box appears (Figure 14.5).

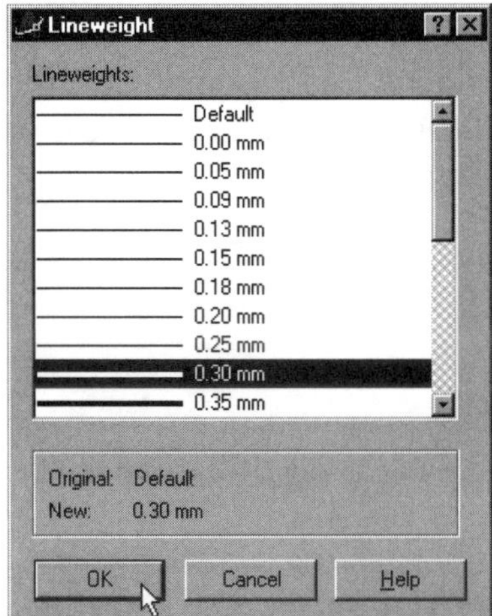

Figure 14.5 *Selecting a line weight*

5. Skip this step if you are using AutoCAD 2000i. Choose a line thickness from the Lineweights list and click OK. You return to the Layer Properties Manager, where the selected line weight appears in the Lineweight box.

The other properties in the Layer Properties Manager are described in the following section.

The On, Freeze, and Lock Options

You can prevent layers from being regenerated with the other layers in a drawing. They can be made visible or invisible, and made available or unavailable for editing. This section describes these options and suggests the circumstances for using them.

Locking and Unlocking Layers in Code

To lock a layer from within VBA code, you set the layer's Lock property to True. Lines 12 and 49 of Listing 14.3 demonstrate the code for locking and unlocking a layer from a macro.

A *locked* layer allows you to create another layer on top of it without having to worry about mistakenly updating any elements of the locked layer. You can still see all the entities in a locked layer, but since a locked layer can never become the active layer, it cannot be selected or edited. You can still add new objects to a locked layer, although you can't update existing ones. For convenience when you're positioning added objects, the object Snap feature in a locked layer will still snap to points.

If you try to make adjustments to entities selected from a locked layer, a message box will let you know that you've been unsuccessful.

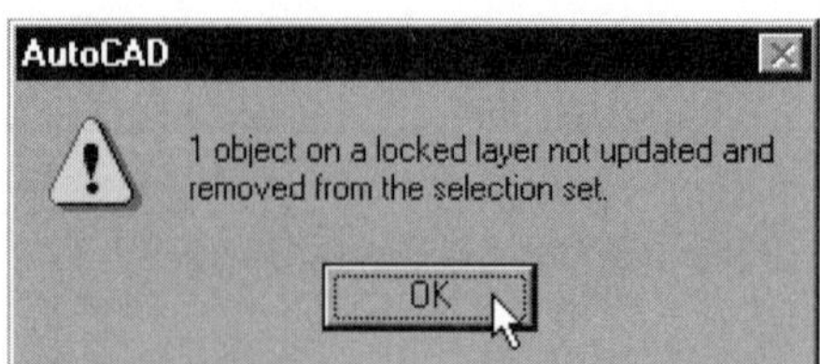

Freezing and Thawing Layers in Code

Freezing (and thawing) of layers is achieved by setting the layer's Freeze property to True (or False). When a layer is frozen, everything associated with it is made invisible, and any requests to regenerate the drawing area will only work on layers that are not frozen.

When a frozen layer is thawed (the Freeze property is switched from True to False), AutoCAD automatically regenerates the whole drawing. Because of the time taken to do this regeneration, the Freeze property is usually set only when a layer isn't going to be needed for a while. If you plan to change a layer's visibility frequently, it is more efficient to set its LayerOn property to True or False.

Exercise 14.1: Draw Floor Plan with Dimensions (continued)

Listing 14.4 contains the FreezeActiveLayer macro, which freezes the active layer. Because VBA doesn't actually allow the active layer to be frozen, the macro must make another layer active before freezing it. Here are the steps for running this macro:

1. Continuing with the Floor Plan project, enter the FreezeActiveLayer macro (Listing 14.4) into the ThisDrawing module's Code window.
2. Select a layer from the Layers box.
3. Run the FreezeActiveLayer macro from the Macros dialog box. After this macro has finished executing, the Freeze icon is updated in the Layers box.

Listing 14.4: FreezeActiveLayer Macro

```
1   Public Sub FreezeActiveLayer()
2       Dim LayerObject As AcadLayer, NewActiveLayerObject ↵
           As AcadLayer
3       Set LayerObject = ThisDrawing.ActiveLayer
4       If ThisDrawing.Layers.Count = 1 Then
5           MsgBox "You cannot freeze the active layer!", ↵
               vbOKOnly + vbCritical, "Freezing Layers"
6       Else
7           If LayerObject.Name = "0" Then
8               Set NewActiveLayerObject = ↵
                   ThisDrawing.Layers.Item(1)
9           Else
10              Set NewActiveLayerObject = ↵
                   ThisDrawing.Layers.Item(0)
11          End If
12          ThisDrawing.ActiveLayer = NewActiveLayerObject
13          LayerObject.Freeze = True
14      End If
15  End Sub
```

Analysis

- Line 1 starts the `FreezeActiveLayer` macro that sets up a reference to the active layer, makes another layer active, and then freezes the original layer.
- Line 2 declares the `LayerObject` and the `NewActiveLayerObject` as being capable of referring to Layer objects.
- Line 3 sets up the `LayerObject` variable as a reference to the active layer.
- Line 4 starts the outer `If...Then...Else...` statement block by checking to see if there is only one layer in the Layers collection.
- Line 5 calls the `MsgBox` function with a warning about not being able to freeze the one-and-only-and-active layer. For the `Buttons` argument, it passes the constants `vbOKOnly` to display the OK button, and `vbCritical` to display the critical icon.

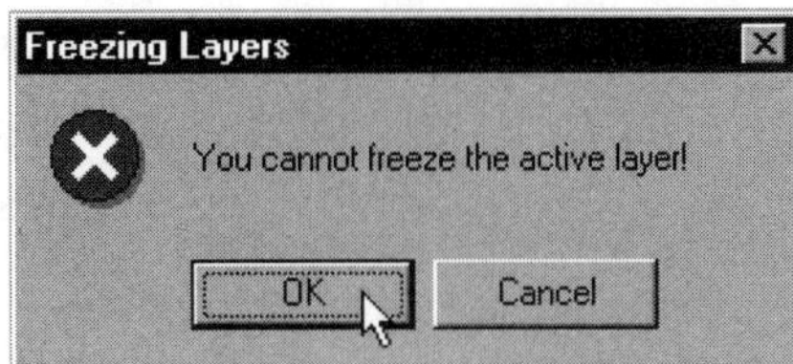

- Line 6 starts the `Else` statement block.
- Line 7 starts the inner `If...Then...Else...` statement block by checking to see if the active layer is named 0, which is the default name for the first layer. VBA will not allow you to rename Layer0.
- Line 8 is executed if the first layer is the active one; the line sets up the `NewActiveLayerObject` variable as a reference to the second item in the Layers collection.
- Line 9 starts the `Else` part, which executes if the active layer isn't the first layer.
- Line 10 sets up the `NewActiveLayerObject` variable to reference the first layer.
- Line 11 ends the inner `If...Then...Else...` statement block that started at Line 7.
- Line 12 makes the Layer object referenced by `NewActiveLayerObject` the active layer.
- Line 13 sets the `Freeze` property of the Layer object referenced by the `LayerObject` variable to True, to freeze it. The `LayerObject` was set up as a reference to the layer that was active when this macro was called (Line 3).
- Line 14 ends the outer `If...Then...Else...` statement block that started at Line 4.
- Line 15 ends the `FreezeActiveLayer` macro.

Turning Layers On and Off in Code

Turning layers on and off is achieved by setting the LayerOn property to True or False, respectively.

When a layer is turned off (LayerOn is False), it becomes hidden. Although the layer can't be seen, it is still regenerated with the rest of the drawing. This means it can be displayed immediately when it is turned on again (LayerOn is True).

If the layer won't be needed for quite a while, it should be frozen rather than just hidden. When a layer is frozen, it doesn't get regenerated until it is thawed, when the rest of the drawing is regenerated with it.

Accessing All Layers from a Macro

The MakeAllLayersVisible macro given in Listing 14.5 shows how to turn on all the layers associated with the active document, ThisDrawing, to make them all visible. To see this macro in action, try Exercise 14.1.

Exercise 14.1: Draw Floor Plan with Dimensions (continued)

1. Continuing with the Floor Plan project, enter the MakeAllLayersVisible macro into ThisDrawing's Code window.
2. Turn off a couple of layers in the Layers drop-down list at the top of the AutoCAD window, by clicking on their light-bulb icons. The light-bulb icon turns gray when you select it to turn off the layer.
3. Run the MakeAllLayersVisible macro from the Macros dialog box. The light-bulb icons in the Layers list all become yellow again to indicate that the layers have all been turned on by the macro.

Listing 14.5: MakeAllLayersVisible Macro

```
1   Public Sub MakeAllLayersVisible()
2       Dim LayerObject As AcadLayer
3       For Each LayerObject In ThisDrawing.Layers
4           LayerObject.LayerOn = True
5       Next
6   End Sub
```

Analysis

- Line 1 starts the `MakeAllLayersVisible` macro, which switches on all the layers associated with ThisDrawing.
- Line 2 declares the `LayerObject` variable as being capable of referencing a Layer object.
- Line 3 starts the `For...Each...Next` statement block that is executed once for every layer in the Layers collection. The `LayerObject` is updated at each iteration to refer to the current layer being processed.
- Line 4 sets the `LayerOn` property to `True` to make the current layer visible.
- Line 5 ends the `For...Each...Next` statement block.
- Line 6 ends the `MakeAllLayersVisible` macro.

Grouping Objects into Blocks

Blocks act as containers, in which you can place as many AutoCAD objects as you like—there is no upper limit. The good news is that after you've created a block, it's reusable as a single entity, so you no longer have to consider the block's individual objects. This allows you to work at a higher level and generate drawings much more efficiently than before.

The Block container is also called the block definition.

Blocks are not limited to ModelSpace and PaperSpace objects; they can also be inserted into another block to form a hierarchical structure of nested blocks.

AutoCAD provides three types of blocks:

Simple Block The simple block is a collection of objects that have been placed into a container and can be referred to as a single entity—a block. You can add this block to a drawing and perform translation and rotation transformations on it, by calling the InsertBlock method with appropriate values for the transformations as arguments. BlockReference objects are used to refer to blocks you've added in this way. Block objects are added to the Blocks collection. The drawings added to a block can come from the current drawing or can be copied from any other AutoCAD drawing. Because copies are used, updating the original will not have any effect on the block.

Xref Block The Xref block is an external link that references drawing objects from another drawing file. If a referenced object in the other drawing changes, the Xref block changes as well. The ExternalReference object is used to refer to these Xref blocks.

Layout Block Layout blocks are used with plotting and are discussed in more detail in Chapter 18 on the CD.

Creating a Simple Block

Listing 14.6 contains the CreateABlock macro that creates a simple block and adds a circle and box object to it.

Exercise 14.2: Creating a Block

1. Start a new project and enter the code shown in Listing 14.6 into the Code window for ThisDrawing.
2. Run the macro from the Macros dialog box in the AutoCAD window. You will be prompted in the command line to enter the details required to create a circle, but nothing will appear in the Model Space.

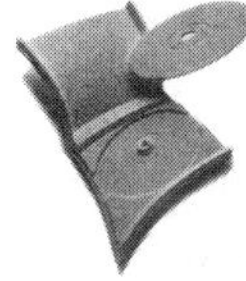

Listing 14.6: CreateABlock Macro

```
1   Public Sub CreateABlock()
2       Dim BlockObject As AcadBlock
3       Dim InputPoint As Variant, Radius As Double
4       InputPoint = ThisDrawing.Utility.GetPoint(, ↵
           "Insert position for block!")
5       Set BlockObject = ↵
           ThisDrawing.Blocks.Add(InputPoint, "MyBlock")
6       InputPoint = ThisDrawing.Utility.GetPoint(, ↵
           "Insert position for circle's center!")
7       Radius = ThisDrawing.Utility.GetDistance(InputPoint, ↵
           "Insert radius!")
8       BlockObject.AddCircle InputPoint, Radius
9       BlockObject.AddBox InputPoint, Radius, Radius, Radius
10  End Sub
```

Analysis

- Line 1 starts the `CreateABlock` macro that prompts the user for the details it requires and creates a block containing a circle and a box.
- Line 2 declares the `BlockObject` variable as being capable of referencing a Block object.
- Line 3 declares the `InputPoint` as Variant so that the three-element array it will contain can be assigned in a single statement. This line also declares the radius for the circle.
- Line 4 prompts the user to enter the position of the block and assigns it to `InputPoint`.

- Line 5 calls the Add method of the Blocks collection to create a new Block object called "MyBlock" at the position entered by the user.
- Lines 6 and 7 call the GetPoint and GetDistance methods to prompt the user to enter the center and radius for the Circle object.
- Line 8 creates a Circle object and adds it to the BlockObject.
- Line 9 creates a Box object based on the radius specified for the Circle object and adds it to the BlockObject.
- Line 10 ends the CreateABlock macro.

This macro only creates a block; it does not display anything in the Model Space. Before you can see what the block contains, it must be added to the current drawing. We'll do that next.

Adding a Block to a Drawing

In this section you'll see how to call the InsertBlock method of the ModelSpace object, with the name of a block as an argument. The InsertBlock method inserts an existing block into the Model Space—don't get it confused with the Add method of the Blocks collection (see Listing 14.6 in the last section), which actually creates and names a block.

Listing 14.7 gives the AddABlock macro that adds the block named "MyBlock" to the current drawing. The CreateABlock macro must be run before you run AddABlock to ensure that the block named "MyBlock" has already been created; otherwise, this macro will terminate abnormally.

LISTING 14.7: ADDABLOCK MACRO

```
Public Sub AddABlock()
    Dim BlockReference As AcadBlockReference
    Dim InputPoint As Variant
    InputPoint = ThisDrawing.Utility.GetPoint(, ↵
       "Input the position for the block!")
    Set BlockReference = ↵
       ThisDrawing.ModelSpace.InsertBlock(InputPoint, ↵
       "MyBlock", 1#, 1#, 1#, 3.14 / 2#)
    BlockReference.Update
    ZoomAll
End Sub
```

ANALYSIS

- Line 1 starts the `AddABlock` macro, which prompts the user to click at the position where the block is to be placed and inserts the block at that position.
- Line 2 declares the `BlockReference` variable as being capable of referencing a Block Reference object.
- Line 3 declares the `InputPoint` as a Variant so that the array it will contain can be assigned in one statement.
- Line 4 assigns to `InputPoint` the position entered by the user.
- Line 5 calls the `InsertBlock` method to insert the block named in the second argument to the Model Space, and sets up the `BlockReference` variable to reference the block. In this example, I've included all the arguments for this method, but only the first two are actually required. The next three arguments specify the scale factors for the x-, y-, and z-coordinates, and the default values are all 1 so that no scaling takes place. The last argument is the angle to be rotated specified in radians (the default is zero).
- Line 6 calls the `Update` method of the `BlockReference` to ensure that the block is drawn in the Model Space (see Figure 14.6).

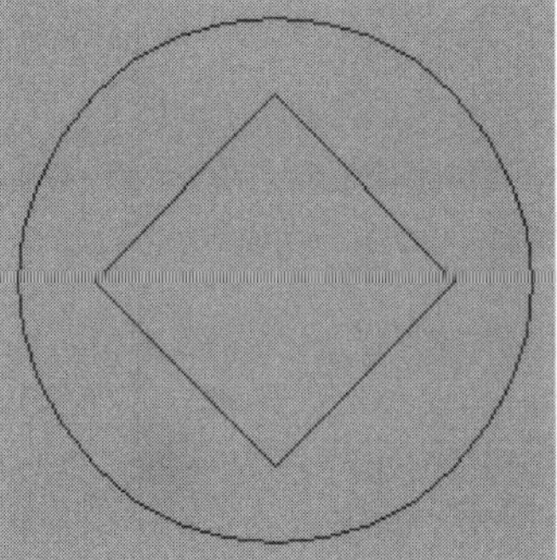

***Figure 14.6** The drawn circle containing a rotated box*

Referencing External Blocks

An Xref block contains external references to drawings from other files. These drawings are not stored in the drawing file with the Xref block, but are retrieved from the external files each time you open the drawing file that refers to them.

Listing 14.8 gives the code for the AddAnXref macro, which adds to the active drawing the map shown in Figure 14.7. This map is included in one of the files provided with AutoCAD; you might find it at C:\Program Files\AutoCAD 2000i\Samples\City Map on you computer.

Enter this macro into the Code window for ThisDrawing, and run it from the Macros dialog box (in line 5, be sure to update the path to the sample map if necessary).

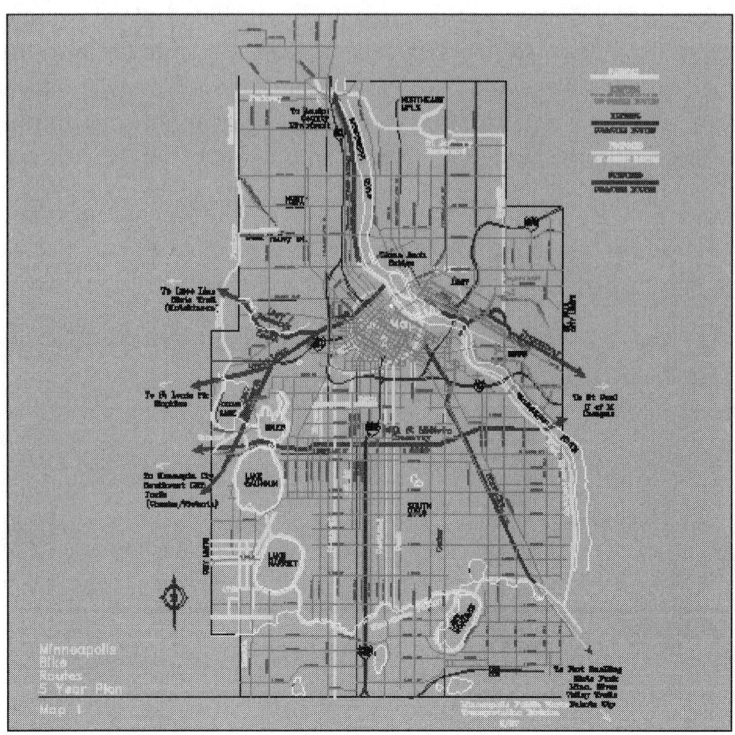

Figure 14.7 *The* `"Xref Map"` *block added by the AddAnXref macro (Listing 14.8)*

Listing 14.8: AddAnXref Macro

```
1   Public Sub AddAnXref()
2       Dim XrefReference As AcadExternalReference
3       Dim InsertPoint As Variant
4       InsertPoint = ThisDrawing.Utility.GetPoint ↵
            (, "Insert position for map!")
5       Set XrefReference = ↵
            ThisDrawing.ModelSpace.AttachExternalReference ↵
            ("c:\Program Files\AutoCAD 2000i\SAMPLE\City Map", ↵
            "XRef Map", InsertPoint, 1#, 1#, 1#, 0#, False)
6       XrefReference.Update
7       ZoomAll
8   End Sub
```

Analysis

- Line 1 starts the `AddAnXref` macro, which adds to the active drawing an Xref block containing a map.
- Line 2 declares the `XrefReference` variable as being capable of linking to an external reference.
- Line 3 declares the `InsertPoint` as a Variant so that the three-array elements defining a point can be assigned in a single statement.
- Line 4 prompts the user for the position to place the Xref block.
- Line 5 calls the `AttachExternalReference` method, with the first argument specifying the full pathname of a drawing file—I've chosen the \SAMPLE\City Map file supplied by AutoCAD. The second argument specifies the name for the Xref object being created. The third argument provides the position where the map is to be placed in the Model Space. These first three arguments are required; the others are optional. The next three arguments specify any scaling that's required on the three coordinates of the `InsertPoint`. The next to last argument specifies the rotation angle in radians. The last argument is passed as True if the external reference is to be an overlay, or False if it is to be an attachment.

External references are overlaid on drawings that are shared by several people who might not be interested in viewing the Xref block material.

- Line 6 updates the external reference to display it in the Model Space.
- Line 7 calls the `ZoomAll` method to adjust the current viewport so that it displays the entire drawing.
- Line 8 ends the `AddAnXref` macro.

Moving Blocks

All the drawing objects from a simple block or an Xref block can be moved, by selecting them to display a single positioning handle that can be dragged to move the block around in the Model Space to the position required.

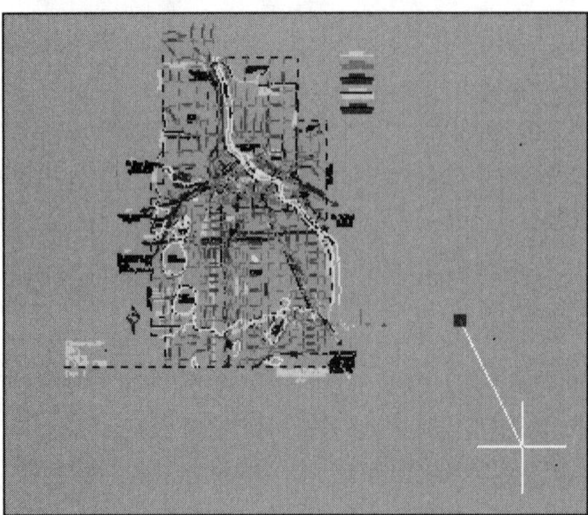

Using Selection Sets

A selection set is a temporary collection of drawing objects that can be treated as a single entity when performing operations such as moving, copying, and deleting. Every AutoCAD drawing has a SelectionSets collection to which you can add as many SelectionSet objects as you want. Any SelectionSet objects that you create exist only while the active drawing is open. Selection sets are normally only added to a drawing whenever they are required for an operation or transformation and are deleted as soon as this has taken place.

Closing a drawing containing a selection set empties out the SelectionSets collection.

In Listing 14.9, a Select Set object is added to the SelectionSets collection. The steps given in Exercise 14.3 show you how to develop the Selection Set application, which allows the user to choose from various selection modes.

Exercise 14.3: Selection Set Application

1. Insert a UserForm in a new project. Add a label-and-text-box pair of controls, a frame containing five option buttons, and two command buttons (see Figure 14.8).

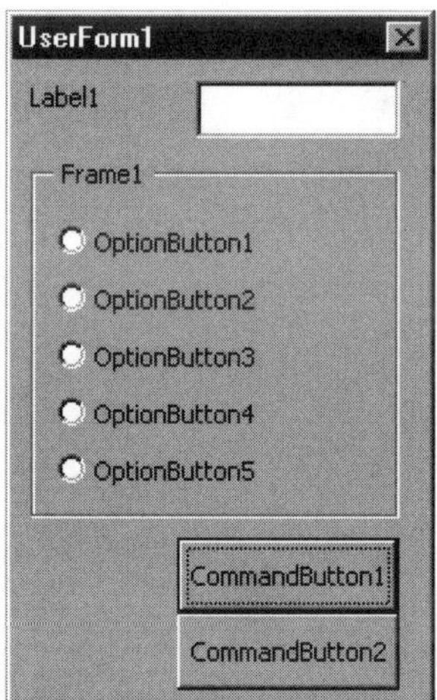

Figure 14.8 *GUI for the Selection Set application*

2. Change the properties of the UserForm and controls as shown in Table 14.1. Change the Accelerator property for CommandButton1 to **o** and for CommandButton2 to **C**.
3. Change the Default property of CommandButton2 to True. A dark border appears around the Cancel button as shown in Figure 14.9.
4. Change the TabIndex property of the text box to 0. The Insertion cursor appears in the text box as shown in Figure 14.9.

Table 14.1 Properties for the Selection Set Application's GUI

OLD NAME	NEW NAME	CAPTION
UserForm1	frmSelectionSet	Selection Set
Label1	—	Name of Selection Set
TextBox1	txtSelectionSetName	—
Frame1	—	Selection Mode
OptionButton1	optWindow	Window
OptionButton2	optCrossing	Crossing
OptionButton3	optPrevious	Previous
OptionButton4	optLast	Last
OptionButton5	optAll	All
CommandButton1	cmdContinue	Continue
CommandButton2	cmdCancel	Cancel

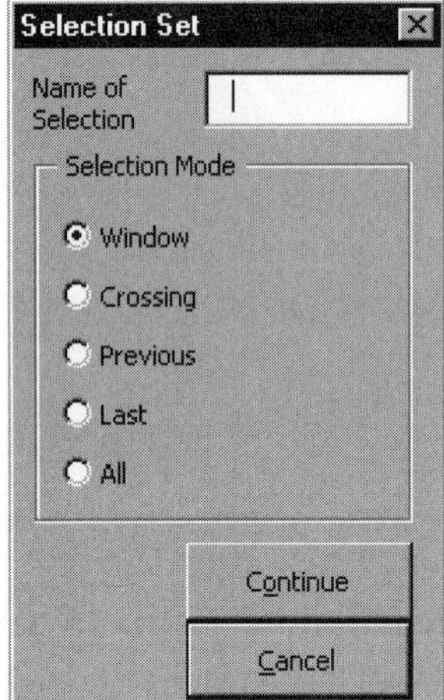

Figure 14.9 *GUI for the Selection Set application*

5. Enter the code given in Listing 14.9 into the UserForm's Code window, placing the three declaration statements into the General Declarations section and the rest into the skeleton event procedures provided by VBA.

6. Enter the following `AddASelectionSet` macro to ThisDrawing's Code window. It enables the Selection Set application to be run from the Macros dialog box accessible from the AutoCAD window.

```
Public Sub AddASelectionSet()
    frmSelectionSet.Show
End Sub
```

7. Create a few drawing objects that can become parts of the selection set. Then run the macro a few times, each time choosing a different selection mode option and following the instructions in the command line.

Figure 14.10 shows the window used as the basis for creating the selection sets containing the objects shown highlighted in Figures 14.11 and 14.12. Figure 14.11 shows the selection set objects as a result of selecting the Window mode option in the GUI, and Figure 14.12 gives the result when the Crossing mode option is selected with the same rectangular window. See the next section for explanations of the selection modes.

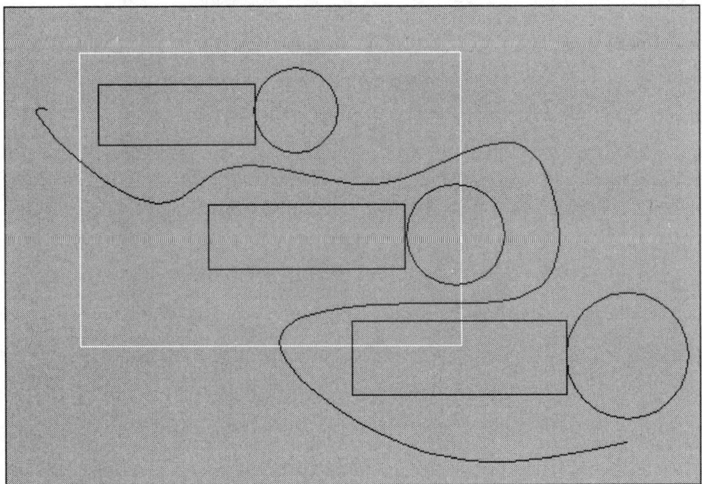

***Figure 14.10** Rectangular window area used as the basis for creating the selection sets of objects shown in Figures 14.11 and 14.12*

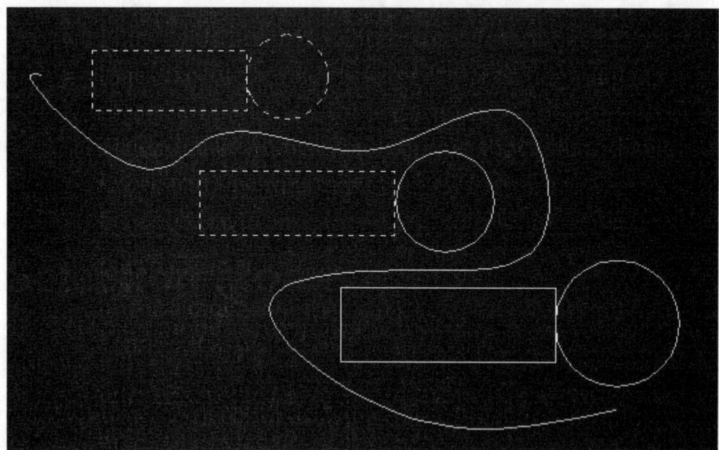

Figure 14.11 *SelectionSet objects when the Window option is selected*

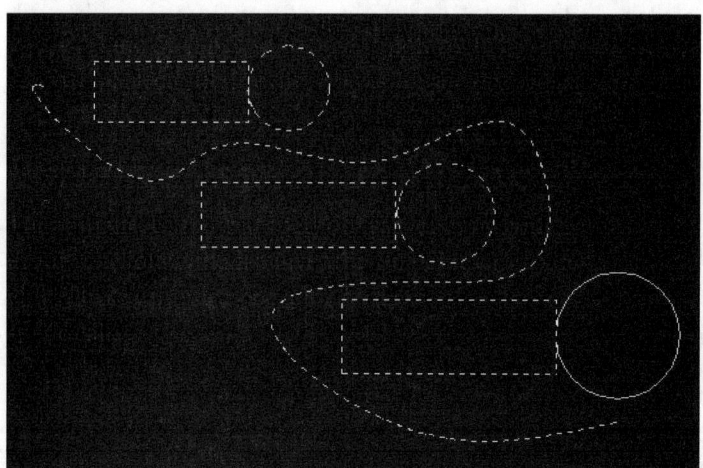

Figure 14.12 *SelectionSet objects when the Crossing option is selected*

Listing 14.9

```
Dim SelectionSetObject As AcadSelectionSet
Dim Point1 As Variant, Point2 As Variant
Dim SelectionMode As Integer

Private Sub cmdCancel_Click()
    End
End Sub

Private Sub cmdContinue_Click()
    frmSelectionSet.hide
    Set SelectionSetObject = ThisDrawing.SelectionSets.Add ↵
       (frmSelectionSet.txtSelectionSetName)
    With ThisDrawing.Utility
        If SelectionMode = acSelectionSetWindow Or ↵
           SelectionMode = acSelectionSetCrossing Then
            .InitializeUserInput 1
            Point1 = .GetPoint ↵
               (, "Enter position of first corner")
            Point2 = .GetCorner ↵
               (Point1, "Enter position for opposite corner")
            SelectionSetObject.Select SelectionMode, ↵
               Point1, Point2
        Else
            SelectionSetObject.Select SelectionMode
        End If
        SelectionSetObject.Highlight True
        SelectionSetObject.Update
        .GetString False, "Hit Enter to finish!"
    End With
    SelectionSetObject.Highlight False
    SelectionSetObject.Update
End Sub

Private Sub optAll_Click()
    SelectionMode = acSelectionSetAll
End Sub

Private Sub optCrossing_Click()
```

```
34      SelectionMode = acSelectionSetCrossing
35  End Sub
36
37  Private Sub optLast_Click()
38      SelectionMode = acSelectionSetLast
39  End Sub
40
41  Private Sub optPrevious_Click()
42      SelectionMode = acSelectionSetPrevious
43  End Sub
44
45  Private Sub optWindow_Click()
46      SelectionMode = acSelectionSetWindow
47  End Sub
48
49  Private Sub UserForm_Initialize()
50      optWindow.Value = True
51  End Sub
```

Analysis

- Line 1 declares the `SelectionSetObject` variable as being capable of referring to a SelectionSet object.
- Line 2 declares the `Point1` and `Point2` variables as Variants so that the three coordinates representing a point can be assigned in a single statement.
- Line 3 declares the `SelectionMode` variable that will be assigned the value of an AutoCAD constant that represents one of the selection modes available.
- Lines 5 through 7 contain the Click event procedure of the Cancel command button.
- Line 9 starts the Click event procedure of the Continue command button.
- Line 10 hides the Selection Set UserForm so that the AutoCAD window becomes active again.
- Line 11 calls the `Add` method of the SelectionSets collection to create a new SelectionSet object with the user-specified name from the text box passed as an argument. Then the new object is added to the collection. This line also sets up the `SelectionSetObject` variable as a reference to this new object.

- Line 12 uses the `With` statement so that the methods of `ThisDrawing.Utility` can be used without fully qualifying them.
- Line 13 starts the `If` statement and determines the selection mode as being Window or Crossing, both of which require the user to specify two points.
- Line 14 calls the `InitializeUserInput` method with an argument of 1 to force the user to input something when prompted in the command line.
- Line 15 calls the `GetPoint` method to prompt the user to enter the position for the first corner of the rectangle for the window.
- Line 16 calls the `GetCorner` method to prompt the user to enter the opposite corner of the rectangle that encloses the drawing objects desired to become part of the selection set.
- Line 17 calls the `Select` method, with the selection mode and with the two points defining the rectangular window that encloses the drawing objects required for the selection set. If the `SelectionMode` variable is set to `acSelectionSetWindow`, then the drawing objects selected will lie completely inside the set. If the variable is set to `acSelectionSetCrossing`, then any objects inside or intersected by the window will be placed in the set.
- Lines 18 and 19 form the `Else` statement block that will be executed if the condition at Line 13 is not met. The `Select` method is called with only the mode as the argument, since none of these modes requires a window to be drawn.
- Line 20 ends the `If...Then...Else...` statement block.
- Line 21 calls the `Highlight` method of the `SelectionSet` object just created, with the argument `True` so that all the drawing objects selected are displayed as dashed lines.
- Line 22 calls the `Update` method to display the selection set as highlighted.
- Line 23 calls the `GetString` method of the Utility object to prompt the user to press Enter to finish. The `GetString` pauses for user input and allows time for the user to examine the screen and make sure that all the drawing objects required in the selection set have been included.
- Line 24 ends the `With` statement.
- Line 25 calls the `Highlight` method of the selection set with the argument `False`, so that the objects it contains are displayed as solid lines.

- Line 26 calls the `Update` method to display the selection set as unhighlighted.
- Line 27 ends the `cmdContinue` event procedure.
- Lines 29 through 47 are the Click event procedures that will respond when the user selects one of the option buttons in the GUI (Figure 14.7). Each event procedure sets the `SelectionMode` variable to the integer value of an AutoCAD constant that denotes how the user is meant to select objects from the Model Space.
- Lines 49 through 51 contain the `Initialize` event procedure of the UserForm that's executed every time the UserForm is loaded; no action is required from the user. This procedure sets the `optWindow` option button's `Value` property to `True` to make it the default option that will be displayed as selected when the UserForm first opens.

Selection Modes

The selection modes determine the technique used for selecting one or more drawing objects.

Window Selects all drawing objects that are completely inside a rectangular window defined by two diagonally opposite points.

Crossing Selects drawing objects that are inside or that cross the boundary of a rectangular window defined by two diagonally opposite points.

Previous Selects the last selection set.

Last Selects the last visible drawing object added to the drawing space.

All Selects all drawing objects in the drawing space.

InitializeUserInput Method

The InitializeUserInput method is used to provide some options during command-line input. The following list gives the Bit values and a description of the options they provide. These values can be added together to allow several options to be instigated in a single call.

Bit Value	Description
0	None
1	Disallows NULL input (such as the user's pressing Enter or the spacebar)
2	Disallows the zero value
4	Disallows negative values
8	Allows the user to select a point outside the current drawing area
16	Not currently used
32	Draws rubber-band lines and boxes as dashed lines when the user is following prompts displayed by the Utility methods
64	Returns the x and y components from the GetDistance method, ignoring the z component of three-dimensional objects
128	Accepts any string input from the user without question

Using Groups

AutoCAD provides a Groups collection that allows you to group objects together just as you do when creating selection sets, except that Group objects are more permanent. Groups have similarities to blocks, too, but groups have the advantage that their objects can still be added and deleted individually using the AppendItem and RemoveItem methods.

Creating a New Group

The Add method of the Groups collection is used to create a new group, and the Item method is used with a name or an index value to access an existing Group object from the collection. Listing 14.10 shows the AddAGroup macro, which creates a group and appends a Circle object and a Line object before setting the group's color to green. Figure 14.13 shows the two objects in the group as a result of running this macro.

To run this macro, enter the AddAGroup macro into the Code window for ThisDrawing. Then return to AutoCAD and run the macro from the Macros dialog box.

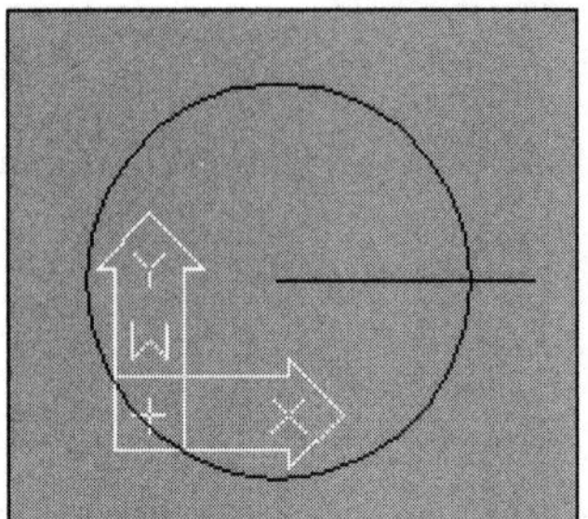

Figure 14.13 *Circle and Line objects added to a group by the AddAGroup macro (Listing 14.10)*

LISTING 14.10: ADDAGROUP MACRO

```
Public Sub AddAGroup()
    Dim GroupObject As AcadGroup
    Dim ObjectsForGroup() As AcadEntity
    Dim CircleObject As AcadCircle
    Dim LineObject As AcadLine
    Dim Center(0 To 2) As Double, Radius As Double
    Dim StartPoint(0 To 2) As Double
    Dim EndPoint(0 To 2) As Double
    Dim Count As Integer
    Center(0) = 1#: Center(1) = 1#: Center(2) = 0#
    Radius = 1.5
    Set CircleObject = ThisDrawing.ModelSpace.AddCircle↵
       (Center, Radius)
    StartPoint(0) = Center(0): StartPoint(1) = Center(1): ↵
       StartPoint(2) = Center(2)
    EndPoint(0) = Center(0) + Radius + 0.5: EndPoint(1) = ↵
       Center(1): EndPoint(2) = Center(2)
    Set LineObject = ThisDrawing.ModelSpace.AddLine↵
       (StartPoint, EndPoint)
    ReDim ObjectsForGroup(0 To ↵
       ThisDrawing.ModelSpace.Count - 1) As AcadEntity
    For Count = 0 To ThisDrawing.ModelSpace.Count - 1
```

```
18          Set ObjectsForGroup(Count) = ↵
               ThisDrawing.ModelSpace.Item(Count)
19      Next
20      Set GroupObject = ThisDrawing.Groups.Add("MyGroup")
21      GroupObject.AppendItems ObjectsForGroup
22      GroupObject.Color = acBlue
23      GroupObject.Highlight True
24      ThisDrawing.Regen acActiveViewport
25      ZoomAll
26  End Sub
```

ANALYSIS

- Line 1 starts the AddAGroup macro, which creates Line and Circle objects and adds them to a group. The group can then be treated as a single entity when setting its attributes, such as color and highlighting.
- Line 2 declares the GroupObject variable as being capable of referencing a Group object.
- Line 3 declares the ObjectsForGroup array as being capable of containing elements that can reference Entity objects. Elements in this array will be assigned references to all the objects in the group.
- Lines 4 and 5 declare the variables that will be set up to refer to the Circle and Line objects that will form the group.
- Line 6 declares the array that will be assigned the coordinates of the center of the circle, and the radius that will define its size.
- Lines 7 and 8 declare the arrays that will hold the two endpoints defining the line.
- Line 9 declares Count as the counter variable used by the For loop.
- Lines 10 and 11 assign values that define the position for the center of the circle and the radius.
- Line 12 calls the AddCircle method to create a new Circle object, passing the center position and radius as arguments.
- Lines 13 and 14 assign the values denoting the coordinates of the two endpoints defining the line.

- Line 15 calls the `AddLine` method to create a new line, passing the arrays containing the two endpoints as arguments.
- Line 16 redefines the `ObjectsForGroup` array so that it will be large enough to contain the number of objects currently associated with the ModelSpace object.
- Line 17 starts the `For` loop that initially sets the `Count` variable to zero, so that it can access the first element in the `ObjectForGroup` and ModelSpace collection arrays. `Count` has a value of 2 at this point, and since both these two element arrays are accessed from the collection with indices of zero and 1, the last item in the collection is the number of items in the collection (`ThisDrawing.ModelSpace.Count`) less 1 to account for starting at zero.
- Line 18 assigns references to the objects in the Model Space to the elements in the `ObjectForGroup` array.
- Line 19 ends the `For` loop.
- Line 20 calls the `Add` method of the Groups collection to create a new Group object, and adds it to the collection. The name `"MyGroup"` is given as the argument. If you run this macro twice, you will need to pass a different name in order to avoid getting the "Group already exists" error message. The `GroupObject` variable is set up to reference this newly created group.
- Line 21 calls the `AppendItems` method to add the drawing objects referred to by the elements in the `ObjectsForGroup` array to the `"MyGroup"` group. The argument expected by this method is an array of drawing objects.
- Line 22 sets the `Color` property of the group to blue, to demonstrate that the group is treated by VBA as a single entity.
- Line 23 calls the `Highlight` property with the argument set to `True`, to display the group members as highlighted.
- Line 24 calls the `Regen` method to regenerate the active viewport and ensure that all changes have been incorporated in the current display.
- Line 25 calls the `ZoomAll` method to ensure that all drawing objects are displayed.
- Line 26 ends the `AddAGroup` macro.

Accessing Individual Drawing Objects from a Group

Using Group objects allows you to access individual drawing objects and update their properties—something that can't be done when using Block objects. To update the line drawn in Figure 14.13 from blue to green, simply insert the following statement at Line 24 of Listing 14.10:

```
GroupObject.Item(1).Color = acGreen
```

Summary

After working your way through this chapter, you should be able to

- Create layers.
- Group drawing objects into layers and generate drawings from various combinations of these layers.
- Lock a layer to prevent editing, and unlock it again.
- Freeze a layer to prevent it from being displayed (and edited), and thaw it again to make it visible and allow editing.
- Turn layers on and off so that they're hidden but can still be regenerated with other unhidden layers.
- Combine drawing objects into a block so that they can be operated on as a single entity.
- Create simple blocks and Xref blocks.
- Create selection sets using the various selection modes that are available with VBA.
- Combine drawing objects into groups.
- Update the properties of individual drawing objects from a group.

Part 5
3D Drawing Techniques

In This Part

Creating and Drawing 3D Solids

AUTOCAD VBA

Chapter 15

In this chapter you'll learn how to add three-dimensional solids to your drawings. AutoCAD provides a variety of methods for creating the kinds of primitive solids that are traditionally used in constructive solid geometry (CSG) techniques. You'll see how to add these to your drawings from macros and view them from different directions. I'll show you how to combine primitive solids to form complex solids, and some ways of creating other solids from planar surfaces using extrusion and revolution. Also covered are techniques for chamfering, filleting, and cross-sectioning from your VBA code.

- Creating 3D solids
- Constructing complex solids
- Creating solids by extrusion and revolution
- Chamfered and filleted edges
- Cross sections

Creating 3D Solids

AutoCAD has a generic type called Acad3DSolid that can represent any 3D solid object that you can add to a drawing using the methods AddBox, AddCone, AddCylinder, AddElliptical Cone, AddElliptical Cylinder, AddExtrudedSolid, AddExtrudedSolidAlong-Path, AddRevolvedSolid, AddSphere, AddTorus, and AddWedge. The Acad3DSolid type declares the solid object that it represents as a free-form surface capable of taking on any shape. Let's take a look at a few of these 3D solids provided by AutoCAD—boxes, wedges, cones, cylinders, spheres, and tori—represented by the Acad3DSolid object type. These solids are typically used in traditional methods to construct complex solids—you'll see how this is done later in the chapter.

All the Acad3DSolids are positioned in the WCS by specifying the position of the centers of their bounding boxes. (A bounding box is the smallest box possible that completely encloses all the edges and vertices of a solid.) By default, these solids are all aligned in some way with the x-, y-, and z-axes. In Chapter 19 on the CD, you'll learn how you can update their orientations.

The center of any solid object is the center of the imaginary bounding box that encloses it.

Exercise 15.1 continues through several sections, developing an application that allows you to add and delete simple solids in a new drawing. Figure 15.1 shows this application after five solids have been added to the Model Space.

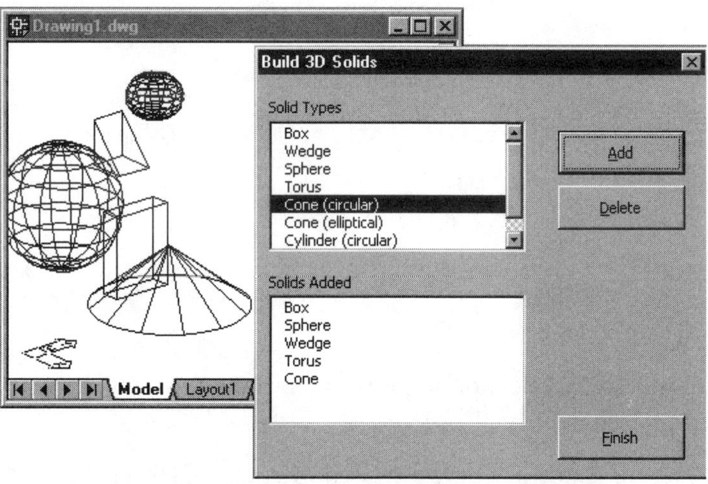

Figure 15.1 *The Build 3D Solids Application in action*

Exercise 15.1: Building the 3D Solids Application

This exercise comprises a series of individual connected procedures that take you through drawing the various 3D solid objects provided by AutoCAD. You'll start by creating the GUI.

1. Start a new project and add a UserForm.
2. Add two list boxes—one to show the types of solids available, and the other to show the solids added to the current drawing session. Figure 15.1 gives you an idea of how to position them.
3. Place a label above each list box to provide a description of its contents.
4. Create three command buttons: to add a solid, to delete a solid that has been added, and to finish running the application and return to the AutoCAD window.
5. Change the properties of the UserForm and the controls to those shown in Table 15.1.

Table 15.1 Properties for the Building 3D Solids Application

Old Name	New Name	Caption
UserForm1	frmBuildSolids	Build 3D Solids
ListBox1	lslSolidTypes	—
ListBox2	lstSolidsAdded	—
Label1	—	Solid Types
Label2	—	Solids Added
CommandButton1	cmdAdd	Add
CommandButton2	cmdDelete	Delete
CommandButton3	cmdFinish	Finish

6. Change the Accelerator property of cmdAdd to **A**, cmdDelete to **D**, and cmdFinish to **F**.
7. Enter the code for the event procedures of the GUI (Listing 15.1).

8. Enter the code for the ChangeViewDirection macro (Listing 15.2) into ThisDrawing's Code window. The default view direction is along the z-axis, which means that solids may often appear two-dimensional (for example, a box may look like a rectangle). To emphasize that the solids are three-dimensional, the ChangeViewDirection macro ensures that the solids are viewed from a different direction. This macro is called by all the macros in this exercise to emphasize the three-dimensional features of the solids being drawn.

LISTING 15.1: EVENT PROCEDURES OF THE BUILDING 3D SOLIDS APPLICATION

```
Private Sub cmdAdd_Click()
    frmBuildSolids.hide
    Select Case lstSolidTypes.ListIndex
    Case 0
        ThisDrawing.DrawBox
        lstSolidsAdded.AddItem "Box"
    Case 1
        ThisDrawing.DrawWedge
        lstSolidsAdded.AddItem "Wedge"
    Case 2
        ThisDrawing.DrawSphere
        lstSolidsAdded.AddItem "Sphere"
    Case 3
        ThisDrawing.DrawTorus
        lstSolidsAdded.AddItem "Torus"
    Case 4
        ThisDrawing.DrawCone
        lstSolidsAdded.AddItem "Cone"
    Case 5
        ThisDrawing.DrawEllipticalCone
        lstSolidsAdded.AddItem "Cone (elliptical)"
    Case 6
        ThisDrawing.DrawCylinder
        lstSolidsAdded.AddItem "Cylinder"
    Case 7
        ThisDrawing.DrawEllipticalCylinder
        lstSolidsAdded.AddItem "Cylinder (elliptical)"
    End Select
    frmBuildSolids.Show
End Sub

```

```
32  Private Sub cmdDelete_Click()
33      If lstSolidsAdded.ListIndex = -1 Then 'no solid selected
34         MsgBox "Please select item from the Solids ↵
              Added listbox.", vbOKOnly, "Building 3D Solids"
35      Else
36          ThisDrawing.ModelSpace.Item ↵
               (lstSolidsAdded.ListIndex).Delete
37          lstSolidsAdded.RemoveItem (lstSolidsAdded.ListIndex)
38          ThisDrawing.Regen acActiveViewport
39      End If
40  End Sub
41
42  Private Sub cmdFinish_Click()
43      Unload Me
44  End Sub
45
46  Private Sub UserForm_Initialize()
47      lstSolidTypes.AddItem "Box"
48      lstSolidTypes.AddItem "Wedge"
49      lstSolidTypes.AddItem "Sphere"
50      lstSolidTypes.AddItem "Torus"
51      lstSolidTypes.AddItem "Cone (circular)"
52      lstSolidTypes.AddItem "Cone (elliptical)"
53      lstSolidTypes.AddItem "Cylinder (circular)"
54      lstSolidTypes.AddItem "Cylinder (elliptical)"
55  End Sub
```

ANALYSIS

- Line 1 starts the Click event procedure for the Add button, which adds the solid selected in the top list box to the Model Space and displays it in the bottom list box.
- Line 2 hides the UserForm so that the user can interact directly with the AutoCAD window to enter the details prompted for in the command line.
- Line 3 starts the `Select Case` statement that uses the `ListIndex` property to identify the selected item from the `lstSolidTypes` list box.
- Lines 4 through 6 contain the code that's run when the Box item from the top list box is selected as the Add button is clicked. Line 5 calls the `DrawBox` procedure (Listing 15.3). Line 6 calls the `AddItem` method to add the string

"Box" to the bottom list box, showing that the solid has been added and allowing the user to select it if they want to delete it.

- Lines 7 through 27 provide code similar to Lines 4 through 6, for the other solids from the top list.
- Line 28 ends the `Select Case` statement.
- Line 29 calls the `Show` method of the UserForm to display it to the user, allowing them to add the next solid or delete an existing one.
- Line 30 ends the `cmdAdd_Click` event procedure.
- Line 32 starts the Click event procedure for the Delete command button, which removes the solid selected in the bottom list box from the Model Space and from the bottom list box.
- Line 33 checks to see if a solid is selected in the bottom list box.
- Line 34 runs if *no* solid has been selected. It calls the `MsgBox` function to instruct the user to select an item from the bottom list box.
- Line 35 starts the `Else` part of the `If` statement block.
- Line 36 uses the Item property with the same index value as the selected item from the bottom list box (`lstSolidsAdded.ListIndex`), to identify the solid to be deleted from the Model Space. The solid is removed using the `Delete` method.
- Line 37 calls the `RemoveItem` method of the `lstSolidsAdded` listbox, supplying the position in the list of the selected item. This removes the item from the list and resets `ListIndex` to –1, so it is important that Line 36 is executed before this line.
- Line 38 calls the `Regen` method to redraw all the solids in the active viewport, to ensure that the deleted solid disappears immediately.
- Lines 39 and 40 end the `If` statement and the `cmdDelete_Click` event procedure, respectively.
- Line 42 starts the Click event procedure of the Finish command button.
- Line 43 uses the `Unload` statement with the `Me` keyword to unload the UserForm, thus closing the Building 3D Solids application.
- Line 44 ends the `cmdFinish_Click` event procedure.

- Line 46 starts the UserForm's Initialize event procedure, which adds all the solid types to the top list box and clears any items from the bottom list box. The application assumes that the Model Space is completely empty when the application is executed, so that the position of the selected item from the bottom list box (`ListIndex` property) can be used to identify the corresponding object from the ModelSpace collection.
- Lines 47 through 54 use the `AddItem` method to add the names of the 3D solids to the top list box.
- Line 55 ends the `UserForm_Initialize` event procedure.

Listing 15.2: ChangeViewDirection Macro

```
1   Public Sub ChangeViewDirection()
2       Dim ViewDirection(0 To 2) As Double
3       ViewDirection(0) = 3#
4       ViewDirection(1) = -2.5
5       ViewDirection(2) = 1.5
6       ThisDrawing.ActiveViewport.Direction = ViewDirection
7       ThisDrawing.ActiveViewport = ThisDrawing.ActiveViewport
8   End Sub
```

Analysis

- Line 1 starts the `ChangeViewDirection` macro, which changes the viewing direction of the WCS.
- Line 2 declares `ViewDirection` as a three-element array.
- Lines 3 through 5 assign values to the three components that make up the view direction vector.
- Line 6 assigns the `ViewDirection` array to the `Direction` property of the active viewport.
- Line 7 assigns the active viewport to itself to regenerate the objects associated with it, in order to ensure that the changes made to the direction vector take effect on the drawing displayed on the screen.

Changes made to a Viewport object are not updated on the screen until that viewport is explicitly made the active viewport again.

- Line 8 ends the `ChangeViewDirection` macro.

Now let's get started creating the different types of solids and incorporating them into the Building 3D Solids application.

Creating a Box

The bounding box for a Box solid has the same vertices and edges as the Box itself. In this section you'll see how to calculate the center of the bounding box and pass it to the AddBox method, to create the Box solid with its edges parallel to the three-dimensional WCS axes.

In Listing 15.3, the AddBox method is called from the DrawBox macro with the following arguments:

BoxCenter A three-element array that defines the coordinates of the center of the box. This is used to position the box in WCS.

BoxLength A positive value representing the length of the box.

BoxWidth A positive value representing the width of the box.

BoxHeight A positive value representing the height of the box.

Exercise 15.1 is continued in this section, taking you through the steps of entering the DrawBox macro and running it. Figure 15.2 shows the Box solid generated by the macro.

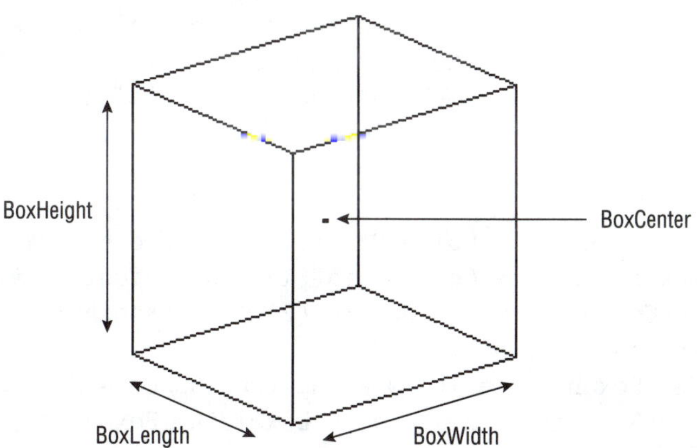

Figure 15.2 *Box generated by the DrawBox macro (Listing 15.3)*

Exercise 15.1: Building the 3D Solids Application (continued)

1. Continuing with Exercise 15.1, enter the DrawBox macro code (Listing 15.3) into the Code window for ThisDrawing.
2. Enter the following statement into the skeleton Click event procedure for optBox:

```
ThisDrawing.DrawBox
```

3. Run your macro from the Macros dialog box in the AutoCAD window, or you can run it from the Visual Basic Editor.
4. Follow the prompts in the command line to enter the position and dimensions required.

Listing 15.3: DrawBox Macro

```
Public Sub DrawBox()
    'draws a box
    Dim BoxObject As Acad3DSolid
    Dim BoxCenter(0 To 2) As Double
    Dim BoxLength As Double, BoxWidth As Double
    Dim BoxHeight As Double
    Dim CornerPoint As Variant
    With ThisDrawing.Utility
        CornerPoint = .GetPoint(, vbCr & ↵
           "Select the position of a corner of the box:")
        BoxLength = .GetDistance(CornerPoint, vbCr & ↵
                          "Enter the distance along the X-axis:")
        BoxWidth = .GetDistance(CornerPoint, vbCr & ↵
                          "Enter the distance along the Y-axis:")
        BoxHeight = .GetDistance(CornerPoint, vbCr & ↵
                          "Enter the distance along the Z-axis:")
    End With
    BoxCenter(0) = CornerPoint(0) + BoxWidth / 2#
    BoxCenter(1) = CornerPoint(1) + BoxHeight / 2#
    BoxCenter(2) = CornerPoint(2) + BoxLength / 2#
    ChangeViewDirection
    Set BoxObject = ThisDrawing.ModelSpace.AddBox ↵
       (BoxCenter, BoxLength, BoxWidth, BoxHeight)
    BoxObject.Update
End Sub
```

Analysis

- Line 1 starts the `DrawBox` macro, which prompts the user for the position and dimensions for the box and then creates it.
- Line 3 declares the `BoxObject` variable as being capable of referencing a 3DSolid object. The 3DSolid object can contain any of the solid objects that are added to the drawing, using `Add` followed by the solid type (such as `AddSphere`, `AddBox`, and `AddCylinder`).
- Line 4 declares the `BoxCenter` array that will be assigned the center of the Box solid, which is also the center of the bounding box.
- Lines 5 and 6 declare the variables that will be allocated the three dimensions of the box along the x-, y-, and z-axes.
- Line 7 declares the `CornerPoint` variable as a Variant type, so that it can be allocated the three-element array containing the coordinates of the position for a corner of the box in a single statement.
- Line 8 uses the `With` statement block, so that the methods of the Utility object for ThisDrawing can be used without having to fully qualify them.
- Line 9 prompts the user to click on the position for a corner of the box. This will be used to determine the center of the box, which in turn defines the position for the box.
- Lines 10 through 12 prompt the user to enter the x, y, and z dimensions for the box by calling the `GetDistance` method to return the three values required.
- Line 13 ends the `With` statement.
- Lines 14 through 16 calculate the three coordinates that define the center of the box based on the corner point and the box's dimensions.
- Line 17 calls the `ChangeViewDirection` macro given in Listing 15.2 so that more than one side of the box will be displayed. Without this step, only the x and y dimensions are visible and the box looks no different from a 2D rectangle.
- Line 18 calls the `AddBox` method to create a three-dimensional box, stores its representation in a 3DSolid object, and sets up the `BoxObject` variable as a reference to it.

- Line 19 calls the `Update` method to ensure that the new box object is displayed on the drawing screen.
- Line 20 ends the `DrawBox` macro.

Creating a Wedge

The AddWedge method is used to create a Wedge solid, given the center of the sloping face and its dimensions in the x, y, and z directions. The center of the sloping face is the same as the center of the bounding box that encloses the wedge. The wedge is normally created with most of its edges parallel to the WCS axes.

Listing 15.4 shows the AddWedge method being called from the DrawWedge macro with the following arguments:

FaceCenterPoint The point at the center of the sloping face, which is also the center of the bounding box that encloses the wedge.

WedgeLength A positive value that represents the length of the wedge.

WedgeWidth A positive value that represents the width of the wedge.

WedgeHeight A positive value that represents the height of the wedge.

In the next series of steps, you enter the DrawWedge macro and run it. Figure 15.3 shows the Wedge solid generated by the macro.

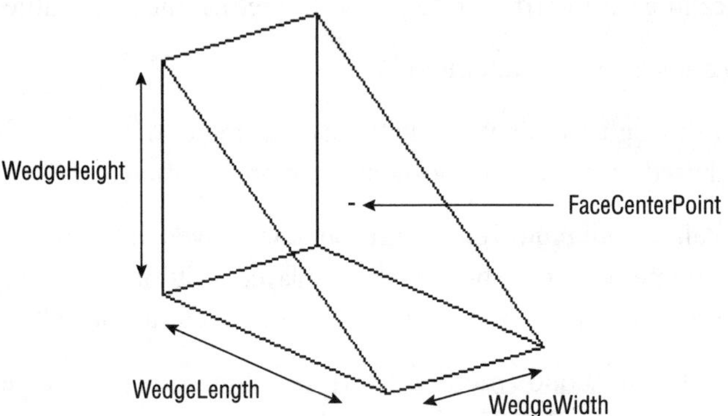

***Figure 15.3** Wedge drawn by the DrawWedge macro (Listing 15.4)*

Exercise 15.1: Building the 3D Solids Application (continued)

1. Continuing with the same drawing, add the DrawWedge macro's code (Listing 15.4) into the Code window for ThisDrawing.
2. Return to the AutoCAD window, choose Tools ➜ Macro ➜ Macros, and run the macro from the Macros dialog box.
3. Follow the prompts in the command line to enter the position and dimensions required.

Listing 15.4: DrawWedge Macro

```
1   Public Sub DrawWedge()
2       'draws a wedge
3       Dim WedgeObject As Acad3DSolid
4       Dim WedgeLength As Double, WedgeWidth As Double
5       Dim WedgeHeight As Double
6       Dim FaceCenterPoint As Variant
7       With ThisDrawing.Utility
8           FaceCenterPoint = .GetPoint(, vbCr & ↵
               "Select the center of the sloping face:")
9           WedgeLength = .GetDistance(FaceCenterPoint, ↵
               vbCr & "Enter the distance along the X-axis:")
10          WedgeWidth = .GetDistance(FaceCenterPoint, ↵
               vbCr & "Enter the distance along the Y-axis:")
11          WedgeHeight = .GetDistance(FaceCenterPoint, ↵
               vbCr & "Enter the distance along the Z-axis:")
12      End With
13      ChangeViewDirection
14      Set WedgeObject = ThisDrawing.ModelSpace.AddWedge ↵
          (FaceCenterPoint, WedgeLength, ↵
          WedgeWidth, WedgeHeight)
15      WedgeObject.Update
16  End Sub
```

Analysis

- Line 1 starts the `DrawWedge` macro, which prompts the user to enter the information required and draws a Wedge solid to the specifications.
- Line 3 declares the `WedgeObject` variable that will be used to reference the 3DSolid object after the Wedge solid has been created.

- Lines 4 and 5 declare the variables used to represent the dimensions of the wedge in the x, y, and z directions.
- Line 6 declares the `FaceCenterPoint` variable as a Variant type so that it can be assigned a three-element array containing the point selected by the user for the center of the sloping face.
- Line 7 uses the `With` statement so that the `GetPoint` and `GetDistance` methods of the Utility object can be used without being fully qualified.
- Line 8 calls the `GetPoint` method to prompt the user to enter the center of the sloping face. This point is also the center of the bounding box for the Wedge object.
- Lines 9 through 11 prompt the user to enter the distances along the x-, y-, and z-axes to specify the size of the wedge.
- Line 12 ends the `With` statement.
- Line 13 calls the `ChangeViewDirection` macro that displays the Wedge solid at an angle, to make its shape more obvious.
- Line 14 calls the `AddWedge` method to create a Wedge solid and set up the `WedgeObject` variable to reference the 3DSolid object that is created to represent the wedge.
- Line 15 calls the `Update` method to redraw the Wedge object on the screen.
- Line 16 ends the `DrawWedge` macro.

Creating a Sphere

The AddSphere method is used to create a Sphere solid, given its center and radius. Listing 15.5 shows this method being called from the DrawSphere macro with the following variables as arguments:

SphereCenter A three-element array representing the center of the sphere, which is also the center of the bounding box.

SphereRadius A positive value representing the radius of the sphere.

In the next series of steps, you enter the DrawSphere macro and run it. Figure 15.4 shows the Sphere solid drawn by the macro.

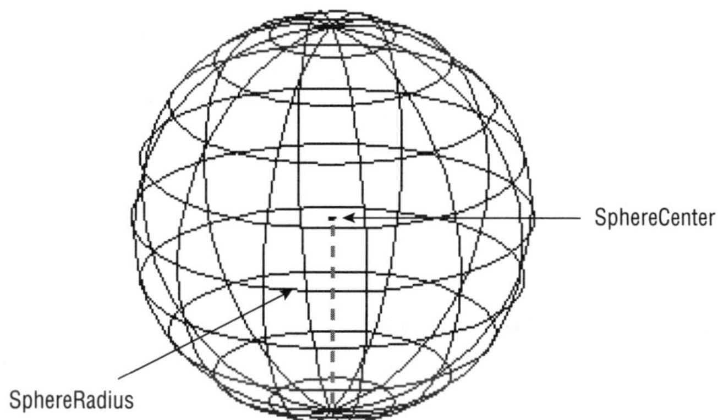

Figure 15.4 *Sphere solid generated by the DrawSphere macro (Listing 15.5)*

Exercise 15.1: Building the 3D Solids Application (continued)

1. Continuing with the same drawing, enter the DrawSphere macro's code (Listing 15.5) into the Code window for ThisDrawing.
2. Return to the AutoCAD window, choose Tools ➜ Macro ➜ Macros, and run the macro from the Macros dialog box.
3. Follow the prompts in the command line to enter the sphere's center and position.

Listing 15.5: DrawSphere Macro

```
Public Sub DrawSphere()
    'draws a sphere
    Dim SphereObject As Acad3DSolid
    Dim SphereCenter As Variant
    Dim SphereRadius As Double
    With ThisDrawing.Utility
        SphereCenter = .GetPoint(, vbCr & ↵
           "Select position for center of sphere:")
        SphereRadius = .GetDistance(SphereCenter, vbCr & ↵
           "Enter radius of Sphere:")
```

```
9       End With
10      ThisDrawing.Preferences.ContourLinesPerSurface = 12
11      Set SphereObject = ThisDrawing.ModelSpace.AddSphere ↵
           (SphereCenter, SphereRadius)
12      SphereObject.Update
13      ChangeViewDirection
14      End Sub
```

ANALYSIS

- Line 1 starts the `DrawSphere` macro, which prompts the user to enter the center and radius, creates the sphere to the user's specifications, and draws it on the screen.
- Line 3 declares the `SphereObject` variable as being capable of referencing a 3DSolid object.
- Line 4 declares the `SphereCenter` variable as a Variant type, so that the three-element array returned by the `GetPoint` method can be assigned to it in a single statement.
- Line 5 declares the `Radius` variable that determines the size of the sphere.
- Line 6 uses the `With` statement so that the Utility object's `GetPoint` and `GetDistance` methods can be used without having to fully qualify them.
- Line 7 calls the `GetPoint` method to prompt the user to enter the center for the sphere solid. This point is also the center of the bounding box for this solid.
- Line 8 calls the `GetDistance` method to prompt the user for the length of the sphere's radius.
- Line 10 updates the number of `ContourLinesPerSurface` property to 12. The number required for a reasonable image depends on the surface's level of curvature and the screen area it covers. Since `ContourLinesPerSurface` is a property of the `Preferences` object of ThisDrawing, all the solids in the active drawing will be updated to reflect any new setting.
- Line 11 calls the `AddSphere` method to create a Sphere solid, and sets up the `SphereObject` variable as a reference to the 3DSolid object that represents the sphere.
- Line 12 calls the `Update` method to draw the sphere on the screen.

- Line 13 calls the `ChangeViewDirection` to view the sphere from a different direction.
- Line 14 ends the `DrawSphere` macro.

The Sphere is the only solid that doesn't change its outline as the viewing direction changes.

Creating a Torus

The AddTorus method is used to create a Torus solid, given its center, its radius, and the radius of its tube. Listing 15.6 shows this method being called from the DrawTorus macro with the following variables as arguments:

TorusCenter A three-element array representing the center of the torus, and also the center of the bounding box that encloses the torus.

TorusRadius A positive value representing the radius of the torus. This is the distance between the center of the torus to the center of the tube.

TubeRadius A positive value representing the radius of the tube of the torus.

In the next series of steps, you enter the DrawTorus macro and run it. Figure 15.5 shows the torus created by the macro. In order to get a clearer view of this torus, I've changed the z-coordinate of view direction vector `ViewDirection(2)` from 1.5 to 4.5 (line 4 of Listing 15.2).

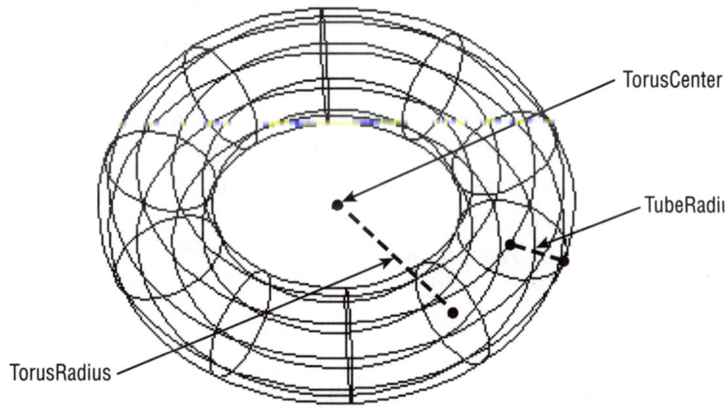

Figure 15.5 *Torus generated by the DrawTorus macro (Listing 15.6)*

EXERCISE 15.1: BUILDING THE 3D SOLIDS APPLICATION (CONTINUED)

1. Continuing with the same drawing, enter the DrawTorus macro's code (Listing 15.6) into ThisDrawing's Code window.
2. Return to the AutoCAD window, choose Tools ➜ Macro ➜ Macros, and run the DrawTorus macro from the Macros dialog box.
3. Answer the prompts in the command line to enter the information required.

LISTING 15.6: DRAWTORUS MACRO

```
1   Public Sub DrawTorus()
2       'draws a torus
3       Dim TorusObject As Acad3DSolid
4       Dim TorusCenter As Variant
5       Dim TorusRadius As Double
6       Dim TubeRadius As Double
7       Dim PointOnRadius(0 To 2) As Double
8       With ThisDrawing.Utility
9           TorusCenter = .GetPoint(, vbCr & ↵
               "Select position for center of Torus:")
10          TorusRadius = .GetDistance(TorusCenter, vbCr & ↵
                                 "Enter radius of Torus:")
11          PointOnRadius(0) = TorusCenter(0) + TorusRadius
12          PointOnRadius(1) = TorusCenter(1)
13          PointOnRadius(2) = TorusCenter(2)
14          TubeRadius = .GetDistance(PointOnRadius, vbCr & ↵
                                 "Enter radius of tube:")
15      End With
16      ThisDrawing.Preferences.ContourLinesPerSurface = 12
17      Set TorusObject = ThisDrawing.ModelSpace.AddTorus ↵
           (TorusCenter, TorusRadius, TubeRadius)
18      TorusObject.Update
19      ChangeViewDirection
20  End Sub
```

ANALYSIS

- Line 1 starts the DrawTorus macro, which prompts the user to enter the position and dimensions of the torus and creates a solid to these specifications.

- Line 3 declares the `TorusObject` variable as being capable of referencing a 3DSolid object.
- Line 4 declares the `TorusCenter` variable as a Variant type so that it can be assigned the three-element array returned by the `GetPoint` method.
- Line 5 declares the `TorusRadius` variable that will be assigned the distance between the position of the center of the hole and any central position along the tube.
- Line 6 declares the `TubeRadius` that will be assigned the radius of the tube, to determine its volume.
- Line 7 declares the `PointOnRadius` array that will be assigned the point at the radius's end that is opposite to the torus's center, which also happens to be at the center of the tube.
- Line 8 uses the `With` statement so that the methods of the Utility object can be used without being fully qualified.
- Line 9 prompts the user for the position of the center of the torus's hole, which is also the center of its bounding box.
- Line 10 prompts the user to enter the radius of the torus.
- Lines 11 through 13 assign to the `PointOnRadius` array the coordinates of the point in the x-axis direction at the distance denoted by the radius. This point is at the center of the tube.
- Line 14 calls the `GetDistance` method with the center of the tube as the first argument, and prompts the user to enter the radius for the tube.
- Line 16 assigns 12 to the `ContourLinesPerSurface` property.
- Line 17 calls the `AddTorus` method to create a Torus solid and sets up the `TorusObject` variable as a reference to the 3DSolids object that represents the torus.
- Line 18 calls the `Update` method to draw the torus in Model Space.
- Line 19 calls the `ChangeViewDirection` macro to display the torus from a different viewing angle. In order to make the shape of the torus even clearer, I changed the z component of the direction vector in this macro from 1.5 to 4.5 (line 5 of Listing 15.2).
- Line 20 ends the `DrawTorus` macro.

Creating a Cone

The AddCone method is used to create a Cone solid, given the center of its box enclosure, its radius, and its height. Listing 15.7 shows this method being called from the DrawCone macro with the following arguments:

ConeCenter A three-element array that defines the coordinates of the center of the bounding box that encloses the cone.

ConeRadius A positive value representing the radius at the base of the cone, which by default lies in the x-y plane.

ConeHeight A positive value representing the height of the cone, which is its length along the z-axis.

In the next series of steps, you enter the DrawCone macro and run it. Figure 15.6 shows the Cone solid generated by the macro, using the default number of contour lines per surface, which is four.

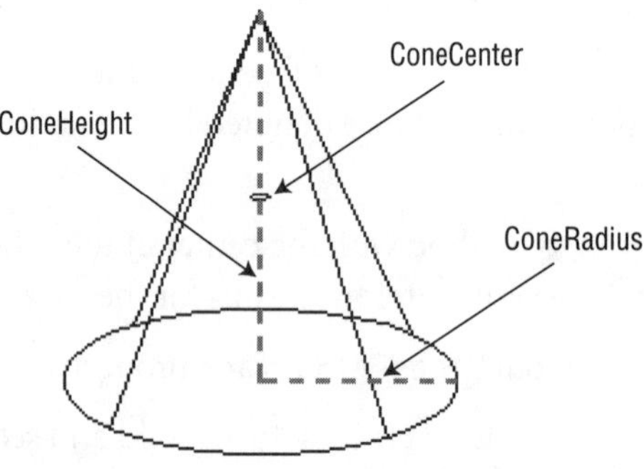

Figure 15.6 *Cone drawn by the DrawCone macro (Listing 15.7), using the default four contour lines per surface*

Exercise 15.1: Building the 3D Solids Application (continued)

1. Continuing with the same project, enter the DrawCone macro's code (Listing 15.7) into the Code window for ThisDrawing.

2. Return to the AutoCAD window and run your macro from the Macros dialog box.

3. Following the prompts in the command line, enter the position and dimensions required.

Listing 15.7: DrawCone Macro

```
1   Public Sub DrawCone()
2       'draws a cone
3       Dim ConeObject As Acad3DSolid
4       Dim ConeCenter As Variant
5       Dim ConeRadius As Double
6       Dim ConeHeight As Double
7       With ThisDrawing.Utility
8           ConeCenter = .GetPoint(, vbCr & ↵
               "Select position for base of cone:")
9           ConeRadius = .GetDistance(ConeCenter, vbCr & ↵
                                 "Enter radius of base:")
10          ConeHeight = .GetDistance(ConeCenter, vbCr & ↵
                                 "Enter height of cone:")
11      End With
12      ConeCenter(2) = ConeCenter(2) + ConeHeight / 2#
13      Set ConeObject = ThisDrawing.ModelSpace.AddCone ↵
           (ConeCenter, ConeRadius, ConeHeight)
14      ConeObject.Update
15      ChangeViewDirection
16  End Sub
```

Analysis

- Line 1 starts the `DrawCone` macro, which draws a Cone solid after prompting the user for its position, the radius at its base, and its height.
- Line 3 declares the `ConeObject` variable as being capable of referencing a 3DSolid object.
- Line 4 declares the `ConeCenter` as a Variant type so that the three-element array returned by the `GetPoint` method can be assigned in a single statement.
- Lines 5 and 6 declare the variables representing the radius of the circular base of the cone, and its height.

- Line 7 uses the `With` statement so that the methods of the Utility object can be used without the need to fully qualify them each time.
- Line 8 calls the `GetPoint` method to prompt the user to select the position for the center of the circular base of the cone. This is used later at Line 12 to calculate the center of the bounding box.
- Lines 9 and 10 call the `GetDistance` method to prompt the user to enter the cone's radius and height.
- Line 12 updates the z-coordinate of the point entered by the user, to represent the center of the base of the cone so that it is positioned halfway between the base and the cone's tip.
- Line 13 calls the `AddCone` method to create a Cone solid, and sets up the `ConeObject` to refer to the 3DSolid object that represents the cone.
- Line 14 calls the `Update` method to draw the Cone object on the screen.
- Line 15 calls the `ChangeViewDirection` macro to change the direction from which the cone is viewed, so that it doesn't look like a 2D triangle.
- Line 16 ends the `DrawCone` macro.

Adding Contour Lines

By updating the `ContourLinesPerSurface` property, you can adjust the number of lines per surface. You simply insert the following statement after line 10 in Listing 15.7:

```
ThisDrawing.Preferences.ContourLinesPerSurface = 20
```

Now when you run the `DrawCone` macro, any cones and other solids in the current drawing plus any added in the future will be generated with the extra contour lines, as shown in Figure 15.7.

Updating the `ContourLinesPerSurface` property of the Preferences object updates all existing 3DSolid objects associated with the current drawing.

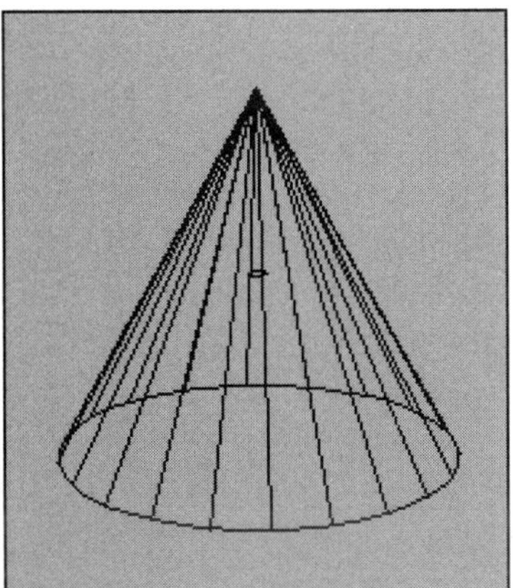

Figure 15.7 *Cone generated by DrawCone macro after including the statement updating the* `ContourLinesPerSurface` *property to 20*

Creating a Cylinder

The AddCylinder method is used to create a Cylinder solid, given the cylinder's center, radius, and height. The edges defining the cylindrical tube are all parallel to the z-axes of the WCS. Listing 15.8 shows this method being called from the DrawCylinder macro with the following variables used as arguments:

CylinderCenter A three-element array defining the coordinates of the center of the cylinder, and also the bounding box that encloses the cylinder.

CylinderRadius A positive value representing the radius of one of the cylinder's flat ends, which both lie in x-y planes.

CylinderHeight A positive value that represents the height of the cylinder. The cylinder's axis is parallel to the z-axis of the WCS.

In the next series of steps, you enter the DrawCylinder macro and run it. Figure 15.8 shows the Cylinder solid generated by the macro.

Exercise 15.1: Building the 3D Solids Application (continued)

1. Using the same project, enter the DrawCylinder macro's code (Listing 15.8) into ThisDrawing's Code window.

2. Return to the AutoCAD window, choose Tools ➜ Macro ➜ Macros and run your DrawCylinder macro from the Macros dialog box.
3. Follow the prompts in the command line to enter the position and dimensions required.

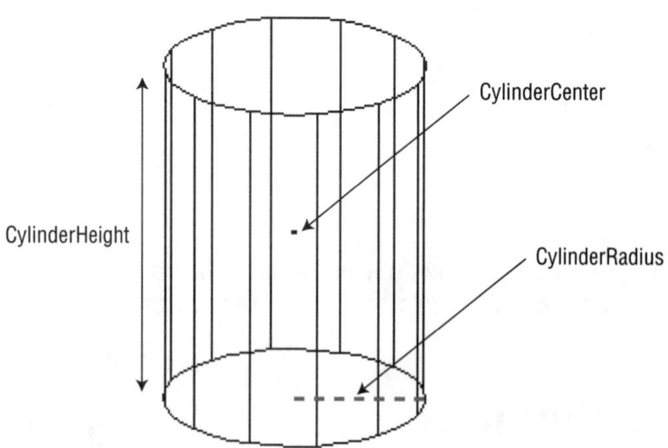

Figure 15.8 *Cylinder produced by the DrawCylinder macro (Listing 15.8)*

LISTING 15.8: DRAWCYLINDER MACRO

```
Public Sub DrawCylinder()
    'draws a cylinder
    Dim CylinderObject As Acad3DSolid
    Dim CylinderCenter As Variant
    Dim CylinderRadius As Double
    Dim CylinderHeight As Double
    With ThisDrawing.Utility
        CylinderCenter = .GetPoint ↵
           (, vbCr & "Select position for center of base:")
        CylinderRadius = .GetDistance ↵
           (CylinderCenter, vbCr & "Enter radius ↵
           of cylinder:")
        CylinderHeight = .GetDistance ↵
           (CylinderCenter, vbCr & "Enter height ↵
           of Cylinder:")
    End With
```

```
12      ThisDrawing.Preferences.ContourLinesPerSurface = 12
13      CylinderCenter(2) = CylinderCenter(2) ↵
            + CylinderHeight / 2#
14      Set CylinderObject = ↵
            ThisDrawing.ModelSpace.AddCylinder ↵
            (CylinderCenter, CylinderRadius, CylinderHeight)
15      CylinderObject.Update
16      ChangeViewDirection
17  End Sub
```

ANALYSIS

- Line 1 starts the `DrawCylinder` macro, which prompts the user to enter the position and dimensions of the cylinder, creates it to the user's specifications, and draws it.
- Line 3 declares the `CylinderObject` variable as being capable of referencing a 3DSolid object.
- Line 4 declares the `CylinderCenter` variable as a Variant type so that it can be assigned the three-element array returned by the `GetPoint` method at Line 8.
- Lines 5 and 6 declare the variables that will represent the cylinder's radius and height.
- Line 7 uses the `With` statement block so that the Utility object's methods can be used without being fully qualified.
- Line 8 calls the `GetPoint` method to prompt the user to select the position for the center of the cylinder's base. This position is initially assigned to the `CylinderCenter` variable; then this variable is adjusted at Line 13, updating it to the center of the bounding box.
- Lines 9 and 10 call the `GetDistance` method to prompt the user to enter the cylinder's radius and height.
- Line 12 updates the number of contours per surface by setting the `ContourLinesPerSurface` property to 12.
- Line 13 updates the z-coordinate of the center of the base, so that the `CylinderCenter` variable contains the coordinates of the center of the bounding box.
- Line 14 calls the `AddCylinder` method to create the cylinder with the attributes specified by the user, and sets up the `CylinderObject` variable as a reference to the 3DSolid object that represents the cylinder.

- Line 15 calls the `Update` method to ensure that the cylinder solid is drawn on the screen.
- Line 16 calls the `ChangeViewDirection` macro so that the cylinder doesn't appear as a 2D rectangle.
- Line 17 ends the `DrawCylinder` macro.

Creating Elliptical Cones and Cylinders

AutoCAD provides the AddEllipticalCone method to create elliptical cones, and the AddEllipticalCylinder method to create elliptical cylinders. These methods differ from the AddCone and AddCylinder methods by replacing their radius argument with the following two arguments:

ConeXDistance, CylinderXDistance A positive value representing the distance along the x-axis for the elliptical base of the cone or cylinder.

ConeYDistance, CylinderYDistance A positive value representing the distance along the y-axis for the elliptical base of the cone or cylinder.

Listings 15.9 and 15.10 contain the DrawEllipticalCone and DrawEllipticalCylinder macros that generate the elliptical cone and the elliptical cylinder shown in Figures 15.9 and 15.10.

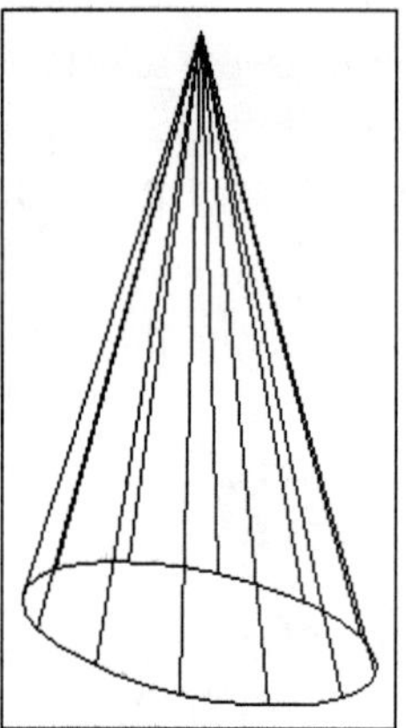

***Figure 15.9** Elliptical cone generated by the DrawEllipticalCone macro (Listing 15.9)*

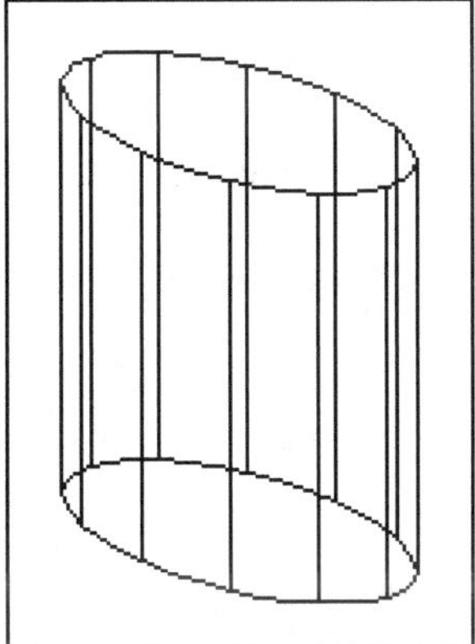

Figure 15.10 Elliptical cylinder generated by the DrawEllipticalCylinder macro (Listing 15.10)

Exercise 15.1: Building the 3D Solids Application (continued)

The following instructions show you where to enter the DrawEllipticalCone macro and how to run it.

1. Continuing with the same project, enter the DrawEllipticalCone macro's code given in Listing 15.9 into the Code window for ThisDrawing.
2. Return to the AutoCAD window, choose Tools ➜ Macro ➜ Macros, and run the DrawEllipticalCone macro from the Macros dialog box.
3. Follow the prompts in the command line to enter the position and dimensions required.

Listing 15.9: DrawEllipticalCone Macro

```
Public Sub DrawEllipticalCone()
    'draw elliptical cone
    Dim ConeObject As Acad3DSolid
    Dim ConeCenter As Variant
    Dim ConeXDistance As Double, ConeYDistance As Double
    Dim ConeHeight As Double
    With ThisDrawing.Utility
```

```
8           ConeCenter = .GetPoint(, vbCr & ↵
               "Select position for center of base:")
9           ConeXDistance = .GetDistance(ConeCenter, vbCr & ↵
               "Enter X distance of base:")
10          ConeYDistance = .GetDistance(ConeCenter, vbCr & ↵
               "Enter Y distance of base:")
11          ConeHeight = .GetDistance(ConeCenter, vbCr & ↵
               "Enter height of cone:")
12      End With
13      ThisDrawing.Preferences.ContourLinesPerSurface = 20
14      ConeCenter(2) = ConeCenter(2) + ConeHeight / 2#
15      Set ConeObject = ↵
           ThisDrawing.ModelSpace.AddEllipticalCone ↵
           (ConeCenter, ConeXDistance, ConeYDistance, ConeHeight)
16      ConeObject.Update
17      ChangeViewDirection
18  End Sub
```

ANALYSIS

- Line 1 starts the `DrawEllipticalCone` macro that prompts the user for the position and dimensions for the elliptical cone, creates it to those specifications, and draws it.

The code for `DrawEllipticalCone` was copied from the `DrawCone` macro and adjusted to include the extra argument. The two macros could be incorporated into one with a message box prompting the user to specify whether or not the solid is elliptical. If an elliptical solid is required, then the `GetDistance` method would be called to get the y distance; otherwise, the x distance is sufficient.

- Line 3 declares the `ConeObject` variable as being capable of referencing a 3DSolid object.
- Line 4 declares the `ConeCenter` variable as a Variant type so that it can be assigned the 3D point returned by the `GetPoint` method.
- Line 5 replaces the `ConeRadius` declaration from the `DrawCone` macro with the two variables that will represent the distances in the x and y directions.
- Line 6 declares the `ConeHeight` variable that will be assigned the value returned by the `GetDistance` method in Line 11.
- Line 7 starts the `With` statement so that the methods of the Utility object can be used without being fully qualified.

- Line 8 prompts the user for the position for the cone's center.
- Lines 9 and 10 prompt the user for the distance in the x and y directions for the elliptical base; these lines replace the prompt for the radius in the `DrawCone` macro.
- Line 11 prompts the user for the cone's height.
- Line 12 ends the `With` statement.
- Line 13 assigns a value to the `ContourLnesPerSurface` variable of the Preferences object.
- Line 14 calculates the y-coordinate for the center of the cone.
- Line 15 calls the `AddEllipticalCone` method with the two arguments passing the x and y distances, replacing the radius argument in the call to the `AddCone` macro.
- Line 16 calls the `Update` method of the `ConeObject` to ensure that the cone is redrawn in the Model space.
- Line 17 calls the `ChangeViewDirection` macro from Listing 15.2 to ensure that the cone is distinguishable from a 2D triangle.
- Line 18 ends the `DrawEllipticalCone` macro.

Exercise 15.1: Building the 3D Solids Application (continued)

The following instructions show you where to enter the `DrawEllipticalCylinder` macro and how to run it.

1. Continuing with the same project, enter the `DrawEllipticalCylinder` macro's code (Listing 15.10) into the Code window for ThisDrawing.
2. Return to the AutoCAD window, choose Tools → Macro → Macros, and run the `DrawEllipticalCylinder` macro from the Macros dialog box.
3. Follow the prompts in the command line to enter the position and dimensions required.

Listing 15.10: DrawEllipticalCylinder Macro

```
Public Sub DrawEllipticalCylinder()
    'draw elliptical cylinder
    Dim CylinderObject As Acad3DSolid
```

```
4       Dim CylinderCenter As Variant
5       Dim CylinderXDistance As Double, ↵
           CylinderYDistance As Double
6       Dim CylinderHeight As Double
7       With ThisDrawing.Utility
8           CylinderCenter = .GetPoint(, vbCr & ↵
               "Select position for center of base:")
9           CylinderXDistance = .GetDistance(CylinderCenter, ↵
               vbCr & "Enter X distance for cylinder:")
10          CylinderYDistance = .GetDistance(CylinderCenter, ↵
               vbCr & "Enter Y distance for cylinder:")
11          CylinderHeight = .GetDistance(CylinderCenter, ↵
               vbCr & "Enter height of Cylinder:")
12      End With
13      ThisDrawing.Preferences.ContourLinesPerSurface = 12
14      CylinderCenter(2) = CylinderCenter(2) ↵
           + CylinderHeight / 2#
15      Set CylinderObject = ↵
           ThisDrawing.ModelSpace.AddEllipticalCylinder ↵
           (CylinderCenter, CylinderXDistance, ↵
           CylinderYDistance, CylinderHeight)
16      CylinderObject.Update
17      ChangeViewDirection
18  End Sub
```

ANALYSIS

- Line 1 starts the `DrawEllipticalCylinder` macro, which prompts the user for the position and dimensions required to create and draw an elliptical cylinder. The code from this macro was copied from the `DrawCylinder` macro and adjusted to suit.
- Line 3 declares the `CylinderObject` variable as being capable of referencing a 3DSolid object.
- Line 4 declares the `CylinderCenter` variable as a Variant type so that it can be assigned the x-, y-, and z-coordinates returned by the `GetPoint` method.
- Line 5 replaces the radius variable from the `DrawCylinder` macro with the two variables that represent the x and y directions for the ellipsis at each end of the cylinder.

- Line 6 declares the `CylinderHeight` variable as Double so that it can be assigned the Double value returned by the `GetDistance` method at line 11.
- Line 7 starts the `With` statement so that the Utility object's methods can be used without being fully qualified.
- Line 8 assigns the `CylinderCenter` variable the point returned by the `GetPoint` method.
- Lines 9 and 10 replace prompts to the user for the radius, with prompts for the x and y distances to define the ellipse.
- Line 11 assigns to the `CylinderHeight` variable the value returned by the `GetDistance` method.
- Line 12 ends the `With` statement.
- Line 13 sets the `ContourLinesPerSurface` variable to 12.
- Line 14 calculates the y value of the cylinder's center.
- Line 15 calls the `AddEllipticalCylinder` method, with the x and y distances replacing the radius argument from the call to the `AddCylinder` method.
- Line 16 regenerates the cylinder to make sure that the current version appears in the Model Space.
- Line 17 calls the `ChangeViewDirection` macro to ensure that the cylinder does not appear as a 2D rectangle.
- Line 18 ends the `DrawEllipticalCylinder` macro.

Now that you've seen how to add a variety of individual solids to your drawings, the next step is to combine them to form a more complex solid.

Constructing Complex Solids

The primitive solids described in the preceding sections can be combined to provide complex solids that are positioned in three-dimensional space using the center point of their bounding boxes. Listing 15.11 contains the CombinePrimitives macro. This macro defines a box and an elliptical cylinder and then calls the Boolean method of the Box object with the CSG operations Intersection, Union, and Subtraction.

Figure 15.11 shows the result of passing the AutoCAD constant acUnion to this Boolean method (see Line 19 of the macro).

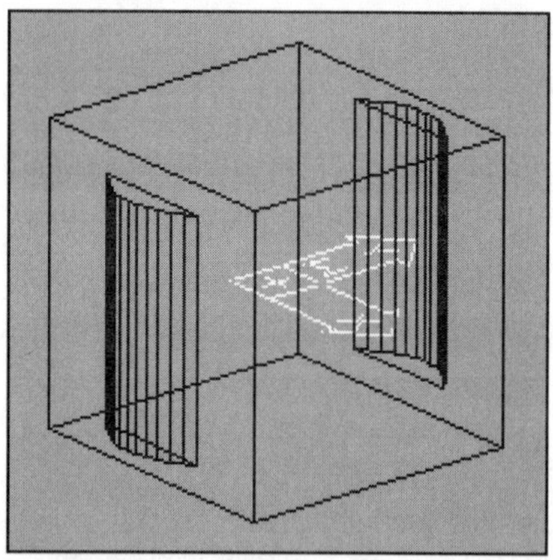

Figure 15.11 *Result of running the CombinePrimitives macro with acUnion passed as an argument to the Boolean method*

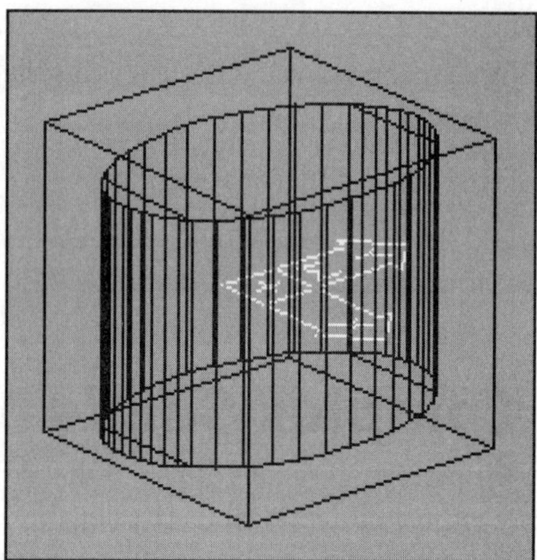

Figure 15.12 *Result of running the CombinePrimitives macro with acSubtraction passed as an argument to the Boolean method.*

Figure 15.12 shows the result of passing the AutoCAD constant acSubtraction to the Boolean method at Line 19 as follows:

```
BoxObject.Boolean acSubtraction, CylinderObject
```

Figure 15.13 shows the result when the acIntersection constant is passed at Line 19 as follows:

```
BoxObject.Boolean acIntersection, CylinderObject
```

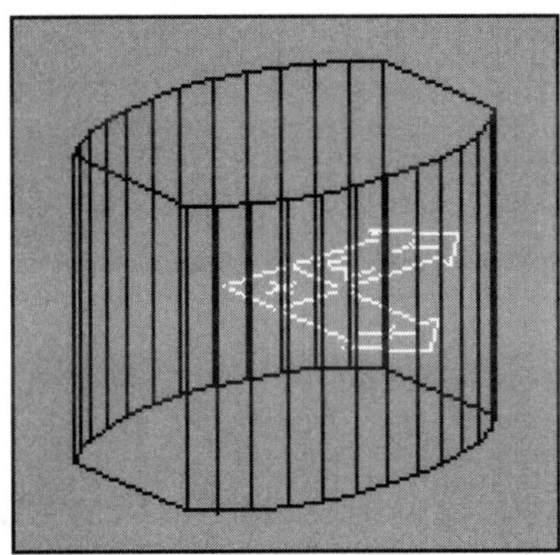

Figure 15.13 *Result of running the CombinePrimitives macro with acIntersection passed as an argument to the Boolean method*

LISTING 15.11: COMBINEPRIMITIVES MACRO

```
1   Public Sub CombinePrimitives()
2       Dim BoxObject As Acad3DSolid
3       Dim BoxCenter(0 To 2) As Double
4       Dim BoxLength As Double, BoxWidth As Double
5       Dim BoxHeight As Double
6       Dim CylinderObject As Acad3DSolid
7       Dim CylinderCenter(0 To 2) As Double
8       Dim CylinderXDistance As Double, ↵
           CylinderYDistance As Double
9       Dim CylinderHeight As Double
10      BoxCenter(0) = 0#: BoxCenter(1) = 0#: BoxCenter(2) = 0#
11      BoxLength = 5#: BoxWidth = 5#: BoxHeight = 5#
12      Set BoxObject = ThisDrawing.ModelSpace.AddBox↵
           (BoxCenter, BoxLength, BoxWidth, BoxHeight)
```

```
13      CylinderCenter(0) = 0#: CylinderCenter(1) = 0#: ↵
           CylinderCenter(2) = 0#
14      CylinderXDistance = 2#
15      CylinderYDistance = 3#
16      CylinderHeight = 4#
17      Set CylinderObject = ↵
           ThisDrawing.ModelSpace.AddEllipticalCylinder↵
           (CylinderCenter, CylinderXDistance, ↵
           CylinderYDistance, CylinderHeight)
18      ChangeViewDirection
19      BoxObject.Boolean acUnion, CylinderObject
20      ThisDrawing.Regen acActiveViewport
21   End Sub
```

ANALYSIS

- Line 1 starts the `CombinePrimitives` macro, which creates a box and an elliptical cylinder and then combines them using the Boolean operations available in AutoCAD.
- Lines 2 through 5 contain all the declarations needed to create a Box solid.
- Lines 6 through 9 contain all the declarations required to create a Cylinder solid.
- Lines 10 through 12 specify the position and dimensions for the Box solid and create it.
- Lines 13 through 17 specify the position and dimensions for the Cylinder solid and create it.
- Line 18 calls the `ChangeViewDirection` macro (Listing 15.2) to change the angle from which the complex solid will be viewed.
- Line 19 calls the Boolean method of the Box solid, with the first argument `acUnion` to denote the Boolean operator required for the construction, and the second argument `CylinderObject` as the solid to be combined with the Box solid. The other enumerated constants `acIntersection` and `acSubtraction` could also have been passed as the first argument.
- Line 20 regenerates the active viewport to display the two solids combined using the Boolean operator.
- Line 21 ends the `CombinePrimitives` macro.

Determining Whether Two Solids Intersect

Suppose you only want to test and see if two solids intersect, without actually performing the intersection. VBA provides a CheckInterference method that belongs to the 3DSolid object. The CheckInterference method calculates the area common to the calling object, plus a second 3DSolid object that is passed as an argument. If you want to try this out, in Listing 15.11 replace Line 19 (which calls the Boolean method) with the following two statements and run your CombinePrimitives macro again:

```
Dim ThreeDSolid As Acad3DSolid, ObjectsIntersect As Boolean
Set ThreeDSolid = BoxObject.CheckInterference(CylinderObject,
ObjectsIntersect)
```

In this example, the ThreeDSolid variable is assigned the area of intersection of the two surfaces, or Nothing if they don't intersect. The 3Dsolid object that is returned by CheckInterference need not be assigned to a variable; instead, you can test the value of the Boolean variable, ObjectsIntersect, passed as the second argument.

Grow Your Own Solids

This section describes how to sweep an outline using *translational sweep (extrusion)* and *rotational sweep (revolution)*. The extrusion effect is useful for objects that get their shape by passing them through a plane, such as door and window frames, and skirting boards. The revolution effect is useful for objects that are created using a lathe or turning machine.

Creating Solids by Extrusion

Extrusion allows you to specify a planar outline of the solid you require, plus a height. This two-dimensional outline is grown into a three-dimensional solid by translating the vertices that define it, in a straight line parallel to the z-axis.

Note that you cannot extrude 3D objects, objects in a block, or polylines that have intersecting edges or are not closed.

The following steps show you how to create a solid by extrusion:

1. Draw a rectangle in the AutoCAD window.
2. Choose Draw ➜ Solids ➜ Extrude.
3. When the command line prompts you to select objects, select the rectangle and press Enter.

4. Enter the height of extrusion, by clicking on two points defining a line the same length as the distance for the extrusion height.
5. When prompted for the angle of taper for extrusion, press Enter to accept the 0 taper angle by default. The rectangle now appears as a box shape.

Extrude Solids by Macro

Extrusion can also be done from a macro. Listing 15.13, for example, contains the DrawExtrudedSolid macro that was used to produce the extruded polygon shown in Figure 15.14. This macro calls the ChangeViewDirection macro given in Listing 15.2, and the GetShape and CloseShape macros given in Listing 7.3 from Chapter 7. The GetShape macro calls the RedrawPolyline macro, also given in Listing 7.3.

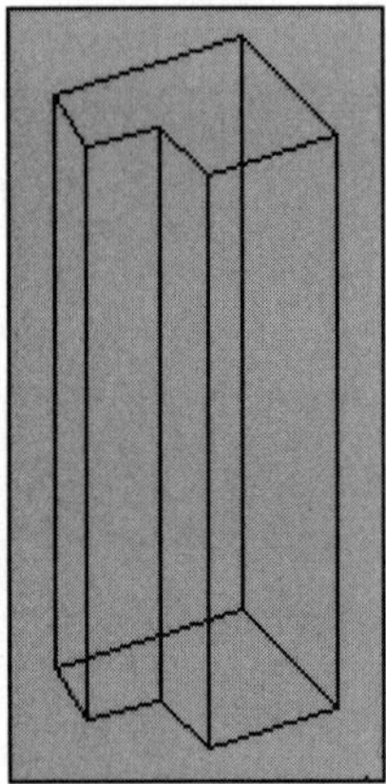

Figure 15.14 *3D solid created from two-dimensional polygon, using extrusion*

To try this macro, enter the code from Listing 15.12 into the Code window for ThisDrawing, along with the code from the other three Chapter 7 macros. You'll also need to copy the following declarations from Listing 7.3 into the General Declarations section of the new project, since these variables are used by all three Chapter 7 macros:

```
Dim PolyArray() As Double
Dim PolygonObject(0) As AcadPolyline
Dim NumberOfElements As Integer
```

LISTING 15.12: DRAWEXTRUDEDSOLID MACRO

```
1    Sub DrawExtrudedSolid()
2        Dim SolidObject As Acad3DSolid
3        Dim RegionObject As Variant
4        Dim Height As Double
5        Dim TaperAngle As Double
6        GetShape
7        CloseShape
8        RegionObject = ↵
            ThisDrawing.ModelSpace.AddRegion(PolygonObject)
9        Height = 3
10       TaperAngle = 0
11       Set SolidObject = ↵
            ThisDrawing.ModelSpace.AddExtrudedSolid ↵
            (RegionObject(0), Height, TaperAngle)
12       ChangeViewDirection
13       ZoomAll
14   End Sub
```

ANALYSIS

- Line 1 starts the `DrawExtrudedSolid` macro. This macro calls the `GetShape` and `CloseShape` macros to prompt the user to enter the points defining a polygon, then closes the polygon and grows the points entered into a three-dimensional polyhedron.
- Line 2 declares the `SolidObject` variable as being capable of referencing a 3DSolid object.
- Line 3 declares the `RegionObject` variable as a Variant type, so that it can be assigned the array returned by the `AddRegion` method.
- Lines 4 and 5 declare the `Height` and `TaperAngle` variables that are assigned the length and taper angle for the extrusion.
- Lines 6 and 7 call the `GetShape` and `CloseShape` macros given in Listing 7.3 from Chapter 7.
- Line 8 calls the `AddRegion` method with the `PolygonObject` passed as the argument. This method creates an array containing a separate `Region` object for every closed loop in the `PolygonObject` array. This array of loops is assigned to the `RegionObject` variable.

- Line 9 assigns a value to the `Height` variable that determines the distance of the extrusion along the z-axis. The direction for the extrusion depends on whether this variable is positive or negative. A positive height grows the shape along the positive z-axis, and a negative value grows the shape along the negative z-axis.
- Line 10 assigns a value of zero to the `TaperAngle` variable. A zero value means no tapering is done. The taper angle can be in the range –90 to +90 and is specified in radians. A positive angle tapers the solid inward starting from the base, and a negative angle tapers the solid outward.
- Line 11 calls the `AddExtrudedSolid` method to create an extruded solid based on planar regions, to a given height and with a specified taper angle.
- Line 12 calls the `ChangeViewDirection` macro given in Listing 15.2.
- Line 13 calls the `ZoomAll` method to ensure that the whole drawing is displayed.
- Line 14 ends the `DrawExtrudedSolid` macro.

Tapering Extruded Solids

Tapering can be included as you extrude a solid. It's done using the same Extrude command described earlier in "Creating Solids by Extrusion." To taper as you extrude, follow the same five steps, but at step 5 type **30** when prompted for the angle of taper for extrusion. Your rectangle will appear similar to the one shown here:

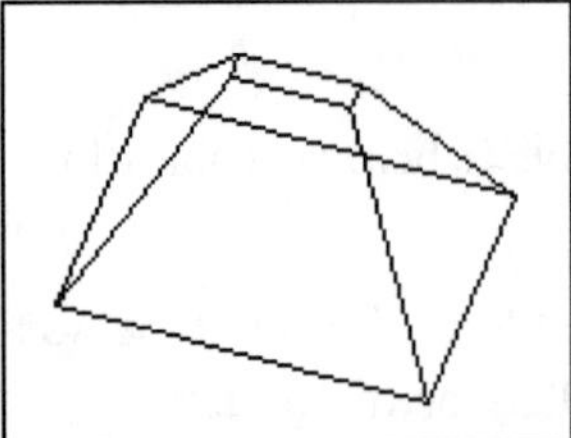

To taper an extruded solid from a macro, all you need do is assign a value to the TaperAngle property passed as the third argument to the AddExtrudedSolid method. The TaperAngle value must be in radians in the range –pi / 2 to +pi / 2. When the TaperAngle is negative, the solid tapers outward from the base; when positive, it tapers inward. You may want to try out negative and positive values to see the results. If you would like to experiment, change Line 10 of the DrawExtrudedSolid macro (Listing 15.12) to (for example) the following:

```
TaperAngle = 10 * Pi / 180
```

Creating Solids by Revolution

Revolved solids are created by rotating a planar outline about an arbitrary axis, collecting the points passed through by the outline at regular intervals. A 3DSolid object represents the new solid.

Listing 15.13 gives the DrawRevolvedSolid macro that prompts the user to enter the points defining a closed outline, and calls the AddRevolvedSolid method with the following four arguments to perform the rotation:

Profile The outline of the shape to be rotated represented by a Region object.

AxisPoint A three-element array of Doubles containing the starting point for the axis of rotation.

AxisDir A three-element array of Doubles containing the direction vector for the axis of rotation.

Angle The angle in radians that the outline is to be rotated, set to 6.28 for a full circle.

Figure 15.15 shows three points being selected for the outline. Figure 15.16 shows the result of calling the AddRevolvedSolid method with the axis starting point at the origin and the direction vector set at (1.0, 1.0, 0.0).

To run the DrawRevolvedSolid macro, you can add it to the same ThisDrawing document as DrawExtrudedSolid and make use of the declarations in the General Declarations section. You will need to add this line:

```
Const Pi = 3.14
```

which is used to convert the degrees of the Angle argument to radians.

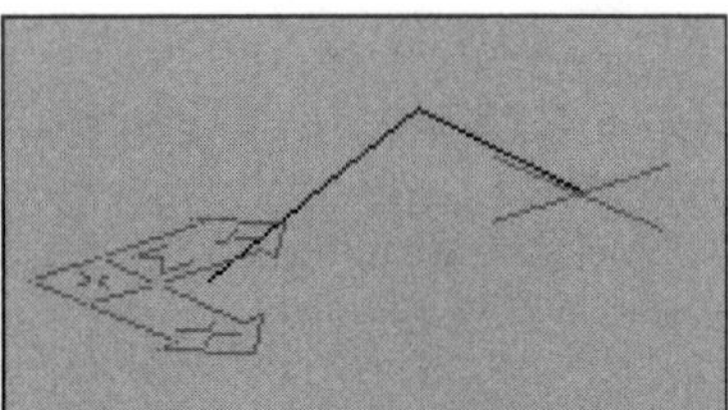

Figure 15.15 *Three points selected to define the outline*

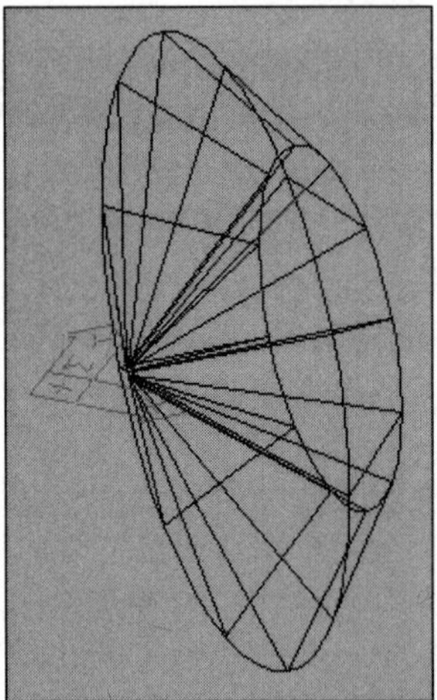

Figure 15.16 *The outline from Figure 15.15 has been revolved 360° about the diagonal from the x-y plane.*

Listing 15.13: DrawRevolvedSolid Macro

```
Public Sub DrawRevolvedSolid()
    Dim SolidObject As Acad3DSolid
    Dim RegionObject As Variant
    Dim AxisPoint(0 To 2) As Double
    Dim AxisDirection(0 To 2) As Double
    Dim Angle As Double
    GetShape
    CloseShape
    RegionObject = ↵
       ThisDrawing.ModelSpace.AddRegion(PolygonObject)
    AxisPoint(0) = 0#: AxisPoint(1) = 0#: AxisPoint(2) = 0#
    AxisDirection(0) = 1#: AxisDirection(1) = 1#: ↵
       AxisDirection(2) = 0#
    Angle = 360# * Pi / 180
    ThisDrawing.Preferences. ContourLinesPerSurface = 12
    Set SolidObject = ↵
       ThisDrawing.ModelSpace.AddRevolvedSolid ↵
       (RegionObject(0), AxisPoint, AxisDirection, Angle)
```

```
15      ChangeViewDirection
16      ZoomAll
17  End Sub
```

ANALYSIS

- Line 1 starts the `DrawRevolvedSolid` macro. This macro calls the `GetShape` and `CloseShape` macros from Listing 7.3 in Chapter 7, to get a closed shape to revolve in steps of 45° around the diagonal line in the x-y plane.
- Line 2 declares the `SolidObject` variable as being capable of referencing a 3DSolid object.
- Line 3 declares the `RegionObject` as a Variant type that allows it to be assigned all the elements from the array returned by the `AddRegion` method in a single statement.
- Lines 4 and 5 declare the `AxisPoint` and `AxisDirection` arrays that define the arbitrary axis that will be used in the rotation.
- Line 6 declares the angle for the amount the outline is to be rotated.
- Lines 7 and 8 call the `GetShape` and `CloseShape` macros that interact with the user to produce a closed shape for the outline.
- Line 9 calls the `AddRegion` method to create an array of Region objects, one for each closed loop in the `PolygonObject` array that's passed to it as an argument. The `RegionObject` is assigned the array containing `RegionObjects` returned by this method.
- Line 10 assigns the coordinates of the WCS origin to the `AxisPoint` array.
- Line 11 assigns the diagonal from the x-y plane to the `AxisDirection` array.
- Line 12 assigns 360° converted to radians as the angle to be rotated.
- Line 13 assigns the `ContourLinesPerSurface` property to 12 so that each point is rotated in steps of 30°. The default is 4, which makes the rotated shape resemble a box.
- Line 14 calls the `AddRevolvedSolid` method with the `RegionObject` variable containing all the Region objects, to rotate the outline around the axis of rotation.
- Line 15 calls the `ChangeViewDirection` so that the rotated shape can be viewed from a better vantage point.

- Line 15 calls the `ZoomAll` method so that the whole shape will appear in the Model Space.
- Line 17 ends the `DrawRevolvedSolid` macro.

Chamfered and Filleted Edges

AutoCAD's Chamfer and Fillet commands under the Modify menu allow you to specify how edges are connected and corners are drawn. The Chamfer command joins two nonparallel lines up to a beveled edge that can be specified by providing two distances (see Figure 15.17). The Fillet command joins up two nonparallel lines with an arc of a specified radius. When the radius is set to zero, the Fillet command will extend or trim the two lines, ensuring that they connect exactly.

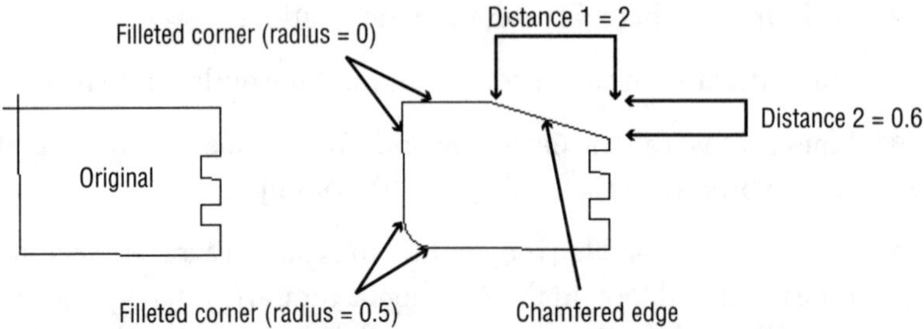

Figure 15.17 *Result of filleting and chamfering a rough shape*

Chamfering and Filleting Edges from a Macro

Although there are no methods named Chamfer and Fillet that you can directly associate with the AutoCAD Chamfer and Fillet commands, you can easily simulate what these commands do from code.

Let's start with chamfering. Listing 15.14 shows how easy it is to chamfer two lines based on two distances—especially when the lines are parallel to the x- and y-axes. Type this code into ThisDrawing's Code window if you would like to try it out. Figure 15.18 shows the result of running the macro, with the original lines given on the left and the chamfered lines on the right.

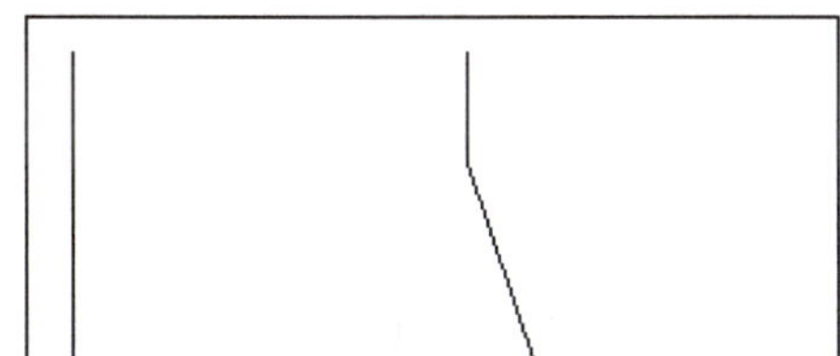

Figure 15.18 Results produced by SimulateChamfer macro

LISTING 15.14: CHAMFERING FROM A MACRO

```
1   Const Distance1 = 2
2   Const Distance2 = 0.75
3
4   Public Sub SimulateChamfer()
5       Dim Line1Start(0 To 2) As Double, ↵
           Line1End(0 To 2) As Double
6       Dim Line2Start(0 To 2) As Double, ↵
           Line2End(0 To 2) As Double
7       Line1Start(0) = 1: Line1Start(1) = 1: Line1Start(2) = 0
8       Line2Start(0) = 0.9: Line2Start(1) = 1.1: ↵
           Line2Start(2) = 0
9       Line1End(0) = 1: Line1End(1) = 4: Line1End(2) = 0
10      Line2End(0) = 4: Line2End(1) = 1.1: Line2End(2) = 0
11      'perform chamfer
12      Line1Start(1) = Line1Start(1) + Distance1
13      Line2Start(0) = Line2Start(0) + Distance2
14      ThisDrawing.ModelSpace.AddLine Line1Start, Line1End
15      ThisDrawing.ModelSpace.AddLine Line2Start, Line2End
16      ThisDrawing.ModelSpace.AddLine Line1Start, Line2Start
17      ThisDrawing.Regen acActiveViewport
18      ZoomAll
19  End Sub
```

ANALYSIS

- Lines 1 and 2 declare the two distances required for the chamfer.
- Line 4 starts the `SimulateChamfer` macro.

- Lines 5 and 6 declare the arrays to contain the start and endpoints of the two lines being chamfered.
- Lines 7 through 10 assign the coordinates defining the two lines to the arrays.
- Line 12 adds `Distance1` to the y-coordinate of the start of `Line1`.
- Line 13 adds `Distance2` to the x-coordinate of the start of `Line2`.
- Lines 14 and 15 add the two lines to the objects in the Model Space.
- Line 16 adds the extra line drawn between the two lines' starting positions, the chamfer.
- Lines 17 through 19 regenerate the active viewport and call the `ZoomAll` method to ensure that the chamfered lines are displayed in Model Space.

Now for filleting: Listing 15.15 shows how the Fillet command's rounded corners can be simulated using simple geometry. Enter it in ThisDrawing's Code window to try it out. Figure 15.19 shows the bathtub drawn as a result of running this code with the constants set at the values listed. You can control the smoothness of the curve by increasing the number of points for the curve to be greater than 3.

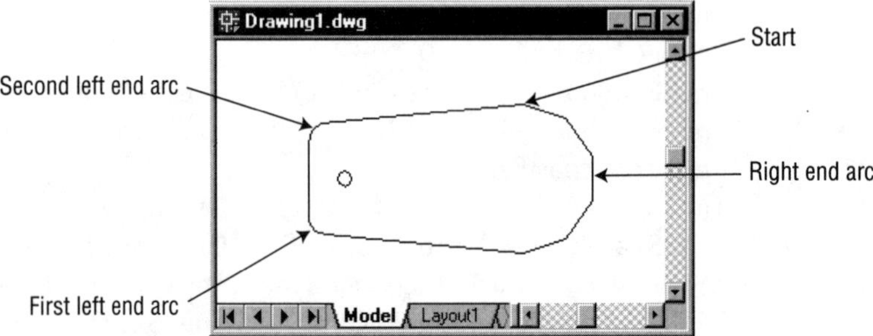

Figure 15.19 *Simulating the Fillet command for drawing corners as arcs*

Listing 15.15: Simulating Fillets in Drawing a Bath

```
Option Explicit
Const BathWidth = 3#
Const BathLength = 5.5
Const NumberOfPointsPer90DegreeTurn = 3
Const pi = 3.141593
```

```

Public Sub DrawBath()
    Dim PolylineObject As AcadPolyline
    Dim CircleObject As AcadCircle
    Dim LineObject As AcadLine
    Dim Points(0 To (↵
       4 * 3 * NumberOfPointsPer90DegreeTurn + 2)) As Double
    Dim AngleInRadians As Double
    Dim CurrentAngle As Double, CurrentIndex As Integer
    Dim Center(0 To 2) As Double
    Dim Count As Integer
    CurrentIndex = 0
    'right end arc (180 degree turn)
    AngleInRadians = pi / ↵
       (NumberOfPointsPer90DegreeTurn * 2 - 1)
    CurrentAngle = pi / 2
    For Count = 1 To NumberOfPointsPer90DegreeTurn * 2
        Points(CurrentIndex) = BathLength / 2# ↵
           + (BathWidth / 2#) * Cos(CurrentAngle)
        Points(CurrentIndex + 1) = (BathWidth / 2#) ↵
           * Sin(CurrentAngle)
        Points(CurrentIndex + 2) = 0#
        CurrentAngle = CurrentAngle - AngleInRadians
        CurrentIndex = CurrentIndex + 3
    Next
    'left end arc
    CurrentAngle = 3 * pi / 2
    For Count = 1 To NumberOfPointsPer90DegreeTurn
        Points(CurrentIndex) = (BathWidth / 8#) ↵
           * Cos(CurrentAngle) - BathLength / 4#
        Points(CurrentIndex + 1) = (BathWidth / 8#) ↵
           * Sin(CurrentAngle) - BathWidth / 4#
        Points(CurrentIndex + 2) = 0#
        CurrentAngle = CurrentAngle - AngleInRadians
        CurrentIndex = CurrentIndex + 3
    Next
    CurrentAngle = pi
     For Count = 1 To NumberOfPointsPer90DegreeTurn
        Points(CurrentIndex) = (BathWidth / 8#) ↵
           * Cos(CurrentAngle) - BathLength / 4#
```

```
39          Points(CurrentIndex + 1) = (BathWidth / 8#) ↵
               * Sin(CurrentAngle) + BathWidth / 4#
40          Points(CurrentIndex + 2) = 0#
41          CurrentAngle = CurrentAngle - AngleInRadians
42          CurrentIndex = CurrentIndex + 3
43      Next
44      Points(CurrentIndex) = Points(0)
45      Points(CurrentIndex + 1) = Points(1)
46      Points(CurrentIndex + 2) = Points(2)
47      Set PolylineObject = ↵
           ThisDrawing.ModelSpace.AddPolyline(Points)
48      PolylineObject.Update
49      Center(0) = Points(↵
           3 * 2 * NumberOfPointsPer90DegreeTurn + 1) + 0.15
50      Center(1) = Points((↵
           3 * 2 * NumberOfPointsPer90DegreeTurn + 1) + Points(↵
           4 * 3 * NumberOfPointsPer90DegreeTurn - 2)) / 2#
51      Center(2) = 0#
52      Set CircleObject = ↵
           ThisDrawing.ModelSpace.AddCircle(Center, 0.15)
53      CircleObject.Update
54      ZoomAll
55  End Sub
```

ANALYSIS

- Lines 1 through 5 declare the constants that you can use to control the bath's appearance. Having all these in the General Declarations section of the Code window makes it easier to update their values—they are easy to find, and you only need to update one value even though they're used in several places through the code.
- Line 7 starts the `DrawBath` macro, which creates the drawing according to the values of the constants.
- Lines 8 through 10 declare the variables that will be set to the various objects used throughout the macro.
- Line 11 declares the `Points` array. The number of points required depends on the number of points to be used for the turn (fillet).
- Line 12 declares the `AngleInRadians` variable as Double. This will be used to increment the `CurrentAngle` variable as the arcs are generated.

- Line 13 declares the `CurrentAngle` as Double. This will be assigned the radians that define the location of the next point on the arc. The `CurrentIndex` variable is also declared to keep tabs on where to put the coordinates of the current point in the `Points` array.
- Line 14 declares the array holding the center point for the fillets.
- Line 15 declares the `Count` variable that keeps tabs on the number of repeats of the `For` loop.
- Line 16 initializes the `CurrentIndex` variable to the first position in the array.
- Line 18 assigns the angle in radians between adjacent pairs of points on the arc.
- Line 19 sets the `CurrentAngle` to 90° converted to radians. This calculates the first point at the top of the right end arc.
- Line 20 starts the `For` loop that calculates all the points in the right end arc. In this loop, the `NumberOfPointsPer90DegreeTurn` is multiplied by two because the arc is 180°.
- Lines 21 through 23 calculate the three coordinates of a point on the arc. Notice how the x-coordinate takes the bath length into account, and the z-coordinate is set to zero.
- Line 24 deducts the increment from the angle as the right end arc makes its way downward.
- Line 25 adds 3 onto the `CurrentIndex` that contains the next free position in the `Points` array, and three coordinates are added at every pass through the loop.
- Line 26 ends the `For` loop.
- Lines 28 through 35 and 36 through 43 contain similar statements for the two left end arcs, as Lines 19 through 26 have for the right end arc.
- Lines 44 through 46 assign the coordinates of the first point in the array to the last point in the array, to ensure that the shape is closed.
- Line 47 creates a Polyline object that makes a polyline based on the `Points` array.
- Line 48 calls the `Update` method to ensure that the polyline appears in the Model Space.
- Lines 49 through 53 define the center of the drainage hole for the bath, create a circle to represent it, and ensure that it is drawn immediately.

- Line 54 calls the `ZoomAll` method to ensure that the bath fits snugly in the Model Space.
- Line 55 ends the `DrawBath` macro.

Cross-Sectioning 3D Solids

AutoCAD provides two commands for cross-sectioning a 3D solid: Slice and Section, both available from the Draw ➜ Solids submenu. The Slice command slices a 3DSolid in half and allows you to specify the part to keep. The Section command allows you to take a cross section of a 3DSolid and save it as a region or anonymous block.

These two commands have equivalent methods in VBA—the SliceSolid and SectionSolid methods. The commands and methods require three points—the origin of the cutting plane, a point to define the positive x-axis, and a point to define the positive y-axis. Here's a quick walk-through of splitting a 3DSolid using the Slice command:

1. Draw a solid object in the Model Space and choose Draw ➜ Solids ➜ Slice.
2. When the command line prompts you, select the solid and press Enter twice.
3. When prompted, enter the three points: the cutting plane's origin, a point defining the positive x-axis, and a point defining the positive y-axis.
4. Select a point on the part of the solid you want to keep. That part will appear if your Slice operation is successful (Figure 15.20).

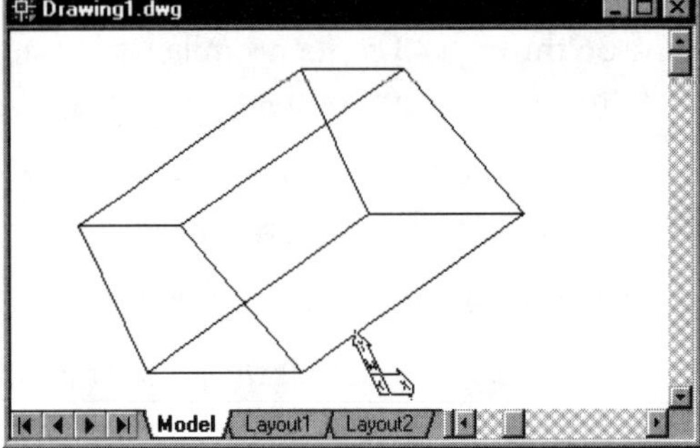

Figure 15.20 *Remaining part of a box solid that has been sliced*

The process is similar for creating a cross section of a solid using the Section command. With a solid drawn in the Model space, choose Draw ➜ Solids ➜ Section. Select the solid when prompted, and press Enter twice. Enter the position for the origin, and the x- and y-axes for the cutting plane. See Figure 15.21 for an example.

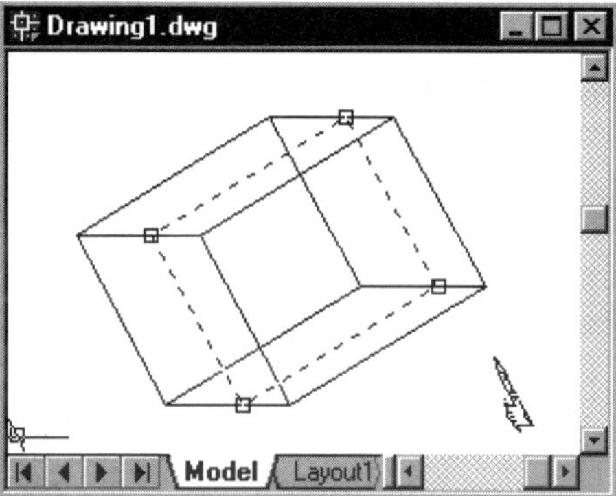

Figure 15.21 *Cross section highlighted to show that it is separate from the box itself*

Now let's take a look at how you can execute these cross-section operations from a macro. AutoCAD VBA's two methods for cross-sectioning solid objects are the SliceSolid method, which returns a 3DSolid object, and the SectionSolid method, which returns a region.

The SliceSolid and SectionSolid Methods

The SliceSolid method allows a 3DSolid object to be split into two pieces by a plane defined by three points. The SliceSolid method returns a new 3DSolid that represents the front or back part. This method has four parameters: three are the points that are needed to define the cutting plane's position and orientation, and the fourth parameter is a Boolean variable that determines whether the solid on the negative side of the plane is kept (True) or if the solid on the positive side is kept (False).

The SectionSolid method allows a cross section to be taken from a 3DSolid object using an arbitrary plane defined by three points as the cutting line. This method has the three points as parameters. It returns a new Region object. Listing 15.16 shows both methods in action. You'll need to draw at least one solid before calling this macro.

LISTING 15.16: SLICEORSECTION MACRO

```
Public Sub SliceOrSection()
    'give user choice of slicing or sectioning
    Dim SolidObject As Acad3DSolid
    Dim SolidNewObject As Acad3DSolid
    Dim RegionObject As AcadRegion
    Dim PlaneOrigin As Variant
    Dim PlaneXAxisPoint As Variant
    Dim PlaneYAxisPoint As Variant
    Dim Pickedpoint As Variant
    Dim Answer As Integer
    On Error Resume Next
    With ThisDrawing.Utility
    .GetEntity SolidObject, Pickedpoint, vbCr & ↵
       "Select solid to cut."
    If Err Then
        MsgBox "Selected solid must be a 3DSolid"
        Exit Sub
    End If
    PlaneOrigin = .GetPoint(Pickedpoint, vbCr & ↵
       "Select point to define origin.")
    PlaneXAxisPoint = .GetPoint(Pickedpoint, vbCr & ↵
       "Select point to define x-axis.")
    PlaneYAxisPoint = .GetPoint(Pickedpoint, vbCr & ↵
       "Select point to define y-axis.")
    Answer = MsgBox("Do you want to splice solid? ↵
       If Yes then solid will be sliced in two. ↵
       If No then cross section will be created.", ↵
       vbYesNo, "Cross-sectioning")
    If Answer = vbYes Then
        Set SolidNewObject = Solid1Object.SliceSolid ↵
           (PlaneOrigin, PlaneXAxisPoint, ↵
            PlaneYAxisPoint, True)
    Else
      Set NewregionObject = SolidObject.SectionSolid ↵
         (PlaneOrigin, PlaneXAxisPoint, PlaneYAxisPoint)
    End If
    End With
End Sub
```

ANALYSIS

- Line 1 starts the `SliceOrSection` macro, which prompts the user to choose between slicing an object or getting a cross-sectioned object.
- Lines 3 through 5 declare the variables that will be set up as references to objects.
- Lines 6 through 8 declare the variables that will store the three points defining a plane entered by the user.
- Line 9 declares the `PickedPoint` variable that is used to refer to the 3DSolid object being sliced or cross-sectioned.
- Line 10 declares the `Answer` variable that is assigned the value returned by the `MsgBox` function.
- Line 11 contains the `On Error` statement so that the macro won't suddenly stop because there are no solid objects in Model Space.
- Line 12 starts the `With` statement block that enables properties and methods from the Utility object to be used without being fully qualified.
- Line 13 calls the `GetEntity` method of the Utility object; this method prompts the user to select the solid to be sliced or cross-sectioned.
- Lines 14 through 17 provide for the fact that the object selected may not be a 3DSolid object, in which case splitting the object must be avoided because both methods can only process a 3DSolid object.
- Lines 18 through 20 prompt the user to enter the three points defining a plane.
- Line 21 asks the user in a message box if they are splicing their solid. If they click No, then cross-sectioning their solid is assumed.
- Line 22 checks to see if the Yes button in the message box was clicked.
- Line 23, which only runs if the Yes button was clicked, calls the `SliceSolid` method.
- Line 24 contains the `Else` statement.
- Line 25 runs if the No button from the message box is clicked. It calls the `SectionSolid` method and assigns the region calculated to the `NewRegionObject` variable.
- Lines 26 through 28 end the `If` statement, the `With` statement, and the `SliceOrSection` macro.

Summary

After working through this chapter, you'll know how to

- Change the angle of view.
- Create a range of primitive solids.
- Combine primitive solids using the CSG Union, Subtraction, and Intersection operators.
- Create solids using extrusion.
- Create solids using revolution.
- Fillet and chamfer edges.
- Taper solids.
- Slice a solid in half.
- Create a cross section of a solid.

ActiveX Controls

AUTOCAD VBA

Chapter 16

In this chapter you'll learn how to build ActiveX controls that exchange data between AutoCAD and the Microsoft applications Excel, Word, and Access.

This chapter covers the following topics:

- ActiveX controls
- Exchange between AutoCAD and Excel
- Exchange between AutoCAD and Word
- ActiveX Database Objects (ADO)
- Exchange between AutoCAD and Access

ActiveX and COM

ActiveX is Microsoft's name for a group of object-oriented programming technologies, principal of which is the *Component Object Model (COM).* COM allows software components to be added or removed across Microsoft platforms without the original applications' having to be recompiled. One software application can talk to another application even if they are written in different languages and run on different platforms. COM technologies were developed by Microsoft in the mid-1990s, primarily to enable interactive content for the World Wide Web. *ActiveX controls* are reusable software components that include the COM technology, allowing the exchange of data between applications.

Using AutoCAD with Other Applications

AutoCAD applications often need to exchange data with other Windows applications. This chapter shows you how to send data from AutoCAD to Microsoft Excel, to Word, and to Access—and vice versa. You've learned in earlier chapters many specific applications for code developed using AutoCAD VBA. So you'll find it easy to transfer your skills and expand your knowledge to include the VBA provided with Microsoft Office applications, and techniques for accessing objects exposed from the object models of these applications.

There are several techniques you can adopt to get items from application A to application B, including simply dragging them from one application to another (cut and paste). The next section shows how easily this is achieved.

To exchange data you can use macros, and once you've set up a reference to the object library of another application, you can work in one application and have data being updated in another. Data exchange can also take place between Access Forms and AutoCAD—you'll see a lot of similarities between these Forms and AutoCAD UserForms. In fact, all applications with VBA capability have Forms or UserForms for building GUIs, and they will all feel very familiar to you.

Dragging Objects into AutoCAD

You can drag-and-drop selected objects from other applications into AutoCAD, provided the other application supports Microsoft ActiveX. The following steps demonstrate dragging and dropping text from a Microsoft Word document into the AutoCAD window.

1. Adjust the positions of the AutoCAD and Word windows so that both are visible.
2. Select some text from the Word document that you want to incorporate into AutoCAD, and drag and drop it into position in the AutoCAD window. The OLE Properties dialog box appears (Figure 16.1) appears.

To copy selected items from another application, hold down Ctrl as you drag them into AutoCAD.

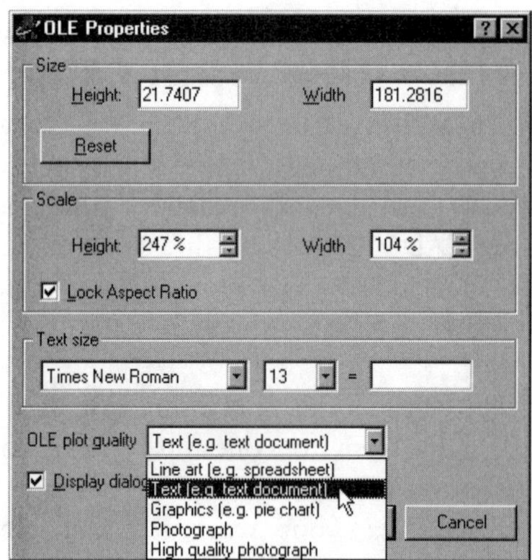

***Figure 16.1** OLE Properties dialog box showing the list of plot qualities available*

3. In the OLE Plot Quality combo box, select "Text (e.g. a text document)" from the drop-down list.
4. Click OK. The selected items are cut from the Word document and pasted into the AutoCAD drawing. Figure 16.2 shows a sphere drawn by the macro that has been copied into the Model Space from a Word document.

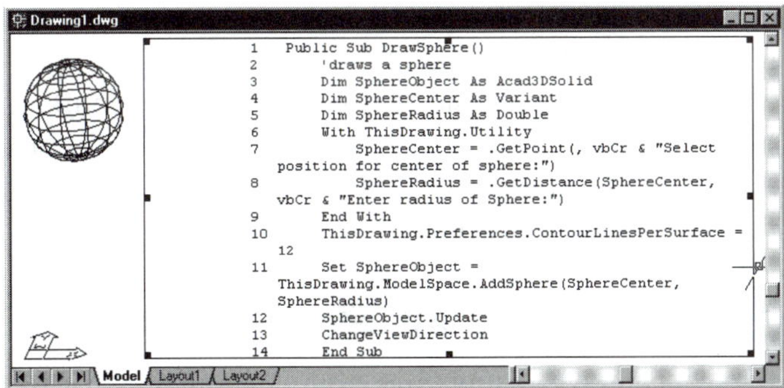

Figure 16.2 *The DrawSphere macro, copied from Word into the Model Space, and a sphere drawn by the macro*

Using ActiveX Controls in Macros

Using the COM technology, you'll find that it's an extremely simple programming task to arrange the exchange of data between AutoCAD and another application.

The VBA CreateObject function creates a new object from another Windows application—you can look into the other application's documentation for further details about the objects, functions, properties, and methods available. (Appendix A provides the object models for Microsoft Excel, Access, and Word.) They're all included in the application's object model, which you can view from the VB Editor's Object Browser.

The VBA GetObject function allows access to existing objects from another Windows application.

The following sections show you how to exchange data from within your VBA code, back and forth between AutoCAD and the Excel, Word, and Access applications. In the exercises of this chapter, you'll exchange some simple data: the coordinates defining a line. It is easy, however, to extend these principles to any data that you can access from AutoCAD—such as all the objects from a drawing, or in a layer, or in a group.

Exchange between AutoCAD and Excel

AutoCAD can send data to Excel, and Excel can send data to AutoCAD. Exercise 16.1 takes you through the steps required to build your ActiveX controls to achieve this.

Listing 16.1 is written in AutoCAD VBA code and uses variables defined as object types available from the Excel object model.

Listing 16.2 is written in Excel VBA. It should look familiar to you, since some things do not change at all between applications. For example, take a look at the call to the MsgBox function and the CreateObject function. Listing 16.1 uses the CreateObject function to return the object representing the open Excel application; and Listing 16.2 uses the CreateObject function to return the object representing the AutoCAD application. Both listings use the objects, properties, and methods associated with the application object returned by CreateObject.

Saving Line Data to an Excel Spreadsheet

To send data from your AutoCAD application to Excel, you call the CreateObject function from a macro run in the AutoCAD window, and that will open Excel. To make the object representing the Excel application accessible from AutoCAD, you must set up a reference to Excel. You'll do this in the first step of Exercise 16.1.

Exercise 16.1: Saving a Line to Excel

1. From the AutoCAD VB Editor, choose Tools → References. The References dialog box appears, containing a list of available references. Select the object library for the version of Microsoft Excel you are using, and click OK. The objects from the Excel Object Library are now accessible from your AutoCAD application.
2. Enter the AutoCADLineToExcel macro (Listing 16.1) into the Code window for ThisDrawing, and run the macro.
3. Open the AutoCAD window and follow the prompts in the command line to enter the two points for the line.
4. Open an Excel workbook. Sheet1 appears, with the row and column headings in bold, and the coordinates of the two points selected in the second and third rows (Figure 16.3).

Book4

	A	B	C	D	E
1	**Line**	**X**	**Y**	**Z**	
2	**Start**	12.38955	2.973214	0	
3	**Finish**	1.800651	2.866071	0	

Sheet1 / Sheet2 / Sheet3

Figure 16.3 *Result of running the AutoCADLineToExcel macro (Listing 16.1)*

5. Deselect the Excel object library in the References dialog box, to free up the memory it required.

Object libraries use a lot of memory. Always remember to deselect any object libraries that you no longer require from the References dialog box.

LISTING 16.1: AUTOCADLINETOEXCEL MACRO

```
Sub AutoCADLineToExcel()
    'sending line data to Excel
    Dim ExcelApplication As Excel.Application
    Dim ExcelWorksheet As Worksheet
    Dim Point3D As Variant 'last point input
    Set ExcelApplication = CreateObject("Excel.Application")
    ExcelApplication.Visible = True
    ExcelApplication.Workbooks.Add
    Set ExcelWorksheet = ↵
       ExcelApplication.ActiveWorkbook.Sheets("Sheet1")
    ExcelWorksheet.Cells(1, 1).Value = "Line"
    ExcelWorksheet.Cells(2, 1).Value = "Start"
    ExcelWorksheet.Cells(3, 1).Value = "Finish"
    ExcelWorksheet.Range("A1:A3").Font.Bold = True
    ExcelWorksheet.Cells(1, 2).Value = "X"
    ExcelWorksheet.Cells(1, 3).Value = "Y"
    ExcelWorksheet.Cells(1, 4).Value = "Z"
    ExcelWorksheet.Range("B1:D1").Font.Bold = True
    Point3D = ThisDrawing.Utility.GetPoint↵
       (, "Click on start of line!")
    ExcelWorksheet.Cells(2, 2).Value = Point3D(0)
    ExcelWorksheet.Cells(2, 3).Value = Point3D(1)
    ExcelWorksheet.Cells(2, 4).Value = Point3D(2)
    Point3D = ThisDrawing.Utility.GetPoint↵
     (, "Click on end of line!")
    ExcelWorksheet.Cells(3, 2).Value = Point3D(0)
    ExcelWorksheet.Cells(3, 3).Value = Point3D(1)
    ExcelWorksheet.Cells(3, 4).Value = Point3D(2)
End Sub
```

ANALYSIS

- Line 1 starts the `AutoCADLineToExcel` macro, which creates a new Excel workbook. It enters row and column headings, along with the coordinates of the line specified interactively by the user.
- Lines 3 and 4 declare the `ExcelApplication` and `ExcelWorksheet` variables as being capable of referencing the `Excel.Application` and `Excel.Worksheet` objects.
- Line 5 declares the `Point3D` variable as Variant so that it can be assigned a three-element array in a single statement.
- Line 6 calls the CreateObject method that creates and returns a reference to an object exposed to the Excel application, and sets up `ExcelApplication` as a reference to the object.
- Line 7 makes the Excel application visible.
- Line 8 uses the `Add` method to create a new workbook in the Excel application.
- Line 9 sets `ExcelWorksheet` up as a reference to the object representing `Sheet1` of the new workbook.
- Line 10 assigns the text for the first row heading to the cell at row 1/column 1 of Sheet1. The `Cells` collection is accessed like a two-dimensional array, with the row number appearing first followed by the column number. The `Value` property is assigned the textual or numerical data that is to appear at the cell—in this case, `Line`.
- Lines 11 and 12 assign `Start` and `Finish` to the cells in the first column of the second and third rows.
- Line 13 uses the `Range` property to return an object representing the range of cells specified in the argument `A1:A3`, which represents the first three cells in column A. Then the Bold property of the Font property of this returned object is set to True, so that the row labels appear in bold text.
- Lines 14 through 16 assign headings to columns B, C, and D in the first row.
- Line 17 sets the Bold property of the Font property of the object representing the `B1:D1` range of cells to True, so that the B, C, and D column headings appear in bold text.

- Line 18 calls the `GetPoint` method of the Utility object, to prompt the user to select a point in the Model Space for the start of the line.
- Lines 19 through 21 assign the `Value` properties of the cells in the B, C, and D columns of the second row, to the x-, y-, and z-coordinates of the point selected by the user.
- Lines 22 through 25 perform the same operations as Lines 18 through 21 for the end of the line. The coordinates are placed in the third row of the worksheet.
- Line 26 ends the `AutoCADLineToExcel` macro.

Now that you can send data from your AutoCAD application to Excel, the next step is to send data from your Excel application to AutoCAD.

Drawing an AutoCAD Line from Excel

In the preceding section, the data defining the endpoints for a line were written to an Excel spreadsheet. At some stage in the future, you will need to read that data back into your AutoCAD application so that you can draw the same line. The following steps show you how to create the DrawAutoCADLine macro shown in Listing 16.2, which does just that.

Exercise 16.2: Drawing the Line from Excel to AutoCAD

1. Open Excel, and choose Tools ➜ Macro ➜ Visual Basic Editor. The Visual Basic Editor window appears, with the Excel icon in the first position of the toolbar, rather than the AutoCAD icon—that's the only difference from the AutoCAD Visual Basic Editor window.
2. From the Excel VB Editor, choose Tools ➜ References. The References dialog box appears, containing a list of available references, just as it did using the same menu command in AutoCAD. Select your version of AutoCAD's object model, and click OK. The objects from the AutoCAD Object Library are now accessible from your Excel application.
3. Return to the Excel window and enter the data shown in Figure 16.4 into Sheet1. These coordinates define the line that will be drawn in the AutoCAD window.
4. In the Excel VBE Project Explorer, open the Code window for ThisWorkbook. Enter the DrawAutoCADLine macro (Listing 16.2).

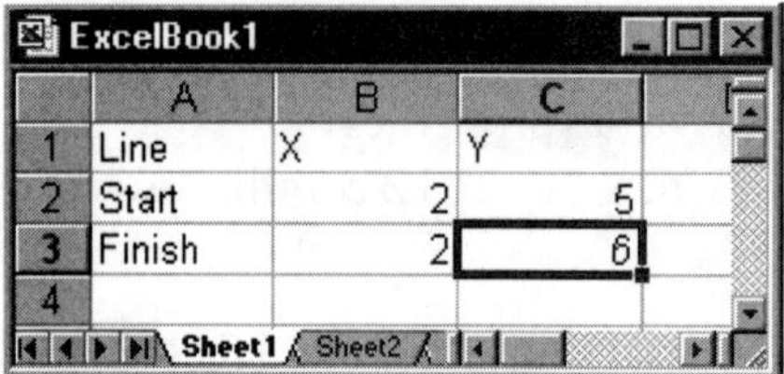

***Figure 16.4** Excel spreadsheet containing the definition of a line*

5. After the macro is in place, choose Run ➜ Run Sub/UserForm to run it. A line is drawn in the AutoCAD window.

6. Remember to deselect the AutoCAD object library again, freeing up the memory it required.

LISTING 16.2: DRAWAUTOCADLINE MACRO

```
1   Public Sub DrawAutoCADLine()
2       'sending line data to AutoCAD
3       Dim AutoCADApplication As AutoCAD.Application
4       Dim StartLine(0 To 2) As Double
5       Dim EndLine(0 To 2) As Double
6       Set AutoCADApplication = CreateObject↵
          ("AutoCAD.Application")
7       StartLine(0) = Cells(2, 2).Value
8       StartLine(1) = Cells(3, 2).Value
9       EndLine(0) = Cells(2, 3).Value
10      EndLine(1) = Cells(3, 3).Value
11      AutoCADApplication.ActiveDocument.ModelSpace.AddLine ↵
          StartLine, EndLine
12  End Sub
```

ANALYSIS

- Line 1 starts the `DrawAutoCADLine` macro, which runs in Excel and draws a line in the AutoCAD window.
- Line 3 declares the `AutoCADApplication` variable as being capable of referring to the AutoCAD Application object.

- Lines 4 and 5 declare the arrays that will hold the two endpoints defining the line.
- Line 6 calls the `CreateObject` method that creates and returns a reference to an object exposed to the AutoCAD application object and sets up the `AutoCADApplication` variable as a reference to the object.
- Lines 7 through 10 assign the coordinate values in the spreadsheet to the `StartLine` and `EndLine` arrays.
- Line 11 creates a new line based on the `StartLine` and `Endline` array values and draws it in the AutoCAD Model tab.
- Line 12 ends the `DrawAutoCADLine` macro.

Exchange between AutoCAD and Word

AutoCAD can send data to Microsoft Word, and Word can send data to AutoCAD. For example, you may want to save your drawing data in a Word document for circulation to people who don't have access to AutoCAD. That drawing data can include images as well as dimensions and any other specifications AutoCAD retains in order to regenerate the drawing.

Word VBA has its own object model containing all the objects, methods, properties, and events needed for creating Word documents. In this section, you'll see how to use the Range method of the Word document to position the insertion point, and then use the InsertAfter method to enter new data into the Word document where it can be saved for future use. When it comes to sending the data back to the AutoCAD application, this exercise shows you how to access items from the Words collection.

Sending Data to Word from an AutoCAD Macro

Listing 16.3 contains the AutoCADDataToWord macro. It prompts the user to enter the endpoints defining a line, and sends the coordinates of the points entered to a Word document. Figure 16.5 shows text placed by the AutoCADDataToWord macro into a Word document window.

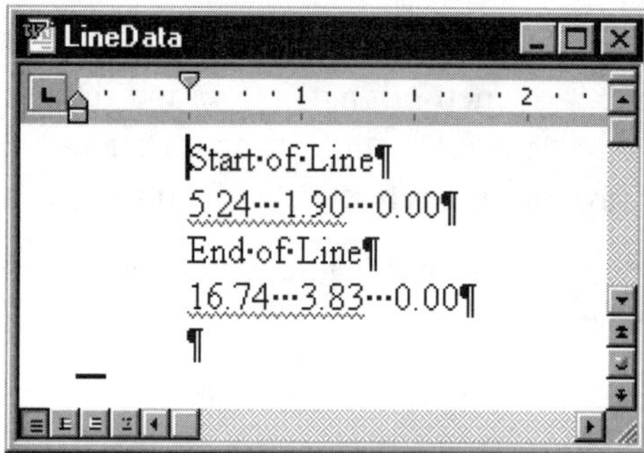

Figure 16.5 Text placed into the Word document window by the AutoCADDataToWord macro (Listing 16.3)

EXERCISE 16.3: SAVING A LINE TO WORD

1. From the AutoCAD VB Editor, choose Tools ➜ References. The References dialog box appears containing a list of available references. Select the object library for the version of Microsoft Word you are using, and click OK. The objects from the Word Object Library are now accessible from your AutoCAD application.
2. Enter the AutoCADDataToWord macro into the Code window for ThisDrawing.
3. Deselect the Word object library item from the References dialog box to free up the memory that it used.

LISTING 16.3: AUTOCADDATATOWORD MACRO

```
Sub AutoCADDataToWord()
    'sending line data to Word
    Dim WordApplication As Word.Application
    Dim WordDocument As Document
    Dim RangeObject As Range
    Dim Point3D As Variant
    Set WordApplication = CreateObject("Word.Application")
    On Error Resume Next
    Set WordDocument = WordApplication.Documents.Open↵
       ("C:\My Documents\LineData.doc")
```

```
10       If Err Then Set WordDocument = ↵
            WordApplication.Documents.Add
11       Set RangeObject = WordDocument.Range(0, 0)
12       RangeObject.Font.Bold = True
13       RangeObject.InsertAfter "Start of Line" + vbCr
14       Point3D = ThisDrawing.Utility.GetPoint↵
            (, "Click on start of line!")
15       RangeObject.InsertAfter Format(Point3D(0), "##0.00") ↵
            + "    "
16       RangeObject.InsertAfter Format(Point3D(1), "##0.00") ↵
            + "    "
17       RangeObject.InsertAfter Format(Point3D(2), "##0.00") ↵
            + vbCr
18       RangeObject.InsertAfter "End of Line" + vbCr
19       Point3D = ThisDrawing.Utility.GetPoint↵
            (, "Click on end of line!")
20       RangeObject.InsertAfter Format(Point3D(0), "##0.00") ↵
            + "    "
21       RangeObject.InsertAfter Format(Point3D(1), "##0.00") ↵
            + "    "
22       RangeObject.InsertAfter Format(Point3D(2), "##0.00") ↵
            + vbCr
23   End Sub
```

Analysis

- Line 1 starts the `AutoCADDataToWord` macro, which prompts the user to select the two endpoints defining a line and sends the coordinates to a Word document.
- Lines 3 through 5 declare the `WordApplication`, `WordDocument`, and `RangeObject` variables. The `WordApplication` variable will refer to the Word Application object, the `WordDocument` variable will refer to the Document object in the Word application, and the `RangeObject` will refer to a Range object that defines a range of characters in the Word document.
- Line 6 declares the `Point3D` variable as Variant so that it can be assigned the three-element array returned by the `GetPoint` method.
- Line 7 calls the `CreateObject` method that creates and returns a reference to an object exposed in the Word application, and sets up Word`Application` as a reference to the Word Application object.

- Line 8 uses the `On Error` statement so that if an error occurs at Line 9, execution will jump to Line 10.
- Line 9 calls the `Open` method of the Documents collection of the Word application, to open the file named in the argument.
- Line 10 tests to see if an error occurred at Line 9. If so, then it could mean that the file being opened does not exist or is already open. This statement overcomes the error by calling the `Add` method of the Documents collection to create a new document.
- Line 11uses the `Range` method to create a Range object that starts at the zero'th character and ends at the zero'th character, as specified by the two arguments. The `RangeObject` is set up as a reference to this Range object.
- Line 12 uses the `RangeObject` variable to set the Bold property of the Font Property of the `Range` object to True.
- Line 13 calls the `InsertAfter` method of the `Range` object, to insert the text string passed to the method as an argument. The plus (+) operator is used to add a carriage return character to the end of the string.
- Line 14 calls the `GetPoint` method to prompt the user to select the position in the AutoCAD window for the start of the line.
- Lines 15 through 17 use the `Format` function to format the coordinates of the selected point as one to three digits before the decimal point, and two digits after. Lines 15 and 16 add a few spaces to separate the three values. Line 17 adds a carriage return to start a new line.
- Lines 18 through 22 perform the same actions as Lines 13 through 17, to enter the details about the end-of-line point into the document.
- Line 23 ends the `AutoCADDataToWord` macro.

Now you can send data from AutoCAD to Word. The next section shows you how to read that data back into AutoCAD.

Drawing an AutoCAD Line from Word

The DrawLineInAutoCAD macro given in Listing 16.4 draws a line in the AutoCAD window, from the Word application.

EXERCISE 16.4: DRAWING THE LINE FROM WORD TO AUTOCAD

1. Continue to run Microsoft Word with the LineData.doc file (Figure 16.5) still the active document. Choose Tools ➜ Macro ➜ Visual Basic Editor. The VB Editor window appears, with the Word icon at the left of the toolbar—that's the only difference from the AutoCAD VB Editor window.
2. From the Word VB Editor choose Tools ➜ References. The References dialog box appears containing a list of available references. Select the object library for the version of Microsoft AutoCAD you are using, and click OK. The objects from the AutoCAD Object Library are now accessible from your Word application.
3. Enter the DrawLineInAutoCAD macro, which is written in Word VBA, into the Code window for ThisDocument in the Word application. You can open this Code window, if it isn't already open, by choosing View ➜ Project Explorer and selecting it from the list.
4. Run the macro, and watch the line specified in the LineData.doc file appear in Model Space.
5. Remember to deselect the AutoCAD object library from the list in the References dialog box to free up the memory it required.

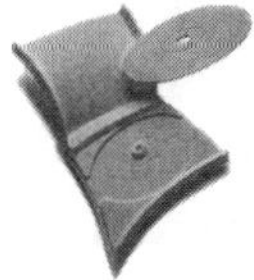

LISTING 16.4: DRAWLINEINAUTOCAD MACRO

```
Public Sub DrawLineInAutoCAD()
    'sending line data to AutoCAD
    Dim AutoCADApplication As AutoCAD.Application
    Dim StartLine(0 To 2) As Double
    Dim EndLine(0 To 2) As Double
    Set AutoCADApplication = ↵
       CreateObject("AutoCAD.Application")
    StartLine(0) = ActiveDocument.Words.Item(0)
    StartLine(1) = ActiveDocument.Words.Item(1)
    EndLine(0) = ActiveDocument.Words.Item(2)
    EndLine(1) = ActiveDocument.Words.Item(3)
    AutoCADApplication.ActiveDocument.ModelSpace.AddLine ↵
       StartLine, EndLine
End Sub
```

ANALYSIS

- Line 1 starts the `DrawLineInAutoCAD` macro, which reads the coordinates defining a line from a Word document, and draws the line in the AutoCAD window.
- Line 3 declares the `AutoCADApplication` variable as being capable of referring to an object.
- Lines 4 and 5 declare the arrays that will be assigned the coordinates of the two endpoints defining the line.
- Line 6 calls the `CreateObject` method that creates and returns a reference to an object exposed in the AutoCAD application, and sets up the `AutoCADApplication` variable as a reference to the object.
- Lines 7 through 10 assign the coordinates stored in the active Word document to the variable arrays.
- Line 11 calls the `AddLine` method to add a line to the Model Space of the active document in the AutoCAD application.
- Line 12 ends the `DrawLineInAutoCAD` macro.

Exchange Between AutoCAD and a Database

One of the primary ways to access a database from AutoCAD is via an ActiveX Data object (ADO). The ADO object model exposes data connection objects, data command objects, and Recordset objects with any other objects, properties, and methods you need in order to access data from databases. Using ADO, most data is exchanged via Recordset objects. Thcsc contain data organized in a table format, with the records of data placed across complete rows and fields of data in the columns.

Before you can access any data in a database from AutoCAD, you have to configure the database first so that the connection can be made. The following steps show you how to configure a database from the AutoCAD window. In this example you'll see how to connect to an Access database, but the same techniques can be used for connecting to other databases.

1. Choose Tools ➜ dbConnect. The dbConnect Manager appears. (If this window is docked, you won't see its title bar; it's the one with a tree view.) Figure 16.6 shows the undocked dbConnect Manager window.

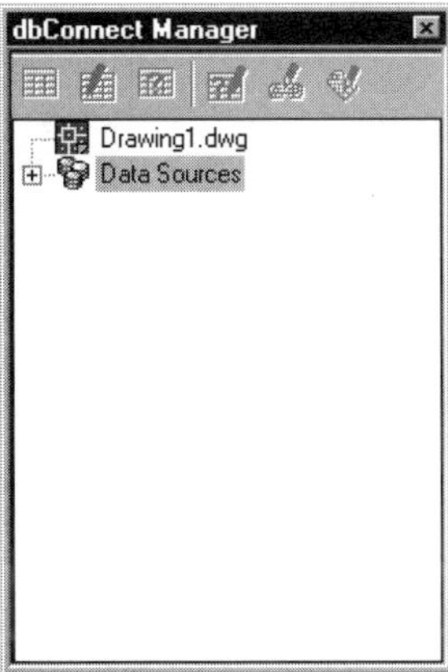

Figure 16.6 *dbConnect Manager containing Drawing1 and Data Sources*

2. Right-click Data Sources from the list in the dbConnect Manager and choose Configure Data Source. The Configure A Data Source dialog box appears (Figure 16.7).

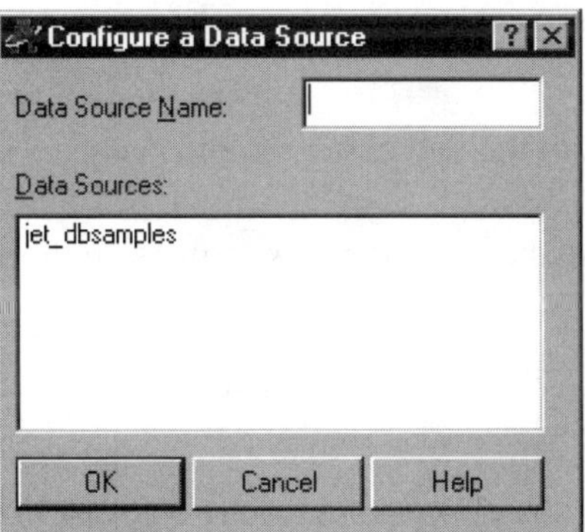

Figure 16.7 *Choosing a data source*

3. From the Data Sources list, choose `jet.dbsamples` and click OK. The Data Link Properties dialog box appears (Figure 16.8).

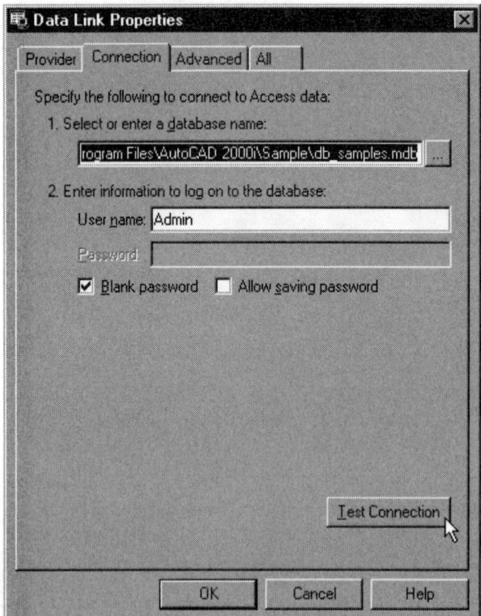

Figure 16.8 *Connecting to the data*

4. Click the Connection tab if it isn't already displayed, and click the ellipsis (...) button at the end of the Database Name text box. The Select Access Database dialog box appears.
5. Choose `db_samples.mdb` from the end of the list and click Open. (If you can't see `db_samples.mdb`, you'll need to navigate to the `Sample` folder in the directory where AutoCAD was installed.) You're now returned to the Connection tab of the Data Link Properties dialog box.
6. Click Test Connection. A message box appears, telling you that the test connection succeeded.
7. Now that you have configured your database, you're ready to view some data. Expand the Data Sources tree view item from the dbConnect Manager window and double-click `jet_dbsamples`.
8. Click on any of the items in the `jet_dbsamples` list to make the buttons along the top of the dbConnect Manager window available for selection. Click on Employee.

9. Click the View Table button (first one on the left). The Data View window opens, displaying employee records (Figure 16.9).

Data View - Employee (Drawing1.dwg) - Read Only

-- New Link Template -- | -- New Label Temp

Emp_Id	Last_Name	First_Name	Gender	
1000	Torbati	Yolanda	F	Programmer
1001	Kleinn	Joel	M	Programmer
1002	Ginsburg	Laura	F	President
1003	Cox	Jennifer	F	Programmer
1005	Ziada	Mauri	M	Product Des
1006	Keyser	Cara	F	Account Exe
1063	Ford	Janice	F	Accountant
1010	Smith	Roxie	M	Programmer
1011	Nelson	Robert	M	Programmer
1012	Sachsen	Lars	M	Support Tec
1013	Shannon	Don	M	Product Des
1016	Miro	Terri	F	Network Adr
1017	Lovett	Greg	M	Programmer
1018	Larson	Steve	M	Programmer

Record 1

Figure 16.9 *Data View window showing the employee data from the jet_dbsamples database*

Now that you are able to view data from a database, let's take a look at how the data got there in the first place. The next section takes data straight out of Excel and creates an Access table.

Saving Line Data in a Database

Let's create a simple application that saves line data to a database. In the example from Exercise 16.5, the database used is Access but the same techniques and code can be applied to any database that has ActiveX capability.

Exercise 16.5: The Line Data Table Application

1. Open Access and choose File → New, select Database from the New dialog box and click OK. The File New Database dialog box appears.
2. Enter **DrawingLines** in the File Name box and click Create.
3. Click the Create Table in Design View option. The Table dialog box appears. Enter the field names **StartX**, **StartY**, **EndX**, **EndY**, and **Color** with their Data Types all numbers, as shown in Figure 16.10.

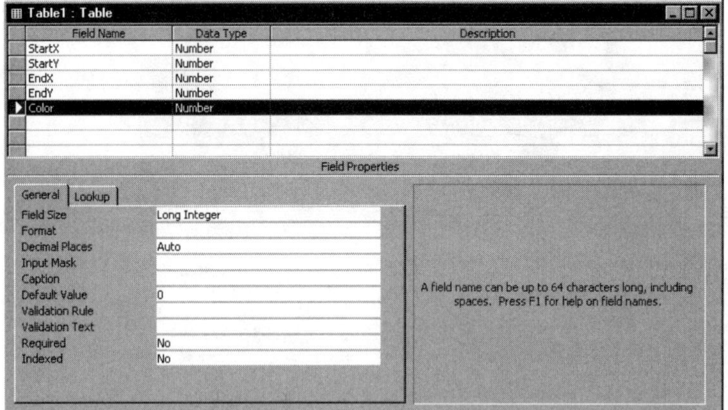

Figure 16.10 *Table dialog box with field names for the Line Data Table application*

4. Choose File ➜ Save As, and save as LineData, accepting Access's offer to create a primary key. This will add `ID` to your list of field names (your database may handle the primary-key matter differently).
5. Choose File ➜ Close to close the database. When you create a table, Access locks it to prevent anyone else from accessing it. Closing the database and reopening it unlocks the database so that AutoCAD can send data to it.
6. Choose File ➜ Open and choose DrawingLines from the list.
7. Run AutoCAD and draw a few lines in the Model Space.
8. In the AutoCAD VB Editor, choose Tools ➜ References and check Microsoft DAO 3.6 Object Library. Click OK.
9. Insert a UserForm with a label and a command button and update their properties to the values shown in Table 16.1. Figure 16.11 shows the UserForm in action.
10. Enter the code shown in Listing 16.5 into the Click event procedure for cmdSave.
11. Run the Line Data Table application and open the table in Access (or your database) to see the results. Figure 16.12 shows my results in Access.

Table 16.1: Properties for the Line Data Table Application

Old Name	New Name	Caption
UserForm1	frmLineDataTable	Line Data Table
CommandButton1	cmdSave	Save to Database
Label1	—	Save line data in database?

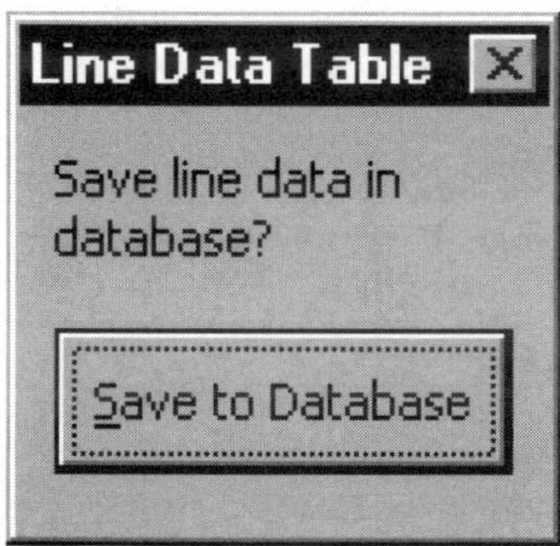

Figure 16.11 *Line Data Table application UserForm*

LineData : Table

ID	StartX	StartY	EndX	EndY	Color
47	4	4	4	4	256
48	4	4	9	5	256
49	9	5	4	4	256
50	4	7	7	1	256
51	2	6	8	4	256
(AutoNumber)	0	0	0	0	0

Record: 1 of 5

Figure 16.12 *The LineData : Table in Access*

Listing 16.5: Coding the Line Data Table Application

```
Private Sub cmdSave_Click()
    Dim DatabaseObject As Database
    Dim LineObject As Recordset
```

```
4       Dim LObject As AutoCAD.AcadLine
5       Dim Count As Integer
6       Set DatabaseObject = OpenDatabase↵
           ("C:\My Documents\DrawingLines.mdb")
7       Set LineObject = DatabaseObject.OpenRecordset↵
           ("LineData")
8       For Count = 0 To ThisDrawing.ModelSpace.Count - 1
9           If ThisDrawing.ModelSpace.Item(Count).ObjectName↵
               = "AcDbLine" Then
10              LineObject.AddNew
11              Set LObject = ThisDrawing.ModelSpace.Item(Count)
12              LineObject!StartX = LObject.StartPoint(0)
13              LineObject!StartY = LObject.StartPoint(1)
14              LineObject!EndX = LObject.EndPoint(0)
15              LineObject!EndY = LObject.EndPoint(1)
16              LineObject!Color = LObject.Color
17              LineObject.Update
18          End If
19      Next
20      LineObject.Close
21      DatabaseObject.Close
22      Set LineObject = Nothing
23      Set DatabaseObject = Nothing
24      MsgBox "Line data save to database!"
25      Unload Me
26  End Sub
```

ANALYSIS

- Line 1 starts the Click event procedure for the Save command button.
- Line 2 declares the `DatabaseObject` variable as being capable of referencing a generic Database object.
- Line 3 declares the `LineObject` variable as being able to reference a Recordset object.
- Line 4 declares the `LObject` variable as a reference to an AutoCAD AcadLine object.

- Line 5 declares the `Count` variable that will be used to count the number of times through the `For` loop.
- Line 6 calls the `OpenDataBase` method from the DAO Object Library to open the database in the file named in the argument. The `DatabaseObject` is set up to reference this open database.
- Line 7 calls the `OpenRecordset` method of the `DatabaseObject` to open the `LineData` table in Access.
- Line 8 starts the `For` loop that accesses all the objects in the ModelSpace collection.
- Line 9 starts the `If` statement that uses the `ObjectName` property to check if the current object represents a line.
- Line 10 calls the `AddNew` method to add a new record to the database table ready for the new data to be assigned.
- Line 11 sets the `LObject` variable to refer to the current ModelSpace item.
- Lines 12 through 16 assign the values from the ModelSpace Line objects to database table elements.
- Line 17 calls the `Update` method of `LineObject` so that the new values are saved to the database.
- Lines 18 and 19 end the `If` statement block and the `For` loop block, respectively.
- Lines 20 and 21 call the `Close` method to close the table and database, respectively.
- Lines 22 and 23 set the `LineObject` and `DatabaseObject` variables to nothing so that they no longer refer to an actual object. This releases the memory and system resources associated with the referenced objects.
- Line 24 calls the `MsgBox` function to let you know that the data has been saved and that the saving to database operation has been completed successfully.
- Line 25 unloads the UserForm and returns you to the AutoCAD window.
- Line 26 ends the `cmdSave_Click` event procedure.

Creating an Access Module from a VBA Macro

As you know, a module is a combination of VBA declarations and procedures that form a separate, individual unit of software. The following steps show you how to create an Access VBA macro that retrieves table entries, and then how to convert your macro into an Access module.

EXERCISE 16.5: THE LINE DATA TABLE APPLICATION (CONTINUED)

1. Continue with the project you created in the preceding section. In the LineData : Database dialog box in the Access window, click Macros from the list of objects on the left. The icon alongside New in the toolbar will change to the Macros icon.

2. Click the New (Macros) icon to open the Macro dialog box. Select the top cell in the Action column and click the down arrow. The drop-down list of actions appears as shown in Figure 16.13.

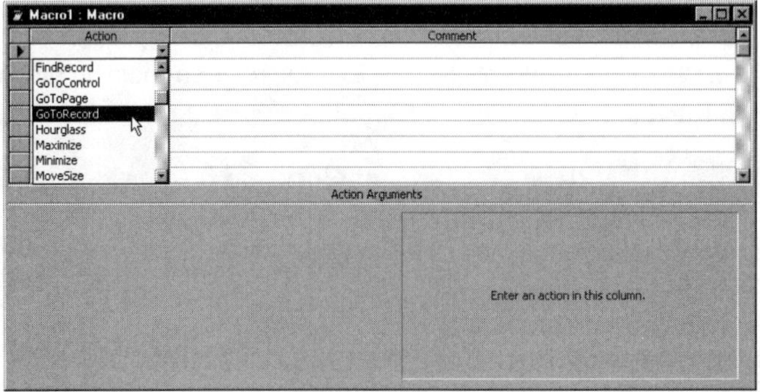

***Figure 16.13** Macro dialog box in Access*

3. Select the GoToRecord entry. The Record field in the Action Arguments section of the Macro dialog box displays `Next`, and gives a description of what the macro does (Figure 16.14).

4. Close the Macro dialog box by clicking its Close button in the upper-right corner. When asked if you want to save the changes to the macro and name it GetNextLine, click Yes.

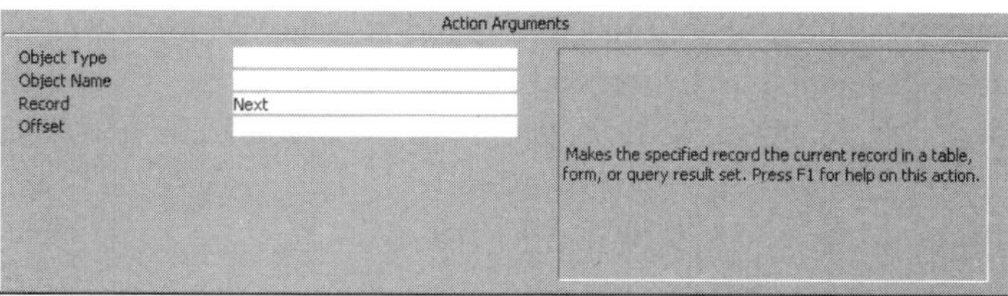

Figure 16.14 *Action Arguments section of the Access Macro dialog box*

5. Open LineData : Table again, select a cell in the top row, and choose Tools ➜ Macro ➜ Run Macro (Access 2000) or choose Tools ➜ Run Macro (Access 97). The Run Macro dialog box appears.
6. Ensure that GetNextLine appears in the Macro Name combo box and click OK. The cursor will now appear in the row below the one you selected.
7. Open the LineData : Database dialog box again and select the GetNextLine macro. Choose File ➜ Save As, select Module from the bottom list, and click OK.

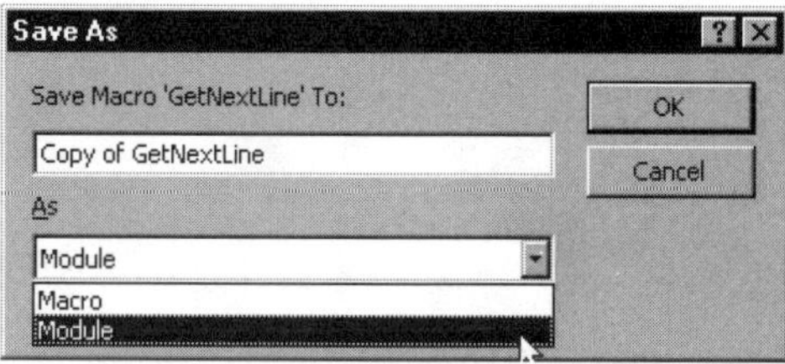

8. In the Convert macro dialog box, leave the check box settings as they are, and click Convert.

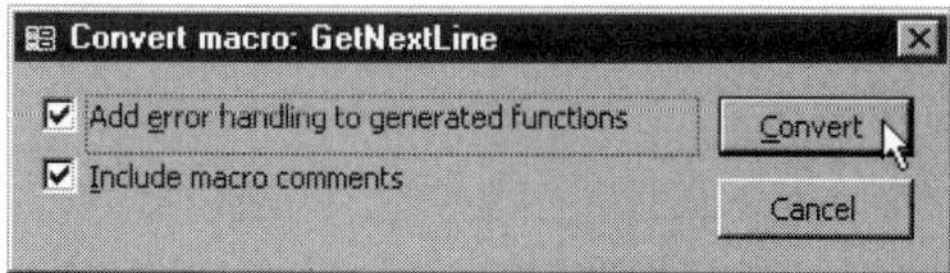

9. A message box informs you that conversion is finished. Click OK to return to the LineData : Database dialog box.

10. Let's take a look at the code created for you in the conversion. In the LineData : Database dialog box in the Access window, select Modules from the Objects list and double-click on Converted Macro - GetNextLine. The Module Code window opens, containing the code shown in Listing 16.6.

LISTING 16.6: GETNEXTLINE FUNCTION

```
1   Option Compare Database
2
3   '------------------------------
4   ' GetNextLine
5   '
6   '------------------------------
7   Function GetNextLine()
8   On Error GoTo GetNextLine_Err
9
10      DoCmd.GoToRecord , "", acNext
11
12
13  GetNextLine_Exit:
14      Exit Function
15
16  GetNextLine_Err:
17      MsgBox Error$
18      Resume GetNextLine_Exit
19
20  End Function
```

ANALYSIS

- Line 1 contains the `Option Compare` statement declaring that the default string comparison method is to be based on the sort order of the database.
- Lines 2 through 6 are comment lines that are ignored by the Visual Basic interpreter.
- Line 7 starts the `GetNextLine` function, which gets the next item from the database.
- Line 8 contains the `On Error` statement, with the `GoTo` being passed a label.

- Line 10 uses the `GoToRecord` method of the `DoCmd` object. The `DoCmd` object allows you to perform any Microsoft Access action from VBA code.
- Line 13 contains the label that the `GoTo` from Line 18 will jump back up to.

You can easily identify labels from variables because of the colon that's appended to them.

- Line 14 uses the `Exit` Function to stop executing the function and jump to the statement after the one where the function was called.
- Line 16 contains the label that the `GoTo` from Line 8 will jump to should an error occur.
- Line 17 calls the `MsgBox` function to provide the user with information about the error that has occurred.
- Line 18 contains the `Resume` statement, which continues execution after the error-handling routine is finished.
- Line 20 ends the `GetNextLine` function.

Displaying Data in Access Forms

Access has Forms, which resemble AutoCAD UserForms. The Access Toolbox contains controls similar to AutoCAD's. Forms can be a quick and easy way of displaying data to a user and providing a means of user interaction with your application. In the next steps, an Access Form is created containing text boxes to allow the user to view the data, a command button for getting the next line, and a Draw Line command button for drawing the line in the AutoCAD window.

Exercise 16.5: The Line Data Table Application (continued)

1. Continue with the same project used in the foregoing procedure. In the Database dialog box, select Forms from the Objects list and click New in the toolbar. The New Form dialog box appears (Figure 16.15).
2. Select AutoForm: Columnar from the list of styles, and choose LineData as the table. Click OK. Next you'll see the LineData Form containing the data from the top row of the table (Figure 16.16).

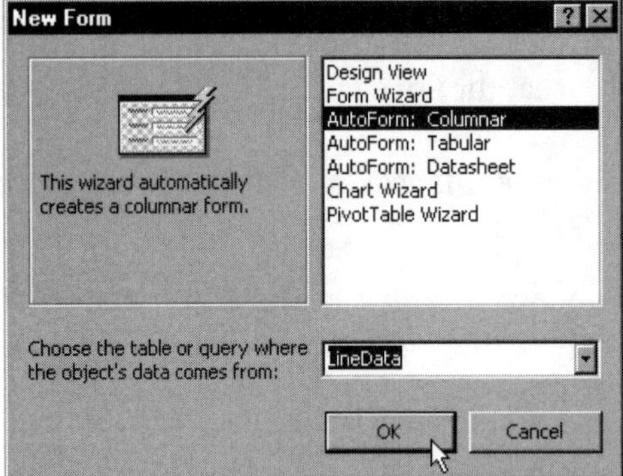

Figure 16.15 *New Form dialog box*

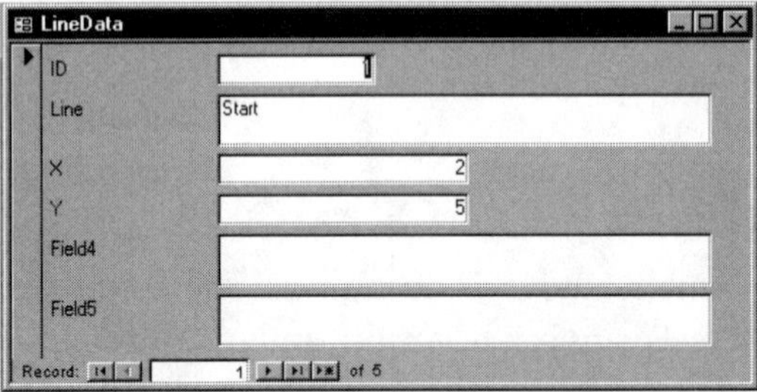

Figure 16.16 *LineData form in Access*

3. Click the Close button in the upper-right corner and when asked, save the Form as LineData.
4. In the LineData : Database window, choose Forms, highlight the new form, and click the Design icon in the toolbar. The Form is displayed with a grid, and a Toolbox alongside (Figure 16.17).
5. Adjust the size of your LineData Form and add two command buttons; use Figure 16.17 as a guide. As you add each button, the Command Button Wizard runs. Click Cancel in each page of the Wizard, because you will be assigning your own actions to the buttons.

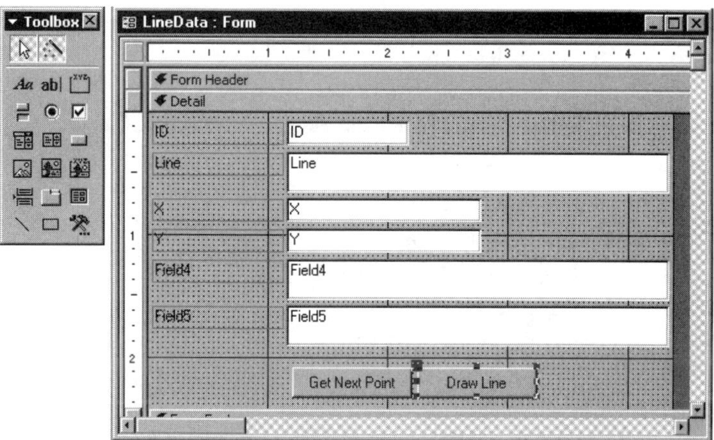

Figure 16.17 *The LineData form as it appears in Design mode with the Toolbox*

6. Change the Caption properties of your command buttons to those shown in Figure 16.17. (You can open the Properties window by right-clicking a command button and selecting Properties from the shortcut menu. You'll find the Caption property in the Format tab.)

7. For the Get Next Point command button, select the Event tab from the Properties window. Select the GetNextLine macro from the drop-down list in the OnClick event box, as shown here:

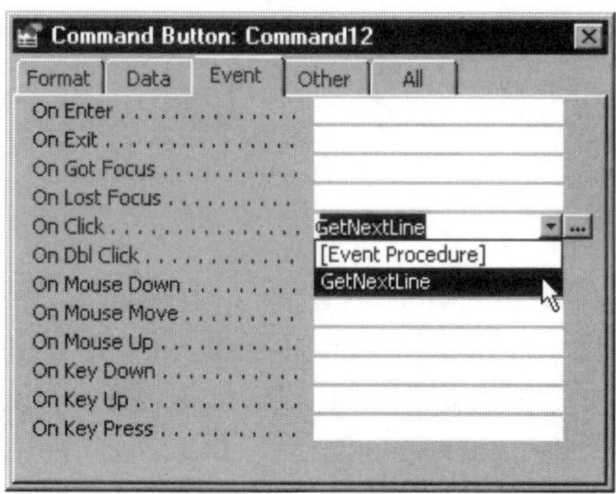

8. In the LineData Form, select the DrawLine command button and choose View ➜ Code. The Code window appears.

9. Now you'll enter the code shown in Listing 16.7 for the Draw Line button. Use the drop-down list of Objects to select Command13, and the drop-down list of procedures to select Click.

Listing 16.7: Sending Data From Access to AutoCAD

```
1   Private Sub Command13_Click()
2   Dim AutoCADApplication As Object
3   Dim StartLine(0 To 2) As Double
4   Dim EndLine(0 To 2) As Double
5   On Error Resume Next
6       Set AutoCADApplication = ↵
           GetObject(, "AutoCAD.Application")
7       If Err Then
8           MsgBox ("Please start AutoCAD before running this ↵
               application!")
9           End
10      End If
11  StartLine(0) = X
12  StartLine(1) = Y
13  GetNextLine
14  EndLine(0) = X
15  EndLine(1) = Y
16  AutoCADApp.ActiveDocument.ModelSpace.AddLine ↵
       StartLine, EndLine
17  End Sub
```

Analysis

- Line 1 starts `Command13_Click` event procedure that is executed when the Draw Line command button is clicked.
- Line 2 declares the `AutoCADApplication` variable as capable of referring to a generic type of object named Object. This allows the variable `AutoCADApplication` to refer to any object, so it's really better to follow the style of earlier macros that declared it as `AutoCAD.Application` and used `CreateObject` in its assignment statement. I have given this alternative style here simply as an example.

- Lines 3 and 4 declare the `StartLine` and `EndLine` arrays that will hold the endpoints of the line.
- Line 5 contains the `On Error` statement so that any error at Line 6 won't terminate the application.
- Line 6 calls the `GetObject` method that creates and returns a reference to an object exposed to the Excel application and sets up `ExcelApplication` as a reference to the object.
- Line 7 starts the `If` statement block that will be executed if an error occurred at Line 6.
- Line 8 calls the `MsgBox` function to inform the user about why the application is being terminated.
- Line 9 calls the `End` method to terminate the event procedure's execution.
- Line 10 ends the `If` statement block.
- Lines 11 through 15 assign the coordinate values in the Access table to the `StartLine` and `EndLine` arrays, calling the `GetNextLine` macro to retrieve the x- and y-coordinates for the `EndLine` array.
- Line 16 creates a new line based on the `StartLine` and `Endline` array values and draws it in the AutoCAD window's Model tab.
- Line 17 ends the event procedure.

With the macro in place, you can run your application:

1. In the Access VB Editor, choose File ➜ Save to save your changes, and then File ➜ Close and Return to Microsoft Access.
2. Now you're ready to run your application. Select Forms from the Objects list in the Database dialog box, highlight the LineData form, and click Open from the toolbar. Your LineData form is loaded and waits for your interaction.
3. Click on the DrawLine command button to draw the line in the AutoCAD window.

Summary

After working through the exercises in this chapter, you will know how to

- Drag items from one application to another.
- Develop ActiveX controls that allow AutoCAD, Excel, Word, and Access to exchange data.
- Use objects from the Excel, Word, and Access object models in AutoCAD statements.
- Write simple Excel, Word, and Access VBA macros.
- Call the CreateObject function to create an object from another Windows application.
- Call the GetObject function to retrieve a generic object.
- Access individual spreadsheet cells in code.
- Draw a line in the AutoCAD window from Excel, Access, and Word.
- Use the RangeObject to set the insertion point for data in the Word document.
- Retrieve Word objects from the Words collection in Word VBA.
- Convert an Access macro to an Access module.
- Develop an Access Form and use it to display data and draw lines in the AutoCAD window.

AutoCAD and the Internet

AUTOCAD VBA

Chapter 17

AutoCAD 2000 and later versions all have the ability to download and open files from Web sites on the Internet, and to save files to Web sites as well. This chapter offers a method of validating URLs entered by users and launching the Web browser from a macro. You'll follow the pages of AutoCAD 2000i's new Publish to Web Wizard that helps you create Web pages containing your AutoCAD drawings—without your ever needing to learn HTML. And you'll see how to add hyperlinks to a drawing.

This chapter contains the following topics:

- Opening and saving Web-based drawings from AutoCAD
- Using the IsURL method to validate URLs entered by users
- Launching a browser from a macro using the LaunchBrowserDialog method
- Downloading and uploading from a macro
- Publishing drawings on the Web
- Adding hyperlinks to a drawing

URL Paths of Files on the Web

AutoCAD 2000 and later versions have the ability to recognize Uniform Resource Locator (URL) addresses for files, in addition to traditional drive\folder\filename combination pathnames. The URL address for a file starts with the access method for the resource, such as File Transfer Protocol (FTP) for files being opened, or Hypertext Transmission Protocol (HTTP) for files being opened or saved. The URLs for AutoCAD files must end with a three-character extension, such as `.dwg` (Drawing files), `.dxf` (Drawing Interchange Files), or `.dwf` (Drawing Web Format files). For example:

```
ftp://autodesk.com/bldgdsgn/ac0111.dxf
http://www.sybex.com/images/MatildaHome.dwg
```

VBA provides an IsURL method to validate that a string is a valid URL. You'll see how to implement this method in Exercise 17.1.

Browsing the Web for Files

AutoCAD provides a toolbar that allows you to run your Internet browser at the click of a button; see Figure 17.1. This Web toolbar may already be on display in your AutoCAD window. If it isn't, choose View ➜ Toolbars, and in the Customize dialog box check the Web Toolbar item. Then click Close, and the Web toolbar will appear on your desktop.

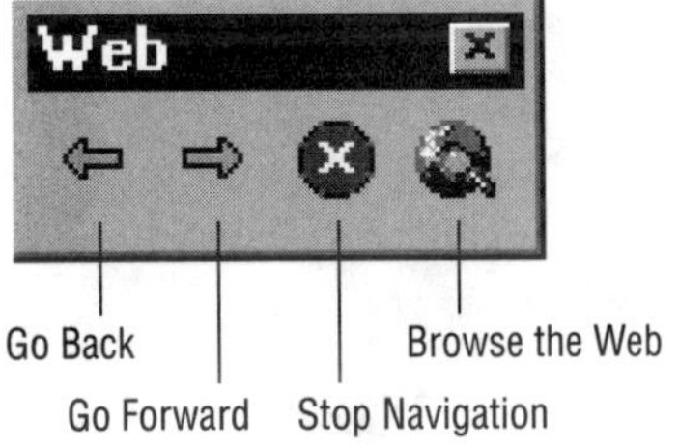

***Figure 17.1** AutoCAD's Web toolbar*

When you click the Browse the Web button on the Web toolbar, AutoCAD's command line displays the string

```
_browser Enter Web location (URL) < … >:
```

Inside the angle brackets is the URL for the current default Internet startup location. A common startup URL—the page that is first displayed when the browser opens—is your home page, or your company's main Web page.

You can set the default Internet location that will be launched as the startup URL by your browser. You can make it any URL of your choosing, but for convenience you'll probably want it set to the Web page you need to access most frequently. The following steps show you where the default startup URL is specified and how to change it to a new URL:

1. From the AutoCAD window, choose Tools → Options. The Options dialog box appears.
2. Click the Files tab and expand the Menu, Help, and Miscellaneous File Names items.
3. Select Default Internet Location, as shown in Figure 17.2, and change the URL to the one you require. Click OK.

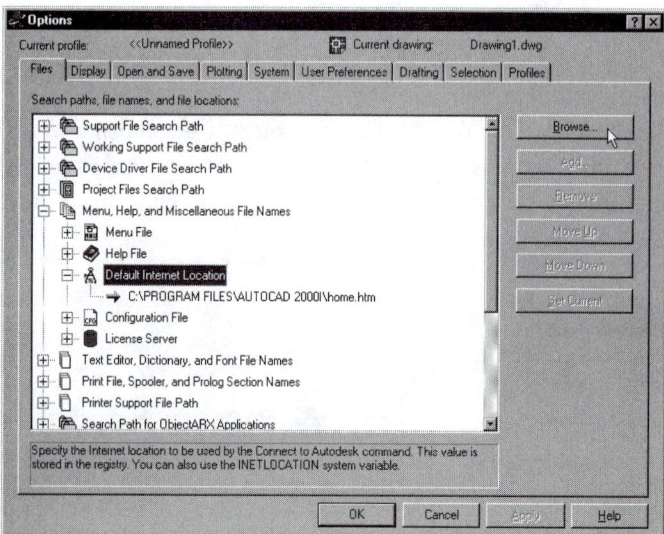

Figure 17.2 *Choosing the Default Internet Location from the list of search paths*

Downloading a Web File Using Macros

If you maintain drawings on a Web site, you may need to develop an application that allows a user to enter the URL address of a file needed for download, and then informs the user of whether the download was successful. The application developed in Exercise 17.1 is done in four stages:

- The first stage develops code that prompts the user for a URL and validates that their input is syntactically correct (Listing 17.1).
- The second stage develops the macro (Listing 17.2) that launches the browser, opening the Web page that is at the URL address entered at stage 1.
- The next stage downloads the file (if there is one) at the URL address on the Web (Listing 17.3).
- In the last stage, you write a macro that informs the user of a successful download of the file at the specified URL (Listing 17.4).

Now let's take a closer look at the four stages of this application.

Getting the URL Using a Macro

This section shows you how to prompt the user to supply a URL for a drawing that is stored at a site with an access method of HTTP or FTP—so you can't really help the user by providing several characters from the beginning of the URL address. The user is prompted to enter the complete URL into an input box, and the macro calls the IsURL method to verify that the string entered is syntactically correct. The code given in Listing 17.1 shows how this is achieved.

Exercise 17.1: Macro-izing the Transfer of Files to a Web Site

Enter the code for the declaration, the GetValidURL macro, and the GetURLFromUser function into ThisDrawing's Code window.

Listing 17.1: The GetURLFromUser Function

```
Dim URLAddress As String

Public Sub GetValidURL()
URLAddress = GetURLFromUser
If ThisDrawing.Utility.IsURL(URLAddress) Then
    MsgBox ("URL is valid.")
Else
    MsgBox ("The URL address should start with ↵
       http:// or ftp://")
     End
```

```
10      End If
11  End Sub
12
13  Function GetURLFromUser() As String
14      GetURLFromUser = InputBox("Enter the required URL:")
15  End Function
```

ANALYSIS

- Line 1 declares the `URLAddress` variable as a string. Since it is declared in the General Declarations section of ThisDrawing's Code window, it will be accessible from all the procedures in the same module.
- Line 3 starts the `GetValidURL` macro that calls the `GetURLFromUser` function, checks if the URL entered is syntactically correct, and reports the result to the user.
- Line 4 calls the `GetURLFromUser` function that prompts the user to enter a URL path, which is returned to the calling statement. The `URLAddress` variable is assigned the value returned.
- Line 5 calls the `IsURL` method of the Utility object, to find out if the string entered by the user has the correct syntax for a URL. (Of course, this doesn't guarantee that it will access an actual Web page.)
- Line 6 calls the `MsgBox` function to let the user know that the URL entered is syntactically correct.

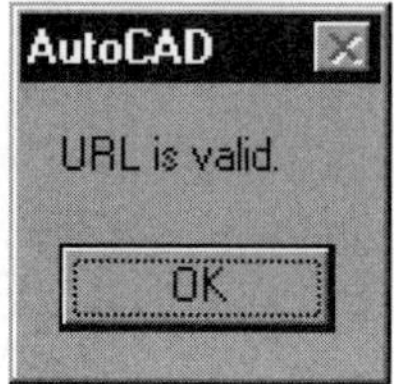

- Line 7 contains the `Else` statement.
- Line 8 calls the `MsgBox` function to inform the user that an invalid URL address was entered.
- Line 9 calls `End` to terminate the application.

- Line 10 ends the `If...Then...Else...`statement block.
- Line 11 ends the `GetValidURL` macro.
- Line 13 starts the `GetURLFromUser` function, declaring the result returned as a string type.
- Line 14 uses the `InputBox` function to prompt the user for a URL address. Then the address is returned to the `GetValidURL` macro, which assigns it to the `URLAddress` variable declared in the General Declarations section.

- Line 15 ends the `GetURLFromUser` function.

Now that the user has entered a valid URL, the next stage is to produce the code to launch the browser and open the requested Web page.

Launching the Browser from a Macro

The LaunchBrowserDialog method of ThisDrawing's Utility object opens the Web Browser dialog box, allowing the user to navigate to the URL of their choice. This method has six parameters; the first five are strings, and the last is a Boolean:

- The first parameter is the URL address of the Web page, if any, selected by the user.
- For the next two parameters, you specify the title caption for the Browser dialog box, and the caption for its command button. Figure 17.3 shows the Browser dialog box produced by Line 4 from Listing 17.2.
- The fourth parameter is passed the URL address of the startup page (the page to be displayed when the browser opens).
- The fifth parameter is assigned the product root key that allows you to set preferences for the settings of the Browser dialog box.
- The last parameter is passed a True value if the Open button is clicked, or False otherwise.

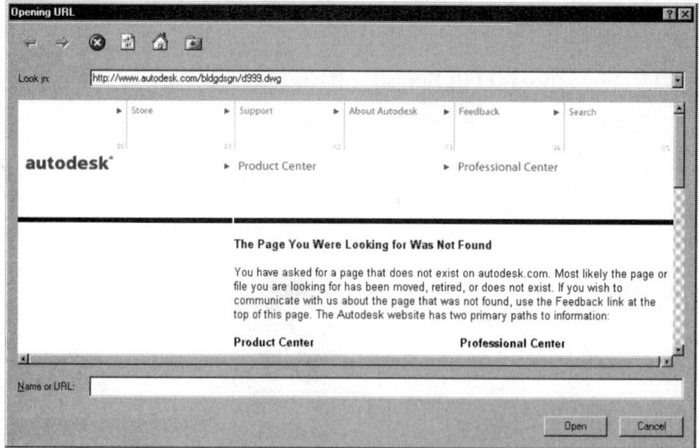

Figure 17.3 *Browser dialog box with title and button captions assigned in the call to the LaunchBrowserDialog method*

Exercise 17.1: Macro-izing the Transfer of Files to a Web Site (continued)

The BrowseTheWeb procedure in Listing 17.2 calls the LaunchBrowserDialog method to open the browser, with the title and button captions passed as the arguments (see Figure 17.3). Add the BrowseTheWeb macro to ThisDrawing's Code window beside the GetValidURL macro (Listing 17.1).

Listing 17.2: Adding the BrowseTheWeb Procedure

```
1   Sub BrowseTheWeb()
2       Dim SelectedURL As String
3       Dim URLSelected As Boolean
4       URLSelected = ThisDrawing.Utility.LaunchBrowserDialog↵
           (SelectedURL, "Opening URL", "Open", URLAddress, ↵
           "ACADBROWSER", True)
5       If URLSelected Then MsgBox "URL " + SelectedURL + ↵
           " has been selected!"
6   End Sub
```

Analysis

- Line 1 starts the `BrowseTheWeb` macro.

- Line 2 declares the `SelectedURL` variable as a string type. The `SelectedURL` variable is assigned the URL that is selected by the user in the Browser dialog box.
- Line 3 declares the `URLSelected` variable as Boolean. This variable will be set to True when the user selects a URL from the Browser dialog box.
- Line 4 calls the `LaunchBrowserDialog` method of the Utility object to open the Browser dialog box shown in Figure 17.3.
- Line 5 verifies that a URL address was selected from the Browser dialog box and, if so, calls the `MsgBox` function to confirm to the user that a URL has been selected.

- Line 6 ends the `BrowseTheWeb` macro.

If everything is going according to plan, the Web page at the URL address entered by the user will now be on display in the browser. The next stage is to write the code to actually download the file from the Web site.

The Code for Getting a Web File

The GetRemoteFile method allows you to get a file from the Web. This method takes the Web file specified by the URL and downloads it to a local destination. GetRemoteFile has three parameters: the URL of the file to be downloaded, the local file's temporary pathname, and IgnoreCache. You pass the URL address in the call, and the method returns the local pathname. IgnoreCache is passed the True value if the file is to be downloaded, or False if the file is only to be downloaded if it hasn't already.

Exercise 17.1: Macro-izing the Transfer of Files to a Web Site (continued)

Listing 17.3 shows the GetRemoteFile method being called by the GetURLFile function. Because the IgnoreCache parameter is passed the True value in this case, the cache of URL files previously downloaded is ignored. Add the GetURLFile function to ThisDrawing's Code window beside the procedures from Listings 17.1 and 17.2.

LISTING 17.3: CALLING THE GETREMOTEFILE FUNCTION

```
1   Function GetURLFile() As String
2       Dim LocalFile As String
3       ThisDrawing.Utility.GetRemoteFile URLAddress,↵
           LocalFile, True
4       MsgBox "File downloaded from the Web to " + LocalFile
5   End Function
```

ANALYSIS

- Line 1 starts the `GetURLFile` function, which downloads the file at the URL entered by the user and lets the user know where to find this file on their local PC.
- Line 2 declares the `LocalFile` variable as a string type.
- Line 3 calls the `GetRemoteFile` method of ThisDrawing's Utility object. This method downloads the Web page from the `URLAddress` to a temporary local file and assigns its pathname to the `LocalFile` variable.
- Line 4 calls the `MsgBox` function to inform the user that a file has been downloaded.
- Line 5 ends the `GetURLFile` function.

The Code for Sending a File to the Web

The `PutRemoteFile` method sends a local file to a Web page identified by a URL address. The `PutRemoteFile` method has two parameters: the URL address to which the local file will be uploaded, and the name of the local file to be uploaded. Listing 17.4 shows this method being called to upload the `Temp.dwg` file to the original source URL.

Listing 17.4 also calls the IsRemoteFile method of the Utility object, to identify whether the file passed to it as the first argument was downloaded from the Web. If so, this method assigns the URL address of the original file to the second parameter and returns True. To test the macro, enter the code from Listing 17.4 into the Code window for the same ThisDrawing module that you've been working with so far.

Listing 17.4: Macro to Verify That the File Was Downloaded

```
1    Sub CheckIfLocalFileIsFromWeb()
2        Dim Answer As Integer
3        Dim URLFileName As String, FileIsFromWeb As Boolean
4        FileIsFromWeb = ThisDrawing.Utility.IsRemoteFile↵
            ("c:\My Documents\Temp.dwg", URLFileName)
5        If FileIsFromWeb Then
6            Answer = MsgBox("File is from " + URLFileName + ↵
                "do you want to save it to the Web?", vbYesNo)
7            If Answer = vbYes Then ↵
                ThisDrawing.Utility.PutRemoteFile URLFileName, ↵
                "c:\My Documents\Temp.dwg"
8        Else
9            MsgBox "File is not from the Web."
10       End If
11   End Sub
```

Analysis

- Line 1 starts the `CheckIfLocalFileIsFromWeb` macro.
- Line 2 declares the `Answer` variable that will be assigned the result of line 6 or 7, according to whether the Yes button or No button is clicked from the message box at Line 6.
- Line 3 declares the `URLFileName` variable as a string, and the `FileIsFromWeb` variable as a Boolean type.
- Line 4 calls the `IsRemoteFile` method of the Utility object, to determine if the `Temp.dwg` file passed as an argument was originally from the Web. If so, the `URLFileName` will be assigned the URL address, and the `FileIsFromWeb` variable will be assigned True.
- Line 5 starts the `If`…Then…`Else`… statement block and checks to see if the `FileIsFromWeb` variable is True.
- Line 6 runs if the file was originally from the Web. This line calls the `MsgBox` functon to ask the user if they want to save the file back to the Web. Calling the `MsgBox` function with the `vbYesNo` constant displays the message box with two command buttons labeled Yes and No. The `Answer` variable is assigned 6 if the Yes button is clicked, and 7 if the No is clicked.

- Line 7: If Answer equals `vbYes` (user clicked the Yes button), then the `PutRemoteFile` method of the Utility object is called to upload the `Temp.dwg` file to the URL address assigned to the `URLFileName`.
- Line 8 contains the `Else` statement.
- Line 9 calls the `MsgBox` function with the message that the file was not downloaded from the Web.
- Line 10 ends the `If...Then...Else...` statement block.
- Line 11 ends the `CheckIfLocalFileIsFromWeb` macro.

Putting It All Together

With everything in place, you can tie it all together. Listing 17.5 contains the TransmitWebFiles macro that calls all the macros in Listings 17.1 through Listing 17.4; together, they make up this transfer-files-to-the-Web application. Did you notice it doesn't have a UserForm associated with it? Here are the steps that finish off your application and run it.

1. Enter the TransmitWebFiles macro into the Code window for ThisDrawing, beside the other macros.
2. Run the application from the Macro dialog box in the AutoCAD window.
3. When prompted by the input box, enter a URL and click OK. A message box tells you whether the URL you entered was syntactically correct.
4. If the URL is valid, the browser opens. It presents the requested Web page containing the drawing from the file if it exists, or perhaps a Web page associated with part of the URL and a message saying that the page wasn't found. What you see will depend on the Web site being accessed. Click Open to return to your application.
5. Now the message box from Listing 17.2 appears, informing you that the file has been selected. Click OK.
6. You'll next be asked if you want to save the file (per Listing 17.4). Click No for this exercise.

LISTING 17.5: TRANSMITWEBFILES MACRO

```
1   Public Sub TransmitWebFiles()
2       GetValidURL
3       BrowseTheWeb
4       GetURLFile
5       CheckIfLocalFileIsFromWeb
6   End Sub
```

ANALYSIS

- Line 1 starts the `TransmitWebFiles` macro, which calls all the other macros and functions that make up this application sans UserForm.
- Line 2 calls the `GetValidURL` macro, which obtains a valid URL from the user.
- Line 3 calls the `BrowseTheWeb` macro, to open up the browser with your specified captions.
- Line 4 calls the `GetURLFile` macro, which gets a file from the specified URL address on the Web.
- Line 5 calls the `CheckIfLocalFileIsFromWeb` macro to see if a local file is from the Web, and if so, asks whether you'd like to send it to the Web again. In reality, you would probably want to update the file in some way before sending it back.
- Line 6 ends the `TransmitWebFiles` macro.

Your application is complete; now you can download files and upload files from and to the Web. Before closing this chapter, we'll walk through a couple of related tasks: how to create your very own Web pages containing data about drawings, and how to add hyperlinks to your drawings.

Preparing Drawings for Publishing on the Web

Preparing drawings for publication on the Web is extremely simple with the Publish to Web Wizard available in AutoCAD 2000i. All you need to do is walk through a series of wizard pages, and at the end of it your HTML pages—containing the DWF or JPG images of AutoCAD drawings—are automatically produced for you.

Exercise 17.2: Using AutoCAD's Publish to Web Wizard

The following steps show you how to get a drawing ready for publication on the Web. To prepare for this exercise, you'll need to run the Tower Block project. This project is created in Chapter 19 on the CD, so go ahead and jump forward to that project now, if you're ready. Use the Orbit control to change the angle of view so that your drawing doesn't look like a collection of two-dimensional rectangles. Save the drawing as `NewDrawing.dwg`.

Drawings must be in a saved file before you can publish them on the Web or post them to the Internet.

1. Choose File ➜ Publish to Web. This runs the Publish to Web Wizard; its Begin page is shown in Figure 17.4. Ensure that the Create New Web Page option button is checked and click Next.

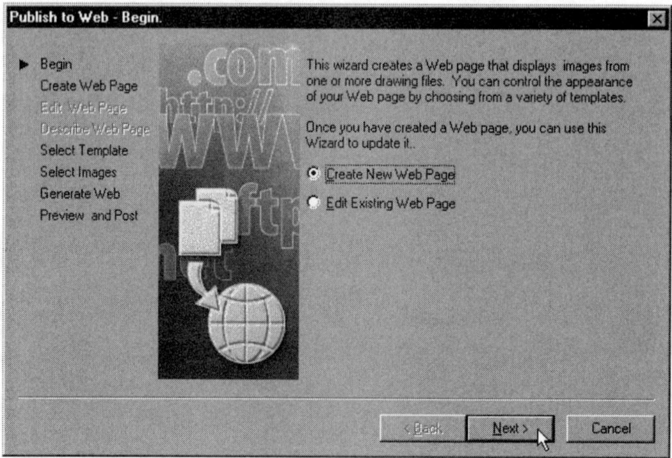

Figure 17.4 *First page of the Publish to Web Wizard*

2. The Create Web Page page of the wizard appears next (Figure 17.5). Enter the name you used to save your TowerBlock drawing, and enter the text description you would like to appear on your Web page along with the drawing. Click Next.
3. In the Select Template page of the wizard (Figure 17.6), try selecting each template one by one. In the preview box, watch the effect each template has on the appearance of the Web page.

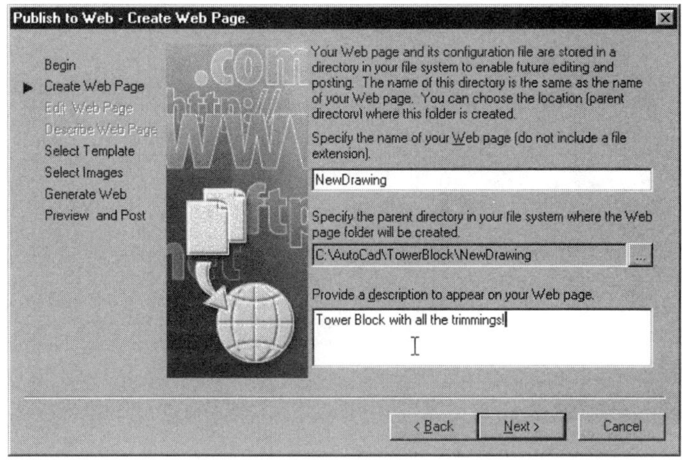

Figure 17.5 *Create Web Page screen of the Publish to Web wizard*

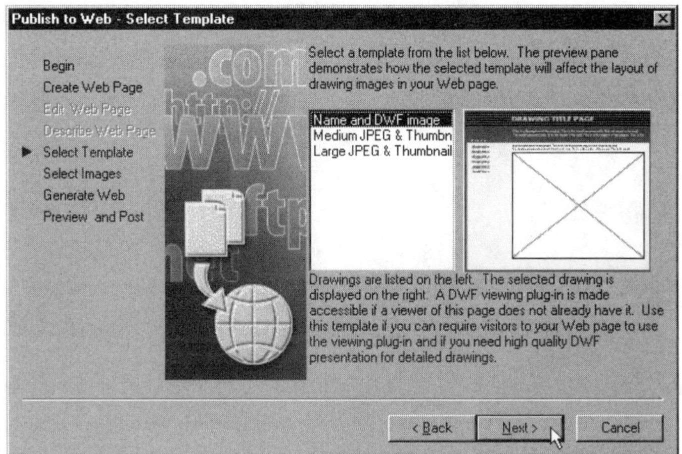

Figure 17.6 *Select Template page of the Publish to Web wizard*

4. Select the top template from the list (Name and DWF Image) and click Next.
5. In the Select Images page of the wizard (Figure 17.7), click Add to add the Model layout to the Image List. Click Next to continue.

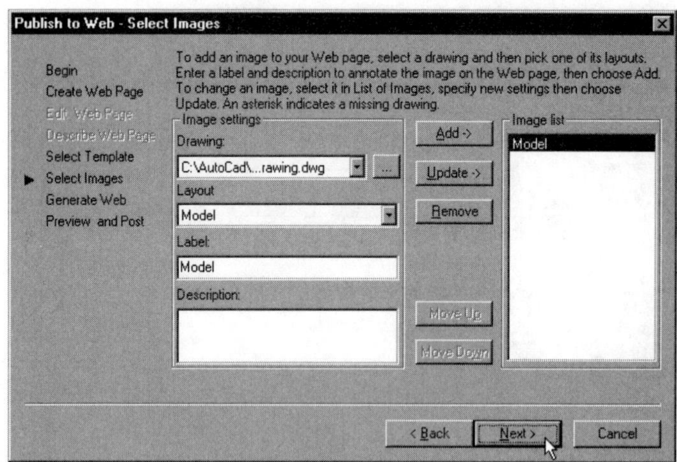

Figure 17.7 *Select Images page from the Publish to Web wizard*

6. Next up is the Generate Web Page screen of the wizard. In that screen, click Next to advance to the Preview and Post page of the wizard (Figure 17.8).

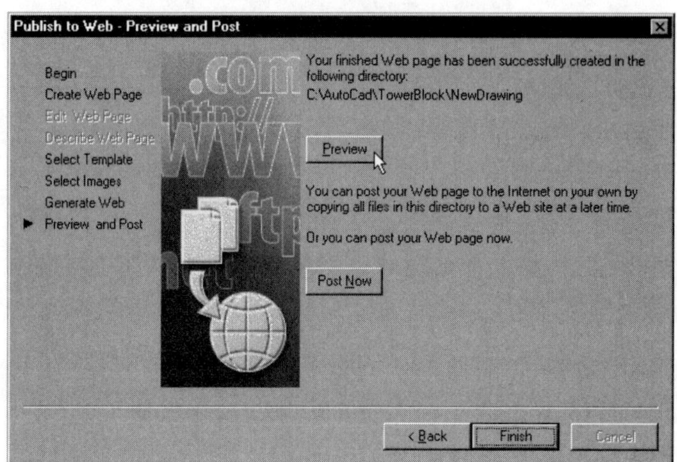

Figure 17.8 *Preview and Post page of the Publish to Web wizard*

7. Click Preview. Your Web browser will open with your new Web page—mine is shown in Figure 17.9.

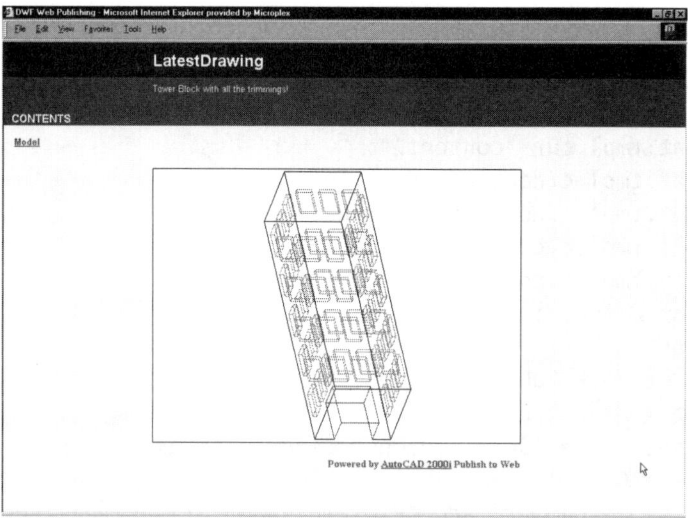

Figure 17.9 *Web browser displaying the Web page created by the Publish to Web wizard*

8. In the Preview and Post page, click Finish. The wizard closes and you return to the AutoCAD window.
9. To view your new Web page again, run Windows Explorer and double-click the `acwebpublish` file in the same directory where you saved your drawing.

You can also view the HTML commands that produced your Web page, using a word processing application such as NotePad, WordPad, or Word. The following HTML code, Listing 17.6, is from the `acwebpublish` file.

Listing 17.6: HTML Code Produced by the Publish to Web Wizard

```
<html>
<head>
<meta name="AcPub2Web" content="v-1-0-1-dwf">
<title>DWF Web Publishing</title>
<!- autodesk Publish to Web ->
<script language="JavaScript">
document.tmpl = new Object;
document.tmpl.h = new Object;
document.tmpl.c = new Object;
```

```
document.tmpl.h.banner="LatestDrawing";
document.tmpl.h.description="Tower Block with all the ↵
  trimmings!";
document.tmpl.c.content1=new Object;
document.tmpl.c.content1.title="Model";
document.tmpl.cur="content1";
document.tmpl.c.content1.dwfFile="IM1.dwf";
document.tmpl.c.content1.thumbnail="";
document.tmpl.c.content1.image="";
document.tmpl.c.content1.description="";
document.close();
</script>
<!- / autodesk Publish to Web ->
</head>
<frameset rows="130,*" framespacing="0" frameborder="0" ↵
  border="0">
<frame name="banner" src="PTWTemplateA3.htm" scrolling="no" ↵
  noresize target="top" frameborder="0" marginwidth="0" ↵
  marginheight="0">
<frameset cols="205,*" framespacing="0" frameborder="0" ↵
  border="0">
     <frame name="contents" src="PTWTemplateA1.htm" ↵
       scrolling="auto" noresize target="main">
     <frame name="main" src="PTWTemplateA2.htm" ↵
       noresize scrolling="auto">
     <noframes>
     <body>
     <p>This page uses frames, but your browser doesn't ↵
       support them.</p>
     </body>
     </noframes>
</frameset>
</frameset>
</html>
```

Adding Hyperlinks to a Drawing

AutoCAD provides a Hyperlinks feature that allows you to associate a drawing object with a hyperlink. Hyperlinks can point to local files, or files at an intranet or Internet location. Hyperlinks are stored as part of the XData of the associated object and can have descriptive text about the contents of the file. To create hyperlinks, you either use the Hyperlink command in the AutoCAD window, or add Hyperlink objects to the Hyperlinks collection. Following are the steps for both methods.

Adding Hyperlinks from the AutoCAD Window

1. Add a few lines to the Model Space. Select one of them and choose Insert → Hyperlink. The Edit Hyperlink dialog box appears (Figure 17.10).

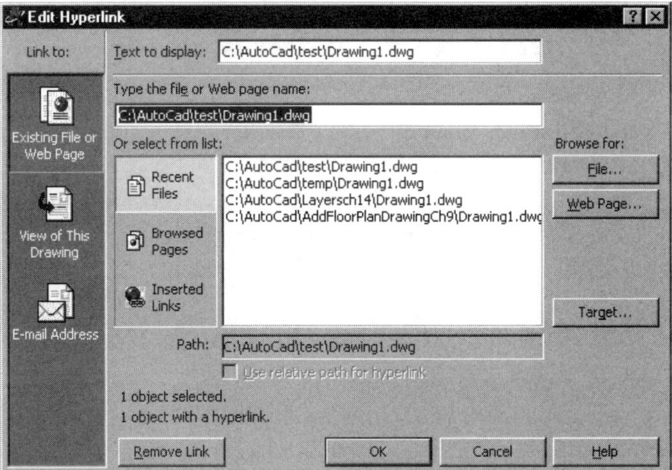

Figure 17.10 *Edit Hyperlink dialog box*

2. Into the Type the File or Web Page Name box, enter the name of the file you want to open when the user follows the hyperlink; or you can select one of the files listed in the panel just below. The selected file will appear in both the Type the File… box and the Text to Display box at the top.
3. Into the Text to Display box, type some text describing the hyperlinked file (type over the filename to replace it). Click OK.
4. Pause the mouse over the now-hyperlinked line in the Model Space. The Hyperlink icon will appear beside the mouse pointer, along with a ToolTip

containing the descriptive text you entered in Step 2 as the Text To Display. Here's an example:

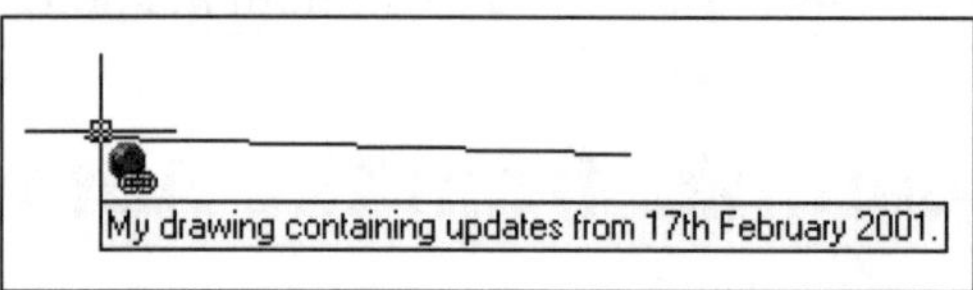

5. Right-click the hyperlinked line, and choose Hyperlink from the bottom of the shortcut menu. In the next flyout menu, select the name of the linked file, and it will open.

Adding Hyperlinks from a Macro

Now let's see how to create a Hyperlink and set its URL address from a macro. AutoCAD's Hyperlink object can be assigned a URL address and descriptive text. The DrawLineWithHyperlink macro shown in Listing 17.7 shows how to set up a hyperlink on a Line object that, when clicked, will open the browser and go straight to the AutoDesk Web site. If you want to try out this macro, enter it into the Code window for ThisDrawing.

LISTING 17.7: MACRO FOR DRAWING A LINE WITH A HYPERLINK

```
Sub DrawLineWithHyperlink()
    Dim StartPoint(0 To 2) As Double
    Dim EndPoint(0 To 2) As Double
    Dim LineObject As AcadLine
    Dim HyperlinkObject As AcadHyperlink
    Dim HyperlinkCollection As AcadHyperlinks
    StartPoint(0) = 1: StartPoint(1) = 1: StartPoint(2) = 0
    EndPoint(0) = 5: EndPoint(1) = 3: EndPoint(2) = 0
    Set LineObject = ↲
       ThisDrawing.ModelSpace.AddLine(StartPoint, ↲
       EndPoint)
    Set HyperlinkCollection = LineObject.Hyperlinks
    Set HyperlinkObject = HyperlinkCollection.Add("AutoDesk")
    HyperlinkObject.URL = "www.autodesk.com"
    HyperlinkObject.URLDescription = "AutoDesk Web site"
End Sub
```

Analysis

- Line 1 starts the DrawLineWithHyperlink macro, which adds a Line object and sets up a hyperlink to the AutoDesk Web site.
- Lines 2 and 3 declare the arrays that will contain the coordinates of the two endpoints of the line.
- Line 4 declares the `LineObject` variable as being capable of referencing an `AcadLine` object.
- Line 5 declares the `HyperlinkObject` variable that will be set up to refer to a new Hyperlink object.
- Line 6 declares the `HyperLinkCollection` that will be set up to refer to the Hyperlinks collection containing the Hyperlink object.
- Lines 7 and 8 assign values to the two endpoints of the line.
- Line 9 adds a Line object to the Model Space and sets up the `LineObject` variable as a reference to the new object.
- Line 10 sets up `HyperlinkCollection` as a reference to the Hyperlinks collection of the Line object.
- Line 11 adds a new Hyperlink object to the `HyperlinkCollection` and sets up the `HyperlinkObject` variable as a reference to the new object.
- Line 12 assigns the URL property of the Hyperlink object to the main AutoDesk Web site address.
- Line 13 assigns text to the `URLDescription` property of the Hyperlink object. This text will appear in the ToolTip text box when the mouse is paused over the line.
- Line 14 ends the macro.

Run your macro, and you'll end up at the AutoDesk site in your default browser. Select the line in the AutoCAD window and choose Insert ➜ Hyperlink. When the Edit Hyperlink dialog box appears, you'll see your Hyperlink object's settings in the Text to Display box and the Type the File or Web Page Name box.

Summary

After completing this chapter, you will be able to

- Download files from sites on the Web.
- Upload files to sites on the Web.
- Verify whether a user-entered URL is valid.
- Launch a browser application from a macro.
- Determine whether a file was originally downloaded from the Web using the IsRemoteFile method.
- Use AutoCAD's Publish to Web Wizard to create your own Web pages containing drawings.
- Add hyperlinks to a drawing.

Object Models

AUTOCAD VBA

Appendix A

Every application that has VBA capability has an object model that shows the relationships between objects. Although each object model's format may look a little different, they all provide basically the same information about their objects and collections and how these can be accessed.

This appendix contains all the object models that comprise the objects and collections referred to throughout this book. It begins with the AutoCAD Object Model, which is used extensively in all the code listings and is described in detail in Chapter 5. Also presented here are other object models of family members in the Microsoft Office suite, including Excel, Word, and Access—and, of course, the Microsoft Office Object Model itself. (Excel and Access were used for examples of exchanging data with AutoCAD in Chapter 16.)

AutoCAD Object Model

The AutoCAD Object Model (see Figure A.1) comprises all the objects that you can access from your VBA code. It also shows which objects provide access to other objects lower in the hierarchy.

- The Application object sits at the very top and can directly or indirectly access all objects in the model. The ModelSpace collection can access any of the listed drawing objects that can be placed in the Model Space section of the AutoCAD window. Collections are groups of objects that usually have something in common.

AutoCAD objects are said to be exposed *if you can access them from your VBA code. Each exposed object represents a specific element of AutoCAD, such as lines and circles, groups and layers, text, and coordinate systems.*

- The Preferences object is used to access the objects that represent the pages of the Options dialog box, as listed in Figure A.2. Each object contains the settings for the options that reside in the Registry. Options that reside in a specific drawing are contained in the DatabasePreferences object. There is only one Preferences object per application.
- The Document object represents the active document, which refers to the current AutoCAD drawing. Only one document can be active at any particular time. In the code, this active document is referred to as ThisDrawing.

In addition to their ability to access other objects in the object model, some objects have properties that provide links to other objects. For example, the Application object can access the object representing the active drawing as follows:

```
Application.ActiveDocument.Name
```

This is a string defining the active drawing file, such as `Drawing1.dwg`.

The object model appears hierarchical and gives the impression that objects are restricted to accessing objects immediately below them in the pecking order. However, the active document has a property named Application that allows it to indirectly access the Application object that is a level above. For example:

```
Application.ActiveDocument.Application.Name
```

would return the name of the application that the ActiveDocument belongs to, such as `AutoCAD`.

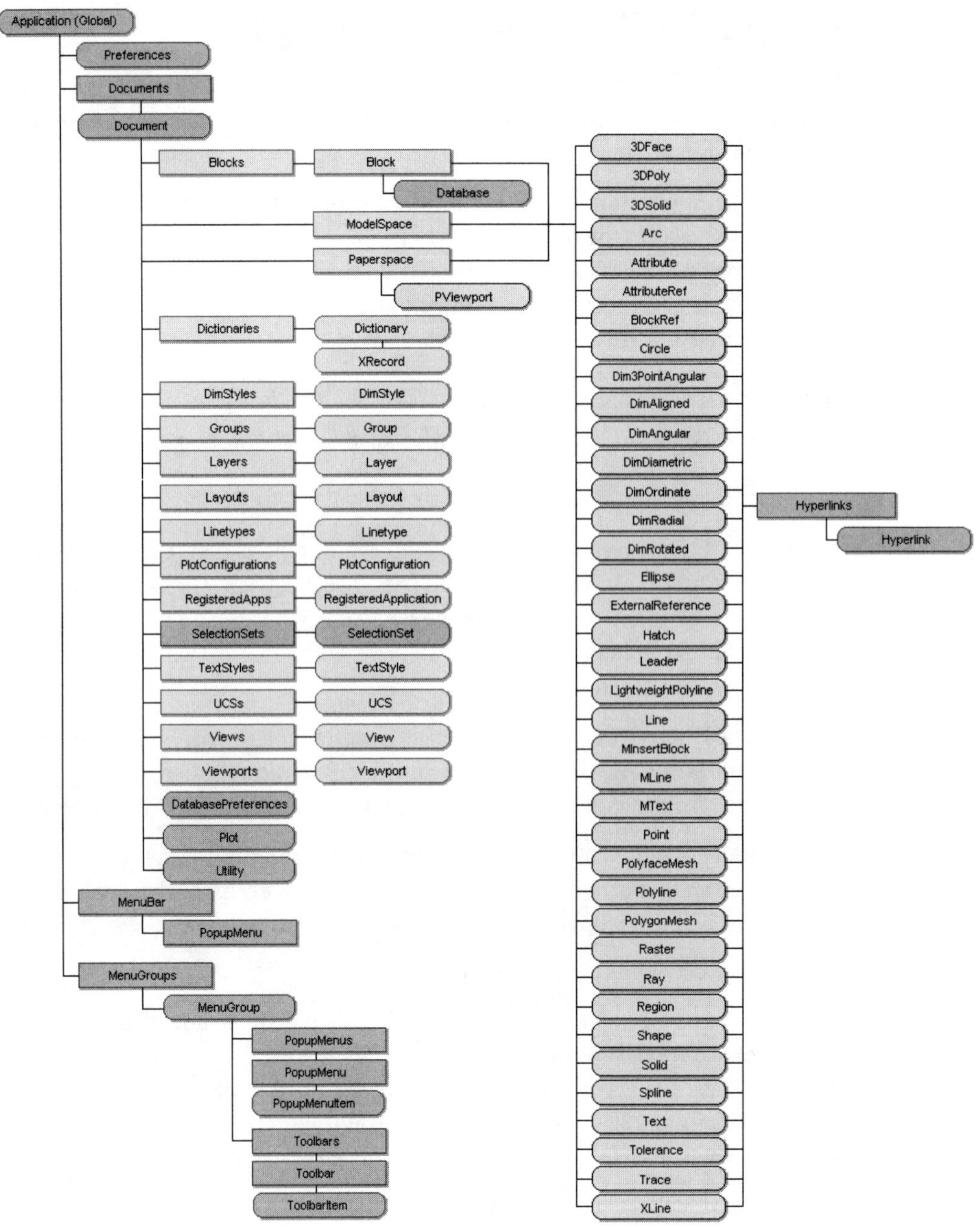

Figure A.1 *Within the AutoCAD Object Model, the shapes with rounded corners are single objects, and the shapes with squared corners are collections of objects.*

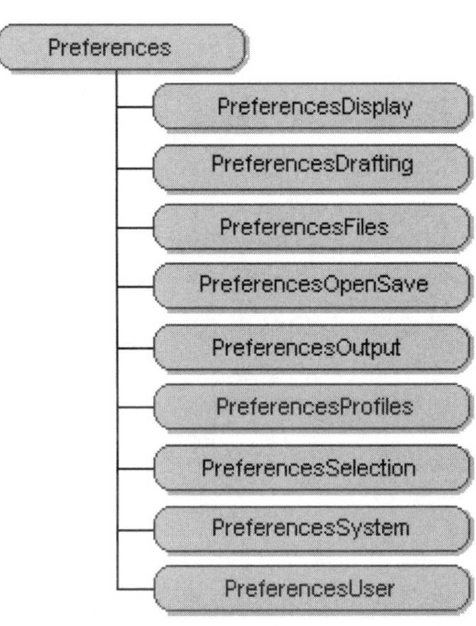

Figure A.2 *Objects accessible from the Preferences object*

The code `Application.ActiveDocument` gives exactly the same results when replaced by `ThisDrawing`. For example, both of the two preceding code statements can be rewritten as follows:

```
ThisDrawing.Name
ThisDrawing.Application.Name
```

Viewing the AutoCAD Object Model

To view the object model from the AutoCAD window:

1. In the AutoCAD menu bar, choose Help ➜ Developer Help. The AutoCAD Help: Developer Documentation dialog box appears.
2. Select the Contents tab from the left-hand side of the dialog box. (You will need to click the Show button if this tab is not already visible.)
3. Expand the list under ActiveX and VBA Reference by clicking the plus symbol, and click Object Model.
4. Use the scroll button to explore the object model that appears on the right.

Microsoft Office Object Model

All the applications from the Microsoft Office Suite can access the Microsoft Office Object Model shown in Figure A.3. It contains collections and objects that are common to all Microsoft Office family members. The light-gray boxes contain collections and objects (in parentheses), and the darker-gray boxes contain only objects. You can access the Help page containing the Microsoft Office Object Model from the VB Editor's Object Browser, by simply selecting Office from the library list and pressing F1.

For example, the Assistant object refers to the Office Assistant help feature. Running the code in Listing A.1 will display the Office Assistant as shown in Figure A.4, regardless of which Office application is being run.

LISTING A.1

```
1   Sub DirectAssistant()
2       With Assistant.NewBalloon
3           .BalloonType = msoBalloonTypeButtons
4           .Icon = msoIconAlertQuery
5           .Button = msoButtonSetCancel
6           .Heading = "What do you want to do?"
7           .Labels(1).Text = "Continue working."
8           .Labels(2).Text = "Save work now!"
9           .Labels(3).Text = "Exit"
10          .Show
11      End With
12  End Sub
```

ANALYSIS

- Line 1 starts the `DirectAssistant` macro.
- Line 2 uses the `With` statement so that the properties of the `NewBalloon` object of the `Assistant` object can be used without fully qualifying them.
- Lines 3 through 9 set the properties of the `NewBalloon` object to produce the balloon shown in Figure A.4.
- Line 10 calls the `NewBalloon` object's `Show` method to display it above the Office Assistant.
- Lines 11 and 12 end the `With` statement and the `DirectAssistant` macro, respectively.

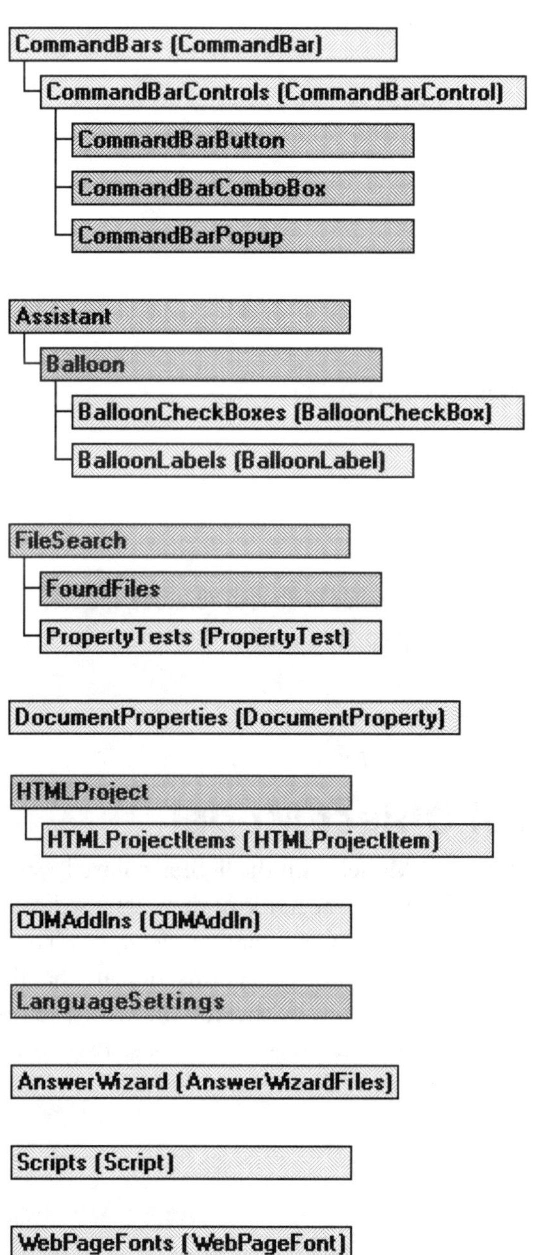

Figure A.3 *Microsoft Office Object Model*

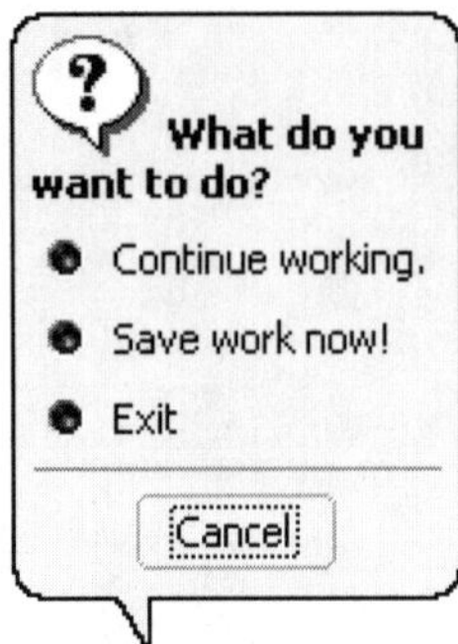

Figure A.4 *Microsoft Office Assistant after running the DirectAssistant macro (Listing A.1)*

Adding New Objects

To create a new object and add it to a collection, you use the Add method in VBA code. The Count property keeps a tally of the number of objects in the collection. The Item property is used with an index value to return the object at the index position in the collection.

Microsoft Excel Object Model

Figure A.5 shows the Excel Object Model, with the lighter-colored rectangles containing the objects in parentheses, following the name of their assigned collections. Objects that don't belong to any collection are shown in darker rectangles. The right-pointing arrows alongside the Worksheets and Charts collections indicate that these collections have additional objects, which you can view by clicking the arrow. To see this Help page, open the Object Browser in the Excel VB Editor, choose Excel from the list of libraries, and press F1.

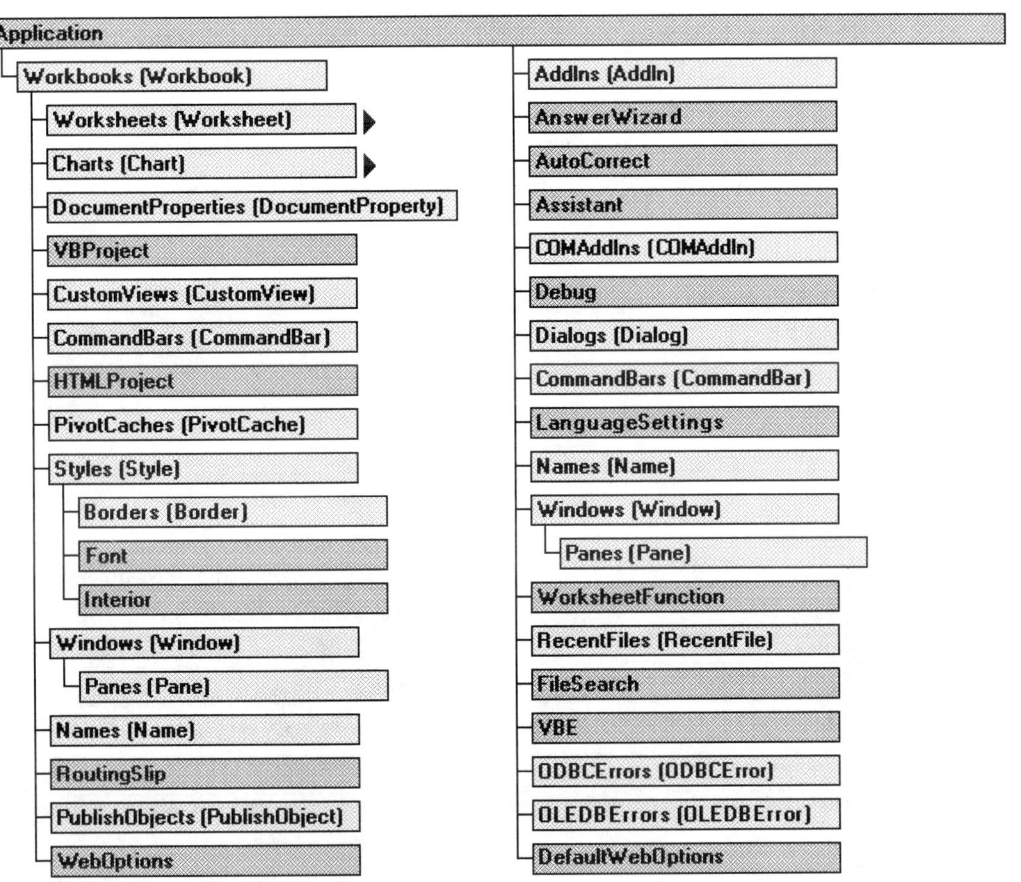

Figure A.5 *Excel Object Model*

Microsoft Access Object Model

The Microsoft Access Object Model shown in Figure A.6 comprises the objects and collections available for you to use in your Access applications. To view this Help page, open the Access VB Editor and search the Help facility for the Application Object's page. Click the See Also hyperlink, and choose Microsoft Access Objects from the list that appears in the Topics Found dialog box; then click Display.

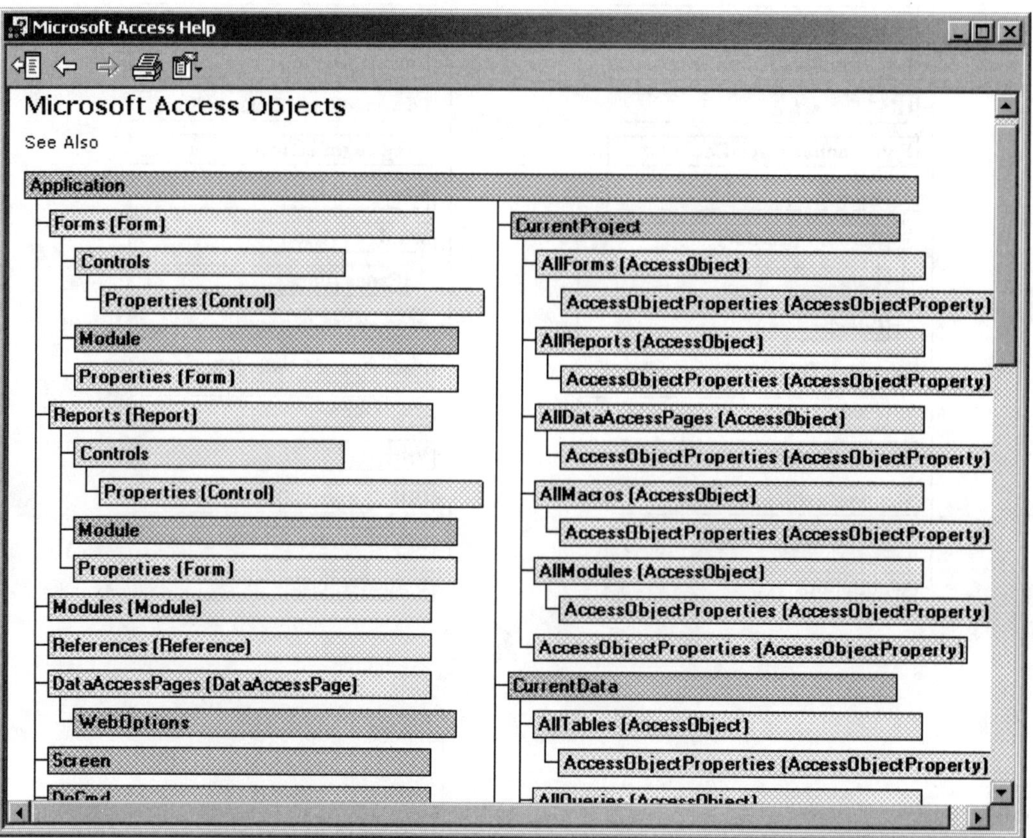

***Figure A.6** Microsoft Access Object Model*

Microsoft Word Object Model

The Microsoft Word Object Model shown in Figure A.7 contains all the objects and collections available in Word. The light-colored rectangles contain collections, followed by the objects these collections contain in parentheses. To view this Help page, open the Word VB Editor; then open the Help window and select Microsoft Word Visual Basic Reference from the Contents tab.

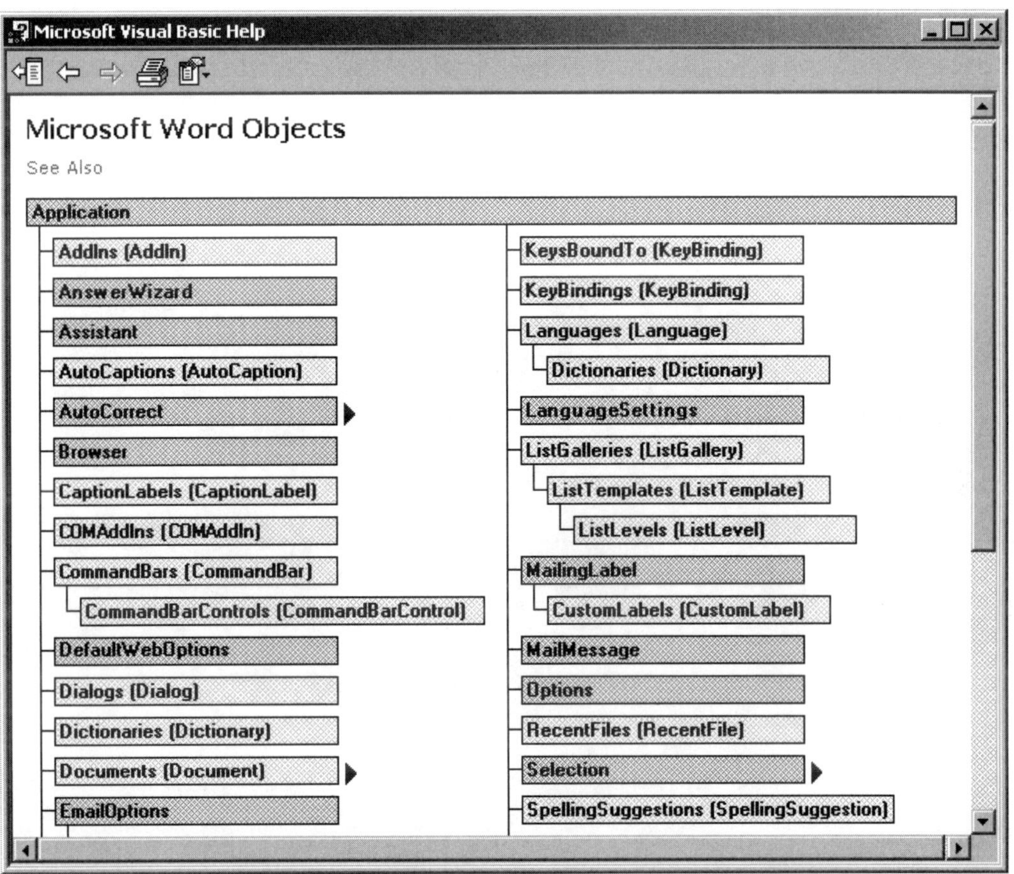

Figure A.7 Microsoft Word Object Model

ASCII Character Set

AUTOCAD VBA

Appendix B

Table A.1: ASCII Character Set (0–127)

0	[null]	**32**	[space]	**64**	@	**96**	`
1	[start of heading]	**33**	!	**65**	A	**97**	a
2	[start of text]	**34**	"	**66**	B	**98**	b
3	[end of text]	**35**	#	**67**	C	**99**	c
4	[end of transmission]	**36**	$	**68**	D	**100**	d
5	[enquiry]	**37**	%	**69**	E	**101**	e
6	[acknowledge]	**38**	&	**70**	F	**102**	f
7	[bell]	**39**	'	**71**	G	**103**	g
8	[backspace]	**40**	(	**72**	H	**104**	h
9	[horizontal tab]	**41**	)	**73**	I	**105**	i
10	[line feed]	**42**	*	**74**	J	**106**	j
11	[vertical tab]	**43**	+	**75**	K	**107**	k
12	[form feed]	**44**	,	**76**	L	**108**	l
13	[carriage return]	**45**	-	**77**	M	**109**	m
14	[shift out]	**46**	.	**78**	N	**110**	n
15	[shift in]	**47**	/	**79**	O	**111**	o
16	[data link escape]	**48**	0	**80**	P	**112**	p
17	[device control 1]	**49**	1	**81**	Q	**113**	q
18	[device control 2]	**50**	2	**82**	R	**114**	r
19	[device control 3]	**51**	3	**83**	S	**115**	s
20	[device control 4]	**52**	4	**84**	T	**116**	t
21	[negative acknowledge]	**53**	5	**85**	U	**117**	u
22	[synchronous idle]	**54**	6	**86**	V	**118**	v
23	[end transmission block]	**55**	7	**87**	W	**119**	w
24	[cancel]	**56**	8	**88**	X	**120**	x
25	[end of medium]	**57**	9	**89**	Y	**121**	y
26	[substitute]	**58**	:	**90**	Z	**122**	z
27	[escape]	**59**	;	**91**	[	**123**	{

Table A.1: ASCII Character Set (0–127) *continued*

28	[file separator]	**60**	<	**92**	\	**124**	|
29	[group separator]	**61**	=	**93**	]	**125**	}
30	[record separator]	**62**	>	**94**	^	**126**	~
31	[unit separator]	**63**	?	**95**	_	**127**	[delete]

Nonprinting characters are described within brackets.
ASCII code characters 0–7, 11, 12, and 14–31 are not supported by Microsoft Windows.

Table A.2: ASCII Character Set (128–255)

128	¤	**160**	[space]	**192**	À	**224**	à
129	¤	**161**	¡	**193**	Á	**225**	á
130	¤	**162**	¢	**194**	Â	**226**	â
131	¤	**163**	£	**195**	Ã	**227**	ã
132	¤	**164**	¤	**196**	Ä	**228**	ä
133	¤	**165**	¥	**197**	Å	**229**	å
134	¤	**166**	¦	**198**	Æ	**230**	æ
135	¤	**167**	§	**199**	Ç	**231**	ç
136	¤	**168**	¨	**200**	È	**232**	è
137	¤	**169**	©	**201**	É	**233**	é
138	¤	**170**	ª	**202**	Ê	**234**	ê
139	¤	**171**	«	**203**	Ë	**235**	ë
140	¤	**172**	¬	**204**	Ì	**236**	ì
141	¤	**173**	-	**205**	Í	**237**	í
142	¤	**174**	®	**206**	Î	**238**	î
143	¤	**175**	¯	**207**	Ï	**239**	ï
144	¤	**176**	°	**208**	Ð	**240**	ð
145	¤	**177**	±	**209**	Ñ	**241**	ñ
146	¤	**178**	2	**210**	Ò	**242**	ò

Table A.2: ASCII Character Set (128–255) *continued*

147	¤	**179**	3	**211**	Ó	**243**	ó
148	¤	**180**	´	**212**	Ô	**244**	ô
149	¤	**181**	µ	**213**	Õ	**245**	õ
150	¤	**182**	¶	**214**	Ö	**246**	ö
151	¤	**183**	·	**215**	×	**247**	÷
152	¤	**184**	¸	**216**	Ø	**248**	ø
153	¤	**185**	1	**217**	Ù	**249**	ù
154	¤	**186**	o	**218**	Ú	**250**	ú
155	¤	**187**	»	**219**	Û	**251**	û
156	¤	**188**	1/4	**220**	Ü	**252**	ü
157	¤	**189**	1/2	**221**	´Y	**253**	´y
158	¤	**190**	3/4	**222**	Þ	**254**	þ
159	¤	**191**	¿	**223**	ß	**255**	ÿ

¤*These characters are not supported by Microsoft Windows.*
The values in the table are the Windows default. However, values in the ANSI character set above 127 are determined by the code page specific to your operating system.
Nonprinting characters are described within brackets.

Index

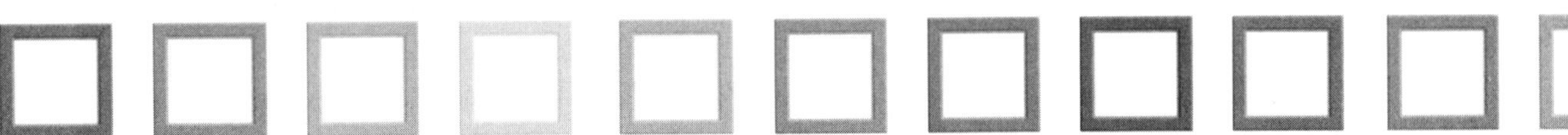

Note to the Reader: Throughout this index **boldfaced** page numbers indicate primary discussions of a topic. *Italicized* page numbers indicate illustrations.

A

B

C

D

E

F

G

H

I

K

L

M

N

O

P

Q

R

S

T

U

V

W

X

Y

Z

What's on the CD-ROM

This CD-ROM is packed with valuable resources in an easy-to-use format to aid in the development of your VBA skills. The resources include

- **Reusable code from the book** We've included every significant code listing presented in the text to help you work through the exercises without having to do a lot of additional typing. Just transfer the code to the Visual Basic Editor to run the macros or to try out code changes.
- **Bonus chapters** The CD-ROM includes two bonus chapters on 2D and 3D drawing techniques, to build on the exercises presented in Parts IV and V of the book. Chapter 18 demonstrates how to plot a drawing using the Plot Table Wizard. It also includes exercises on how to create a macro to automate plotting tasks. Chapter 19 exercises show you how to use code to shade and render 3D drawings and do hidden-surface removal.
- **Adobe Acrobat Reader** This program is included for your convenience so you can read the .PDF files that are on the CD-ROM.